LEVANT SUPPLEMENTARY SERIES
VOLUME 15

LANDSCAPE AND INTERACTION
The Troodos Archaeological and Environmental Survey Project, Cyprus

---

VOLUME 2
The TAESP Landscape

By
Michael Given, A. Bernard Knapp, Jay Noller, Luke Sollars and Vasiliki Kassianidou

with contributions by

Iain Banks, Alexis Boutin, Hugh Corley, Stephen Digney, Ian Evans, Sevina Floridou, Ruth Smadar Gabrieli, Erin Gibson, Angus Graham, Marios Hadjianastasis, Mara T. Horowitz, Jean Humbert, Tracy Ireland, Sarah Janes, Abel Lufafa, Carole McCartney, Maria Ntinou, Chris Parks, Colin Robins, Charlotte Schriwer, Sheila Slevin, Gary Tompsett, Neil Urwin, Joanita Vroom and Kristina Winther-Jacobsen

and

Stephen Digney, Myrto Goergakopoulou, Abel Lufafa, Emmanuel Moutafov, Danielle Parks†, Colin Robins, Sheila Slevin and Gary Tompsett

OXBOW BOOKS
Oxford and Oakville

Published jointly by
the Council for British Research in the Levant
and
Oxbow Books, Oxford, UK

CBRL Honorary Editor: Thomas F. Tartaron

ISBN 978-1-78297-188-7

Front cover: The Karkotis Valley looking south, with the church of Panayia Kousouliotissa in the foreground, the village of Korakou, and the Troodos Mountains in the background with Mount Olympus (Michael Given)

This book is available direct from:

Oxbow Books, Oxford, UK
(Phone: 01865-241249; Fax: 01865-794449)

and

The David Brown Book Company
PO Box 511, Oakville, CT 06779, USA
(Phone: 860-945-9329; Fax: 860-945-9468)

or from our website

www.oxbowbooks.com

A CIP record for this book is available from the British Library

Printed and bound in Great Britain by
Short Run Press, Exeter

To the people of the Survey Area, past and present

Abstract

The fieldwalkers and specialists of the Troodos Archaeological and Environmental Survey Project investigated a wide variety of physical and cultural landscapes on the northern edge of the Troodos Mountains in central Cyprus over six field seasons. These landscapes range from the cultivated Mesaoria Plain in the north to the forested Troodos Mountains in the south, and from the rich and fertile Karkotis Valley in the west to the drier and narrower Lagoudhera Valley in the east. Across this physical topography lie the cultural landscapes of food and fibre production, natural resource extraction, water conveyance and industry, ritual and burial, and the structures associated with villages, farms and copper mines.

Our regional perspective and time span, of at least 12,000 years, mean that the research issues are inevitably wide-ranging. At the core is the complex and dynamic relationship between people and their landscape, as it was played out in resource extraction, communication, settlement, social organisation, and the manipulation of soils, plants and water. This conceptual focus opens out onto a wide range of case studies, both chronologically and thematically.

Volume 1 of this publication contains a full explanation of the project's research context, research philosophy and methodology, and detailed analyses of the archaeology, material culture, architecture and environmental record of the Survey Area as a whole. This is followed by a series of period-specific analyses (Prehistoric, Iron Age, Hellenistic–Roman and Byzantine–Modern), and a conclusion that addresses our primary research goals and offers an evaluation of the project.

Volume 2 presents the results of our fieldwork and research, area by area. The analysis of this material is organized geographically, thematically and chronologically, and focuses on explicit research questions: the volume is data-rich but not merely descriptive. The emphasis throughout is on the integration of the work of our field teams and interdisciplinary specialists: this integration began in the field, was carried through the analysis and into the publication.

Our findings cover all periods from the Aceramic Neolithic to the present day. In the Aceramic Neolithic there was seasonal exploitation of the plains for cereal cultivation. We have established a pattern of substantial valley settlements and smaller foothill agricultural sites from the Late Chalcolithic to early in the Late Bronze Age. Particularly important are two Early Bronze Age settlements in the Karkotis Valley, clearly exploiting the copper mines of Skouriotissa and the rich and well-watered alluvial soils of the valley. Our most notable finds from the Iron Age to Classical period consist of two Archaic rural sanctuaries and several cemeteries.

In the Late Roman period we have an industrial landscape centred on the massive-scale production of copper at Skouriotissa, supported by intensive cultivation in the valley and a network of farmsteads spreading further afield. There is also a separate mining and agricultural system to the south-east, as well as isolated sites in the mountains producing timber, charcoal and other forest products. After an apparent gap in the Byzantine period, we have a system of Medieval estates, intense cultivation in the fertile Karkotis Valley in the Medieval and Ottoman periods, and a complex of small settlements, churches and paths in the mountains. Our work in the modern period has focused on the history and archaeology of mining and agriculture, and includes a substantial series of interviews with local villagers.

Contents

Preface

For a full account of our thanks to the many people and institutions that have supported us in fieldwork, research and publication, please see the Preface to Volume 1. Here, we would like to emphasize our gratitude to the successive directors and staff of the Department of Antiquities, who have given us permission to carry out our survey and supported us in many other ways; to the Cyprus American Archaeological Research Institute in Nicosia, for their invaluable logistical, academic and moral support over the years; and to the people of the Survey Area for their welcome, friendship and support.

We are very happy to acknowledge the many funding bodies that have made the project possible:

- Arts and Humanities Research Council
- British Academy
- Council for British Research in the Levant
- Institute for Aegean Prehistory
- Carnegie Trust for the Universities of Scotland
- Mediterranean Archaeological Trust
- Oregon State University
- University of Glasgow
- Society for the Promotion of Roman Studies
- American Schools of Oriental Research

Since our first season in 2000, 95 individuals have carried out the fieldwork, analysis and publication work. They are listed in full in Volume 1, and our heartfelt thanks go to them.

List of Colour Plates

List of Figures

List of Tables

List of Contributors

Iain Banks (University of Glasgow)
Alexis Boutin (Sonoma State University)
Hugh Corley (English Heritage)
Stephen Digney
Ian Evans (University of Newcastle, NSW)
Sevina Floridou
Ruth Smadar Gabrieli (University of Western Australia and University of Sydney)
Myrto Georgakopoulou (British School at Athens)
Erin Gibson (University of Northern British Columbia)
Michael Given (University of Glasgow)
Angus Graham (University College London)
Marios Hadjianastasis (University of Birmingham)
Mara T. Horowitz (Alalakh Excavations)
Jean Humbert
Tracy Ireland (University of Canberra)
Sarah Janes (University of Glasgow)
Vasiliki Kassianidou (University of Cyprus)
A. Bernard Knapp (University of Glasgow)
Abel Lufafa
Sturt W. Manning (Cornell University)
Carole McCartney (University of Cyprus)
Emmanuel Moutafov (Institute for Advanced Study, Berlin)
Jay Noller (Oregon State University)
Maria Ntinou (Hellenic Open University)
Chris Parks (Indiana University)
Danielle A. Parks†
Colin Robins (Claremont McKenna, Pitzer and Scripps Colleges)
Robert Schon (University of Arizona)
Charlotte Schriwer (National University of Singapore)
Sheila Slevin
Luke Sollars (University of Glasgow)
Gary Tompsett
Neil Urwin
Joanita Vroom (Leiden University)
Kristina Winther-Jacobsen (University of Copenhagen)

1. Introduction

Michael Given

The fieldwalkers and specialists of the Troodos Archaeological and Environmental Survey Project investigated a wide variety of physical and cultural landscapes on the northern edge of the Troodos Mountains over six field seasons. These landscapes range from the cultivated Mesaoria Plain in the north to the forested Troodos Mountains in the south, and from the rich and fertile Karkotis Valley in the west to the drier and narrower Lagoudhera Valley in the east. Across this physical topography lie the cultural landscapes of food and fibre production, natural resource extraction, water conveyance and industry, ritual and burial, and the buildings assocated with villages, farms and copper mines.

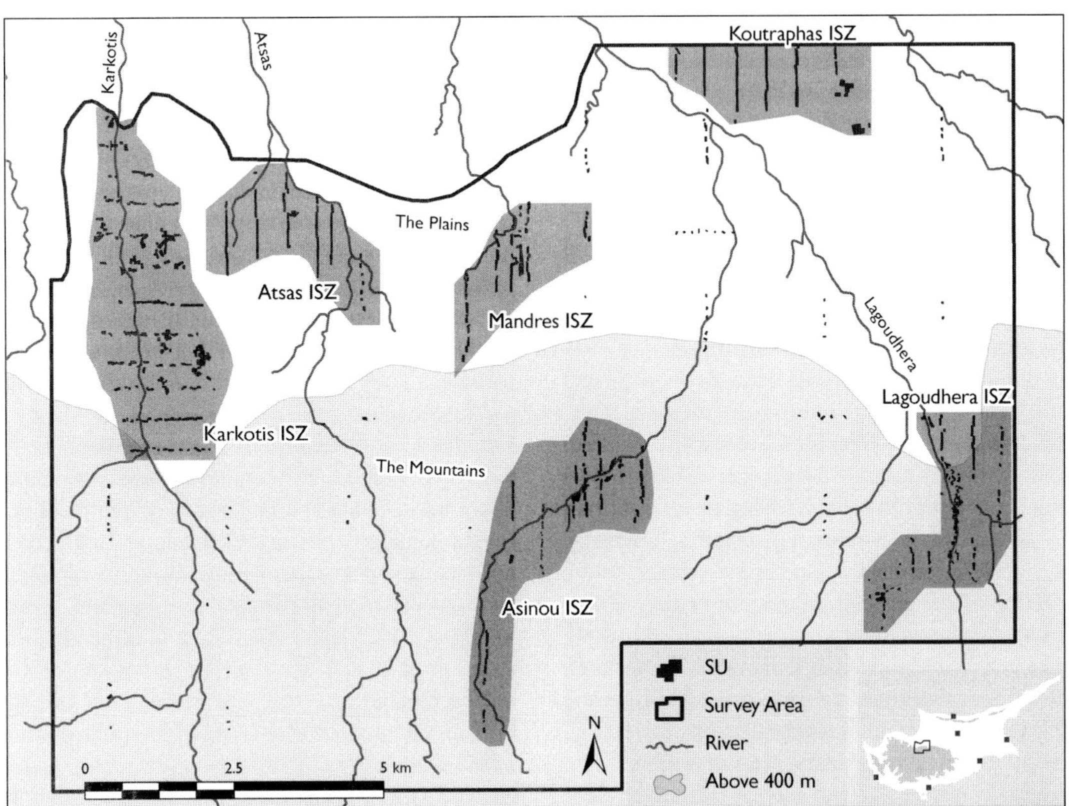

Fig. 1.1. Map of the TAESP Survey Area, with regions (Plains, Mountains, Karkotis Valley, Lagoudhera Valley), Intensive Survey Zones (ISZ), Survey Units (SU) and extensive transects (Luke Sollars)

This volume presents the results of that fieldwork and research. The analysis of all this material is organized geographically, thematically, and chronologically, and focuses on explicit research questions: our intention has always been that the volume should be data-rich but not merely descriptive. Our regional perspective and time span, of at least 12,000 years, mean that the research issues are inevitably wide-ranging. At the core is the complex and dynamic relationship between people and their landscape, as it was played out in resource extraction, communication, settlement, social organisation, and the manipulation of soils, plants and water. This conceptual focus opens out onto a huge range of case studies, from Late Epipalaeolithic seasonal harvesting on the Koutraphas plateau (Chapter 2.13), to Late Roman copper production on an industrial scale at the Skouriotissa mine (Chapter 3.12), to the impact of colonial forest boundaries on the mountain inhabitants of the late 19th and 20th centuries AD (Chapter 5.8).

Volume 1 of this publication contains a full explanation of the project's research context and methodology, detailed analyses of the archaeology, architecture, material culture and environmental record of the Survey Area as a whole, and overviews and analyses of the Survey Area by period. Volume 2, the present one, presents the results of our fieldwork and analysis, area by area.

For analytical purposes we have divided the Survey Area into four regions (Fig. 1.1). The Plains region (Chapter 2) incorporates the shallow and relatively dry Atsas Valley, the Pleistocene fluvial terraces round Mandres, and the Koutraphas Plateau, all of them across the north of our Survey Area. The Karkotis Valley (Chapter 3) runs down the western edge of the Survey Area, and is remarkably rich, fertile and well watered. The Lagoudhera Valley (Chapter 4) in the east, by contrast, is poorer in both soils and water, but supported a flourishing copper production industry during the Roman period. The mountains (Chapter 5) across the south of the Survey Area are very distinctive culturally as well as physically, and show clear and important interactions with the communities of the plains and valleys from the Roman period onwards.

Within these four regions we carried out transect survey and a range of other, more intensive methods in six Intensive Survey Zones: Atsas, Mandres and Koutraphas (in the Plains region); Karkotis Valley; Asinou (Mountains region); and Lagoudhera Valley. The rationale for choosing these zones is explained in Volume 1, Chapter 2.2. Because they were selected purposively, to give a representative range of the physical and cultural terrain of the Survey Area, we supplemented them with a grid of 1-km long 'extensive transects' (explained in Volume 1, Chapter 2.2). The analysis from these transects is discussed within each chapter to give context to the Intensive Survey Zones (e.g. Chapter 3.15, 'The Karkotis Valley in Context').

Within the Intensive Survey Zones, our core field method consisted of fieldwalking in individual Survey Units, typically 25 x 50 m, which were placed in and formed key parts of long transects running across the Intensive Survey Zone, normally at right angles to the main water course. From each Survey Unit the field teams collected a representative sample of pottery, all chipped stone, and a selection of other cultural material (metals, slag, roof tiles, etc). In areas where there was a broad spread of material, we carried out block survey of normally contiguous Survey Units; these areas were termed Special Interest Areas (SIAs), and are summarised in Appendix 1. Specific features or locations were recorded as Places of Special Interest (POSIs), initially with a pro forma and subsequently, if required, by a variety of techniques such as site gridding, standing building survey and topographic survey. They are listed in Appendix 2. Our methods for fieldwalking and artefact collection are explained in full in Volume 1, Chapter 2.3, and the raw data are available in our online data archive (TAESPdata 2007).

All this archaeological fieldwork was carried out under strict geomorphological control, and every field team included a geomorphologist (Volume 1, Chapter 2.4). Geomorphological Units were recorded with all Survey Units, partly so that features such as soil colour and degree of erosion could be analysed, and partly to make sure that every Survey Unit was internally consistent and coherent, rather than straddling geomorphological boundaries. In this way we achieved control over the contexts of the surface archaeological record. Additional geomorphological analysis was carried out on specific POSIs as required, and Morphostratigraphic Units were recorded across the entire Survey Area for analysis at a broader scale.

Much of our interpretation depends upon the chronological, functional and distributional analysis of artefacts. All artefacts brought back by the field teams were examined and recorded by the relevant specialists. This analysis, at the 'Finds' level, forms the basis of our GIS mapping and hence our interpretation of human activity in the landscape. The artefact data at this level are summarised in this volume where relevant, usually at the SIA or POSI level.

The artefact specialists made a selection of the most informative, interesting or representative pieces, which make up the analysis at the Inventory level. Most of these are published in the artefact catalogues in Volume 1. Catalogue numbers prefixed 'TCP' ('TAESP Catalogue Pottery) refer to the pottery catalogue (Volume 1, Chapter 3.6); 'TCS' numbers refer to the special finds catalogue (Volume 1, Chapter 3.7); and 'TCL' numbers refer to the lithics catalogue (Volume 1, Chapter 3.8). The complete artefact data set at both Finds and Inventory levels can be viewed in our online data archive (TAESPdata 2007).

This core analysis – consisting of archaeological survey, geomorphological mapping and artefact analysis – was complemented by a range of work by various specialists. Our archaeometallurgists focused on investigating the mining operations at Skouriotissa (Chapter 3.12), Ayia Marina *Mavrovouni* (Chapter 4.6) and Alestos (Chapters 4.3 and 4.4), as well as examining slag and other relevant finds from the whole Survey Area (for methodology see

Table 1.1. TAESP acronyms and abbreviations. For full explanation, see Volume 1, Chapter 2

Acronym	Explanation
AU01	Archaeometallurgical POSI Unit
BU0001	Building Unit
GI	Geomorphological Intern
GU0001	Geomorphology Unit
IP0001	Image Print (field map based on georegistered aerial photo)
ISZ	Intensive Survey Zone
NU01	Geobotany Unit
POSI	Place of Special Interest; ID numbers prefixed 'TP'
PU01	POSI Unit (sequential system)
PUE0N0	POSI Unit (coordinate system: E2N5, E3N5, etc.)
SE01	Structural Element (for architectural analysis)
SIA	Special Interest Area; ID numbers prefixed 'TS'
SU0001	Survey Unit
TCL001	TAESP Catalogue: Lithics
TCS001	TAESP Catalogue: Special Finds
TCP001	TAESP Catalogue: Pottery
TIA001	TAESP Inventory: Archaeometallurgy
TIL001	TAESP Inventory: Lithics
TIS001	TAESP Inventory: Special Finds
TIP001	TAESP Inventory: Pottery
TM001	TAESP Sample
TN001	TAESP Geobotany transect or block
TP001	TAESP Place of Special Interest
TS01	TAESP Special Interest Area
TT	TAESP Transect, e.g. TT3880000N (east–west); TT497000E (north–south)
XU	Experimental Unit, with details of seeded sherds
XSU	Experimental Survey Unit, with details of sherds recovered by teams

Volume 1, Chapter 2.12; for results across the Survey Area as a whole, see Volume 1, Chaper 3.9).

Our team of architectural historians recorded Building Units across the Survey Area, and made specific investigations of watermills, irrigation channels and weirs, construction materials, and the relationship between architecture and colonialism. This work involved close collaboration with our oral and documentary historian (for methodology, see Volume 1, Chapter 2.14; for results across the Survey Area as a whole, see Volume 1, Chapters 3.11 and 3.12).

Our geobotanist investigated Medieval–Modern olive trees (Chapter 3.16) and the fuel supply for ancient copper mining (for methodology, see Volume 1, Chapter 2.11; for results across the Survey Area as a whole, Volume 1, Chapter 4.7 and 4.8). Other specialists investigated communication routes (Volume 1, Chapter 3.13) and tombs (Volume 2, Chapter 3.14), carried out geophysical survey and topographical survey, conducted fieldwalking experiments to test our methodology (Volume 1, Chapters 2.8 and 2.9) and constructed, maintained and queried the database and GIS (Volume 1, Chapter 2.7).

Virtually all of TAESP's formal statistical and spatial analysis was carried out via our relational database and GIS. The analytical procedures are discussed in Volume 1, Chapter 2.10. The extensive use of GIS maps in this volume demonstrates the centrality of this analysis to our interpretation of human activity in the TAESP landscape. Some of these maps represent data from over 30,000 sherds, and so are not intended to be schematic or simplistic. As with any presentation of data-rich material, they repay a certain investment of time on the part of the reader.

Nevertheless, our GIS maps operate within the confines of the broad-brush approach of regional survey: they show trends and patterns of artefact distribution across the landscape, rather than precise statistics for every Survey Unit. It does not matter, for example, if a particular Survey Unit is half-obscured by a circle representing pottery density: what matters is the overall pattern across a broad area and its interpretation.

Following principles of design discussed by Tufte (1997) and Monmonier (1996), and in an effort to avoid confusing graphics, we have endeavoured to apply a reasonably intuitive and consistent style to all of our maps. The more familiar a reader becomes with our style, the easier it will be to see past the graphical representation to the data contained within.

Table 1.2. Pottery periods

Code	Period	Period Span
PH	Prehistoric	before 750 BC
CHAL	Chalcolithic	3900–2600 BC
LChPh	Late Chalcolithic/Philia	2700–2500 BC
BA	Bronze Age	2600–1050 BC
PeB	Prehistoric Bronze Age	2700–1650 BC
PoB	Protohistoric Bronze Age	1650–1050 BC
PoBAR	Late Bronze Age to Archaic	1600–475 BC
GA	Cypro-Geometric to Archaic	1050–475 BC
GAC	Cypro-Geometric to Classical	1050–312 BC
AR	Cypro-Archaic	750–475 BC
AC	Cypro-Archaic to Classical	750–312 BC
HA	Historical Antiquity (Archaic to Late Roman)	750 BC–AD 650
CL	Cypro-Classical	475–312 BC
CLH	Classical to Hellenistic	475–31 BC
HEL	Hellenistic	312–31 BC
LH	Late Hellenistic	150–31 BC
HR	Hellenistic to Roman	312 BC–AD 650
HER	Hellenistic to Early Roman	312 BC–AD 200
LHER	Late Hellenistic to Early Roman	200 BC–AD 200
ER	Early Roman	31 BC–AD 200
ROM	Early to Late Roman	31 BC–AD 650
MR	Mid Roman	3rd–4th c. AD
LR	Late Roman	AD 400–650/800?
RM	Roman to Modern	31 BC– Present
HIS	Historical (Archaic to Modern)	750 BC– Present
BYZ	Byzantine	AD 650–1191
MEDUI	Medieval utility period I	Late 12th–late 14th/early 15th c. AD
MED	Medieval	AD 1191–1571
MEDOTT	Medieval to Ottoman	AD 1191–1878
MM	Medieval to Modern	AD 1191– Present
MEDB	Byzantine to Medieval	AD 12th–13th c.
MEDF	Medieval-Frankish	AD 14th–15th c.
MEDUII	Medieval utility period II	AD 15th–mid 16th c.
MEDUIII	Medieval utility period III	15th c.–end 20th c.
OTT	Ottoman	AD 1571–1878
OTTMODI	Ottoman to Modern I	AD 1571–beginning 20th c.
MEDVOTT	Medieval-Venetian to Early Ottoman	AD 16th–17th c.
OTTMODII	Ottoman to Modern II	AD 18th–mid 20th c.
MOD	Modern	AD 1878– Present
UN	Unknown	Unknown

Because of the complexity of our analytical procedures, the material and the landscape itself, as well as our long familiarity with them, it is very much our responsibility to explain and interpret these maps (Mattingly and Witcher 2004, 177). That is what we do in the accompanying text. The data, however, are open to other interpretations. Again, the complete database and GIS files are available for download from our online data archive (TAESPdata 2007). It is also possible for readers to query the database and GIS and create their own analytical maps using the online GIS presented in our article in Internet Archaeology (Given *et al.* 2007). We would warmly welcome any dialogue on the analysis and interpretation of the TAESP landscape.

It is inevitable that a project of this size and complexity should generate its own specialized language and abbreviations, not least because of the 27 different recording forms and corresponding database tables used by project members. A full explanation of these can be found in Volume 1, Chapter 2.1, but for convenience we summarise the main abbreviations and project-specific terms that the reader will meet in this volume in Table 1.1, and list the chronological periods we use to classify our pottery in Table 1.2.

The writing in this volume represents the collaboration of 30 team members: the project directors, specialists, team leaders and Geomorphological Interns (see List of Contributors). Rather than having each specialist write a separate chapter with little reference to the others, we have chosen to integrate the work of all these colleagues throughout the book. This principle of working on the material together during fieldwork and writing it up together for the publication is fundamental to our research philosophy. Equally important is the role of team leaders and Geomorphological Interns in interpreting and writing about the landscape they know better than any other project members (Volume 1, Chapter 1.4). All contributors are listed at the beginning of each chapter with their specialism.

This volume embraces a wide range of often contrasting perspectives. The engagement with a working watermill and its miller (Chapter 3.4) is clearly very different from a typological and distributional analysis of pottery and chipped stone from a Bronze Age settlement (Chapter 3.5), and that is different again from the investigation of Holocene river movement through the recording of a soil section (Chapter 3.5). Similarly, the Intensive Survey Zones within our Survey Area are intentionally very diverse, with very different physiography, material culture and historical development. These specific characteristics drive the more thematic structure of our chapter on the mountains (Chapter 5), for example, compared with the south-to-north organisation of our discussion of the Karkotis Valley (Chapter 3). To a reader working through the entire volume, this variety may come across as being apparently uneven in approach. Taken together, however, these wide-ranging and interdisciplinary perspectives are intended to give a more nuanced and sensitive approach to a strikingly multi-facetted landscape. We discuss the epistemological rewards of this integration of approaches more fully in Volume 1, Chapter 1.4.

This integration of the writing of a large team of researchers also makes for long lists of authors in references. We do not apologise for this: as well as generating a more nuanced and informed interpretation of the landscape, it is a better acknowledgment of the collaborative work of a large team of researchers. We suggest that each chapter is referenced as follows:

Boutin, Alexis, Michael Given, Iain Banks, Stephen Digney, Ian Evans, Sevina Floridou, Ruth Smadar Gabrieli, Marios Hadjianastasis, Mara T. Horowitz, Tracy Ireland, Sarah Janes, Vasiliki Kassianidou, A. Bernard Knapp, Carole McCartney, Charlotte Schriwer, Sheila Slevin, Neil Urwin, Joanita Vroom, and Kristina Winther-Jacobsen

2013 The Karkotis Valley. In *Landscape and Interaction: Troodos Archaeological and Environmental Survey Project, Cyprus*, edited by Michael Given, A. Bernard Knapp, Jay Noller, Luke Sollars and Vasiliki Kassianidou, Volume 2: 51–151. Levant Supplementary Series 15. London: Council for British Research in the Levant.

2. The Plains

Edited by Michael Given (Atsas and Mandres) and Luke Sollars (Koutraphas)

with contributions by Alexis Boutin (team leader, Atsas), Stephen Digney (team leader, Team X), Ian Evans (architecture), Sevina Floridou (architecture), Ruth Smadar Gabrieli (pottery), Erin Gibson (team leader, Mandres), Michael Given (historical periods; team leader, Koutraphas), Marios Hadjianastasis (oral history), Mara T. Horowitz (pottery), Tracy Ireland (historical archaeology), Sarah Janes (pottery, figurines), A. Bernard Knapp (prehistory), Carole McCartney (lithics), Jay Noller (geomorphology), Colin Robins (geomorphology), Charlotte Schriwer (watermills), Sheila Slevin (geomorphology), Neil Urwin (botany and geobotany), Joanita Vroom (pottery) and Kristina Winther-Jacobsen (pottery)

2.1 Introduction

The northern third of our Survey Area is distinguished by a striking diversity of landforms, natural resources and patterns of human activity. A series of northward-flowing rivers dissect broad mid-Pleistocene fluvial terraces, which themselves overlie igneous pillow lavas and limestone reefs (Fig. 2.1). Where the pillow lavas are exposed, they exhibit copper ores and thin soils, which contrast with the ancient, fertile soils of the Pleistocene terraces and the more recent fluvial deposits in the valley bottoms. Human interaction with this landscape has varied from seasonal exploitation to intensive estate agriculture, exploiting not just the soils and water but the jasper outcrops and copper ores, the wild plants and the pastures.

Our research in this region sought to investigate the relationship between human activity and the environment in an area that contrasted greatly with the rich and densely used Karkotis Valley, which lies immediately over the watershed to the west (Table 2.1). Investigating seasonal activity was a particularly important issue, and turned out to be relevant across a broad array of periods, with likely summer subsistence in the Late Palaeolithic or Aceramic Neolithic, possible seasonal or occasional use in the Roman period, and a highly organized system of mountain villages growing cereals here in the 19th and early 20th centuries AD. We also investigated an impressively long-lived ad hoc lithics industry that exploited local materials rather than importing exotic ones, discovered the traces of an extensive network of Bronze Age rural settlements, detected a clear shift in the settlement pattern between the Bronze Age and Iron Age, and compared the archaeological and historical evidence for a 15th-century AD agricultural estate.

We investigated this large and diverse region primarily by means of three separate Intensive Survey Zones (Plate 2.1): Atsas; Mandres; and Koutraphas. In each of these we carried out transect survey along north–south transect lines, complemented by block survey of Special Interest Areas and more detailed investigation of specific POSIs, structures, and environmental features. Because the Intensive Survey Zones were purposively chosen for their known features and representativeness, the team working in this region (Team 'X') also surveyed a series of 1-km transects on a kilometre grid across the whole area outside of the Intensive Survey Zones (for methodology see Volume 1, Chapter 2.3).

Fig. 2.1. Looking south-east over the Plains area from the lime kiln on Koronia hill (BU0141), with the Troodos range beyond. Mandres is just off the photograph to the right (Michael Given)

Table 2.1. The Plains: chronological summary

Period	Activity	Name/ID number	Chapter
Prehistoric	Late Epipalaeolithic/Aceramic Neolithic chipped stone	Kambos tou Lemonari	2.13
	Bronze Age settlement	Petrera	2.14
	Bronze Age settlement	Mandroudhes	2.9
	Bronze Age pottery & lithics scatter	Lemonas	2.7
Iron Age–Classical	Archaic sanctuary & cemetery	Khalospitia & Kamilaries	2.4
Hellenistic–Roman	Roman settlement	Lithosourka	2.7
	Roman farmstead	Vrysi tou Haji Christophi	2.5
	Roman farmstead	Phoukasa	2.6
	Roman jasper industry		2.7
	Agricultural settlements	Sanidhia, Katalasharis	2.15
Byzantine–Modern	Medieval–Modern villages	Kato & Pano Koutraphas, Potami	2.16
	2 Ottoman water mills (Atsas)	BU0053, BU0059	2.7
	4 Ottoman water mills (Koutraphas)	BU0104, BU0096, BU0109, BU0073	2.16
	Ottoman–Modern satellite settlement	Lemonas	2.7
	Ottoman–Modern satellite settlement	Mandres	2.10
	Medieval Modern agriculture	NW Koutraphas plateau	2.16
	Ottoman–Modern water management		2.2
	Colonial bridges	TP004, TP020, BU0114	2.11, 2.16

The Atsas Intensive Survey Zone is a dry-cropped valley on the eastern edge of Skouriotissa mine, and was distinctive for its clear peaks in artefact density in an otherwise empty landscape. Its northern part had the added attraction of lying in the United Nations Buffer Zone, so the archaeological preservation was excellent. The Mandres Intensive Survey Zone was of great interest for its transitional position between the mountains and the plains, which is one of the reasons for the location there of one principal site of interest, the Ottoman–Modern satellite settlement of Mandres. The Pleistocene fluvial terraces above the Medieval–Modern villages of Pano and

Kato Koutraphas had ancient, red soils but comparatively little water, and again provided some scarce but relatively clear patterns of artefact distribution and land use.

This chapter begins by giving an overview of the environment of this area, and then deals with the three Intensive Survey Zones, working from Atsas in the west to Koutraphas in the East. For each of them we give an introduction and overview, followed by a series of thematic sections and finishing with a summary and conclusions. At the end of the chapter we step back and consider the Plains region as a whole, first by examining the data from the 'Team X' transects and other investigations outside the Intensive Survey Zones, and then by integrating all of these data to give an interdisciplinary and multi-period analysis of the relationship between human activity and the environment in this very diverse region.

2.2 Environmental Setting

The Atsas, Mandres and Koutraphas Intensive Survey Zones provide us with a replicated study of the interactions of people and environment at three different locations within the same biophysical setting. These three areas provide a range of environmental variability from which we can make statistically reasoned conclusions about the relationships between the material cultural record and uses of the landscape that we describe as 'the Plains'.

The Plains are low-lying areas of gentle slope and undulating topography that today have few trees or landforms that would disrupt one's view of the distant flat horizon. Of the three Intensive Survey Zones, Koutraphas matches this definition best and Mandres the least, a reflection of their proximity to the steep mountain front of the Troodos. Koutraphas is farthest from the Troodos, while Mandres actually lies astride the boundary between the Troodos and the Mesaoria, the great central plain of Cyprus (Plate 2.2). This distance may seem trivial in terms of magnitude, but within 1 km north of the mountain front the mean annual precipitation diminishes by 20% from 355 to 290 mm, and the number of individual storm events by 50% (Cyprus Meteorological Service). In other words, Mandres is wetter than Koutraphas, and probably has been for most of the cultural past.

When we look at the geological past, we see the Plains as a much gentler and less dissected landscape of broad, coalescing fluvial fans that front a sweeping shoreline along an ancestral Morphou Bay. The time is almost a million years ago when Cyprus was still a group of smaller islands (see Volume 1, Chapter 4.3). Since then, erosion of the major rivers and their tributaries has exacted a toll on the stores of sediments and soils of these old fans. Dependent on the rate of down-cutting by their master stream, the tributaries seek new, lower levels with significant delay because they do not have the same means of water capture in their headwaters. The large, mountain streams capture more rainfall that occurs more often and with greater intensity. The Plains rivers, by contrast, may not approach this capacity because of the lesser water supply and the loss of any precipitation that does occur by infiltration to the soils. On the Plains, then, we surveyed a biophysical setting removed from a natural and perennial source and flow of water. We should then consider the Plains as semi-arid desert, a drought-susceptible landscape that is prone to crop failures and other maladies that affect agrarian society.

In spite of these risks, the Plains offer an incomparable advantage to cereal growers, with rich, thick soils that are easily seeded. These soils capture rain and hold it well through the growing season, so that significant yields of cereal are attained. Further, the cereal seed stock generated from Syria and the Levant, the likely birthplace of this industry, would be varietals bred for similar soils and climate. In other words, from the beginning, imported seeds would prosper in the Mesaoria. Compared to the development and maintenance costs of the major river valleys with their potentially frequent floods, the Plains represent a sustainable resource easily converted to cereal cropland and easily maintained as such for millennia.

Irrigation and Management of Water Supply

The Atsas Intensive Survey Zone is the one area of the Plains with generations of irrigation and water supply works. In part, this distinction stems from where we chose to bound our Intensive Survey Zones, as the Koutraphas zone lies well above and away from what could be diverted from the Koutraphas river system. This distinction also results from watershed size and elevation, as the local streams are of insufficient and ephemeral discharge to warrant construction of water collection, storage and conveyance facilities.

The oldest of the extant works in the Atsas are the water channels supplying mills along a tributary and mainstream of the Ayii Saranta stream (BU0002–04, BU0053, BU0059). The mills utilize the same flow source, using the accumulated water head in succession (see Chapter 2.7). At each mill, overflow channels lead to local, small landholdings on Holocene fluvial terraces. These lands are today dominantly planted with fruit, nut and olive groves. There are short channels, disconnected by infilling, erosion or destruction of causeways, along the eastern slope of Skouriotissa. We identified fragments of irrigation channels documented by the early 20th-century cadastral map, particularly at Skouriotissa *Kapati* (TT491000E), Petra *Merras* (near TP217–18), and Petra *Phoukasa* (TP236). The last carries water from a weir (no longer functioning) near TP236, along the eastern bank of Ayii Saranta stream, thence across the Atsas River and zig-zagging north through the fields of the Buffer Zone and into Petra where it supplies the village centre and surrounding fields and groves.

The Karkotis watershed has been significantly and artificially expanded into the Atsas basin (for discussion and map, see Volume 1, Chapter 3.12 and Fig. 3.51).

Ayii Saranta and nearby streams were each channelized, probably into a metre-wide, dug trench along the stream bank where bedrock exposure would lessen drainage loss of conveyed water. The number of channels and potential magnitude of flow in this system would have diverted significantly and correspondingly lowered discharge in the Karkotis River north/downstream of the village of Phlasou. Three canals cross the Karkotis/Atsas drainage divide, two at Katydhata *Varys* and one at Katydhata *Pamboula*. A possible fourth crossing lies near Linou *Appidhes* on the south slopes of Ayii Saranta hill, but this would drop water into a landscape relatively unproductive for cereals agriculture, for about 500 m, before reaching the nearest substantial field where it could be used. This network of canals shows that agriculture and communities in the Atsas plain, from mountain front to well north/downstream of Petra, were dependent on sufficient discharge in the Karkotis (a weather-climate vulnerability) and the communities upstream, particularly Katydhata and Linou (a political vulnerability?).

The dependence on the Karkotis River for water supply would have been lessened by the construction of two mid-20th century concrete and rock-fill dams. These supply, or rather did supply prior to 1974, water to the village of Petra. Located near the Troodos–Nicosia highway, along TT493250E and near TP130, these reservoirs also feed a network of irrigation canals along the eastern fluvial terraces of the Atsas. A temporary impoundment, one of several seen over the years along intermittent rivers in the area, had about 500–1000 m^3 of water in 2003 and contained several dozen carp. This pond was situated behind a 3–4 m earthen dam at TP205. Ephemeral impoundments such as this are typically used for irrigation, with gasoline-powered pumps feeding a network of black plastic irrigation pipe.

Land Sculpting

By definition (almost) the Plains are plough-ready. Little in the way of preparation or maintenance need be performed, compared with other areas. It is unknown what the first inhabitants and those converting the land to agricultural use might have faced in terms of vegetative cover. The Plains would have had steppe-shrubs, grass, conifer (pine-dominated is most likely), or a mix of those. Burning off the native vegetation would have been the simplest means of land clearance. Following this, large stones, some very large at 1 m diameter and some 2–3 tons mass, would need to be removed. For the flat, gentle treads of most of the surveyed Plains transects, this activity would probably have been an obligatory effort prior to the first seeding. Because the density of large stones in the Pleistocene fluvial fan deposits is relatively low (<25%), the use of an ard, whether powered by human or draft-animal, and/or other tillage implements would have been useful in preparing a seed bed.

As documented by the survey, particularly along transects in the Koutraphas Intensive Survey Zone, field walls, structures, field corners and rock piles are present-day features created by past land clearance activities. Inspection of these stones reveals at least three classes of aging amongst all of their uses. The oldest surviving in situ stones are fully covered with lichens and have reddened patina on hidden (within wall) surfaces. Field corners are marked by these large stones, which have a patina below ground, including silica growths, and tool marks from generations of ploughs and other field tools/machinery. The second class of field stones are those with a lesser amount of lichen cover and patination. Typical locations for these are in upper parts of field walls and piles.

A third class of stones consists of those associated with two modern mechanized stone-harvesting methods: deep ploughing and potato (stone) harvester. The deep plough is a one- to three-toothed implement inserted to 0.5–1.0 m depth and dragged behind a large bulldozer. It breaks through the petrocalcic or other type of hardpan that restricts root penetration into the subsoil. This tool also uproots large stones that the bulldozer pushes, with soil, into a pile at field edge. The Plains are commonly cropped in potatoes. Stones interfere with the harvest and may be mistaken for potatoes by field harvesters. So the growers first run a special potato harvester through the top soil to harvest potato-size and larger stones. Once cleared, with piles of >10 cm stones, a potato field can be safely and fully mechanized for potato production. Piles of harvested stones are fairly common in the Koutraphas Intensive Survey Zone. To a lesser extent piles of field stones have been shaped into check dams in the gullies and valleys of the Plains. Rare hillslope terraces serve as another resting place for field-harvested stones.

Vegetation

The Plains are, for ecological and land use reasons, wholly non-diverse in vegetation. The area is broadly cropped today in cereals and pulses, with potato, watermelon and other specialty or market crops. Along inset fluvial terraces and the rare, constructed agricultural terraces, orchards of olive, fruit and nut trees are planted. It is an agricultural landscape.

The Koutraphas Intensive Survey Zone is an archetype of the Plains agro-ecosystem. Consisting of nearly 70% 'Grass + grassy batha + cereal crops' land cover, this area remains true to the definition of the prairie/savannah ecological zone (see Volume 1, Chapter 4.4). Only 7.3% of the Koutraphas comes under the class of Open Mediterranean Forest or what we call 'Batha + pine' (10%), due to the presence of a few pines (*Pinus nigra* or *Pinus brutia*) amongst the low-lying grasses and small shrubs. 'Garigue + batha' and 'Batha (Open Heath)' together cover more than 20% of the Intensive Survey Zone on the steep slopes of gullies and in the lower reaches of drainages of the large Lagoudhera fluvial fan complex that underlies the entire Intensive Survey Zone.

Located just inside the northern boundary of the Troodos Ophiolite bedrock (Upper Pillow Lavas, top of section), the

Atsas Intensive Survey Zone is more diverse in lithology and landforms, and yet retains much of the 'Grass + grassy batha + cereal crops' land cover (56.1%) associated with the Plains (see Volume 1, Chapter 4.4). A higher percentage of hilliness and the presence of ore-bearing pillow lavas leads to a greater proportion of 'Garigue + batha + isolated pine trees' (c.27%), and 'Disturbed surface and built-up areas' (mines at Skouriotissa) (c.11%). A few orchards round out the major land cover types in the Atsas.

At the other end of the Plains spectrum, the Mandres Intensive Survey Zone includes the modern zone of pine forest encroachment on the grass- and cereal-dominated landscape of the past few millennia. Pine-forested lands account for 40.8% of this area, nearly equal to that of the 'Grass + grassy batha + cereal' (44.2%). Pines are kept in check from further expansion onto the level treads of Pleistocene fluvial fans and terraces by annual field burning by the Cyprus Department of Forestry along a 200+ m buffer strip bordering the forest lands. Encroachment in this zone has occurred by means of the unchecked succession of pine forest over former Garigue and Batha land cover (<8%) along drainage side slopes and interspersed hills. In particular, we noted that the forest favours lands abandoned from traditional use of cereal cropping on narrow, constructed agricultural terraces.

2.3 Atsas Valley Intensive Survey Zone: Introduction and Overview

The initial impetus for our research in the Atsas Valley (Fig. 2.2) was a request in July 2003 from the Department of Antiquities to carry out a survey of the Lemonas area, where the Hellenic Mining Company had applied to extend their operations and where a preliminary survey by the Department of Antiquities had discovered significant prehistoric and medieval material. We quickly discovered that this area was of great interest because of its striking contrast with the adjacent Karkotis Valley. In particular, we found field after field with absolutely no trace of cultural materials, and then sudden and very clear dense patches of artefacts. This is a relatively unusual occurrence in the lower-lying levels of the Survey Area.

In addition, part of the area lay within the United Nations Buffer Zone. Thanks to the support of the Department of Antiquities and the United Nations, we were able to work in this area, which has lain relatively untouched since 1974. Agricultural work still continues in parts of it, but there has been no development, road building, deep ploughing or bulldozing. As a result, archaeological remains survived in strikingly better condition than in areas to the south.

One of the major research questions we addressed in this area was the organisation of agriculture in the Roman period. The pattern of large tracts of apparently unused land, with a few small farmsteads and occasional larger settlements, was in total contrast to the intensive and continuous human activity across the entire Karkotis Valley over the watershed to the west. Was this just a matter of natural resources such as water supply and soil fertility? Or was it part of the complex organisation that supported the massive copper production operation at Skouriotissa, which in visual terms, at least, dominates the entire Atsas area? Material from other periods included Chalcolithic to Late Bronze Age finds at Lemonas, an Archaic sanctuary and cemetery, and an Ottoman/early Modern seasonal settlement. In many respects these concentrations of activity in an otherwise empty landscape connected the Atsas valley more closely with the Mandres and Koutraphas areas, farther east along the plains, than they did with the Karkotis Valley over the watershed to the west.

The core of our methodology consisted of five north–south transects of Survey Units, plus some block survey round the Roman farmstead of Linou *Vrysi tou Haji Christophi*, to determine whether there was a halo of material from manuring or dumping round it. We also

Fig. 2.2. The Atsas area viewed from the south. The edge of Skouriotissa mine appears on the left, with Morphou Bay beyond; Lemonas is just beyond the bright patch in the centre, with the Kyrenia Mountains beyond (Chris Parks)

mapped the architectural remains of that same farmstead, and recorded a variety of individual POSIs. To get a clearer picture of the geomorphological development of the area in a short time, we walked systematically along all gullies, checking for material eroding out of gully walls and examining ancient soils and surfaces along their edges. Because we had special permission to work in the Buffer Zone, we took the opportunity to do some broader reconnaissance survey, which resulted in the discovery of an Archaic sanctuary (TP215) and cemetery (TP248), as well as a Roman settlement (TP216).

The section of the Atsas valley that we surveyed encompasses the confluence of three rivers (Atsas, Arodhaphnas, and Haji Christophi) that cross the Upper Pillow Lava bedrock formation, as well as numerous smaller tributary streams (Plate 2.3). The rivers are flanked by narrow terraces ranging from 5 to 40 m wide, underlain by fluvial sediments and overlying topsoil. Beyond the terraced fringe of the rivers lie ridges of exposed bedrock (ancient eroded surfaces) and interspersed depressions filled with colluvial sediment and soil now planted with grain.

Most of the river terraces have strongly developed havara soils, which are resistant to erosion. The river banks are thus resistant to erosion, and rivers in this area have been constrained mainly to channel deepening for many thousands of years. The narrow, deep channel form of the rivers and gullies is largely due to this property of bank stability. Agricultural and industrial modification of the landscape has been minimal. Check dams, terraces and roads are few in number, particularly compared to nearby areas. Overall erosion and landscape modification for the past 2000 years is significantly low here. This means that the potential for the preservation of cultural materials in areas between the gullies and rivers is relatively high.

Survey activities were conducted around the time of straw baling. Most fields had standing stubble that was partially covered with rows of raked straw. The rocky ridges were characterized by good survey visibility, while the grain fields had relatively poor survey visibility. River channels also had poor visibility because of cover from dense stands of bamboo and other vegetation, whereas the smaller gullies generally had good visibility.

2.4 Archaic Sanctuary and Cemetery at Evrykhou *Khalospitia* and *Kamilaries*

The sanctuary of Evrykhou *Khalospitia* (TP215) lies on a slight rise above and north of a bend in the Atsas River, on rolling land with good views in all directions. The soil in the immediate area consists of residuum from bedrock with minor fluvial materials, being in the low section of a Pleistocene channel (ancestral Atsas?). In the section exposed in a modern well on the north side of the sanctuary, the topsoil is 20–30 cm deep, lying on bedrock. As agricultural land, this is relatively poor, though it is rather better up the hill to the north-west.

The sanctuary is clearly visible as a substantial rectangular structure, with four walls expressed as linear rubble piles overgrown with jujube (*Zizyphus lotus*). The enclosure is approximately 19 × 12 m, which is too big to have been a roofed structure, and so was clearly a temenos, or sanctuary precinct. There is a 6-m wide gap in the north wall, a 2-m gap at the south end of the west wall, and a 2-m gap at the east end of the south wall, although these may result at least partly from the action of the plough in breaking through into the interior of the temenos. Most stone is imported, and consists of microgabbro, limestone, diabase and eroded coral heads originally from Koroni, presumably picked up from the Koutraphas River. Some stones show colouring from red soils on the hill to the north-west, a Middle Pleistocene fluvial fan terrace.

The centre of the temenos has been ploughed out, which exposed large quantities of figurines, terracotta sculpture, Iron Age pottery, and some Roman pottery and tile (collected as PU01). There are more figurines at the north end, and some ground stone. Just north of the temenos lie a microgabbro rubber and a stone mortar. We found several figurine fragments dating to the Archaic–Classical periods, including small and large, handmade and mouldmade terracotta figurines. As with most materials retrieved through surface survey, the figurines are fragmentary and exhibit varying degrees of preservation. The smaller items, which constitute just over half of the finds recorded, are more highly weathered than the larger fragments.

The smaller items include individual limbs (TCS051; see Volume 1, Chapter 3.7 for catalogue) and fragments of freestanding handmade 'snowmen' figurines (TCS049; TCS052). Of particular interest is a small Classical torso with drapery, a belt and the arm held across the chest (TCS046). This mouldmade piece has traces of blue and red paint making it one of only two pieces in the collection with signs of original painted decoration. The other decorated find is a fragment from the base of a medium hollow figure or stand, decorated with painted black zig-zags and lines (TCS047). There are two zoomorphic fragments, a well-preserved horse's head (TCS048), and the torso of an unidentified quadruped, possibly a horse (TCS050). It is likely that both of these pieces were originally part of horse and chariot groups. There are slightly fewer fragments of larger figurines in the collection. They include parts of large, hollow freestanding figures (TCS054; TCS056) and possible stand fragments (TCS055).

The repertoire is similar to that of specific Archaic–Classical Cypriot rural sanctuaries on Cyprus such as Ayia Irini (Gjerstad *et al.* 1935, 797–810) and Tamassos *Frangissa* (Buchholz 1991). The finds are not great in quantity but are interesting for their diversity in both type and date. The fragmented nature of the finds and the small numbers, however, make it difficult to offer any firm statement about the cult or cult activities at this site.

The pottery corresponds well with the figurines, and includes Cypriot White Painted and Plain White Ware (Table 2.2). A number of rolled lug handles with black

Table 2.2. Evrykhou Khalospitia *(TP215): pottery. TCP numbers refer to Pottery Catalogue in Volume 1, Chapter 3.6*

Period	Fct	Type	No.	Weight
Bronze Age	HU	HU	2	185g
Prehistoric Bronze Age	LU	RPO	1	2g
Late Bronze Age to Archaic	HU	HU	2	260g
Cypro-Geometric to Classical	HU	HU	1	175g
	HU	Pit12	2	450g
	HU	WP	3	284g
	LU	LU	2	20g
	LU	LUB04	1	70g TCP700
	LU	RS	1	21g
	LU	WP	3	87g
Cypro-Archaic to Classical	HU	Pit	1	220g
Historical Antiquity (Archaic to Late Roman)	HU	HU	5	965g
	LU	LU	24	484g
	TW	TW	2	12g
Hellenistic	TW	Lag	1	87g TCP699
Hellenistic to Roman	CW	CW	1	3g
Hellenistic to Early Roman	TW	BS	1	5g
Early to Late Roman	Ar	Ti	1	330g
	Ar	TiCA	1	120g
Late Roman	TW	ERSAI	1	30g TCP701
Historical (Archaic to Modern)	HU	HU	1	20g
	LU	LU	2	105g
Medieval to Modern	TW	G	1	12g
Medieval utility period III	U	TtaB	1	10g
Ottoman to Modern I	U	ID04A	1	12g
Modern	TW	TW	1	10g
Unknown	HU	HU	1	50g

Table 2.3. Evrykhou Kamilaries *(TP248): pottery. TCP numbers refer to Pottery Catalogue in Volume 1, Chapter 3.6*

Period	Fct	Type	No.	Weight
Cypro-Archaic to Classical	CW	CW	5	238g TCP708
	HU	HU	1	80g
	LU	BcC	3	62g
	LU	BORC	3	80g
	LU	BORO	3	20g
	LU	LU	5	93g
	LU	WPC	4	78g TCP707
	TW	BORBc	3	30g

paint accents clearly came from large painted jars or jugs (amphorae or hydria) with the typical painted handle tails.

This is the standard form of open-air Archaic and Classical rural sanctuary throughout Cyprus. A very similar example from the northern Troodos is Frangissa, 30 km to the east (Buchholz 1991). There are many other examples in the region with similar material, but where the built structure is not so clear as at Khalospitia (Given and Knapp 2003, 275–76; Karageorghis 1977; Loulloupis 1989).

In a field boundary wall 40 m west of the temenos was some more terracotta sculpture, most notably a foot (collected as TP215.PU02), as well as a tile rim. Another 30 m to the south-west was a possible rock-cut pit, with some sherds of a Hellenistic cooking pot and Roman tile in its vicinity. The rubble lines and rough walls, possibly no more than field boundaries, continue for 100 m to the north-west, north and north-east, though there are minimal artefacts associated with them and no clear structures.

The Archaic cemetery of Evrykhou *Kamilaries* (TP248) lies on a shallow uncultivated spur, 450 m to the south-east. On the west of the spur are ploughed fields gently sloping towards the north, and on the east is a steep incised gully. Immediately to the south is a prominent hill, but otherwise there is a clear view, with Skouriotissa and Morphou Bay visible to the north-west and north. At least 25 tombs have been cut into fossiliferous limestone; one example has a clear dromos and collapsed chamber. They were clearly looted some time ago. There was a good scatter of Archaic pottery of fine quality, some with relatively fresh breaks (Table 2.3). This included Archaic–Classical cookware, Bichrome ware, Plain wares, Black-on-Red ware and Cypriot White Painted ware. The material was freshly exposed and in many cases joins were identified. Bichrome wares were common in the assemblage.

2.5 Roman Farmstead at Linou *Vrysi tou Haji Christophi*

Vrysi tou Haji Christophi (TP201) is a natural spring probably controlled by north- and west-trending faults in the Lower Pillow Lava formation. The association of the Roman farmstead with the spring could indicate a long-lived water source for the area. The spring is covered with dense stands of rushes, myrtle and jujube. This made it impossible to search the spring for structures or cultural materials. Forty metres to the north lie two small structures, with a substantial concentration of Roman tile and pottery fragments (Fig. 2.3; TP202).

Fig. 2.3. Roman farmstead at Linou Vrysi tou Haji Christophi, *viewed from the spring (Michael Given)*

Table 2.4. Linou Vrysi tou Haji Christophi *(TS18: SU2161–65): pottery. TCP numbers refer to Pottery Catalogue in Volume 1, Chapter 3.6*

Fct	Type	No.	Weight
Historical Antiquity (Archaic to Late Roman)			
Fct	*Type*	*No.*	*Weight*
HU	HU	12	856g
LU	LU	5	73g
TW	TW	1	1g
Hellenistic to Roman			
Fct	*Type*	*No.*	*Weight*
CW	CW	2	10g
Tr	Am07	1	19g
Tr	Mav01	1	105g
Early to Late Roman			
Fct	*Type*	*No.*	*Weight*
Ar	Ti	5	945g
HU	HU	4	400g
TW	ARS	1	1g
Late Roman			
Fct	*Type*	*No.*	*Weight*
Ar	TiSk01	3	335g
Ar	TiSk02	17	4.485kg TCP373
Ar	TiSk05	1	650g
Ar	TiSkC01	4	181g
Ar	TiSkC03	4	805g
CW	CW	2	9g
Tr	LR1	2	36g
TW	LRC	1	5g
Historical (Archaic to Modern)			
Fct	*Type*	*No.*	*Weight*
CW	CW	1	9g
HU	HU	2	87g
Medieval-Frankish			
Fct	*Type*	*No.*	*Weight*
TW	CGS05	1	2g
Unknown			
Fct	*Type*	*No.*	*Weight*
Un	Un	1	135g

Six Survey Units were sufficient to investigate the surrounding pottery scatter (TS18; Plate 2.4). Taken with the adjoining Survey Units from Transect TT492000E, the earliest specifically dated material in the area surrounding the farmstead was Late Roman, in substantial quantities (Table 2.4). This was accompanied by smaller quantities of material that could only be dated to the relatively broad periods of Roman, Hellenistic/Roman or Historical Antiquity. Taking all Hellenistic and Roman pottery together, the densest Survey Units were on the eastern edge of the farmstead and between there and the stream, with 15.1 and 9.0 sherds/100 m^2 respectively. On the other sides the density was between 1 and 4 sherds/100 m^2, and beyond 50 m from the farmstead cultural materials dropped off completely.

From the same area came a fragment of a millstone (discussed below), but no chipped stone or slag. The tile count, by contrast, was substantial, peaking at 70 fragments in one Survey Unit; its distribution pattern was identical to that of the Hellenistic to Roman pottery. All these finds have parallels in the Late Roman material from Skouriotissa. The only definite post-Roman piece was a single sherd of sgraffito.

The structures themselves (Fig. 2.4) lie on a small rocky spur above the stream. This spur forms a narrow crescent of slightly steeper ground between two large fields that slope gently down toward the gully to the south-east. Much of the crescent is covered in impenetrable patches of wild jujube (*Zizyphus lotus*). Between these patches was a covering of thick, coarse grass and thistles. One rectangular structure is very clear, measuring approximately 8 × 6 m (PU01; see Table 2.5). Immediately north of it is another substantial area of rubble and tile fragments, which almost certainly represents another structure, although it is obscured beneath an impenetrable jujube bush (PU04; PU06). We carried out some rudimentary clearing and cleaning of obvious structural remains to facilitate the mapping, which was done in the course of a single day.

PU04, a small depression surrounded by rubble, was especially rich in tiles (10 within less than 2 m^2), with

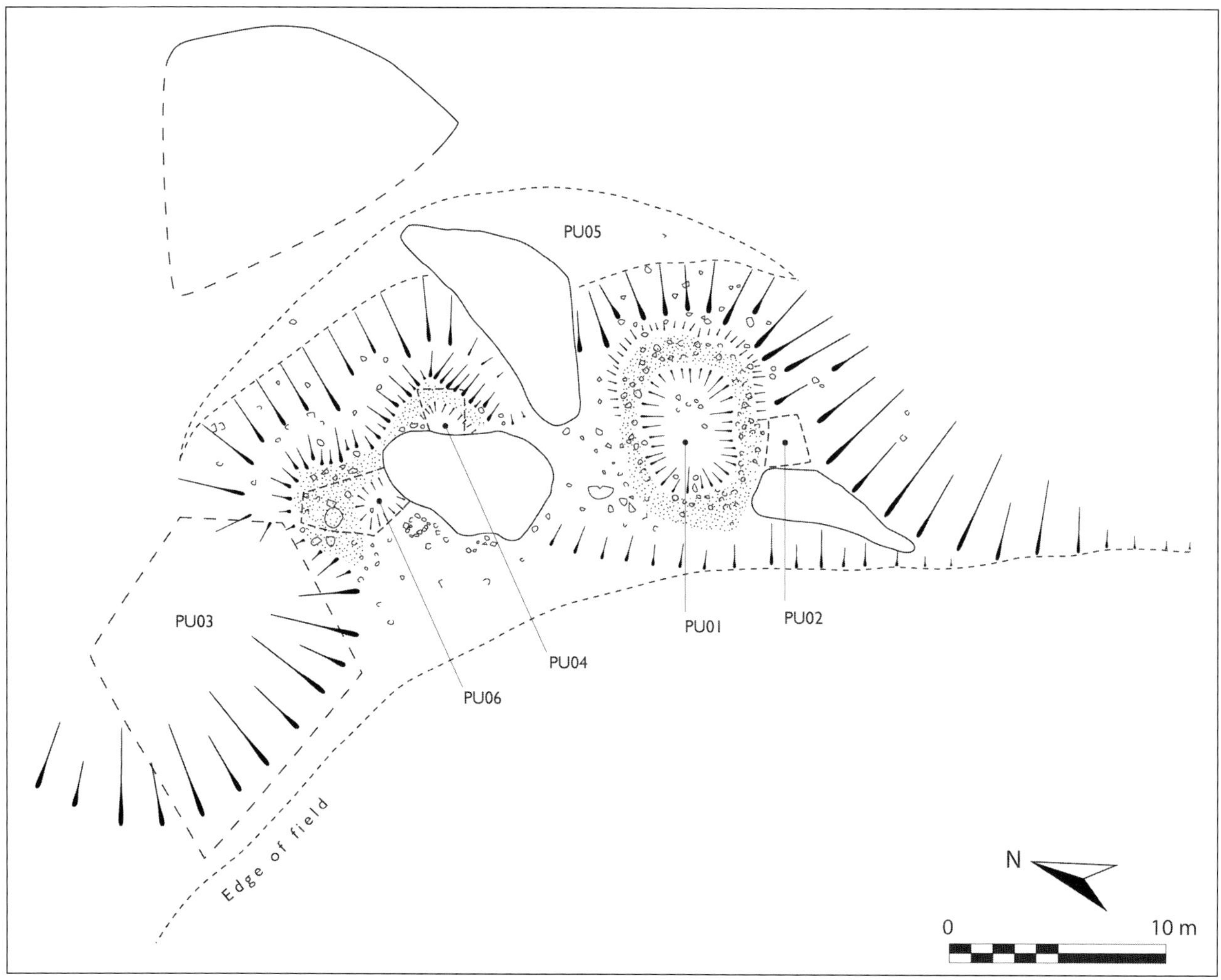

Fig. 2.4. Linou Vrysi tou Haji Christophi *(TP202): map of Roman farmstead (Julie Candy, finalised by Jean Humbert)*

Table 2.5. Linou Vrysi tou Haji Christophi *(TP202): description of POSI Units*

PU01	Rectangular structure dug into slope. Walls made from mixture of large pieces of bedrock and smooth river boulders. Interior full of rubble. No clear wall faces discernable.
PU02	Small rectangular area of rubble; tumble from the walls of PU01.
PU03	Smooth area running down the slope between the two fields.
PU04	Small depression surrounded by stones. Much of the soil was fine with few inclusions, suggesting that it was wind-blown and had settled since the collapse of the structure. Many tile fragments.
PU05	Strip along bottom edge; the final shallow slope before the cultivated field.
PU06	Small, flat area with ground stone.
PU07	1-m strip at edge of cultivated field.

many large fragments. Initially we thought the rubble might represent walls in situ, but there were substantial amounts of soil around and between them. The quantity of large tile fragments and the depression likely indicate a collapsed roof, with the tiles atop the building rubble.

The architecture of the site must have been substantial, as several fragments of water pipe were collected. The pipes differ slightly from the single fragment collected at Skouriotissa, but the diameter is the same and the fabric is very similar. The transport amphorae (LR1, Mav1, Am7) are all types identified at Skouriotissa, Ayia Marina *Mavrovouni* and Xyliatos *Litharkies*. A variety of Late Roman Table Wares is represented, mostly Cypriot Red Slip but also some Phocaean and African fragments. In total only three sherds (one sgraffito) may belong to the post-Roman period and there is no conclusive evidence for occupation before the Late Roman period.

As well as pottery, all of the units collected (PU01–07) had large amounts of tiles, as measured both by sherd count (37 out of 96 fragments) and by weight (Table 2.6); there are a further 34 tiles from the surrounding Survey Units (Table 2.3). All of these figures refer to our representative collection, rather than the total number discovered. PU06 on the eastern slope of the knoll had the highest concentration, including a large fragment of a

Table 2.6. Linou Vrysi tou Haji Christophi *(TP201–202): pottery. TCP numbers refer to Pottery Catalogue in Volume 1, Chapter 3.6*

Historical Antiquity (Archaic to Late Roman)			
Fct	*Type*	*No.*	*Weight*
HU	HU	16	1.209kg
LU	LU	15	166g
Tr	Am	3	345g
TW	TW	1	5g

Hellenistic to Roman			
Fct	*Type*	*No.*	*Weight*
TW	RS	1	2g

Late Hellenistic to Early Roman			
Fct	*Type*	*No.*	*Weight*
TW	CS	3	20g TCP689

Early to Late Roman			
Fct	*Type*	*No.*	*Weight*
Ar	Ti	10	2.965kg
Ar	TiP	1	725g
CW	CW	5	22g
LU	LU	1	10g
Tr	Am13	2	1.8kg TCP691
CW	CWCR02c	1	9g TCP688
CW	CWPDh	1	6g TCP692
HU	Mor	1	380g TCP690
LU	LU	3	24g
Tr	LR1	2	25g

Late Roman			
Fct	*Type*	*No.*	*Weight*
Ar	TiP	11	3.885kg
Ar	TiSk02	4	6.43kg TCP693
Ar	TiSk03	3	575g
Ar	TiSkC01	4	491g
Ar	TiSkC04	3	180g
CW	CW	2	5g

Roman to Modern			
Fct	*Type*	*No.*	*Weight*
Ar	Ti	1	39g

Historical (Archaic to Modern)			
Fct	*Type*	*No.*	*Weight*
HU	HU	1	19g
LU	LU	1	10g

Fig. 2.5. Linou Vrysi tou Haji Christophi *(TP202): millstone (Michael Given)*

well-preserved Late Roman spouted mortarium (bowl for the grinding and preparation of food) and a Dhiorios pot rim of similar date. An almost complete tile was collected from PU03. Only one tile fragment did not have a completely flat reverse, which is indicative of their Late Roman date and contrasts completely to the tiles found at Xyliatos *Litharkies*. Generally the Table Wares collected appear to be Early Roman, and there is no secure identification of Late Roman Table Wares on the knoll itself.

Between the two structures is a large gabbro millstone 95 cm in diameter with a square socket 11 cm wide and 5 cm deep (Fig. 2.5). There was also a large basalt quern (over 50 cm^2) in PU06. Another broken millstone was found in the field immediately to the east of the farmstead (SU2162). This is particularly interesting as it is made of highly vesicular basalt, a material unavailable on Cyprus and imported from the Late Bronze Age onwards for use as grinding equipment (Elliot 1985, 313). We also observed several building stones of which at least one had a square corner cut into it, and a small piece of slag.

The material collected at the Roman farmstead is chronologically consistent with that collected at Skouriotissa and dated to the Late Roman period. There is also some evidence for Late Hellenistic to Early Roman activity similar to that seen at Ayia Marina *Mavrovouni*. Post-Roman material is sparse, and there is none round the actual buildings.

There is a broad range of pottery functions, with the exception of storage, as there are no pithos fragments. Generally the number of Heavy Utility vessels appears to be much lower than at Ayia Marina *Mavrovouni*, Xyliatos *Litharkies* and Katydhata *Pano Limna*. This may have resulted from the thick rubble in PU04. The majority of Heavy Utility vessels would have been inside the building and thus lying beneath the collapsed material. This scenario would also explain the absence of Late Roman table wares on the knoll and the very high number of tiles coming from the collapsed roof. The number of tile fragments is conspicuous. To some extent it confirms the picture gathered from other sites in the Survey Area (Litharkies, Mavrovouni, Skouriotissa), which indicates that tiles were used for several types of building, including some domestic ones. Unlike these other sites, the three grinding stones provide ample evidence for the agricultural function of the site. Even if the same types of pottery have been identified at mining sites, the proportional distribution of pottery functions at Vrysi tou Haji Christophi appears to be unique. This is partly explained, however, by the unique state of preservation at the site.

Vrysi tou Haji Christophi is our best example of a Roman farmstead, as defined by the extant architecture, the pottery, the millstones, and the halo of material round it. It was a relatively small working unit based on one or two structures, and presumably produced olive oil and perhaps cereals and other crops. The results of the block survey show a classic 'halo' pattern of material in the area immediately around the farmstead, falling off within 50 m (Bevan 2002; Pettegrew 2001). In this case the halo is more likely to derive from dumping and post-

Table 2.7. Linou Vrysi tou Haji Christophi *(TP202): average weight of sherds collected from surrounding Survey Units, compared to Sanidhia and Katalasharis on the Koutraphas plateau*

	Vrysi	**Sanidhia**	**Katalasharis**
Architectural	217 g	55 g	105 g
Other	46 g	18 g	19 g

depositional spread than from manuring, as the sherds are, on average, more than twice as large as the those collected at Sanidhia and Katalasharis on the Koutraphas plateau (Table 2.7; Chapter 2.15). The high number of tiles on the knoll reflects the post-depositional history of the site, but the units surveyed around the knoll also produced a proportionally higher number of tiles, which may indicate that the 'halo' is largely post-depositional. Phoukasa, however, a farmstead 900 m to the north-west, also produced a proportionally higher number of tiles than other sites in the Survey Area.

Vrysi tou Haji Christophi may have formed part of a network of other similar farmsteads, also interacting with local medium-sized settlements such as Lithosourka (TP216), and with the broader system encompassing the town of Soloi and the massive copper production enterprise at Skouriotissa (see also the next two sections). The structure itself is probably well preserved under the thick collapse and presents a regionally unique opportunity to study a Roman farmstead within a reasonably intact ancient landscape.

2.6 Roman Farmstead and Cistern at Petra *Phoukasa*

The Roman farmstead at Phoukasa (TS20) lies 900 m north-west of Vrysi tou Haji Christophi, and is clearly situated to make best use of local natural resources. Two streams are located nearby, though as the farmstead maintained a large water cistern, their output may have been seasonal or occasionally non-drinkable. During our survey, for example, the stream flowing through a gully on the north-west was contaminated by the mining operations at Skouriotissa. The farmstead is located on a Pleistocene fluvial terrace, now a ridgetop, along the west bank of the Ayii Saranta stream, near the base of Phoukasa hill. Soil cover and sediments are thin over the Lower Pillow Lava formation. The contact between the Lower and Upper Pillow Lava formations, typically a telling sign where ore-bearing rocks might be found, underlies it.

The farmstead itself included several architectural features (TP221; Petra *Phoukasa*). A circular cistern, c. 2.5 m in diameter and c. 1.5 m in its greatest surviving depth, was dug into the western part of the ridgetop. Although mostly worn away, some plaster still coated its stone lining. Just to the north is a circular depression filled in with bedrock chunks and many tile fragments, which is most likely a collapsed structure. It is unsurprising to find a cistern conveniently placed next to a tile roof to collect the water runoff. In the centre of the ridgetop was a small patch of concrete paving, with the small-pebbled matrix characteristic of the Roman period. The ridgetop was terraced at some point in the past, which (as with the Roman settlement at Pano Limna) probably facilitated the building of structures.

The farmstead can be dated by its abundant pottery, and characteristically for the Atsas area this contrasts with the almost total absence of pottery in the surrounding area (Plate 2.4). For this reason, the entire pottery assemblage on the ridgetop, almost all of which dates to a single period, can be associated with the farmstead (Table 2.8). It represents a full array of functions, including architectural, cooking, Heavy and Light Utility wares, Table Wares, and a single fragment of a LR1 transport amphora. All functions are represented among the Late Roman pottery, which is the main phase of occupation here. A small collection of pottery from the Early Roman period, however, suggests that the later settlement probably replaced one that existed a few centuries earlier. This consists of Table Wares only, which makes it impossible to speculate further as to the function of the earlier phase of occupation. As with the farmstead at Vrysi tou Haji Christophi (TS18), the proportion of tiles to pottery is very high compared to other Late Roman settlements in the Survey Area.

Table 2.8. Petra Phoukasa *(TS20: SU2187): pottery. TCP numbers refer to Pottery Catalogue in Volume 1, Chapter 3.6*

Fct	*Type*	*No.*	*Weight*
Historical Antiquity (Archaic to Late Roman)			
Ar	TiP	10	3.025kg
HU	HU	22	1.74kg
LU	LU	14	121g
TW	TW	3	10g
Late Hellenistic to Early Roman			
TW	Sig	3	11g TCP391
Early Roman			
TW	CS12	1	10g
Early to Late Roman			
Ar	Ti	6	1.335kg
Ar	TiCS	3	540g TCP389
CW	CW	17	101g
Late Roman			
Ar	TiSkC01	8	1.2kg
Ar	TiSkC03	4	625g
CW	CWPR06	1	11g TCP388
HU	HUR10b	1	80g TCP387
LU	LU	1	10g
Tr	LR1	1	14g
TW	CRS	3	45g
TW	LRC	1	4g
Roman to Modern			
HU	HUC	1	400g TCP390
Historical (Archaic to Modern)			
HU	HU	1	15g
LU	LU	2	15g

Eight chipped stone artefacts were collected from the ridgetop where the farmstead is located (SU2187): one amorphous flake core; three blank fragments; a chunk; and three tools. The tools consist of a notch, a flake with rectilinear retouch, and an unretouched utilized flake. All of these (except the flake with rectilinear retouch) are made from local jasper, which is consistent with the material from Roman-period sites such as Skouriotissa *Pseftas* in the northern Karkotis Valley (TS13; Chapter 3.13). The tool with rectilinear retouch is made on translucent Lefkara chert, a material not locally available in the TAESP area. The presence of flat invasive retouch on one lateral edge and the well prepared facetted butt are features that suggest an early prehistoric date for this object, implying that this artefact is intrusive to a sample that would otherwise be at home in the Roman period.

In terms of its architecture and ceramic assemblage, Phoukasa bears many similarities to the farmstead at Vrysi tou Haji Christophi (TP202; see above). The material collected is consistent with it, but there are some differences that may result from a different post-depositional history. There was a much greater depth of soil here, as evidenced by more complete remnants of this Pleistocene depositional unit present nearby. Another similarity is the appearance of Late Hellenistic to Early Roman Table Wares, but no other pottery securely datable to the earlier period. Phoukasa is clearly part of a Late Roman network of farmsteads linked to the intensive contemporary exploitation of mineral resources at Skouriotissa mine, which begins just 100 m to the west.

2.7 Diachronic Analysis of the Atsas Valley

The distinguishing factor in the pottery distribution of the Atsas Valley as a whole is the relative dearth of pottery in most areas, punctuated by discrete concentrations. This stands in stark contrast to the Karkotis River Valley to its west, where there are varying, yet continually present, quantities of pottery. The lack of cultural materials is clearly not due to erosion or other processes that have removed them from the landscape. The other striking feature of the valley, particularly its western edge, is the exploitation of its abundant sources of red jasper. This section reviews the broader landscape of the valley in chronological order.

Prehistoric There is a clear Chalcolithic and Bronze Age presence in the north-east of the area, between the Ottoman–Modern settlement of Lemonas and the Atsas river 350 m to its north. The contrast with the areas to the west shows that this scatter of pottery and lithics is centred on the deep soils of fluvial terraces along the Atsas river (Plate 2.4). The densities are light, never rising above 0.9 sherds/100 m^2, but the concentration in the northern half of the eastern transect is unmistakeable.

Five of these Survey Units (SU2171–74, SU2177) contain Chalcolithic (Red Monochrome and Red-on-White), Late Chalcolithic/Philia (Red Monochrome/Red Polished hybrid), and Prehistoric Bronze Age (Red Polished) pottery, at low but significant levels. The Chalcolithic wares were generally in poor condition as a result of their soft firing. The Red Monochrome/Red Polished hybrid ware was harder and better preserved, as was the classic Red Polished. The combination of material of these three periods is interesting, as it contrasts with the pattern in the Karkotis Valley, where the chronological phases are geographically separated (Late Chalcolithic/Philia at Koutroullis, Middle Bronze Age at Laonarka). This area also contained evidence for the Protohistoric Bronze Age, including low densities of White Slip ware and pithos sherds. The White Slip sherds were too worn to assign a specific type, while the pithos sherds were consistent with a date of Late Cypriot II, possibly late in that period.

Two gabbro ground stone mortars were collected in the northernmost Survey Unit of the transect running past Lemonas (SU2171), and 13 chipped stone artefacts were recovered from the Survey Units running 300 m on each side of the settlement. All but three chipped stone artefacts were made of local jasper. These included four fragments of knapping debris, a core trimming element, two amorphous flake cores and a utilized flake tool. The three pieces made on non-local Lefkara cherts consisted of an unworked chip, an unretouched utilized flake and a *dhoukani* flake. The utilized flake is quite small and would not be inconsistent with the sample of utilized tools collected from Phlasou *Koutroullis* (Chapter 3.5). It is, however, a poorly diagnostic type, like the sample as a whole, and although it does not contradict association with the prehistoric sherds collected from Lemonas and its vicinity, the chipped stone provides little information that can be specifically assigned to any particular period.

Iron Age and Roman The most striking evidence from the Iron Age consists of the Archaic rural sanctuary of Khalospitia (TP215) and the Archaic cemetery at Kamilaries, with at least 25 tombs (TP248) (Chapter 2.4). The other substantial concentration of Iron Age material lies on the opposite, southern side of the river Atsas, in the area of the later settlement of Lemonas. Unlike the prehistoric material between the settlement and the Atsas River to the north, the Iron Age pottery is concentrated immediately round Lemonas, peaking at 1.6 sherds/100 m^2 for all Iron Age pottery immediately adjacent to the settlement, with a thinner scatter to its south. This material includes some figurine fragments, possibly associated with the sanctuary at Khalospitia across the river, or else perhaps from another sanctuary or tombs closer to Lemonas.

The Iron Age pottery recovered from the Lemonas area includes both Light and Heavy Utility vessels, along with a single fragment of a transport amphora. The majority of the pieces are undecorated body sherds. The few decorated pieces come from White Painted, Black Slip, Black on Red and Red Slip wares, dating the pottery scatter to the Late Geometric–Classical era. Three figurine fragments were found in the same area: an Archaic–Classical human figure fragment with black paint; an unidentified Geometric–Classical piece; and an amorphous piece with an incised 'x' whose fabric looks more Bronze Age than Iron Age.

The substantial Roman settlement of Petra *Lithosourka* (TP216) lies above the north-east bank of the Atsas River, 750 m north of Vrysi tou Haji Christophi and 800 m east of Phoukasa. The remains are densely covered with overgrowth, and consist essentially of an extensive area of rubble piles, tile and pottery, some 200 m in diameter. The site lies astride a riser between strath terraces of the Atsas, where the river had cut down to bedrock. The upper terrace is Late Pleistocene and the lower of later age, quite possibly Early Holocene. Such a location would have avoided building on valuable agricultural land, as well as giving an unhindered view of the eastern plain below Skouriotissa; any farther upstream and the rugged Pleistocene fluvial fan terrain would impede this view. The material continues down the slope to the south as far as the river Atsas. This is clearly not the core of the site however, and seems to consist mostly of a 'halo' of pottery dumped outside the settlement, as well as an area of more recent terracing close to the river.

The site is outside the Intensive Survey Zone, but the pottery observed there shared the most important characteristics of Phoukasa and Vrysi tou Haji Christophi. All functions were represented and the date is mainly Late Roman with a small assemblage of Late Hellenistic to Early Roman Table Wares. Even though a single fragment of a LR1 amphora was found at each of these three sites, only Lithosourka had fragments of the transport amphora type dumped at Skouriotissa (Chapter 3.12). Only rarely was this type of amphora collected in the rest of the Survey Area, which may reflect a close connection between Lithosourka and the Skouriotissa mine.

The pottery distribution across the Atsas area in the Hellenistic to Roman period shows clear concentrations at Phoukasa and Vrysi tou Haji Christophi (Plate 2.4). In addition, there is a light scatter round Lemonas, peaking at 2.4 sherds/100 m^2 close to the settlement, and trailing off to the north and south. This is a similar picture to that we get for the Iron Age, and suggests there might well be earlier structures under the ruined Ottoman–Modern houses of Lemonas. The pottery that can be dated more precisely trends towards Late Roman rather than Hellenistic or Early Roman. Other than this there is a very light scatter of Hellenistic–Roman pottery in the west of the Atsas area: eight Survey Units have very light scatters of less than 0.5 sherds/100 m^2, and another reaches 2.9. Given that this area is highly dissected, this might be the result of later erosion, or it may suggest non-intensive agriculture in the general area.

When all this material is combined with Roman farmsteads at Vrysi tou Haji Christophi (Chapter 2.5) and Phoukasa (2.6), it is clear that the Atsas area had an organized if not very intensive system of agricultural production during the Roman period (see also Volume 1, Chapter 5.3). Similar systems with networks of farmsteads are known, for example, in the hinterland of Roman Kourion (Swiny and Mavromatis 2000), and in the wide fluvial plain and smaller valleys around Roman Tamassos (Given and Knapp 2003, 199–200, 310). This type of system contrasts with the much more continuous and intensive cultivation seen in the Karkotis Valley (Chapter 3).

Judging by its proximity and the easy communication route, the Atsas area was dependent on the town-kingdom of Soloi, however remote it may seem today. Soloi clearly had a substantial urban population and import/export trade to support (des Gagniers and Tinh 1985). Even more demanding, however, was the massive copper production that took place immediately to the west of Phoukasa farmstead. Given the amount of labour required for smelting operations at Skouriotissa alone (Chapter 3.12), the supporting agricultural production must have been large-scale and intensive, and these farmsteads are certainly contemporary with the smelting. The presence of a medium-sized village at Lithosourka suggests a relatively complex hierarchical system of exchange, with middle-ranking settlements redistributing food onwards either to Soloi or possibly direct to Skouriotissa. There is more evidence for this system farther east in the plains area, and a rather different system within the well-watered and intensively cultivated Karkotis Valley.

Lithics One of the most distinctive features of the north-west of the Atsas area, immediately adjacent to the Roman farmstead of Phoukasa, is the abundance of red jasper outcrops in the pillow basalts. The ridgetop on which the farmstead is situated possesses poorer quality jasper. Interestingly, many of the culturally modified jasper cores and flakes found around the farmstead (SU2187) were browner in colour and of a high quality. They may have been carried up to the ridgetop from one of the other local jasper sources in nearby gullies.

At the base of the spoil heaps of Skouriotissa mine, 80 m to the north of the farmstead, is a series of abundant red jasper outcrops in a gully (TP237; Petra *Phoukasa*). Four POSI units (PU01–04) were collected from the southern slopes of this gully. Another jasper outcrop 150 m south-east and downslope of the farmstead produced abundant red jasper of high quality (TP236; Petra *Phoukasa*). Here we observed an entire *chaîne opératoire* of tool production, from cores to flakes to tiny debitage. We collected one area (PU01) directly downslope of TP236. Although the stone knapping activities cannot yet be dated securely because of a lack of typological specificity, this, undoubtedly, is a favoured area for the local production of chipped stone tools.

Both TP236 and TP237 can be described as lithic workshops located at raw material outcrops. The chipped stone material from both samples is exclusively local jasper and is dominated by artefacts associated with flake production: abundant cores (including a core trimming element at TP236); unworked flake blanks; and knapping debris (Table 2.9). An unretouched utilized flake is the only tool from TP236, while there are five such utilized flakes

Table 2.9. Petra Phoukasa *(TP236–37): lithic category counts and percentages of chipped stone categories*

	TP236		TP237	
	Count	*%*	*Count*	*%*
Cores	23	12%	18	21%
Blanks	75	38%	8	9%
Debris	99	50%	53	62%
Tools	1	1%	7	8%
Total	**198**	**100%**	**86**	**100%**

and two flake scrapers from TP237. All of these items represent a core technology consistent with the sample collected from Petra *Phoukasa* (TS20) and other sites dominated by jasper and dated by pottery to the Roman period. Only one ground stone tool (a grinder made on gabbro) was recovered from TP237. As such both of these jasper workshops reflect the utilization of localized raw materials characteristic of the Atsas area generally.

Other less productive jasper outcrops and occasional flakes and cores were found sporadically across the rest of the area (e.g. TP206, TP207). These included two unworked jasper flakes, a flake of non-local translucent Lefkara chert, a jasper chunk, and a tested jasper flake core. These single finds, though broadly consistent with the chipped stone materials elsewhere in the valley, particularly the use of local jasper, are not diagnostic to any specific period.

Medieval–Modern The most striking feature of the Medieval–Modern periods in the Atsas Valley is Lemonas village, the remains of a seasonal settlement from the Late Ottoman and Modern periods (TP209; Evrykhou *Tanayies*). The structures that remain partially intact have foundations of river boulders, stone and potsherd chinking, and mudbrick superstructures. The extent of the extant mudbrick walls suggests a relatively recent date of abandonment, probably in the mid-20th century. Prehistoric ground stone tools were incorporated into the structures, presumably taken from the Chalcolithic–Bronze Age settlement that was situated immediately to the north of the village or even underneath it (see Chapter 2.10 for other examples). Structurally, the settlement has the same organic and complex plan as the core of Kato Koutraphas *Mandres* (Chapter 2.10); either there were no outlying structures, in contrast to Mandres, or they were destroyed during more recent cultivation.

In 1963 aerial photographs of this area, several threshing floors encircle the village. Although they no longer exist their paving stones seem, as a result of cultivation practices, to have been pushed into rubble piles or strewn throughout adjacent fields. There was a single *dhoukani* flake from a Survey Unit 150 m north of the settlement. This lack of *dhoukani* flakes associated with surviving or destroyed threshing floors is not uncommon in the Survey Area, suggesting that sledges were often curated and stored away from the threshing floors.

The earliest post-Byzantine material from close to the settlement is a single piece of 14th–15th-century sgraffito 150 m to the south, though there are further fragments in another broad fluvial terrace 1100 m to the south-east. For all periods afterwards there is a very slight concentration immediately south-west of the settlement, never rising over 0.8 sherds/100 m^2 for a specific period (18th–mid-20th century), or 3.2 for all Medieval–Modern periods together. The same transect shows a gradual fall-off both north and south, giving a clear 'halo' from manuring and dumping of about 500 m north–south. The main area cultivated was clearly limited to the fluvial terrace.

What is most striking about the Medieval–Modern pottery from Lemonas is the lack of Cooking Ware: it is very largely Heavy Utility and Light Utility, with some Table Ware. The absence of Cooking Ware may be an expression of the seasonal nature of the settlement, with a much more limited range of cooking activity during the periods of cultivation and harvest when people stayed there.

Judging by a nearby transect, there was a similarly cultivated fluvial terrace 1100 m to the south-east, farther up the Atsas River and on the opposite side. This terrace has a similar square area, and has similarly low but continuous levels of pottery from the same periods. A bedrock hill in the centre of the area has a series of anthropogenic terraces on it, although with so little soil it seems unlikely that they were agricultural in purpose (TP131). There is a clearly artificial cut in the bedrock, and a large number of river cobbles that must have been brought up to build a structure. Each of the terraces or platforms must have had a building or possibly threshing floor associated with it. Again we see the use of a rock outcrop for buildings, saving the tillable soils for crops. This is not a settlement on the same scale as Lemonas, but there is a clear focus on these pockets of fluvial land within the wider, deeply incised landscape of the pillow lavas. Throughout the rest of this deeply incised and fragmented Atsas area west of Lemonas, only two isolated Survey Units contained a single Medieval sherd.

In the north-west of the Atsas area there is a different type of evidence for Medieval–Modern activity, in the form of two watermills (BU0053, BU0059) on the Ayia Saranta stream, a tributary of the river Atsas. Both of these use water diverted from the Karkotis drainage (Chapter 2.2) that was also used to power the three 'pink mills' (BU0002–04; Chapter 3.10). The grain to feed them likely came from the thickly settled and intensively cultivated Karkotis Valley, rather than from the very sparsely settled and cultivated Atsas Valley.

The penstock and leat of Mylos tou Ahmed Agha (BU0053) are still visible, but the bulldozed dirt track has destroyed what may have been an arch carrying the water channel to the penstock. The penstock is two-tiered on the north-east and south-west sides, and four-tiered on the south-east face (Fig. 2.6). Construction material is of irregular basalt rubble with some coursing using large stones as edging at the top of each tier. There is basalt and limestone chinking in the plaster. The penstock base measures 4.2 × 7.9 m, and the leat is 11.5 m long by 1.45 m wide externally; the internal channel width is 0.55 m. The section demolished by the road is 9.5 m long; the leat

Fig. 2.6. West face of Mylos tou Ahmed Agha (BU0053) (Chris Parks)

curves and is wider at the highest gradient of the hill before it straightens in the approach to the penstock. The owner was a Turkish Cypriot named Ahmed Agha; according to the miller of the Evrykhou mill, this is one of seven mills that was in Ahmed Agha's ownership.

Just 50 m downstream is a second of Ahmed Agha's mills (BU0059). This is a multiple level mill of irregular coursed basalt construction with an exterior lime plaster. It is 10 m in length, 1.57 m wide and 2.3 m high. The side walls of the leat have crumbled, leaving the channel floor as the highest level of construction at 0.8 m above the penstock height. There is some tile and white sandstone chinking in the plaster. The penstock has a mostly decayed upper chute, which could have been of the hopper type. The outflow is submerged in earth, and the millhouse is c. 10 m farther north-west; only the south-west corner of the river boulder courses is visible, as well as the scant outline of the west wall. Special features of this mill included an undatable quern, located on the north-west side of the water race, 8 m from the penstock. A niche on the north face of the penstock is in the shape of an irregular half-sphere. An incised basalt stone was found on the north-east corner of the front face of the penstock.

Just to the south-east of the Atsas Intensive Survey Zone, 1.5 km south of Lemonas village, is a colonial period bridge with two arches resting on abutments and made from regular cut sandstone blocks (TP004; Evrykhou *Atsas*). The bridge is 25 m long and 4 m wide, and the road that crosses it is 2.8 m in width. The bridge runs from north-east to south-west across the deep channel of the Atsas River. According to an engineer's report of 1901, the bridge was difficult to construct because of the high banks of the river, and the builders needed to cut deeply into the bank on the Evrykhou side of the river. The stone for this and the other bridges along the same stretch of road came from the quarries of Koronia, 4.2 km to the north-east, and Phoukassa, part of Skouriotissa mine, 4.0 km north-west (SA1/1922/1899, Red 79). The role British roads and bridges played in the colonial rule of Cyprus during the 20th century is discussed in Volume 1, Chapter 3.13.

Geobotany We carried out geobotanical analysis of two POSIs where the vegetation had been relatively little disturbed: the Roman farmstead of Linou *Vrysi tou Haji Christophi* (TP202; geobotanical unit NU052); and the more extensive Roman settlement of Petra *Lithosourka* (TP216; geobotanical unit NU053). These were used to generate light signatures for the supervised classification of ASTER satellite imagery (see Volume 1, Chapter 2.11 for methodology). The imagery classification was deliberately limited to this area in order to extrapolate the chosen indicator areas within a geomorphologically homogeneous area (Urwin 2003, 300).

The vegetation indicators from TP202, when extrapolated over the Atsas Intensive Survey Area and its immediate surroundings, show a distinct correlation with recorded POSIs lying in uncultivated ground (Plate 2.5). This is particularly clear with TP248 (Archaic cemetery), TP208 (slag and pottery), TP206 and TP207 (lithics scatters), and TP201 (spring). The Archaic sanctuary (TP215) is not predicted, probably because it has been ploughed both inside and outside the walls. There is also some close grouping with a number of other POSIs, and some more examples are indicated in unsurveyed areas.

The vegetation indicators from the quadrat at TP216, when extrapolated over the Atsas Valley, show little correlation with recorded POSI sites, though they do suggest the substantial size of TP216 itself (Plate 2.6). The wider extrapolation over unsurveyed areas, however, may indicate the existence of similar sites to TP216 in areas within the green line buffer zone and in the batha-dominated area in the north-central part of the Survey Area.

Given the likelihood of a substantial network of Late Roman farmsteads and settlements in the Soloi hinterland, and their potentially excellent survival in the relatively undisturbed Buffer Zone, it would be well worth checking these predicted sites and further refining the indicators. Because of the inaccessible nature of much of the Buffer Zone and its immediate surroundings, that will have to wait for a political settlement. Given the very substantial area covered by the Buffer Zone across the island, however, this could be an invaluable tool for the cultural resource management of its enormously rich archaeology.

Conclusion One of the most interesting aspects of the Atsas Valley Intensive Survey Zone lies in its environmental contrast to the adjacent Karkotis Valley to the west, and how this plays out in different periods. For the Chalcolithic period and Bronze Age there is no real difference in the cultural landscape. In both areas there are individual pockets of settlement in the Chalcolithic period (Koutroullis and Lemonas), and a much wider spread of material in the Early Bronze Age with specific focuses, in the case of the Atsas Valley a presumed settlement near Lemonas. In the Roman period, the need for intensive and large-scale agricultural and copper production produces a much stronger contrast between the two areas. The abundance of water and the extent of irrigated, arable soil in the Karkotis Valley allow for dense settlement and continuous agricultural production. The Atsas Valley, by contrast, which is no farther from the mines and Soloi, is limited to a network of isolated farmsteads, about 1 km apart, with occasional larger settlements presumably functioning as redistribution points. The Medieval to Modern period is not dissimilar to the Roman period, with single isolated settlements on patchy remnants of fluvial terraces, in contrast to the dense estates and villages of the extensive, preserved fluvial terraces of the Karkotis Valley.

2.8 Mandres Intensive Survey Zone: Introduction and Overview

The core of the Mandres Intensive Survey Zone is the ruined satellite settlement of Kato Koutraphas *Mandres* (TS07), abandoned in the mid-20th century. Our research there was an interdisciplinary effort that combined structural analysis of the surviving mudbrick and stone structures, examination of the manipulation of the fluvial terraces, analysis of pottery and chipped stone, and extensive interviews with people from associated villages who remembered using Mandres. Of particular interest was the role of this satellite settlement in growing and processing cereals for mountain villages, and in providing a base for goatherds and shepherds outside their villages. The large number of threshing floors and goat pens, along with its agglomerated core and dispersed structures on the periphery, made material remains at Mandres of great interest.

Investigating the surrounding area was an integral part of our research on the settlement of Mandres (Plate 2.7). A central concern was the way in which the settlement exploited its hinterland, whether for cultivation, grazing or foraging. Communication between Mandres and its users' own villages was also important, and is in clear opposition to the main road and stone bridge built by the British colonial power at the beginning of the 20th century. The surface pottery also gave us some very useful information about the time depth and predecessors of the settlement.

We can also see glimpses of the settlement and land use patterns of earlier periods, in the areas of well-preserved surface between the incision caused by the gullies and the manipulation of the fluvial terraces in and around the Mandres settlement. A small-scale but very distinct Prehistoric and Protohistoric Bronze Age settlement at Kato Koutraphas *Mandroudhes* (TP239) has a light halo of pottery suggesting land use within a kilometre radius, and there might have been another such settlement north-east of Mandres. There is a substantial shift in the Iron Age and Roman period, with what seems to be the main centre of activity largely obliterated by Mandres itself.

The Mandres Intensive Survey Zone lies at the foot of the Troodos Mountains, here represented by steep slopes on the Sheeted Dyke Complex formation, on a series of terraces of Middle to Late Pleistocene fluvial fan deposits (Plate 2.7; see also Chapter 2.2). Beneath the deposits, and widely exposed in the stream and gully side slopes, are outcrops of Basal Group formation of altered basalt and andesite flows and diabase dykes, and farther north, outcrops of Lower and Upper Pillow Lava formations. Accumulated within the deep petrocalcic horizons of the terrace soils, at the interface between the deposits and bedrock, calcium carbonate cements and forms a hardpan that laterally diverts subsurface water to side-valley seeps during and following the rainy season. The nearby diabase dyke outcrops to the south and limestone (Koronia Formation) outcrops to the north provide ample sources for construction stone and lime for mortar and other building uses.

This position at the interface between mountains and plains (Plate 2.1) gives the area a particular character and, at different times, an important role in the region as a whole. With an elevation of 280 m asl, it is a level and breezy location, which with its gullies and arable soils make it good for growing and processing grain, including the vital wind-powered winnowing. As a satellite settlement in the 18th or 19th century onwards, these qualities were easily accessible to the mountain dwellers to the south. To the north lie the Mesaoria plain and major communication

Fig. 2.7. Fieldwalking on the Koutraphas plateau in November 2003, looking north to Koronia hill (Michael Given)

Fig. 2.8. Kato Koutraphas Mandroudhes *(TP239): site gridding in progress (Michael Given)*

routes, both east–west and connecting the mountains with the Bay of Morphou and the import/export network.

Our transect survey in the Mandres Intensive Survey Zone consisted of five north–south transects that crossed and bracketed the Mandres settlement, plus some block survey in the immedate area of Mandres. In our normal summer seasons we experienced the same visibility problems as we did in the Koutraphas area, because of unusually dense stubble. As at Koutraphas, we were able to compensate for this by returning in November 2003 to carry out some additional transect survey on ploughed soil (Fig. 2.7).

2.9 Bronze Age Settlement at Kato Koutraphas *Mandroudhes*

Kato Koutraphas *Mandroudhes* (TP239) is a Bronze Age rural settlement, right on the interface between the Troodos Mountains and the fluvial plains. Its most striking characteristic is the excellent preservation of the surface on which it lies, with only minimal disturbance from ploughing, erosion and other post-depositional processes. Combined with careful gridding, this surface preservation allowed us to examine the spatial variation of activities across the area of the artefact scatter.

Mandroudhes was discovered during regular transect survey. As soon as it became clear there was a substantial scatter of pottery and ground stone in the ploughsoil, we stopped the Survey Unit (SU3005) to allow the gridding of the main concentration. The grid consisted of 26 squares on a 5 × 5 m grid. We counted all material in the squares and collected a representative sample, and then carried out a grab of chipped stone and feature sherds in four quadrants extending beyond the grid on all sides (Fig. 2.8). We mapped the geomorphology of the area, and our survey transect, as well as informal scouting, demonstrated that there was no more detectable cultural material in the adjoining fields or in the gully along the eastern side.

Mandroudhes lies almost entirely on Pleistocene fluvial fan deposits, with a small area to the south-west on the

Table 2.10. Kato Koutraphas Mandroudhes *(TP239): pottery. TCP numbers refer to Pottery Catalogue in Volume 1, Chapter 3.6*

Bronze Age

Fct	*Type*	*No.*	*Weight*
HU	HU	5	200g
HU	RS	1	47g
LU	LU	7	69g
LU	RS	6	65g

Prehistoric Bronze Age

Fct	*Type*	*No.*	*Weight*
CW	RPC	1	7g
HU	RMP	4	127g
HU	RP	7	130g
HU	RPC	3	60g
HU	RPOL	1	8g
LU	LU	2	15g
LU	RP	7	69g
LU	RPC	30	304g
LU	RPO	33	326g
LU	RPOL	2	31g
LU	RPOS	2	4g
TW	RPT	1	8g
TW	RPTO	3	36g

Protohistoric Bronze Age

Fct	*Type*	*No.*	*Weight*
HU	Pit	25	2.745kg
LU	RS	2	7g
TW	WS	5	31g
TW	WSCL	1	14g
TW	WSCS	1	12g
TW	WSO	5	35g
			TCP706

underlying basalt of the Upper Pillow Lava Formation. Contact between the basalt and sediments is marked by white outcrops of the petrocalcic soil horizon. The outcrop pattern of the petrocalcic horizon indicates that this modern contact trace must be within several metres of the original valley's western edge when the sediments were deposited. The fluvial deposits are composed of pebble- to boulder-sized clasts (fragments) of basalt, andesite and, to a greater amount, diabase of bedrock formations. These rocks, along with the petrocalcic horizon, are more resistant to erosion than the surrounding basaltic bedrock. Over the past several hundred thousand years the landscape has essentially reversed its topographic form, from valley to ridge top, leaving the alluvium stranded 8–12 m above the modern stream course.

The Holocene period is conspicuously absent here, as all of the local streams have been in a state of incision since at least the Late Pleistocene (some 12,000 years ago). Mandroudhes is bounded on the east by a narrow, straight-reached and V-shaped stream valley. In places the upper 2–4 m of the valley wall have slopes of more than 40°; this is because of the resistant nature of the petrocalcic soil horizon which readily forms cliffs. Two apparently natural stream terraces, converted to agricultural terraces in the past millennia, are narrow (<10 m) and short (<25 m along the stream). There is no apparent connection between the level on which Mandroudhes sits and the potentially contemporaneous fluvial deposits in the valley bottom.

Surface water drainage across the spread of cultural material is particularly restricted to the site, with no area upslope to contribute potentially erosive flow, and there is virtually no probability that this material could have originated from anywhere upslope. Off-site drainage is by sheet flow and by two gullies, heading into the eastern margin of the site, that were controlled some centuries ago by the installation of check dams. Lichens, microbiotic soil crusts around the check dam stones, and the typology of the stones all suggest that these check dams were constructed in the Ottoman period.

Overall the POSI rests on a landscape of great antiquity, far older than when the cultural materials were deposited by the inhabitants. The rate of erosion has been low and tillage disturbance relatively shallow and benign, which is why the cultural material is still present after so many millennia. The two gullies may have been a focal point for movement of materials off the terrace, and the artefacts found in them could have originated from upslope.

There is some spatial variation in the distribution of material across the grid, and because of the relative stability of the surface this may suggest different activity areas. This is clearest with the Prehistoric Bronze Age material and ground stone (Plate 2.8). The main concentration of Heavy Utility sherds (consisting entirely of Red Polished wares) is clearly in the centre and west of the grid. Apart from one piece, the ground stone is all in the north-west, and we found another 20 pieces to the west of the grid. Light Utility ware is spread throughout, and there is too little Table Ware and Cooking Ware (3 and 1 sherds respectively) to be confident about any distribution patterns. But it does appear that there was a food processing and storage area on the west side of the site. During the Protohistoric Bronze Age the Table Ware is much more widespread, albeit concentrated mainly on the west side. The main concentration of Heavy Utility, which this time consists entirely of pithos sherds, extends from the west to the centre of the grid.

The Mandroudhes area contained a wide spectrum of prehistoric pottery, from Chalcolithic through to Protohistoric Bronze Age (Table 2.10). Low numbers of worn Chalcolithic sherds identified as Red-on-White and Red Monochrome wares occurred in these Survey Units, but no clear concentration was identified. Significant amounts of Prehistoric Bronze Age Red Polished sherds also appeared at Mandroudhes, making up 60% of the 132 sherds collected during the gridding. From the sample collected in the field there is more than double the number of open Red Polished vessels than closed. The general lack of incised or highly decorated pieces suggests a domestic rather than mortuary source for this material, although the more delicate nature of fine ware pieces could lead to differential rates of preservation on the surface. Some of the Red Polished Ware sample consisted of large fresh pieces, suggesting a source in the immediate vicinity.

The Protohistoric Bronze Age pottery (27% of the total collected) suggests that there was a small settlement during that period as well. The material was significantly worn, making it likely that some movement on the surface had occurred, although as explained above this is unlikely to have been across any significant distance. This material seems to be exclusively ProBA 1 (LC I) in date, including the very beginning of that phase. The pottery consisted

Table 2.11. Kato Koutraphas Mandroudhes *(TP239): ground stone types*

Axe	2
Adze	1
Mortar	1
Rubber	9 (+ 4 not collected)
Quern	1 (+1 not collected)
Grinding Slab	(1 fragment, not collected)
Rubbing stone	1
Grinder	3
Pecking stone	1
Pounder	1
Pounder\hammerstone	1
Hammerstone\pounder\rubbing stone	1
Hammerstone\rubbing stone	1
Hammerstone\grinder	1
Hammerstone\axe	1
TOTAL	25 (+ 6 not collected)

of White Slip ware, Plain White Handmade ware, and distinctive LC I pithoi with 'pie-crust' and raised banded decoration. Overall, 10 sherds of White Slip were collected, three of which retained paint. Most of the sherds of White Slip ware were too worn to identify specifically, although two were identifiable as Proto-White Slip by the reddish sandy fabric and decorative motifs (TCP485, TCP706).

Two pieces of chipped stone were found at Mandroudhes – a jasper hammerstone (another was found 350 m to the north) and a discoidal flake core. The latter is interesting in that it is made of non-local Lefkara chert. These artefacts suggest that there was a chipped stone industry in use at Mandroudhes, although as at Katydhata *Laonarka* (Chapter 3.9) it is poorly represented. It is unclear whether the paucity of chipped stone artefacts represents a true reflection of a depleted industry during the Late Bronze Age in the Survey Area, or whether it merely indicates recovery bias.

The ground stone component of Mandroudhes is by far the most significant lithic element of the site, with 25 items (Table 2.11) collected or recorded in situ. Nearly all of the artefacts in the sample were made of the heavy basal rock types that derive from the Troodos range. The exceptions consist of a quern of dense sandstone, and a quern and flat grinding slab fragment, both made of diabase. The sample is dominated by 21 items of grinding equipment, typically associated with 'domestic' use in processing cereals. Large heavy rubbers are particularly numerous (nine collected, with a further four recorded in the field). Of interest is the presence of two distinct types of rubber: one has 'upturned' handles for using on a narrower quern, while the second is a heavier and thicker type with a flat base. Both types are also notably present at the ProBA site of Aredhiou *Vouppes*, 23 km to the east, and other Bronze Age sites across the island, for example at Maa *Palaeokastro* (personal observation; see also Karageorghis and Demas 1988, 418).

In sum, there is clear evidence at Mandroudhes of two distinctive periods, the PreBA and the ProBA, the earlier of which seems to have had different activity areas, with a food processing area on the west side. During the ProBA, the distribution of the material, and its nature, points to the existence of a small settlement with substantial food storage activity. Like the site of Aredhiou *Vouppes* located by the Sydney Cyprus Survey Project (Given and Knapp 2003, 179–82; see also Steel 2009), Mandroudhes seems to provide crucial evidence for the existence of an agricultural village, which with its distinctive array of fine Table Wares, may have been of more than local significance.

2.10 Ottoman–Modern Settlement at Kato Koutraphas *Mandres*

Mandres is an abandoned settlement located within the territory of the village of Kato Koutraphas. Mandres's role as a seasonal settlement has been previously discussed by Ionas (1988, 20) and Given (2000, 218), although as we discuss below it would be more appropriate to term it a satellite settlement. It was used in the spring and summer by people from villages higher in the mountains, such as Tembria and Kalliana, to grow grain and then to harvest and winnow it, and during the winter by goatherds. The settlement therefore possesses a very high number of *alonia*, or threshing floors, as well as dwellings, goatfolds and storage facilities. There is also evidence to suggest that goatherders occupied Mandres throughout the year.

A central aim of our research at Mandres was to analyse the surviving architecture to establish how it evolved over time and how these physical changes might reflect continuities or changes in its use. The analysis of the architecture was combined with a consideration of the pottery and chipped stone collected from Survey Units both within and around the settlement site. This combination allowed us to establish a chronological framework for the material remains at Mandres. This framework could not be established on purely historical or architectural/stylistic grounds, because of the longevity of vernacular rural building styles in the region. Documentary research and oral history interviews added depth to the analysis and enabled us to investigate the social and historical context of Mandres and its relationship with the broader cultural landscape.

Mandres was occupied throughout the 18th and 19th centuries and abandoned in the mid-20th century, with a likelihood that occupation stretched back into the 17th and 16th centuries (see below). Goodwin (1984, 1060) claims that Mandres had a population of 50 in the late 19th century and that it was a village of Greek Cypriots only.

The settlement of Mandres has a central nucleated core of dwellings, with a number of streets and 20 surviving (or partly surviving) threshing floors clustered to the north and east of the village (Fig. 2.9). The central village is surrounded by 14 outlying buildings, two with surviving associated *mandres* or goatfolds (BU0005–06) and eight with surviving, associated threshing floors (BU0007, BU0010, BU0013–14, BU0016, BU0018–19, BU0042). Most Building Units at Mandres are preserved to roof height, and four retained flat earthen roofs at the time of the field survey. There is also evidence (derived from the 1963 aerial photograph and from observations of foundations

Fig. 2.9. Kato Koutraphas Mandres *(TS07): aerial photograph from 1963 showing structures and threshing floors. Based upon the aerial photograph taken by the Department of Lands and Surveys with the sanction of the Government of the Republic of Cyprus; State copyright reserved (Luke Sollars)*

on the site) of several completely demolished and robbed out structures within the central village.

There is no evidence for a church or mosque in the village, despite Goodwin's claim that he observed ruins of a church there (1984, 1060). Our interview data (discussed further below) stressed that, as a seasonal settlement, there was no church in Mandres and that priests would not visit the village except to visit their family members.

The remains of Mandres village have not stood untouched since the mid-20th century, and there have been several post-abandonment uses. In the 1960s Goodwin (1984, 1060) recorded that two Greek Cypriots were living there, and local people that we interviewed recalled that in 1974 refugee shepherds moved in. In recent years, most of the surrounding agricultural fields have been enlarged, ploughing through the natural risers of the river terraces, and creating one large agricultural field instead of several smaller ones. These actions reflect the use of large-scale farm machinery rather than the ox-drawn plough: the roadways and paths associated with the village have been altered by bulldozing, while threshing floors to the east of the village have been destroyed by mechanized ploughing.

More recently, the Cypriot National Guard has used the site for military training. They have made alterations to the fabric of the settlement, including the addition of mock roofs, walls and windows made from galvanised iron, light timbers and masonite. Unfortunately such construction work, along with military activities, has resulted in substantial destabilisation and degradation of the increasingly vulnerable earth and stone structural remains.

Fig. 2.10. Kato Koutraphas Mandres *(TS07): general view over settlement looking south-east; threshing floors under the eucalyptus tree on the left; BU0020 is the farthest house on the left, with the main agglomeration on its right; outlier BU0006 is on the far right (Chris Parks)*

Fig. 2.11. Kato Koutraphas Mandres *(TS07): outlying structure: north-west and south-west walls showing calcrete chinking (BU0016; TP027) (Chris Parks)*

Environmental Context

Mandres is located on the southern boundary of the Mesaoria, in the western region of long, narrow plains between incised valleys below the northern foothills of Moutti tou Dhia of the Troodos Mountain Range. It lies at the confluence of two unnamed tributary gullies, which form the Argaki ton Mandron gully. The latter is a tributary of the Elaia River that drains north into Morphou Bay. The Argaki ton Mandron confluence comprises a T-shaped landform with three steep gullies. The settlement developed on a series of gentle fluvial terraces. The distinctive local pillow lavas form the basalt bedrock, which is visible in small portions on many of the terrace treads.

Mandres is an ideal location for the harvesting of grains. At 280 m asl, it is a level and breezy location, surrounded by numerous alluvial terraces ideal for agriculture (Fig. 2.10). Agricultural fields were constructed using the terrace treads, with the risers as field divisions. Threshing floors again made use of the flat terrace treads, while the risers formed the walls and boundaries of these floors.

The gully on the western side of the village contains three wells and an olive grove with trees no more than 50 years old. Two older olive trees, however, are situated closer to the settlement. A feature of interest relating to Mandres' threshing floors, discussed further below, is that nine of them have mature eucalypts (Murray River Red Gums/*Eucalyptus camaldulensis*) planted immediately adjacent to them, as if to mark their location amidst the sweeping fields of the plain.

Architectural Analysis

The aim of the architectural analysis was to provide an understanding of the relationship between the structures, their construction styles and the history of their development, use and re-use. Particular attention therefore was paid to the style of construction of the built units and the relationship between, or 'superposition' of, the structural elements, to determine phases of construction and adaptation.

<u>Identification of Building Units</u> The settlement was divided into numbered 'Building Units' (BUs) (Plate 2.9). In the central village it could not be determined if the Building Units (as numbered) were equivalent to single dwellings, or dwelling and storage complexes; however, the identification of contiguous structures, which were added to, divided or altered by later construction phases, tended to reveal contemporaneous construction events, rather than actual dwelling spaces. Several freestanding houses (e.g. BU0007; see Fig. 2.15), as well as a number of intact central village houses (e.g. BU0037), can be interpreted confidently as having been used as houses, or dwelling/storage complexes, in their final period of occupation. We use the term 'Building Unit' rather than 'houses' for the purposes of this analysis.

The constructions covered in this analysis include the standing Building Units of the central village, as well as the 14 buildings that surround the core settlement. Other

Fig. 2.12. Kato Koutraphas Mandres *(TS07): fireplace in centre of wall (BU0037, SE06) (Chris Parks)*

Fig. 2.13. Kato Koutraphas Mandres *(TS07): built-in manger (BU0007, SE09) (Chris Parks)*

Fig. 2.14. Kato Koutraphas Mandres *(TS07): corner shelf made from* dhoukani *plank (BU0020) (Chris Parks)*

structures or features present in the village include three external, dome-shaped stone ovens (next to BU0006, BU0026 and BU0043), 20 extant threshing floors and a number of roads leading to and from the village, as well as streets within the central village (Plate 2.9).

Construction Features Mandres features the use of masonry and mudbrick construction to form the walls and foundations of the structures. In some cases, it appears that abandoned and partially collapsed masonry was added to or repaired with mudbrick to rebuild a dwelling/storage space. The masonry walls are made mostly of basalt (red and bluestone) or limestone boulders with chinking of calcrete (sourced at the site), limestone, river pebbles, pottery and some red jasper (Ionas 1988, 146). The walls were left unplastered, and so the chinking was used to create a decorative effect, some walls showing distinctive white horizontal bands of calcrete chinking (Fig. 2.11). Some re-used stone querns and other large stone tools have also been incorporated into the masonry walls.

Fireplaces are constructed of mud, timber and stone: two in the centre of their walls (e.g. BU0037; Fig. 2.12) and four in corners having survived (Ionas 1988, 84–86). Fireplaces made largely of mud would not survive long following abandonment, so it is likely that they reflect the most recent periods of occupation. The fireplaces and internal walls feature plasters of varying qualities, from coarse mud to finer lime-based plasters. Surviving chimneys in the village are constructed from re-used broken pottery water jugs and Shell oil cans.

The mudbricks used on the site are well made and tempered with stone, gravel, straw, bone and pottery. The surviving flat earthen roofs are constructed of reeds, gorse, timber and earth, in the vernacular rural style of the region (Volume 1, Chapter 3.11). Local informants stressed that the earth used for roofs, called *konnos,* was sourced especially for its waterproof qualities. The timber posts and joists that support the roofs are hand-adzed or simple unfinished rounded timber poles. Some machine-sawn timbers are also used in the outlying houses and in BU0037.

Many of the houses display 'built-in' features such as stone benches, mangers (Fig. 2.13), stone constructed niches for holding lamps, and timber and stone 'pegs' from which to hang things or to support a timber shelf. BU0020 features an in situ corner shelf constructed from a plank of re-used *dhoukani* (Fig. 2.14).

Classification into Style Groups Each numbered Building Unit has been classified according to the main stylistic features of its construction. The two most basic stylistic divisions are the *makrinari* and *dikhoro* forms, as identified by Ionas (1988, 47–48). The *dikhoro* (here termed Type A) is a double-width structure that requires a supporting beam and posts to carry a double parallel row of roof joists for the wider internal space. The *makrinari* (Type B) is a narrow rectangular unit, which can be roofed by a single row of timber joists. At Mandres these built forms are created using a variety of construction techniques, which can be classified into four stylistically distinctive groups (Table 2.12).

Questions remain as to whether the distinctions identified in construction styles imply differences in the time of construction, diversity in construction practices derived from village or family customs, or simply expediency in

Table 2.12. Kato Koutraphas Mandres *(TS07): distribution of style groups*

Construction Technique	**Type A (Dikhoro)**	**BUs of Type A**	**Type B (Makrinari)**	**BUs of Type B**
1. High stone socle (>1 m) + mud brick superstructure	A1	BU0008, BU0013, BU0019, BU0021, BU0025, BU0030, BU0032–33	B1	BU0005, BU0017, BU0028–29, BU0036
2. Low stone socle (<1 m) + mud brick superstructure	A2	BU0020, BU0039, BU0041–42	B2	BU0010–11, BU0014, BU0018, BU0031, BU0051–52
3. High back/low front stone socle + mud brick superstructure			B3	BU0007, BU0015
4. Constructed all of stone (except roof)	A4	BU0009, BU0012, BU0016, BU0022, BU0027, BU0037, BU0038, BU0040, BU0043	B4	BU0006, BU0023–24
Total numbers		*21*		*17*

Fig. 2.15. Kato Koutraphas Mandres *(TS07): structure with stepped stone socle, from the south-east (BU0007, SE01, SE03, SE06; style group B3) (Chris Parks)*

Fig. 2.16. Kato Koutraphas Mandres *(TS07): structure with low unstepped socle and mudbrick superstructure, from the west (BU0020; style group A2) (Chris Parks)*

the availability of materials. An informant, who lived and worked in Mandres prior to the Second World War, told us that stone houses were more expensive as the stone had to be carried by donkey from quarries in the mountains. He believed the stone houses, therefore, belonged to the richer families. Another informant, who now farms the land around the village, felt that the stone houses were older and that the use of mudbrick was a newer form of construction in the village. He stated that the making of mudbricks required specialist artisans who had to be brought in, and that this form of construction was, therefore, more expensive than stone.

The distinctive form of Style Group B3, where the stone socle is higher on the rear elevation than the front, is seen in only two Building Units, both of which are outlying structures (BU0007, BU0015). This construction style can be seen partly as a response to a sloping building site, but this regular stepped form of stone construction (see for instance Fig. 2.15) is stylistically quite distinct from the other, mostly mudbrick, Building Units constructed on sloping sites, such as BU0020 (Fig. 2.16). It seems likely that Style Group A3 represents a signature form of construction employed by a single builder, or building team, and that these Building Units are contemporary.

Building Unit Analysis Building Units were further divided into structural elements that were given sequential numbers and described in detail. Following Davies, structural elements were defined as component parts of a structure, such as walls, beams, lintels and so on (Davies and Buckley 1987, 7). Structural element numbers were also attributed to infill, repair or alterations to the building. Davies's method is particularly appropriate for identifying phases in the life of a structure and for the analysis of vernacular architectural forms, where stylistic or technological changes in construction are not apparent. The limitation of this form of analysis is that the time depth between separate construction events is not readily indicated. In the case of Mandres, complexity of changes to, and re-use of, structural elements are generally assumed to represent longer periods of use and occupation of a structure. Structures that show less evidence of change

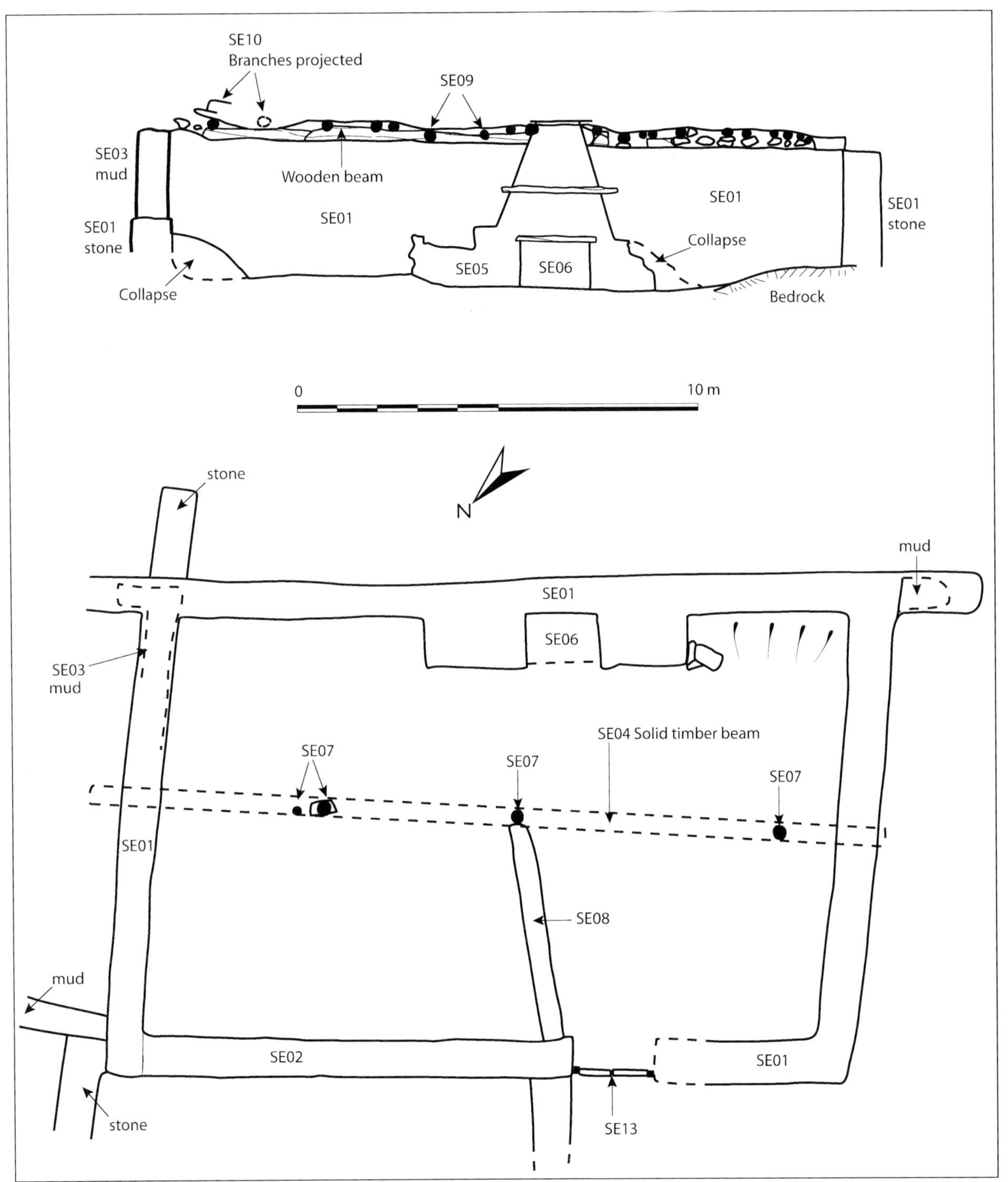

Fig. 2.17. Kato Koutraphas Mandres *(TS07): plan and section of BU0037 with structural elements (Sophie Pullar, finalised by Luke Sollars)*

and alteration are generally assumed to have had fewer occupation phases and to have been abandoned after a shorter period of time.

An example of the identification and numbering of structural elements for BU0037 is shown in the plan and section in Fig. 2.17. The structural element analysis of BU0037 shows that individual Building Units were subject to phases of adaptation and re-use as the village expanded. BU0037 had a complex history of re-use, adaptation and alteration, demonstrating at least four occupation phases, including one of quite recent, mid- to late 20th century use, represented by the recent hearth (SE06) and intact roof (SE09–10). The earlier changes made to the structure include the creation of an internal dividing wall (SE08), perhaps to create a separate hay storage area, and the incorporation of a relict and abandoned structure (SE01).

Table 2.13. Kato Koutraphas Mandres *(TS07): evolution of related Building Unit (BU) groups in the central part of the settlement. The arrows connect one BU with another that abuts and post-dates it; the dashes connect BUs that abut but appear to have been built at the same time. BUs on the same line are likely to be approximately contemporary, resulting from successive periods of expansion in the population of the settlement*

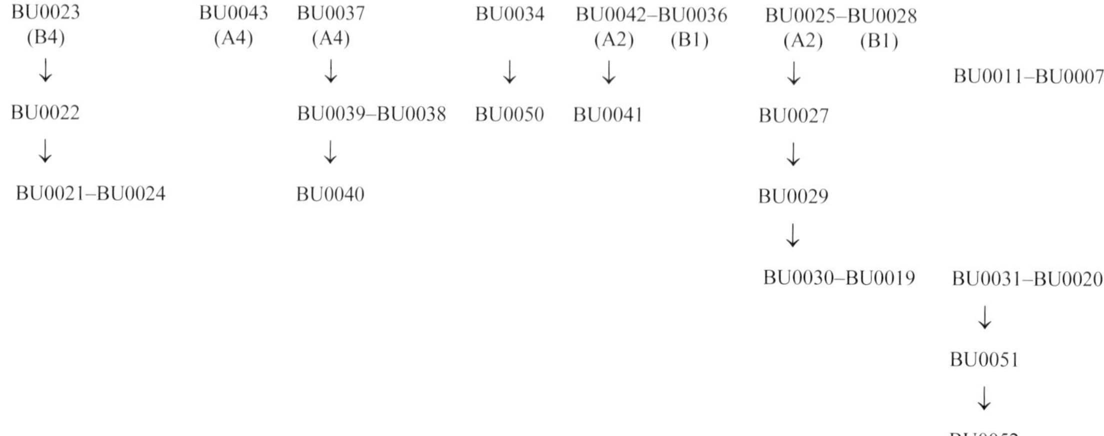

Once structural elements for a Building Unit were identified, numbered and described, the relationships between these elements were described in terms of superposition, in other words the stratigraphy of construction events. The relationships between the Building Unit and adjoining units were also described at this point, which yielded an understanding of the way a number of the Building Units in the central village evolved.

Table 2.13 shows how the related groups of Building Units in the central settlement evolved, starting from an original structure that was added to and abutted by subsequent structures, as is commonly observed in Cypriot villages (Ionas 1988, 45). This analysis suggests that the oldest structures in the village are largely, but not exclusively, of masonry construction (Types A4 and B4).

Threshing Floors

As mentioned above, Mandres features a very large number of threshing floors or *alonia* (TP122), many of which are clearly visible in the 1963 aerial photograph (Fig. 2.9). The 1:1250 village plan, probably made in the 1920s, shows 42 *alonia* (Fig. 2.18), but only 20 of these have survived the recent expansion of machine cultivation in the land surrounding the village. These floors are all roughly circular, even though the plots that contain them are mainly rectilinear (Fig. 2.18). They range in diameter from 14.2 to 9.5 m. Twelve are paved with basalt cobbles, two with limestone flagstones, while the remaining six generally have a hard, compacted earth surface.

Threshing floor 1 is paved with basalt cobbles arranged in a sunburst pattern and has random rubble retaining walls to the west and east, where it is cut into the slope. It also possesses a raised stone lip on the western side where the land falls away. This is the only surviving threshing floor at Mandres where a distinct pattern can be observed in the paving; most are simply characterized by an irregular though neat arrangement of flattish cobbles (Fig. 2.19). Limestone flags would seem to provide an excellent threshing surface, being flatter than the basalt cobbles; limestone flags and lime plaster are commonly used on threshing floors in other parts of Cyprus (Whittaker 1999, 16–17). Basalt, however, was a more readily available resource in the vicinity of Mandres, where it is also used as the main building material. There is no surviving evidence that plaster was used on the threshing floors at Mandres.

The circular threshing floors of Mandres were designed for use with the *dhoukani*, a wooden threshing sledge with an underside studded with stone flakes and pulled by oxen, donkeys or horses (Whittaker 1999, 13). Of the 46 lithic artefacts collected from these threshing floors, 44 were *dhoukani* flakes (see Table 2.17 and discussion below). A remnant fragment of a broken *dhoukani* sledge was found in BU0020, where it had been re-used as a corner shelf (Fig. 2.14)

Threshing floors in the recent historic period in Cyprus were generally individual family assets rather than communal facilities (Given 2000, 215). The larger villages in the Survey Area, such as Katydhata, Phlasou, Linou and Evrykhou, have only a small number of threshing floors associated with them today. This is partly explained by the encroachment of recent development on village threshing floors that are no longer in use. At Mandres, several of them are clearly associated with outlying dwellings (Table 2.14); there are so many surrounding the core of the village that each one was, presumably, owned by particular individuals or families. Interviews with men who remember life at Mandres before the Second World War confirm that each family had their own threshing floor.

Whittaker (1999, 22) noted that despite the clear demarcation of individual properties, threshing floors in Cyprus tend to be located in clusters, to facilitate cooperative labour and socialisation as a part of the annual task of threshing grain. The cluster of threshing floors around the perimeter of the central settlement of Mandres confirms this pattern. Families occupying the outlying

Fig. 2.18. Kato Koutraphas Mandres *(TS07): Village Plan of 1920s (revised 1967, 1993) showing structures and threshing floors. Ov = oven. PDF = public distribution fountain. TF = threshing floor. Based upon the map prepared by the Department of Lands and Surveys with the sanction of the Government of the Republic of Cyprus; State copyright reserved*

Table 2.14. Kato Koutraphas Mandres *(TS07): threshing floors (TP122). See Plate 2.9 for locations*

No.	Building Unit	Eucalyptus	Dhoukani flakes	Diameter (m)	Features
1	BU0018		23	14.2	Paved with basalt cobbles in sunburst pattern. Most chipped stone around S edge. Retaining walls where cut into slope. Stone lip on W side where land slopes away.
2		Yes	2	14.0	Paved with basalt cobbles. Retaining walls where cut into slope.
3		Yes	1	13.0	2/3 destroyed by road construction.
4		Yes	2	10.1	Paved with some limestone flags. 2/3 destroyed by ploughing.
5				12.0	Damaged from ploughing. Unpaved, but stones may have been removed during ploughing.
6	BU0022/23	Yes	14	?	Mostly destroyed by road works and ploughing. Some stone paving survives in the road surface.
7	BU0034			10.2	Unpaved, but very hard compacted gravel surface. Earthen embankment to W.
8	BU0017		1	11.0	Unpaved; compacted surface.
9	BU0036		2	13.0	Paved. Some large limestone flags. Similar to No. 4.
10			1	11.2	Basalt cobble paving. Retaining wall on N.
11	BU0043	Yes		14.0	Basalt cobble paving mostly destroyed. Retaining wall on W.
12				10.5	Unpaved, compacted surface
13	BU0041/42			10.5	Unpaved, compacted surface. Standing stone slabs form perimeter. Retaining wall to NW.
14	BU0009	Yes		13.5	Basalt cobble paving.
15	BU0010	Yes		11.5	Paved with unusually large basalt cobbles.
16		Yes		12.5	Basalt cobble paving. Retaining wall and lip to N.
17	BU0013/14			12.2	Basalt cobble paving.
18	BU0013		1	9.5	Basalt cobble paving. Some damage from ploughing/grading.
19	BU0016			11.8	Basalt cobble paving. Upper and lower retaining walls.
20	BU0007	Yes		12.8	Unpaved, compacted surface. Retaining walls on upper and lower sides.

Fig. 2.19. Kato Koutraphas Mandres *(TS07): threshing floor from the north, showing paving, retaining wall in foreground, and eucalyptus tree (TP122, threshing floor 9) (Chris Parks)*

dwellings with associated threshing floors may, therefore, have come from different villages, or belonged to different extended family groups than those occupying the core village. It also seems likely, however, that these dwellings represent the most recent period of construction at Mandres, when the availability of buildings sites was limited, and new buildings were accordingly forced into more remote sites.

Another interesting feature is that 9 of the 20 surviving threshing floors at Mandres have mature eucalypts (*Eucalyptus camaldulensis*) planted alongside them (Table 2.14). There is a total of twelve mature eucalypts growing around Mandres, with nine located adjacent to surviving threshing floors. There is also evidence of several further trees that have been cut down. One cut eucalypt stump 120 m north of the centre of the settlement has 65–70 growth rings and a girth of 2.13 m. It is burnt on the outside and has no bark, which means that up to five growth rings may be missing from the outside. This tree is therefore estimated to have been between 70 and 75 years old when cut down. The extant trees have a similar girth to the cut stump, which suggests that the stump is relatively recent (within 10 years) and that the age of the currently growing trees is, therefore, in the range of 75–85 years. Thus it would seem that the eucalypts were all planted at the same time, probably in the 1910s or 1920s.

Eucalypts are not ideal shade trees, and these particular trees are not well sited to provide shade. As threshing was often done in the cool of the evening, their original purpose or intent is unclear. It is unlikely that the arrangement of the eucalypts in the landscape could be the result of natural dispersal. Eucalypts were introduced into Cyprus by the British in 1879, both to dry out swampy regions and therefore help to control malaria, and also as a source of fast growing timber (SA1/1840/1880–83). Today eucalypts abound along river beds and in the towns and cities of Cyprus, but their specific, planted locations in the rural landscape at Mandres is a curious feature. It is interesting to speculate about the reasons for this planting pattern, which appears to mark the location of threshing floors, including those floors located with the outlying buildings surrounding the central settlement core. Whether the trees are linked to the presence of the threshing floors, to provide some shade, or to identify or mark them in some way, or whether they were simply planted to enhance the quality of the environment, they reinforce the fact that Mandres was a busy and well cared for seasonal settlement in the early decades of the 20th century, perhaps at the height of its use for intensive agricultural production.

Pottery and Dating

Pottery was collected from Survey Units surrounding Mandres (Table 2.15), from smaller POSI Units between the buildings (Table 2.16), and from the Building Units themselves, including examples used as chinking in masonry. The majority of this pottery may be dated between the 15th and 20th centuries. There was also a small number of Hellenistic and Roman sherds found within the settlement area, and a larger concentration of this earlier material in SU0345 and SU0352 to the east of Mandres (Chapter 2.11).

The settlement of Mandres, and logically the area which was the source for its building materials, therefore yielded pottery dated from antiquity and from between the late 15th and early 20th centuries. Informants suggest that the stone for construction in Mandres was brought to the site from quarries in the region, but it is likely that the mud, calcrete and pottery (the latter two used in chinking), as well as other artefactual material such as broken querns, were opportunistically sourced at or near the settlement site. The presence of late 15th–17th-century pottery around the site and in the Building Units suggests that this area was occupied from the late 15th or early 16th centuries, with subsequent building phases through the Ottoman period and into the late 19th–early 20th centuries. Some of this

Table 2.15. Kato Koutraphas Mandres *(TS07: SU0009–11, SU0321–54, SU1381–88, SU2024): pottery from block survey. See also Table 2.16. TCP numbers refer to Pottery Catalogue in Volume 1, Chapter 3.6*

Fct	*Type*	*No.*	*Weight*
Prehistoric Bronze Age			
HU	RPOL	1	35g
LU	RPOM	1	5g
LU	RPOS	1	10g
			TCP128
TW	RPOL	2	30g
Cypro-Geometric to Classical			
LU	BcB	1	5g
			TCP129
LU	BORO	1	5g
LU	RS	1	5g
LU	WP	1	25g
LU	WPC	6	65g
			TCP131, TCP132
Historical Antiquity (Archaic to Late Roman)			
Ar	Ti	1	100g
Ar	TiP	2	110g
HU	HU	23	830g
LU	LU	16	96g
TW	RS	2	2g
TW	TW	1	15g
Hellenistic			
TW	BS	2	15g
TW	BS01	1	5g
			TCP135
TW	RS	1	2g
Hellenistic to Roman			
CW	CW	4	10g
Tr	Mav01	2	105g
			TCP311
Tr	Mav02	1	325g
			TCP133
TW	SRS	2	10g
Late Hellenistic to Early Roman			
TW	CS	1	30g
TW	Sig	2	4g
Early to Late Roman			
Ar	Ti	2	225g
CW	CW	15	52g
CW	CWFPWh01	1	55g
			TCP268
HU	HUR01	1	29g
HU	HUR06	1	80g
			TCP136
Late Roman			
Ar	TiSkC01	1	80g
HU	HUR10	1	225g
			TCP019
Tr	Am	1	20g
Tr	LR1	3	223g
TW	CRS	2	18g
TW	CRS02	5	143g
TW	CRS09	2	27g
TW	RS	1	25g
Roman to Modern			
CW	CW	8	50g
HU	HU	3	370g
Historical (Archaic to Modern)			
Ar	Ti	2	400g
			TCP134
CW	CW	9	119g
HU	HU	158	5.892kg
LU	LU	146	1.178kg
LU	LUB01	1	75g
Medieval utility period I			
U	UL01	1	110g
			TCP312
Medieval			
TW	Ug	1	3g
Medieval to Modern			
Ar	Brk	1	80g
CW	BGW	3	35g
CW	CW	3	30g
CW	Tta	2	67g
HU	BGW	1	93g
HU	HU	27	1.399kg
LU	LU	27	391g
U	BUPSJa	2	95g
U	UFB01	1	40g
			TCP020
Medieval utility period III			
U	ID03	1	50g
			TCP021
Ottoman			
TW	G04	1	42g
TW	Ug	1	58g
Medieval-Venetian to Early Ottoman			
TW	CGS06	1	7g
			TCP130
TW	G03	1	10g
TW	MP01	4	52g
Ottoman to Modern II			
HU	BuH	25	900g
LU	BuL	10	110g
TW	G01	1	5g
TW	G02	2	95g
TW	G03	3	50g
TW	G06	1	5g
TW	MP01	2	15g
TW	SP01	1	20g
TW	SP02	2	35g
Modern			
Ar	Brk	2	310g
Ar	TiCh	7	285g
CW	BGW	1	30g
CW	BGW01	1	5g
HU	HU	12	550g
			TCP018
LU	LU	1	7g
TW	BGW02	1	20g
TW	G03	2	40g
TW	G05	1	2g
TW	G07	1	2g
TW	SP01	2	12g
Unknown			
HU	HU	2	42g
LU	LU	1	5g
Un	Un	2	575g

material provides useful *termini post quem* dates for several of the related groups of Building Units.

BU0021.SE02 (a mudbrick wall) contained a sherd of Cypriot Green Painted Sgraffito Ware of the Medieval-Frankish period (late 15th to early 16th century), a sherd of pale green Monochrome Glazed Ware (MedVOtt; c. 16th–17th centuries), and some coarse ware of indeterminate date. BU0021.SE05 (collapsed roof and wall material) also contained a piece of c. 16th–17th-century pale green Monochrome Glazed Ware.

BU0022, which abuts and predates BU0021 in terms of the stratigraphic relationship between the structural elements, contains an Ottoman–Modern sherd in SE01 (a stone wall). BU0024, which is the last phase in the construction sequence of BU0023–22–21–24, contains a fragment of pale green Monochrome Glazed Ware of the Ottoman period (late 16th–late 19th centuries) in SE02 (a stone wall), two sherds of c. 16th–17th-century Monochrome Glazed Wares, and coarse wares in stone wall SE04.

Table 2.16. Kato Koutraphas Mandres *(TP008, TP021): pottery from round buildings. See also Table 2.15. TCP numbers refer to Pottery Catalogue in Volume 1, Chapter 3.6*

Hellenistic

Fct	*Type*	*No.*	*Weight*
TW	BS	1	2g

Early to Late Roman

Fct	*Type*	*No.*	*Weight*
CW	CW	3	5g

Late Roman

Fct	*Type*	*No.*	*Weight*
TW	CRS	1	5g

Roman to Modern

Fct	*Type*	*No.*	*Weight*
LU	LU	3	35g

Historical (Archaic to Modern)

Fct	*Type*	*No.*	*Weight*
Ar	Ti	1	65g
CW	CW	1	5g
HU	HU	14	480g
LU	LU	16	96g
TW	TW	1	5g

Medieval to Modern

Fct	*Type*	*No.*	*Weight*
U	BUPSJa	7	895g
U	UPSJu	6	590g

Ottoman

Fct	*Type*	*No.*	*Weight*
PO	Pipe	1	10g TCP571
TW	PP05	2	10g

Ottoman to Modern I

Fct	*Type*	*No.*	*Weight*
CW	G04	1	2g
TW	G02	1	3g
TW	MP01	4	67g
TW	SP02	1	2g

Medieval-Venetian to Early Ottoman

Fct	*Type*	*No.*	*Weight*
TW	CGS06	1	1g
TW	MP01	1	1g

Ottoman to Modern II

Fct	*Type*	*No.*	*Weight*
HU	BuH	11	242g
LU	BuL	3	17g
TW	G03	5	35g
TW	MP01	1	65g TCP570
TW	SP01	1	3g
TW	SP02	1	1g

Modern

Fct	*Type*	*No.*	*Weight*
Ar	Brk	1	20g
Ar	TiCh	4	260g
HU	BGW	2	35g
TW	Por	2	15g
TW	SP02	1	10g

Thus, these structures are no earlier than the 16th century, but the mixture of possibly later pottery suggests that they were constructed in the 19th century. The presence of the pottery and re-used stone tools in the Building Units strongly suggests, however, that these items were derived from the remains of earlier occupation at this site, either from rubbish dumps or from earlier construction that was in ruins by the time the present structures were built. This pattern also suggests that occupation at Mandres dates from the late 15th century.

This date is supported by the documentary sources. Mandres appears on the Venetian village list of 1565 with 14 *francomati* (free peasant farmers), which implies a resident population of at least 14 households (Grivaud 1998, 470). In the Ottoman census of 1831 it was lumped together with Vyzakia (Theocharides and Andreev 1996, 43), perhaps indicating the anomalous, or seasonal, nature of its settlement. It does not appear in the list of wheat and barley paid in kind by the villages of Morphou district in 1832, although Vyzakia does (Papadopoullos 1965, 187). This situation implies that the inhabitants of Mandres paid their tithes through their permanent villages, rather than as residents of this seasonal village.

A sherd of Monochrome Painted Ware, with added brown paint, imported from Çanakkale in western Turkey, was collected from SE03 (a mudbrick wall) in BU0030, a Building Unit in the central village. This pottery is 19th century and later in date. SE03 (the mudbrick wall) also included a Hellenistic sherd. Other Building Units containing 16th–17th-century sherds include BU0037, BU0040 and BU0025. Most glazed and decorated Table Wares found in the Building Units at Mandres consist of painted wares (55%), followed by glazed wares (43%) and sgraffito (2%).

Lithics

The largest number of lithic finds (100 pieces) was collected from the central area of the Mandres settlement (TP021); of these, 93 are chipped stone and 7 are ground stone. The majority of the ground stone items recorded were incorporated into the walls of the Building Units, clearly representing a secondary use of these tools (of potentially Roman and/or Medieval date) as building materials. These artefacts include three querns, located in BU0017, BU0028 and BU0033, and a grist stone incorporated into BU0024. Three pieces of portable ground stone were collected: a rubber fragment from TP021.PU09 (TCL348); a small quern from BU0012 (TCL352); and a pounder from BU0028 (TCL330) (see Volume 1, Chapter 3.8 for a discussion of the lithics).

In the large sample of chipped stone, there was a relatively high percentage (44%) of tools; this figure is broadly parallel to the village samples from Ayios Epiphanios, Katydhata and Phlasou, where *dhoukani* flakes dominate the tool samples. Cores and unworked blanks belonging to the TP021 sample are comparatively less frequent (6% and 10% respectively), while knapping waste represents a significant percentage of the sample (40%).

Interestingly, there is a difference between the materials collected from within the centre of the village and those from the POSI Units on the road (Table 2.17): artefacts from within the village are more heavily dominated by tools (69%), primarily *dhoukani* flakes (9 of 11 tools, or 82%); in contrast samples from the road include more significant percentages of cores, knapping debris and blanks and a relatively lower percentage of tools. This latter group is dominated by flake tools, especially utilized flakes (21 pieces; 70%), providing a contrast to the sample from the settlement. It is worth considering, therefore, whether

Table 2.17. Kato Koutraphas Mandres *(TS07): chipped stone artefacts*

	Village centre TP021 PU01–03, PU10	Road TP021 PU04–09	Threshing floors TP122	Outlier & threshing floors TP008	Outlier & threshing floor TP027	SUs on E edge of settlement (SU0344–54)	Transect E of settlement (SU1372–90)	Jasper outcrop TP240
Cores	2	4	10	–	1	1	5	4
Debitage	2	35	17	–	–	–	5	4
Blanks	1	8	15	–	–	–	5	2
Tools	11	30	46	1	4	2	5	4
Chipped stone total	**16**	**77**	**88**	**1**	**5**	**3**	**20**	**14**
Ground stone	7	–	1	–	–	1	–	–

Table 2.18. Kato Koutraphas Mandres *(TS07): non-local cherts used in the manufacture of the major tool groups. Figures show number of tools made with non-local cherts followed by the number of tools made with local and non-local cherts in brackets*

	Village centre & road TP021	Threshing floors TP122	Outlier & threshing floors TP008	Outlier & threshing floor TP027	SUs on E edge of settlement (SU0344–54)	Transect E of settlement (SU1372–90)	Jasper outcrop TP240
Dhoukani flake	14 (18)	27 (44)	1 (1)	–	1 (1)	1 (2)	–
Utilized flake	2 (18)	–	–	1 (2)	0 (1)	0 (3)	0 (3)
Flake tool	3 (5)	2 (2)	–	0 (2)	–	–	0 (1)
Totals	**19 (41)**	**29 (46)**	**1(1)**	**1 (4)**	**1 (2)**	**1 (5)**	**0 (4)**

the material from the track, which is certainly not in situ, may represent background material reflecting an initial occupation phase of the site during the Roman period, as suggested by the presence of a background scatter of Roman pottery in the same POSI Units.

A very substantial sample of 88 lithic artefacts was collected from 11 of the 20 extant threshing floors that encircle the Mandres settlement. Here again the tools are the dominant artefact category (46 pieces; 52%), of which nearly all (44 pieces; 96%) were *dhoukani* flakes (Table 2.17).

One striking feature among the various samples from Mandres (TS07) is the strong preference for non-local, predominantly Lefkara cherts, used in particular for the production of *dhoukani* flakes (Table 2.18). Samples located in or near the Mandres settlement itself show a high percentage of non-local cherts; these are used in the manufacture of nearly all tools, but for *dhoukani* flakes in particular. This clear preference in raw material selection shows that threshing sledges were purchased at markets outside the TAESP Survey Area, since these cherts do not occur locally. Indeed, one local informant suggested that sledges were obtained from Kyrenia.

Nevertheless, the presence of significant numbers of *dhoukani* flakes made of local jasper and chalcedony materials requires the consideration of two alternative interpretations. First is the probable use of local jasper for the production of threshing tools during the Roman period (as suggested by samples elsewhere in the Survey Area). The alternative is the replacement of worn or broken sledge 'teeth' (probably by locals) with materials close to hand. A very large jasper core, c. 28 cm in diameter, collected between buildings within the centre of the village (TCL351, from TP021.PU10) suggests that at least some sledge repair at Mandres may have been done by the villagers themselves, rather than by travelling *athkiakathes* (flint knappers) (cf. Fox and Pearlman 1987, 229; Whittaker 2000, 65–66). That some sledge repairs also occurred at the threshing floors, potentially by travelling *athkiakadhes*, is suggested by the significant numbers of *dhoukani* flakes made of Lefkara cherts found across the Mandres *alonia* (TP122); many of these were in a heavily worn or fragmentary state.

Elsewhere, the distribution of artefact types, like the low number of Lefkara cherts in the block survey (SU0344–54), the material from TP021.PU04–09, and the samples of TP027 and TP240, argues for an early historic characterization in these areas (Table 2.18). When non-local cherts appear in these samples they typically correspond to the presence of *dhoukani* flakes, implying a degree of mixing with later historic threshing materials.

Oral History

We had the opportunity to interview a number of individuals who had lived at Mandres before the Second World War (for methodology see Volume 1, Chapter 2.14). All interviewees agreed that Mandres was used by farmers from Tembria and Kalliana; a number also mentioned the villages of Galata and Kato Koutraphas. The men interviewed also agreed that the houses around the outskirts of the village were inhabited by goatherders, who lived in Mandres all year-round, while the central village was occupied by farmers who visited in the summer. The informants suggested that Mandres was generally a village of men, but at sowing and harvesting time women shared in the labour, bringing their children and babies with them to Mandres. The goatherders, who reportedly lived in the outlying houses at Mandres, would have needed the space for their goatfolds. They made cheese, and sometimes families would collaborate in this task. Both herders and farmers were considered to be 'villagers' (*khoriani*). As mentioned above, the informants also agreed that most families had their own threshing floors at Mandres, accounting for their large number.

A similar situation was recorded in oral history interviews during the Akamas Survey. Shepherds and their families lived at the settlement of Ayios Kononas during the winter and early summer, while three families who grew wheat remained there all summer to look after the crop (Hayes and Thomsen 1995, 52). The animal folds are not necessarily evidence for full-scale pastoralism, however. On the Methana peninsula in the Peloponnese, Greece, families would have to bring their sheep and goats with them when they spent a few days at a seasonal settlement to work on agricultural activities, and so needed a small animal fold (Forbes 2007, 58).

Informants recounted clearly perceived activity-based divisions within the essentially open space of both the *makrinari* and *dikhoro* Building Units. These included a space for tethering animals, often with a trough for their feed (Fig. 2.13), a space for storing hay, and spaces for cooking, eating and sleeping. If a house consisted of a number of rooms, the separate space was often used as a store for hay. One informant described how storerooms would be filled with hay by throwing it in though a hole in the roof (*volikotrypa*). These informants suggested that dwellings in Mandres were generally owned by single families, but also mentioned that two-storey houses, which are still identifiable (Fig. 2.16), may have belonged to two families.

One informant told us that the British regime appointed a *moukhtar* (mayor) for Mandres, even though it was not considered to be a 'community' (*kinotita*) by the local inhabitants. This same logic applied in eastern Crete: however many months a year families might spend at their *metokhia*, they were not considered proper family residences (Brumfield 2000, 58). Similarly, and as already noted, our informants explained that Mandres had no church, and that priests only visited Mandres to visit their relatives. The men interviewed agreed that Mandres was abandoned after the Second World War, because people sought to supplement their agricultural activities with paid work in the mines that were then opening.

Conclusions

This analysis has investigated how the settlement of Mandres grew and how the density of occupation of the nucleated settlement intensified. It suggests that the oldest surviving structures in the settlement were built in stone. The more marginal, steep, gully sides around the central settlement were developed later as space became more limited. These later structures tended to be of mudbrick. Local informants have suggested that the outlying structures belonged to goatherds, while the farmers lived in the central village. This seems to apply to BU0005 and BU0006, which do not show evidence of threshing floors, but do have evidence for associated goatfolds. All except one (BU0008) of the other outlying houses, however, do possess closely associated threshing floors, suggesting that their inhabitants were involved in grain production as well as pastoralism.

The substantial surviving stone and mudbrick structures at Mandres reflect the year-round use of this settlement by herders and crop growers, rather than simply its seasonal, summertime use for growing grain. It may be more accurate, therefore, to see at least the later periods of occupation at Mandres, those for which we have oral information and which the extant remains most clearly reflect, as an agricultural satellite settlement rather than a seasonal settlement. Some men would overwinter at Mandres, while their wives and children stayed in the village. Families with vineyards, however, spoke of working six months in the vineyards and six months, in the summer, at Mandres. The presence of hearths in the Building Units suggests wintertime occupation, and many of the interviews confirm that the village was occupied year-round by herders, who were visited by their families from time to time, and for the two periods of sowing and harvesting. Indoor fires were not solely restricted to the distinctive mud-plastered fireplaces: in BU0025 a broken water jug, embedded directly in the earthen roof, has been used as a simple chimney over an open hearth (Ionas 1988, 86).

It is likely that Mandres was used by nearby villages for agriculture and herding, for some time before the present structures were built. The pottery collected suggests occupation of the site from the 15th century, while documentary records go back to the mid-16th century. It is hard to know whether this early settlement was seasonal or permanent, although seasonal settlements or *metokhia* in Crete are known from documentary sources as far back as the 15th century (Brumfield 2000, 57–58). Workers may have sheltered in less substantial, or even temporary, field shelters that disappeared prior to the construction of the extant settlement. This interpretation is strengthened by the presence of recycled building materials, such as the pottery, stone querns and re-used *dhoukani* in the extant building fabric, indicating that occupation on the site probably predates most of the extant buildings.

The construction of the more substantial dwellings that survive may have resulted from a range of imperatives. The creation of a permanent, satellite settlement represents a substantial investment in time and resources for subsistence transhumant pastoralists and agriculturalists. It seems likely that agricultural intensification stimulated the production of a larger surplus, which then enabled the construction of a permanent infrastructure, which subsequently could be used as a base for a range of activities. The enhancement of the treeless plain environment, with introduced eucalypts in the early 20th century, reflects continued investment in Mandres, while the chipped stone evidence reflects the sourcing of specialist materials and specialist tradesmen to support the intensive agricultural production carried out there.

Given (2000, 228) has argued that, despite historical characterisations of the 17th and 18th centuries in Cyprus as periods of depopulation and abandonment of rural settlements, seasonal settlements of the northern Troodos provide evidence for the intensification of rural production at this time. The evidence from Mandres supports this interpretation.

The village morphology suggests a sustained period of growth, followed by a period of reduced occupation within the central settlement: some of the old stone houses in the centre were abandoned and crumbled, and the focus perhaps changed to the well-built mudbrick outliers. As the central settlement area became filled it was necessary to construct new houses, with fewer occupation phases, on the marginal, steeply sloping land along the edges of the village. An olive tree planted some 120 m west of the settlement in the early 18th century would have belonged to this phase of intensification.

The village occupation then contracted to the oldest, central part of the village, where the most recent occupation phases re-used older structural elements. It is unlikely that any of the extant built fabric predates the late 18th or 19th centuries, and some appears to have been constructed as late as the first half of the 20th century. Nonetheless stone querns re-used in house walls, and the predominance of bone and ceramic in the locally sourced mud used for bricks and plaster, are suggestive of occupation, predating the houses containing these features, on or near the site.

According to those who lived at Mandres prior to the 1940s, its abandonment was the result of people moving away from rural areas to find paid work in factories and mines. The men whose testimonies we have characterize the final period of occupation of Mandres as one of extreme poverty. The industrialisation and public works programmes promoted by the British colonial administration in the first decades of the 20th century appear to have had a significant impact on rural life in the study area. Perceptions of the quality of a largely subsistence rural lifestyle, with limited access to cash and consumer products, must have changed very rapidly during that period. One of our informants, born in 1928, left Mandres in 1945 to work for the Water Supply and Irrigation Department, for a wage of 9 grosha a day. He had a clear image of rural poverty, recalling that 'our trousers were like a map of Europe, they had so many patches'.

Perceptions of life in pre-war Mandres vary from who tell stories of abject and wretched poverty, to those that speak of a greater sense of community cohesion. Mandres reflects both these themes. A community of families worked side by side, year after year, to expand their food production beyond the resources available to them in their home villages. Mandres also reflects the impact of British colonialism, the industrialisation of the region with the opening of the mines, and the changes the introduction of a cash economy wrought, both on the landscape and on people's perceptions of the quality of a largely subsistence agricultural lifestyle.

2.11 Mandres in Context: Transect Survey across the Plain

To investigate patterns of human activity across this area of fluvial terraces and incised gullies, we walked six north–south transects, as well as some block survey immediately to the east of the Mandres settlement (Plate 2.10). Difficulties of access and visibility meant that their spacing was somewhat uneven, and beyond this the second and third transects from the west suffered from major visibility problems. To some extent this issue was resolved by carrying out survey in November 2003 when most of the fields were ploughed. Surfaces are, in general, stable, with incision limited to the Late Pleistocene–Holocene gullies that cross the area, and with some sheet erosion east and south-east of the Mandres settlement (Plate 2.7).

Prehistoric

Apart from the rural settlement at Kato Koutraphas *Mandroudhes* (TP239), there is a very light scatter of Prehistoric Bronze Age material across the whole of the Mandres Intensive Survey Zone (Plate 2.10). This scatter comes to just 50 pieces, excluding those collected from the grid at Mandroudhes. Most of the sherds were, unsurprisingly, found on stable, mainly tilled surfaces, and there were none in the eroded area south of Mandres settlement. If we take the surviving sherds as a partial picture, then it seems that there are two very broad scatters, each of them c. 1 km wide from north to south: one surrounding Mandroudhes; and one, with a centre at the higher densities in SU3016 and SU3018, c. 600 m north-east of Mandres. The latter could represent traces of another small settlement, like Mandroudhes, whose edge we only touched. The geomorphological indicators of long-term stability are strong here, so the possibility of our transect running through an eroded site core is an unlikely explanation.

Can we detect a similar pattern elsewhere on the Plains? There is another, quite similar case of a halo of material round what was presumably a Prehistoric, and probably also a Protohistoric, Bronze Age settlement at Lemonas in the Atsas Valley, 1.9 km to the north-west of Lemonas (Chapter 2.7). At Nikitari *Petrera* (TP242), 3.3 km north-east of the SU3016/SU3018 concentration, there is a more substantial surface scatter of pottery and ground stone, most likely from a Bronze Age settlement, although this could also be interpreted as a specific activity site (Chapter 2.14). Some of these concentrations seem *prima facie* to have very low densities of material, while some are surrounded by areas of relatively poor surface stability. Taken together, however, they imply a surprisingly dense pattern of small, rural, Bronze Age sites in this relatively well-watered transitional zone between the foothills and the Plains (Chapter 2.17). Given that during most of the Prehistoric Bronze Age, the inhabitants of Cyprus remained rural and self-sufficient, not much different from their Neolithic and Chalcolithic ancestors, such site patterning is not surprising, although it has seldom been demonstrated quite so clearly elsewhere on the island.

Iron Age to Roman

The Iron Age suggests a focus on the immediate area of the later Mandres settlement. This is a very different pattern to that visible in the Bronze Age, and seems to continue through to the Roman period and beyond. The striking concentration from Iron Age through to the Roman period is on the south-east margin of the later settlement (SU0345–52); this is partially but not entirely due to a ploughed strip that offered much better visibility than the surrounding areas. Four pieces of White Painted Ware were clearly diagnostic of the Iron Age, although there was other material that could have belonged anywhere between the Iron Age and Roman period. Only three sherds of pre-Medieval pottery were retrieved from the actual structures of Mandres: two Hellenistic sherds (BU0037.SE16, floor; BU0030.SE3, mudbrick wall); and one Late Roman sherd (BU0031.SE3, stone socle). These were evidently incorporated during the structures' most recent construction phase, using materials lying to hand.

The most chronologically specific concentration is, as so often in the Survey Area, the Late Roman period, with densities of up to 5.4 sherds/100 m^2. This is accompanied by smaller amounts of Hellenistic pottery, and there might well be an almost invisible Hellenistic and Early Roman component – again as often encountered elsewhere in the Survey Area. The transect running 100 m to the east shows a very light scatter of Late Roman sherds, and there is a handful of other sherds within a radius of 500 m. Problems of erosion to the south and east of Mandres make this difficult to assess securely. If we do have a Roman-period farmstead or some such under the later settlement of Mandres, this would constitute its halo from dumping or manuring, or both.

Mandres in the Roman period could then be a largely obliterated version of either the farmstead at Vrysi tou Haji Christophi in the Atsas valley, 3.5 km to the west (Chapter 2.5), or of the pottery scatter at Sanidhia on the Koutraphas plateau, 4.5 km to the north-east (Chapter 2.15).

An outcrop of red jasper 1.4 km north-east of Mandres had a few worked pieces in its immediate vicinity (TP240; Kato Koutraphas *Khalospidhia*). This material included unworked flakes and a number of flake cores, including amorphous and change-of-orientation types. Unretouched utilized flakes found with a notched flake dominate the small number of tools found in the sample. Together these artefacts share more in common with the samples associated with Roman pottery, both at Mandres and elsewhere. They are more likely to represent the Roman ad hoc industry than the small-scale replacing of *dhoukani* flakes from local sources in the Medieval–Modern period.

Medieval–Modern

Judging from the pottery and the documentary sources, there was substantial activity at the site of Mandres by the 15th or 16th centuries. It was clearly playing its role of satellite settlement for mountain villages by the beginning of the 19th century, and very likely before that. Across the Intensive Survey Zone as a whole are found occasional sherds from the Medieval period, including one from the 12th or 13th century, there is, however, no particular focus on Mandres: at this time the area was presumably on the periphery of some neighbouring estate and settlement, perhaps Koutraphas 3.5 km to the north-east.

From the Early Ottoman period, the pottery distribution shows more of a focus on the settlement of Mandres. Densities are still very low, although this is partly due to tightly-defined periods and difficulties in dating wares precisely: less than 1.0 sherds/100 m^2 on the edge of the settlement; and less than 0.5 sherds/100 m^2 within 300 m of the settlement. This represents much less intensive activity than the haloes round the Medieval–Modern villages of the Karkotis Valley, such as Phlasou (Chapter 3.8) and Katydhata (Chapter 3.10), which tend to be between 1 and 5 sherds/100 m^2. Clearly, a satellite settlement such as Mandres involved a much more limited range of domestic and agricultural activities, and so did not produce as much domestic waste or manure.

A three-arched colonial period bridge (TP020) crosses the Argakin tou Vromonerou 800 m north of Mandres. It is approximately 18 m long, 4 m wide (road width) and 2.8 m high. It is constructed from pale yellow sandstone blocks, with plaster on the inside parapet of the bridge to reduce weathering and to increase its visibility to traffic. The blocks are of the same type found in 19th–20th-century quarries in Nicosia Formation (sandstone) south-east of the old walled city of Nicosia. This bridge was part of the Nicosia–Troodos road constructed in 1900, and provides important evidence for our analysis of British colonial road building policies and the maintenance of colonial rule during the 20th century (see Volume 1, Chapter 3.13).

2.12 Koutraphas Intensive Survey Zone: Introduction and Overview

The aim of our survey work in the Koutraphas Intensive Survey Zone was to examine a hitherto neglected area in the north-east of the Survey Area (Fig. 2.20). Today the Koutraphas area, located on the southern edge of the fertile Mesaoria plain, is almost entirely taken up with large fields dedicated to the production of cereals, although

Fig. 2.20. Elaia Valley from the south, with the Koutraphas pediment behind. The village of Kato Koutraphas is just beyond the photo to the left, and Nikitari Petrera *(TP242) is exactly in the centre (Hugh Corley)*

some smaller plots are given over to annual fruit and vegetable crops such as potatoes and watermelons. There are no modern villages within the Intensive Survey Zone, but several lie close to it, to the south, east and west. We were interested to see if the apparently fertile soils of the area had always been worked in this way, or if earlier periods had seen quite different patterns of occupation and exploitation in the landscape.

The Koutraphas Intensive Survey Zone has some of the oldest, most stable surfaces in the Survey Area. These surfaces result from the deposition of fluvial fans during the Pleistocene; they are made up of thick deposits of brown to reddish sand, pebbles, cobbles and boulders 30–50 m deep. The surface zone overall is highly weathered and oxidised, producing a cobbled, clayey soil with a distinctive red colour. Agricultural terracing on the shoulder, back and foot slopes of the landform has created younger surfaces from the exposed older sediments. The substrata of these younger surfaces are, accordingly, less weathered, yet retain organic matter to greater depth than the older soils. Locally, these terraces tap into deeply buried, red, clayey palaeosols that have similar management properties as the extant soils on the treads of the landform.

While the surface is cut by many broad swales and streams as well as gullies, no permanent water courses flow through the Koutraphas Intensive Survey Zone. Modern wells, like earlier hand-dug versions, are limited to the lowest elevations along swales and streams where the depth to bedrock is minimal (<20 m) and thus allowing perched water tables, suitable for exploitation, to develop on the bedrock. The Elaia River, however, runs along its south-western boundary (Plate 2.11). To the south and west of the river the deeply dissected Early(?) to Middle Pleistocene fluvial fans and underlying bedrock of the foothills begin to disrupt the landscape, forcing a very different approach to the exploitation of the land, before they too are replaced by the steep, now densely forested mountains. The Elaia River is the obvious communication route from the Lagoudhera and Asinou valleys to the plains. Whether as a path for copper being brought from Mavrovouni, or for timber, pitch and other mountain or forest resources being carried from the Asinou valley, the Elaia River traverses the plains to Skouriotissa in the north of the Karkotis Intensive Survey Zone, and beyond to Morphou Bay.

We worked in the Koutraphas Intensive Survey Zone during 2002 and 2003, achieving a very systematic coverage of the zone with a combination of transect and block survey (Plate 2.11). This combination of survey methods reflects changes in the surface condition at different points in the agricultural calendar. Block survey took advantage of small pockets of ploughed ground when most of the area was covered in wheat, while transects were possible between one harvest and the next year's planting. While ground visibility did not appear to affect the efficiency of our fieldwalkers (Volume 1, Chapter 2.10), we felt that the disturbed soil of ploughed ground was potentially more fruitful than the hard-packed stubble surfaces of newly harvested fields (Fig. 2.7). The decision was justified as we collected a good distribution of material, and identifiable areas of concentration, within the zone: aceramic Neolithic chipped and ground stone in the east; Hellenistic–Roman and Medieval–Modern pottery in the west; and a noticeable decrease in pottery density in the middle and east of the area.

While it may never have been densely, or even permanently, settled, the material evidence recovered suggests that the Koutraphas area has, to a greater or lesser extent, been occupied or exploited at various times during the last ten thousand years. Centres of activity and evidence for land use from the Neolithic, Roman and Medieval–Modern periods were all identified within the area.

2.13 *Ad Hoc* Stone Industries

A thin blanket of chipped stone is spread across the whole Koutraphas Intensive Survey Zone, much of it representing the production of cutting and chopping tools from local materials. The chipped stone, in conjunction with the rather smaller quantities of ground stone, suggests that cereal crops have been exploited seasonally in the area since the Neolithic, an activity attested in later periods by pottery distributions (Chapter 2.15) and 19th–20th-century architecture and agricultural facilities (Chapter 2.10).

Occasional or seasonal cereal and plant processing was evident in the chipped and ground stone tools found in the west of this Intensive Survey Zone, at Pano Koutraphas *Katalasharis* (TP256) and Pano Koutraphas *Sanidhia* (TP245). This material was recorded on stable surfaces and was probably in situ, although the same cannot necessarily be said for further items recorded on the eroded and unstable surfaces to the east of Sanidhia (Plate 2.12).

An ad hoc approach to tool making is suggested by the use of local diabase for making the rubbing stones, querns and pounders, and the local jasper employed to produce most of the chipped stone. At the same time a transitory element is introduced to these activity areas by the presence of higher quality, non-local Lefkara cherts and chalcedony.

The majority of evidence for stone technology appears, perhaps unsurprisingly, to date from the Neolithic. There is evidence, however, which suggests that an ad hoc lithic industry associated with cereal production and processing continued in the area into the Roman (Chapter 2.15) and, perhaps, Medieval (Chapter 2.16) periods. The variety of chipped stone items recorded around Katalasharis and on transects to the east of Sanidhia was similar to other samples where Roman pottery dominated. Retouched and utilized flake tools and flake scrapers made on jasper, found some 500 m north of Sanidhia, broadly resemble artefacts associated with Roman period activity elsewhere in the TAESP area. Furthermore, two ground stone rubbers collected in same area would not be inconsistent with such an interpretation, but the unstable ground surface in these Survey Units precludes a definite dating (Plate 2.13; Table 2.19). At Sanidhia itself, while the pottery was predominantly Roman, cores, trimming elements and blanks of local jasper indicated a Neolithic ad hoc production of flakes similar to that identified at Kambos tou Lemonari (TP095) and elsewhere in Cyprus (e.g. McCartney and Gratuze 2003; McCartney and Todd 2005).

A handful of *dhoukani* blades found in the Koutraphas Intensive Survey Zone provides evidence for the exploitation of local materials in the Roman (Chapter 2.15) or Medieval–Modern (Chapter 2.16) periods. These were made from imported Lefkara cherts and from local jasper and chalcedony in equal numbers, while the remains of earlier manufacturing were dominated by local material. It seems that the stone-workers' presence was temporary and when they moved on, they took most of their valuable, high quality, imported chert with them. The impermanence of their occupation is further underlined by the domination of chipped stone tools, rather than core reduction debris, in the material record.

Prehistoric seasonal activity is most clearly illustrated by a significant concentration of material at Nikitari *Kambos tou Lemonari* (TP095), in a gently sloping, ploughed field to the west of the road running north from Vyzakia (Fig. 2.21). In this location, only tillage and sheet erosion could have any impact on the position of the artefacts, and in both cases their effect is minor. An unusual density of ground stone was accompanied by a more diffuse but fairly even spread of worked jasper. A few further pieces of chipped stone in an east-sloping olive grove on the opposite side of the road were clearly peripheral to the main scatter. All of the pottery dates to post-prehistoric periods (Table 2.20).

The ground stone at Kambos tou Lemonari was representative of the wider distribution across the

Table 2.19. Pano Koutraphas Sanidhia *(TP245): lithic counts in SUs to north and south*

	SU3033–41	**SU3045–46**
Surface	*Stable*	*Unstable*
Cores	5	1
Blanks	2	1
Debris	2	0
Tools	8	3
Ground Stone	4	2
Total	**21**	**7**
Suggested Period	Aceramic Neolithic	Roman

Table 2.20. Nikitari Kambos tou Lemonari *(TP095; SU1328–38): pottery*

Period	*Fct*	*Type*	*No.*	*Weight*
Early to Late Roman	La	La	3	20g
Roman to Modern	CW	CW	1	1g
Historical (Archaic to Modern)	HU	HU	3	35g
	LU	LU	2	30g
Medieval to Modern	HU	HU	1	10g
	LU	LU	3	65g
Modern	LU	LU	1	1g

Fig. 2.21. Nikitari Kambos tou Lemonari *(TP095): view looking north-west to Morphou Bay (Michael Given)*

Koutraphas area, despite appearing rougher than Bronze Age examples recovered from Mandroudhes (Chapter 2.9) in the Mandres Intensive Survey Zone and Koutroullis (Chapter 3.5) in the Karkotis Valley. These early prehistoric querns, rubbers, grinders and one mortar suggest that the exploitation of cereals and other plants was the prime concern at Kambos tou Lemonari. This conclusion is supported by the prominence of utilized flakes in the chipped stone record, suggesting that simple cutting tools were the ones most frequently produced. Examples with abraded edges, as well as heavily battered 'chopping' edges, suggest a wide range of activities, the specifics of which could only be determined through use-wear analysis. The cutting and shredding of plant materials, however, would fit well with the abundant sample of ground stone tools found.

The ad hoc production of tools is indicated initially by the use of local materials. The ground stone tools were all made from local basal rocks, while the chipped stone record was dominated by poor quality, local jasper. It is worth noting, however, that in comparison with samples from elsewhere in the TAESP area, the jasper used at Kambos tou Lemonari was of comparatively high quality. Additionally, the low level of Lefkara cherts used here, compared to other prehistoric localities, such as Phlasou *Koutroullis* (Chapter 3.5), implies that the individuals who so intensively worked the local jasper at Kambos tou Lemonari were temporary occupants. Lefkara cherts do not occur naturally in the TAESP area, but begin to outcrop farther east; such high quality, valuable material would only have been left behind if it was exhausted or lost.

The chipped stone tools and significant number of cores (Table 2.21) point toward occasional occupation and expedient tool production at Kambos tou Lemonari. The presence of core trimming elements and jasper hammer stones define the simple core technology necessitated by the use of poor quality raw materials. The prevalence of chipped stone tools and tested nodules, rather than core reduction debris and unworked blanks, illustrates the relatively ad hoc character of activity, in which flakes were struck and used in the immediate vicinity. A similar pattern was observed at two other early lithic scatter sites 15–20 km to the east, at Agrokipia *Palaeokamina* and Politiko *Kelaïdhoni* (Given and Knapp 2003, 182–86; McCartney 2005).

Table 2.21. Nikitari Kambos tou Lemonari *(TP095 and SU1330): chipped stone category counts and percentages*

	No.	%
Cores	15	25%
Blades	5	8%
Tools	38	62%
Debitage	3	5%
Total	**61**	**100%**

Prismatic blades (e.g. TCL173) made from the good quality Lefkara chert, combined with an ad hoc flake *chaîne opératoire*, is a feature of assemblages belonging to the Cypriot Aceramic Neolithic (McCartney and Gratuze 2003). This combination of tool types and the systematic exploitation of local jasper are, however, also typical of sites likely to predate the Cypriot Aceramic Neolithic (McCartney 2005; McCartney and Todd 2005). Conversely, while *pièces esquillées* made on local jasper (TCL389) are seen frequently in assemblages covering the same time span, they can also occur later (Briois *et al.* 1997; McCartney 2003, 2005; McCartney and Gratuze 2003). It is interesting in this context to note the absence of obsidian from Kambos tou Lemonari; it is similarly absent in Late Epipalaeolithic assemblages such as that from Akrotiri *Aetokremnos*, which defines the 'Akrotiri' phase (McCartney 2005; Simmons 1999, 127; McCartney and Todd 2005).

The ad hoc manufacture of stone tools, while apparently continuing into later periods, points on the whole toward small task groups or mobile foragers in the Early Aceramic Neolithic. They would have worked seasonally in the area to exploit cereal crops, with permanent bases at larger settlements elsewhere, as yet unidentified, perhaps close to chert sources like the activity sites at Politiko *Kelaïdhoni* and Agrokipia *Palaeokamina* (Given and Knapp 2003, 182–86; McCartney 2005).

2.14 Bronze Age Activities at Nikitari *Petrera*

While it seems likely that the majority of the lithic material discussed above was of Neolithic origin, there is evidence to suggest that ad hoc stone processing continued through

Table 2.22. Nikitari Petrera *(TP242: SU3097, SU3100): pottery. TCP numbers refer to Pottery Catalogue in Volume 1, Chapter 3.6*

Prehistoric

Fct	*Type*	*No.*	*Weight*
HU	HU	16	1.02kg
HU	Sla	2	84g TCP509
Un	Sla	3	145g TCP505

Bronze Age

Fct	*Type*	*No.*	*Weight*
HU	HU	30	1.734kg TCP508
LU	LU	5	33g

Prehistoric Bronze Age

Fct	*Type*	*No.*	*Weight*
LU	LU	1	4g

Cypro-Geometric to Classical

Fct	*Type*	*No.*	*Weight*
LU	LU	1	12g

Historical Antiquity (Archaic to Late Roman)

Fct	*Type*	*No.*	*Weight*
HU	HU	1	55g
LU	LU	14	217g
TW	TW	1	2g

Hellenistic to Roman

Fct	*Type*	*No.*	*Weight*
CW	CW	1	7g
TW	SRS	3	19g

Early to Late Roman

Fct	*Type*	*No.*	*Weight*
TW	ARS	1	8g

Historical (Archaic to Modern)

Fct	*Type*	*No.*	*Weight*
LU	LU	18	200g

Medieval to Modern

Fct	*Type*	*No.*	*Weight*
TW	G	1	6g
U	Uju	2	12g

the Bronze Age and into the Roman period. An isolated perforated weight (TCL301) found at Sanidhia (TP245) is similar to a type reported in Protohistoric Bronze Age contexts elsewhere on Cyprus (e.g. Elliot 1985, 307). More tellingly, just outside the Intensive Survey Zone at Nikitari *Petrera* (TP242) was a considerable concentration of ground stone spread over approximately 50 m from east to west. The general background scatter of basal rocks at this locality suggests that the sample recorded represents only a small portion of the ground stone at the site. Associated with the ground stone was a small amount of Bronze Age pottery and a handful of chipped stone.

Petrera is situated on a side-valley fluvial fan of Late Pleistocene age, on the southern banks of the Elaia River (Fig. 2.20). The fan edge has been shaped by two streams and the Elaia River itself into a steep, cliff edge that ranges in height from 2–5 m and sweeps in an arc from the south-west clockwise around to the east-south-east. The only level entry to the site area is from the south-east. Appropriate, for millennia, for the dry cropping of cereals, its stable surface overlies thick sediments and soil with a mollic (organic-rich) ploughsoil (Plate 2.11).

Querns and pounding stones suggest that intensive cereal production took place at Petrera during the Protohistoric Bronze Age period (Fig. 2.22). So too do well-worn rubbers with up-turned handles, and a variety made from thick, lightly pecked or unshaped, elongated boulders that were also found at Kato Koutraphas *Mandroudhes* (Chapter 2.9), another plains site 4.9 km to the south-west. Further evidence for cereal processing and a Protohistoric Bronze Age date comes from ground stone collected from Survey Units close to Petrera (Fig. 2.22). They included a quern and a pounder, but were dominated by well-made rubbers. One, which had been re-used as an anvil, perhaps suggests that temporary occupation does not necessarily mean short-term or fleeting occupation.

The Bronze Age date for Petrera is supported by the chipped stone, as well as the pottery. While very small and inconclusive, the chipped stone assemblage was in keeping with Bronze Age assemblages elsewhere in the Survey Area, notably at Kato Koutraphas *Mandroudhes* (Chapter 2.9) and Katydhata *Laonarka* (Chapter 3.9). All periods were represented in the pottery assemblage, but the clear majority consisted of prehistoric Light and Heavy Utility wares with no preserved finish, made from a coarse fabric (Table 2.22). Some of the material was assigned to the Bronze Age; the utilitarian functions suggest an activity site rather than anything more permanent, so perhaps, like the Neolithic workers elsewhere in the Koutraphas area, the Bronze Age occupants of Petrera were working away from a larger, more permanent base. It seems, however, that the production and processing of cereal crops did not occupy all their time. An almost complete senet board (TCL323), a type fossil of the Bronze Age in Cyprus (Falconer *et al.* 2005; Swiny *et al.* 2003, 231–33), suggests that game playing was one activity of at least some people at Petrera (Sebbane 2001; Swiny 1980). By the Late Bronze Age, however, senet boards were occasionally built into structures, so its presence here might be due to a secondary use (Steel and McCartney 2008, 30–32).

Fig. 2.22. Nikitari Petrera *(TP242): ground stone (Hugh Corley)*

Table 2.23. Nikitari Sanidhia *(TP245: SU3033–46): pottery. TCP numbers refer to Pottery Catalogue in Volume 1, Chapter 3.6*

Historical Antiquity (Archaic to Late Roman)			
Fct	*Type*	*No.*	*Weight*
HU	HU	97	3.153kg
LU	LU	151	1.96kg
Tr	Am	1	21g
TW	TW	3	15g

Hellenistic			
Fct	*Type*	*No.*	*Weight*
TW	BS	3	12g TCP492

Late Hellenistic			
Fct	*Type*	*No.*	*Weight*
CW	CWL03	1	9g TCP490

Hellenistic to Roman			
Fct	*Type*	*No.*	*Weight*
CW	CW	34	183g
HU	HUR24	1	40g
LU	LUR19	1	5g TCP493
Tr	Am	1	50g
Tr	Mav03	3	65g
TW	SRS	26	168g
TW	TW	3	19g

Hellenistic to Early Roman			
Fct	*Type*	*No.*	*Weight*
TW	CS	1	14g

Early Roman			
Fct	*Type*	*No.*	*Weight*
CW	CWJ03	3	55g TCP489
TW	CS06	2	11g
TW	CS11	5	39g
TW	CS12	2	33g

Early to Late Roman			
Fct	*Type*	*No.*	*Weight*
CW	CW	41	283g
CW	CWCR02a	3	23g
CW	CWCR03	2	22g
CW	CWFPWh	2	43g
CW	CWPR04	1	5g
CW	CWPR12	1	6g
HU	HUR01	6	254g
HU	HUR03	2	33g
HU	HUR08	1	30g
Tr	AmSk01	13	452g
Tr	AmSk02	2	50g
Tr	AmSk03	3	33g
TW	ARS	6	34g

Mid Roman			
Fct	*Type*	*No.*	*Weight*
Tr	Pin	2	145g TCP491
TW	ARS50A/B	1	3g

Late Roman			
Fct	*Type*	*No.*	*Weight*
Ar	TiP	1	55g
CW	CWCR06	1	10g
CW	CWPR04a	1	10g
CW	CWPR06	1	6g
HU	HU	1	15g
HU	HUR22	1	38g
LU	LU	1	6g
TW	CRS	6	155g
TW	CRS01b	1	12g
TW	CRS02	1	6g
TW	CRS09	2	17g
TW	CRS09A	1	16g
TW	LRC	3	12g

Roman to Modern			
Fct	*Type*	*No.*	*Weight*
CW	CWB01	1	10g

Historical (Archaic to Modern)			
Fct	*Type*	*No.*	*Weight*
HU	HU	21	1.075kg
LU	LU	16	212g
LU	LUR15	1	16g

Medieval-Frankish			
Fct	*Type*	*No.*	*Weight*
TW	CGS04	1	4g

Ottoman to Modern I			
Fct	*Type*	*No.*	*Weight*
TW	G03	1	2g

Ottoman to Modern II			
Fct	*Type*	*No.*	*Weight*
TW	G02	1	11g
TW	MP01	2	34g

It seems odd that while Bronze Age activity is evident throughout the northern Troodos, there is no evidence that the Koutraphas area was occupied, or even exploited, on a large scale at this time. Perhaps it was impractical to exploit an area that lay this far from centres of settlement or industrial activity, such as the copper workings at Skouriotissa just to the west or Tamassos far to the east. Perhaps the Koutraphas area fell into some kind of activity shadow in the regional network of landscape exploitation – a point between centres of population or other activities that was too far from any of them to be practically inhabited or exploited.

2.15 Temporary Occupation and Exploitation in the Roman Period

While there seems to have been more widespread activity in the Koutraphas area in the Hellenistic to Roman periods, it is noticeable that the eastern part of the zone, where much of the Neolithic evidence had been recorded, was almost devoid of material from these later periods, apart from a very small amount of Cooking Ware that could have been made at any time since the Roman period. By contrast, there was a definite carpet of pottery containing a full range of types spread across the four westernmost transects (Plate 2.14). This carpet had relatively well-defined edges, and there were two distinct peaks in artefact density on the edge of the small plateau above the Elaia River, one at Pano Koutraphas *Katalasharis* (TP256), and another at Pano Koutraphas *Sanidhia* (TP245).

Sanidhia and Katalasharis are both ploughsoil assemblages greatly affected by tilling, producing the smallest average size of sherds at any of the identified Hellenistic–Roman sites. Very few individual fragments of pottery can be securely dated either to the Late Hellenistic or the Early Roman period, yet they clearly indicate activity at

Table 2.24. Nikitari Katalasharis *(TP256: SU3070–76): pottery. TCP numbers refer to Pottery Catalogue in Volume 1, Chapter 3.6*

Historical Antiquity (Archaic to Late Roman)

Fct	*Type*	*No.*	*Weight*
HU	HU	50	2.014kg
LU	LU	93	1.23kg
Tr	Am	1	70g

Hellenistic

Fct	*Type*	*No.*	*Weight*
TW	BS	2	8g
TW	FP	1	7g
			TCP500

Hellenistic to Roman

Fct	*Type*	*No.*	*Weight*
CW	CW	44	273g
HU	HUR24	1	90g
Tr	KoaP	1	60g
TW	SRS	11	53g
TW	TW	3	11g

Late Hellenistic to Early Roman

Fct	*Type*	*No.*	*Weight*
TW	CS	3	50g
TW	ESA	1	20g

Early Roman

Fct	*Type*	*No.*	*Weight*
CW	CWJ02	1	19g
			TCP501
TW	CS11	2	23g
TW	CS12	1	8g

Early to Late Roman

Fct	*Type*	*No.*	*Weight*
Ar	TiP	1	110g
CW	CW	2	4g
CW	CWCR01	1	12g
CW	CWCR02a	3	39g
CW	CWFPWh	1	17g
CW	CWPR04	1	25g
CW	CWPR15	2	20g
HU	HUR01	6	189g
HU	HUR03	3	105g
Tr	AmSk01	8	193g
Tr	AmSk03	2	28g
TW	ARS	5	17g

Late Roman

Fct	*Type*	*No.*	*Weight*
Ar	TiP	2	210g
Ar	TiSk01	1	100g
CW	CWCR01	1	12g
CW	CWPR06	2	25g
LU	LU	1	26g
TW	CRS	1	20g
			TCP502
TW	CRS01b	1	11g
TW	CRS02	1	10g
TW	CRS09A	1	14g
TW	CRS09b	2	32g
TW	CRS09c	1	9g
TW	LRC	2	7g
TW	LRC01a	1	10g
TW	LRC01B	1	3g
			TCP499
TW	LRC10A	3	37g

Historical (Archaic to Modern)

Fct	*Type*	*No.*	*Weight*
HU	HU	14	614g
HU	Tri	1	21g
LU	LU	21	228g
TW	TW	6	37g

Medieval

Fct	*Type*	*No.*	*Weight*
TW	GS05	1	8g

Medieval to Modern

Fct	*Type*	*No.*	*Weight*
CW	BGW	9	196g
CW	Tia	5	256g
CW	Tta	4	64g
HU	HU	42	2.96kg
LU	LU	60	957g
TW	G	1	18g
TW	G04	1	11g
U	BuHK	2	180g
U	ID	12	379g
U	ID04A	2	20g
U	Tta02	1	70g
			TCP497
U	U	1	7g
U	Uju	3	19g
U	UPSJa	1	40g

Medieval-Frankish

Fct	*Type*	*No.*	*Weight*
TW	CGS05	4	32g

Medieval utility period III

Fct	*Type*	*No.*	*Weight*
LU	IDWF	1	9g
			TCP498
U	ID03	4	49g
			TCP496

Ottoman to Modern I

Fct	*Type*	*No.*	*Weight*
TW	CGS06	2	28g
TW	G03	6	100g
TW	UnG	2	18g
U	ID02	6	95g
U	UJa07	1	65g
			TCP495
U	ULSJ01	2	112g

Medieval-Venetian to Early Ottoman

Fct	*Type*	*No.*	*Weight*
TW	CGS06	2	22g
TW	G03	1	3g
TW	MP01	6	55g

Ottoman to Modern II

Fct	*Type*	*No.*	*Weight*
LU	BuL	2	28g
TW	SP01	1	12g

Modern

Fct	*Type*	*No.*	*Weight*
HU	HU	2	50g

Sanidhia and Katalasharis during those periods. At Sanidhia a few undiagnostic Black Slipped sherds, several Cypriot Sigillata fragments and a few sherds of Mid Roman pinched handled amphorae were collected, suggesting that there was intermittent occupation of the site over the entire Roman period (Table 2.23).

At Katalasharis we collected two Black Slipped sherds, a few Cypriot Sigillata fragments, a single fragment of Eastern Sigillata A, another imported type – possibly western – and a fish plate (Table 2.24). No fragments of Late Hellenistic or Early Roman transport amphorae were collected at either site, and only two Cooking Ware fragments could be securely dated to this period. The near absence of earlier Cooking Ware is probably explained by its friable texture making it very prone to breaking down with the frequent ploughing in this area.

It is unlikely that the peaks at Sanidhia and Katalasharis represent the outer edges of a single, large settlement bracketed by the two transects. Such a settlement would have been more than 500 m across, making it the size of a very substantial town. The pottery levels, while substantial, do not reflect a settlement of such proportions in either number or character, and we discovered no traces of large-scale architecture. Even medium-size rural settlements in Cyprus, such as Kalavasos *Kopetra* (Rautman *et al.* 2003) and Panayia Ematousa (Jacobsen 2006a), have large quantities of transport amphorae. The evidence is far more suggestive of two smaller establishments, a pattern of occupation similar to that in the Atsas Valley (Chapter 2.7). Across the entire western part of the Intensive Survey Zone areas with peak pottery densities were surrounded by a thin layer of Hellenistic to Roman pottery. This could be the result of manuring or simply the dispersal of material from the two concentrations through constant, ongoing agricultural activity across the area.

No structural evidence was identified at either Sanidhia or Katalasharis, but the pottery spread indicates that they might have been larger than Vrysi tou Haji Christophi in the Atsas Valley, where the remains of two stone structures were recorded (Chapter 2.5). The differing pottery spreads may, at least in part, be due to the different conditions under which the two areas were surveyed — Koutraphas in November over ploughed fields, Vrysi tou Haji Christophi and environs in the height of summer over wheat stubble. If any structures at Sanidhia or Katalasharis were built from mudbrick or wood, they would not have survived as well as the stone-built buildings at Vrysi tou Haji Christophi. Repeated construction or reconstruction of less substantial buildings might also account for the wider spread of pottery at Sanidhia and Katalasharis (Dewar and McBride 1992, 234, fig. 1). The scarcity of building materials, including tiles, and the broad spread of material could equally be due to their dispersal by constant ploughing, especially modern deep ploughing.

The scarcity of tile in the area also points toward less substantial structures, which might have been roofed with less durable materials such as wood or reeds. Again, there is a marked contrast with Vrysi tou Haji Christophi (Chapter 2.5), where large amounts of tile were clearly associated with two small structures. It is quite possible that the differences between the two sites result from their very different post-depositional history. The small knoll on which Vrysi tou Haji Christophi was found has served to collect loose material disturbed by ploughing, particularly once the thick vegetation was established on it, whereas Sanidhia was located in the middle of a field that is still ploughed today. Very little tile was collected anywhere in the Koutraphas area, and just one self-slipped, Late Roman fragment at Sanidhia. At the same time, there is no evidence for systematic field clearance of large fragments. The three Roman fragments recovered from Katalasharis may suggest it was the more permanent of the two settlements. A peak of later pottery at the site indicates that activity there continued into the Medieval–Modern period, although it is likely that there were long gaps between periods of occupation.

The pottery assemblages at Sanidhia and Katalasharis suggest a continuing settlement throughout the Hellenistic to Roman period. Sanidhia is one of the few places in the entire TAESP area where mid-Roman pottery in the form of African Red Slip wares and pinched handled transport amphorae have been collected. This pattern it shares with Ayia Marina *Mavrovouni* (TS02) and Xyliatos *Litharkies* (TS10), two areas associated with the exploitation of copper. In fact, most of the broad range of Table and Cooking Wares occurring at Sanidhia and Katalasharis also occur at Mavrovouni and Litharkies. There was a full range of Cooking Wares and a considerable amount of utility ware at Sanidhia and Katalasharis, both of which are indicative of settlement. The Light Utility ware was not particularly distinctive, but all the Heavy Utility items were basins rather than closed vessels. Although it is possible that cloth covers could have been used on them for short periods, basins are more suited to food preparation than to long-term storage. None of them showed signs of internal wear, again suggesting either short-term use or else the use of other, perhaps stone, vessels as mortarium types for the grinding and preparation of food. The absence of large, long-term storage vessels is unusual, but not in itself sufficient to identify these sites as seasonal settlements.

Ethnoarchaeological studies on the Aegean island of Keos indicate that there is a significant distinction between proper farms and limited activity locations and structures (Whitelaw *et al.* 1994, 169). The dispersed, limited-use facilities are usually the foci of a restricted range of activities, leaving a potentially distinctive range of debris leading to only minor accumulations of material. It was observed, however, that such an accumulation was usually below the recovery threshold of most surface surveys. Consequently, Whitelaw and colleagues believed it was impossible to distinguish between seasonal and permanent occupation (Whitelaw 1991, 416; Whitelaw *et al.* 1994, 168–69). Whitelaw was writing in the first half of the 1990s, basing his results on Aegean surveys carried out in the 1970s and 1980s, when collections were much less intensive. The assemblages at Sanidhia and Katalasharis are well above any such postulated recovery threshold, but the absence of vessels for long-term storage may indeed suggest seasonal occupation. At the only excavated and published Late Roman farmstead of Pyrgouthi, Greece, the absence of large storage vessels was interpreted as a sign of self-sufficiency and diversified production (Hjohlman 2002, 117). At Sanidhia, the lack of pithoi, normally used for storage in a permanent settlement, is unusual but not in itself sufficient to identify it as a seasonal settlement. A few transport amphorae were identified, some of them locally made, so it is possible they were strictly production sites.

If Sanidhia and Katalasharis were agricultural settlements, we must consider how they might have fitted into any wider system that operated in the area, such as that in the hinterland of Kourion (Swiny and Mavromatis 2000). They lie on the western edge of the Koutraphas pediment, which would seem to link them to the Atsas farmsteads, Skouriotissa, the Karkotis Valley and the city of Soloi, rather than Tamassos to the east (Given and Knapp 2003, 199–200). They also lie conveniently on the route between the copper production areas of Alestos and Mavrovouni, where a large number of pithoi have been found, and the port at Morphou Bay. If this route followed the Elaia River Valley, as seems reasonable, it would have passed immediately below the agricultural area of Koutraphas. The location of Sanidhia and Katalasharis, close to the mountains, might also suggest a connection, seasonal or otherwise, with the small Roman settlements in the Rotson Valley to the south (Chapters 4.1, 5.9; Sollars 2005, 133).

2.16 Agriculture and Milling in the Medieval–Modern Periods

Beyond the concentrations at Katalasharis and Sanidhia there was a thin layer of Roman pottery across the Intensive Survey Zone, particularly in the west. The pattern suggests

Table 2.25. Koutraphas Intensive Survey Zone: Medieval–Modern glazed and decorated wares

	Glazed	*Sgraffito*	*Painted*
NW corner	1	9	5
Katalasharis	6	5	6
SE corner	3	2	1

that the pottery fragments were distributed in the course of manuring. A similar pattern is visible in the Medieval–Modern pottery record, and includes material in the east of the area (Plate 2.15). Seven *dhoukani* blades were amongst the pottery in the east and the west. These too were perhaps spread on the fields with the manure, but it is surprising that so few were recorded in a landscape so dominated by agriculture. This could reflect differing patterns of use, disposal or loss between pottery and stone, and perhaps depends on the locations in which each was used.

The two surviving villages closest to the Intensive Survey Zone, Kato Koutraphas and Potami, appear in the 16th-century Venetian village lists (Grivaud 1998, 469), and Kato Koutraphas, at least, was in existence earlier than that. By 1832 Pano Koutraphas (TP140) was a Turkish Cypriot village, which in that year produced 32 bushels of barley and just under 20 of wheat; the highest figures of any village in the Survey Area (Papadopoullos 1965, 187–89). It was abandoned after the inter-communal violence of 1964 (Koutraphas 1987), and has since been demolished. Save for the still-standing water fountain of the 1950s, it is now virtually indistinguishable from the surrounding fields.

Kato Koutraphas was the focus for a feudal estate that was certainly established by the 1460s, and which continued well into the 16th century (Aristeidou 1994, 145; Bustron 1884, 418; Grivaud 1998, 370–71). The current village church, Panayia Chryseleousa (TP244), was built in the 18th century, but contains re-used elements from the original Medieval structure (Gunnis 1936, 293).

In 1512 Kato Koutraphas included a total of 237.3 ha of irrigated, dry cultivated and uncultivated land (Grivaud 1998, 370; see Volume 1, Chapter 5.4 for a full discussion). Depending on the precise configuration of this land, it is possible that this included the pottery concentration in the north-west of our Intensive Survey Zone. This consisted of a relatively large amount of very fine sgraffito (Table 2.25), along with some Cooking Ware and utility wares. Pottery types identified included Cypriot Brown and Green Sgraffito Ware of the Medieval-Frankish period (late 14th–15th century), Cypriot Green Painted Sgraffito Ware (late 15th–early 16th century) and Monochrome Green Painted Ware (16th century onward).

A second, rather larger peak of Medieval–Modern pottery, especially Ottoman and Modern, coincided with the concentration of Roman material at Katalasharis (TP256). The assemblage had a similar chronological pattern to the material retrieved in the north-west of the Intensive Survey Zone, and included fragments of Cypriot Brown and Green Sgraffito (late 14th–15th centuries) as well as monochrome green painted ware (16th century onward), Ottoman to Modern monochrome glazed wares, and a single piece of green, slip-painted ware either from Didymoteicho in northern Greece or from Çanakkale in western Turkey, dated to the late 19th/early 20th centuries (Vroom 2005, 186–87). There was, by contrast, virtually nothing recorded at Sanidhia (TP245) for these later periods.

No structural evidence was found at either location, but the pottery record indicates considerable activity at Katalasharis during the Medieval–Modern periods. On its own the Ottoman–Modern pottery, consisting largely of Light Utility vessels, suggests that there was storage and/or consumption there, but not cooking. The less precisely dated Medieval–Modern pottery included Cooking Wares and a surprisingly large amount of Heavy Utility sherds. Despite the absence of structures, the combined pottery of this quite focused distribution suggests a rural household with large-scale, perhaps long-term storage facilities. The high proportion of Heavy Utility, compared to the Light Utility and Table Wares, is unusual, and perhaps indicates an emphasis on storage over occupation at Katalasharis. As no structures survive and none of the village lists (Grivaud 1998, 469) record any settlement other than the known villages in the area, this might be seen as primarily a storage site for one of them, with occasional, perhaps seasonal occupation. This re-use of the same area as the Hellenistic–Roman site at Katalasharis is the only sign of long-term continuity in the Koutraphas Intensive Survey Zone.

In the west of the Koutraphas Intensive Survey Zone, then, there appears to be a thin spread of Medieval–Modern pottery on the broader, flatter ground on top of the plateau to the north of the river, typically about 1–2 sherds/100 m^2, but rising up to 10, or in one case 13 sherds/100 m^2. The lower end of this corresponds to what we interpret as manuring levels of pottery density between the Medieval estates in the Karkotis Valley (e.g. Plate 3.6). On the evidence of a single transect, the general spread of pottery was even sparser on the lower and more accessible ground to the south of the river, consistently less than 1 sherds/100 m^2. Presumably the well-watered alluvial soils of the valley floor would have been more intensively cultivated (see Volume 1, Chapter 5.4).

TAESP collected more evidence on the plateau, away from the villages, where the thin spread might be attributed to sparse manuring centred upon occasional settlements, or at least gathering points, indicated by the peaks in the pottery record. In addition to the two in the west of the Intensive Survey Zone, there was another small concentration of Medieval–Modern pottery in a flat, fertile area to the south-east (Plate 2.15). The mix of pottery types in these few Survey Units included Light and Heavy Utility in addition to Cooking Ware, and glazed ware dated from the late 15th to 20th centuries. It is suggested once again that the thin scatter of sherds in the block survey may be the result of manuring.

Perhaps the fields on the edge of the Mesaoria needed less fertilizer, or were farmed less intensively, incorporating more fallow periods into the agricultural cycle. There is

Fig. 2.23. Watermill in Vyzakia village (BU0104): turbine wheel and water jet outlet in the wheel room (Chris Parks)

also evidence of smaller fields, sited opportunistically, using terracing or check dams to take advantage of local topography and conditions, like the 7 m-wide check dam at Potami *Strata Oritissas* (TP204) in the east of the Intensive Survey Zone. The considerable effort required to take manure any great distance from a village, let alone across the river and up the steep northern bank, may also account for the low densities of material across the zone. The small halo around the peak in pottery at Katalasharis may indicate some kind of seasonal activity, but this short-term occupation and/or less intensive farming techniques meant that there was never enough material generated to carpet the landscape.

While it is clear that activity in the fields did not cease at the end of the Roman period, it would seem that such occupation as had taken place decreased even further. The majority of the pottery came from the west of the zone, although a small amount was recorded in block survey to the east (Plate 2.15). Densities were too low to be the residue of permanent settlement, but perhaps represented low-level manuring (see below) or items discarded or lost by workers from the nearby villages. These include Potami and Nikitari in the east, Kato Koutraphas in the west, and Pano Koutraphas, also in the west, but abandoned in the 1960s and now demolished. All of them appear on Medieval lists from the first half of the 16th century onward (Grivaud 1998, 74, 469).

The Elaia River will not have been used to irrigate any of the fields within the Intensive Survey Zone. It may, however, have played a role in processing the cereal crops produced there; at least four mills lie on or close by the 4 km stretch of the river before it meets the zone's south-western boundary (Plate 2.16).

There was no clear evidence to date any of the mills; they almost certainly predate the British colonial period and were probably constructed during the 17th or 18th century, although they, or their predecessors, may date back to the Medieval period. All were built to a reasonably standardized design, with leat, penstock, and turbine/milling house (Volume 1, Chapter 3.11). Similar mills were built across the Levant, using equivalent materials and construction methods (McQuitty 1995). These examples were built mostly from coursed rubble masonry that included a high proportion of basalt river boulders, and walls were finished with lime plaster.

The watermill in Vyzakia village (BU0104) was a multiple level construction, with a penstock, leat and a ruined millhouse. The five tiers of the penstock were built from irregular coursed basalt masonry finished with a smooth, white, lime plaster face. Most of the corner quoins used irregular basalt blocks, although limestone blocks were incorporated in the lower tiers of the penstock. The majority of mills recorded in the Survey Area had circular penstock chutes, but at Vyzakia this was, unusually, square. A large metal horizontal turbine wheel, almost identical to the one still in use in the Stylianides mill in Evrykhou, was in place in the vaulted wheel chamber (Fig. 2.23). The millhouse was built in stone, but had been subsequently repaired with mudbrick.

As at Vyzakia, the mill at the abandoned village of Pano Koutraphas (BU0096) was conveniently situated on the edge of the village, close by a concentrated customer base

Fig. 2.24. Pano Koutraphas: watermill (BU0096) (Chris Parks)

(Fig. 2.24). A nearby modern wheat farm underlines the mill's processing function and its ideal location between source and consumer. A five-tiered penstock and substantial mill room were well preserved, but much of the leat was destroyed by the road from Kato Koutraphas, which runs along the plain on the margin of the village. An unusual feature in this mill was the fan-shaped entry point to the leat, and a sluice system that controlled the overflow from the penstock chute on the eastern side. The chute was also relatively large, measuring 1.75 m in diameter, suggesting that the mill once had a sizeable, reliable source of water for energy, which perhaps would have given it the capacity to cater to a wider community. The wheel chamber was long and narrow, measuring approximately 2.5 × 2.0 m, and was a rare example of a fully extant wheel chamber in the Survey Area. The millhouse was less well preserved, and the broken remains of millstones were scattered in one of its three rooms.

The variety of materials used in the construction and repair of this mill suggest that it had an important place in the community over an extended period. The structure was predominantly built with river stones and cobbles, which still bore the remains of a plaster covering, on both the interior and the exterior of the structure. The wheel chamber and the archway leading into it were built in finer limestone masonry; red plaster covering the uppermost layer of masonry around the millhouse appears to be an attempt at restoration or preservation. Pano Koutraphas was a Turkish village when it was abandoned in 1974, and the mill was built close to the mosque, suggesting perhaps the mosque's ownership or control of the milling process (Schriwer 2006, 296–97).

The mill at Vyzakia *Muttokambos* (BU0109) lay approximately 800 m upstream of the village, on the road between Vyzakia and Xyliatos and other villages farther up into the foothills. The cadastral map identifies it as a corn mill, something supported by its location close to the plains. The five-tiered penstock was built of roughly coursed rubble masonry using identical construction methods to the mill on the edge of the village (BU0104). Here, however, the chute was round with a smaller diameter. The top courses of the penstock and leat may be a rubble masonry extension. The wheelhouse was still extant with the usual arched opening, and the water outlet inside it was still visible.

Most pertinent, perhaps, to the Koutraphas Intensive Survey Zone is the mill at Nikitari *Mersinia* (BU0073), which stands beside a river crossing almost equidistant between Vyzakia and Pano Koutraphas. The crossing leads from the Asinou valley directly up into the broad, flat fields of the plateau, making the mill well positioned for grinding the large quantities of grain produced here. Here, too, two distinct phases of construction are visible, possibly indicating additions to increase the height of the leat as part of a wider programme of watermill renovation within in the Lagoudhera valley.

A four-arched colonial bridge (BU0114) across the river at Kato Koutraphas *Vouphas* attests to the route's continuing use into the 19th and 20th centuries, and it is still crossed by the modern road running down to join the main route between Nicosia and the Troodos mountains. Archival accounts describe the bridge as having six arches, including five with a 6-m span and one with a 3-m span (SA1/1922/1899). There are now only four arches, but a stretch between the 3-m arch on the north and the next 6-m arch has clearly been rebuilt as a solid causeway with a facing of river cobbles. This presumably replaced the original two arches. The original sections of the bridge are made of margined limestone quarried from Koronia hill c. 1.7 km to the south-west. When it was built as part of the Nicosia–Troodos road in 1900, it was the longest bridge in Cyprus (SA1/1922/1899, Red 79). This bridge played a significant role in British colonial road building policy (Volume 1, Chapter 3.13).

2.17 Conclusions: Settlement and Seasonality in the Plains Landscape

In environmental terms, the plains provide something of a paradox (Chapter 2.2). The soils are rich and thick and hold the rainfall well; in a year with average rainfall they are ideal for the dry cropping of cereals. That average, however, is less than 300 mm per year for much of this area, so drought and crop failure is a constant risk. Irrigation was clearly used throughout the Karkotis and adjoining valleys and plains; it was limited, however, by what supplies could be exported from the Karkotis, as well as by water loss, occurring chiefly through infiltration and to a lesser amount evaporation. The shape of the mountain front constrains the distribution of irrigation water, so that those areas farthest from the Karkotis must necessarily tap into its resources at a higher elevation. Villages in the mountains have a direct 'umbilical cord' of canal water that is fed to fields and attendant mills on the plains.

It is hardly surprising that we do not see the same intensity and continuity of settlement and agriculture as in, for example, the well-watered Karkotis Valley and its artificial (irrigated) distributaries. The relationship between environmental constraints and cultural initiatives, however, is a complex and dynamic one. When we discard modern notions of fixed and permanent settlements with year-round inhabitants, a whole new range of landscape strategies and experiences becomes possible: forays for gathering and harvesting; regular connections between several mountain villages and a single, satellite settlement on the plains; small-scale farmsteads dependent on larger settlements elsewhere; and complex systems of travel, labour and short-term accommodation.

Our principal way of exploring these issues consisted of intensive and detailed examination of three different areas within the plains, consisting of the Atsas, Mandres and Koutraphas Intensive Survey Zones. Because these were chosen purposively, we complemented them by the systematic survey of 1 km-long 'extensive' transects every 2 km outside the Intensive Survey Zones, carried out by our 'Team X' (for methodology see Volume 1, Chapter 2.3; for map, see Plate 2.1). The following discussion examines the results of the three Intensive Survey Zones in the context of the wider Team X transects.

The only prehistoric material discovered in the Team X transects consisted of two Prehistoric Bronze Age Red Polished sherds and one Bronze Age Light Utility sherd found in adjacent Survey Units, 1.7 km north-east of Mandres, and an isolated fragment of Phorades-type slag, presumably dating to the Protohistoric Bronze Age, 1.2 km south-west of Nikitari (SU2914).

In the Iron Age, the plains make up, so far as we can tell, an almost empty landscape. Apart from the Archaic sanctuary at Evrykhou *Khalospitia* in the Atsas Valley and a nearby cemetery (Chapter 2.4), we found no identifiable Geometric–Classical material across this whole area. The sanctuary and cemetery are presumably associated with the more abundant Archaic material in the Karkotis Valley some 3 km to the west, or the contemporary city-kingdom of Soloi 10 km to the north-west, or both.

There are some interesting variations in the distribution of Hellenistic and Roman material across the plains. This comes out particularly clearly in the contrast between the small settlements or farmsteads with manuring and dumping haloes round them in the Koutraphas area, and the almost total lack of material in the Team X transects to the south and east. This lack of material is clear even in transects with good visibility and access, such as TT3882000X, which lies 3 km east of Mandres. There are no obvious environmental reasons for this distribution: if anything, we would expect more activity farther south towards the mountains where rainfall and river flow are higher.

It seems clear from the well-preserved Atsas material that Roman activity consists mainly of isolated farmsteads, with occasional rather larger settlements. This seems to be the case in the Koutraphas and perhaps Mandres areas as well, although later cultivation and disturbance have been greater and we are only dealing with ploughsoil scatters. The Atsas farmsteads lie in the shadow of the Skouriotissa mine, and judging from the correspondences of their material culture with that of the Skouriotissa slag heap and associated settlements, they were clearly linked very closely to the production of copper. The arrangement presumably involved the supply of agricultural staples, such as wheat and olive oil, to the workforce, whether via middle-ranking settlements such as Lithosourka (Chapter 2.7), or via the city-kingdom of Soloi 9 km to the north-west. Areas east and south of Koutraphas and Mandres, however similar their soils and water availability, were apparently too far for this to work.

The mines and smelting installations at Mavrovouni and Alestos in the Lagoudhera Valley had a similar need for food, given the clear lack of agricultural production in their immediate area (Chapter 4.6). The Roman farmsteads or small settlements of Katalasharis and Sanidhia in the Koutraphas Intensive Survey Zone are 7.5 km from Mavrovouni along the most obvious communications route, the Lagoudhera and Elaia Valleys. These relationships between the Roman farmsteads and settlements of the plains, the mines at Skouriotissa and Mavrovouni, and the city-kingdom of Soloi are clearly highly complex. Because of the division of the island, unfortunately, we have very limited data from the northern components of this system.

It may even be that some of these farmsteads and small agricultural settlements were seasonally worked. Katalasharis and Sanidhia have no associated tiles, unlike Vrysi tou Haji Christophi in the Atsas Valley, and the Heavy Utility pottery mostly consists of open shapes, as opposed to the closed shapes needed for substantial storage, such as pithoi (Chapter 2.15). The clearer of the two structures at Vrysi tou Haji Christophi measures 8 × 6 m, and the other is of a similar size. For comparison, the known 19th- and 20th-century seasonal residences at Mandres typically fall between c. 7 × 4 m and 9 × 6 m. It would certainly make sense for such small-scale agricultural enterprises with a significantly poor water supply to be occupied only when needed. In particular, it would be well worth avoiding the driest and hottest time of year between the grain and the olive harvests, when springs and cisterns would be at their lowest.

The distribution of Medieval–Modern pottery across the Plains also shows considerable variation. There is a clear halo of material resulting from dumping and manuring round Mandres, and a considerable spread on the plateau round Katalasharis immediately east of Kato Koutraphas. We may also have clipped the western and southern edges of a halo extending c. 1.5 km from Potami. Most of this material is generically Medieval–Modern, though some of it can be dated more precisely: 14th- and 15th-century material is restricted to the Katalasharis area, and 16th- and 17th-century material to Mandres and Katalasharis. It seems reasonable to assume some sort of connection between the material in and around Katalasharis and the Medieval estate located on the site of Kato Koutraphas village (Chapter 2.16; see also Volume 1, Chapter 5.4). There is a clear discontinuity between the two, however, and there is an unusually high proportion of cooking ware, so Medieval Katalasharis might be some sort of production site dependent on the estate 1.1 km to its west.

The distribution of the *dhoukani* flakes is very similar to that of the Medieval–Modern pottery, and like that is clearly associated with Mandres, Kato Koutraphas and Potami. The raw materials show a high proportion of imported Lefkara chert, suggesting that these are part of the Medieval–Modern *dhoukani* industry, rather than being a local ad hoc Roman production (see Volume 1, Chapter 3.8). The possible exception is the area west of Potami, where there are several jasper pieces, but the nearest substantial concentration of Roman pottery is 1.6 km away.

Beyond the three areas of Mandres, east of Kato Koutraphas, and south and west of Potami, there is virtually no Medieval–Modern material in the plains. This includes our Team X transects, even in the ones with good visibility. One low concentration of mainly Ottoman and Modern material lies 1 km south-west of Nikitari, in a transitional zone between plains and mountains, not unlike the position of Mandres.

The watermills, which are almost certainly Ottoman in date, show a markedly different distribution from the pottery. Four of them are spaced every 1.0–1.4 km along the middle reaches of the Lagoudhera/Elaia River, but no farther north. They are clearly positioned to take advantage of the greater water flow before it is lost from evaporation and infiltration as it slowly crosses the plains. This is clearly more important than proximity to agricultural areas and villages such as Kato Koutraphas and Potami. A consequence is that regular movement perpendicular to the land's contours is a common experience in this landscape – as people carry grain to the mills and flour back to their settlement.

Rather than trying to impose a static and rigid 'settlement pattern' on this diverse material, it might be better to think of a flexible network of small, satellite settlements; exploiting good soils where possible, but still dependent on bigger centres with better water supplies and some sort of administrative role. A Medieval example of this is Katalasharis with its emphasis on production and storage, dependent on the feudal estate of Koutraphas (see above; Volume 1, Chapter 5.4). An example from the Late Ottoman and early colonial period is Mandres, which had no administrative status or identity as a community; its seasonal residents 'belonged' in a fuller sense to particular mountain villages.

The experience of someone living and working in this landscape, then, was very different to that of a permanent town dweller or even villager. As with transhumant pastoralist societies, seasonal rhythms of movement defined the agricultural and social year, connecting mountain village and satellite settlement on the plains, or connecting storage facility and watermill. These rhythms were enacted by means of complex and intersecting routes across this landscape, particularly those running between north and south (see Volume 1, Chapter 3.13).

This landscape, flexible in terms of time, space and identity, was inimical to the British colonial project of bringing order and definition to its new colony (Given 2004, 69–92). To them, Mandres needed a headman and the status of a 'full' community (Chapter 2.10). The new colonial road, built contouring around the base of the Troodos in 1900, cut east–west across rivers, paths and rhythms connecting the mountains and the plains. Like another new road round the Methana peninsula in Greece (Forbes 2007, 89–91), it brought new routes, markets and connections, it altered the axis of people's movements across the plains and at the same time changed the perceptions they held of their landscape.

3. The Karkotis Valley

Edited by Alexis Boutin and Michael Given

with contributions by Iain Banks (geophysics), Alexis Boutin (Team West team leader; tombs), Stephen Digney (Team X team leader), Ian Evans (architecture), Sevina Floridou (water distribution system), Ruth Smadar Gabrieli (pottery), Michael Given (Medieval–Modern periods), Marios Hadjianastasis (oral and documentary history), Mara T. Horowitz (pottery), Tracy Ireland (historical archaeology), Sarah Janes (figurines, sanctuaries), Vasiliki Kassianidou (archaeometallurgy), A. Bernard Knapp (prehistory), Carole McCartney (lithics), Jay Noller (geomorphology), Maria Ntinou (charcoal analysis), Charlotte Schriwer (watermills), Sheila Slevin (geomorphology), Neil Urwin (botany and olive trees), Joanita Vroom (pottery) and Kristina Winther-Jacobsen (pottery)

3.1 Introduction

The Karkotis Valley Intensive Survey Zone has continuous artefactual evidence from six millennia, from the Chalcolithic to the Modern period (Plate 3.1; Table 3.1). Moreover, while some artefact concentrations are temporally and spatially localized, many parts of it feature pottery assemblages from multiple time periods. The primary and secondary distribution of artefacts must be interpreted in concert with three major, interrelated factors: the Karkotis River; the Morphou Bay area; and Skouriotissa mine. Not only has the river directly affected artefact distribution through incising and flooding, but these cyclical actions have also made the valley exceptionally fertile (Fig. 3.1). Consequently, the agriculturally rich Karkotis floodplain has been the setting for reiterative human occupation across the millennia.

The rich copper deposits of the Troodos pillow basalts have been exploited for thousands of years at and around the Skouriotissa mine. The agricultural fertility of the Karkotis valley was able to support the substantial populations required by the mining infrastructure, notably in the Prehistoric Bronze Age, the Roman period and the 20th century. The Karkotis River empties into Morphou Bay, and at many different periods the communities and resources of the Karkotis Valley are clearly closely connected with the more cosmopolitan ports to the north. In fact, the most direct riverine access route for people and goods coming from the highest point on the island (modern Mt. Olympus) to the north coast is the Karkotis Valley.

Before our survey, the known prehistory of this valley was confined essentially to the excavation of a series of Prehistoric Bronze Age tombs around the villages of Katydhata (Markides 1916) and Linou (Flourentzos 1989). Further tombs from the Iron Age, Hellenistic and Roman periods have been excavated by the Department of Antiquities in the valley, including some richly furnished Roman tombs at Evrykhou (Jacobsen 2007), while the Cyprus Survey records show several funerary cippi and inscriptions from Evrykhou and elsewhere in the valley (Nicolaou 1984; see Chapter 3.14 for mortuary landscapes, and Plate 3.1 for a map). Apart from general assumptions that there might have been Roman, as well as earlier, settlements under the modern villages of Evrykhou and Katydhata, no synthetic or analytical work had been done. As for the crucially important ancient copper mines of Skouriotissa, they are known mainly from the observations

Table 3.1. The Karkotis Valley: chronological summary

Period	Activity	Name/ID number	Chapter
Prehistoric	Late Chalco/early PreBA 1 settlement	Koutroullis	3.5
	PreBA 2 settlement and tombs	Laonarka	3.9
Iron Age–Classical	Sanctuary	Pano Limna	3.11
Hellenistic–Roman	Settlement	Pano Limna	3.11
	Copper mine & slag heaps	Skouriotissa	3.12
	Pottery scatter, ground stone, olive mill	Pseftas	3.13
	Pottery scatter	Dodekaskala	3.6
	Land levelling		3.10
	Tombs		3.14
Byzantine–Modern	Medieval–Modern villages	Katydhata, Agroladhou, Evrykhou	3.3, 3.10, 3.15
	Medieval & Turkish Cypriot village	Ayios Epiphanios	3.7
	Medieval estate, Ott & Mod village	Phlasou	3.8
	Monasteries	Panayia Kousouliotissa, Skouriotissa	3.6, 3.12
	Rural churches	BU0088, BU0103, TP251	3.3, 3.7
	Working water mill	Mylos tou Stylli	3.4
	Water mills	BU0002–04, BU0044, BU0046, BU0060–62, BU0064, BU0070, BU0075–76, BU0098–99	3.3, 3.8, 3.10, 3.15
	Threshing floors	At Phlasou, Katydhata	3.8, 3.10
	Medieval–Ottoman olive trees		3.8, 3.16
	20th century copper mine	Skouriotissa	3.12

Fig. 3.1. Looking eastwards across the Karkotis Valley from Ayios Epiphanios, along the line of Transect TT3881000N (Chris Parks)

of mining engineers in the 1920s and 1930s, as well as from ancient documentary sources (Bruce *et al.* 1937; Kassianidou 2000).

The ancient name of the Karkotis River was 'Karios', first attested in the graffito of a Cypriot mercenary at Karnak, Egypt, in the 4th century BC, who described himself as 'Kariyopotames', 'from the area of the River Karios' (Masson 1979). A probable variant on this is 'Klarios', used by Plutarch to refer to a river near ancient Soloi (*Life of Solon* 26). The Medieval–Modern versions of this were variously 'Kares', 'Karyotis' and 'Karkotis' (Masson 1979, 220). The region also took its name from Soloi, the Archaic–Roman city on the coast immediately north-west of the TAESP area within the Karkotis Valley. 'Soliopotames' is an adjective showing a person's origin, appearing in another mercenary's graffito in Karnak (Masson 1979, 218). From the Medieval period onwards the valley was referred to as the 'Solea Valley', even though this was never an administrative area (Paulides 1990, 245).

Although the city of Soloi is relatively well attested in the ancient literature (des Gagniers and Tinh 1985), virtually nothing is said about the fertile and well-watered valley that was clearly a vital part of its hinterland. This reflects the expected bias in the sources, which focus on the urban and political at the expense of the rural and social. The greater detail and better preservation of Medieval and Ottoman written administrative texts give us much fuller information, so we have some useful historical sources that talk about villages and estates such as Phlasou (Chapter 3.8) and Agroladhou (Chapter 3.3).

Another useful set of documentary sources consists of travellers' accounts. Even though the valley was little known to outsiders in the 20th century, before then it had considerable fame for its natural resources. In the 18th century, for example, the Solea Valley was proverbial among foreign travellers in Cyprus for its fertility, intensive cultivation, numerous villages, and above all for its water. These three quotations graphically demonstrate the richness of this physical and human landscape:

> We crossed into the delightful country of Solea, which is a vale about a mile wide, and winds between the hills for seven or eight miles: it is much improved with gardens and buildings, and is very well watered with springs and rivulets. ... Two streams [at the church of St Nicholas tis Steyis near Kakopetria] come rushing down the hills, and are carried all through the country of Solea in many rivulets. (Pococke in 1738; Cobham 1908, 262)

> The Valley of Sollia or Soglia I think the finest in the island; Massaria [the Mesaoria plain] indeed is a rich, extensive, and would be a plentiful country, were it not wholly destitute of trees and villages, which the other has in plenty, together with abundance of water and wood from the adjacent hills. (Drummond in 1750; Cobham 1908, 296)

> We now entered the vale of Soulea, the most beautiful we had yet seen in the island; well watered and richly cultivated. Green meadows contrasted with the corn now ripe, hamlets shaded with mulberry-trees, and healthy peasantry busily employed with their harvest, and the care of their silk-worms, enlivened the scenery. (Sibthorp in 1787; Cobham 1908, 330)

The core of our methodology consisted of transect survey, which provided comprehensive coverage of the broad lower part of the valley (Plate 3.1). The transects crossed the north–south valley at right angles, providing a cross-section between the western and eastern ridgelines and across the alluvial terraces surrounding the river channel. In total, we carried out twelve east–west transects, 500 m apart. Three of them (TT3880000N, TT3880500N, TT3881000N) in the southern part of the area actually were conducted c. 100 m south of the intended transect line because of a different map projection used during the 2001 field season. But, because their Survey Units and Geomorphological Units were digitized at the correct locations in the GIS, all descriptions and conclusions relevant to them are still valid.

For all other transects we followed the designated transect line, except where access, visibility or context problems arose. Access to certain areas along survey transects was sometimes obstructed by the Karkotis River and its tributaries, as well as by major irrigation channels. Land adjacent to these watercourses tended to be heavily overgrown. Intensive agricultural land use in this fertile river valley has led to the creation of extensive terrace systems through levelling, ploughing and (only to a minor extent) the importation of soil. To adjust for these problems in the field, we moved our survey off the designated transect line to avoid poor visibility, obviously imported surface materials, or other significantly disturbed contexts. Initially, our field methodology allowed us to move the centre line of the Survey Unit a maximum of 20 m away from the transect line (Volume 1, Chapter 2.3). Due to poor ground visibility in much of the Karkotis Valley, many transects would have been insufficiently sampled, so we relaxed this guideline to allow teams to move transects up to 50 m away from the transect line.

A further complication was that the northern boundary of the Intensive Survey Zone forms part of the United Nations Buffer Zone. This area was host to the San Martin United Nations camp, opposite the Roman slag heap at Skouriotissa, and there was a marked military presence of the National Guard of the Republic of Cyprus and the United Nations. Both of these kindly granted us permission to survey.

This chapter is organized both geographically and thematically. After giving an overview of the environment and physical landscape (Chapter 3.2), we discuss and analyse a series of areas, starting with Agroladhou, in the southern higher part of the surveyed valley, then work our way downstream and northwards to Skouriotissa *Pseftas*, immediately south of the Buffer Zone. Each area has its own particularly significant periods, themes and research questions. We discuss the tombs and mortuary landscapes of the valley as a whole (Chapter 3.14), examine the valley in its wider context, incorporating the data from our extensive 'Team X' transects (Chapter 3.15), and finish with a series of period and thematic summaries (Chapter 3.16). Broader analyses of the Survey Area by period can be found in Volume 1, Chapter 5.

3.2 Environmental Setting and Description

Our survey transects inspected the middle segment (reach) of the narrow Karkotis watershed, drained by the perennially flowing Karkotis River and tributaries (Plate 3.2). This watershed drains half the land lying above 1650 m, including the highest points of the island, and does so with the shortest path to the seashore. Such a steep slope and high catchment are the primary reasons the environment, and its use by people, are so special on Cyprus, and make up the themes often revisited in this chapter.

For at least 500,000 years, the Karkotis has been eroding out an ancient mid-ocean rift valley, the Cretaceous Solea Graben, where relatively softer rocks have been removed, leaving behind the less erodible ones. From south (high summits) to north (sea), the Karkotis cuts across the north-tipped layered strata of the Troodos Ophiolite, the upper half of which is exposed in the Intensive Survey Zone as Pillow Lavas and Basal Group Formations. The Karkotis stream network is the realm of fluvial processes involving channel erosion (surface lowering) and floodplain deposition (surface raising). Between the channels, including gullies, is the hillslope where colluvial (sheetwash) and gravity (creep) processes predominate. The landscape may seem quite varied, but actually is a simple set of three landforms present on both sides of a stream channel. Along any given cross-section of a stream valley in this watershed one may note the seven-step division of landform: ridge–hillslope–floodplain–channel–floodplain–hillslope–ridge.

The main channel of the Karkotis is unusually, perhaps unnaturally, straight; it has a few angular bends, and is of even width along the reach between Kakopetria and Skouriotissa. This flume-like channel is similar in cross-section along much of its 12 km length: it is trapezoidal in shape, about 250 m wide at the top and about 185 m wide at the base (Fig. 3.2). Thus, the Karkotis looks more like a flume to transport water than a natural river. The basal width, i.e. the useable valley floor, is the length of a Roman furlong, which makes this even more curious.

At this point of our analysis the Karkotis channel could be either geological or anthropogenic, or both. If this flume-like channel is purely a geological erosion feature, then the bedrock geology would have to be the controlling factor. The Karkotis runs down the middle of the Cretaceous Solea Graben (Bettison-Varga *et al.* 1992), and that alone could explain its unusual morphology. Weak fault zones down the graben's axis could be influencing this, but there are no known faults that parallel any part of this watercourse. So it is unlikely that the valley bottom is due to fault orientation in the bedrock. The channel could be a consequence of the shapes and orientations of the rock bodies themselves; but none of the geological maps show bedrock boundaries parallel to features of the Karkotis. Alternatively, the flume-like channel could be anthropogenic. We could hypothesize that the channel was straightened for hydrological reasons – irrigation or mining, or both. A major problem with the valley dimensions solely being an engineered feature, i.e. a flume, is that we would have to identify material dumps extensive enough to accommodate the volume of excavated debris. These points are examined further below (see section 3.10, Land Levelling and the Karkotis).

The two bedrock formations underlying the Intensive Survey Zone impart a difference in valley width: the distance between ridges is less in the southern part of the valley where the erosion-resistant Basal Group underlies the steep slopes. Here we find an agricultural system dominated by steep, narrow terraces that contour the hillslopes, with a stepped set of narrow floodplains long since abandoned by the Karkotis. The ancient floodplains, called fluvial terraces, are typically continuous downstream to the narrows, located in the Buffer Zone. These terraces, as well as the valley, widen over the Pillow Lavas, forming uniquely shaped, stepped landforms: these special terraces are crossed by lateral tributaries of the Karkotis that have eroded out wide-floored side valleys. Ridgelines separating the side valleys jut out on the banks of the Karkotis, forming the bedrock foundations for villages such as Katydhata, Linou, Phlasou and Evrykhou. The criss-cross of side-valley terraces with those in the main valley created a variably stepped mosaic of sediments, wherein sufficiently deep soils have formed whose moisture and nutrients are available for plant uptake. Hillslopes are mantled with thin (<1m) colluvial deposits and immature soils that neither hold water well nor offer nutrients for plants.

So, from these geological and geomorphological subdivisions of the landscape, we see the template with which our story builds: ridge-river intersections for settlement, terraces for primary agricultural use and hillslopes for pasture, wild plant gathering, marginal crops and woodland. Overall, we have a mosaic against which to interpret the surface archaeological record, and geomorphology provides a consistent explanation for the distribution of artefacts.

Because the Karkotis River runs from the highest peak to sea level over the shortest distance, it has the highest potential energy (i.e. the ability to carry the most water) of any river on the island. It will be the last river to dry up in times of drought and will flood the most readily. For the 16th-century chronicler Florio Bustron (Bustron 1884, 28), it is the first of the four great rivers in Cyprus, and he makes a point of listing the 14 villages that it 'waters'. In a Cypriot proverb recorded in the mid-19th century, it is clear that the river's primacy was well known (the Karkotis here has its medieval name of Kares): 'Kares, Koures and Diorizos, but above all Kares' (Masson 1979, 219–20). In sum, the Karkotis is a unique river with a unique archaeological scenario.

Over its history the bed elevation of the Karkotis has fluctuated, following the pace of the global glacial-interglacial cycle. During the last glacial (c. 40,000–12,000 BP) and during the Little Ice Age (16th–early 19th century AD), the Karkotis headwaters were fed by permanent icefields. Although no evidence of glaciers has been observed (Noller, unpublished data), the Karkotis is the only watershed to have nivation features; these are present on the northern slopes of Mt. Olympus and are suggestive of permanent icefields. Ice was collected for ice houses in Nicosia during the 18th–late 19th centuries, and structures to embank the snow can still be found there (Scott-Stevenson 1880, 241; SA1/3644/1889; Michaelides 1981, 98).

The Little Ice Age, occurring during the Ottoman period (in political terms, 1571–1878), was the last major climatic event in the region. Glacials, and periods like the Little Ice Age, would be times of high discharge in the Karkotis. Peak floods on the Karkotis moved large boulders out of the Troodos and downstream, depositing them in bars still visible today. The average mass of individual boulders in these deposits ranges from 5 tons (south) to 0.3 tons (north) across the Intensive Survey Zone. Since the end of the Little Ice Age, the island and the general surrounding region have been under a period of intensified aridity.

Response of the watershed to post-glacial changes during early human settlement is best exemplified in the lower Koutroullis field-terrace cut (TP246; Chapter 3.5). Prehistoric Bronze Age 1 (c. 2600–2400 BC) pottery appears in a buried soil c. 4 m below the modern surface and c. 12 m above the modern river channel. The exact

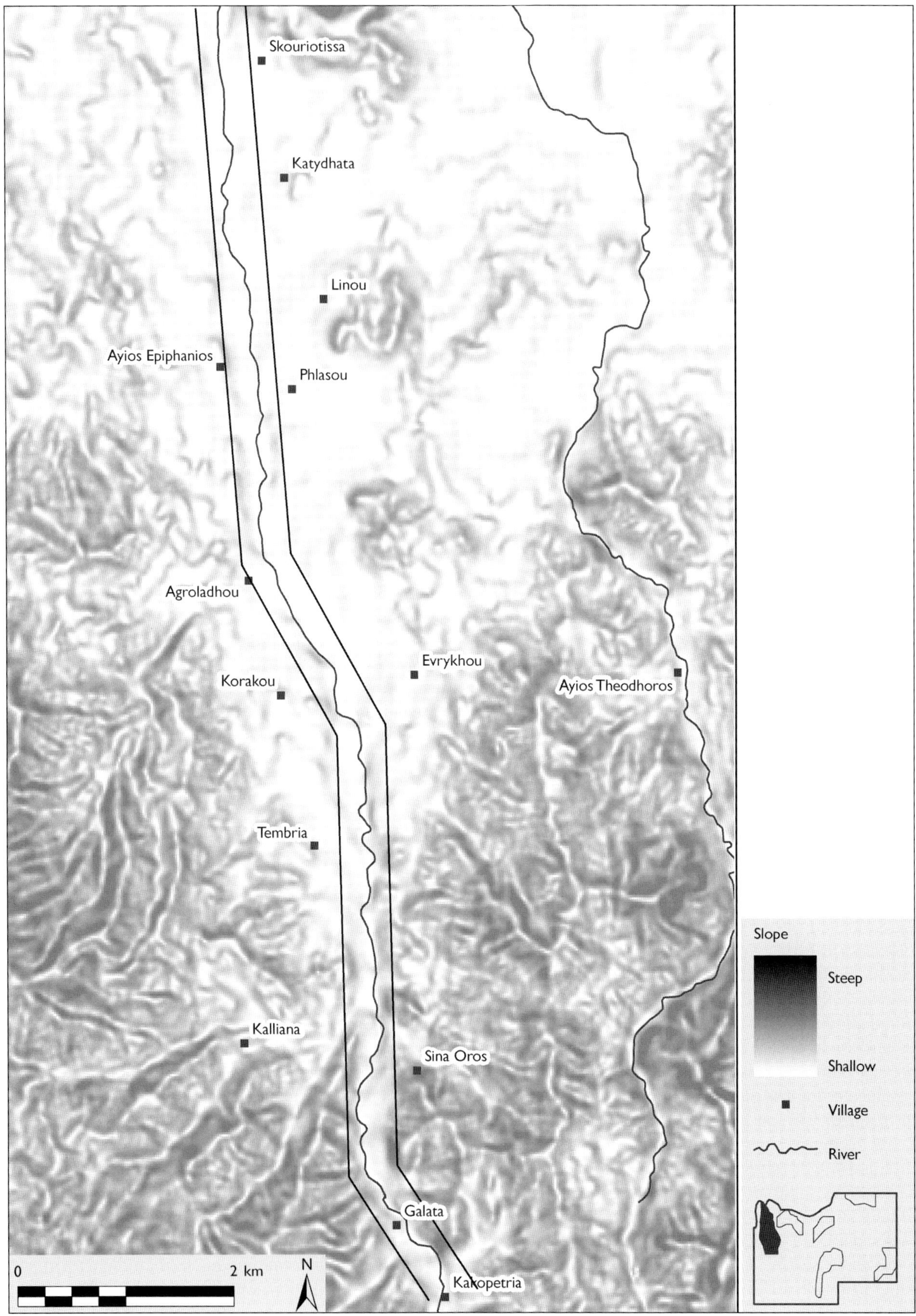

Fig. 3.2. Map of percent slope of the Karkotis River between Kakopetria (south) and Skouriotissa (north). The parallel lines indicate the outer rim of the river's single channel (Jay Noller, finalised by Luke Sollars)

timing is yet to be resolved, however, we can definitely conclude that the river had aggraded to +12 m after 2600 BC and at least an additional 4 m before incising down to its current level. The magnitude of these changes is large for Cyprus, but not exceptionally so compared to the amount of post-Byzantine alterations in floodplain elevation (4–8 m) on the Gialias River (Cyprus's second largest river) near Dhali. The implications of this are highly significant for our full understanding of the prehistoric and early historic landscape. Given the paucity of +12 to +16 m fluvial terraces, most Bronze Age materials are either too deeply buried to be turned up by ploughing on the extant fluvial terraces, or else they have been eroded away by the river. Or, as we will argue below, human agency has played a dominant role.

We observed differences in terrace construction and in field shape and use, depending on the natural contour of the land. In the southern part of the Intensive Survey Zone, where the river valley is narrower, valley walls are steeper, terraces near the river are smaller and the risers between them are higher. In the northern part, the valley near the current level of the river is broader, which results in wider terraces that support large cultivated fields. Thus, the chances of finding surveyable land here were good, because the Geomorphological Units were of a size large enough for TAESP standards (minimum 20 m length on transect), while the larger area of the fields provided a greater likelihood that some portion of them would have at least 20% visibility. The land immediately adjacent to the river usually does not lend itself to survey because it consists of narrow, steep terraces often choked with flora.

Vegetation

The valley is settled and extensively cultivated with vegetables and orchards from the river banks to the upper terraces. The cultivated strip averages about 1.0–1.5 km in width on either side of the present river channel. The valley walls, however, are naturally vegetated.

Northward from a line bisecting the river valley in the area of Evrykhou/Korakou, the foot slopes support a mosaic of grassy batha, garrigue/batha and batha/pine savannah, in ascending order of elevation from the valley floor. Batha is a low open heath dominated by *Sarcopoterium spinosum* and *Thymus capitatus*. Garrigue is a higher and denser heath, dominated by *Zyziphus spina-Christi*, *Cytisus* and *Rhamnus oleoides*. On the upper slopes are isolated patches of dense pine forest at 30–60% canopy cover, but in general, the slopes in this portion of the valley are dominated by some form of batha.

South of Evrykhou, the lower slopes consist of pine woodland (10–30% canopy cover). These become thicker on the upper slopes, culminating in dense forest stands with greater than 60% canopy cover. The pine forests are virtually monotypic stands of *Pinus brutia var. halepensis* (the Aleppo or Cyprus pine) The co-dominants of higher altitude conifer forests (cedar, cypress and black pines) are absent on the Karkotis Valley walls. On some slopes in the southern reaches of the Karkotis Valley, however, *Pinus brutia* shares dominance with *Pistacia terebinthus* (terebinth) and *Quercus infectoria* (Aleppo oak). The forest understorey is usually a mixture of *Cistus creticus, Sarcopoterium spinosum* and *Noaeo mucronata*.

The vegetation of the riverine corridor itself is significantly altered from the natural community in the lower reaches (between Skouriotissa mine and Phlasou), with dense eucalypt plantings (*Eucalyptus camaldulensis*) among reeds (*Arundo donax*) and bamboo. Upstream from Agroladhou, remnants of the natural riverine forest are more common. These include *Alnus orientalis* (oriental alder), *Platanus orientalis* (oriental plane) and *Quercus infectoria*, accompanied by a number of feral trees that have escaped from cultivation (carob, walnut and olives).

Much of the area is taken up with intensive cultivation, thanks to the alluvial soils and plentiful water. Data and figures from 1825 and 1833 show that this has been the case for at least two centuries: if we include the territory of Evrykhou village, just to the south, the Intensive Survey Zone had in 1833, 990 olive trees, 508 mulberry trees, 27 carob trees, 24 almond trees, 9 walnut trees and 1 fig tree (Given and Hadjianastasis 2010; Sarınay 2000). During this period, wheat and barley were grown mainly in the upper part of the valley, from Evrykhou southwards. The main crops in the late 20th century were fruit trees (soft fruit and vines in the upper part of the valley, mainly citrus in the Intensive Survey Zone), olives, nuts (mainly almonds), vegetables, pulses and cereals (mainly in the upper valley) (Paulides 1990, 242–43).

Irrigation and Artefact Movement

The Karkotis watershed stands out as one in which, with minimal construction, a series of diversion weirs and canals could irrigate all of the potential arable soils on fluvial terraces. From the narrows upstream of the Intensive Survey Zone (north of modern Kakopetria), the terrace treads emanate and diverge; major (feeder) irrigation canals follow the natural breaks in slope between the fluvial terraces. Construction and maintenance of the canals would mix (bury and expose) artefacts. In fact, the issue of large-scale movement of sediment is highly significant in the Karkotis Valley, given the large amount of terracing and ploughing that occurs while cultivating this fertile area. On the whole, the natural landscape has been extensively levelled to maximize the arability of the soils (for example, east of the river along Transect TT3879500N). These practices potentially move a great deal of soil, sediment and the artefacts held within them.

Growers have extensively irrigated the fluvial terraces, affecting material distributions in the process. Irrigation can result in silt deposition that potentially covers up artefacts. This silt often dries and cracks, forming a hard crust. It should be noted, however, that subsequent ploughing can bring the artefacts back to the surface. In one type of irrigation scheme, small earthen channels dug into the treads of terraces direct water flow from the principal irrigation canals to the trees, resulting in sediment and artefact movement within the terrace. Water flow in the channels tends to move fine sediment, and residually concentrate pottery sherds and slag (especially the smaller pieces) (see also Volume 1, Chapter 2.9). Irrigation networks may also facilitate the movement of artefacts between terraces; these small earthen channels are connected to larger (often also earthen) irrigation canals. These larger canals cut through the terraces as they travel through, dislodging sediment and artefacts and transporting them downstream. The amount of material carried, the distance travelled and where it is deposited, depend on the volume and speed at which the water moves and the morphology of the irrigation network.

For example, on Transect TT3883000N, the principal irrigation canals largely run north and have canals running from them at regular intervals in a westerly direction. These western-oriented canals were then breached at various intervals to irrigate individual terraces (diverted north again). The water flowing north was also breached at various intervals and redirected across the tread by small earthen channels and rills (largely in a westerly direction). The main direction of artefact movement in channels would, in other words, be westward from higher terraces. This is a conservative and cautious argument that can be allayed if we assume that the immense and well-engineered network of canals is designed to flow at velocities that do *not* erode sediment. If sherds were, or are, moving at significant rates, then the canal system would be bankrupt in short order. In the end it can reasonably be argued that field-to-field transmission of artefacts is moot. Transport within and across field boundaries through land-levelling activities is of more significant and real concern.

3.3 Soil, Water and Production in the Medieval–Modern South Karkotis Valley

The southern part of the Karkotis Valley Intensive Survey Zone forms a complex network of fields, terraces, irrigation systems, tracks and settlements. In spite of the difficulties of ground visibility, access and extensive human modification of the surface, the data produced by transect survey and related fieldwork and research give considerable insights into the development of land use and social organisation in the Medieval and Ottoman periods. Particularly significant are the management and control of soil, water and agricultural production.

In terms of pottery densities from the 16th century onwards, a key location comprised the four Survey Units in the south-west, at the base of the ridgeline running along the western side of the valley (Plate 3.3). This area was reported to be the location of the Medieval–Modern village of Agroladhou (TP253), well known from historical sources and still remembered by local people.

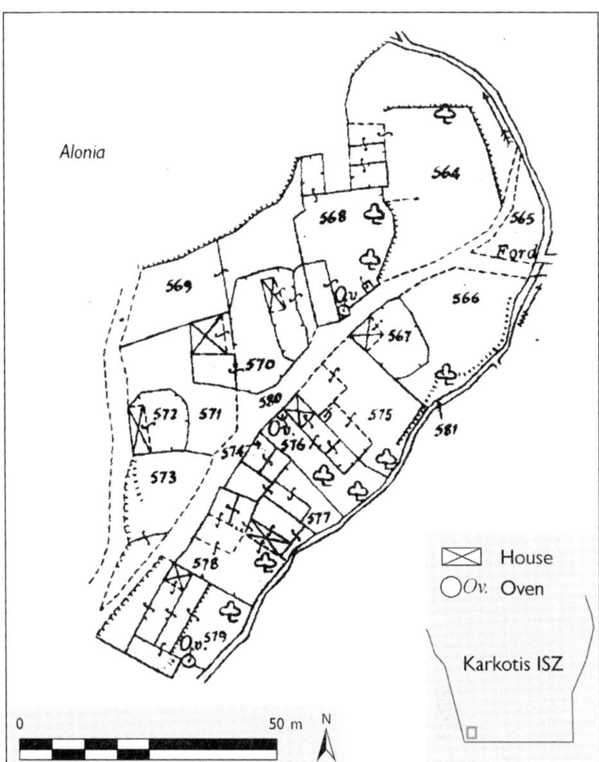

Fig. 3.3. Agroladhou: village plan (1926; revised 1967). Based upon the map prepared by the Department of Lands and Surveys with the sanction of the Government of the Republic of Cyprus; State copyright reserved

In the late 15th century, Agroladhou is recorded as a *casal* (village) belonging to the Grand Commandery of the Knights of St John, and in 1565 it is listed as a *prastio* (dependent hamlet) with seven *francomati* (free peasant farmers) (de Mas Latrie 1852–61 III, 502; Grivaud 1998, 469). In the 1825 tax register, it was a mixed village with only seven taxpayers (heads of household) (Papadopoullos 1965, 123). Its population declined from 19 in 1881, to 13 in 1960, and it was finally abandoned after 1974 (Karouzis 1984a). According to local memory, it was mainly a Turkish Cypriot village consisting of pastoralists. A woman (born c. 1948), who now occupies the land where Agroladhou once stood, told the team that her great-grandfather lived in the village, and she remembers the decrepit remains of its structures from her childhood.

Informal scouting by the survey team failed to produce any extant architectural remains of Agroladhou, which seem to have been obliterated by modern construction. The village plan, made in 1926 and revised in 1967, shows seven small houses, with associated courtyards and other structures, on either side of a track immediately north-west of the river (Fig. 3.3). Three of them also had ovens. Immediately to the west is the locality name Alonia, presumably the location of the village threshing floors, while two cemeteries are marked to the south.

The four Survey Units conducted along the transect in this area produced significant amounts of pottery from the

Table 3.2. Agroladhou village: pottery from SU2062–65. TCP numbers refer to Pottery Catalogue in Volume 1, Chapter 3.6

Historical Antiquity (Archaic to Late Roman)

Fct	*Type*	*No.*	*Weight*
HU	HU	11	261g
LU	LU	10	116g
Un	Un	1	9g

Hellenistic to Roman

Fct	*Type*	*No.*	*Weight*
CW	CW	3	16g

Early to Late Roman

Fct	*Type*	*No.*	*Weight*
Ar	Ti	3	290g
Ar	TiP	2	300g
TW	ARS	1	5g

Late Roman

Fct	*Type*	*No.*	*Weight*
TW	CRS	2	14g
TW	CRS02	2	12g
TW	LRC10A	1	10g

Roman to Modern

Fct	*Type*	*No.*	*Weight*
Ar	Ti	1	60g

Historical (Archaic to Modern)

Fct	*Type*	*No.*	*Weight*
HU	HU	13	740g
LU	LU	25	363g
TW	TW	2	11g

Medieval to Modern

Fct	*Type*	*No.*	*Weight*
Ar	Ti	2	90g
CW	BGW	1	6g
U	BuLK	2	35g
U	ID02	1	19g
U	ID04A	1	20g

Byzantine to Medieval

Fct	*Type*	*No.*	*Weight*
TW	CGS02	1	11g

Medieval utility period III

Fct	*Type*	*No.*	*Weight*
U	ID04	2	37g

Ottoman to Modern I

Fct	*Type*	*No.*	*Weight*
LU	BuL	2	16g

Medieval-Venetian to Early Ottoman

Fct	*Type*	*No.*	*Weight*
TW	G02	1	7g
TW	G03	1	9g
TW	MP01	7	82g

Ottoman to Modern II

Fct	*Type*	*No.*	*Weight*
HU	BuH	8	281g
LU	BuL	6	90g
TW	MP02	2	37g TCP326
TW	PP07	1	2g TCP325
U	UPL01	1	15g

Modern

Fct	*Type*	*No.*	*Weight*
TW	Por	2	10g
TW	SP02	1	4g

Medieval–Modern periods, with a clear increase of both pottery and tile fragments downhill toward the presumed site of Agroladhou (Plate 3.3). There was no material at all from the Frankish period. From the Venetian period to the mid-20th century there was a scatter of material, which at c. 4 sherds/100 m^2 was never very heavy, but stood out clearly from the rest of the transect. This material was a characteristic Late Medieval and Ottoman domestic mix: Table Wares; Heavy and Light Utility jugs and jars, many of them burnished; and Cooking Ware (a single piece of Brown Glazed Ware).

The oldest of the Table Wares found near Agroladhou is a fragment of Incised Sgraffito Ware, possibly made on Cyprus, of Byzantine–Medieval period (c. 13th century?). There also are a few sherds of Monochrome Green Painted Ware from Lapithos (c. 16th century onward) and Monochrome Yellow Glazed Ware of the Medieval-Venetian to Early Ottoman periods. The rest of the Table Wares are later, among them a handful of Monochrome Glazed Wares in various colours of Ottoman to Modern times (c. 18th–mid-20th centuries). Imported fragments from western Turkey in this same, later time range include one piece of a Polychrome Painted coffee cup from Kütahya, with a black circle inside, and blue and black paint on the outside (TCP325; c. 18th century), as well as one sherd of Monochrome Brown Painted Ware from Çanakkale (c. 19th century onward) (Vroom 2005, 168–71, 180–81). Painted wares are the most common types of glazed and decorated Table Wares found in the Agroladhou area: 64% are painted, 29% glazed, and 7% sgraffito.

Two chipped stone artefacts were collected from SU2064: one piece of debris and one *dhoukani* (threshing sledge) flake. A somewhat larger sample was collected across Transect TT3878500N (SU2066–70), including a second *dhoukani* flake, two debris chunks, one flake and five flake cores. All of this material, made of local jasper and chalcedony, may represent a background scatter of ad hoc flake production. In the absence of other flake tools or utilized pieces, however, this collection may simply indicate the local manufacture of *dhoukani* replacement flakes using local material.

Immediately to the west of these four Survey Units, some 200 m from the site of Agroladhou, was a row of four aged olive trees, planted along a drainage running eastward from the base of the ridge toward the Karkotis River. After being bisected by a modern road, the line continued with two olive trees in a ploughed agricultural field and then extended onto the next two lower terraces. This strategy of planting along a gully, at right angles to the river, is not uncommon on the west side of the valley, as it permits the maximum utilization of water runoff and

Fig. 3.4. South Karkotis Valley looking north from Korakou, with the church of Ayia Varvara (BU0087) on the left (Chris Parks)

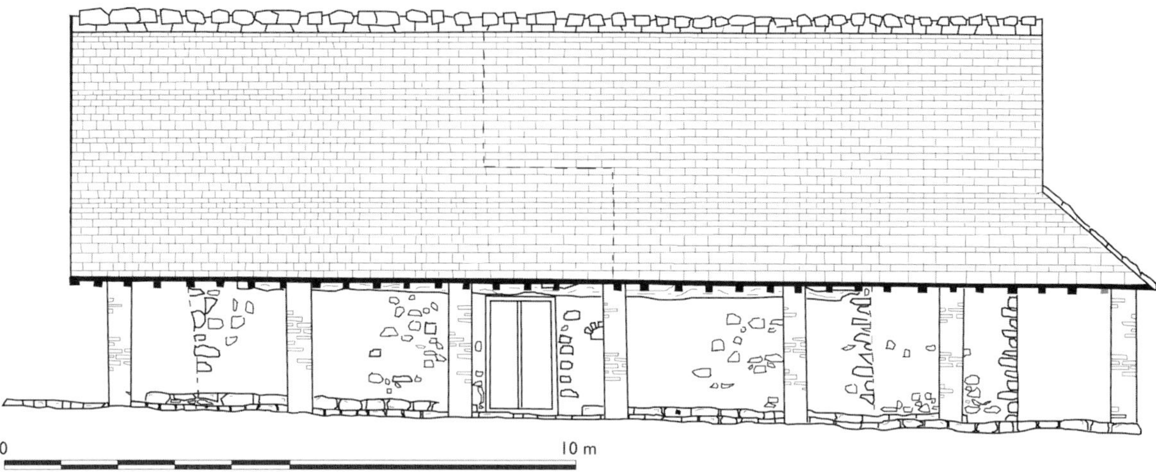

Fig. 3.5. Ayios Yeoryios church (BU0088): elevation of north side, showing foundations of earlier church, quoins of original west wall, and two phases of tiling (Amanda Gow)

sediment from the slope. There were rows of stones placed at the base of the trees to trap water and sediment, and tree-roots had been exposed by soil erosion where the stones had been removed (to facilitate recent grain cultivation). The two oldest trees were estimated to be about 290 and 208 years old respectively (see Volume 1, Chapter 2.11 for dating methods). Approximate planting dates, therefore, are in the first and last decades of the 18th century and suggest a broader economy for Agroladhou than simply the pastoralism of oral memory.

On a ridge 350 m to the north-west of Agroladhou is the early 17th-century church of Ayia Varvara (BU0087) (Gunnis 1936, 149). Although not large (12 × 5 m), it has a prominent position on the ridge, aurally as well as visually. As with many of these churches, it is seen more clearly from across and up the valley, than from down the valley to the north (Fig. 3.4). Beside the west door is a limestone edge-runner from a crushing mill, probably for olives. This association between olive production and the church is common throughout the Survey Area and beyond, although in this case the association might date to a recent period, with the millstone being brought in from elsewhere. There is a similar juxtaposition at Tembria, 2.5 km up the valley. A more datable example comes from the church of Ayios Loukas, on another ridge 1.2 km to the south-east (BU0089). According to an inscription, this church was built in 1697; it has a similar millstone cut in half and incorporated very visibly into its south wall (Volume 1, Chapter 3.11, Plate 3.3, Fig. 3.48).

On the next major ridge to the north is the church of Ayios Yeoryios (Fig. 3.5; TP139; BU0088). This church probably dates to the 16th or 17th century, although it was rebuilt in 1842, according to an inscription, and renovated in 2003. Sherds are used as chinking in the rubble walls, including a pithos rim with a red-painted wavy line. Although the overall dimensions are now 17 × 6 m, including a 2-m porch over the west end, lines of cornerstones on both the north and south faces show that its predecessor was only 11.9 m long (these are visible between the 5th and 6th brick piers on Fig. 3.5). The apse is also a later addition. The neo-classical influences in the west doorway and the column in the apse window indicate a 19th-century date, suggesting that these were part of the 1842 rebuilding. Some painted plaster on the exterior survives near the frame of the door in the southern wall and on the east wall predating the apse. A course of limestone blocks protruding from the foot of the north wall may suggest an even earlier predecessor. The interior has been totally renovated, and on the northern wall is a new mural of St. George, within an arched setting. The church's dramatic position, on a ridge overlooking the valley, clearly echoes that of Ayia Varvara, 0.7 km to the south, and Ayios Epiphanios, 1.1 km to the north.

The survey transect running between Ayia Varvara and Ayios Yeoryios contained virtually no Medieval–Modern material on the west side of the river (Plate 3.3). This is a striking contrast to the Agroladhou area to the south, and also to the transect 150 m north of Ayios Yeoryios, where there was substantial Late Medieval, Ottoman and early 20th-century material. The widespread terracing in this area means that all surfaces are only subject to human mixing of the soil, and there are no obvious morphological patterns in the terraces to suggest that one area has been under terracing longer than any other. The artefact distribution, in other words, is reliable when viewed at this relatively coarse resolution. Immediately north of Ayios Yeoryios, we clearly see the edge of the substantial artefact scatters resulting from intensive cultivation around the villages of Ayios Epiphanios and Phlasou.

Fig. 3.6. Lachistos mill (BU0070): north facade, with penstock on the right and buttresses supporting the leat. Behind is the church of Ayios Loukas in Korakou (BU0089) (Chris Parks)

Mylos tis Varvaras (BU0099) lies 520 m south-east of Ayia Varvara church and carries the saint's name. A millhouse, penstock and leat survive, but the construction material and technique used are very different from those of the other mills in the TAESP area, and the mill may date to the Late Medieval rather than Ottoman period. The millhouse was built using river boulders in irregular courses with tile and basalt chinking. The interior has a wooden post supporting a wooden beam. The penstock is four-tiered, supported by three-tiered fan-shaped buttresses north and south of the penstock. The penstock is of the square hopper type with sloping plastered walls on either side. The millrace is 12 m long and was constructed using irregular courses of river boulders.

Lachistos mill (BU0070) lies 490 m south-east of Mylos tis Varvaras, on the east bank of the Karkotis river (Fig. 3.6). Because it was both well preserved and characteristic of many of the mills in the Survey Area, we recorded it in some detail. The name 'Lachistos' was explained by Mr Styllis, the Evrykhou miller (Chapter 3.4), as being

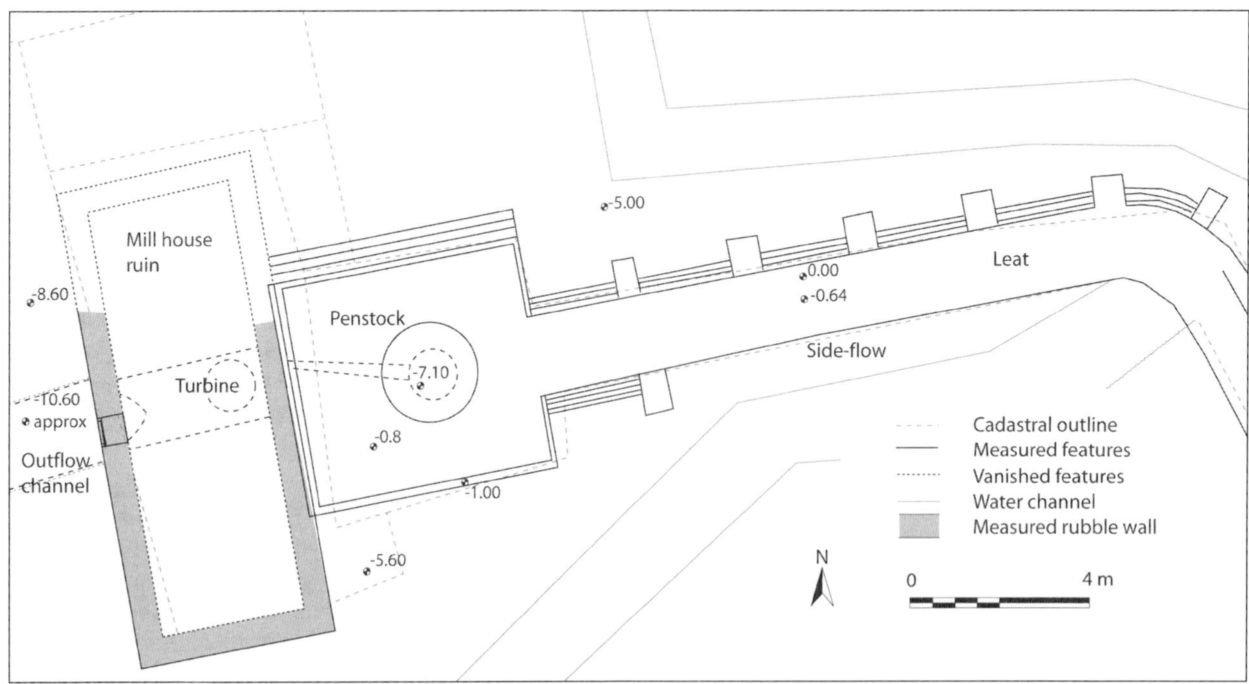

Fig. 3.7. Lachistos mill (BU0070): plan (Sevina Floridou)

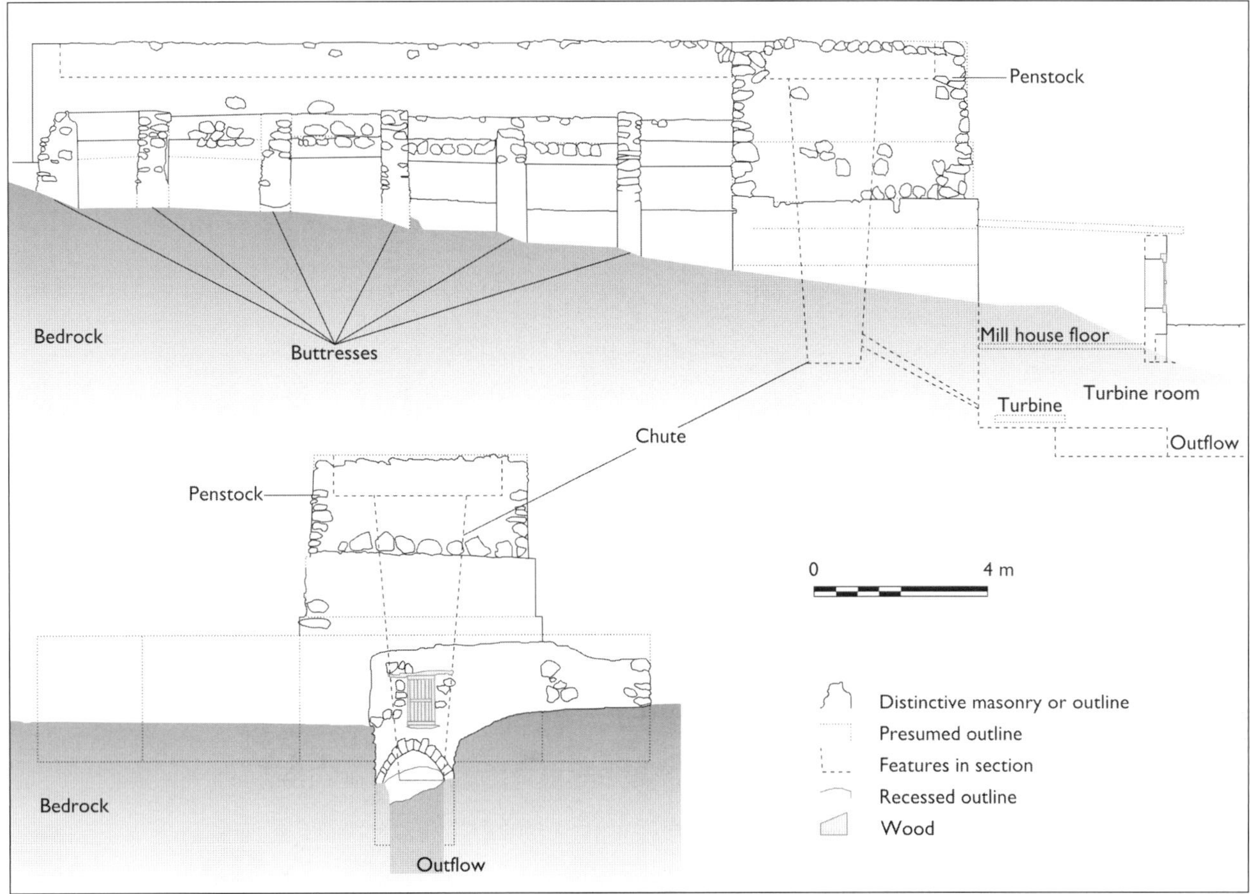

Fig. 3.8. Lachistos mill (BU0070): north (above) and west (below) elevations (Sevina Floridou)

derived from *lakchia*, or ravine, because of its low position in relation to the river. An alternative name that we heard, 'Mylos tis Panayias' or 'Mill of the Virgin Mary', was attributed to its Ottoman-period owners bequeathing it to the church in order to avoid paying taxes. As with Mylos tis Varvaras, this close connection between church and watermill can work at both a practical and an ideological level (Volume 1, Chapter 5.4).

The Lachistos mill is linked into the Karkotis Valley's intensive irrigation network, based on the principle of receiving water for irrigation purposes, letting it flow onwards or else allowing its diversion, according to a strictly observed schedule of water sharing (see Volume 1, Chapter 3.12). The mill receives water diverted from the Karkotis River at the Avrouliatis weir (BU0101), located 480 m to the south and directly opposite the Koumis mill (BU0074). The aqueduct, 5.6 m high where it joins the penstock, is a robust structure, built up in four tiers on its north face. It has supporting buttresses every 2.6 to 3.0 m (Figs 3.6–3.7), mostly on the north face.

The Lachistos penstock is c. 5.6 m high, with well-defined courses of basalt river boulders and cobbles, and four very narrow tiers on the north face, two on the west and one each on the other sides. In some of the lower courses large, rectangular, fired clay tiles are used instead

Fig. 3.9. Lachistos mill (BU0070): west facade, with wheel room through arch, grinding room through window, and penstock above (Chris Parks)

of quoins. Tiles are also used as chinking and to create a levelled topmost edge (Figs 3.8–3.9). Traces of lime plaster covering this stonework can still be seen, and like other

Fig. 3.10. Wheel room of Lachistos mill (BU0070), with wheel hub, some loose paddles, and the spout for the jet of water behind (Chris Parks)

mills of the area there are several phases of construction, or reconstruction. The water chute is one of the widest in the Survey Area, with an upper diameter of 2.17 m. It is circular, set into the rectangular penstock tower. Round it is a rectangular basin, the width of the penstock, and with walls 80 cm high. The chute itself is 6.30 m deep, tapering conically downwards, in a smooth plastered wall, towards the siphon located at the bottom.

The wheel room is intact, with the horizontal millwheel still in situ. This wheel is made of wood, with diagonal slots for wooden paddles in the frame (Fig. 3.10). The outflow arch has two phases: the vaulted dressed stones visible behind the outer voussoirs are clearly earlier, and seem to have slipped out of position (Fig. 3.8; Fig. 3.9). The rest of the millhouse above the wheel room is mostly destroyed, although a part of the west side, which has a window with dilapidated wooden latticing and shutters, located above the arched outflow, still survives. The wooden millwheel indicates that this mill stopped functioning well before the mid-1920s or 1930s, when metal turbines began to replace wooden wheels.

These mills were clearly capable of supporting (and being supported by) the large-scale production of cereals grown on the alluvial soil and elaborate terraces of the valley floor. In the Medieval and Early Ottoman period agricultural production was largely estate-based, but during the 18th and 19th centuries it increasingly came to be based on smallholders, with the mills owned by institutions such as the church, or associations of wealthier villagers. Either way, their monumental size and careful finishing clearly made them rather imposing: their construction resembled a village church more than the mudbrick houses of the villagers waiting to have their grain ground.

Continuing the survey transects up the valley sides, we discovered a very different form of cultivation from that on the valley floor on its eastern side. These involved very slight traces of Z-shaped terraces on the hillslope (Plate 3.3), which are similar to those described by Rackham and Moody (Rackham and Moody 1996, 141) as being a distinctive terracing technique in Crete. The terraces systematically use bedrock outcrops as terrace risers and follow the zig-zag pattern of basalt dykes across the hillslope. The resultant terraces are very narrow and, from a distance, resemble goat paths. Upon closer inspection, they actually are broader and flatter than one would expect simply from the movement of flocks. No artefacts were found in association with them, but ground visibility was extremely poor. The terraces are hard to date precisely, though clearly they are not modern. Other such terraces have been observed elsewhere in the Survey Area and in Cyprus.

Why cultivate such a steep and thin-soiled area when the well-watered and fertile alluvial soils of the valley floor are so close? It is clear from historical sources and from the huge amounts of labour spent in constructing the terrace and irrigation systems that the valley floor was dominated by large-scale cash-cropping during the Medieval and Ottoman periods, particularly cereals, flax and cotton. The feudal system of the Medieval period, however, depended on giving serfs the use of land for subsistence cultivation; this is fully evident from the Kato Koutraphas accounts of 1512 (Volume 1, Chapter 5.4). Most of this land was necessarily of poorer quality than the land cultivated for the estate and needed a greater input of labour. The Z-shaped terraces on the upper slopes of the Karkotis Valley represent exactly the sort of land that might be used in this way. The contrast is all the more striking because of the broad sweep of irrigated and terraced lands on the valley floor immediately below.

Closer examination of the soils in these terraces shows that they are not as unsuitable for agriculture as they might at first appear. Soils on hillslopes are relatively deeper (generally >0.3m) where colluvium and residuum accumulate upslope behind resistant basalt dykes. Soil development is enhanced in these natural terraces as water is more readily available and plants are more successful as a result. Although not as easily cultivatable, nor as moist as the valley floor, hillslope soils in the natural and anthropogenic terraces can provide nearly equivalent crop yields during wet years, if nutrients are properly managed. Such a management scheme could be as simple as leaving more than half of the crop biomass (chaff, stalks) on the field and allowing judicious grazing to cycle the biomass as plant-available manure. Such fields would likely do well under a crop–fallow rotation, which would be easy to manage and not require the effort given to the irrigated fields downslope.

In terms of Medieval–Modern artefact distribution and known settlements, the southern part of the Karkotis Valley Intensive Survey Zone shows distinctly less human activity than the Phlasou and Katydhata areas discussed later in this chapter. The complexity of the activity that does exist, however, is very clear. In the valley bottom is an intensive system of terracing, served by an elaborate network of irrigation channels. These were clearly controlled by the feudal estates based in Korakou, Evrykhou and Phlasou, and later by Ottoman cash-cropping estates apparently on the same sites. The system of churches on each ridge along the western side of the valley seems to have supported this production, by the visual and aural domination of the valley, as well as the more pragmatic mechanism of owning the olive presses and grain mills (see also Given and Hadjianastasis 2010).

The steeper hillslopes of the valley edges formed a very different type of resource. Dry cropping of the terraces and the deeper soils behind the basalt dykes allowed the maximisation of cereal yields, particularly in good years, and an opportunity to serfs and free peasant farmers to produce their own crops outside the estate-controlled valley floor. The hillslopes also provided good grazing, which in turn helped to fertilise the terraces and patches of arable land. The abundance and variety of herbs, roots and berries were highly valued for nutrition, flavouring and medical uses. This so-called 'wasteland' would more appropriately be called a 'gardenscape' (Forbes 1997). It was just as productive and played just as important a social role as the elaborate walled terraces, water channels and churches of the estate system in the valley floor below.

Fig. 3.11. Mylos tou Stylli, Evrykhou (BU0049): north-west facade, showing the outflow from the turbine room and the penstock above the roof (Michael Given)

3.4 Mylos tou Stylli, Evrykhou: Technology and Religion in a Working Watermill

Sevina Floridou

Mylos tou Stylli, just beyond the south-eastern margins of the village of Evrykhou, is one of the few working watermills that still survive in Cyprus. The aim of investigating this complex was to document the functioning and use of the mill, not just as a physical mechanism, but as a series of complex subjectivities governing the beliefs and practices of its users and impacting on the physical structure (for analysis of watermills in their landscape context, see Chapter 3.10 and Volume 1, Chapter 3.11). We also wanted to determine the phases that both building and equipment had undergone, from the day of their construction to the date of our own documentation. The greatest fortune in this enterprise was the presence of both the miller and his wife, particularly because our fieldwork coincided with a major turning point in the mill's biography (see below).

It was also significant that the mill had already been documented and published by Robert Morris (1984; see also Ionas 2001, 190–200). This provided an opportunity to verify his observations and also to document what had altered since that time. What came to light was the rich and extensive vocabulary the miller used in his craft, in the local Greek Cypriot vernacular. We made detailed sketches of the milling equipment, which were then assembled, with each part named, in a schematic drawing. The plan of the millhouse was made using the scanned cadastral drawing, to scale, while incorporating our own and Morris's observations.

Fig. 3.12. Mr Stelios Alexandrou ('Styllis o Mylonas') being interviewed by Sevina Floridou, 26 July 2001 (Chris Parks)

History and Architecture of the Mill

Mr Stelios Alexandrou, known locally as Styllis o Mylonas, was at the time of our research (2001–2003) the last miller in the area, if not in Cyprus overall (Fig. 3.12). Born in 1917 or 1918, he was an orphan, and had been adopted by the miller Hadjistyllis Hadjichristophis to serve as his apprentice (*chiraki*). In 1950 Hadjichristophis had bequeathed the mill to Styllis rather than to his own blood relatives, a source of great pride for Styllis. He had moved to Alexandria for 40 years before deciding to return and renovate the mill that had belonged to his father.

The mill complex, founded in 1878, has witnessed considerable alterations and renovations over the years, in keeping with its function, habitation and long use, as well as the changing technology of milling during the last 125 years (Fig. 3.13). It is situated just south of Evrykhou, and is set on a north-west by south-east axis. The mill is accessed via a steep path leading off the road entering the village from the south, and stands on a steep east bank of the Karkotis River; it was built on four levels amongst fruit orchards irrigated by water channels. One of these channels diverts water from the Klarios River (a tributary of the Karkotis), feeding the leat of the mill that is located on the uppermost level, together with the penstock.

The leat (Fig. 3.13, E) was constructed in irregular stone basalt and river boulders, but has since been cemented. In place of the side by-pass channel (*aloupos*), which in older mills is constructed in stone, there is a concrete rectangular opening fitted with a wooden, paddle-type, sluice-board that has a circular 'head', used as a lifting handle, on top. This is one in a sequence of monitoring nodes that need to be checked prior to letting the water turn the turbine. This aperture is used to let water escape should it flow too forcefully, or else for carrying debris to prevent it from falling down the penstock.

The penstock (Fig. 3.13, C), as it stands today, was built in 1926, and drops down over 10 m to the lowest level. It is a monumental construction, built of uniform stonework, with a vertical exterior face of about 3.5 m in height, proceeding downwards in four stepped tiers that incline outwards. On top it has a distinctive flat surface, without the stone hopper that is common in some mills of the area. Other mills with this type of leat and penstock are the Krommidos (BU0062) and Shaban Bey (BU0075) mills in Phlasou.

A conical downflow reservoir fills the interior of the penstock, tapering, towards the bottom, into a slanted chute, which in turn leads into a nozzle. Three different nozzles can be fitted, with apertures ranging in diameter from 6.5 to 9.0 cm (Morris 1984, 167). The forces exerted by the water following such compression, determines the tower-like penstock exterior. The corners are shaped in finely dressed limestone ashlar, creating a contrast to its basalt boulder walls. The same edging is used for the arched opening below the leat, where it joins the penstock. A framed inscribed limestone plaque set on the north-east face bears the date of the 1926 renovation.

Adjacent and east of the penstock is the miller's residence, set on two levels (Fig. 3.13, B). The *dichoro* or milling room (A) is lower down, on the third level, located between the penstock and the lower level of the house. It was constructed, in 1922, by the previous owner Hadjistyllis Hadjichristophis. The fourth and lowest level consists of the vaulted outflow chamber where the water, after falling down the penstock, drives the horizontal turbine before flowing out into a pool. The water is channelled further downhill and used for irrigation, as well as serving an adjacent mill, before ultimately returning back to the Karkotis.

New millstones were brought from the Greek island of Melos in 1926. In 1950, the floor of the milling room was cemented and the wooden, horizontal, paddle wheel was replaced with the metal turbine still in place today. A number of further technological alterations were also made, namely the importing of a second pair of milling stones from France and the addition of a timber platform upon which the millstones are secured (Morris 1984, 166). A diesel-powered turbine was added in 1961 in a rear storeroom with corrugated roof (K).

Interior, Milling Equipment and Furnishings

The milling room consists of a *dichoro*, or room of double width with a double-pitched roof. The foundation, at the lowest tier, is of irregular coursed, unplastered basalt, while the mill walls are in mudbrick, originally only plastered on the inside. The back wall of the milling room is, in fact, the base wall of the penstock and the stonework visible in the interior is unplastered. On the exterior, older pictures show plaster only around the window frames (Morris 1984, 170; Panayiotou 2001).

An I-beam, supported by engaged buttresses in the walls, supports the *tsappes* (rectangular timber roof rafters). The ceiling is laid with bamboo canes, with a tiled roof above. Mr Styllis cut the canes from the nearby river bed in 1998, and they were strung together by Mrs Aphrodite, the miller's wife; together they then re-laid the ceiling. 'Εν του επίεννεν να' ν με σέλοτεξ. Το σέλοτεξ εν' για τα σπίθκια, τούτον εν εργοστάσιον, πάν' του τα καννιά...' ('It didn't look good in sellotex [chipboard], that's nice for houses; this is a factory, it looks better with canes'), explained Mrs Aphrodite. Valuing modern, imported building materials more highly than traditional, local materials in this way is common throughout the Cypriot countryside.

The rectangular milling room is entered from a north-east covered porch (G), through a double door, which leads into the front part of the *dichoro* (A). A similar door opposite leads to an open terrace facing south-west (F), where washed wheat was laid to dry on cotton bed-sheets before being ground. A fireplace is situated in the right-hand corner, beside the entrance (H). Two windows on the facade overlook the village, with the mill outflow directly below the south-western one. The vault is constructed in basalt, unlike most mills where it is found in dressed limestone ashlar.

In the milling room there are two pairs of millstones set into a raised wooden platform (Fig. 3.14). The older pair, imported from Melos, were used to grind wheat from 1926 until 1950, when Myltis in Kalliana set up his mill with new French millstones (BU0060) (for imported millstones see Rizopoulou-Egoumenidou and Myrianthefs 2003, 179–81). Styllis recalled that the new mill had 'stopped' his own millstones – an ominous event when the millstones had to cease grinding. The Kalliana mill ground finer flour, so Styllis also went to France for new millstones (Mrs Aphrodite said he went two weeks after they were married). The stones he brought back from France were '*kseres*', undressed. The old millstones continued grinding pig meal until 1970, catering to demand from Skouriotissa mine. Pig farming declined, however, and the old millstones went out of use – referred to as 'worthless', but still kept in situ.

About halfway along the back wall of the milling room, the paddle brake (*statis*) protrudes out of an opening in the floor (Fig. 3.13, no. 8; Fig. 3.18). The vertical wood shaft possesses a knob, secured by inserting a Y-shaped stick against it, with the other end of the stick secured in a hollow in the stone wall.

The timber trestle table (Fig. 3.13, no. 3; Fig. 3.15, no. 27) is raised about 1 m from the floor, and is situated in the central part of the room, accessed by four steps set along its narrow side and rounded at one end. A vacant space between the two doors and the wooden platform allows all the milling activity to take place below the table at floor level: opening the sacks of grain; tipping the grain into containers; emptying the flour into calico sacks as it comes out of the grinding process; storing the sacks with flour and empty grain containers. Since everything is done by hand, the grain is transferred in containers, up the steps, onto the platform and tipped into the hopper (Fig. 3.15, no. 9), itself held in place by a trestle (10) nailed directly onto the hopper.

A vertical revolving pole passes through the trestle table (Fig. 3.15, no. 1), secured both to the floor and the roof rafters (7). It serves to remove the upper millstone (11) when the bedstone (12) needs to be dressed. The lower stone is incised with particular groove markings (13), allowing the wheat to be crushed in a scissor-like motion when the top wheel rotates over the fixed lower one. The bedstone must be secured with a sturdy timber frame (34) underneath the table, to prevent it being dragged round by the rotating runner stone.

At our visit on Sunday 1 July 2001, the belt of the old millstones from Melos had been removed and lay in a heap, in the corner beside the drive wheel. The French millstones, however, were grinding wheat for 'resi', a traditional wheat and lamb stew, in preparation for a wedding in Korakou. The oldest millstones, of the 1878–1922 phase (not on the premises any more), had been situated directly above the horizontal wooden paddle, in place of the independent horizontal drive wheel. During this first phase, the milling room may have been separated from the front room, with the second room possibly added at a later date.

In the turbine room underneath, the outflow is situated directly beneath the west facade window, its axis slightly displaced in relation to the penstock outflow. The nozzle, a pierced rectangular block of stone into which a wooden nozzle jet is set, is located on the easternmost corner of the back wall so that the jet of water hits the horizontal turbine wheel and turns it anti-clockwise. The floor of the turbine room is dissected by a deep channel, with narrow ledges left and right, allowing access to the brake on the left and to a wider platform to the right where the turbine sits, to the right of the nozzle, upon a raised stone platform. The height of the chamber is about 2.5 m, measured from the peak of the vault to the bottom of the channel.

The 'water brake', or engaging mechanism, is a simple wooden stick with a *faouta*, a spade-shaped horizontal wedge, threaded onto the stick and secured just below the nozzle (Fig. 3.16). The paddle break (*statis*) can be manipulated from the millroom upstairs (Fig. 3.18), raising it away from the nozzle and allowing the jet to drive the turbine. When the wedge is lowered directly in front of the nozzle, the water jet shoots upwards away from the paddles of the turbine, thus stopping its rotation. The *faouta* was missing from the brake; instead, a makeshift wooden plank had been nailed perpendicularly to the vertical shaft.

Mr Styllis told us that his mill could, at maximum speed, grind 6 *ttenekedes* (tins) per hour. Mrs Aphrodite explained that a tin weighed 13 kg. This would mean that the mill could grind c. 79 kg of grain per hour. Morris cites an average of four tins (at 12.30 kg each), coming to 49 kg per hour, with a maximum of 5–5.5 tins per hour (1984, 168).

A Sanctification Ritual

In 1984 Morris reported that the French Burr millstones had lost only half an inch in 34 years, and still had another four inches of working surface left. From this he estimated that they could continue unaltered for another 278 years (Morris 1984, 169). In 2002, however, the millstones needed re-

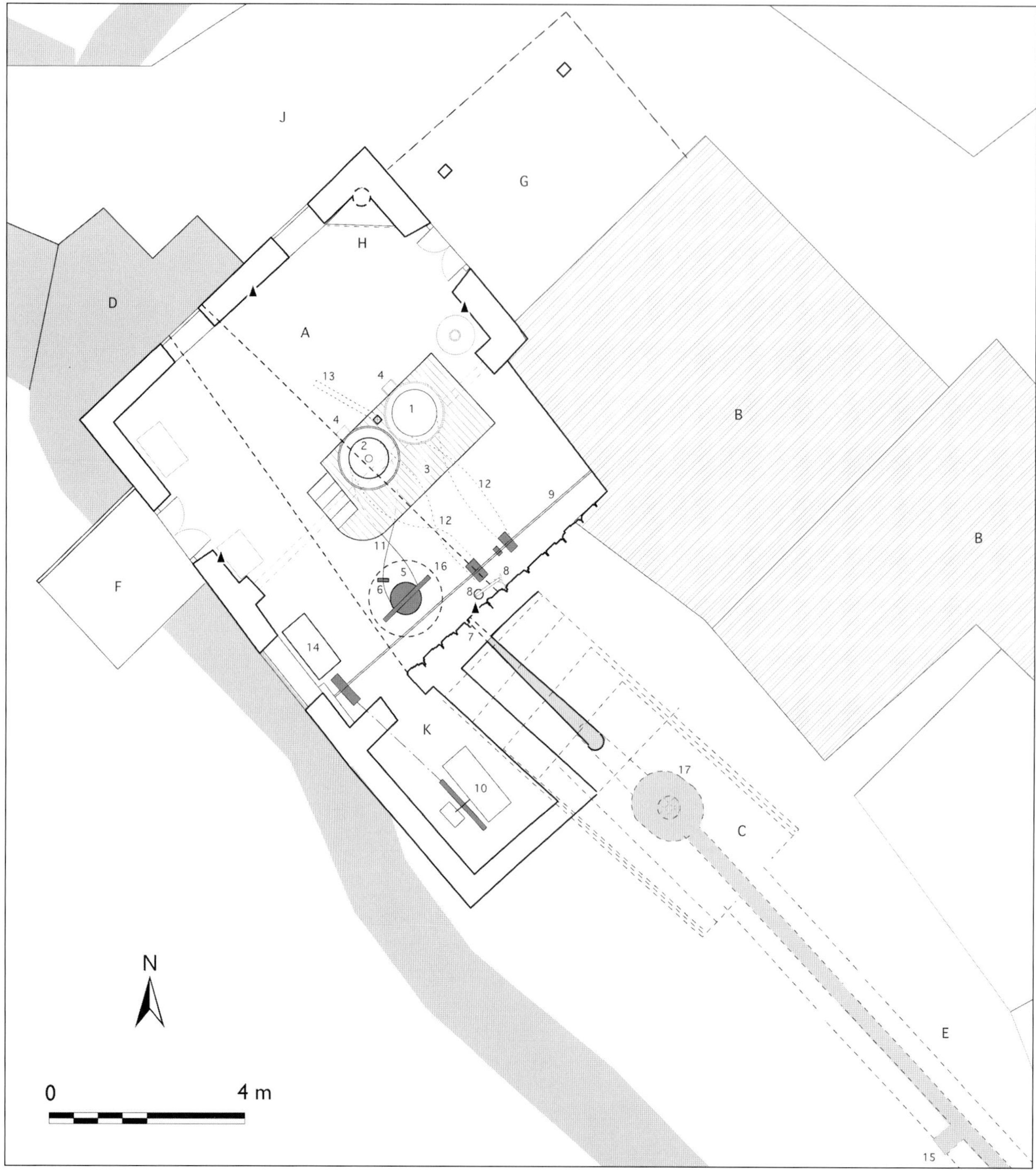

Fig. 3.13. Mylos tou Stylli, Evrykhou (BU0049): plan (from Morris 1984, with alterations from cadastral plan and TAESP survey in 2001 and 2002; illustration: Sevina Floridou). Key below and on opposite page

ENGLISH

A.	Milling room (1922)
B.	Miller's residence
C.	Penstock (1926)
D.	Outflow pool from turbine room
E.	Leat or race
F.	Open air verandah
G.	Covered porch
H.	Fireplace
J.	Access path
K.	Engine room in ex-store room
L.	Turbine room below milling room floor

Black triangle = Icon(s)

1.	Melos millstones (1926)
2.	French Burr stones (1950)
3.	Timber trestle table (1950)
4.	Flour chute
5.	Drive wheel on turbine axle (after 1998 modification)
6.	Secondary belt support and drive
7.	Water chute
8.	Engaging mechanism (water brake)
9.	Line shaft
10.	Engine mounting pod (1961)
11.	Current main driving belt

12. Alternate belts (1961)
13. Pivoting pole (1950)
14. Cotton machine
15. Bypass channel opening
16. Turbine position under milling room floor
17. Water downflow

CYPRIOT
A. Μύλος
B. Κατοικία μυλωνά
C. Γρεμμήστρα
D. Αυλάτζιν Πουκατοστέγης
E. Πετραύλακο
F. Ακάλυπτη βεράντα
G. Στέγαστρο
H. Νισκιά
J. Μονοπάτι
K. Μηχανή του πετρελαίου στο πρόην Σώσπιτο
L. Πουκατοστέγην

Red square = Εικόνισμα
1. Ζεβκάρι μυλόπετρες που νήσον Μύλον για το κλιθθάριν
2. Ζεβκάριν πέτρες Γαλλικές για το σιτάριν
3. Πάγκος
4. Καταπαχτή
5. Τροχαλίας
6. Στερέωση του κολανιού
7. Σιφούνι
8. Στάτης (Φτεροστάτης)
9. Άξονας
10. Μηχανή του πετρελαίου
11. Κολάνι
12. Κολάνια για να δουλεύκουν οι πέτρες όταν έν έσει νερόν
13. Άξονας
14. Παμπακομηχανή
15. Αλουπός
16. Φτερωτή
17. Βερκίν

Fig. 3.14. Mylos tou Stylli, Evrykhou (BU0049): Mrs Aphrodite with the millstones. The French millstones are on the right, with the hopper above; the older millstones from Melos are on the left (Chris Parks)

dressing to an extent that required their total dismantling from the central boss around which they were assembled. On 24 July 2002, milling had ceased and the millstones had been opened (Fig. 3.17). The mill had been 'protected' by the shape of the cross, with icons on each wall, and a whole iconostasis had been set up against the back wall, abutting the penstock, just above the hand-operated brake.

The iconostasis consisted of a tryptich icon (that had been in the mill during previous visits), with a second row of icons hung on nails hammered into a long wooden board set beneath it (Fig. 3.18) This had been in place during our visit in 2001. On this occasion, however, there was a *kandili*, or small oil lamp, made out of a glass jar containing water and oil with a wick floating on top, sitting below the iconostasis on a small, stone ledge, protruding from the wall. An open bible had been laid upon the metal frame support of the axle shaft that led down to the turbine beneath the floor. Seven wax church candles had been secured to the horizontal wooden bar of the handbrake (Fig. 3.18).

The icons in the millhouse for the sanctification ritual were located on the south wall, directly above the point where the water enters the mill building, through the nozzle of the penstock chute, into the vaulted turbine room under the workroom floor. This is also the point where the flow of water, and through that, the rotation of the turbine, can be humanly controlled through the handbrake. The icon arrangement in the millhouse was of a domestic arrangement, with apparently no particular significance to the saints arrayed left and right of the two principal icons. Christ and the Virgin were located in the centre of an array of icons, with the icon of Christ on the right.

Icons 'protect' and sanctify both the water and the space (Stewart 1991, 1994). Whenever sanctification rituals are deemed necessary, more icons may be placed, one on each wall, towards the four cardinal points (Fig. 3.13). This is the ritual of *stavroma*, thus shaping the cross and enveloping the space within a 'magic circle' (Kyriakidou-Nestoros 1989, 31).

The seven candles placed on the horizontal bar of the handbrake (Fig. 3.18) may have signified the seven days of the week. The candles and Bible completed all the required items necessary for a sanctification ritual. In Greek Christian Orthodox tradition, demons live and danger lurks in water and the place where it flows (Stewart 1991). Water continues to be exorcised in the Orthodox Church, during the baptism ceremony, as well as at Epiphany on January 6, when water is ceremonially sanctified by the priest, who throws a cross into a lake, sea or river. Water is considered easily polluted, particularly by death, and so needs to be sanctified by the exercise of some form of ritual cleansing and purification. The local bishop conducted the ritual in order to 'expel demons' and bestow divine protection on the miller.

Twice I asked the miller what the icons were for. He did not reply. His wife said that the Bishop of Morphou had performed an *agiasmos* (sanctification). When I insisted on asking why they had performed the *agiasmos*, Mr Styllis began patiently explaining the mill structure, item by item, naming each separate component and its function. Leaning over the lower millstone, lying exposed

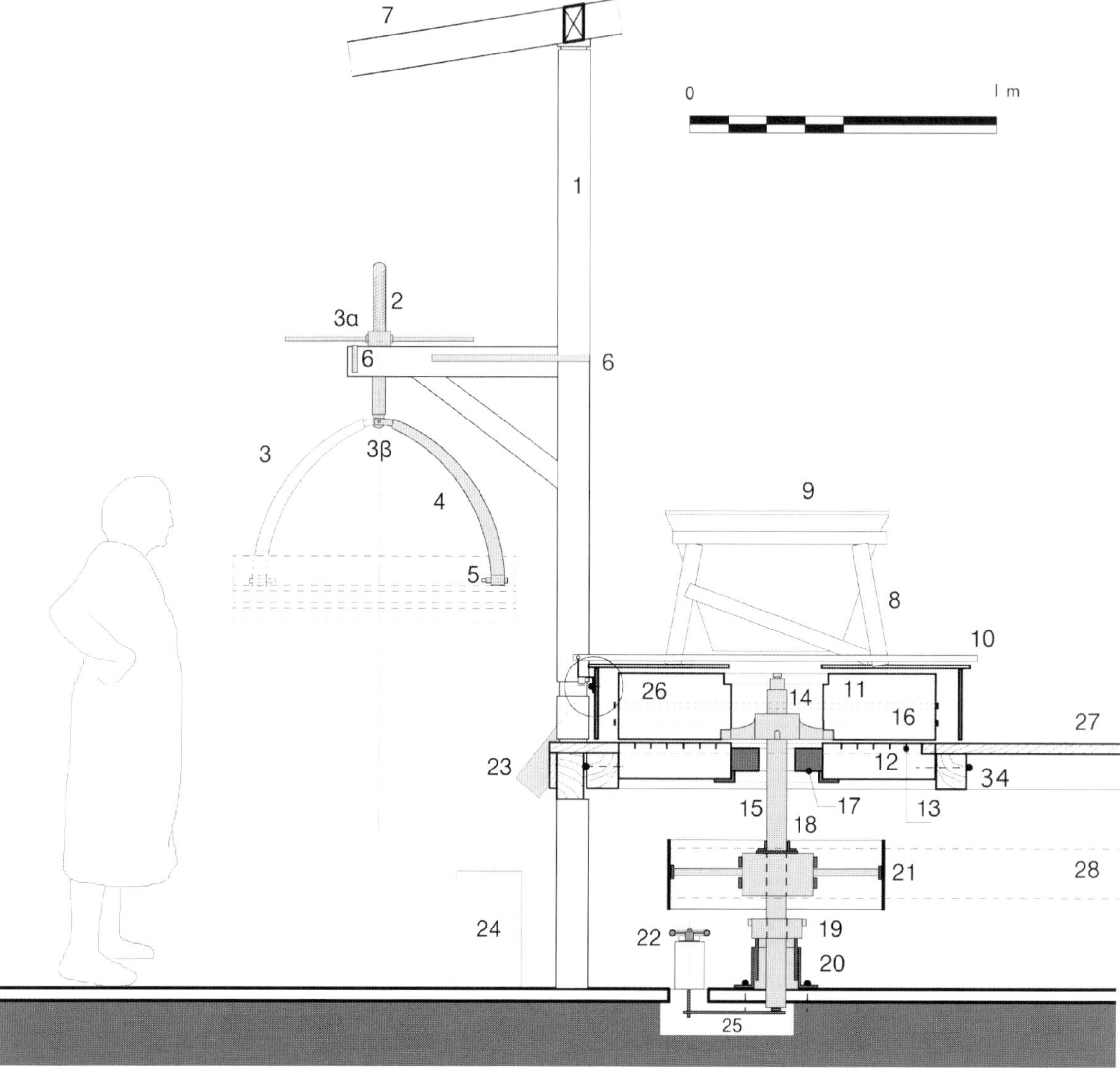

Fig. 3.15. Mylos tou Stylli, Evrykhou (BU0049): schematic section of mill mechanism and French millstones (set up c. 1950) (Sevina Floridou). Key below and on opposite page

1. Timber pivot post supporting the crane used to lift, open and dress the millstones.
2. Screw
3. Lifting crane. 3a: 'Head of crane'. 3b: Pivot screw
4. Braces, supported on the screw with pivots (5) which are secured into orifices in the stone.
5. Pivots
6. Metal supporting bands
7. Roof beam
8. Trestle, nailed onto hopper
9. Hopper
10. Perimetrical drum made of galvanised sheets and wooden lid
11. Runner stone (both stones made from radially assembled segments)
12. Stationary lower millstone
13. Grooves incised into bedstone
14. Steel 'adze' shaped support
15. Axle
16. Cast iron braces
17. Ball bearing, holds axle in place and allows motion through the stone
18. Screwed flange, a smaller ball bearing through which the axle passes down.
19. Ball bearing
20. Cast iron flange screwed to the floor
21. Belt wheel, loosened at some time by a plumber (miller was not happy about this)
22. Breyer lever, according to the miller, '...the wheel to raise stone by means of a metal rod: this pushes up the ball bearing, the ball bearing raises the axle and the axle raises the stone when the belts have to be put on the wheel so that the stone becomes lighter (ie easier to turn and slow down).
23. Flour outlet of galvanised sheet metal
24. Corrugated metal flour container
25. Moving rod under floor
26. Screw operated grain regulator from hopper to mill, literally '...That which feeds the mill...'
27. Timber trestle table
28. Belt

b. Index of transcribed Cypriot terms as described by the miller Mr. Styllis

1. Περιστρεφόμενος στύλλος '...Στύλλος του βιντζιού για άννοιμαν των μυλόπετρων, σήκωμα τζαι χάραξην...'
2. Βίδα
3. Βίντζιν. 3α. Τζεφάλιν του βιντζιού. 3b. Καβίλια
4. Αγκώνες εφαρμοσμένες πα' στην βίδαν τζαι που κάτω έχουν καβίλιες (5) που εφαρμόζουν με' στην πέτραν
6. Λάμες στερέωσης
7. Βολίτζιν οροφής
8. Τριστέλλιν '...έναν σώμα με την κοφινιάν...'
9. Κοφινιά

10. 'Καππάτζιν ξύλινον τζαι γυροί που λαμαρίναν πιντωμένην'

'Ζεφκάριν πέτρες (11 & 12) Γαλλικές για το σιτάριν... μόνον οι πέτρες ξερές εν' που την Γαλλίαν... 'κομμάθκια ολογερής'

11. Πουπανολίθαρον
12. Κατολίθαρον
13. Κανάλια '... Μετά τζαιρόν βαθυνίσκω τα...'
14. Ξινάριν
15. Άξονας
16. Βρασιόλια
17. Βούλλας '...Βαστά τον στύλλον να γυρίζει μέσον του λιθαρκού...'
18. Φλάντζα βιδωμένη '...που κάτω έσιει βουλλίν με ρουλεμάν που κατεβαίνει ο άξονας μέσα...'
19. Βουλλίν με ρουλεμάν
20. Φλάντζα με ματέμι βιδωμένη στο πάτωμα
21. Τροχαλία, ή '...τροχός για το κολάνι... '
22. Μουκλός, '...Τζείνον που ξιουλλά την πέτραν τζαι ψηλώνει την με λάμα - κουντά το βουλλίν πάνω, το βουλλίν κουντά τον στύλλον τζαι ο στύλλος την πέτραν, άμαν θέλει να βάλουμεν τα κολάνια να αλαβρύνει τζαι ύστερα γυρίζει για να κάτσει η πέτρα στο φάδιν της για να αλαβροποιήσει...'
23. Χωνί αλευριού
24. Ττενεκκές
25. Λάμα στο πάτωμα
26. '...Τζείνον που διά τροφή στον μύλον...'
27. Πάγκος
28. Κολάνι

*Fig. 3.16. Mylos tou Stylli, Evykhou: the nozzle and paddle break (*statis*) in the turbine room (Chris Parks)*

Fig. 3.17. Mylos tou Stylli, Evrykhou: Styllis and Aphrodite Alexandrou, with the French runner millstone lifted out (Sevina Floridou)

Fig. 3.18. Mylos tou Stylli, Evrykhou (BU0049): row of icons on the wall, above the penstock outflow, and the water brake (below) with candles and a Y-shaped stick holding it in place; 24 July 2002 (Sevina Floridou)

with the runnerstone and hopper removed, he showed me the problem, spoke of his enormous dilemma and asked me what, in my opinion, he should do.

The grooves of the lower millstone had worn down to less than 0.5 cm in relation to the boss (*voullin*), so the wheat, thrown in from the hopper above, was unable to disperse over its surface when the upper stone was set in motion. The miller needed to dress the stones with deeper grooves, but that meant dismantling the lower millstone, composed of radial stone segments around the steel boss. He was deeply troubled because, in order to provide the necessary depth the grooves required, he would have to lower the *voullin* by about 1–1.5 cm, which would require dismantling the bedstone. He was afraid he would be unable to reassemble the stones with the boss correctly, and then re-set it in relation to the correct height of the wheels and belt mechanism, without impairing the rotational movement from the water-powered paddle. Furthermore, stone had fused to metal, having been cemented together with a binding mortar made from decades of fine flour. The old miller was afraid he would injure, or even break, the stones in his attempt to separate them from the boss.

The miller's dilemma resulted from having to face both the end of his life and the end of his mill, which was what kept him going. The mill had reached its end before he had. By intervening, he could perhaps give a new lease of life to the mill (and hence continue milling for his remaining life), or maybe he would ruin the mill forever. Either way, he had to come to terms with the finality of both his life and his profession, for he felt there was no one to turn to for technical expertise.

Conclusions

How a mill functions can be understood by determining factors of gravity and water flow, and by the analysis of the mechanics of thrust, span and support. Just as importantly, religious beliefs and mythical associations can be seen to determine their architectural shape and layout; just as much for mills as for religious buildings. The structures used for other pre-industrial activities, such as threshing, and wine and olive pressing are similarly governed by the symbolism of 'divine circles'.

Sanctification, through the ideological hierarchy of the 'triumph of life over death', is performed by numerous rituals involving motion in a cyclic, anti-clockwise direction. Inside a mill, the point of water entering the building is at the nozzle. Therefore, the jet of water striking the paddle wheel must always come from the left of the wheel, initiating its anti-clockwise rotation. This explains why the horizontal axis of the chute is displaced in relation to that of the vaulted chambers below. In Greek rituals, movement towards the right is always understood to be anti-clockwise (Stewart 1994), however, the anti-clockwise, cyclic motion symbolising life is an archaic custom, existing long before it was incorporated into Orthodox Christianity.

The anti-clockwise rotation of the horizontal turbine wheel has been observed in all the mills in the study area, wherever we have had access to the vaulted turbine chamber. The nozzle of the water outflow inside the turbine room is always located on the left of the turbine paddle wheel (Fig. 3.16).

Throughout his life, the last miller of the Karkotis Valley kept making alterations and minor adjustments to the mill equipment, always trying to address issues of stability, productivity, reducing friction on the stones, helping the wheels rotate more smoothly and with more 'streamlined lightness' (*alavrokopima*). Some alterations were informed from the time when milling was a thriving competitive business, with enough colleagues to exchange know-how and enough innovative ideas to copy. Later, however, alterations became hasty, like the nailing of a plank of wood against the shaft of the paddle brake to direct water away from the nozzle. Perhaps there were no more craftsmen in associated professions to whom he could turn to for spare parts – for example, the ironmongers specializing in farming equipment, who disappeared early.

He was disappointed that his son did not follow the trade, and earlier in his life had faced the dilemma, just as his father had done, of getting an apprentice himself. But, so that the mill would not pass into hands outside the family, he had decided not to, thereby acknowledging the transformation of the value of his trade into real estate property. Yet, he broke down when greeted by a picture of ruin at Koumis mill, which belonged to Mr. Styllis's adopted aunt. His father had built the penstock in the 1930s. The mill had remained disused for 30 years and was completely ruined. 'Without man,' he lamented, 'there is devastation'.

Acknowledgements (Sevina Floridou)

Mr Styllis, himself unable to read or write, had the presence of mind to pass on as much milling knowledge of the whole area, as I, in my limited understanding, was able to receive. Contrary to the Orthodox ideological hierarchy he dared to share his craft with a woman, for which I am forever grateful. I would also like to express my thanks to Marios Sarris, social anthropologist, for the religious interpretations.

3.5 Prehistoric Settlement at Phlasou *Koutroullis*

The earliest evidence of distinctive settlement activity in the Karkotis Valley Intensive Survey Zone comes from Koutroullis (TS06), a ridge rising above the landscape just south-east of Kato Phlasou. The concentration of pottery and chipped stone at Koutroullis, which dates to the Late Chalcolithic–Prehistoric Bronze Age 1 transition (Late Chalcolithic/Philia), is virtually the only material of these dates in the Karkotis Valley. This assemblage is also distinguished in having the largest group of ground stone artefacts in the Survey Area. Overall, the artefacts point strongly to the presence of a Late Chalcolithic and Early PreBA 1 settlement. Such a settlement, located atop the ridge trending westward from the valley edge (Fig. 3.19), would have enjoyed an excellent, northerly view of the entire Karkotis Valley down to Morphou Bay and, on clear days, to the coast of Turkey (Fig. 3.20).

During transect survey, the team observed prehistoric pottery and ground stone tools eroding out of a road-cut (TP135) on the south-east slope of the Koutroullis ridge (Fig. 3.21). Comparable sherds and chipped stone material were distributed along the dirt road leading east from the cut, which had been created by a bulldozer no earlier than 2002, according to the farmer who maintains a sheepfold on top of

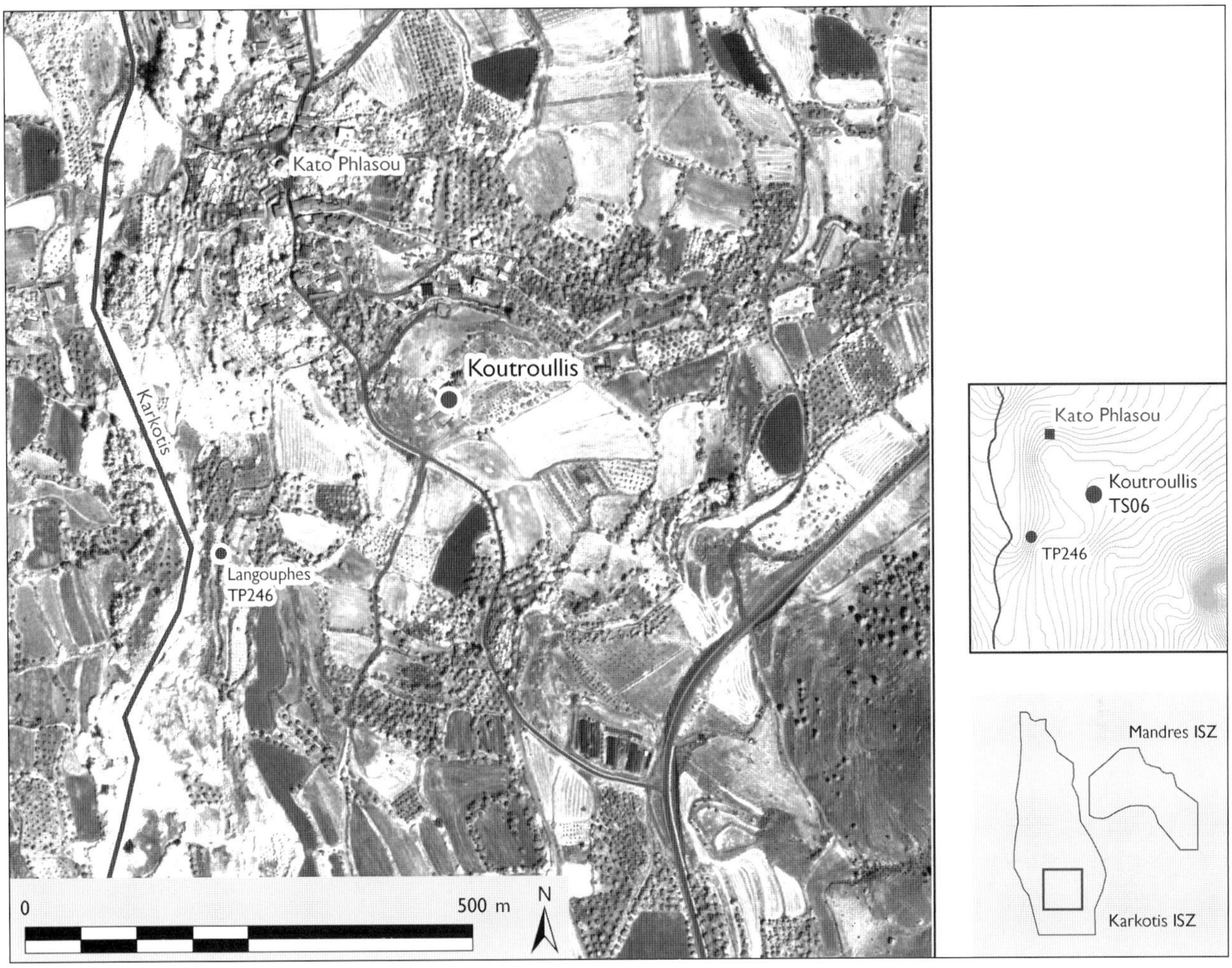

Fig. 3.19. Phlasou Koutroullis *(TS06) and its context: corrected satellite image (2003) courtesy of the Cyprus Geological Survey Department (Luke Sollars)*

Fig. 3.20. Phlasou Koutroullis *(TS06), looking north-east down the Karkotis Valley (Chris Parks)*

Fig. 3.21. Phlasou Koutroullis *(TP135): road-cut (Chris Parks)*

the ridge. The road-cut itself has maximum dimensions of c. 35 m (length) by 3 m (height). After distinguishing areas of intact soil and slopewash, we divided the intact soil into layers based on relative amounts of carbonate (Fig. 3.22), which then were established as POSI units.

To complement the artefactual data collected from the road-cut, we conducted block survey on the surface of the ridge and in the cultivated fields below it (to the south-east). The topography of the ridge is characterized by a series of small, irregular terraces. The only area where poor ground visibility prevented block survey was the steep western slope. Most of the ridge, which is an outcrop of pillow basalt, is overlain with thin soil or has none at all. Its southern and eastern portions have the thickest soil cover, a mixture of

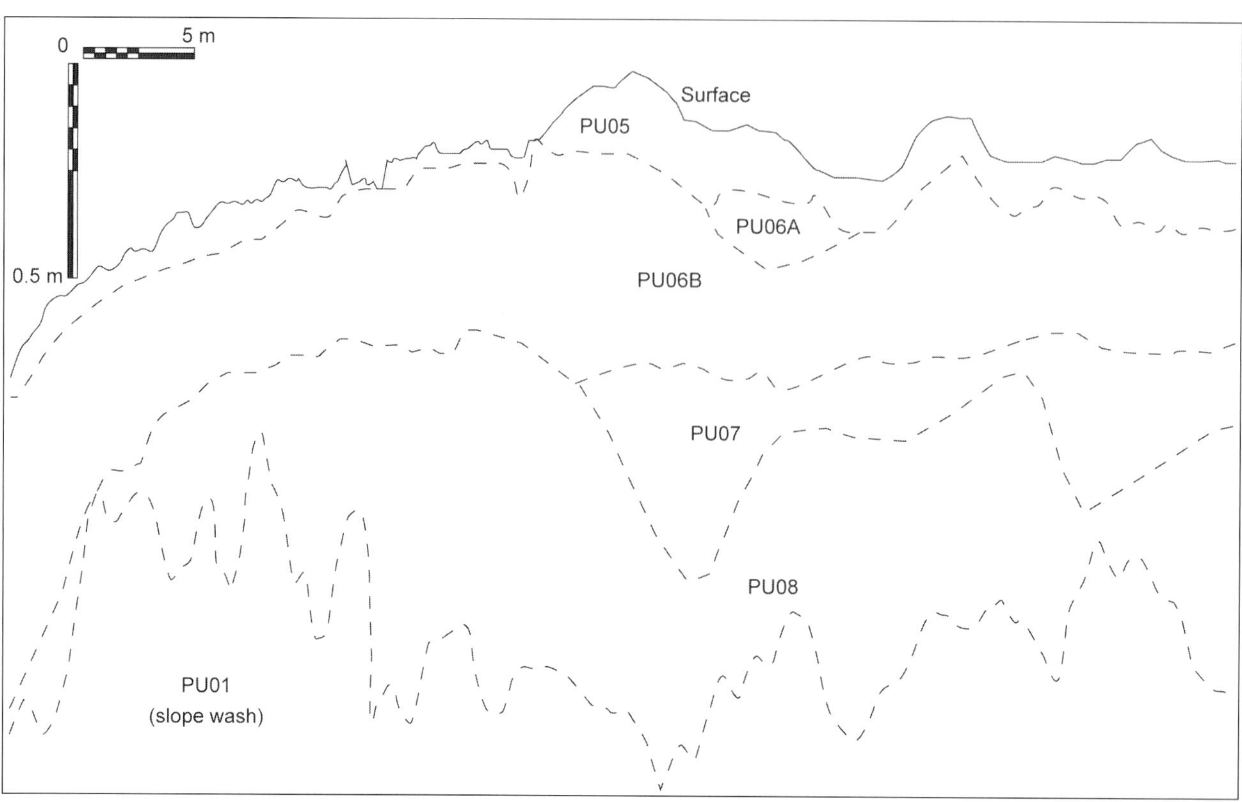

Fig. 3.22. Phlasou Koutroullis *(TP135): section drawing of road-cut. Horizontal scale has been compressed by a factor of 20 (Jay Noller, finalised by Luke Sollars)*

colluvium (i.e. eroded remains from the top of the ridge, which could include remnants of human occupation, such as decomposed mudbrick) and fluvial sediments. These deposits lie 18–21 m above the modern Karkotis channel.

The prehistoric course of the Karkotis River also is suggested by a vertically excavated terrace riser (TP246) at Phlasou *Langouphes*, located c. 325 m south-west of Koutroullis. A cross-section of the ancient river channel, consisting of discrete, stratified layers of artefact-bearing flood deposits, is visible in the riser (Plate 3.4). A representative sample of pottery, chipped stone, ground stone and picrolite was collected from each of five POSI units that correspond to the flooding episodes. Also collected were four samples for phytolith analysis: the dark brown palaeosol yielded high concentrations of cereal silica plant parts (Patricia Anderson, pers. comm.). The pottery in this palaeosol was homogenous and of the same date as the material from Koutroullis. Sherd fragments were large and minimally worn, suggesting that they had not spent a significant amount of time in the river prior to being buried in the flood deposit.

The location of this palaeosol at c. 12 m above the level of the current river channel suggests that the river was at, or below, this elevation while people were living at Koutroullis. At this time of occupation, Koutroullis would have been some 7 to 10 m higher, on the east bank of the Karkotis. During prehistoric periods, the site would have lain adjacent to the floodplain of the Karkotis River, much as the modern villages were positioned in the Medieval–Modern periods. TP246 deposits are located west and upstream of a bedrock ridge. Such a position in the landscape obviates any possibility of direct connection with Koutroullis by geomorphic processes. In other words, water could not have flowed down the local trunk stream carrying artefacts from Koutroullis to the main channel of the Karkotis and then flowed upstream against gravity and current to the TP246 site. The contemporaneity of artefacts is the result of at least two distant loci of site formation processes.

The northern slope of the Koutroullis ridge is low and has little evident disturbance from modern activity. Because the soil here is thinner, the pottery and substantial ground stone and chipped stone tool assemblages are probably in situ. One notable Survey Unit (SU2104) yielded a high quantity of large, freshly broken fragments of domestic pottery. The most common vessel shapes were related to storage, and include very large, open-mouthed jars with short necks and smaller, hole-mouth jars with flaring rims (e.g. TCP339). The northern face of the ridge also is strewn with abundant building stone. Additional archaeological remains may already have eroded from, or still be lying immediately under, the surface of the northern side. The largest quantity of pottery came from another Survey Unit (SU2085) on the ridge's southern side. This unit encompassed a steep slope whose surface soil is regularly churned up by sheep as they make their way to the sheepfold. These characteristics

Table 3.3. Phlasou Koutroullis *(TS06): pottery from TP135, TP177, TP246. TCP numbers refer to Pottery Catalogue in Volume 1, Chapter 3.6*

Chalcolithic

Fct	Type	No.	Weight
HU	RM	444	6.52kg TCP650, TCP651, TCP653
HU	RMCL	11	478g TCP652
LU	RM	281	1.272kg TCP654, TCP657, TCP658
TW	RM	67	193g TCP643

Late Chalcolithic/Philia

Fct	Type	No.	Weight
HU	RM	9	90g
HU	RMP	42	3.265kg TCP644, TCP645, TCP646
LU	RMP	104	402g TCP648
TW	RM	14	30g
TW	RMP	21	85g

Prehistoric Bronze Age

Fct	Type	No.	Weight
HU	HU	4	25g
HU	RM	4	468g
HU	RMP	14	396g
HU	RP	4	134g
LU	LU	4	17g
LU	RMP	29	395g
LU	RP	13	54g
LU	RPC	1	5g TCP649
LU	RPOM	1	10g TCP647
TW	RP	12	45g
TW	RPT	62	252g TCP655, TCP656

Late Bronze Age to Archaic

Fct	Type	No.	Weight
LU	LU	1	5g

Cypro-Geometric to Classical

Fct	Type	No.	Weight
TW	BS	1	2g

Historical Antiquity (Archaic to Late Roman)

Fct	Type	No.	Weight
HU	HU	15	29g
LU	LU	10	59g

Hellenistic

Fct	Type	No.	Weight
TW	RS	1	2g

Early to Late Roman

Fct	Type	No.	Weight
Ar	TiP	1	400g

Late Roman

Fct	Type	No.	Weight
Ar	TiP	2	460g

Roman to Modern

Fct	Type	No.	Weight
Ar	Ti	3	130g

Historical (Archaic to Modern)

Fct	Type	No.	Weight
LU	LU	30	139g
TW	TW	1	2g

Medieval to Modern

Fct	Type	No.	Weight
HU	BuHK	1	16g
HU	HU	2	105g
LU	BuLK	1	19g
U	BuLK	1	1g

Medieval-Frankish

Fct	Type	No.	Weight
TW	CGS05	2	5g

Medieval-Venetian to Early Ottoman

Fct	Type	No.	Weight
TW	G03	1	4g

Ottoman to Modern II

Fct	Type	No.	Weight
LU	BuL	3	27g

Modern

Fct	Type	No.	Weight
Ar	TiCh	3	95g
HU	HU	2	29g

Unknown

Fct	Type	No.	Weight
LU	LU	1	1g
LU	Un	5	40g

suggest that more active movement of artefacts downslope from the summit occurs on the southern side. Because this side of the ridge also boasts the thickest deposits of sediment, there is a very real chance that archaeological remains are intact under the surface.

Pottery

The pottery from Koutroullis (Table 3.3–3.4) presents a challenge to classification because it falls into a transitional phase where firm identifications and chronologies are still debated (Peltenburg 1991). While the red burnished surfaces of most sherds might readily be labelled as Red Polished (RP) wares, an examination of the fabric, firing, thickness and vessel forms points instead to the Red-and-Black Lustrous and Red Monochrome (RM) wares of the Prehistoric Bronze Age 1 period (c. 2600–2000 BC). This type of pottery appears, *prima facie*, to be similar to that commonly found at Ambelikou *Ayios Yeoryios*, a site that lies just north of the Survey Area. For the sake of clarity, all pottery with Chalcolithic fabric and monochrome burnished surface has been categorised here as 'Red Monochrome' (RM) and assigned to the earliest phase of the PreBA 1 period (Late Chalcolithic/Philia, c. 2600–2400). Until a fully stratified site spanning this phase is excavated and published, it is impossible to be more specific.

The RM pottery from Koutroullis has thick walls and relatively soft fabric consisting of a mixed, rather poorly sorted, clay tempered with chaff (e.g. TCP643; for pottery catalogue, see Volume 1, Chapter 3.6). Firing was uneven, which resulted in a reddish-brown range of surface colours. Finishing was medium- to well-burnished with few strokes visible; such strokes usually show a streaky range of colours, from red to black, rather than matt versus shiny. Vessel types include bowls of various sizes and large jars with open mouths and partly finished interiors.

Some fragments of a smaller, finer type of bowl have a glossy black interior and slightly thinner walls (e.g.

TCP658). Whereas in standard RP ware these bowls would be expected to have a fine calcareous fabric, the TAESP material is universally of a tan-pink, poorly sorted fabric, tempered with chaff. This resulted in small fine bowls with glossy surfaces, pock-marked by burned-out chaff, and with a coarse dark reddish brown-to-black section producing a jagged fracture. Analogous RP ware bowls typically are made of fine calcareous clay with a very smooth fracture (Barlow 1991).

Several sherds with soft, powdery, tan-white fabric and faint traces of either a cream coloured or washy red slip were found at Koutroullis. Because of their soft firing, they tend to be very worn and small (e.g. TCP646). The fabric shows some similarities to both Chalcolithic Red-on-White ware and Philia ware, and it was not possible to identify them more accurately. No diagnostic Early–Middle Chalcolithic material was identified at Koutroullis. One possible interpretation, therefore, is that the site does have an earlier phase, but deposition and erosion factors have only enabled us to recover very worn, non-diagnostic sherds. Conversely, these sherds may be contemporary with the rest of the assemblage and, if so, would represent the last expressions of a changing ceramic tradition in the transitional PreBA 1.

Also found at Koutroullis were some examples of what seem to be very early RP ware, possibly of the Philia facies (Webb and Frankel 1999). This material consists of tan-to-grey, fine fabrics with tiny burned-out specks, coated with brilliant red slip and given a streaky burnish. Several smaller vessels, whose finish has largely worn off, have a fabric tempered with small, rounded, white chunks. These sherds (e.g. TCP336) feature the plug-through handle technique typical of the RP ware horizon, an innovation introduced to Cyprus at the beginning of the Philia phase (Peltenburg 1996, 25, n.10; Frankel *et al.* 1996, 42–43). Some of the large jar fragments (e.g. TCP303) found at Koutroullis also were consistent with the RP tradition, having a distinct neck, hard firing and thinner walls, although the fabric still resembled RM ware and contained large amounts of chaff temper. There was also a single example of the scratch-through technique, where a red underslip or self-slip was exposed by scraping away a greyish overslip. This sherd (TCP648) had a fine, calcareous fabric, consistent with RP fine wares, although with a higher organic content than might be expected. No examples of incised and lime-filled fine ware, slashed handles or other typical RP I–III diagnostics were found at Koutroullis.

In a separate visit to the site during 2004, Giorgos Georgiou (Department of Antiquities, Cyprus) recovered a large plug-through handle made in RM fabric. The plug-through handle is a hallmark of RP ware and of the Cypriot Bronze Age generally. If this handle is among the first of its kind ever produced on Cyprus, as we believe it to be, then it neatly illustrates the transitional nature of PreBA 1 material culture at Koutroullis, when new and old ideas and technological traditions intermingled and eventually formed the classic RP canon.

A set of three Survey Units (SU2029–31) located c. 300 m south-west of Koutroullis contained an assemblage of prehistoric artefacts comparable to that from the ridge. These included moderate densities of Chalcolithic and PreBA 1 pottery and a concentration of chipped stone (consisting almost entirely of cores, blanks and debris made of local jasper, although there was one translucent Lefkara hammer stone). Very little Chalcolithic and Early PreBA 1 material was found east of Koutroullis along this transect. When considered alongside the material from the bulldozed terrace riser (TP246), it is evident that the Koutroullis ridge and the area immediately to its south-west constitute the only significant concentration of artefacts in the TAESP Survey Area dating to this era.

Chipped Stone

A substantial amount of lithic material was collected from Koutroullis, the vast majority of which represents prehistoric activity at the site. These samples constitute one of the most comprehensive prehistoric chipped and ground stone assemblages collected by TAESP, giving a clear glimpse of those industries in use at the end of the Chalcolithic and the beginning of the Prehistoric Bronze Age.

No finds were discovered on the threshing floors (TP176, TP187), which suggests that the *dhoukani*-bearing sledges were housed elsewhere rather than left to decay on site. One *dhoukani* flake recovered from the Koutroullis road-cut (TP135) represents an element that probably fell out or was discarded during the use of these threshing floors and subsequently became incorporated into the earlier prehistoric material.

Forty chipped stone and 24 ground stone artefacts were collected from the road-cut (Tables 3.5, 3.7). These samples represent the main stone artefact assemblages from Koutroullis, with an additional four ground stone tools and a single chipped stone tool found near the summit of the ridge (collected as TP177). Two further chipped stone and two ground stone artefacts were recovered from flood deposits at Langouphes (TP246). The POSI samples are augmented by significant numbers of both chipped stone (n=25) and ground stone (n=40) from Survey Units conducted on the Koutroullis ridge.

A number of interesting features are apparent in the Koutroullis chipped stone assemblage. There is clear spatial variation in the distribution of the artefact types, assuming there has been no significant post-depositional movement here. More tool use seems to have taken place in the vicinity of the road-cut, in contrast to the rest of the transect where there was more evidence for core reduction (Table 3.5). The cores used for the production of tool blanks invariably represent cores for the production of flakes, represented by a variety of types including amorphous, alternating platform cores, change-of-orientation and single platform examples. A significant number of heavily exhausted cores-on-flakes, splintered pieces or core fragments show a high degree

Table 3.4. Phlasou Koutroullis *(TS06): pottery from SU2006–12, SU2078–85, SU2104. TCP numbers refer to Pottery Catalogue in Volume 1, Chapter 3.6*

Chalcolithic

Fct	Type	No.	Weight
HU	RM	59	2.814kg
	TCP328, TCP329, TCP330, TCP331		
HU	Un	1	65g
LU	RM	25	295g
	TCP335, TCP339		
LU	RMCS	6	140g
	TCP332, TCP333		
TW	RM	13	49g

Late Chalcolithic/Philia

Fct	Type	No.	Weight
HU	RMP	12	1.285kg
			TCP340
LU	RMP	6	37g

Bronze Age

Fct	Type	No.	Weight
LU	BS	1	6g

Prehistoric Bronze Age

Fct	Type	No.	Weight
HU	RP	3	98g
HU	RPC	3	175g
	TCP295, TCP337		
HU	RPS	1	50g
			TCP289
LU	RP	7	60g
			TCP336
LU	RPC	3	63g
	TCP278, TCP338		
LU	RPS	1	28g
			TCP290
TW	RP	10	60g
			TCP334
TW	RPC	1	2g

Cypro-Geometric to Classical

Fct	Type	No.	Weight
HU	HU	1	55g
HU	Per	1	26g
LU	LU	3	23g

Historical Antiquity (Archaic to Late Roman)

Fct	Type	No.	Weight
HU	HU	18	523g
LU	LU	54	579g
LU	LUR14	1	12g
TW	BS	1	2g
TW	TW	2	14g

Hellenistic

Fct	Type	No.	Weight
TW	RS	1	2g

Hellenistic to Roman

Fct	Type	No.	Weight
CW	CW	7	21g
LU	LUR06	1	15g
Tr	Mav01	1	160g
TW	RS	1	14g

Late Hellenistic to Early Roman

Fct	Type	No.	Weight
TW	Sig	2	8g

Early to Late Roman

Fct	Type	No.	Weight
Ar	Ti	5	855g
Ar	TiP	7	1.045kg
LU	LUR01	4	220g
TW	ARS	2	5g
TW	TW	1	8g

Late Roman

Fct	Type	No.	Weight
Ar	Ti	1	55g
Ar	TiP	4	455g

Roman to Modern

Fct	Type	No.	Weight
Ar	Brk	1	250g
Ar	Ti	6	696g
HU	HU	1	35g
HU	Pit13	1	380g
			TCP293

Historical (Archaic to Modern)

Fct	Type	No.	Weight
Ar	TiCS	1	71g
HU	HU	23	1.136kg
HU	Pit	3	590g
LU	LU	18	189g
TW	TW	3	38g

Byzantine

Fct	Type	No.	Weight
TW	G07	2	27g
			TCP285

Medieval utility period I

Fct	Type	No.	Weight
CW	Tta02	1	20g
CW	TtaB	1	20g
			TCP286
U	UAA98	3	55g
U	UL01	1	70g
			TCP280

Medieval

Fct	Type	No.	Weight
TW	BGW	1	10g
TW	G02	3	21g
TW	G04	1	2g

Medieval to Modern

Fct	Type	No.	Weight
CW	BGW	38	395g
CW	Tia	4	119g
CW	TtaB	1	25g
HU	BuHK	1	245g
HU	HU	70	2.56kg
LU	BuLK	4	28g
LU	G	1	16g
LU	LU	84	1.125kg
TW	BGW	1	10g
TW	G01	1	20g
U	BuLK	1	4g
U	BUPSJa	1	76g
U	UH02	1	25g

Byzantine to Medieval

Fct	Type	No.	Weight
TW	CGS03	1	7g
TW	MP06	1	10g
			TCP282
TW	SP03	2	16g
			TCP327

Medieval-Frankish

Fct	Type	No.	Weight
TW	CGS02	3	68g
			TCP287
TW	CGS05	35	193g
			TCP283

Medieval utility period II

Fct	Type	No.	Weight
CW	Tta02	2	68g

Medieval utility period III

Fct	Type	No.	Weight
CW	BGWCC	1	15g
CW	Tia03	1	15g
U	ID04	15	233g
U	UJa02	12	160g
	TCP279, TCP284		
U	UPSJu	1	18g
			TCP292

Ottoman

Fct	Type	No.	Weight
TW	G03	3	18g

Ottoman to Modern I

Fct	*Type*	*No.*	*Weight*
HU	HU	1	330g
LU	LU	8	100g
TW	G03	6	90g
TW	G04	1	5g
TW	G05	4	55g
TW	MP01	1	5g
TW	MP02	1	9g
U	UBR01	1	37g TCP291
U	ULSJ01	1	65g TCP294

Medieval-Venetian to Early Ottoman

Fct	*Type*	*No.*	*Weight*
TW	MP01	8	80g

Ottoman to Modern II

Fct	*Type*	*No.*	*Weight*
HU	BuH	19	707g TCP288
HU	BuP	1	290g
LU	BuL	82	967g
TW	SP01	2	22g
U	ID01	1	35g
U	UPL01	1	20g TCP281

Modern

Fct	*Type*	*No.*	*Weight*
Ar	Brk	1	425g
Ar	TiCh	18	368g
CW	BGW	1	8g
TW	BGW02	1	6g
TW	Por	1	5g
TW	SP01	3	38g
TW	SP02	1	3g

of raw material conservation. The reason for employing a knapping strategy designed to conserve raw material is indicated by the high percentage of exotic Lefkara cherts present in the Koutroullis assemblage. This is the only prehistoric assemblage from TAESP to demonstrate such a concentrated utilization of exotic chert types.

Table 3.6 illustrates the overwhelming preference for Lefkara cherts in the production of tools at Koutroullis. The greater overall percentages of Lefkara chert belonging to all artefact categories from the road-cut show a more intensive utilization of better quality chert in this part of the site, in contrast to more ad hoc flake production using local, poorer quality jasper and chalcedony elsewhere. Overall, the presence of such significant percentages of Lefkara cherts in the Koutroullis samples demonstrates a significant degree of contact with other areas of the island where such materials could be obtained. One such area lies to the east, where broadly contemporary sites occur on the north-eastern side of the Troodos range, notably at Politiko *Phournia/Kokkinorotsos* and Marki *Alonia*, both of which have assemblages exhibiting abundant Lefkara chert (Smith 1996, 104; Given and Knapp 2003, 196–97; Webb *et al.* 2009, 209–18).

The presence of a single picrolite flake fragment in the road-cut sample (PU02) is also significant, considering the importance of this material for the manufacture of cruciform figurines during the Chalcolithic and ornaments in both the Chalcolithic and subsequent PreBA 1 period. It should be noted that Georgiou collected two additional unworked picrolite pieces at Koutroullis (CS 2957) during his visit in 2004.

Tools present in the different Koutroullis samples are dominated by retouched flake tools (63%; 12 of 19 collected). This stands in contrast to the unretouched utilized flake implements (31%) and the single, probably intrusive *dhoukani* flake (6%). The types of retouched tools in this sample include a variety of marginally retouched flakes, three truncations, a notch, a perforator and a scraper. Such flake tools are typical of Chalcolithic and Early Cypriot assemblages elsewhere (Smith 1996; McCartney

Table 3.5. Phlasou Koutroullis *(TS06): counts of chipped stone categories from POSIs and Survey Units*

	TP135	*TP177*	*TP246*	*Survey Units*	***Totals***
Cores	4	--	--	12	**16**
Blanks	12	--	1	5	**18**
Debris	9	--	--	6	**15**
Tools	15	1	1	2	**19**
Totals	**40**	**1**	**2**	**25**	**68**

2003; Finlayson and McCartney 1998; Given and Knapp 2003, 196). The significant number of utilized flakes in the Koutroullis sample was also a feature at Politiko *Phournia/Kokkinorotsos* (Webb *et al.* 2009, 213). At Koutroullis, however, and judging from the diminutive and fragmentary character of the Koutroullis artefacts in general, those may have more to do with the desire to fully exploit imported Lefkara cherts (Given and Knapp 2003, 196, table 4.34).

Broadly agreeing with this characterization is the sample of 11 pieces collected from the western half of Transect TT3879500N, c. 100 m south of Koutroullis. This includes five cores (45%), one flake (9%), three pieces of debris (27%) and two tools (18%): all made of local jasper, apart from a retouched flake and a *dhoukani* flake made of non-local Lefkara cherts. As suggested for the Koutroullis samples, the *dhoukani* flake is probably intrusive, belonging to some historic period. The material from the eastern half of the same transect is consistent both with the western half and with the industry shown at Koutroullis. It is all jasper or chalcedony, dominated by cores for the production of flakes (five: one amorphous, three change-of-orientation and one tested nodule), five flakes and seven pieces of debris.

Ground stone

Ground stone artefacts from Koutroullis similarly represent one of the most significant assemblages collected by TAESP: a total of 70 artefacts. A large mortar and a large quern fragment also were noted, but not collected, near the road-cut. We collected a small sample near the ridge's summit (TP177), and photographed others where they lay embedded in the ground. They are dominated by hand tools, including numerous grinders, rubbers, and rubbing stones, which, along with grinding slabs and querns, provide parallels to broadly contemporary settlement sites such as Marki *Alonia* or Sotira *Kaminoudhia* (Webb 1996; Swiny *et al.* 2003). A possible differentiation in the use of space may be indicated by the greater numbers of pounding tools, relative to the number of grinding tools, collected from the road-cut (Table 3.7). Only two stone vessel fragments were collected from the Survey Units, which demonstrates further the relative paucity of this class of ground stone artefact. Georgiou also collected a sample of 15 ground stone tools (CS 2957), which contained parallel grinding and pounding tools, as well as an additional vessel fragment, confirming or at least reflecting the TAESP results.

One possibly intrusive artefact in the Koutroullis collection of grinding tools is a rubber made of vesicular basalt. While vesicular basalt is locally available in the form of the Lower Pillow Lavas, it represents a material type very seldom seen at broadly contemporary Marki *Alonia*, where it was used predominantly for the manufacture of small mortars and vessels, not rubbers (Webb 1996, 73–74). Highly vesicular basalt used to make durable rubbers represents an imported material type recorded elsewhere in Late Cypriot (ProBA) contexts (Elliot 1985, 313). Another tool type worthy of note is represented by two well-made axes: one recovered from the road-cut and the other from a Survey Unit (SU2104). Both examples represent the type of short, wide, wedge-shaped axe recorded for Bronze Age assemblages elsewhere, while their low number also is a post-Chalcolithic trait (Swiny 1986, 3–4; Webb 1996, 73, 80–81; Swiny *et al.* 2003, 222). Georgiou collected two additional cutting tools and a small axe very similar to those recorded by TAESP, as well as an adze (CS 2957).

Table 3.6. Phlasou Koutroullis *(TS06): relative percentages of Lefkara cherts for each major artefact category*

	TP135	*TP177*	*TP246*	*SUs*
Cores	25%	–	–	8%
Blanks	58%	–	100%	0%
Debris	56%	–	–	17%
Tools	80%	0%	100%	100%

Conclusions

The main era of activity around Koutroullis dates to the Late Chalcolithic–early Prehistoric Bronze Age transitional period (through the Philia phase). Collected artefacts such as stone tools for grinding and pounding, Table Ware bowls and large storage jars all suggest the existence of a settlement here. This suggestion seems to be confirmed by the presence of building stone strewn across the surface of the ridge, as well as substantial deposits of colluvium that may consist, at least partly, of decomposed mudbrick. The ridge's wide-ranging views and its apparent proximity to the ancient river course may have influenced prehistoric peoples' decision to settle there.

The high proportions of ground stone tools used for grinding and pounding also suggest a possible role in copper ore processing, which is of great interest given the presence of excellent ore sources some 3 km to the north at Skouriotissa. The only other noteworthy concentration of Chalcolithic or PreBA 1 material in the Survey Area – although less localized than at Koutroullis – was found at Lemonas in the Atsas Valley Intensive Survey Zone, and consisted of worn, painted, Early–Middle Chalcolithic wares and PreBA 2 Red Polished wares, all non-diagnostic (Chapter 2.7). The substantial copper resources around Skouriotissa may, therefore, have been instrumental in the decision to settle nearby. Along with Laonarka, Koutroullis represents one of the two most significant loci of prehistoric activity in the Survey Area.

Elsewhere in Cyprus during the PreBA 1 period, both the size and number of settlements were greater than during the (Early–Middle) Chalcolithic period. More than simple population growth was involved in these changes: the demand for arable land had increased and subsistence production would have placed stress on resources and land alike. Settlement spread into areas previously unoccupied: arable zones such as the western *Mesaoria* or the coastal plain north of the Kyrenia range; along the eastern rim of the Troodos; the southern and western coastal fringes and immediate hinterlands; and in the Troodos foothill zone around the upper reaches of the Pedhieos, Yialias and Kouris Rivers (Knapp 2008, 70). To these last areas we can now add the Karkotis Valley. Most of these regions, and in particular those of the river valleys, lent themselves well to the use of intensified plough agriculture, while those in the Troodos foothill region were ideally situated to tap into the copper deposits of the Lower Pillow Lavas. Koutroullis thus conforms well to the known patterning of settlements

Table 3.7. Phlasou Koutroullis *(TS06): counts of major ground stone classes*

	TP135	*TP177*	*TP246*	*Survey Units*	***Totals***
Cutting tools	3	–	–	1	**4**
Grinding tools	7	3	2	25	**37**
Pounding tools	14	1	–	12	**27**
Vessels	–	–	–	2	**2**
Totals	**24**	**4**	**2**	**40**	**70**

Fig. 3.23. Phlasou Dodekaskala *(TS11) from the north with Panayia Kousouliotissa on the left and Korakou village in the background (Chris Parks)*

in the PreBA and would have been ideally situated to take advantage of nearby copper resources.

3.6 Phlasou *Dodekaskala*: Roman–Modern Pottery Scatters and Monastery

East of Phlasou village, substantial drainages have created a broad area of alluvial terraces that form a plain between two ridges on the eastern side of the Karkotis Valley (TS11; Fig. 3.23). Its flat relief means that it has not been so heavily terraced and manipulated as the lower terraces closer to the river. On the hillslope immediately above the valley floor is the church of Panayia Kousouliotissa, around which is a bulldozed area marking the site of its 18th-century monastery. We carried out block survey below the church and across the olive groves and grain fields that now occupy this alluvial extension of the valley floor. Context was provided by three transects, one running straight into this plain and another two running up the ridges to the north and south.

The agricultural fields comprising Dodekaskala lie at the eastern extent of the Karkotis Valley's fluvial terraces and occupy the oldest, most elevated of these landforms. The field divisions are all heavily vegetated earthen terrace walls, the highest of which appear to follow the natural fluvial terrace risers. Concrete irrigation canals are prevalent, with very few earthen channels remaining. The steepness of the hill to the east suggests that, if the extant material culture represents the remains of a settlement, it is most likely in situ and has been disturbed by ploughing. A less likely scenario is that the remains were washed down from some location on the hill itself.

When the Ukrainian monk Basil Bars'kyj arrived by foot at the church and monastery of Panayia Kousouliotissa in 1735, its construction was still unfinished (Bars'kyj 1996, 40–41). The building project was sponsored by the Bishop of Kyrenia, who exercised direct authority over the monastery from his residence at the monastery of Panayia Skouriotissa, 3 km to the north. As always in

Fig. 3.24. Church of Panayia Kousouliotissa (BU0094), with children's clothing tied to eucalyptus tree (Chris Parks)

Bars'kyj's descriptions of monasteries, the water supply plays a central role:

> From it [the Karkotis River] a small channel runs near the wall of the monastery, and from this the monks drink and water their fruit trees. They have plenty of olive trees and eight date palms, seven growing in a clump together, and the eighth separately. In the middle of the monastery there stands by itself a very small stone church, with a round roof and two entrances, one from the north and the other from the west, while a third is being made on the southern side. (Bars'kyj 1996, 41)

The property of the monastery is listed in the late 18th-century Kyrenia Codex (Kousoulia 2004). In addition to religious equipment, such as a sacred chalice, holy gospel and bronze incense burner, the monastery possessed a range of pottery, including two cooking pots, a frying pan, a roasting pan and ten *pitharia*. The local villagers believe that Panayia Kousouliotissa has the ability to cure sickness in babies and small children and, to this day, they tie pieces of their sick child's clothing to a large eucalyptus tree next to the church (Fig. 3.24; Paraskevopoulou 1982, 119).

As well as our standard east–west transects placed at 500 m intervals, we carried out block survey over several seasons in the olive groves and cereal fields west of the church. The ploughed olive groves provided good visibility, and the terrain and material were relatively straightforward; therefore, we used this area for experimental fieldwalking in the 2000 pilot season and as a team training area at the beginning of the 2001 and 2002 seasons. This situation also provided opportunities for experimenting with re-surveying the same units in successive seasons. The main research goals of this work were to characterize the broad spread of Roman pottery in the area and to investigate the monastery by means of the artefact scatter around it. Thanks to the banks and terracing, the surface is stable throughout the area. The main post-depositional factor to bear in mind during the following analysis is the dumping of soil along the eastern side of the road below the church.

The area shows a total of just 17 Bronze and Iron Age sherds, mainly consisting of Red Polished, White Painted and Black-on-Red sherds, as well as some Heavy Utility pieces. The distribution of Hellenistic–Roman pottery shows much greater densities and more meaningful patterns. Taking the period as a whole, there is a relatively even scatter across the centre and southern parts of the area (Plate 3.5). Densities rarely rise above 5 sherds/100 m^2, which for these periods tend to signify intensive cultivation over a broad area. The Phlasou area to the west shows exactly the same broad spread of relatively low densities.

There is rather more of a peak in the northern part of the block-surveyed area, with figures rising to 31.5 sherds/100 m^2. This could well have continued to increase to the north of our surveyed area, and is particularly evident in the Late Roman period (15.7 sherds/100 m^2). As is often the case in the Survey Area, however, the Late Roman peak coincides with a few Hellenistic and Early Roman period pieces (Table 3.8). These do not appear elsewhere in Dodekaskala, which suggests some sort of continuity in this location from Hellenistic to Late Roman. The Late Roman pottery consists mainly of Table Wares (especially Cypriot Red Slip), pan tiles and some Cooking Wares. The concentration of tiles of all periods (which, coincidentally, is also 15.7 sherds/100 m^2) is particularly intense, one of the highest in the Karkotis Valley Intensive Survey Zone. There is an unusual lack of Heavy Utility wares, often found elsewhere in the Karkotis Valley.

Overall, the assemblage is not complete enough in terms of functions to identify it as the primary remains of a settlement, nor are the density levels anywhere near those of known settlements such as Pano Limna and Katydhata. The assemblage is not funerary in nature since Late Roman tombs contained very little pottery. Most likely, the Hellenistic–Roman assemblage represents manuring or dumping material derived from a settlement somewhere in the area. This is also suggested by the high proportion of tile fragments. The slight increase in the north-west corner implies that the settlement lies c. 100–200 m in that direction. Some 500 m to the north-west, around the modern village of Pano Phlasou, the densities return to their background level of c. 5 sherds/100 m^2.

When taken as a group, the Medieval–Modern pottery shows a general and rather even scatter across Dodekaskala, again with slightly greater densities in the north-west. There was a substantial estate and settlement at Pano Phlasou from at least the 14th century, with a dense halo of pottery around it (Chapter 3.8). Dodekaskala differs from Phlasou in the scarcity of early material, no Byzantine pottery and only a thin scattering of 14th- and 15th-century sherds. The 16th and 17th centuries show a broader scatter in the centre and south, rising to a relatively low peak of 2.1 sherds/100 m^2 immediately below the church. But even this concentration contrasts with the densities of up to 6 and 7 sherds/100 m^2 around the villages of Phlasou and Linou.

The striking pattern at Dodekaskala is the 18th- to mid-20th-century material (OttModII), which coincides with the life of the monastery (Plate 3.6). The southern part of the area shows a light-density carpet of up to 3 sherds/100 m^2, while in the north there is a very clear peak, rising to 18.7 sherds/100 m^2. This matches anything found at Phlasou, where 16.8 is the highest density, and is, in fact, the second highest value for this period in the entire Survey Area (the highest, at 19.8, is on the edge of Katydhata). This peak, however, is clearly separate from the monastery, given that the very low-density fields between it and the road have not been affected either by dumping or erosion. There are no clear correlates between this period and the Ottoman, OttModI or Modern periods. If anything, the pattern looks most similar to the Hellenistic–Roman and tile distributions.

The earliest diagnostic Medieval–Modern coarse ware from this area, dating to the 12th/13th–early 15th centuries AD, consists of a small quantity of kitchen-size storage vessels and Cooking Ware (Table 3.8). The rest of the coarse ware dates to the 15th century onwards. It comes from storage vessels, such as jars and jugs, and also includes several varieties of glazed wares. There are also pithoi, whose date cannot be determined. Of the 26 Table Ware sherds that could be specifically dated to the Medieval period (pre-16th century), most were sgraffito, including one piece from Paphos, probably dating to the early 13th century (TCP017), and another late 14th–15th-century piece from Lapithos (TCP014). Another sherd of Paphian slip-painted ware probably dates to the early 13th century. The 58 Table Ware sherds from the 16th–17th centuries (MedVOtt) were dominated by monochrome glazed wares, particularly green, but also yellow and pale green (e.g. TCP269 and TCP270, both 16th century, from Lapithos).

The Ottoman to early 20th-century pottery was dominated by burnished Heavy and Light Utility vessels (271 sherds), mostly from OttModII (c. 1700–1950). Many of them are clearly storage vessels, including at least five pithos fragments, which would be expected from the monastery and are actually recorded in the 18th-century inventory. There were only 17 pieces of Cooking Ware from the Medieval–Modern periods, consisting of five frying pan fragments and a range of glazed and unglazed cooking pots. These are perfectly in keeping with the two cooking pots, frying pan and roasting pan of the 18th-century monastery inventory.

The Ottoman-period Table Wares stand in a much lower proportion to utility wares than was the case in the Medieval period: six monochrome painted; three monochrome glazed; five slip-painted (e.g. a late 19th/early 20th-century rim from Didymoteicho: TCP031; for pottery catalogue, see Volume 1, Chapter 3.6). The Ottoman-period imports in this area are noteworthy, including two 'spirali verdi' Maiolica bases from Tuscany, dating to the 17th/18th centuries (TCP032, TCP185), and an 18th-century polychrome painted ware rim from Kütahya (TCP102). Also intriguing

Table 3.8. Phlasou Dodekaskala *(TS11): pottery from SU0001–20, SU1001–04, SU1302–04, SU1602–05, SU2087–98, SU2964–65. TCP numbers refer to Pottery Catalogue in Volume 1, Chapter 3.6*

Prehistoric Bronze Age

Fct	*Type*	*No.*	*Weight*
LU	RP	2	10g
LU	RPC	1	5g

Late Bronze Age to Archaic

Fct	*Type*	*No.*	*Weight*
HU	HU	6	350g

Cypro-Geometric to Classical

Fct	*Type*	*No.*	*Weight*
LU	WP	1	20g
TW	BOR	1	1g

Cypro-Archaic

Fct	*Type*	*No.*	*Weight*
TW	BS	1	5g

Historical Antiquity (Archaic to Late Roman)

Fct	*Type*	*No.*	*Weight*
Ar	Ti	23	2.475kg
Ar	TiP	2	305g
HU	HU	31	1.375kg
HU	HUSW	1	100g
LU	LU	52	616g
LU	LUSW	1	20g
Tr	Am	57	3.468kg
TW	RS	2	2g
TW	TW	1	2g
U	U	7	105g

Classical to Hellenistic

Fct	*Type*	*No.*	*Weight*
TW	TW	1	5g

Hellenistic

Fct	*Type*	*No.*	*Weight*
PO	Ug	1	20g TCP012
TW	RS	1	5g

Hellenistic to Roman

Fct	*Type*	*No.*	*Weight*
CW	CW	1	1g
CW	CWFPWh	1	60g TCP015
LU	LUR06	1	15g TCP028
Tr	Am01	1	220g TCP010
Tr	Am11	1	206g TCP011
TW	RS	2	5g TCP013

Hellenistic to Early Roman

Fct	*Type*	*No.*	*Weight*
CW	CW	3	10g
Tr	KoaP	1	110g TCP009
TW	SRS	2	20g

Late Hellenistic to Early Roman

Fct	*Type*	*No.*	*Weight*
TW	CS	1	5g
TW	ESA	1	80g TCP005

Early Roman

Fct	*Type*	*No.*	*Weight*
TW	CS11	2	10g
TW	ESB	1	7g

Early to Late Roman

Fct	*Type*	*No.*	*Weight*
Ar	Ti	57	6.285kg
Ar	TiC	1	75g
Ar	TiCA	6	240g
Ar	TiP	47	4.79kg
CW	CW	8	32g
CW	CWFPWh	1	19g
HU	HU	1	200g TCP004

Late Roman

Fct	*Type*	*No.*	*Weight*
Ar	Ti	2	200g
Ar	TiC	4	205g
Ar	TiP	20	1.92kg
Ar	TiSk02	14	2.5kg TCP003
Ar	TiSkC03	1	35g
CW	CWCR01	1	90g TCP022
CW	CWPR11	1	15g TCP001
HU	HUR10	1	225g TCP019
HU	Pit01	1	25g
Tr	Am	1	15g
Tr	LR1	4	180g
TW	CRS	5	101g
TW	CRS09	5	50g TCP025, TCP026
TW	CRSK01	1	20g TCP024
TW	LRC	2	10g
TW	LRC03F	1	10g TCP023
TW	LRC10	1	20g TCP027
TW	LRC10A	1	10g TCP016
TW	RS	8	75g

Roman to Modern

Fct	*Type*	*No.*	*Weight*
Ar	Ti	1	41g

Historical (Archaic to Modern)

Fct	*Type*	*No.*	*Weight*
Ar	Ti	38	1.615kg
Ar	TiCA	1	65g
Ar	TiP	2	435g
CW	CW	40	305g
HU	HU	271	12.398kg
LU	LU	292	3.58kg
Tr	Am	2	150g
TW	TW	5	30g
U	U	43	740g

Medieval utility period I

Fct	*Type*	*No.*	*Weight*
U	UBR02	1	30g TCP030

Medieval

Fct	*Type*	*No.*	*Weight*
TW	G04	1	5g

Medieval to Modern

Fct	*Type*	*No.*	*Weight*
Ar	Brk	1	160g
Ar	Ti	1	490g TCP271
Ar	TiC	1	160g TCP253
Ar	TiF	3	550g
CW	CW	5	50g
CW	Tia	1	13g
HU	HU	6	203g
LU	LU	5	50g
TW	G	2	70g
TW	G05	1	5g
U	UFB01	1	40g TCP020
U	Uja	1	90g TCP007

Byzantine to Medieval

Fct	*Type*	*No.*	*Weight*
TW	CGS02	1	20g TCP254

Fct	Type	No.	Weight
TW	CGS07	1	10g
			TCP017
TW	CSP02	1	20g
Medieval-Frankish			
Fct	*Type*	*No.*	*Weight*
TW	CGS	1	20g
TW	CGS05	6	60g
			TCP014
TW	CGS07	3	40g
Medieval utility period III			
Fct	*Type*	*No.*	*Weight*
U	ID03	1	50g
			TCP021
U	ID04	1	18g
Ottoman			
Fct	*Type*	*No.*	*Weight*
TW	PP01	1	30g
			TCP032
Ottoman to Modern I			
Fct	*Type*	*No.*	*Weight*
HU	HU	3	60g
TW	G07	1	2g
TW	UnG	1	12g
U	UFB02	1	58g
			TCP008
Medieval-Venetian to Early Ottoman			
Fct	*Type*	*No.*	*Weight*
TW	CGS06	3	30g
TW	CMP01	1	2g
TW	G01	4	90g
TW	G02	3	30g
TW	G03	19	230g
TW	MP01	28	399g
			TCP029, TCP269, TCP270
Ottoman to Modern II			
Fct	*Type*	*No.*	*Weight*
CW	BGW	1	5g
HU	BuH	49	1.603kg
LU	BuL	34	435g
TW	BGW02	1	25g
TW	MP01	4	110g
			TCP002
TW	MP02	1	20g
TW	SP01	2	15g
			TCP031
Modern			
Fct	*Type*	*No.*	*Weight*
Ar	Brk	8	830g
Ar	Ti	5	130g
Ar	TiCh	37	847g
CW	BGW	1	5g
CW	BGW01	4	30g
CW	BGW02	1	62g
			TCP006
HU	HU	33	910g
			TCP018
LU	LU	5	60g
TW	BGW02	1	20g
TW	G	1	2g
TW	G03	1	2g
TW	Por	19	122g
TW	SP01	2	45g
TW	SP02	1	10g
Unknown			
Fct	*Type*	*No.*	*Weight*
Un	Un	1	320g

was a fragment of Medieval–Modern tile with a circular embossed stamp apparently showing a cross in one half and three bosses (TCP271).

Clearly, the association of this material with the monastery is not certain, given that the main peak of OttModII material is 200 m to its west and that there has been considerable disturbance during the building of the new road. One of the Survey Units immediately below the monastery, however, had a stable surface and no imported soil (SU1605). With respectable densities of 3.8 OttModI sherds/100 m^2 and 12.3 sherds/100 m^2 for all Medieval–Modern periods, this was clearly denser than the units immediately around it. It showed a good range of the Cooking Wares, storage vessels and Table Ware just discussed, including the embossed tile and the 16th-century Lapithos Table Wares.

For the Roman period, Dodekaskala provides an excellent example of the carpet of material that spreads across most of the central and lower Karkotis Valley, probably representing intensive cultivation and manuring associated with a substantial settlement nearby. This settlement either could be a relatively small one between Dodekaskala and Pano Phlasou, or else the more substantial settlement of Evrykhou. Perhaps the most likely situation, given that Evrykhou is the closest major centre, is that a Late Roman estate existed close to Dodekaskala. The peak of Medieval–Modern material in the north-west suggests a similar dependence on a substantial settlement in that direction, but in this case we know it to be the estate and village of Pano Phlasou. That said, there is clearly material associated with the monastery and church of Panayia Kousouliotissa, representing not just spread from the ruins, but also a halo, suggesting activities such as the cultivation of fruit trees and the dumping of domestic waste.

Chipped Stone and Ground Stone

A total of 41 chipped stone artefacts and five ground stone tools was collected from Survey Units in Dodekaskala. The chipped stone material was distributed in low numbers across the area (Table 3.9). The diffuse distribution of material makes it impossible to recognize any specific assemblage, suggesting instead a generalized background spread of material. A relatively small sample of 11 chipped stone artefacts was collected from two blocks of Survey Units where Roman pottery predominated. All these artefacts were made of local jasper and reflect the simple

Table 3.9. Phlasou Dodekaskala *(TS11): chipped stone counts in Survey Units (SUs)*

	Roman SUs	*Medieval–Modern SUs*	*All SUs*
Cores	4	5	9
Blanks	2	6	8
Debris	1	5	6
Tools	4	14	18

ad hoc flake industry seen at other sites in the TAESP area where Roman artefacts are prominent. The only *dhoukani* flake in the sample, also made of jasper, is consistent with other Roman samples in the Survey Area.

Thirty of these artefacts, a very substantial figure, were recovered from four blocks of Survey Units dominated by Medieval–Modern pottery. These artefacts were characterized by the use of local jasper and again illustrate an expedient flake-based industry. Of interest is a single *dhoukani* flake made on non-local Lefkara chert, which is characteristic of other Medieval–Modern samples in the Survey Area, notably at Mandres (Chapter 2.10). Other tools in this sample include a retouched flake, two flake scrapers and nine utilized flakes. This range of tool types would be consistent with other samples of the Late Roman period or earlier, but may suggest that a simple flake industry (to be distinguished from *dhoukani* manufacture) was in use during the historic to recent past. The prevalence of such flake tools and the general paucity of *dhoukani* flakes, however, provide a contrast with chipped stone samples collected in other areas dominated by Medieval–Modern pottery, for example, at Ayios Epiphanios or at Phlasou and Katydhata villages, where *dhoukani* flakes are prominent. The latter feature argues against a later historic attribution for the material, suggesting instead that the diffuse scatter of lithics from Dodekaskala represents disturbed material that technically and typologically fit best within the chronological time frame of the Late Roman period.

The five ground stone tools were also collected in Survey Units dominated by Medieval–Modern pottery, although it is impossible to assign these artefacts to any particular period with certainty. Most of these – a rubber, one rubbing stone, one polishing stone, and an anvil/grinding slab – are made of basal rocks typical of grinding and pounding tools recovered throughout the Survey Area. The final tool, a perforated hammer made of diabase, is more diagnostic: it is traditionally characteristic of Bronze Age assemblages and may broadly correspond to the presence of Bronze Age pottery in the area (Swiny 1986, 15; Webb 1996, 79–80).

3.7 Ayios Epiphanios: a Medieval and Turkish Cypriot Village

The western side of the Karkotis Valley in our Intensive Survey Zone is composed of much narrower alluvial terraces and provides a far narrower strip of arable land than the broad expanses of the eastern side (Plate 3.6). For that reason, and because the main communication routes all lie to the east, the modern villages in this stretch are all on the eastern side of the valley. It is clear, however, that this distribution is very different to the Medieval period. Our work around the abandoned village of Ayios Epiphanios and the churches in the vicinity showed a major centre of settlement and agricultural production. Ground visibility was poor, and much of the area fell between two survey transects, so our analysis is based on the recording of structures and other POSIs as much as transect survey itself.

The abandoned Turkish Cypriot village of Ayios Epiphanios lies on a flat-topped ridge that projects from the valley's western ridgeline; from that prominent location, it has a commanding view of much of the Karkotis Valley. It is well known locally as the birthplace of Rauf Denktash, the 'president' of the self-proclaimed Turkish Cypriot state from 1976–2005. It was completely abandoned in 1975 when the United Nations Forces in Cyprus transferred the last of its residents to the Turkish Cypriot occupied areas. Apart from the church, the village was then bulldozed and used as a Greek Cypriot National Guard camp, which has now also been abandoned.

Ayios Epiphanios appears in the 16th-century village lists, mainly referred to as the *casal* (village) of San Pifani; in 1565 it had a population of 48 (Grivaud 1998, 469). There is no clear evidence that this settlement was located on the same plateau as the later village. The current church of Ayia Mavri (BU0090) is modern, and almost all evidence of domestic structures has been obliterated by demolition and bulldozing. There are extant foundations of one large (c. 6 × 7 m) and two smaller buildings on a terrace on the eastern side, showing socles of river cobbles, some with a deteriorating plaster facing, and mudbrick walls (TP043). These clearly relate to the recent village, not to its Medieval predecessor.

The survey transect (TT3880500N) continued eastwards from the base of the plateau towards the river, with significant amounts of Medieval pottery (SU0066–70), including nine pieces of Cypriot Brown and Green Sgraffito Ware from Paphos and Lapithos dating to the late 14th–15th centuries AD, and 27 Monochrome Glazed Ware and Monochrome Green Painted Ware sherds dating to the 16th–17th centuries. This assemblage breaks down as 42% painted, 39% glazed and 19% sgraffito. With similar amounts of Ottoman and Modern pottery, however, these Survey Units differed little from the rest of the transect on the eastern side of the river, and indeed from our survey across this entire section of the valley. These transects provide evidence for substantial Medieval activity in the area, but nothing specifically associated with a settlement.

The 1831 census records Ayios Epiphanios as a mixed Turkish and Greek Cypriot village, like all the villages of this part of the valley, although by 1825 there were only five Christian poll-tax payers (Papadopoullos 1965, 123; Sarınay 2000). The 1881 census shows 27 inhabited houses, with a population of 95 (Census 1882, 26). By this time,

Fig. 3.25. Ayios Epiphanios church (BU0103) (Alexis Boutin)

the village was situated on the southern part of the plateau, and the 1926 cadastral plan shows some 15 courtyard structures, ten of them with ovens, and six threshing floors. The church seems to be the predecessor of the present one and is labelled 'Ayios Andronikos' rather than the current 'Ayia Mavri'. As is common with small Turkish Cypriot villages, there is no mosque.

So where was the Medieval settlement, if not on the plateau? A local story tells of the 'King of Ayios Epiphanios' and how he lost his water rights to the 'Queen of Linou' on the other side of the river (see Chapter 3.10 for a similar story from Katydhata). Interestingly, the storytellers locate Ayios Epiphanios not on the plateau, but around the church of the same name 550 m to the north. Substantial remains of this church still stand, and even though a track has been pushed through its nave, we were able to record its architecture and context (Fig. 3.25; BU0103; TP002).

Two upstanding sections of wall survive: the south-east corner, including part of the apse; and part of the north wall. The walls are 1.0–1.5 m thick, composed of a double skin of river cobbles, filled with rubble and bound with thick, lime-ash mortar. The interior is plastered, and while no traces of painting were visible, great numbers of small sherds had been impressed into the surface, apparently for decoration. A stretch of walling to the south may be part of an enclosure. A circular quern stone for grinding grain lay just to the north-west.

The closest Survey Units were at the base of the hillslope, 85 m to the east (SU0040–41). The bulk of the material (115 sherds) consisted of Heavy and Light Utility wares that only could be dated to the 'historical' period; this pattern is certainly in keeping with the storage needs of a substantial settlement. There was little that could be called Medieval, the bulk of the fine wares dating later. These included, for instance, three pale yellow sherds of Monochrome Glazed Ware of the Medieval-Venetian to Early Ottoman periods (c. 16th–17th centuries) and a brown sherd of Monochrome Glazed Ware of Ottoman to Modern periods (c. 18th–mid-20th centuries). Finally, there was a very typical scatter of Ottoman burnished wares and a fragment of a cooking jar or casserole with a brown glazed interior. Informal exploring to the south of the church, in the direction of Ayios Epiphanios village up on the plateau, showed much more convincing concentrations of clearly Medieval and post-Medieval pottery.

One striking concentration lies exactly between the village and the church, some 250 m south of the latter. As well as sgraffito, this concentration included a fragment of a large sugar mould, with a broad profile and a slight flare around the hole at the base of the cone. This form and the substantial height of the mould (surviving to 18 cm) suggest that it was of the tall type used for coarse crystal sugar (von Wartburg 1983, 310–11). Even though the Medieval sugar industry is most familiar from the south coast of Cyprus, there are reports from the 15th and 16th centuries of plantations at Lefka, 5 km to the north, and perhaps of a refinery as well (von Wartburg 2000, 389). This was the only fragment of sugar mould identified in the Survey Area, however, so in itself it is insufficient evidence for sugar plantations in this part of the Karkotis Valley.

On a steep terrace riser just 50 m south of that concentration, there is a substantial building foundation eroding out of the slope (TP254). Large amounts of pottery and a few animal bone fragments also are eroding from this wall, including 14th–16th-century sgraffito, cooking pots with large strap handles and other utility pieces. Judging by the morphology of the terrace, this is the exterior wall of a substantial in situ structure, well protected by the deeply filled terrace lying above. This observation was only made after the end of fieldwork, hence the summary nature of this report, but it offers an exciting opportunity for geophysical survey and the excavation of a Medieval domestic structure.

The evidence for the Medieval settlement is further complicated by the remains of a second church, 180 m north-west of the church of Ayios Epiphanios. This church was dedicated to the Panayia (Virgin Mary), and its locality name is unsurprisingly Paleokklishia or 'old church' (TP251). The remains were recently bulldozed, during the construction of the same track that cuts through Ayios Epiphanios church. Vestigial rectilinear and curvilinear wall foundations made of large cobbles and small boulders can still be seen, along with a few flagstones bound with mortar. There are fragments of painted plaster in the collapsed walls, as well as associated pottery ranging from the late 13th–early 16th century, but mostly from the 14th and 15th centuries. Most of the sherds are from sgraffito ware, small open bowls, used for drinking, but there are also some plates and open bowls. One Paphian piece from the late 13th or early 14th century has traces of mortar in it, and so was presumably built into a wall. This implies that the church was constructed or re-mortared after that date.

We discovered no chipped stone in the village or around the two churches. Several lithic artefacts (29) were, however, collected across the transect directly east of Ayios Epiphanios (TT3880500N). This collection was dominated by 12 tools (41%), with rather less evidence for core reduction: five cores (17%), six unworked blanks (21%) and six pieces of debris (21%). All but five artefacts represent the reduction of local jasper and chalcedony materials for the production of flakes, including three flake tools and four utilized flakes. Lefkara cherts imported to the area are represented by a single unretouched spall and, more typically, by four *dhoukani* flakes. In general, this sample is very similar to the other Survey Area samples dominated by pottery of Medieval–Modern date.

The Medieval settlement of Ayios Epiphanios was clearly substantial, spreading over an area perhaps some 400 × 200 m, although not necessarily continuously. Two churches suggest two separate foci. This area was at least as large as the better-known estates and villages on the east side of the river, such as Linou and Phlasou. The myth of the King of Ayios Epiphanios suggests that the rivalry between these two sides of the river has been very significant in the local conception of the landscape. As happened frequently between the Late Medieval period and the 19th century, the settlement moved and changed its character substantially. This shift may have been the result of Anatolian Turks settling here after 1571. By the early 19th century the village had become a mixed one. By the 20th century, it was entirely Turkish Cypriot until its abandonment in 1975 (Karouzis 1984b) and its demolition and subsequent occupation by the Greek Cypriot army. Seen from this long-term perspective, it is no paradox that a Turkish Cypriot village should have a church dedicated to one Christian saint and be named after another whose church lies 550 m away, in the heart of what was once a large and thriving settlement.

3.8 Phlasou: From Medieval Estate to Modern Twin Village

The modern villages of Kato (Lower) Phlasou and Pano (Upper) Phlasou have an unusual and, at first sight, inexplicable layout (Plate 3.7). Kato Phlasou consists of three agglomerations some 500 m apart, lying on slightly raised ridges immediately to the east of the Karkotis River. Above and 300 m east of the central conglomeration are two apparently isolated churches, Ayios Yeoryios and Ayios Dhimitrianos, and a further 200 m east of them is the village of Pano Phlasou. This last is administratively a separate entity, but has no churches, coffee shops or other public institutions. What are the reasons for these unusual developments? How did Phlasou change from Medieval estate to Ottoman-period village to the twin villages of the Modern period? What role did the landscape play in the lives and worldviews of the estate workers and villagers?

According to a forged document, supposedly dating to 1198 AD, a series of privileges was given, in that year, by King Amaury to the Commune of Marseille (i.e. the association of Marseillaise merchants operating in Cyprus) in return for their support of the Crusader cause in the Holy Land and Jerusalem (de Mas Latrie 1852–61, II, 24–25; Roberts 2000, 66). In 1250, by which time the document had been forged, the Pope was persuaded to confirm the supposed privileges, which included the *casal* (village) of 'Flacie' or Phlasou (Coureas 2005, 122).

In the 1460s, 'Flassu' was given as a fief by James II to Fra Francesco Sabat (Bustron 1884, 419), but by the late 15th century it was once again a royal village in the Baliazzo delle Marathasse real (de Mas Latrie 1852–61, III, 506). It is recorded in the 16th-century village lists as 'Flasu', 'Flassu', and 'Flassou', appearing twice as a *prastio* (hamlet) and once as a *casal*. In 1565, it had 84 *francomati* (free peasant farmers) (Grivaud 1998, 469). In 1826, 30 Christian householders paid the *cizye* (poll-tax), which amounted to 945 Turkish piastres (Papadopoullos 1965, 123). In 1832, the annual compulsory purchase of wheat and barley to supply the inhabitants of Nicosia amounted to 4.5 *kafiz* (just over half a bushel) of barley, with Phlasou indicated as a Turkish village (Papadopoullos 1965, 189). The property register of 1833 recorded 40 houses (20 Muslim, 20 non-Muslim), 16.1 ha of fields (of which 96% belonged to non-Muslims) 3 walnuts, 72 mulberries, 101 olives (20 owned by Muslims, 81 by non-

Fig. 3.26. Phlasou, looking south-south-west. Foreground, from left to right: Ayios Yeoryios and cemetery; school; Ayios Dhimitrianos. Part of Kato Phlasou beyond (Chris Parks)

Muslims), 4 almonds, and 0.05 ha of citrus trees (Sarınay 2000, 155, 182, see Volume 1, Chapter 5.4).

The oldest known monument in Phlasou is the church of Ayios Yeoryios (BU0084), which lies between Pano Phlasou and the southern segment of Kato Phlasou (Fig. 3.26). It dates to the 17th or 18th century, possibly 1722 (Phlasou 1989, 259) or 1735, although it may well have had a Medieval predecessor. As with many such village churches, a rising population in the late 19th and early 20th centuries made it too small for its community, and a larger replacement was completed in 1906. This new church is dedicated to Ayios Dhimitrianos (BU0080) and lies 150 m to the north-west, almost exactly in the centre of the component parts of Kato and Pano Phlasou. The old church of Ayios Yeoryios, being extra-mural, then became a cemetery church, and still serves that function today. The position of both of these churches outside the built-up area is one more peculiarity of the Phlasou settlement complex.

Pottery Distribution

Our main tool for investigating the development and distribution of settlement and human activity in the Phlasou area consisted of intensive survey in transects across the valley, as well as block survey centred on the area of the two churches. The block survey (TS04; Phlasou *Koutroullis tou Ayiou Yeoryiou*) covered a series of broad anthropogenic terraces that seem to have been created at a variety of times. Some of the terraces are armoured with tall, stone-built risers and may be dated by old olive trees associated with their boundaries, others are encircled by modern, concrete irrigation channels. These fields were variously used for olive orchards, grain and vegetable cultivation.

Pottery distribution in some Survey Units near the river should be regarded critically, either because of Little Ice Age deposition and burial of pre-17th-century surfaces, or because the material might have been deposited from further upstream. Otherwise, most of this area is relatively free from substantial surface artefact movement, due to the dense patchwork of anthropogenic terraces.

Charting the changing densities of pottery from the Byzantine period onwards gives a good general sense of the shifting focus of the estate and village(s) of Phlasou (Plate 3.8). The Early Medieval material ('Medieval-Byzantine'; 12th–13th centuries) shows a clear scatter immediately north-east of Ayios Dhimitrianos and west and south of Ayios Yeoryios. Although never denser than 1.2 sherds/100 m^2, this area in fact holds 10 out of the 36 Early Medieval sherds in the entire Survey Area. The earliest imported Table Wares found here include a few pieces of Glazed White Ware II (GWWII) from Byzantine-period Constantinople (c. late 11th–12th centuries; Vroom 2005, 74–77) and Islamic Lustre-Painted Ware, perhaps from Syria, of the Medieval-Byzantine period (c. 12th–13th centuries). There also are some fragments of Cypriot Incised Sgraffito Ware and Slip-Painted Wares (from the production centre of Paphos?) of the Byzantine to Medieval periods (c. early 13th century?)

The material from the 14th–15th centuries ('Medieval-Frankish') has more substantial densities of up to 7.8

sherds/100 m^2. Apart from one dense outlier by the middle agglomeration of Kato Phlasou, there is again a clear focus around the two churches. This clearly is the site of the Medieval estate. The material might result from destruction and subsequent ploughing, or else from dumping of rubbish immediately around the estate grounds. The Table Wares of the Medieval-Frankish period found here include sherds of Cypriot Brown and Green Sgraffito Ware (c. late 14th–15th centuries), Cypriot Brown and Green Incised Sgraffito Ware (c. late 14th–15th centuries) and Green Painted Sgraffito Ware from Lapithos (c. late 15th–early 16th centuries).

The utility pottery whose date is limited to the Late Medieval period (Medieval Utility 2; 15th–mid-16th century) has very low densities, but the small amount present shows precisely the same focus around the churches, with nothing at all at Kato Phlasou. The generic 16th–17th-century material (MedVOtt: Medieval-Venetian to Early Ottoman) is, by contrast, much more widespread. While relatively substantial around the churches (up to 3.3 sherds/100 m^2), there are much denser areas adjacent to the north and middle agglomerations of Kato Phlasou. These areas include the two densest Survey Units of this period in the entire Survey Area, as well as the four Survey Units with the highest raw counts of MedVOtt sherds (up to 20). This area also yielded some MedVOtt Table Wares. These consist mostly of Monochrome Green Painted Ware fragments from Lapithos (c. 16th century onward) and Monochrome Glazed Wares. There is a light scatter of MedVOtt pottery across the entire central part of the Karkotis Valley. Because of the integrity of the material on each terrace, this pattern probably derives from 16th–17th century manuring and dumping practices based on several dispersed settlements, rather than a single central estate.

The Ottoman material generally shows a broad distribution like that of the Medieval-Venetian/early Ottoman, although with some continuing focus around the two churches. This is particularly clear in the Ottoman–Modern 1 (1571–early 20th century) and Ottoman–Modern 2 (18th–mid-20th centuries) periods. The unambiguously Modern material shows no remaining focus around the churches at all: there is a broad carpet of 1–3 sherds/100 m^2 across the entire valley, with only one clear density peak by the middle agglomeration at Kato Phlasou.

The most striking feature of the Medieval–Ottoman coarse wares is the dominance of Cooking Wares in the earlier part of the period and the dominance of storage wares in the later part. In general there is little material before the 15th century AD. Exceptions are an open tray with a thin base, which is most probably a cooking vessel, possibly the *gastria* (Bakirtzis 1989, 131), and the profile of a cooking pot (which, however, could also be used as storage container). It is striking that three large Survey Units in the north-east of the area (SU2014–16) and another immediately west of the church of Ayios Dhimitrianos (SU2002) have substantial amounts of Medieval material, but no early coarse wares.

Most of the storage wares that predominate from the 15th century onwards are small- and medium-sized vessels, such as water jars and water jugs for the table. There are also a few pithos fragments 125 m south-west of the church of Ayios Yeoryios (SU2007). In general there is little Cooking Ware from this period, though there are exceptions.

The Table Wares of these later periods include a substantial amount of Monochrome Glazed Wares in various colours. In addition, there are remnants of Monochrome Painted Ware in brown from Çanakkale in western Turkey (c. 19th century), Slip-Painted Ware in green and yellow from Didymoteicho and/or Çanakkale (c. late 19th–early 20th centuries) and Polychrome Painted Ware from Grottaglie in southern Italy and/or imitations from Corfu (c. 19th century onward) (Vroom 2005, 180–87).

In general, the material from the 13th and 14th centuries is relatively minor, although it may be buried under either of the churches, or has otherwise been removed. It seems that cooking was the dominant activity during this phase. From the 15th century onwards the main activity was clearly storage, and perhaps some transport of produce into the area, while the Table Wares suggest consumption of produce.

Agriculture and Food Processing

We recorded and dated 34 olive trees between Phlasou and Evrykhou (for methodology see Volume 1, Chapter 2.11). These ranged in date from the 15th to the late 19th centuries, with a single late 14th century example at Pano Phlasou (Fig. 3.27; for map see Plate 3.26). All of these olives are on relic terraces on both sides of the river. Two olive trees on the southern side of Koutroullis hill date to c. 1540 and c. 1610. This fits well with the high population and intensive production of the 16th and early 17th centuries, and with the wide distribution of Medieval-Venetian/Early Ottoman pottery in this area. The relatively small number of trees seems normal for individual estates and monasteries of the period, as is seen, for example, at Asinou Monastery (Chapter 5.5), in contrast to the extensive olive groves known from the 20th century. By 1833, 101 olive trees were recorded for Phlasou village as a whole (Sarınay 2000, 155, 182).

There are unexpectedly few *dhoukani* flakes, even on the outskirts of the modern villages and on the known threshing floors (Plate 3.9). This may be because the flakes were considered to be valuable, worth the effort of finding and replacing in the sledge. This activity is reported in numerous ethnographic studies (e.g. Whittaker 2000, with references). There is a clear concentration of nine pieces 400 m west-north-west of the northern section of Kato Phlasou. There is no clear explanation for this distribution: no threshing floors still extant or marked on the cadastral map. In terms of correlation with the pottery in the same Survey Units, the Medieval–Modern period offers the most likely date. It is possible that they relate to threshing in the Medieval period that has left no other trace in the archaeological and historical record. The chipped stone

Fig. 3.27. Olive tree at Pano Phlasou dating to the late 14th century (Neil Urwin)

pieces all are made of imported Lefkara chert, rather than local and poorer quality jasper or chalcedony. Another three pieces lay on the northern edge of the northern section of Kato Phlasou, which conforms to the normal pattern for the Ottoman–Modern period of threshing immediately outside the settlement.

Just 150 m north of Ayios Dhimitrianos church, we found four *dhoukani* flakes, in addition to three flake tools and an unworked flake (TP132; Phlasou *Strongilo*; SU2016–17). One additional blank fragment was collected from SU2015, as well as an axe and a pestle/rubbing stone from SU2004 and SU2012 respectively. The concentration at Strongilo coincides exactly with the density peak of Medieval pottery immediately north-east of the church of Ayios Dhimitrianos. The 1963 aerial photograph of the two fields in which they were found shows a group of about 20 circular features some 5–7 m across (TP132), although nothing is now visible. It is tempting to see these features as threshing floors, but their small size and apparent overlapping could, perhaps, make this unlikely.

Whatever these features may represent, the presence of typical *dhoukani* flakes here helps to confirm the earlier presence of threshing floors that have since been destroyed by ploughing activity. These artefacts, of which two are heavily worn and two are broken, imply the maintenance of sledge 'teeth' around the threshing floors. Of interest in this context is a *dhoukani* flake made of chalcedony, adding support to the idea that local raw materials were periodically used to repair threshing sledges. The presence of possible mastic traces on a utilized jasper flake, recovered from SU2017, may represent similar patching activity of threshing sledge lithic elements, a possibility that needs to be confirmed by use-wear analysis.

There are two very well preserved threshing floors on the hill at Phlasou *Koutroullis*, just south of the southern part of Kato Phlasou. The prominence of this hill on the valley floor makes it an excellent spot to catch the wind for winnowing. One of these floors (TP176) is on the summit, shaded by a row of eucalyptus trees. Unusually, it is rectangular, measuring some 18 × 9 m, and is paved with river cobbles. The second lies on the north-east slope and is semicircular in shape (TP187). It is paved with stones, and the terrace on which it sits is retained with a dry-stack wall made of chunks of local basalt and some ground stone tools, presumably from the adjacent Late Chalcolithic/early Prehistoric Bronze Age settlement of Koutroullis (TS06). A local informant remembered TP176 being in use during the 1960s, but the other had already fallen out of use. Both places fit the normal pattern of family-owned threshing floors on the outskirts of the village.

A Phlasou resident born in 1919 provided a vivid image of the basic diet of his childhood and early adulthood. 'We were reduced to living by our own hands', he told our oral historian Marios Hadjianastasis (August 2002). They ground barley with a hand quern and used the flour to make pitta bread, cooked on a *pittoplaka*, a clay disk placed over the fire. They baked leaven bread once a week, with barley bread for the family and a couple of wheat loafs in case they had guests. To improve the flavour, they spread pig lard and sugar on the bread, and during the harvest ate bulgur wheat with pork fat. Their clothes were made at home on the loom with cotton grown in their own fields.

Another indicator of the changing agricultural economy around Phlasou is the series of four watermills on the east bank of the Karkotis River (Plate 3.7). The Molos mill (BU0076) is dated to 1690 by an inscription, and the three others were probably constructed in the 17th or 18th century (Krommidhos, BU0062; Shaban Bey, BU0075; Mylaria, BU0098). In 1833, three of these mills were owned by non-Muslims and one by Muslims (Sarınay 2000, 155, 182). The Muslim-owned mill may have formed part of an Islamic religious endowment (Evkaf), as there were eight such Evkaf-owned mills in the Lefka subdistrict (Sarınay 2000, 345). By the earlier 20th century and in living memory, the Hadjidemetriou family of Phlasou owned three of the mills (Krommidhos, Shaban Bey and Molos). According to the miller of the Evrykhou mill (Chapter 3.4), the Shaban Bey mill was famous as the most productive in the area, and was in use till the 1940s (for full descriptions of these mills see Volume 1, Chapter 3.11, and TAESPdata 2007).

Conclusions

The general development of Phlasou in the Medieval–Modern periods is now clear. Its beginnings lay in the Late Byzantine period, and by the 15th century AD it was a substantial agricultural estate belonging at different times to the Lusignan dynasty and to Frankish landlords. The centre of the estate was in the area of the modern school (see below), most likely around the predecessor of the church of Ayios Yeoryios. Its economy depended on cereals and other intensively produced crops on the well-watered soils of the Karkotis River alluvial terraces. Phlasou was clearly part of the dynamic Medieval Cypriot exchange network, selling cash crops and importing Table Ware from abroad. There is a strong focus on the area immediately around the estate, with continual commuting to fields, cultivation, manuring and dumping.

In the 16th century, there was an increase in activity across the whole of the central Karkotis Valley, and the area immediately around the estate does not stand out so sharply. This expansion continued through the Ottoman period, and by the 18th century there were at least two new centres of population and settlement that lay closer to the river and adjacent to the watermills. By the 19th century, the old estate had lost all primacy in the area, and it was becoming difficult to define the village of Phlasou. In the first British census of 1881, the population was counted as a single entity, with 311 inhabitants of 'Phlasou'. In the second census of 1891, there were 229 inhabitants of 'Kato Phlasou' and 69 of 'Pano Phlasou' (Phlasou 1989). This marks the beginning of the administrative division of the two Phlasou villages, even though the three elements of Kato Phlasou were as far from each other as from Pano Phlasou. In the 1911 census, they were once again combined, but in all others the populations were counted separately.

An additional complication is that, at least in the 19th and most of the 20th centuries, there were both Greek Cypriot and Turkish Cypriot inhabitants. In the 1833 property register, 20 Muslim and 20 non-Muslim houses were recorded (Sarınay 2000, 155, 182). This is not at all in proportion to the land ownership, where Muslims held 0.6 ha and non-Muslims 16.1 ha, or 96%. The British colonial census of 1921 records 275 Greek Cypriots and 26 Turkish Cypriots in Kato Phlasou, and 72 Greek Cypriots and 42 Turkish Cypriots in Pano Phlasou (Phlasou 1989).

A mosque and associated boys' school are marked by the cadastral plan on the southern edge of the northern element of Kato Phlasou, providing a focus for the Turkish Cypriot community within the larger Phlasou community. According to village tradition, the mosque was originally a church dedicated to Ayios Yeoryios. When Turkish Cypriots settled in the area, the church became their mosque, and the Greek Cypriots built the current church of Ayios Yeoryios as a replacement, possibly in 1735. The Turkish Cypriot community, according to the same tradition, originally lived on the western side of the mosque, down towards the river.

The Greek Cypriot population faced a similar problem of focus in the early 20th century. The old church of Ayios Yeoryios was too small to hold the entire community, but in which of the four sections of the village(s) should the replacement be built? The solution was to build it, unusually, outside the settlements, but exactly in the centre of all four of them, providing a hub for their dispersed elements. This church was finished in 1906 and dedicated to Ayios Dhimitrianos, while the church of Ayios Yeoryios became a cemetery chapel. A large neo-classical school was built in the 1930s exactly between them, and in the last two decades these have been joined by the church hall and the village playschool. This area has become the new focus for the community and brings together its scattered elements. In a neat cyclical process, these unifying institutions are in exactly the same place as the original estate buildings that provided the focus for the landscape in the Medieval period.

3.9 PreBA 2 Settlement and Tombs at Katydhata *Laonarka*

The Bronze Age tombs in and around the modern village of Katydhata have formed an essential part of the literature on prehistoric Cyprus for nearly 100 years. The settlement associated with this extensive prehistoric cemetery, however, has always proved elusive. The nearest known, at least partly contemporary, settlement is the Prehistoric Bronze Age 2 (Middle Cypriot I–II) site at Ambelikou *Aletri*, some 8 km to the north-west (Merrillees 1984; Frankel and Webb 2012). A range of work undertaken by TAESP, including transects, block survey, gridded collections and geophysical survey, cannot confirm that the Laonarka locality (TS09) is indeed the long-sought Bronze Age settlement. Nevertheless, it certainly formed part of the mortuary complex of PreBA Katydhata, and sufficient evidence exists to suggest that the associated settlement was located nearby, perhaps beneath the modern village. It must be pointed out, moreover, that PreBA tombs also occur beneath the modern village at its north and south ends (see below).

Katydhata village is situated on Upper Pillow Lava basalts, in the northern sector of the Karkotis Valley

Fig. 3.28. Katydhata Laonarka *(TS09), showing the ridge in the foreground, and the field and olive grove, from the west (Michael Given)*

Intensive Survey Zone. Laonarka lies approximately 1 km south of the Skouriotissa mine, on the eastern extent of the alluvial terraces of the Karkotis River. The alluvial deposits around Laonarka are thin compared to other parts of the valley.

One of the most striking geographical features in this area is the Katydhata Park Ridge, largely composed of exposed pillow lava bedrock but with some areas of thin, gravelly colluvium supporting limited batha vegetation. The remnants of Bronze Age Laonarka are located just south and east of this bedrock ridge, which forms the eastern boundary of contemporary Katydhata village (Plate 3.10). In the late 1990s, the top of the ridge was terraced by bulldozing, and foreign soil was imported to facilitate the growth of newly planted trees on the downslope terraces. The only pottery visible along the transect (TT3882000N) that ran over the ridge derived from the imported soil. Below the ridge is another recently terraced area on the lower slope where bedrock is covered by a thin, gravely, colluvial layer, largely unstable, while the hill itself is dissected by rills and gullies. All tombs recorded by TAESP at Laonarka, of whatever time period, have been excavated into the basaltic bedrock. The bedrock visible within the tombs contains a high percentage of malachite (a copper ore), as is typical of Upper Pillow Lava around ore bodies.

A flattened, arable, straw stubble field lies at the base of Katydhata Park Ridge's eastern slope (Fig. 3.28). This field slopes to the south-east and has a sandy loam texture. Bulldozed areas surround it to the north, south and east (a road and tank blinds have been cut in). To the south-east of the straw stubble field is an anthropogenic terrace containing a large, comparatively recent olive grove. The Geomorphological Units encompassing the straw stubble field and olive grove are characterized by transitional alluvial and colluvial units: that is, their sediments were deposited (1) by gravity and sheets of surface water from the adjacent hillslope and (2) by alluvial sediment from the river when the original alluvial terrace was formed. We came to refer to the area encompassing the straw stubble field and olive grove as the 'primary concentration' (Boutin *et al.* 2003, 338), because it seemed to be the focus of Prehistoric Bronze Age activity.

Between 1883 and 1885, Ohnefalsch-Richter excavated three 'Late Bronze Age' tombs in Katydhata (Gjerstad 1926, 8) and in Linou (Ohnefalsch-Richter 1893, 356, 463, 498, pl. CLXXII). Myres and Ohnefalsch-Richter (1899, 4) described them as a 'Bronze Age necropolis east of the villages of Katydata and Linu'. During the second decade of the 20th century, Markides (1916) excavated over 100 tombs in and around the village of Katydhata, dating them from the Middle Cypriot to Hellenistic periods. Markides kept a field notebook (now in the Cyprus Museum) with stratigraphic observations on successive burials in tombs. This was copied in its entirety and used by Åström (1989) in his publication of Katydhata. Gjerstad (1926, 8) added that Markides excavated these tombs in a field (Gjerstad termed it a necropolis) at the southern end of the modern village and, also using Markides' notebooks and reports, gave an account of the tombs' morphology, dating and contents (1926, 48–87). In the centre of Katydhata village, close to the church and opposite what was then a coffee shop, Markides excavated eight more tombs (Nos. 100–107) of 'beehive type', all dated to the Late Cypriot period (Åström 1989, 9); some of their pottery is catalogued by Åström (1972). By comparing historical photographs from Markides' expedition to the modern landscape, we were able to identify tentatively the site of the expedition's encampment, on the grounds of the Katydhata village school (Given *et al.* 2002, 35).

Amongst the Katydhata burials excavated by Markides, there were two possible Early Cypriot III (PreBA 2) tombs (Tombs 73, 75). Overall, however, Åström felt that the tomb groups reflected Middle Cypriot occupation nearby, perhaps contemporary with the settlement and mines at Ambelikou *Aletri*. Åström (1989, 6–8) described burials dated throughout the Middle–Late Cypriot periods,

Table 3.10. Katydhata Laonarka *(TS09): pottery from TP035, TP040, TP127, TP243. TCP numbers refer to Pottery Catalogue in Volume 1, Chapter 3.6*

Prehistoric Bronze Age

Fct	*Type*	*No.*	*Weight*
HU	RP	5	79g
HU	RPC	5	403g
HU	RPOL	21	629g
LU	RP	8	35g
LU	RPC	62	945g
LU	RPIC	1	14g
LU	RPO	2	12g
LU	RPOL	12	218g
LU	RPOS	1	5g
TW	RP	1	2g
TW	RPC	2	17g TCP576
TW	RPIC	4	22g
TW	RPIO	4	11g
TW	RPOS	3	11g
TW	RPT	5	9g
TW	RPTC	2	4g
TW	RPTO	15	79g

Cypro-Geometric to Classical

Fct	*Type*	*No.*	*Weight*
LU	BS	1	6g

Historical Antiquity (Archaic to Late Roman)

Fct	*Type*	*No.*	*Weight*
HU	HU	3	204g

Hellenistic to Roman

Fct	*Type*	*No.*	*Weight*
HU	HU	2	165g
LU	LU	1	118g
Tr	Am	1	110g

Late Hellenistic to Early Roman

Fct	*Type*	*No.*	*Weight*
TW	CS	1	95g

Early Roman

Fct	*Type*	*No.*	*Weight*
CW	CW	1	10g
La	La01	1	3g
La	La02	2	20g
LU	LU	1	10g

Early to Late Roman

Fct	*Type*	*No.*	*Weight*
Ar	TiAn	1	1.1kg
CW	CW	2	68g

Roman to Modern

Fct	*Type*	*No.*	*Weight*
HU	HU	1	20g

Historical (Archaic to Modern)

Fct	*Type*	*No.*	*Weight*
HU	HU	2	27g
LU	LU	3	33g

Medieval to Modern

Fct	*Type*	*No.*	*Weight*
LU	LU	1	55g
LU	MP	2	14g

Modern

Fct	*Type*	*No.*	*Weight*
Ar	Brk	2	53g
TW	G07	4	15g

Unknown

Fct	*Type*	*No.*	*Weight*
Un	Un	2	15g

including a LC I (ProBA 1) tomb recovered in 1957 with a hoard of bronze weapons (see also Linou *Ayii Saranta* below). Tomb 81 is described as 'rich', with cylinder seals and gold, faience, bone and other objects. Tomb 100, the 'Tomb of the Ladies', contained terracotta figurines along with bronze and gold earrings. Late Helladic III A1–III B imports were found in Tombs 11, 26, 50, 81, 90, 100 and 102, along with 'early Cypro-Mycenaean' wares. Åström (1973) provided basic statistics on these Mycenaean wares from Katydhata, which Fortin (1980) interpreted, somewhat precipitously, as indicating a Mycenaean settlement. Keswani (2004, 72, 135–36) also gives a brief account of the Katydhata tombs, noting that the Katydhata 'community' shared in the region's mortuary practices and prestige symbolism.

In 1965, the Cyprus Survey recorded a looted Late Cypriot tomb in Katydhata (CS 1403), but we were unable to relocate it. Flourentzos (1989) published several tombs from Linou, south-east of Katydhata village and south of the Katydhata cemetery excavated by Markides. Tombs 1, 2 and 3 were in the locality Alonia, in the northern part of Linou village. Their ceramic contents suggest that the tombs were first used during the Middle Cypriot (PreBA 2) period, with possible re-use during the Late Cypriot (ProBA). Tomb 4, Cypro-Archaic in date, was in the locality Dimistavros. Tombs 1–4 were excavated by the Cyprus Survey under M. Loulloupis. Tomb 5, found by the National Guard in 'excavations' at their camp, was in the locality Ayii Saranta and was excavated by Flourentzos; it contained a hoard of diversely shaped bronze objects. Swiny (1989) dated the metal objects of Tomb 5 to a late phase of the Middle Cypriot period. Flourentzos (1989, 62) observed that Tomb 5 appeared to be part of a looted necropolis.

Pottery

The primary concentration, as well as the stable alluvial agricultural fields to the south and east, was explored by means of block survey, transect survey and fixed grid collections (TP035, TP243), to establish the boundaries and nature of prehistoric activity at Laonarka. Fixed grid collections in the straw stubble field defined the distribution of PreBA pottery at a finer resolution and confirmed the high density of these wares, particularly at the northern end of the collection grid (Plate 3.11). This peak coincides with some of the possible structures revealed by geophysical survey in the northern part of the central geophysics grid (Fig. 3.29; see discussion below). In considering the overall spatio-temporal distribution of pottery at Laonarka, it is apparent that a north-east by south-west oriented swath represents the heaviest densities of PreBA 2 pottery (11–19 sherds/100 m^2) (Plate 3.12). This swath, which roughly parallels the Katydhata Park Ridge, consists of the primary concentration, as well as Survey Units in cultivated fields to the south-west.

The predominantly Red Polished (RP) III ware sherds in the north-east by south-west swath displayed characteristics not unlike the Markides tomb assemblages, with Heavy and Light Utility wares as well as Table Wares (Table 3.10; Table 3.11). The presence of small incised juglets and fine ware bowls could indicate either a mortuary assemblage or the scattered remains of domestic assemblages. Pottery from Markides' tombs was highly variable; some even contained primarily coarse and Cooking Wares. Consequently, those Survey Units (e.g. SU1066) containing a higher proportion of Heavy and Light Utility RP III wares (usually more typical of domestic assemblages) could still represent the remains of a looted tomb. Over 100 tombs have been excavated in the area, both by archaeologists and looters, and small discard piles of broken pottery might well be expected near tombs.

Vessel types recovered in sherd form by TAESP included incised lime-filled juglets (e.g. TCP076) and bowls (e.g. TCP069), small fine ware bowls with black interiors polished to a very glossy finish, large bowls (e.g. TCP078) or basins with a brick-like fabric that were likewise very well finished, a number of medium-sized jar/jugs with thin walls and scraped interiors (e.g. TCP068), and a smaller quantity of thick, coarser pieces that appear to be from very large jars with lightly finished interiors (TCP199 is probably a very large tripod leg). Several slashed and/or twisted handles also were found, including both round-sectioned, vertical strap handles and flat, horizontal, wishbone-shaped bowl handles (e.g. TCP111). Fabrics generally were hard-fired, especially the small, fine ware bowls with black interiors.

White Painted (WP) II–VI wares are rare in the Laonarka area and unknown from our survey work. This stands in contrast to many contemporary tomb groups in the Mesaoria or northern Troodos (e.g. Dhenia *Kafkallia*, Marki *Alonia* and Politiko *Troullia*). The most common type of WP ware found in the Markides tombs is the small bottle, such as one found in Tomb 42, a WP III string-hole style tripod jug (42.6) (Åström 1989, 26, pl. 35). It should be noted, however, that much WP II–IV ware is relatively soft and does not survive well on the ground surface. The lack of WP finds in the Survey Area may simply reflect this taphonomic factor.

Several tombs recorded on the slopes of the Katydhata Park Ridge also indicate the mortuary nature of some PreBA 2 activity at Laonarka (Table 3.12). Consisting of chambers with dromoi, the morphology of these tombs suggests that they were Bronze Age in date (though no artefacts were found in direct association with them). Human skeletal remains (including cranial fragments and maxillary dentition) found during block survey in the primary concentration (SU0073–74) may be the remains of looted tombs nearby.

Chipped Stone and Ground Stone

Neither the chipped stone samples nor the ground stone artefacts (see below) collected from Laonarka represent lithic material strongly diagnostic of the Bronze Age. The chipped stone artefacts were made predominantly on local jasper and chalcedony, a typical feature of the Survey Area overall. Most of these artefacts represent certain elements of a simple flake-based core technology, characteristic of assemblages from the Chalcolithic onwards. Chipped stone was absent from the intensive gridded collection, and was prevalent most notably in the western block (SU1053–65: 28 pieces).

All major categories of chipped stone artefact are represented in these block survey samples, suggesting that tool production was carried out in this area. The 30 pieces broke down as 5 cores, 1 blank, 9 pieces of debitage and 15 tools. Although the high number of tools does recall village samples dominated by *dhoukani* flakes, the prominence of other tool types in the Laonarka samples suggests that they could provide an outline of a Bronze Age industry at this locality (see below). Only one chipped stone artefact, a well-made flake core produced on jasper, was collected from the re-survey of the olive grove (SU1098).

The 15 tools collected offer some additional detail on the chipped stone technology of the area. Two flake tools made on local jasper represent generalized tools (one notch and one denticulate). These latter, together with the eight unretouched utilized flakes, dominate the tool sample, demonstrating a feature characteristic of samples where prehistoric and early historic pottery dominates. These tools include three examples made of non-local cherts, a feature that also compares well with the more substantial assemblage recovered from Phlasou *Koutroullis* (TS06). Against the latter association are five *dhoukani* flakes, three of which were made on local jasper recalling examples associated with Roman period materials elsewhere in the Survey Area. Although threshing tools clearly existed prior to the modern *dhoukani* sledge, the two final examples made on non-local Lefkara cherts are more in keeping with the high numbers of such artefacts recovered across historic village contexts within the Survey Area, for example in the villages of Phlasou, Katydhata and Linou or at the seasonal village of Mandres.

Only one ground stone tool (a rubbing stone) was recovered from the straw stubble field (in TP243). A significant number of additional ground stone artefacts were, however, collected during re-survey of the olive grove (SU1097–98): these include a hammer stone/grinder, two rubbing stones, a grinding slab and a fragment of a well-made stone disc from SU1097, as well as a hammer stone, a grinder and an anvil stone re-using a grinder from SU1098. While all of these tools would be at home in a Bronze Age settlement context (e.g. Swiny *et al.* 2003; Webb 1996), the absence of a large assemblage of ground stone artefacts with significant numbers of agricultural tools such as rubbers and querns is conspicuous.

Although the distribution of ground stone tools in Laonarka is diffuse, and of only low to moderate density, it nevertheless represents a concentration in this part of the Karkotis Valley Intensive Survey Zone. In the primary concentration, tools for grinding (e.g. rubbing stones, a

Table 3.11. Katydhata Laonarka *(TS09): pottery from SU0071–78, SU0099–0104, SU1012–14, SU1053–81, SU1086–99, SU2188–91. TCP numbers refer to Pottery Catalogue in Volume 1, Chapter 3.6*

Prehistoric

Fct	*Type*	*No.*	*Weight*
CW	Sla	3	27g
			TCP242
LU	Sla	2	55g

Bronze Age

Fct	*Type*	*No.*	*Weight*
CW	CW	6	37g
HU	HU	15	1.103kg
LU	BS	2	10g
LU	LU	4	23g
			TCP395
LU	RS	8	16g
			TCP115, TCP116
LU	Un	4	13g
TW	BRX	3	9g
TW	RS	1	2g
Un	Un	1	2g

Prehistoric Bronze Age

Fct	*Type*	*No.*	*Weight*
HU	HU	1	80g
HU	RP	15	421g
			TCP195, TCP199
HU	RPC	68	1.181kg
			TCP120
HU	RPO	1	5g
HU	RPOL	78	1.182kg
			TCP071, TCP072, TCP073, TCP078, TCP086, TCP087, TCP121
HU	RPS	5	144g
LU	RP	20	103g
			TCP124
LU	RPC	237	1.812kg
			TCP068, TCP074, TCP111, TCP196, TCP197, TCP198
LU	RPO	28	239g
LU	RPOL	14	147g
			TCP088
LU	RPOM	46	199g
LU	RPOS	6	16g
			TCP117
TW	BPO	1	2g
TW	RPIC	11	33g
			TCP076, TCP113
TW	RPIOS	5	6g
			TCP069
TW	RPT	2	4g
			TCP112
TW	RPTC	9	17g
TW	RPTOM	45	162g
			TCP077, TCP085, TCP123
TW	RPTOS	21	41g
			TCP070, TCP075, TCP114
TW	RS	2	8g

Protohistoric Bronze Age

Fct	*Type*	*No.*	*Weight*
HU	HU	1	35g
LU	BS	1	2g
LU	LU	3	20g
LU	RLU	1	12g
			TCP079
LU	RLUC	1	2g
			TCP119
LU	WPBC	2	15g
			TCP108, TCP109
TW	BRI	1	2g
			TCP392
TW	BRIIC	1	18g
			TCP241
TW	BS	2	4g
TW	Mo	1	2g
			TCP393
TW	RLU	1	2g
TW	RS	1	2g
			TCP394
TW	WSO	8	15g

Late Bronze Age to Archaic

Fct	*Type*	*No.*	*Weight*
CW	CW	1	55g
			TCP398
HU	HU	6	220g
LU	LU	2	16g
LU	RS	1	4g

Cypro-Geometric to Archaic

Fct	*Type*	*No.*	*Weight*
HU	WPC	4	45g
			TCP229
LU	BORC	1	35g
LU	WPC	10	68g
			TCP230
LU	WPO	1	5g

Cypro-Geometric to Classical

Fct	*Type*	*No.*	*Weight*
HU	BOR	1	25g
HU	CAmS	3	180g
HU	HU	9	323g
HU	RS	2	78g
HU	WP	3	65g
HU	WPC	4	110g
LU	Bc	1	5g
LU	BOR	4	23g
			TCP192
LU	BORC	3	48g
LU	BORO	3	17g
LU	BS	1	6g
LU	BSC	2	17g
			TCP193
LU	CAmS	2	140g
LU	LU	7	67g
			TCP110
LU	RS	3	30g
LU	WP	28	337g
			TCP082, TCP083, TCP084, TCP122
LU	WPC	18	187g
			TCP200, TCP227
LU	WPO	1	22g
Tr	Cam	1	92g
TW	BcBO	1	2g
			TCP081
TW	BOR	1	4g
			TCP118
TW	BORO	2	10g
			TCP397
TW	BSO	1	3g
			TCP194
TW	RS	5	18g
TW	WP	2	6g
TW	WPC	1	2g
TW	WPO	1	5g
			TCP396

Cypro-Archaic to Classical

Fct	*Type*	*No.*	*Weight*
TW	BORO	1	3g

Historical Antiquity (Archaic to Late Roman)

Fct	*Type*	*No.*	*Weight*
Ar	Ti	11	737g
Ar	TiP	2	275g
CW	CW	9	40g
HU	HU	206	6.85kg
HU	HUR08	2	85g
LU	LU	183	1.892kg
TW	RS	4	23g
TW	TW	8	36g
U	Loom	1	27g
			TCP243

Cypro-Classical

Fct	*Type*	*No.*	*Weight*
TW	BS	1	4g

Classical to Hellenistic

Fct	Type	No.	Weight
TW	BS	2	9g TCP239
TW	RS	2	16g

Hellenistic

Fct	Type	No.	Weight
PO	Ug	2	22g
TW	BS	15	80g
TW	BS02	1	6g TCP240
TW	CC	2	6g
TW	RS	13	60g
TW	TW	1	35g

Hellenistic to Roman

Fct	Type	No.	Weight
CW	CW	17	70g
CW	CWFPWh	2	35g TCP105
CW	CWPR	2	16g
CW	CWPR08	1	12g TCP244
HU	HUR03	1	35g TCP080
LU	LU	1	25g
Tr	Am07	4	67g TCP245
TW	RS	1	3g
TW	SRS	29	164g
TW	TW	1	3g

Late Hellenistic to Early Roman

Fct	Type	No.	Weight
TW	CS	3	13g
TW	ESA	18	83g
TW	Sig	15	43g TCP234

Early Roman

Fct	Type	No.	Weight
CW	CW	1	2g
CW	CWC	1	5g
CW	CWPR04a	3	15g TCP235
La	La01	1	1g
La	La02	2	6g TCP232
La	La04	1	3g TCP238
TW	CS11	1	8g
TW	CS12	1	4g
TW	CS22A	3	8g
TW	CS28	1	7g
TW	CS31A	1	2g TCP233
TW	SigW	1	10g TCP236

Early to Late Roman

Fct	Type	No.	Weight
Ar	Ti	7	491g
Ar	TiP	4	435g
CW	CW	89	504g
CW	CWCR02a	1	15g
CW	CWFPWh	2	21g
CW	CWPR04	3	37g
CW	CWPR08a	1	5g
HU	HU	1	12g
HU	HUR01	2	78g
HU	HUR08	3	96g
LU	LU	1	5g
Tr	AmSk01	2	48g
TW	ARS	4	24g

Mid Roman

Fct	Type	No.	Weight
Tr	Pin	1	15g TCP228

Late Roman

Fct	Type	No.	Weight
Ar	Ti	3	610g
Ar	TiCS	1	18g
Ar	TiP	7	803g
CW	CWCR01	1	10g
CW	CWCR06	1	8g TCP231
HU	HUR05	1	55g TCP106
Tr	LR1	1	40g
TW	CRS	10	130g
TW	CRS02	5	54g
TW	CRS09	2	22g
TW	LRC	1	7g

Roman to Modern

Fct	Type	No.	Weight
Ar	Ti	18	1.015kg
CW	CW	1	25g
HU	HU	44	1.119kg
La	La	1	20g TCP237
LU	LU	177	1.878kg

Historical (Archaic to Modern)

Fct	Type	No.	Weight
Ar	Ti	3	140g
HU	HU	337	10.631kg
LU	LU	605	5.675kg
TW	TW	2	30g

Medieval utility period I

Fct	Type	No.	Weight
U	UAA98	6	124g

Medieval

Fct	Type	No.	Weight
TW	G05	1	10g

Medieval to Modern

Fct	Type	No.	Weight
CW	BGW	21	119g
CW	MP	1	30g
CW	Tia	4	120g
CW	Tta	1	46g
HU	HU	13	496g
LU	BuLK	4	16g
LU	G	1	1g
LU	LU	44	528g
LU	LUR03	1	35g TCP252
LU	LUS	1	50g TCP107
TW	BGW	2	25g
TW	G	1	10g
TW	G01	1	10g
TW	MP	1	6g
TW	UnG	3	55g
U	BuLK	11	225g
U	ID02	4	58g
U	UPSJu	1	11g

Medieval-Frankish

Fct	Type	No.	Weight
TW	CGS05	14	165g
TW	CGS06	1	3g
TW	CGS07	1	10g

Ottoman

Fct	Type	No.	Weight
TW	G01	2	12g
TW	G02	2	10g
TW	G03	2	10g
TW	G05	1	5g
TW	MP01	1	5g

Ottoman to Modern I

Fct	Type	No.	Weight
CW	TiaB	1	50g
TW	G02	1	10g
TW	MP01	1	15g

Medieval-Venetian to Early Ottoman

Fct	*Type*	*No.*	*Weight*
TW	CGS06	4	42g
TW	G03	5	55g
TW	GS06	1	10g
TW	MP01	6	33g

Ottoman to Modern II

Fct	*Type*	*No.*	*Weight*
CW	BGW	2	4g
HU	BuH	38	941g
LU	BuL	111	1.205kg
TW	BGW	1	7g
TW	BGW02	2	20g
TW	G03	4	32g
TW	G04	3	12g
TW	G05	2	15g
TW	G07	3	15g
TW	MP01	6	35g
TW	MP02	4	39g
TW	SP01	1	8g
TW	SP02	9	82g
TW	UnG	1	12g

Modern

Fct	*Type*	*No.*	*Weight*
Ar	Brk	5	375g
Ar	TiCh	27	609g
HU	HU	5	149g
LU	LU	8	165g
TW	BGW01	1	2g
TW	BGW02	1	8g
TW	G02	1	45g
TW	G05	1	7g
TW	G07	13	148g
TW	MP01	1	20g
TW	POR	24	183g

Unknown

Fct	*Type*	*No.*	*Weight*
CW	CW	8	75g
CW	Un04	1	7g
HU	HU	12	620g
LU	LU	23	91g
Un	UN	2	97g

Table 3.12. Katydhata Laonarka *(TS09): recorded tombs and associated features (see POSI catalogue in Appendix 2 for details)*

TP044	Shaft or pit, c. 90 x 80 cm, c. 45 cm deep. Filled in antiquity, revealed in bulldozer cut. No artefacts.
TP063	Circular chamber tomb with dromos (probably Bronze Age). Dromos c. 0.70 m wide, facing SSW. Chamber c. 2.0 m in diameter and c. 1.5 m high.
TP111	Circular chamber tomb with dromos (probably Bronze Age). Dromos c. 2.0 m wide, facing NW. Chamber c. 2.2 m diameter and c. 1.6 m high.
TP166	Collapsed dromos facing NW. None of chamber is visible.

grinding slab, a stone disc) were proportionately only slightly more abundant than pounding tools (e.g. hammer stones, an anvil). In this context, it is perhaps worth mentioning that Markides' excavations of tombs in and around Katydhata produced some stone spindle whorls in Tomb 26 (Åström 1989, 20) and stone mace heads in Tombs 27 and 62 (1989, 21, 37), but no mention is made of either ground stone or chipped stone items. Finally, it should be noted the number of ground stone objects found during the re-survey of the olive grove indicates that other, similar objects may have been overlooked in other Survey Units within Laonarka.

Transect survey helps to put this material in context. The sample of chipped stone from Transect TT3881500N, running from east to west 300 m south of Laonarka, is broadly comparable to that from Laonarka itself, with 52% consisting of tools, dominated by eight unretouched utilized flakes (53% of the sample). All of these were made of local jasper, apart from one piece of silicified umber. The single flake tool in the sample is represented by a perforator, similarly made of local material, while all but one of the six *dhoukani* flakes (83%) were made on Lefkara cherts, a pattern that reflects the Laonarka sample. The same transect produced five ground stone objects: a basalt grinder (SU1315); a small spherical hartzburgite gaming piece (SU1307); a flat diabase pebble engraved with an 'x' or crude cross (SU1307); a diabase fragment exhibiting polish and striations probably struck during the re-sharpening of an axe (SU1317); and a rubbing stone made by re-using a perforated microgabbro hammer (SU1305). While rubbing stones are rather commonplace, perforated hammers are representative of a tool type associated with crushing ore in Bronze Age contexts (Swiny 1986, 15–16).

Two additional artefacts (a core trimming element and a tool) were collected from Transect TT3882000N, which passed through the village of Katydhata. The tool, a utilized flake made of non-local chert (like the core trimming piece on local jasper), fits well with other chipped stone artefacts recovered from the area of Laonarka.

Geophysical Survey

During the 2002 and 2003 field seasons, Iain Banks conducted a resistivity survey, using a Geoscan RM-15 and a 0.5 m probe separation, in the primary concentration. He tested 21 20-m squares using a 1 × 1 m sampling interval, all arranged on a grid leading southward through the straw stubble field and entering the north-east edge of the olive grove (Fig. 3.29).

Linear anomalies immediately highlighted the possibility of architectural features, while further examination of the geophysical data plot revealed two separate groups of anomalies (Fig. 3.29). The first group is associated with geological features seen on a 1960s aerial photograph and seems to underlie the second group of anomalies. Although this might be taken to indicate that the second group was of anthropogenic origin, geophysical results must be regarded as tentative until tested through excavation (hence we use the term 'anomaly' rather than 'feature'). Bearing this caveat in mind, the geometrical element in their shapes suggests that the second group of anomalies might represent architectural remnants. Most of the anomalies are located in the straw stubble field and appear to form a rough T-shape towards the northern end of the area, roughly on a north-east by south-west/ north-west by south-east alignment. If these anomalous readings do represent a building complex, its dimensions would be approximately 40 × 20 m on the north-east by south-west axis and about 20 × 20 m on the north-west by south-east axis (Fig. 3.29).

There also are several other rectangular, sub-rectangular and small circular anomalies, which could indicate either buildings or a mixture of buildings and enclosure walls. Further anomalies include a faint linear band running across the south-west grid (the 1960s boundary of the olive grove) and, at the north end of the central grid, a sub-circular anomaly evident as a darker band of readings (Central interpretation/A in Fig. 3.29), representing a very tight range of data and strongly suggesting yet another structure. It is this area, the northern end of these central plots, where grid collection found the densest concentrations of prehistoric pottery (Plate 3.11).

Geophysical survey during the 2003 season, on either side of the 2002 grids, revealed further anomalies in the primary concentration that could be associated with structural remains. The full plot gives some indication of this, although the range in the data means that the detail is more reduced than when we focused on particular areas (Fig. 3.29). As was the case with the southern grids in the 2002 survey, the track is seen as a white strip of dummy readings running across the grids.

The most interesting results of the 2003 survey lay in the grids on the south-west side of the plot. This group of four grids, comprising two pairs offset by 20 m, produced a rather faint, large oval anomaly, which lay on a north-east by south-west axis. The oval anomaly, which appeared to represent a large enclosure (south-west interpretation/A), measured at least 30 m on the long north-east by south-west axis, and over 20 m on the shorter axis. In addition, there was a circular anomaly in the lower, south-western end of the oval, with a diameter of about 10–12 m (B). This may represent a structure within the enclosure. There were also faint linear anomalies running north-east by south-west which might represent plough marks, or else indicate false patterns created by the processing of the data. Both anomalies were fairly well defined, however, and we are reasonably confident that they represent structural remains. This potential enclosure also resembled an anomaly that was evident in the south-central area (E in Fig. 3.29), which opens up the possibility that there were two oval enclosures within the straw stubble field. Because anomaly E appeared to cut, or be cut by, anomalies C and D, it is possible that the structural remains, if such they are, represent more than one period within the primary concentration.

On the east side, toward the olive grove, the four grids surveyed in 2003 added relatively little (Fig. 3.29). This area showed considerable disturbance, and most anomalies within it probably derive from the underlying geology. Certainly one can see an effect similar to the 2002 grids close to the track. There were two anomalies of interest within the eastern surveyed area. The first (East interpretation/C in Fig. 3.29) appeared to be roughly delta-shaped and was represented by low readings (hence shown in white on the interpretive plot). This reading implies a higher moisture level and normally is indicative of a negative feature such as a ditch. In view of the extreme conditions for resistivity survey, considerable caution must be exercised in interpreting this feature. It measured roughly 10 m across in both directions and could represent the foundation of a structure, or else a small ditched enclosure. Further downslope of this anomaly was another, similar but less well defined one (D). Another roughly delta-shaped feature was apparent, but was slightly smaller than 'C', measuring roughly 9 × 5 m.

Geophysical survey in the olive grove itself produced little in either season indicative of anomalies that could be considered anthropogenic. Of the four grids in the area surveyed during 2002, only the north-west one revealed an anomaly that might suggest human activity (Central interpretation/G in Fig. 3.29). This was a medium-dark, curving linear anomaly running north-east by south-west adjacent to the dummy readings alongside the modern track. The remainder of the survey carried out in the olive grove produced no results indicative of structural remains. The remaining linear anomalies most likely relate to the olive grove itself, while a few patches of very dark anomalies would seem to be geological rather than anthropogenic in origin.

Two seasons of geophysical survey at Laonarka produced some very intriguing anomalies in the primary concentration. Combined, these anomalies suggest the possible existence of structural remains within the stubble field, perhaps representing two distinct periods of activity. If this is the case, then one period is represented by oval and circular elements, while the other is represented by largely rectilinear elements. Indeed, settlement architecture in the Chalcolithic and earlier periods was generally circular, while that of the PreBA was rectilinear (Keswani 2004, 148). If the rectangular geophysical anomalies are in fact structural elements, we might expect them to date to the PreBA, as we found no substantial amounts of pottery from another distinctive chronological period.

There is some disjunction between the high pottery density and limited number of geophysical anomalies in the olive grove to the south-east. This may be explained by the slight downward incline from the straw stubble field toward the olive grove. Here, modern land use – including intensive agricultural exploitation and constant ploughing (especially in the olive groves and orchards) – is a main contributing factor. Artefacts originally relating to a possible settlement on the slope may have migrated, through ploughing and/or soil creep, down into the flatter ground of the olive grove. It must be reiterated, however,

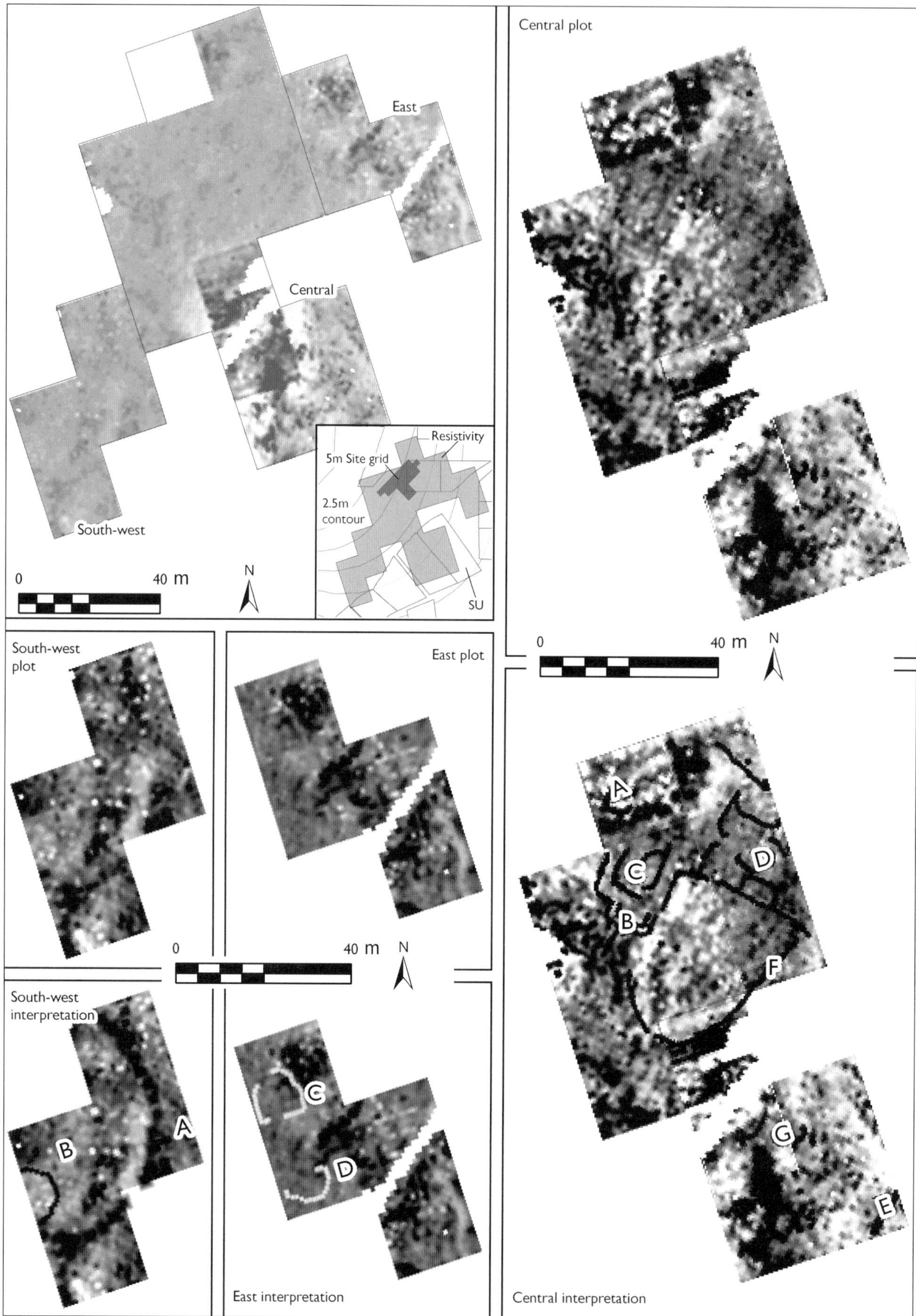

Fig. 3.29. Katydhata Laonarka *(TS09): resistivity survey (Iain Banks, finalised by Luke Sollars)*

that conditions in both seasons were at the extreme end of the resistivity meter's operational parameters, and the interpretations must be treated with due caution. Excavation, in other words, is the only way to demonstrate the existence of any structural remains.

Conclusions

The concentration of PreBA 2 pottery at Laonarka is surrounded on three sides by a halo of prehistoric artefacts. In this halo, PreBA 2 pottery appears consistently, but only in moderate or low densities. The halo also features significant concentrations of flake and utilized chipped stone tools. In addition, a few Protohistoric Bronze Age (ProBA) sherds, including Base-Ring, White Slip, Red Slip, Monochrome and Red Lustrous Wheelmade wares, were found at Laonarka. This ProBA material most likely represents the remains of tomb assemblages. Indeed, the Markides excavations had revealed that some PreBA 2 tombs were used into the LC IIC phase (i.e. ProBA 2). The ProBA pottery found by TAESP would seem to corroborate a scenario of continuous human activity at Laonarka from the PreBA into the Iron Age. In general, the distribution of ProBA material is distinctly further west (i.e. closer to the Karkotis River) than that of the PreBA.

During the PreBA, the dead were usually buried in extramural cemeteries located at least several hundred meters from inhabited areas (Keswani 2005, 248). Other known necropoleis and settlements in the northern foothills of the Troodos were established in the Philia–Early Cypriot I (PreBA 1) phases and continued into the Middle Cypriot phase (PreBA 2), for example at Marki *Alonia* (Frankel and Webb 2001, 115–16; 2006). PreBA villages such as Marki, Alambra *Mouttes* and Politiko *Troullia* (Falconer *et al.* 2005; Fall *et al.* 2008) were typically situated on high ground directly above a significant watercourse and separated from their necropoleis either by the river, smaller ravines or other natural topographical features. These necropoleis are commonly within a direct line of sight of their settlement and usually border agricultural land.

In the case of the Karkotis River, the broad alluvial fan between Katydhata and Linou, plus the terraces east of the river, form a possible 'core territory' on a scale similar to that at Marki, Politiko and Alambra. This area of the Karkotis Valley is also separated from the Mesaoria by enclosing hills. If there is any common pattern here, then the core of the PreBA settlement contemporary with the tombs around Laonarka might be sought either beneath the modern village, or on the ridge west of the river (unfortunately in a heavily eroded zone at the very edge of the Survey Area). A concentration of pottery and stone tools just north of the Phlasou ridge might have been a relic of settlement activity there, adjacent to the earlier settlement on the east side of the river, at Phlasou.

Laonarka seems to represent the remains of at least one part of a PreBA 2 habitational and mortuary complex known from previous excavations in and around Katydhata village. The proliferation of RP III juglets and fine ware bowl sherds in good condition, together with the lack of settlement materials such as mudbrick and wall plaster chunks, coarseware installations such as basins, and the low density of ground stone in the primary concentration, might lead to the conclusion that the PreBA 2 remains at Laonarka represent a cemetery rather than a settlement. If this is the case, the oval anomalies apparent in geophysical survey could indicate the filled remains of PreBA 2 tombs. Equally, however, the rectilinear anomalies could represent structures from the settlement or (less likely) the remains of later animal pens, which would account for the lack of significant pottery from other time periods. The human remains and shaft cuts found at the foot of the Katydhata Park Ridge's north-east slope suggest that this area of the ridge also was used for mortuary activity, perhaps in association with the RP pottery III found thereabouts. The presence of an associated settlement may, however, be indicated by the notably dense and wide halo of prehistoric pottery and chipped stone in and around Laonarka. Thus, as we have emphasized before, excavations alone can resolve these lingering questions.

3.10 Katydhata Village and Landscape

The modern village of Katydhata occupies a potentially strategic position, both economically and socially (Fig. 3.30). It lies towards the northern end of the broader area of valley terraces that includes Phlasou, but also controls a major constriction in the valley 2.5 km to its north. Towering above it to the east and north-east is the massive ore body and modern copper mine of Skouriotissa, which has been of major importance to the local economy and social structure probably since the Bronze Age (Chapter 3.12). Here, before passing through the foothill narrows to the coastal zone, with its own issues of climate such as seasonal fog, humidity, wind and sea spray, one finds the longest frost-free growing season in the valley, along with the attendant richness of soil and water. The local growers are able to sow earlier and get crops to market earlier, even by weeks, than fellow growers higher up in the valley.

Yet these resources have not produced a continually thriving settlement. Katydhata is the only modern village in the Karkotis Valley Invensive Survey Zone with no historical records before the 16th century. Today, after the economic boom produced by the copper mines in the early and mid-20th century, it is a quiet village with a substantial proportion of its population made up of weekenders from Nicosia. In communication terms, it is nowadays essentially a dead end: the major communication route down the Karkotis Valley that joins the Troodos range with Lefka and the Bay of Morphou is blocked by the Buffer Zone, running across the valley at its constriction north of the village. Our work in the Katydhata area aimed to chart this changing relationship between natural resources and social organisation.

Hellenistic–Roman Katydhata

Activity at Katydhata *Laonarka* (TS09) during the Hellenistic–Roman period is suggested by tombs and corroborated by heavy concentrations of pottery, particularly on the west side of the village (for map see Plate 3.10). The high proportions of Hellenistic–Early Roman Table Wares suggest that a significant amount of this pottery comes from tombs. This is supported by the absence of chronologically diagnostic utility wares. On the west side of the village, the high proportions of Hellenistic–Early Roman Table Wares are accompanied by fragments of lamps and unguentaria, classes of objects most common in mortuary contexts (see Chapter 3.14), which is consistent with the multiple tombs recorded as POSIs in the area. In 1915, Markides excavated seven Hellenistic and Roman chamber tombs immediately south of the village. These were rectangular in form, with a flat or slightly arched roof. They were entered by a long narrow dromos with up to eight steps and often contained niches for offerings (Markides 1916, 5–8).

The density of Hellenistic–Roman pottery is consistently higher on the western side of the village, as is pottery of the Late Roman period (when tombs contained very little ceramic material). Consequently, mortuary practices alone cannot explain the total number of sherds. Other than the tombs, however, we found no evidence for a major rural Hellenistic–Roman settlement at Laonarka. In order for post-depositional processes to obliterate traces of such a settlement, a substantial amount of earth-moving would have to be involved, but not so much as to remove the well-preserved evidence for the Bronze Age settlement and mortuary complex. Some Hellenistic–Roman activity nonetheless is logical, given Laonarka's location directly east of the Roman settlement at Katydhata *Pano Limna* (TS15) and south of the Skouriotissa mine.

Katydhata Village

Simos Menardos (1970, 24) suggests that the name and location are both ancient, with a Ptolemaic settlement in the area, although the first written record of the name Katydhata comes from the 16th century AD. Louis de Mas Latrie (1852–61, III, 506) mentions the *casal* as part of the 'Baliazzo delle Marathasse real', that is a hamlet belonging to the part of Marathassa valley owned by the crown. The legend, based on which the village took its name, probably comes from the medieval period, and was recounted to us by a villager:

> In the old days there were downriver some houses which were called 'Riatika' [the queen's] where the queen lived. A rich man who lived upriver and owned the water rights fell in love with her but she was not interested in him. To tempt her he gave her water rights in return for her sleeping with him. She agreed but on the crucial night she sent in her place her maid, a girl who looked like her and also had her hair in braids like the queen. The rich man did not understand the trick but cut the girls' braids as proof that he slept with the queen. When later on he claimed that he and the queen slept together and produced the braids to prove it, the queen turned up and showed her braids, thus ridiculing him. He became very angry and said 'Κάτω τα ύδατα!' ['Kato ta ydhata' or 'Down with the waters!'], which meant that he would give her no more water. And the village name came from that.

In 1565 Katydhata had a total of 54 *francomati* (Grivaud 1998, 470). There seems to be a considerable lack of evidence for the earlier part of the Ottoman period. A

Fig. 3.30. View from the eastern edge of Katydhata looking north down the Karkotis Valley, with the southern end of the slag heap appearing behind the three-doored garage in the centre (Luke Sollars)

reference to a court dispute between villagers in 1709 can be found in the documents of Kykkos Monastery (Theocharides 1993, I, 390–91). Marina Kyriacou, a woman from Katydhata, accused Papa-Thanasis, the local priest, of unlawfully appropriating some animals which belonged to her late mother, 16 years earlier, and claimed the amount of 32 *gurush* (piastres). The priest claimed he had bought the animals, consisting of an ox, a cow and a calf, for the amount of 28 *gurush*, and produced witnesses to prove his claims. The case was dismissed.

In 1824 we have a record of permission being given by the landowner for the cultivation of lands neighbouring the Kykkos Monastery estates in the area (possibly near Korakou) (Theocharides 1993, IV, 1987). Katydhata belonged to the district (*kaza*) of Lefka, one of the larger and more significant districts of the island. The village appears in the Ottoman tax register of 1825–26. It contained 20 taxable households, generating an annual tax revenue of 945 piastres (Papadopoullos 1965, 123). In the 1831 Ottoman tax register it is found to have a total of 49 adult males eligible for taxation, of which 8 were Muslim and 41 non-Muslim (Sarınay 2000, 119). According to the same source, these people and their families lived in 24 houses and owned 343.5 *dönüm* of arable land, 1 goatfold, 72 mulberry trees, 1 orchard, 101 olive trees and 2 almond trees. The village also had 1 mill, belonging to a Christian (Sarınay 2000, 155, 182). The main village church of Ayios Ioannis O Theologos was built in 1870, probably replacing an older church. Inside are two ancient columns with Corinthian capitals, quite likely from Soloi or Skouriotissa, and a stone panel showing a cypress between two lions (Gunnis 1936, 259). According to the first British census, undertaken in 1881, the village had 123 inhabitants and 28 inhabited houses (Census 1882, 26).

The village's proximity to the regional administrative centre of Lefka, as well as its position directly on the route between the mountains and the town along the Karkotis valley, meant that it was part of a trade route which brought products from the mountain to the lowlands, Lefka and Morphou, and vice versa. The architecture of the village, like that of Linou 1 km to the south, is particularly interesting: it contains a large number of average and large Ottoman houses, some including their own private Turkish bath. This suggests that in the Ottoman period the area was the home of particularly wealthy regional figures, perhaps Ottoman officials involved in trade and wealthy landowners. The village was part of an area that attracted the interest of foreign merchants trading in raw materials. In 1691 we have the case of Edward Stafford, an English consular official who was based in Galata and was active in money lending and trade of cotton and silk (*No. 3 Şer'i Sicil Defteri*, Kyrenia Archives, 32/428; published in facsimile in Merkelbach 1991, 399).

According to local tradition, during the 19th century an Ottoman official, perhaps a dragoman, called Oikonomidis lived in the village. His house was an *arhontiko*, a rich Ottoman house, and had its own private *hamam* (Turkish bath). Most of the complex was renovated in 2000–2001 to make a village community centre and mining museum (Fig. 3.31). Some Ottoman manuscripts were found when the house was being renovated, but unfortunately these are now inaccessible.

The *hamam* measures 3.9 × 2.9 m, and is built of rubble masonry and cut limestone quoins, with a plastered exterior (Fig. 3.32). The striking domed roof is built of stone, and has a terracotta ventilator, partly formed out of the neck of a storage jar. There is a collapsed mudbrick room on its southern side, and a collapsed stone-built room and a stone oven on its western side.

The village's economy and population remained largely agricultural until 1914, when the Skouriotissa mine opened (see also Chapter 3.12). This meant an influx of workers to the area, which forced the population of the village to adjust, or intensify, their crops in order to supply the miners. The villagers took their produce to the miners' settlement on Saturdays, as it was their payday. Any surplus was then sold in Morphou. In addition, the village provided rented housing to the miners. It also brought a significant shift to the population's distribution: at one point, according to one of our informants, up to 90% worked in the mines. The village's proximity to the coast at Morphou Bay and the construction of the Cyprus Railway to connect the area's mines changed the face of the landscape.

Before 1974 the village's population rose to about 500. The Turkish invasion and the division of the island, with the Buffer Zone passing just 2 km north of the village, meant that the its position changed from being on a major route to a dead end. Employment opportunities dwindled, which led to a mass exodus to the cities, mainly Nicosia. In 2003 the population was only 186. The progressive attitude of the current village council and its president, along with their efforts for improving the village, have, among other successes, secured funding for a highly imaginative museum of the mining history of the area.

Fields, Terraces and Pottery Distribution

The Katydhata area was one of the most difficult sections of the Karkotis Valley in which to carry out transect survey, with high terraces, steep field banks, poor ground visibility and frequent houses and gardens. These factors also make it a particularly interesting area, with centuries of human manipulation of the landscape clearly visible in the archaeological and geomorphological record.

The lowest reach of the Karkotis in the Survey Area is geomorphically defined as a broad, terrace-stepped plain between a constriction in the bedrock valley walls between Laonarka/Pano Limna and the narrows north-west of Skouriotissa. The plain is asymmetric. From east to west, the sequence consists of: (1) the east bedrock ridge abutting a long slope marked by several ancient fluvial terraces from Katydhata to the river; (2) a relatively broad series of low fluvial terraces and historic floodplains

Fig. 3.31. The new community centre at Katydhata, with part of the Oikonomides house on the right restored as a mining museum (21 November 2003) (Michael Given)

Fig. 3.32. Katydhata hamam (BU0132) from the south, with domed roof and vent, and collapsed room in the foreground (Chris Parks)

around and west of the modern river channel; and (3) the west bedrock ridge. Agriculture is focused on the alluvial soils in two distinct domains: cereals and irrigated crops in older, more-developed, clayey- to silty-textured soils east of the river; and orchards in younger, immature sandy soils west of the river. This follows the need for orchards to be in better-drained soils. Fields are continuous up to the boundary of industrial activity at Skouriotissa, and field layouts predating the modern mine indicate that this is a long-lived relationship: there does not appear to be a buffer or intermediate class of land use between the metal industry and agriculture.

Pano Limna, Laonarka and Katydhata are founded on bedrock ridges, with the latter two on opposite sides of the same hill, well above (>10 m) what are impressive hyper-concentrated flood-flow deposits in the low-lying terraces and floodplain. These fluvial deposits include boulders deposited in bars that are present along the length of the river in the Karkotis Valley Intensive Survey Zone. Here the boulders have a mean size of c. 0.5 m diameter, less than half of that at the upper part of the Intensive Survey Zone. Their relative age characteristics are consistent with floods during the Little Ice Age (Ottoman Period). The youngest set of flood sheets contains cultural materials that must have been eroded from upstream contexts. Without fail, vertical sections cut into these Late Holocene (<4000 years BP) fluvial deposits reveal a range of historic and non-diagnostic artefacts.

In this dramatically transformed landscape, the date of the surface artefacts is limited by the age of that surface. One clear example is the westernmost Survey Unit in Transect TT3881500N (SU1321), which in many ways is representative of the agricultural fields on the slopes of the ridgeline along the western edge of the valley. This Survey Unit was situated in a large, rocky and shallow agricultural field that had been partially ripped into bedrock. Levelling along the western boundary had exposed the subsoil. The eastern portion of the field had been filled, and therefore most pottery was located in the field's centre where the former land surface intersects the tread (plane) of the modern field. The location of this field along the ridgelines, means that its surface has been abandoned by fluvial processes longer than those closer to the river. Indeed, any such context up and away from the river channel by more than 20 m elevation difference is likely Pleistocene in age and predates the human occupation of the island. Accordingly, almost all of the pottery in SU1321 dates between the Prehistoric Bronze Age and Late Roman period (although pottery quantities were low overall).

A distinctive characteristic of the local cultural landscape is a number of walls and terraces built of slag cakes. A good example is a terrace wall on the edge of a track 400 m west of the village, just east of the Karkotis River (TP120). The wall is 3 m long and 1 m high, built of complete slag cakes up to 50 cm in diameter. The threshing floors north-west of the village also have retaining walls built of slag (TP102; see next sub-section), and there are similar small walls within the village itself built of slag and often whitewashed. According to a Katydhata resident, the mine used to sell slag cakes for building purposes.

In spite of the lack of historical documentation from the early and middle Medieval period, the Katydhata area contained almost one-third of all diagnostic Byzantine and Medieval-Byzantine pottery from the entire Survey Area (17/43 fine ware sherds; 9/43 utility ware sherds). Bearing in mind the difficulties of dating the utility wares precisely, there seems to be a slight but significant scatter within a radius of 900 m from Katydhata village, particularly on its north-western edge and on the west side of the river just below the Iron Age and Roman site of Pano Limna. Typical examples of the Table Wares include fragments of Cypriot Brown and Green Sgraffito Ware of the Byzantine to Medieval periods (c. 13th century?). The nine utility ware pieces are all UAA98, flat vessels with thin bases from which the rim rises directly. They belong to a series of vessels with in-turned rim, but due to the absence of a wall, the lip is in fact upright (cf. TCP062, TCP313). The shape is similar to the *gastra* or *gastrion*, the clay base for the *klibanos*, which is a dome-shaped mobile oven used to bake the *klibanikios* or *klibanites* – bread or small pieces of meat (Bakirtzis 1989, 131, pl. 11, 3–4).

Land Levelling and the Karkotis

In the Cypriot agricultural norm, field terraces are developed on hillslopes, generally exceeding 15%, and field check dams are constructed along gullies and minor drainages. Field levelling for hillslope terraces and check dam construction are labour-intensive activities requiring a relative abundance of stone for dry-stack wall construction. In Noller's (2010) survey of the entire island, he notes that these two disparate anthropogenic landforms are constructed largely of stone. In addition, he finds that fields developed on fluvial deposits, including fans and stream terraces, are all plane-parallel with the original geological deposit and surface. All, that is, except for this reach of the Karkotis, where surface slopes cross lines of contour at low angles and are broadly separated by earthen, not stone, risers. Natural terraces of Troodos rivers parallel the main channel bed, with lines of contour crossing at high angles to the surface slope. So, these Karkotis surfaces cannot be entirely natural (we have considered and ruled out meanders and other floodplain morphologies; see Volume 1, Chapter 4.6).

The fields around Katydhata best exemplify this unusual morphology, and are proposed as cultural in construction, in other words due to land levelling (Plate 3.13). Here, the fields are divided into ranks of levels or terraces that contour *away* from the river channel. An individual plot or field is a subset of an agricultural terrace. Groups of agricultural terraces developed by land levelling, bounded by high cut-and-fill slopes, with attendant irrigation canals, form a *rank*. Each terrace rank tapers upstream to meet the straight-wall of the channel. This is close to the point where the irrigation-canal intake is located within the channel.

So, when did all this land levelling occur? The age distribution of artefacts provides the best indication. Given the scope and depth of land levelling, measuring 5 m in some places, the probability is very low for any earlier cultural materials to survive at the surface with all this digging and depositing (Volume 1, Chapter 4.6). Thus, the oldest prevalent materials we find at the surface ought to be related to the time of land levelling. The clear preponderance of Roman artefacts points to this as the period of levelling activity. The ranks would need irrigation water otherwise what is the point of creating slopes that most efficiently carry water for distances away from the river? It then follows that the irrigation scheme of the Karkotis was set at this time: the Roman period. Earlier artefacts and cultural materials and sites now lie buried within a double-thick layer in the lower half of each terrace and rank (Volume 1, Chapter 4.6). Since the Roman period, cultural materials have accumulated on the Roman fields assured of little disturbance by overland erosion or transport away because of the near-level and isolated fields and terraces of the equally level and isolated ranks. The context for the Roman and later materials is excellent here, some of the best in the Survey Area.

The spatial relationship of these levelled ranks of terraces and the Karkotis channel might offer some measure of explanation for the dimensions of this giant 'flume' (see Chapter 3.1 above). The 12-km reach of a c. 200 m-wide Karkotis 'flume' would have a volume across its entire extent of two million cubic metres for every metre of excavated depth. Our evidence at Phlasou *Langouphes* (TP246; Volume 1, Figs 4.5–4.6) requires the deepening of the Karkotis channel by between 5 and 8 m since the Bronze Age or later. This channel could have been eroded by the Karkotis unaided by humans, with the dislodged sediment deposited downstream of Skouriotissa; but the geometry of this incision remains to be explained.

Given the history of engineered structures on Cyprus, the Roman period would be the most likely candidate for significant diversion, or other engineered constructions, aimed at controlling the Karkotis (Wilson 2012). That the channel is a furlong in width adds to the Roman character of its excavation. From these initial attempts at hydrological control, we would expect later activities to lead to changes in channel morphology within the 'flume'. The alignment of extensive mining and agriculture activity during the Roman period in the Survey Area is a hypothesis that has been clearly demonstrated by this study (Volume 1, Chapter 4.6). So it is a reasonable hypothesis that the spoils of channel excavation or dredging during the Roman period could have been incorporated into the contemporary land-levelling schemes on the surrounding valley sides. The depth and extent of sediment and soils displaced to level the ranks of terraces within the Karkotis Valley are not fully known, but can be estimated with our GIS to be in the order of one to three million cubic metres, at minimum. So, within the uncertainties of our current understanding of the surficial strata and soils in the valley, the levelled land along the Karkotis could be holding one or more metres of excavated channel gravel from the Karkotis. This would be in addition to the soils and rock already present on the valley sides that would have just been moved around locally (cf. Volume 1, Fig. 4.5).

In summary, it might be possible to account for the volumes of fill required to satisfy the 'flume' hypothesis, and so the inner flume of the valley could be largely engineered – most likely a Roman channel with side walls largely unchanged for more than a millennium. Future study is required to test the 'Roman flume' hypothesis, and then, if it holds, to develop firm estimates of the amount of debris and the timing of its accumulation.

The hypothesis of an original geological origin for the Karkotis 'flume' would be strengthened with a disproved 'Roman flume' hypothesis. This 'flume', however, cannot be the Pleistocene channel, carved during higher discharges of the glacials. We know from our investigation of Phlasou *Langouphes* that the Pleistocene Karkotis was several, to many, metres above its current level (Chapter

3.5; Volume 1, Chapter 4.6), and so could have only assumed its 'flume' shape after the Bronze Age. Natural incision of the flume-like channel could occur. The problem for us has been, and in the future is going to be, making the distinction between natural and engineered origins. At this time the most parsimonious answer is that both extensive engineering and natural erosion are responsible for the form of the Karkotis River channel through our Survey Area, the former for its shape, and the latter for its depth.

Medieval Katydhata

The pottery from the 14th and 15th centuries in the Karkotis Valley is decidedly patchy, and all extant material lies east of the river (Plate 3.14). Unlike Phlasou (Chapter 3.8), Katydhata has almost no pottery from this period, which accords with the lack of historical documentation for the village in the same period. There are rather greater densities of 14th- and 15th-century pottery starting 500 m to the south of the village, which continue southwards towards Linou.

By the 16th and 17th centuries, Katydhata had a broad spread of pottery all around it, albeit not quite as dense and continuous as around Phlasou. Table Wares include Monochrome Green Painted Ware of the Medieval-Venetian to Early Ottoman periods (c. 16th century onward). The densest areas are to the south near Linou and the village's northern outskirts. Further north, the pottery tails off, and at the constriction in the valley where the Buffer Zone crosses, there is no pottery at all. This suggests that the particularly well-watered and fertile stretch of valley from Korakou to Katydhata is a relatively distinct zone, separate from its neighbours in terms of economy, daily activity and visibility.

In the Ottoman and Modern periods, the pottery distribution around Katydhata is identical to that of the other villages of the Karkotis Valley Intensive Survey Zone. There is a broad, low-density carpet across all cultivatable areas of the valley, which is rather denser on the valley's outskirts due to dumping and intensive cultivation. This is particularly clear on the north and south-west edges of Katydhata. In the areas of greatest density, the functional types represent a full array of uses, including tiles, Cooking Wares, Table Wares and Heavy and Light Utility wares. The more recent Table Wares include Monochrome Glazed Wares in various colours, Monochrome Painted Ware in brown from Çanakkale in western Turkey (c. 19th century onward) and Slip-Painted Ware in green and yellow from Didymoteicho in northern Greece and/or Çanakkale (c. late 19th–early 20th centuries) (Vroom 2005, 180–83, 186–87). This breaks down as 22% painted, 59% glazed and 19% sgraffito.

This distribution of pottery in the Medieval–Modern periods is supplemented by our location, measurement and dating of old olive trees (see Volume 1, Chapter 4.7). There are 46 individual trees, dating from the late 15th century to the late 19th century, distributed on relic terraces on both sides of the Karkotis River between Linou and Skouriotissa. The oldest olive trees are distinctly grouped in clusters at Linou and Katydhata. Later plantings are closer to the river and occupy both banks north of Katydhata.

Chipped Stone and Threshing

The transect crossing the valley immediately to the north of Katydhata (TT3882500N) provides a substantial sample of diagnostic lithic artefacts, consisting of five flake cores, one unworked flake, one blank fragment and 21 tools. Of the core reduction artefacts, it is notable that two pieces were produced on Lefkara cherts. The tools are more heavily dominated (67%) by Lefkara cherts and also include one utilized flake of obsidian; this is the only example of obsidian recovered by TAESP.

The tool types across this transect suggest the presence of numerous threshing floors in the area, as 15 (71%) of them are *dhoukani* flakes. This provides one of the most numerically significant samples of such flakes in the Survey Area. Moreover, SU1043's five *dhoukani* flakes represent the largest number in a single Survey Unit, of which four were made on Lefkara cherts. The presence of examples made from non-local chert, together with a single jasper *dhoukani* flake, may imply, yet again, the local use of this inferior material for threshing sledge production and management.

Some of these pieces may have spread from their areas of use to fields along with manure and dumped material (Given *et al.* 2003a, 309). At the eastern end of the transect, there is a marked concentration in the two Survey Units (SU1048–49) immediately adjacent to a series of terraces with threshing floors (TP102; Fig. 3.33). The terraces are built into the north-west side of the ridge and support several paved and unpaved threshing floors. Some of the dry-stack retaining walls are still preserved; they are composed of river cobbles and, in some cases, the slag cakes that are such a characteristic building material around Katydhata and Skouriotissa. They are clearly visible on the 1963 aerial photograph, and were the main group of threshing floors for the inhabitants of Katydhata.

The three Survey Units on the north-western side of these threshing floors contained six *dhoukani* flakes, plus an additional unworked flake and a fragment of a ground stone vessel made of white marble (SU1047–49). Two of the *dhoukani* flakes were made of translucent Lefkara chert, one of Moni chert, one of translucent chert, one of red jasper and one of chalcedony. The Lefkara chert is non-local, which is typical of similar tools recovered elsewhere from historic contexts in the TAESP Survey Area. Of particular interest is the flake of translucent chert, which has traces of the mastic used to insert it into the sledge (TCL113).

Watermills

Just over the Karkotis/Atsas watershed, 900 m south-east of Katydhata, are three watermills located within 350 m of each other, remembered today as 'the mills of Ahmed Agha' (BU0002–0004; Fig. 3.34). This group of watermills has two particularly striking features of (for full descriptions see TAESPdata 2007). The first is that their masonry is finished with a characteristic pink-coloured plaster that is unique in the Survey Area. The second is that they are fed by water channelled in across the watershed from Deimma Asprallou-Linopsa (BU0105), a weir and diversion node on the Karkotis River in Phlasou, 2.5 km to the south-west. This channel was one of two major aqueducts supplying the village of Petra in the Atsas Valley, a much smaller catchment than the Karkotis Valley (the other passed to the west and north of Skouriotissa mine). The precision of our dating does not allow us to discern whether the mills were built at the same time as the aqueduct, or after; either way, controlling a share in this major water transfer was clearly crucial to the operation of the mills.

The construction of the highest mill (BU0002; Fig. 3.35) took advantage of a natural bedrock spur, using the immediately available natural resource of the pillow basalt of the local landscape as its main construction material; this was also the material used for the two mills below it (BU0003, BU0004). As with the majority of watermills in the Karkotis valley, this one was built against a steep, terraced slope that helped to maximize the potential energy of the water power through the momentum it gained by the drop in height. Although its penstock is intact, the mill is cut by the road leading to Katydhata, which has destroyed most of its leat. On the opposite side of the road lie more cultivated fields with irrigation networks running through them, but no remains of the leat are now visible.

This mill is aligned south-west to north-east, and is the only one of the three to have a visible wheel chamber, although there is no sign of a wheel in situ. The last known owner was a landowner named Ahmed Agha who, according to local farmers, owned at least seven mills in this area, including BU0003 and BU0004.

The central mill of the three, BU0003, is located c. 300 downslope of BU0002, and has the longest surviving leat of the three, although in a ruinous state. The construction of this mill reflects a relative lack of geomorphological constraint compared to other mills in the TAESP landscape, as it was not built against any terraced slope. It may have relied on the momentum of the water flowing from BU0002, although this was unclear when we retraced the channel and irrigation network around the mills. It was constructed using roughly coursed masonry on bedrock, again using the locally available pillow basalt, which is overlaid with thin pinkish-white lime plaster. An arch springer was located on the lower side of the north face of the penstock, along with some very eroded and so indecipherable letters in Arabic script. The springer could have been a later addition to the mill, from the time of the mill's Ottoman or Turkish Cypriot ownership.

The last of this group of mills, BU0004, is situated another 230 m downstream from BU0003. The mill faces north-west, toward the Skouriotissa mines, and thus has a slightly unusual orientation in relation to the previous two mills. The use of the pink-toned plaster and the identical construction materials and building techniques suggest that these three mills all had a similar construction date.

Fig. 3.33. Katydhata Pamboulia *(TP102): threshing floors (Chris Parks)*

There is another mill on the east bank of the Karkotis River, 1.3 km west of the three pink-plaster mills and 400 m west of Katydhata village (BU0044; Fig. 3.36). Aligned from east to west, this mill is situated in an extensively terraced landscape consisting of old and new terracing. It is constructed of rubble in rough courses, with stone foundations and a soft very light pink, lime plaster finish, similar to that used in the construction of the previous three mills. An interesting point to note is that the foundations are made of limestone, a resource not available in the immediately surrounding landscape, rather than the pillow basalt used for BU0002–0004. The wooden wheel is in situ in the partially ruined wheelhouse beneath the mill.

This mill most likely dates to a later period than the three Linou mills, probably to the 18th century. According to local information, it was yet another of the seven belonging to Ahmed Agha. Its position near the other three watermills helped to create a network of mills supporting the surrounding grain fields of the Skouriotissa area, as well as those of Katydhata and Linou villages.

The modern irrigation channels surrounding the watermills in Linou and Katydhata showed signs of repeated repair and renovation using previously existing, older channel systems. This suggests a long history of irrigation routes (Volume 1, Chapter 3.12) as well as new and old terraced agriculture, with which the mills were always associated. This complex network of irrigation channels and terraced agriculture may, as previously suggested, account for the fact that the water supplied to the watermills was diverted and channelled from higher up the Karkotis River, rather than being fed directly by the river, as is the case with other watermills in the Karkotis valley.

The position of these four watermills is strategic in terms of the economic landscape (see also Volume 1, Chapter 3.12). They are situated between the wheat-producing areas

Fig. 3.34. 'Pink mills' between Linou and Katydhata: BU0002 and BU0003, with Skouriotissa mine in background (Chris Parks)

of the Atsas plains and the well-watered alluvial soils of the Karkotis Valley, where cereals have formed the basis of an agricultural economy since ancient times. The position of Katydhata, on a trade route between the cereal-producing lowlands and the highlands, also indicates the importance of the exchange of products and services; lowlanders, who did not have the available services of watermills to grind their grains, could take it to the watermills in the Upper Karkotis region. This basic need may have stimulated the general growth of trade and cooperation between various economic production zones of the highland and lowland areas. Their central location in the Karkotis landscape indicates that these watermills were also easily accessible by surrounding settled communities, such as Ayios Nikolaos, Ayios Yeoryios and Ayios Epiphanios.

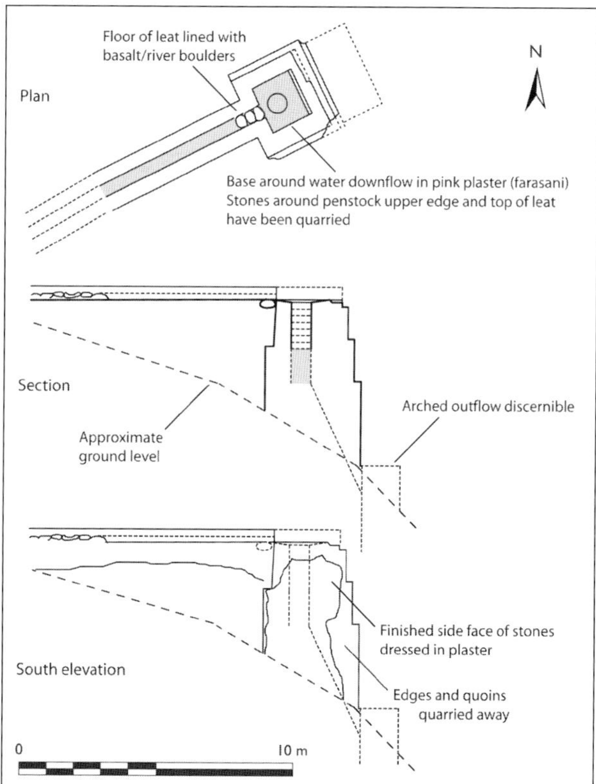

Fig. 3.35. Watermill at Linou Kapati *(BU0002): plan, section and elevation (Sevina Floridou, finalised by Luke Sollars)*

Conclusions

Katydhata has a distinctive location in a rich agricultural area, controlling movement between the upper valley and the coastal plain. These environmental factors are clearly crucial for understanding its unusual trajectory through the Medieval–Modern periods, but they by no means determine it. One of Katydhata's striking features is, in fact, the great variety of configurations in the same landscape. Unlike the other villages examined in the Karkotis Valley, the Katydhata area is rich in pottery from the Late Byzantine and Early Medieval periods, but not from the 14th and 15th centuries. It was clearly prominent in the Ottoman period, and played an important role in the 20th century mining operation at Skouriotissa. Today it lies on a dead-end road leading to the Green Line and, to a large extent, supplies weekend housing for villagers who have migrated to Nicosia.

The Medieval and Ottoman watermills clearly made Katydhata something of a local powerhouse, with villagers from the plains coming south to have their grain ground. Yet social and political factors often distorted what might seem to us to be the most efficient or cost-effective configuration. It is interesting that oral memory ascribes the complexity of the water distribution system not to the most functional or practical solution, but to the revenge of a jilted lover. The Katydhata landscape is an intricate network made up of personal, social, technical and environmental threads, which relate to each other in complex and ever-changing ways.

Fig. 3.36. Watermill at Katydhata Mylos *(BU0044): exterior (Chris Parks)*

3.11 Archaic Sanctuary and Roman Settlement at Katydhata *Pano Limna*

Pano Limna (TS15) was a substantial sanctuary during the Archaic period, perhaps with a small settlement immediately to its south-east, and then a rather larger settlement and cemetery during the Roman period. Apart from a newly bulldozed field at one edge and some looting of tombs and the sanctuary, it has been little disturbed, and sub-surface preservation seems to be excellent. It lies on the western edge of the Karkotis Valley opposite Katydhata (Plate 3.15; Fig. 3.37), exactly at the transition between the deep-soiled alluvial terraces of the valley floor and the thin-soiled basalt slopes. There are excellent views across the valley to Skouriotissa mine in the north-east and to Linou and Phlasou in the south-east (Fig. 3.38).

We addressed the wealth of material at Pano Limna with a wide range of methods, including topographical survey, intensive gridding and collecting, resistivity survey, soil depth mapping and contextual mapping and survey. Our first aim was to characterize the cult at the sanctuary and interpret its location in the wider landscape. Our second was to assess the role of the Roman settlement in the settlement hierarchy and production system of the area, particularly in relation to the massive copper smelting operation at Skouriotissa, just 1300 m to the north-east, on the far side of the Karkotis Valley.

A village called 'Limna' is recorded in this region on the Venetian village lists, with 13 *francomati* (free peasant farmers) in 1565 (Grivaud 1998, 468). It also appears on a series of 16th- and 17th-century maps (e.g. Stylianou and Stylianou 1980, 273, 295, 304). Despite these references and village memories of a settlement here, we found nothing of any significance belonging to the Medieval or post-Medieval period. It has no relation with the village of Limnitis, 7 km west of Soloi, where according to the 7th-century *Life of Saint Auxibios* the saint landed on his voyage from Rome (Gjerstad *et al.* 1937, 407–409; Noret 1993, lines 56–58).

The sanctuary we discovered at Pano Limna seems to be the one investigated by Max Ohnefalsch-Richter in 1882 (Myres and Ohnefalsch-Richter 1899, 4–5; Ohnefalsch-Richter 1893, 20–21, 218, 255, 351, pl. XVI; Reinach 1891, 185). He describes it as being near the 'villages of Katydhata-Linou', 8 km south-east of Karavostasi, which fits the location of Pano Limna exactly. His finds included groups of figures dancing round male or female flute players, fragments of a silver bowl with flowers in relief, and fragments of a silver *patera* with a battle of Greeks and Amazons.

Because the main part of the site was clearly cut into terraces, with distinct risers and treads, we decided to use organic POSI Units that respected these terraces (TP119). The terraces were numbered A to H consecutively, beginning from the base of the slope immediately above the modern road (Plate 3.16). According to the cadastral plan, our terrace B was the predecessor of the modern road. In each of the 87 squares, we counted all the pottery and tile, and collected a representative sample.

In the same area, resistivity survey was carried out over three 20-m grid squares, taking readings at 1 × 1 m intervals using a Geoscan RM15 resistivity meter. Grids 1 and 2 are discussed below. Grid 3, which was immediately west of TP252 in Plate 3.15, revealed only geological features. Context was provided by block survey in the fields immediately to the east (TS15) and by recording as POSIs several features such as soil sections (TP118; TP252) and tombs (TP129; TP197).

Environment and Geomorphology

Pano Limna (TS15) encompasses a narrow band of ancient fluvial terraces sandwiched between bare bedrock hillslope and the historic floodplain of the Karkotis River (Plate 3.16). These terraces represent the northernmost extant landforms of the Pleistocene courses of the Karkotis along the east-facing slope of a north-trending basalt ridge (GU1066; GU2115). This area is distinct, both because of the high densities of pottery present, and because of the exceptionally mixed characteristics of rock and soil on this geomorphological boundary. Where this boundary passes Pano Limna, by contrast, the contact between bedrock and

Fig. 3.37. Katydhata Pano Limna *(TS15), looking westwards across the valley from Katydhata (Chris Parks)*

Fig. 3.38. Katydhata Pano Limna *(TS15), looking south-east from the ridge above the site towards Katydhata and Linou (Chris Parks)*

fluvial sediments is stark. A thin (<10 cm) layer of gravely sandy loam colluvium covers bedrock with common, large (>50 m^2) areas of exposed bedrock.

The soil in the fluvial terraces ranges from sandy clay loam to loam, with substantial amounts of bedrock gravel in some areas, and the soil colour varies from 10YR 5/3 (brown) to 2.5Y 4/3 (olive brown). The soil depth is approximately 0.5 m. Elsewhere on the fluvial terraces soil texture is predominantly silt loam. The anomalous soil texture in the Pano Limna area must be due to importation, probably the result of decomposed mudbrick structures (see further below). Although mudbrick can be used for manuring, this has yet to be identified in the region, and thus it is more likely to be the remnants of an in situ settlement.

These hillslope terraces are unusual in that they have been cut down into the bedrock, and many of them have a comparatively thick soil cover, up to 35 cm, that is not supported by the discontinuous nature of soil cover on the pillow lavas; this can be seen on the contours in Plate 3.16. A number of factors indicate that these may be settlement terraces and house platforms, rather than agricultural terraces. It is uncommon for agricultural terraces to be cut all the way back to bedrock over the entire area of the tread. It is also apparent from the large size and good preservation of the sherds that the terraces have not been ploughed; ploughsoil pottery assemblages tend to be more homogenised and have mechanical abrasion. The large quantity of soil on these terraces is a dramatic anomaly in comparison with the surrounding exposed bedrock. Most likely the soil is almost entirely imported and results from the decomposition of mudbrick structures. There is a sharp transition between the soil-covered terraces and the bedrock slope along the contour.

On the lower part of this slope there are five fairly distinct terraces with a larger riser above them (3–6 m high), followed by further series of less distinct levels and terraces. The five well-defined terraces (A–E) slope down to the east and north. On average, the terrace treads are 6–7 m wide and the risers are 0.5–1.5 m high. Above these terraces are at least three other, less distinct terraces (F, G and H). There appears to be more soil in the north-east, on top of, and on the north slope of, a small and flattish spur that runs to the north-east, where POSI Units G9–G12 and R11–R12 have soil c. 30 cm deep. In the same area is a concentration of imported river-worn cobbles (ophiolite and limestone rocks); these are eroding down the slope and sprinkled over the entire site. This configuration indicates that some type of structure(s) existed in this area, perhaps corresponding to the sanctuary discussed below. Another area with thick deposits of soil lies at the south end of terrace G.

As a whole, there is still a substantial amount of soil on the terraces and slopes, indicating that the remains of structures and artefacts are largely in situ. Generally, the upper area of the slope is more stable than the lower area. There are, however, areas of sheetwash, rills and gullies that concentrate water flow within the site, moving soil and artefacts. The area most affected by sheetwash is probably to the north and, to a lesser extent, the east of the flattened spur area. Soil and artefacts that once were on this platform have moved downslope, c. 10 m maximum in the north, c. 1 m in the north-east and c. 5 m in the east. Another example of artefact movement is a small gully that collects water from upslope and cuts through F6, E6–8 before dropping onto D07, where it continues north along the rest of the tread of terrace D. In sum, some artefact movement can be expected downslope at Pano Limna.

Archaic–Classical Sanctuary and its Context (TP119)

The presence of some 250-figurine fragments demonstrates the presence of an Iron Age sanctuary, perhaps including a *bothros* or pit for the sacred disposal of offerings. Pano Limna lies on a low, but well-defined, east-facing spur, with a dramatic view directly across the valley to the Skouriotissa mine. The distribution map comparing Iron Age pottery and figurines shows a very clear correlation in the north-west part of the gridded area (Plate 3.17). In contrast to the terraces of the main settlement, this is a steep-sided spur flanked by a gully on its northern side (Fig. 3.39). It is exactly in this area that the soil map shows the thickest depths of soil, clearly imported, and a concentration of imported river cobbles.

We tested this correlation further using resistivity survey consisting of a 20-m grid square (Fig. 3.40, Grid 1). Ground conditions were very dry and the soil generally shallow, which meant that the overall dataset was very low, with a highest reading of 165 ohms. In the arid conditions of a Cypriot summer, these values are relatively good, but it means that the resistivity meter was operating at the extremes of its capabilities and caution should be exercised when interpreting the results. The bedrock was fairly close to the surface, and at various points there was no soil to make an electrical contact. In the bottom corner of the plot, a shelf of rock emerged above the soil; it can be seen as a white stripe across the bottom of the survey square.

There are two faint sub-circular anomalies in the data. The first is on the east of the plot and measures about 12 × 10 m, while the second is more oval and is c. 10 m across. These suggest a circular feature surrounded by an oval enclosure. There is little indication of any internal features, although a linear anomaly runs diagonally across the smaller anomaly. Based on the nature of the anomalies, the two features indicated may be negative ones, where a ditch is the surviving feature. As the data are in a tight range and uniformly of a low resistance it is, however, possible that the anomalies represent stone features, which are less resistant to the current than the surrounding material.

Because of their association with a dense scatter of Archaic–Classical figurines (see below), these features may be interpreted as two overlapping temenos walls, possibly from consecutive periods. This hypothesis is further strengthened by apparent similarities to the cult centre at Ayia Irini and the sanctuary of Anat-Aphrodite in Idalion (Gjerstad *et al.* 1935, 821). Both consist of open temenoi with encircling walls and central altars, and date from the Cypro-Geometric period (CG) onwards (1935, 462, 527). The oval temenos at Ayia Irini is particularly comparable in both size and composition, consisting of an earthen wall enclosing a roughly oval, open area measuring 11.5 × 7.9 m (1935, 671). The sanctuary at Khalospitia (TP215) in the Atsas valley, 4.5 km to the east (Chapter 2.4), has what seem to be the remains of a temenos wall showing above the surface. These remains are more or less rectangular and, at 19 × 12 m, slightly larger than the anomalies at Pano

Fig. 3.39. Katydhata Pano Limna *(TP119): view of sanctuary area from the north (Chris Parks)*

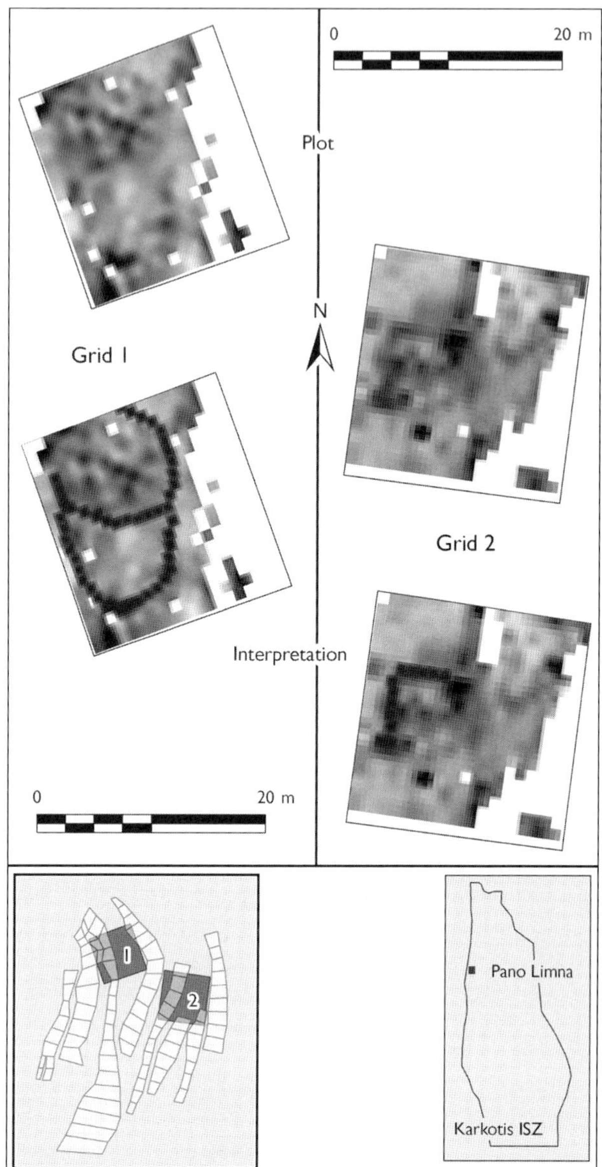

Fig. 3.40. Katydhata Pano Limna *(TP119): resistivity survey. Grid 1: sanctuary. Grid 2: possible Roman structures (Iain Banks, finalised by Luke Sollars)*

Limna. Small, but noticeable, developments in temenos architecture were made during CG III at both Ayia Irini and Idalion, including heightened walls, a raised floor and new altar at Ayia Irini (Gjerstad *et al.* 1935, 671, 822), and rebuilding at Idalion (1935, 529). These developments may parallel the perceived shift in position of the features under discussion at Pano Limna.

The distribution map shows that a few figurines have clearly drifted down the slope as a result of the sheetwash observed in the northern part of the area (Plate 3.17). Sherd densities ranging up to 10 per 100 m^2, even some 50 m east of the main concentration, suggest that the activities indicated by sherd debris were more widely spread, perhaps consisting of houses, workshops or temporary structures that grew up around the sanctuary. There is evidence of industrial and storage activities, for example, around the contemporary sanctuary and *bothros* of Peristeries on the eastern edge of Marion (Smith 1997, 90–91).

The figurines recovered are highly characteristic of survey finds: they are all fragmentary, many are highly eroded, and almost 30% of them cannot be precisely identified. Most of the fragments are from handmade anthropomorphic figures, although some mouldmade pieces are represented by figurines and plaques of a late Archaic–Classical date. All are terracotta except for one small limestone piece that was noted north of the gully, on the north side of the sanctuary. All pieces were worn and showed some lichen growth. Most figurines had a ferrous, well-levigated fabric; a few were softer and more mixed or calcareous. The fragments of larger figures were generally more hard-fired and a few had bright grey cores. The surfaces were mostly unfinished, and only one showed possible red paint.

The majority of identifiable fragments are from small ring dancer groups (see Volume 1, Chapter 3.7 for catalogue and illustrations). These include ring bases (flattened and semicircular in section, and ranging from 9–13 cm in diameter; e.g. TCS029), tubular bodies with bottoms shaped to fit on ring bases (e.g. TCS018), and sets of arms with clasped hands (e.g. TCS038, TCS036). Also represented are fragments of flat-bottomed, freestanding tubular figurines (e.g. TCS009) and flat, strap-like torsos and body fragments (e.g. TCS012). A significant quantity of detached limbs was recovered, almost half of which are arms. Larger figurines (ranging from an estimated 60–120 cm tall) are represented by fragments of hollow statues and by leaning figurines, none of which can be identified as a specific subject or figure type (e.g. hand: TCS013; fragment: TCS037).

The collection includes a single fragment from a zoomorphic figurine, consisting of a horse's head (TCS034). There are no clear examples of riders or chariot groups, although some of the unidentifiable fragments and small body parts, including a variety of small heads, may have come from this type of figurine (e.g. TCS022,

TCS010). At least two small rectangular plaques were found with mould-impressed figures in profile, probably Classical as opposed to Archaic (TCS011, TCS044). The figures face to their right and have their left arms holding something in front of them. A unique form of plaque figurine was found with a frontal, female torso preserved (TCS043).

The range of terracotta figures represented at Pano Limna is consistent with other Archaic–Classical sanctuaries across the island. The combination of small, tubular and strap-shaped figurines, and large, leaning and hollow statues is particularly reminiscent of Ayia Irini (Gjerstad *et al.* 1935, 642–824), Tamassos *Frangissa* (Buchholz 1991) and the sanctuary of Apollo Hylates at Kourion (Buitron-Oliver 1996; Young and Young 1955). Smaller figures predominate, but this may be because any larger statues lying on the surface are more likely to have been removed. Similarly, chariot and rider figurines, which are a major component at the above sites, are noticeably absent from the material recovered at Pano Limna. Only further investigation, particularly excavation, can determine whether these survey-based observations actually reflect the absence of such material at this site.

The quantity of ring dancer figurines suggests that the cult would have been similar to that of Apollo Hylates at Kourion (Soren 1987, 35). Much of the material recovered from Pano Limna has parallels in the material from that site (Buitron-Oliver 1996; Young and Young 1955). It may be that the figurines derive from a disturbed *bothros*, a pit where temple offerings are ritually buried. Further investigation would be beneficial to establish the nature of the geophysical anomalies and to collect more information on the nature of the cult activities and affiliations of this rural sanctuary.

There was comparatively little Archaic–Classical pottery recovered from the area of greatest figurine density (Table 3.13). Diagnostic material was limited to a single strap handle of Cypriot White-Painted Ware with typical black paint along the length of it. One black-slipped and two small red-slipped fragments found in the survey were so worn that they could only be assigned to the Geometric–Archaic periods generally. There was also a small number of Wheelmade Plain White Ware sherds (assigned to 'Historical Antiquity' because of the lack of diagnostic features) that could well be Archaic–Classical. The rest of the gridding, beyond the immediate area of the sanctuary, had rather more in the way of identifiable Iron Age pottery: two Black-on-Red fragments; five fragments of White-Painted Ware; one piece of a coarse ware basin (Persian Bowl); and one red slip sherd of general Geometric–Archaic date.

In addition to gridding and mapping in the area of the terraces and sanctuary, we also carried out block survey across the road to the east, in order to provide a broader context – both archaeological and geomorphological. This work contributed a more complete range of Archaic–Classical pottery (Table 3.14), including White Painted Ware, Heavy Utility, Black-on-Red and Bichrome of both large and small vessels. Most of the Iron Age pottery collected during block survey came from the southern end of the area (SU2132–38). These Survey Units were carried out in a large, triangular field located at the confluence of two shallow gullies. The pottery concentration at the confluence of the gullies raises the possibility that Iron Age activities may not have been restricted to the sanctuary area. A wider spectrum of Iron Age vessel types (including amphorae) and functions (Table Ware and utility wares) was represented in this assemblage, but there was only one Archaic–Classical figurine.

Three Survey Units on the hillslope just north and north-east of the sanctuary (SU2125–27) contained much smaller amounts of utility Iron Age pottery, as well as three Archaic–Classical figurines, presumably originating from the sanctuary. Transect survey heading eastwards across the valley showed that the density of pottery fell significantly as one moved east of Pano Limna toward the Karkotis River.

Roman Settlement and its Context (TP118; TP119; TP252)

A range of evidence points to a substantial Roman settlement in the same area as the Archaic–Classical sanctuary, although extending much further to the south and west. As well as trying to establish its size, date and character, analysis focused on the possible relationship of such a settlement to the massive Late Roman copper production site at Skouriotissa.

The clearest evidence for a settlement could be seen in the uncultivated ground immediately south of the Iron Age sanctuary, where a series of what appeared to be house terraces coincided with a significant density of Roman pottery. In this area, we carried out resistivity survey in two, 20-m grid squares. In both cases there were outcrops of bedrock that reduced the amount of ground available for geophysical investigation.

Only one grid-square appeared to have the potential for indicating traces of a settlement (Fig. 3.40, c–d). At the top of this plot were two straight anomalies of higher resistance. These might indicate the presence of two walls of an otherwise destroyed structure. The anomaly running parallel with the top of the grid measured c. 7 m in length, the other c. 6 m in length. The dataset was even tighter than for the sanctuary, with a range of around 40 ohms, excluding spikes. The linear anomalies, however, were significantly different to the adjacent readings. Furthermore, as might be expected of destroyed buildings, the ends of the linear anomalies appeared to be in spreads of higher resistance, which might represent rubble at the ends of walls. There may well have been a rectangular building at this location, with just the traces of two walls left below the surface after its destruction. It is difficult to see a natural explanation for the anomalies.

The other resistivity grid was less productive, with a stripe of disturbance probably due to geological features,

Table 3.13. Katydhata Pano Limna *(TS15): pottery from TP119, TP129, TP252. TCP numbers refer to Pottery Catalogue in Volume 1, Chapter 3.6*

Bronze Age

Fct	*Type*	*No.*	*Weight*
LU	LU	1	2g

Prehistoric Bronze Age

Fct	*Type*	*No.*	*Weight*
HU	RPC	1	39g
LU	RPO	1	5g

Cypro-Geometric to Classical

Fct	*Type*	*No.*	Weight
HU	BOR	1	6g
HU	CAmS	3	468g
HU	HU	1	28g
HU	Per	6	386g TCP630, TCP632
HU	Pit12	2	665g TCP624
HU	WP	1	35g
LU	BOR	2	58g
LU	BORC	1	8g
LU	BS	2	49g
LU	LU	7	42g
LU	RS	3	11g
LU	WP	3	95g
Tr	CAm	3	487g
Tr	EGAm	3	153g TCP635
TW	BORO	1	5g TCP638
TW	RS	2	11g

Historical Antiquity (Archaic to Late Roman)

Fct	*Type*	*No.*	*Weight*
Ar	Brk	1	150g
Ar	Ti	30	5.898kg TCP625, TCP640
Ar	TiC	2	95g
Ar	TiP	6	865g
HU	HU	175	10.937kg
HU	HUB03	1	660g TCP627
HU	HUR26	1	105g TCP642
LU	LU	164	1.607kg
Tr	Am	2	255g
TW	TW	5	38g

Hellenistic to Roman

Fct	*Type*	*No.*	*Weight*
CW	CW	4	27g
CW	CWPR09	1	4g TCP637
La	La	1	5g
TW	RS	2	7g
TW	SRS	3	16g

Late Hellenistic to Early Roman

Fct	*Type*	*No.*	*Weight*
TW	CC	1	2g TCP633
TW	ESA	6	9g
TW	ESA04A	1	4g
TW	RS	1	3g
TW	Sig	2	7g
TW	Sig01	1	2g

Early Roman

Fct	*Type*	*No.*	*Weight*
La	La01	3	6g TCP626
TW	CS12	2	11g
TW	SigW	1	3g

Early to Late Roman

Fct	*Type*	*No.*	*Weight*
Ar	Ti	29	5.495kg
Ar	TiC	1	65g
Ar	TiCA	14	1.224kg TCP628
Ar	TiCS	2	345g
Ar	TiP	25	5.638kg
CW	CW	34	173g
LU	LUR01	1	82g TCP631
Tr	AmSk01	1	28g TCP639
TW	ARS	2	11g

Late Roman

Fct	Type	No.	Weight
Ar	Ti	1	190g
Ar	TiP	7	1.135kg
Ar	TiSk01	10	1.665kg
Ar	TiSk02	1	295g
Ar	TiSk05	1	225g
Ar	TiSkC01	7	610g
Ar	TiSkC02	1	70g
Ar	TiSkC03	3	500g TCP641
Ar	TiSkC04	5	468g TCP634
CW	CW	1	1g
HU	HU	4	327g
HU	HUR01A	1	31g TCP629
LU	LU	2	16g
Tr	Am	1	25g
Tr	LR1	4	175g
TW	CRS	4	63g
TW	CRS09	1	8g

Roman to Modern

Fct	*Type*	*No.*	*Weight*
Ar	Ti	12	678g
LU	LU	1	9g

Historical (Archaic to Modern)

Fct	*Type*	*No.*	*Weight*
HU	HU	78	5.08kg
HU	HUR25	1	48g TCP636
LU	LU	152	1.078kg

Medieval to Modern

Fct	*Type*	*No.*	*Weight*
Ar	Brk	1	112g
CW	BGW	1	4g

Byzantine to Medieval

Fct	*Type*	*No.*	*Weight*
TW	CGS01	1	90g

Ottoman to Modern I

Fct	*Type*	*No.*	*Weight*
TW	G03	1	16g

Medieval-Venetian to Early Ottoman

Fct	*Type*	*No.*	*Weight*
TW	G05	1	3g

Modern

Fct	*Type*	*No.*	*Weight*
HU	HU	3	136g
LU	LU	1	5g

Unknown

Fct	*Type*	*No.*	*Weight*
HU	HU	3	147g
U	Un	2	11g
Un	Un	1	35g

Table 3.14. Katydhata Pano Limna *(TS15): pottery from SU1082–84 and SU2124–41. TCP numbers refer to Pottery Catalogue in Volume 1, Chapter 3.6*

Bronze Age

Fct	Type	No.	Weight
TW	RS	1	25g
			TCP354

Prehistoric Bronze Age

Fct	Type	No.	Weight
HU	RPOL	1	24g
LU	RP	2	17g

Late Bronze Age to Archaic

Fct	Type	No.	Weight
HU	HU	3	177g
HU	Pit19	2	270g
			TCP343
HU	Pit20	1	140g
			TCP344

Cypro-Geometric to Archaic

Fct	Type	No.	Weight
HU	HU	1	105g
LU	LU	6	100g
			TCP363, TCP364

Cypro-Geometric to Classical

Fct	Type	No.	Weight
HU	BOR	3	225g
			TCP348, TCP358
HU	CamS	2	190g
HU	HU	1	32g
HU	Per	1	62g
HU	Pit12	1	230g
HU	Sh	2	365g
			TCP361
HU	WPC	3	175g
			TCP350, TCP359
LU	Bc	1	65g
			TCP360
LU	BOR	1	30g
			TCP351
LU	LU	4	45g
LU	LUR16	1	2g
LU	LUR17	1	5g
LU	RS	2	10g
LU	WP	4	80g
LU	WPC	4	140g
			TCP362
Tr	CAm	7	1.74kg
TW	TW	1	20g
			TCP367

Historical Antiquity (Archaic to Late Roman)

Fct	Type	No.	Weight
Ar	Ti	5	1.018kg
Ar	TiCS	2	125g
Ar	TiP	4	480g
HU	HU	203	13.324kg
HU	Pit21	1	190g
			TCP370
LU	LU	134	2.713kg
Tr	Am	4	467g
TW	BS	1	20g
TW	RS	1	8g
TW	TW	6	40g
			TCP355
Un	Un	1	120g

Classical to Hellenistic

Fct	Type	No.	Weight
TW	BG	1	5g

Hellenistic

Fct	Type	No.	Weight
PO	Ug	1	2g
PO	Ug01	1	30g
			TCP346
Tr	Rho	1	117g
			TCP347
TW	BS	3	10g
TW	FP	1	10g
			TCP353

Hellenistic to Roman

Fct	Type	No.	Weight
CW	CW	29	305g
CW	CWFPWh	1	20g
			TCP369
CW	CWPR02	3	18g
HU	HUR24	1	80g
LU	LUR08	1	4g
Tr	Am	2	170g
Tr	Am07	5	107g
Tr	Mav01	1	160g
			TCP356
TW	SRS	11	132g

Late Hellenistic to Early Roman

Fct	Type	No.	Weight
TW	CS18A	1	5g
TW	ESA	4	10g
TW	Sig	10	60g

Early Roman

Fct	Type	No.	Weight
TW	CS12	2	29g
TW	ESA48	1	10g
			TCP349
TW	SigW	1	5g
			TCP345

Early to Late Roman

Fct	Type	No.	Weight
Ar	Ti	30	5.693kg
Ar	TiCS	1	85g
Ar	TiP	13	3.285kg
CW	CW	21	138g
CW	CWFPWh	2	14g
HU	HUR01	1	34g
HU	HUR03	1	70g
LU	LU	1	13g
Tr	AmSk01	3	92g
Tr	AmSk02	1	70g
			TCP357
TW	ARS	2	7g
TW	RS	1	22g

Late Roman

Fct	Type	No.	Weight
Ar	Ti	3	475g
Ar	TiC	1	90g
Ar	TiP	62	7.936kg
Ar	TiSk02	1	310g
Ar	TiSk03	1	415g
Ar	TiSkC01	2	115g
Ar	TiSkC03	2	215g
HU	HU	2	90g
HU	HUR21	1	16g
HU	Pit01	1	245g
HU	Pit22	3	725g
			TCP371
LU	LUB03	1	40g
			TCP352
Tr	Am	4	210g
Tr	LR1	8	438g
Tr	Pal	1	19g
			TCP365
TW	CRS	8	180g
TW	CRS01	1	11g
TW	CRS02	3	26g
TW	CRS09	3	62g
TW	CRS11	1	18g
TW	LRC	1	4g
TW	LRC03	2	17g

Roman to Modern

Fct	Type	No.	Weight
HU	HU	1	665g

Historical (Archaic to Modern)

Fct	Type	No.	Weight

HU	HU	114	8.116kg
LU	LU	85	1.691kg
TW	TW	1	2g
Un	Un	1	140g

Medieval utility period I

Fct	*Type*	*No.*	*Weight*
U	UAA98	3	105g

Medieval to Modern

Fct	*Type*	*No.*	*Weight*
CW	Tta	1	16g
HU	HU	3	142g
LU	LU	5	177g
U	BuHK	3	196g
U	BuLK	45	1.199kg
U	ID	1	14g

U	ID04A	1	45g
U	UL02	2	146g
U	UPSJu	1	11g

Byzantine to Medieval

Fct	*Type*	*No.*	*Weight*
TW	GS02	2	52g
		TCP366, TCP368	

Ottoman

Fct	*Type*	*No.*	*Weight*
TW	G03	2	24g

Ottoman to Modern I

Fct	*Type*	*No.*	*Weight*
TW	G02	1	6g
TW	MP02	1	8g

Medieval-Venetian to Early Ottoman

Fct	*Type*	*No.*	*Weight*
TW	MP01	2	24g

Ottoman to Modern II

Fct	*Type*	*No.*	*Weight*
HU	BuH	9	405g
LU	BuL	28	413g

Modern

Fct	*Type*	*No.*	*Weight*
Ar	TiCh	3	130g
LU	G	2	11g

Unknown

Fct	*Type*	*No.*	*Weight*
HU	HU	2	88g
LU	LU	1	28g

and so is not illustrated here. It is unlikely that there are any settlement traces in this area.

The Hellenistic–Roman pottery from the collection grid over the area of the terraces shows much greater densities than the Iron Age material, as well as a wider spread across the area (Plate 3.17). There are two main peaks, in both cases with densities up to 30 sherds/100 m^2: (1) the area of the sanctuary; and (2) the broader terraces on the south-east. The densities around the sanctuary suggest some sort of re-use or continuing use. Rural Roman sanctuaries in Cyprus are difficult to identify, as there are no objects specifically related to them, so this re-use might have been domestic. Even in the major sanctuaries Roman terracotta figurines and miniature altars are rare (Maier 2000, 502). The best argument for the presence of a sanctuary during the Roman period is the tendency for cult continuity (e.g. at Palaepaphos and Apollo Hylates; see Maier 2000 and Soren 1987). Since very little soil has eroded from this area, those who lived here in Roman times could not have been ignorant of the existence of an old sanctuary at the site.

Four out of a total of the 29 Hellenistic–Roman lamps found in the entire Survey Area came from this collection grid, suggesting that post-depositional processes have been less destructive here. The assemblage is well rounded, with all functional categories represented. It contains, however, a high proportion of residual material (37 Iron Age sherds, 13 Late Hellenistic–Early Roman sherds, 73 Roman sherds and 24 Late Roman sherds), which obscures patterns in the composition.

Approximately 50 m to the south of the terraced area was a section some 25 m long, cut recently by a bulldozer as part of a newly levelled olive grove. Most of the western part of this field is cut out of bedrock, hence the almost total lack of archaeological material in it, but the wall of

Fig. 3.41. Katydhata Pano Limna *(TP252): exposed wall from Roman-period structure (Chris Parks)*

a structure was exposed in the section (Fig. 3.41; TP252). The main layers visible in the section consist of: topsoil; 30–40 cm of slope wash, with Roman pottery eroding out of it; melted mudbrick; and a two-course rubble foundation wall. The section also shows two infilled channels: one a rill, the other a c. 0.8 × 3 m channel, with accretionery pebble beds and finer grained beds.

Of the 159 sherds collected from this section, most identifiable pieces were Late Hellenistic–Early Roman (5), Roman (24) and Late Roman (25) in date. Only two pieces were of Iron Age date, and one of these was in the topsoil. It seems most likely that this wall represents part of a structure from the Roman-period settlement. The relatively high number of Table Wares and the almost complete absence of Cooking Wares suggest that the pottery is redeposited refuse, probably from the settlement.

The distribution map of Hellenistic–Roman pottery from the block survey to the east of the terraces (Plate 3.18) shows a much greater density and wider spread than that of the Iron Age. The whole area shows a carpet of pottery on both sides of the river, up to c. 7 sherds/100 m^2. There is a very clear peak at Pano Limna in the terraces on the east side of the road, with six Survey Units having between 7 and 28 sherds/100 m^2, and one having the substantial number of 48 sherds/100 m^2. This dense area stretches for some 150 m, north to south, and is notably denser than that surrounding Katydhata village.

Most of the diagnostic pottery from the block survey belongs to the Roman and Late Roman periods, which is consistent with the pottery from the terraces (Table 3.13; Table 3.14). Close ties with the Skouriotissa mine are suggested by the appearance of the same types of tile in both areas and fragments of amphorae from the Skouriotissa dump (TP171; see Chapter 3.12). On the whole, however, the block survey revealed a wider time-range of pottery (i.e. significant sherd densities from the Iron Age and Hellenistic–Roman periods) than the evidence from the occupational terraces initially suggested. Thus, the extant Late Roman settlement may represent the latest occupation of an area that had been settled, more or less continuously, since the Iron Age. The huge concentrations of tiles confirm that Pano Limna was a locus of significant settlement activity. The low to moderate densities of pottery dating to the Ottoman through Modern periods found across TS15 is fairly typical of amounts found elsewhere in the Karkotis Valley Intensive Survey Zone and probably represents the historical and current agricultural use of the terraces.

Pano Limna produced the second highest number of imported Eastern Sigillata A fragments in the Karkotis Valley Intensive Survey Zone. Its high proportions here (in comparison to other types of imported sigillata and Cypriot Sigillata) provoke two possible explanations. Either, the settlement at Pano Limna should be dated to the earlier part of the Roman period (c. 1st century BC), or, the introduction of Cypriot Sigillata in the Survey Area occurred at a very slow pace, as is also seen in eastern Cyprus (Lund 2006b, 37). Overall, the high proportions of Eastern Sigillata A and lamp fragments suggest that washed-out tomb material has mixed in with material on the occupational terraces.

The samples of chipped and ground stone collected from Pano Limna are relatively small and non-diagnostic. No lithics were recovered from the tombs or the exposed stretch of wall. The gridded collection over the sanctuary and settlement produced a jasper blank fragment and a 15 cm long, flat pebble that was used successively as pounder and grinder (TCL418). The grinder comes from the south-eastern part of the sample, in the centre of the heaviest concentration of Roman pottery. The Survey Units to the east and south-east of Pano Limna produced a more substantial sample of chipped stone, including two cores and a core trimming element, one flake, a flake fragment and two chunks, all of them made on local jasper or chalcedony. Overall, these samples generally fit with the background scatters of lithics found across the Survey Area at localities exhibiting prominent concentrations of Roman pottery, thus reinforcing the idea that during the Roman period there was an *ad hoc* industry employing sharp cutting edges.

The evidence given by the artefact scatter for a substantial settlement is complemented by the soil data. The soil texture of GU1066 in particular (i.e. the field lying between the road and TP118 in Plate 3.18) contains more clay than would be expected at this position in the landscape. Coupled with the variability of soil colour along the terrace, this suggests that the soil has been modified by imported material, particularly mudbrick that has dissolved over time. The exposed Roman-period wall (TP252) and a stratigraphic section visible in the riser at the eastern edge of GU1066 (TP118), both show layers of melted mudbrick, including pottery sherds. In addition, the two Survey Units conducted in GU1066 (SU1082–83) produced a complete assemblage of functional pottery types (Table Wares and utility wares). These points suggest a minimum extent of 500 m for the settlement, running from the terraces south-east past the wall at TP252 to the section at TP118. By local standards this is a substantial settlement. It clearly had close relations with the nearby contemporaneous copper production operation at Skouriotissa, which it could have supported by much larger scale agricultural production than the farmsteads of the Atsas valley (Chapter 2.3).

A further component of the Roman-period settlement at Pano Limna consists of a series of 13 collapsed and/or robbed tombs (Fig. 3.42). Twelve of them lie across a gully to the south of the house terraces (TP129), with another example just north of the terraces (TP197). All of the tombs are cut into bedrock covered with a layer of colluvium, and lie on an anthropogenic terrace between the western ridgeline and the road to the east. In terms of their surviving morphology, the tombs range from depressions overgrown with vegetation, to collapsed dromoi attached to multiple collapsed chambers, to collapsed dromoi connected to intact chambers that have mostly filled in with soil and chunks of bedrock. Most of the tombs have overgrown spoil heaps immediately adjacent, presumably the result of looting. Many of the spoil heaps include cobbles and small boulders, which may have been used to seal the tombs.

All except three of the tombs had associated pottery in their spoil heaps or interiors, generally with fewer than ten sherds each, though one example (TP129.PU07) had 53 sherds. Most of the diagnostic pieces were Late Roman, a period during which tombs tended to have very little pottery, so it is possible that this pottery came from the adjacent settlement. Two fragments of Iron Age Heavy Utility vessels and a Red Polished fragment from the Prehistoric Bronze Age were collected from PU02. Based on the pottery from the tombs themselves, then, a date is uncertain. On the other hand, their orientation, which is almost exclusively in a north–south line, could have followed an ancient road, as was common practice in the Roman period.

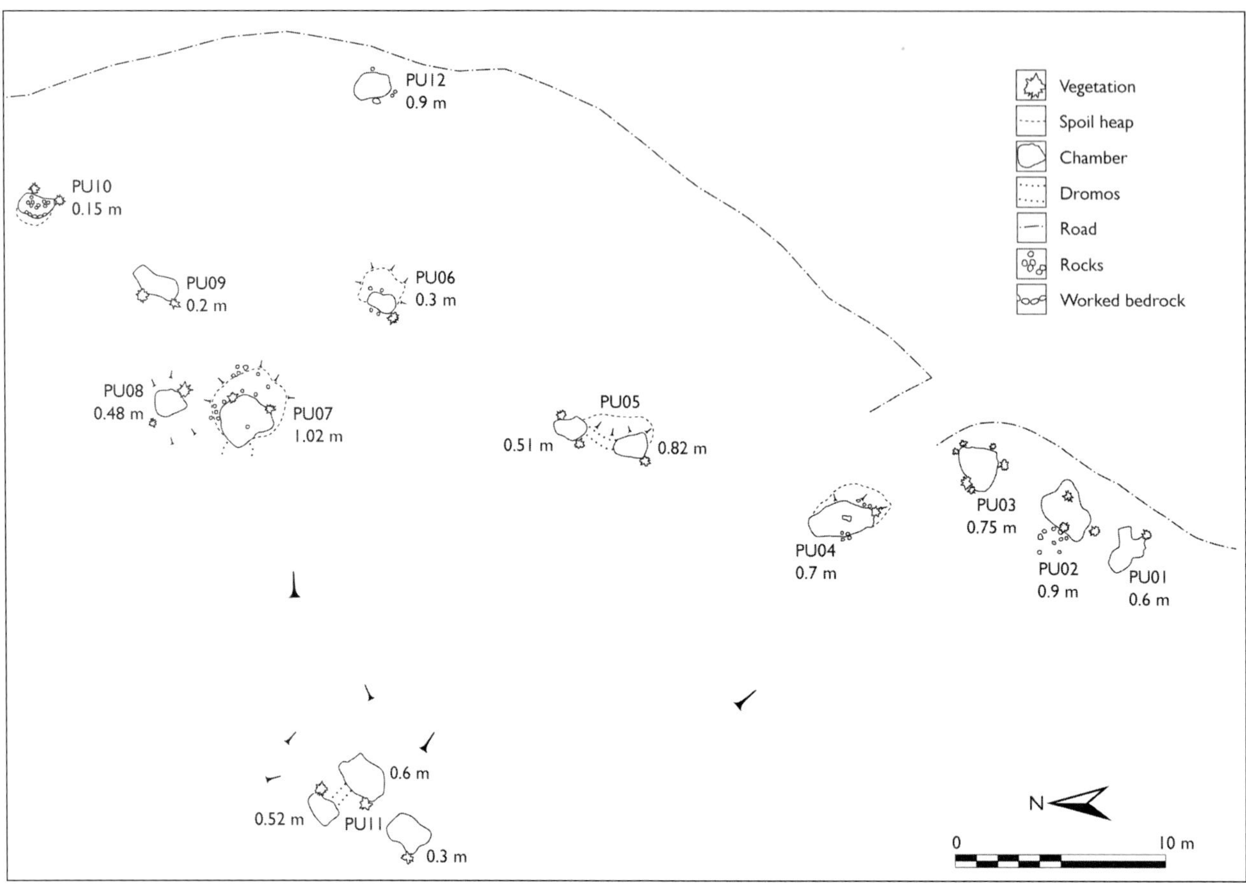

Fig. 3.42. Katydhata Pano Limna *(TP129): plan of tombs. Figures refer to depth (Rebekah Merriman, finalised by Jean Humbert)*

Conclusions

The pottery seems to suggest as many as three phases of occupation at Pano Limna. During the Archaic period, the number of terracotta figurines clearly points to a sanctuary, probably associated with some type of settlement. The cult of the sanctuary is clearly similar to that of Apollo Hylates at Kourion, with ring dancing and the veneration of new life as expressed in trees and vegetation. There is a similar sanctuary at Khalospitia 4 km to the east, on the far side of Skouriotissa mine and visually dominated by it in a similar way. Judging by its adjacent cemetery, Khalospitia also had an associated settlement (Chapter 2.4).

During the Late Hellenistic to Early Roman period, there appears to have been a settlement in this area, but it is possible that some of the pottery derives from looted or washed-out tombs. Since utility wares of the Late Hellenistic to Early Roman period are rarely recognized in the Survey Area, and the tiles appear to be indistinguishable from later periods, it is very difficult to postively identify Late Hellenistic to Early Roman settlements in the Survey Area.

Significant occupation of the area during the Late Roman period is unequivocal. Although Late Roman funerary customs in Cyprus suggest that the pottery associated with the tombs is unlikely to have come from them, the tombs may still have been re-used during this period. The settlement was closely linked to the contemporary copper production at Skouriotissa, 1.3 km to the north-east, and presumably to the other settlements and estates spread across this part of the Karkotis Valley and beyond. This network is very clear from the tile and amphora types, so common in these settlements (Volume 1, Chapters 3.3, 5.3).

3.12 Ancient and Modern Copper Production at Skouriotissa *Vouppes*

Skouriotissa (TS01) is one of the largest copper ore deposits of the island, and the only mine still operating today (Fig. 3.43). Furthermore, it is the location of the largest slag heap recorded on the island, which gives the locality its name. *Skoria* or *skouria* is the Greek word for slag, and in the vicinity of the ancient slag heap there is a church, once part of a monastery (see below), dedicated to the Virgin Mary of the slag (Panagia Skouriotissa). The slag heap appears in early photographs taken by the Cyprus Mines Corporation, the American company that first owned a mining lease for the modern exploitation of the ore deposit (Fig. 3.44).

The slag heap was estimated to contain two million tons of copper slag, and in the 1920s it covered an area of about 800 m in length, 30–90 m in width and 20 m in height (Lavender 1962, 63). Although much of the slag has

Fig. 3.43. Skouriotissa mine from the hilltop church of Prophitis Elias, looking north, with the village of Linou in the foreground (Michael Given)

Fig. 3.44. Skouriotissa slag heap (Bruce et al. *1937, 640, fig. 326)*

since been quarried away for use as road metal, the heap is still impressive. This, together with the fact that the mine of Skouriotissa may be the only one that is specifically mentioned in the ancient sources (see below), led to the decision by the Department of Antiquities of Cyprus to declare it an ancient monument in 1991. This also meant that from the very beginning of academic interest in the production of Cypriot copper in antiquity, the Skouriotissa mine and heap have been visited by virtually every archaeometallurgist who has ever worked on the island, many of whom sampled and analysed the slag.

Analyses of slag samples from Skouriotissa were published as early as 1861 by Terreil (Davies 1928–30, 75, note 1), and then by Cullis and Edge (1922). Charles Godfrey Gunther, the prospector hired to investigate the possibility of copper mining in Cyprus, visited Skouriotissa in 1912 and was the first to identify and interpret the remains of the ancient copper industry, from both the mining and the smelting stages of production that he observed there. His descriptions, recounted in Lavender's book (1962, 66–77), are invaluable and offer critical information regarding some of the features recorded by TAESP and discussed below. His efforts eventually led to the formation of the Cyprus Copper Mines Corporation (CMC), the American company that had the lease to exploit Skouriotissa until the Turkish invasion of 1974, after which their operations there ceased. Bruce, the resident director of CMC, published a paper on the ancient artefacts and remains uncovered in the mines operated by his company (Bruce *et al.* 1937, 643). Even today his paper remains the best and most complete publication on the remnants of the island's ancient mines.

The mines and slag heaps were also visited and sampled by Koucky and Steinberg (1974, 1982), who tried to create a typology of Cypriot slags for use in the field (1982, 117). Zwicker together with his colleagues also sampled and analysed a number of samples from Skouriotissa (Zwicker *et al.* 1972, 40). More importantly, in his effort to estimate the scale of copper production in Cyprus during different archaeological periods, Zwicker (1986, 96) collected charcoal and mining timbers from various locations, in order to radiocarbon date them. Among them were three mining timbers from the mine of Skouriotissa and three charcoal samples from the slag heaps (Zwicker 1986, 102–103).

The ore deposit and slag heap of Skouriotissa are often mentioned in the publications by the Oxford group on Lead Isotope Analysis. Skouriotissa, together with the mines of Mavrovouni and Apliki, forms the so-called Solea axis ore deposits (Stos-Gale *et al.* 1997, 98) which is credited with being the source of copper for almost all copper oxhide ingots in the Mediterranean and even as far as Germany dating from the 13th century BC onwards (Gale and Stos-Gale 1999, 272–73). Furthermore, Gale and Stos-Gale (1986, 89) mention four fragments of an oxhide ingot (Inv. Number 1976-I-20/7a–7d), stored in the Cyprus Museum, that were said to be from Skouriotissa together with fragments of crucibles and tuyères. In another paper, they state that there are at least seven fragments from Skouriotissa (Stos-Gale *et al.* 1997, 107).

A wider study of oxhide ingot fragments from Cyprus (Kassianidou 2009) showed that these fragments most probably formed part of the well-known Mathiatis hoard, which was accidentally discovered during operations of CMC at the mine of Mathiatis South and which came into the possession of the owner of the company Harvey Mudd (Catling 1964, 283). Bruce (1937, 641) published a photograph of the ingot fragments said to be from Mathiatis, and which Catling identified as the fragments exported by Mudd (Catling 1964, 283). A closer look at this photograph revealed that six of the seven fragments thought to be from Skouriotissa are included in this photograph. Thus, at least six of the seven ingot fragments are, in fact, not from Skouriotissa, but instead, form part of the Mathiatis hoard.

The overall impression one gets is that ancient activities at Skouriotissa were well recorded by previous scholars. This, however, is not the case. As noted in the past (Kassianidou 2004, 95), all previously published archaeometallurgical studies, such as the ones listed above, rarely give information on the provenance of analyzed samples within a slag heap, which is a stratified deposit built over several decades, if not centuries. For the Sydney Cyprus Survey Project we designed a systematic methodology for recording slag heaps (Kassianidou 2003a, 44–46; 2004, 96–99). Skouriotissa's large size, however, demanded a different approach, and the methodology applied was slightly modified and improved in order to be able to record the remains in the best possible way (Volume 1, Chapter 2.12).

The following section first discusses what is known about the ancient mines of Skouriotissa, and then discusses a large deposit of amphorae fragments (TP171). This is followed by a discussion of the mine itself and the different parts of the slag heap (TP007) that we systematically recorded. To conclude, all the information gathered is used to form a comprehensive picture of what we know about copper production in this, perhaps the most important of all Cypriot mines.

Skouriotissa in the Ancient Sources

The mine of Skouriotissa may be the only mine specifically mentioned in ancient sources. A fragmentary text attributed to Pseudo-Aristotle contains the following passage:

> Boukasa is a mountain with gold mines and is situated at the foot of the Troodos toward the northern parts of the island and in relation to the sea, it is on the west… It has various mines of gold and silver, and copper, and *stypteria*, split and white, and true *stypteria*. And *sory* and yeast of gold, and *misy* and *khalkitis* and other metals. (Wallace and Orphanides 1990, 54–55).

Boukasa can only be Phoukasa, the local name for the copper-rich hill on the outskirts of Katydhata village and the location of the Skouriotissa mine. A mineral deposit rich in gold and silver, known by modern miners as 'Devil's Mud', was extracted from Skouriotissa in the 20th century (Ingham 1959, 169–70). From this a total of 1862 kg of gold and 12,142 kg of silver was produced between 1933 and 1942 (Panayiotou 1990, 233). It is, however, highly doubtful that this type of mineral would have been identified as a precious metal ore and exploited in antiquity (Kassianidou 2012, 244). This is because the precious metals are in colloidal form (Bear 1963, 185) and they are not visible, nor can they be collected by panning. Instead they have to be extracted through a series of fairly complex metallurgical procedures, none of which are recorded on the island. Furthermore, it is clear that this geological stratum was of no interest to the ancients: their galleries usually cut through it, in an effort to reach the copper deposits below (Bear 1963, 186).

Together with Mavrovouni and Apliki, Skouriotissa is the best candidate to be identified as the mine of Soloi that Galen visited in 166 AD, in order to collect minerals for the manufacture of medicaments, and described in his books. According to Galen, the mine was located at a distance of 30 stadia (5.5 km) from the town (*De Simplicium Medicamentorum Temperamentis ac Facultatibus Libri* XI. 12. 214.12–15; Wallace and Orphanides 1990, 227). Mavrovouni, Apliki and Skouriotissa are 5 km, 8 km and

9 km from Soloi respectively. In front of the mine there was a building, while below it there was a village. He describes the terrible smell of the air in the mine, the lack of oxygen which led to the extinction of the oil lamps used to light the passages and the foul taste of the water (XI. 12. 240.4–11; Wallace and Orphanides 1990, 227). This sounds extraordinarily similar to the descriptions of conditions described by modern miners at Skouriotissa and Mavrovouni (Varnava 1993, 35–45) and recorded in a recent film documentary by Paschalis Papapetrou (2008).

In the same book Galen describes how *chalcanthos*, the copper sulphate, was produced in the mine. Water rich in this mineral percolated through the walls of the mine and was collected in amphorae placed in a tunnel that inclined and descended to a distance of 1 stadium (184 m). When full, the amphorae were carried to the surface, and in a room in front of the mine their contents were transferred into square shallow basins, where the water was left to evaporate, leaving behind the crystallized salts. Modern scholars have made much of this text. Some used it as an indication that copper production had ceased on the island by the time of Galen's visit (Davies 1928–30, 84; Raber 1984, 144; Bruce *et al.* 1937, 640; Bear 1963, 2). The work carried out by SCSP and now TAESP has now shown this to be incorrect (Kassianidou 2004, 99). Koucky and Steinberg (1974, 168; 1989, 292) also used this text to support their theory of copper production using hydrometallurgy, but this has now been contested (Kassianidou and Van Lokeren 2003, 227).

Skouriotissa Mine

The ore deposit of Skouriotissa consists of two parts: Phoukasa hill, which rises to a height of 400 m; and Phoenix, which lies 300 m to the west. The Phoukasa ore deposit once consisted of c. 6 million tons of cupriferous pyrite. This deposit was covered by strata rich in umber and yellow ochre, both of which were exploited in the recent past and surely in antiquity (Ingham 1959, 141). Almost all of the ore body has now been mined away, initially by underground galleries, and since 1960 with the opencast method (Panayiotou 1990, 232). This factor unfortunately means that little is left of the hill once riddled with ancient and modern galleries, and that much of the surrounding area is now covered by the extensive modern spoil heaps (Fig. 3.45).

Although remains of galleries are still visible in the section of the opencast mine (Fig. 3.46), it is impossible to know whether they are ancient or modern. Furthermore, as the mine was active during the course of our fieldwork it was impossible for us even to try and record these remains.

Nevertheless, when it comes to the study of the ancient mine at Skouriotissa, we are in a much better position, because many of the features and artefacts uncovered by the modern miners are mentioned in Gunther's reports. These are reproduced by Lavender (1962, 67–72) and are carefully described by Bruce *et al.* (1937, 662–64). Furthermore, the ancient galleries are recorded in published plans and sections of the mine of Skouriotissa (Fig. 3.47; Cullis and Edge 1922, fig. facing p. 10; Bruce *et al.* 1937, 666–67, figs 376–78).

When Gunther first arrived at Skouriotissa in 1912, he noted the presence of two large excavations 3–5 m in height and more than 30 m wide. He identified these as stopes (defined by Bruce *et al.* (1937, 671) as 'a room or wide working space in ore') that may have been collapsed entrances to the mine (Lavender 1962, 67). When CMC started operations, they uncovered many more underground galleries and shafts which were entered from the surface through adits, which are horizontal or gently sloping passages driven from the surface into the ore body (Bruce *et al.* 1937, 648). The size and shape of the galleries varied according to the nature of the rock they penetrated. In hard rock the size was as small as possible, while in softer rock it could reach as much as 2 m in height (1937, 649). Where necessary wooden posts were used (1937, 653–55). These were well preserved and often contained native copper that had formed within the grain of the wood (1937, 650).

Three such wooden supports from the Skouriotissa mine were radiocarbon dated by the University of Heidelberg (H3675-2890, H6157-5855, H3676-2892) and published by Zwicker (1986, 102–103). The dates published by Zwicker were as follows: H3675-2890 was dated to 620±50 BC; H6157-5855 was dated to 580±60 BC; and H3676-2891 was dated to 485±50 BC. With the help of Sturt Manning we were able to retrieve the original results for two of the samples, which are as follows: H3675-2890 dates to 2590 ± 36 years BP; and H3676-2891 dates to 2455 ± 47 years BP. Using the OxCal radiocarbon calibration programme provided by the Oxford Radiocarbon Accelerator Unit, we recalibrated these two dates. The version of the programme used is OxCal v4.1.7 by Bronk Ramsey (2010). According to the recalibrated results, the wooden support H3675-2890 dates to between 828 and 748 BC (2σ), in other words in the Cypro-Geometric period, while the wooden support H3676-2891 dates to between 671 and 408 BC (2σ), the Cypro-Archaic to Cypro-Classical period. These results are extremely important as they indicate that the mine was active throughout the Iron Age and the time of the Cypriot kingdoms.

Small cuts along the sides of the galleries were used to support oil lamps that would have helped to illuminate the area. In an effort to reach the deeper levels of the ore deposit, many of the galleries were inclined and in some cases they were even spiral in form. In the steeper ones, steps were cut on their floor (Bruce *et al.* 1937, 649). Within the ancient galleries of Skouriotissa fragments of wooden ladders were found, together with reed baskets, three iron tools, Roman lamps and pipes (Bruce *et al.* 1937, 662–64).

Fig. 3.45. The opencast pit of Skouriotissa mine looking south, with ore and patches of slag visible on the right (Chris Parks)

Fig. 3.46. Remains of a gallery within the modern opencast mine of Phoukasa. Height of opening from top of collapsed material to top of gallery c. 1 m (Vasiliki Kassianidou)

Amphora Dump at Skouriotissa *Phoukasa* (TP171)

One of the most intriguing finds of the 20th-century miners was noted by Gunther outside one of the stopes. This was a large concentration of broken amphorae, estimated to cover an area of one acre (0.4 ha), and standing almost 7 m high (Lavender 1962, 67). Bruce *et al.* (1937, 663, figs 368–69) published two photographs of this pottery dump, showing it near a house built on top of the foundations of an ancient structure. The location of the pottery dump is noted in the published plans of the ancient mine (Fig. 3.47). Gunther was interested by this find as he thought it indicated that the ore deposit was not exhausted in antiquity. He explained:

> The only use the writer can assign to these earthenware vessels, all discarded at one place, was to bail water. It is manifestly impossible to follow an ore body to any important depth below water level with no other means of raising water than men carrying jars! (Lavender 1962, 67).

Ground water would have been one of the most serious problems that mining engineers had to solve, and bailing was one of the methods used towards this effect. The technique was employed in the mines of Iberia, and is described in the following passage by Pliny:

> One of these mines, now called after Baebelo, furnished Hannibal with 300 pounds weight of silver a day, the tunnelling having been carried a mile and a half into the mountain. Along the whole of this distance watermen are posted who all night and day in spells measured by lanterns bale out the water and make a stream. (Pliny, *Natural History*, Book XXXIII, xxxi. 97)

As Healy (1978, 96) pointed out, however, this method of drainage would have been practical only in those cases where the flow of water was limited. Alternatively, it

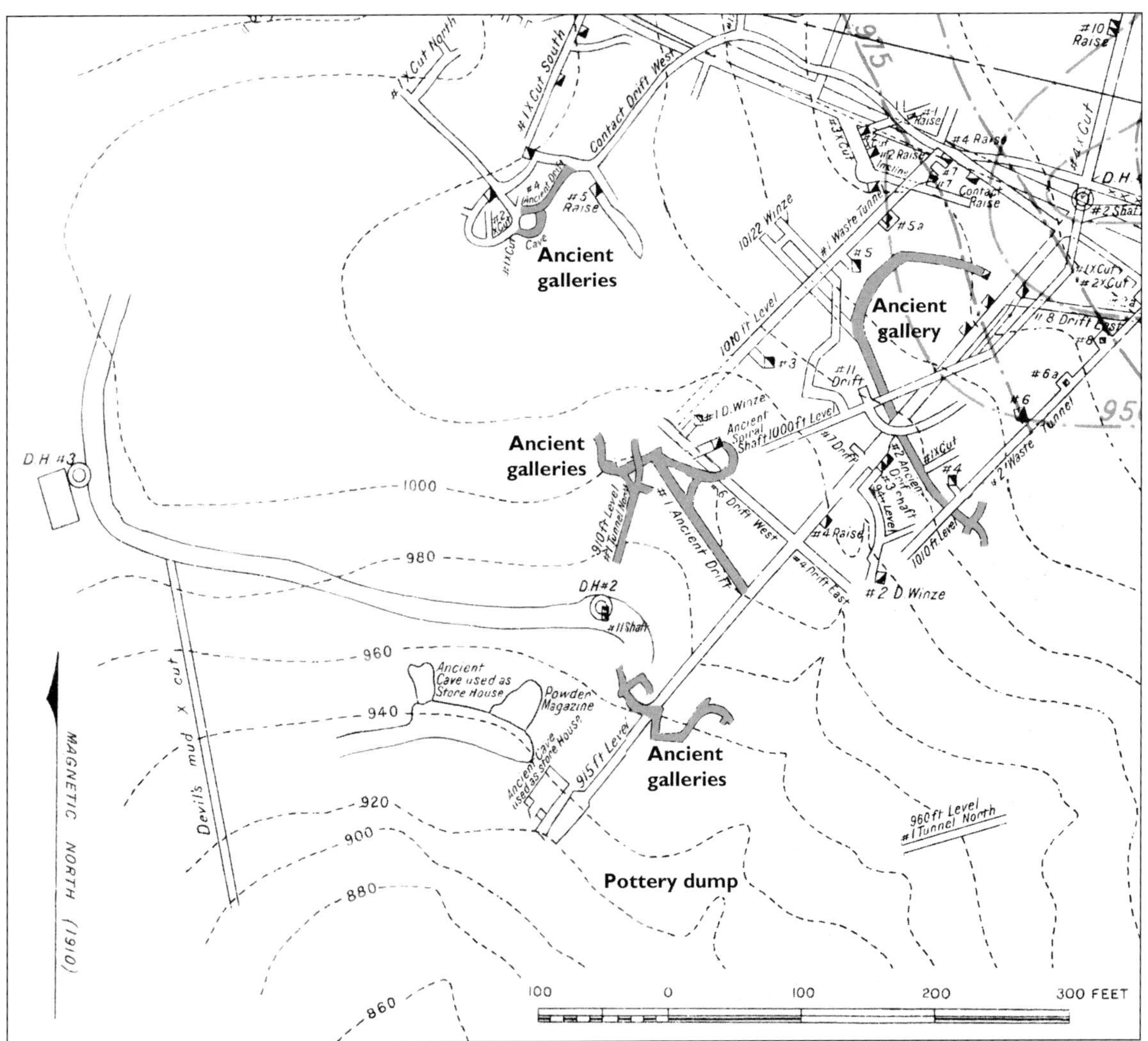

Fig. 3.47. Plan of Skouriotissa showing the location of the ancient galleries and the amphora dump (Cullis and Edge 1922, fig. facing p. 10)

could have been applied in those cases where the water was actually of some value. Thus Bruce *et al.* (1937, 663) suggested that the amphorae were used to collect the water that was rich in copper sulphates, as described by Galen.

In 1996 exploratory work was carried out by the Hellenic Mining Company, which since 1975 had the lease to exploit Skouriotissa, in the area between Phoukasa and Phoenix. During this work the pottery dump was rediscovered, and was recorded by the Cypriot Department of Antiquities before its removal (Plate 3.19; Cyprus Museum inventory CS 2845). The photograph shows the floor and one of the foundation walls of the modern house, which lie above the layer of badly corroded and broken pottery (at the bottom of the photograph).

Because the area was going to be exploited by opencast methods, the mining company moved some of the pottery that was still in situ to a safe location near its offices. Thanks to the help of the Director of Skouriotissa mine, Constantinos Xydas, we were able to study and sample this mixed and unstratified deposit of pottery fragments (TP171; Fig. 3.48).

The deposit is made up entirely of sherds from two or possibly three types of closely related, locally produced transport amphorae. The sherds are badly damaged by mineral accretions, which to a large extent are post-depositional: one of the by-products of the exposed minerals that surrounded this deposit for centuries is sulphuric acid, which is extremely corrosive. The most common type by far is like the vessel illustrated in the photograph published by Bruce *et al.* (1937, 327), while the others appear to be smaller versions of the same type. The amphorae have an everted thickened rim with a flattened sloping lip, vertical handles with two vertical ribs and a solid round knob base/toe, though there is quite a lot of variety in the detail (Fig. 3.49).

The toe is very distinctive. It has a tendency to be twisted, which appears to be a regional characteristic (Volume 1, Chapter 3.3; Jacobsen 2004, 146–48). All

Fig. 3.48. Skouriotissa: relocated amphora dump (TP171), with (inset) it being dumped in its new location (Vasiliki Kassianidou)

three types of amphorae are remarkably thin-walled and seem unsuitable for long distance transport. On the other hand the large handles and the toes provide a good grip for lifting.

Although no wasters have been found, their local origin has been confirmed by petrographic analyses (Volume 1, Chapter 3.3). Interestingly, although several fragments of transport amphorae were found around the slag heap, no fragments of the Skouriotissa amphorae were identified there (see below). Some fragments of the dominant type have also been found in small quantities at the Roman sites of Litharkies (Chapter 4.4), Sanidhia and Katalasharis (Chapter 2.15). The only fragments of Skouriotissa amphorae identified outside the Survey Area are two possible rim fragments found at Ayia Irini in the Morphou bay area (Quilici 1971, fig. 52.III:33, fig. 83.III:56). This may reflect not so much the distribution of the vessels, as the state of research and publication in this area of Cyprus. The possible fragments found at Aiya Irini suggest a date no later than the 2nd century AD.

Their distribution may indicate that the amphorae served multiple purposes. The vessels' morphology seems to have been modified to facilitate manhandling rather than long distance transport; perhaps the vessels were produced for this particular purpose. The vessels may have been used to transport food from local support villages and farmsteads to the people working at the mine. The remains of such a network have been identified on the plain south-east of the mine (Chapter 2.3).

As discussed above, however, the amphorae were found in direct association with the mining galleries, which suggests a primary use inside the mine itself. It has already been suggested that the amphorae may have been used to drain the mine by bailing, or to collect the mineral rich water for further treatment and production of valuable salts. Equally possible is that the amphorae were used to carry drinking water to the miners: due to the high temperatures within the underground galleries and the hard physical labour, the miners would certainly have had to consume substantial amounts of water. Considering the size of the slag heap, one can envision a considerable work force employed in the mine. During the Roman period, at least, the work force would most certainly have consisted largely of slaves (Kassianidou 2000, 753), who most probably spent the majority of their day underground. Thus food and more importantly drinking water would have had to be carried underground. The absence of this type of amphora from the slag heap presumably results from the fact that the preserved sections of the slag heap date to the Middle and Late Roman periods, and so post-date the Early Roman amphora dump.

Main Slag Heap at Skouriotissa *Vouppes* (TP007)

During our pilot season in 2000 we observed that, because of a variety of mining company activities such as quarrying for slag, cutting roads or installing piping, the slag heap had been sectioned at various points. We decided that visible sections in the slag heap would be designated as separate Archaeometallurgical Units (AU). Our topographic scientist used metric photography to record the sections,

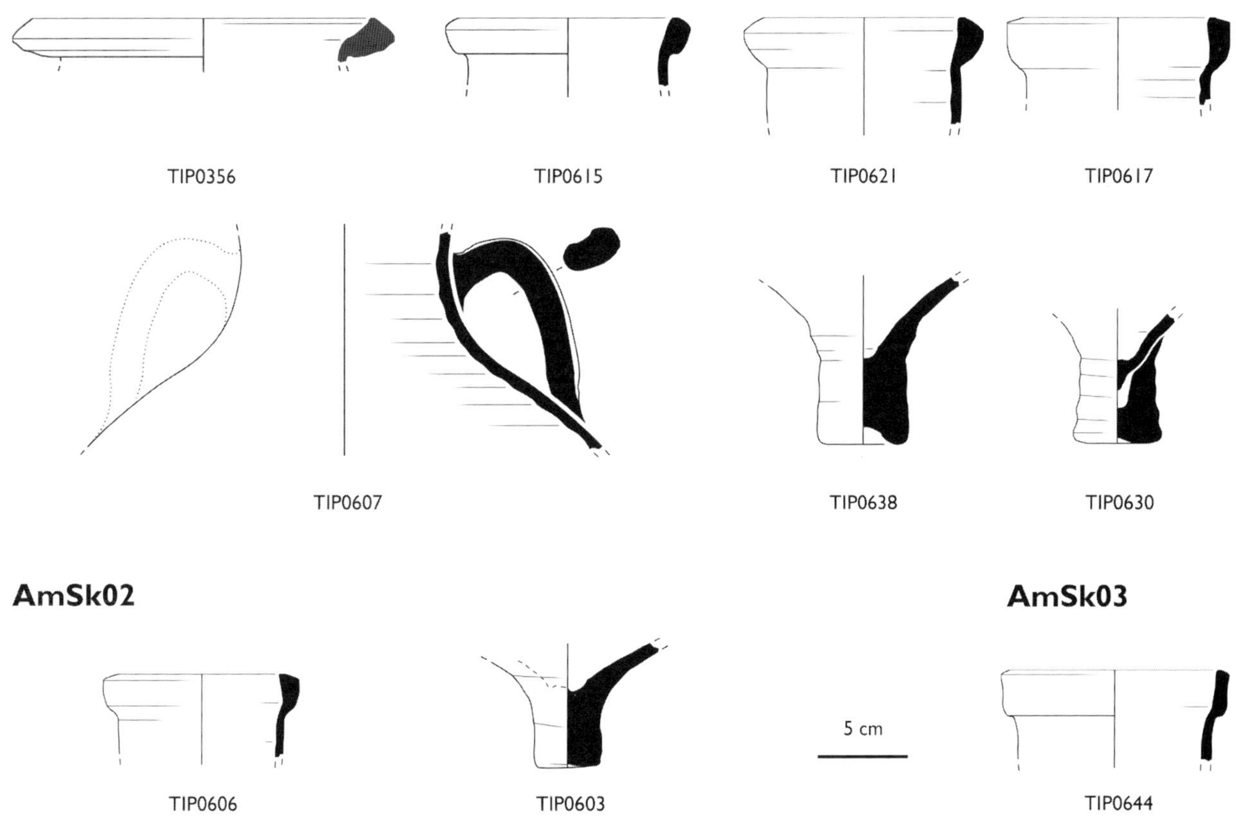

Fig. 3.49. Skouriotissa amphorae profiles (illustration: Jean Humbert)

and a total station to produce a topographic map of the slag heap (Fig. 3.50).

Smaller sections were simply photographed with a digital camera. The Archaeometallurgical Units that were important or undisturbed by modern mining activities were also drawn, and their layers described in detail. Samples of slag, charcoal and, if present, pottery were subsequently collected from all layers accessible to us (many of the layers in the larger sections were simply too high to be reached). As we explain for specific Archaeometallurgical Units below, some of the more inaccessible sections were noted but not recorded; their locations are marked on Fig. 3.50. We were assisted in this laborious work by Myrto Georgakopoulou and Thomas Tselios.

The main pottery collections at TP007 took place in 2000 and in 2002. The first collection was representative while the follow up was a grab sample. TP007, however, was selectively re-sampled several times due to the continuous appearance of large well-preserved fragments eroding from around the slag heap. None of these fragments were observed while still embedded in the slag heap, but several fragments are discoloured by traces of slag, indicating their likely proximity to smelting activities when they were discarded. For the collection, the ground along the exposed section of the slag heap was divided into two long strips, subdivided according to the vertical sections of the slag heap. Pottery collected at the foot of the vertical sections was assigned to the given AU, while pottery found at a distance – where it was uncertain which section it came from – was assigned to a PU.

AU01 The large vertical section along the road and in front of the United Nations San Martin camp (Fig. 3.50) is over 30 m long and has multiple well-defined layers of slag, furnace material and crushed minerals (Fig. 3.51; Fig. 3.52; Table 3.15). We collected samples from all layers that could be reached standing on the talus. Although only a handful of sherds was found within the layers of the section, the area in front (PU01) had considerable quantities of sherds and tile fragments. The 35 sherds collected consisted of mostly tile, Light Utility wares, Table Wares and transport amphorae, including TCP542–44, as well as fragments of Cypriot Red Slip Ware form 2 and Late Roman amphora type 1, all suggesting a Late Roman date.

The form of the stratified deposit offers an indication of the processes that formed it. The lower strata are almost horizontal and were clearly used as work surfaces, as among them are three layers (Y34–Y36) consisting entirely of crushed furnace material. Many of the layers are composed of slag crushed to a size smaller than 5 cm.

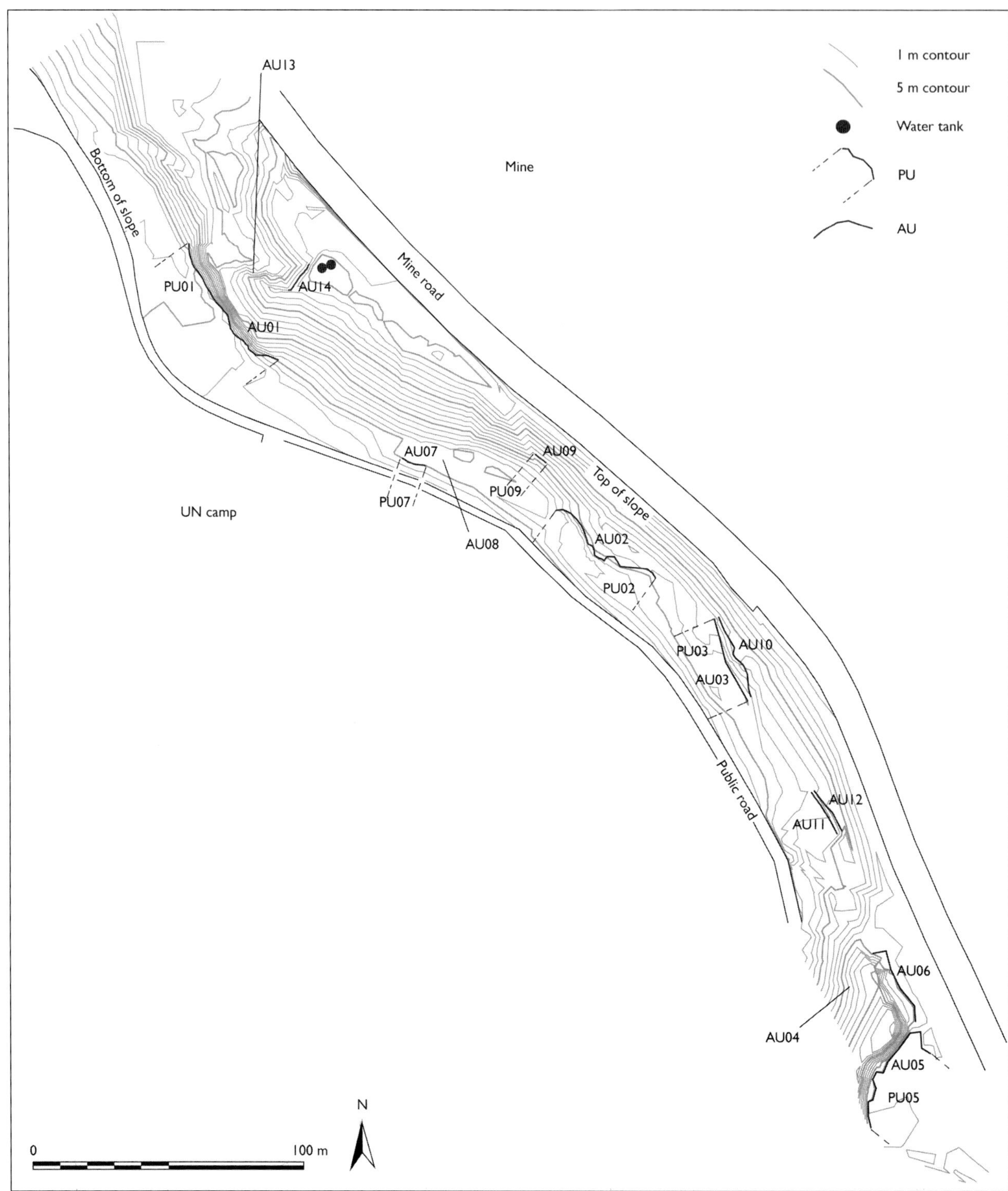

Fig. 3.50. Skouriotissa Vouppes *(TP007): topographic map. AU = Archaeometallurgical Unit (slag heap sections). PU = POSI Unit (artefact collection area in front of the sections) (Gary Tompsett; finalised by Luke Sollars)*

This phenomenon was also observed in the Roman slag heaps at Mitsero (Kassianidou *et al.* 2003, 92). Given that by this period the smelting technology had advanced to such a level that less than 1% of copper was left in the slag, it has already been argued (Kassianidou and Van Lokeren 2003, 223) that crushing the slag was clearly not done in order to separate the slag from the metal, as would have been necessary in the Bronze Age. This suggestion seems to be further supported here. It is clear that crushing the slag was part of a deliberate effort to manage this huge amount of waste material by creating stable heaps. The upper layers have a much steeper inclination (e.g. Y6 and

Y51) and consist predominantly of slag cakes that have clearly been tipped from above: they all face downwards.

A sample of charcoal collected from Layer Y27 was radiocarbon dated (OxA 16813 RY1001-1010 and OxA 16814 RY1011-1021) to AD 220–350 (94.3% main range). Since the sample preserved no bark or outer ring, the tree must have been cut at a date somewhat later than the one determined by radiocarbon. Y27 is one of the lower layers in this section, found in the bottom part of the enormous slag heap. A second sample of charcoal collected from Layer Y39, the lowest visible section in the section, was also radiocarbon dated (Wk-25879). The determined date is AD 235–331 (1SD or 68%) or AD 140–381 (95.4%). This indicates the earliest known activities in this part of this copper producing area, although it clearly began earlier than this, as the lowest strata remain buried under the talus.

Charcoal analysis was carried out by Maria Ntinou (for further discussion, see Volume 1, Chapter 3.10). The samples from AU01 (Table 3.16) included a few charcoal pieces that in all cases were identified as *Pinus brutia*.

Fig. 3.51. Skouriotissa Vouppes *(TP007): southern half of slag section AU01 (Chris Parks)*

Bark fragments would probably correspond to timber of the same species.

AU02 To the south of AU01 and parallel to the road there is another exposed section (AU02), which has been greatly disturbed by two very large, thick plastic pipes: this section was not recorded in detail. The pottery collected from PU02 included tile fragments (TCP545, TCP550–51), Late Roman Cooking Wares (TCP547), Late Roman Heavy Utility wares (TCP548–49), Late Roman Cypriot Red Slip Table Wares, and fragments of transport amphorae such as Late Roman type 1 (TCP546). These generally suggest a Late Roman date.

AU03 Further south is another section in the slag heap (Fig. 3.53; Table 3.17). A track had been cut through it, creating another small section (AU010; see below). A tile fragment was collected from the stratified layers of AU03, but it could not be dated specifically. In front of the section (PU03), however, 21 sherds were collected, including tiles, Late Roman Cooking Wares (TCP552), Heavy and Light Utility wares, Late Roman Table Ware (e.g. a Cypriot Red Slip Ware, form 9 sherd), a sherd of imported Phocaean Red Slip Ware, Form 10 (TCP553), and transport amphorae. All these suggest a date in the late 6th–early 7th centuries AD.

A sample of charcoal collected from layer Y20 at the base of this section was radiocarbon dated (OxA16815+16816 RY1000-1010, OxA 16818 RY1001-1010, OxA 16819 RY1011-1022). This calibrated date falls after AD 595–665 (95.4%); because the sample preserved no bark or outer ring, the tree must have been cut at a somewhat later date than the one provided by radiocarbon. This rather modest and low-lying section of the slag heap clearly indicates that production was active well into the 7th century AD. This is extremely important as it shows the chronological extent of production in the area of Skouriotissa.

The charcoal pieces from this section (Table 3.18) were relatively abundant, but as with the other sections the best

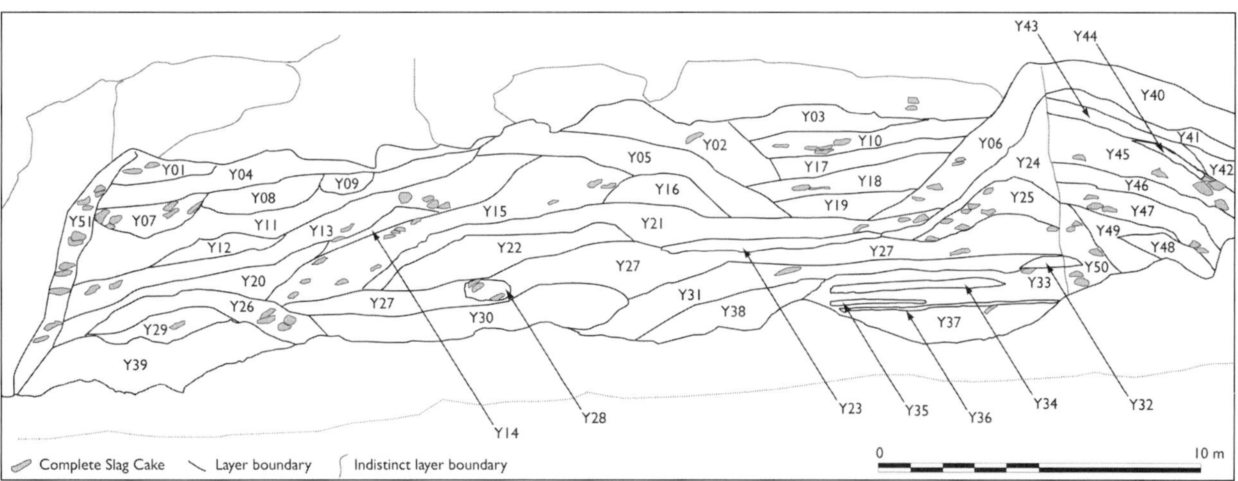

Fig. 3.52. Skouriotissa Vouppes *(TP007): N–S section drawing of AU01 (Vasiliki Kassianidou)*

Table 3.15. Skouriotissa Vouppes *(TP007): description of AU01 layers*

Layer	Layer material	Sherds	Comments
Y01	Slag – Cakes		Matrix sediment is rich in fine charcoal.
Y02	Slag – Cakes		Slag cakes mixed with small pieces of slag. Inaccessible.
Y03	Slag – Small		Inaccessible.
Y04	Slag – Small		Slag cakes mixed with small pieces of slag.
Y05	Slag – Cakes		Matrix sediment is rich in fine charcoal.
Y06	Slag – Cakes		Bulk sediment material collected with slag for botanical analysis.
Y07	Slag – Cakes		Crushed gossan. Inaccessible.
Y08	Slag – Medium/Small		Inaccessible.
Y09	Slag – Small		
Y10	Slag – Cakes		Slag cakes mixed with small pieces of slag.
Y11	Slag – Cakes		Crushed gossan.
Y12	Slag – Small		Crushed gossan. Inaccessible.
Y13	Slag – Cakes	1	Very small slag. Charcoal furnace slag amongst the finds.
Y14	Slag – Small	2	Slag cakes mixed with small pieces of slag.
Y15	Slag – Cakes		Slag cakes mixed with small pieces of slag.
Y16	Slag – Small		Bulk sediment material collected with slag for botanical analysis.
Y17	Slag – Large/Small		Brown sediment. Sample of sediment collected.
Y18	Slag – Cakes		Slag cakes mixed with large pieces of slag. Inaccessible.
Y19	Slag – Medium		Inaccessible.
Y20	Slag – Small	5	Small and medium pieces of slag. Inaccessible.
Y21	Slag – Small		Inaccessible.
Y22	Slag – Large/Medium		Inaccessible.
Y23	Ground Ore/Flux		Inaccessible.
Y24	Slag – Small		Slag cakes mixed with small pieces of slag. Inaccessible.
Y25	Slag – Cakes		Inaccessible.
Y26	Slag – Large		Slag cakes mixed with large pieces of slag.
Y27	Slag – Small		Inaccessible.
Y28	Slag – Cakes		
Y29	Slag – Cakes		Inaccessible.
Y30	Slag – Cakes		Inaccessible.
Y31	Slag – Cakes		Inaccessible.
Y32	Other		Small and very small pieces of slag.
Y33	Slag – Small		Inaccessible.
Y34	Furnace Material		Inaccessible.
Y35	Furnace Material		Inaccessible.
Y36	Furnace Material		Inaccessible.
Y37	Slag – Cakes		Inaccessible.
Y38	Slag – Cakes		Inaccessible.
Y39	Slag – Small		Inaccessible.
Y40	Slag – Cakes		Inaccessible.
Y41	Ground Ore/Flux		Inaccessible.
Y42	Slag – Large/Small		Inaccessible.
Y43	Slag – Small		Inaccessible.
Y44	Ground Ore/Flux		Slag cakes mixed with large pieces of slag. Inaccessible.
Y45	Slag – Cakes		One bag of slag is bulk sample.
Y46	Slag – Small		Inaccessible.
Y47	Slag – Cakes		Inaccessible.
Y48	Slag – Small		Inaccessible.
Y49	Ground Ore/Flux		Inaccessible.
Y50	Slag – Cakes		Slag cakes mixed with small pieces of slag.
Y51	Slag – Cakes		Very small slag. High proportion of iron oxides or sulphates.

represented taxon was *Pinus brutia*. The other taxa present were olive, oak, some species of the mint family, oriental plane and oriental alder.

AU04 Unlike the other Archaeometallurgical Units, AU04 is not a vertical section but the surface of the southern end of the slag heap, covered in low vegetation. The vegetation and the deposit form a very stable surface. Since this side of the heap had not been sectioned, the stratigraphy is not visible and could not be recorded. Only towards the bottom had some of the layers been exposed. Amongst the sherds collected here were tiles (TCP527), Late Roman Cooking Wares (TCP530), Late Roman Heavy and Light Utility wares (TCP528–29) and Late Roman 1 amphora fragments. More pottery dating to the Late Roman period was collected in front of the section (PU04) including tiles, Heavy and Light Utility wares, Cypriot Red Slip Ware and Late Roman amphora type 1 fragments.

Table 3.16. Skouriotissa Vouppes *(TP007): charcoal analysis from section AU01*

	Layer Y27, A002	Layer Y31, A003	Layer Y33	Layer Y37, A002
Pinus brutia	1	2	1	2
Bark	1			

AU05 This south-east facing section of the slag heap currently lies within the property of the mining company (Fig. 3.54). It is one of the highest sections and one of the best that we were able to record by metric photography. The section was drawn, and samples were taken from the layers we could reach (Table 3.19). The fact that we were able to climb to the top of the section meant that we could sample the top layer, which presumably corresponds to the very last phase of smelting in the area. Unfortunately, recent landscaping of the area in front of the section meant that the lowest layers, and therefore the earliest phases, were no longer visible or accessible.

As with the case of AU01, the lower strata are almost horizontal and would have been used as work surfaces. A layer consisting entirely of furnace material (Y17) probably indicates the position of smelting installations. The higher strata are, again, inclined and often consist of large pieces of slag or complete slag cakes.

A group of mortar stones, found within the fenced area that encompasses this section, probably represents the simple tools used to crush the slag into the small pieces that form many of the layers (TCL334). They were clearly collected and deposited there by the personnel of the mining company, and may come from different parts of the slag heap, not just AU05. Similar examples were recovered from the Mitsero slag heaps (Kassianidou and Van Lokeren 2003, 223, figs 5.18–19).

Table 3.17. Skouriotissa Vouppes *(TP007): description of AU03 layers*

Layer	Layer material	Sherds	Comments
Y01	Slag – Small		Slag cakes mixed with small pieces of slag.
Y02	Slag – Large/Medium		Very small slag.
Y03	Slag – Small		Slag cakes mixed with large pieces of slag. Inaccessible.
Y04	Sediment		
Y05	Slag – Large/Medium		Inaccessible.
Y06	Slag – Medium/Small		Inaccessible.
Y07	Slag – Medium		Inaccessible.
Y08	Slag – Small		Inaccessible.
Y09	Other		Slag cakes mixed with small and large pieces of slag. May also contain some furnace material.
Y10	Sediment		Inaccessible.
Y11	Slag – Large/Medium		Inaccessible.
Y12	Slag – Small		Slag cakes mixed with large pieces of slag. Inaccessible.
Y13	Slag – Medium		Slag cakes mixed with small pieces of slag. Inaccessible.
Y14	Slag – Medium		Very small slag. Inaccessible. May contain some furnace material.
Y15	Slag – Medium		Stones. Inaccessible.
Y16	Slag – Large/Medium		Slag cakes mixed with large pieces of slag.
Y17	Slag – Large/Medium	1	Contains a very small layer of crashed furnace material and very fine charcoal.
Y18	Slag – Small		
Y19	Slag – Medium		Unlike other small slag layers this does not have much matrix sediment.
Y20	Slag – Small		Slag cakes mixed with small pieces of slag.
Y21	Sediment		
Y22	Slag – Small		Ground furnace material. Possible work floor. Material is dark brown and very fine.

The pottery collected from the stratified layers (AU05) mainly consisted of tiles (TCP532), Heavy and Light Utility wares, and some fragments of Late Roman amphora type 1 (TCP531) and Late Roman Red Slip Table Ware. Among the pottery collected from PU05 were examples of water pipe fragments (TCP556), Cooking Wares and transport amphorae, including Late Roman amphora type 1 fragments (TCP554) dating to the Late Roman period. There was also what appears to be a fragment of a Levantine transport amphora of a type dated to the mid-Roman period (TCP555).

A piece of charcoal collected from layer Y29 was radiocarbon dated (OxA 16820 RY1001-1011, OxA 16821 RY1014-1025, OxA 16822 RY1027-1037, OxA 16823 RY1039-1049, OxA 16824 RY1050-1064, OxA 16825 RY1076-1085). This had a total of 86 rings and included a piece of the bark. This is important as it gives a much more precise date for this specific layer. The date for this sample lies within AD 395–440 (95.4% range). A second piece of charcoal from layer Y39, which lies to the south of Layer Y29 and is clearly part of a later dumping phase, was also radiocarbon dated (Wk-25880), producing a date of AD 420–555 (95.4%). Considering that both these samples come from layers located at the base of the section, with more than 5 m of slag lying above them, the chronological extent of production in Skouriotissa becomes clear, as does the intensity of production in the Late Roman period. It also shows how the epicentre of the smelting operations slowly shifted from the north (AU01) to the south-east (AU05).

The three pieces of charcoal identified in this section (Table 3.20) belong to the Cyprus pine and the black pine, the latter usually growing on the higher elevations of the Troodos Mountain.

<u>AU06</u> AU06 is the east-facing section of the slag heap, and lies within the property of the mining company (Fig. 3.55). It is parallel to the road, leading from the opencast to the processing plant, which was in constant use by large

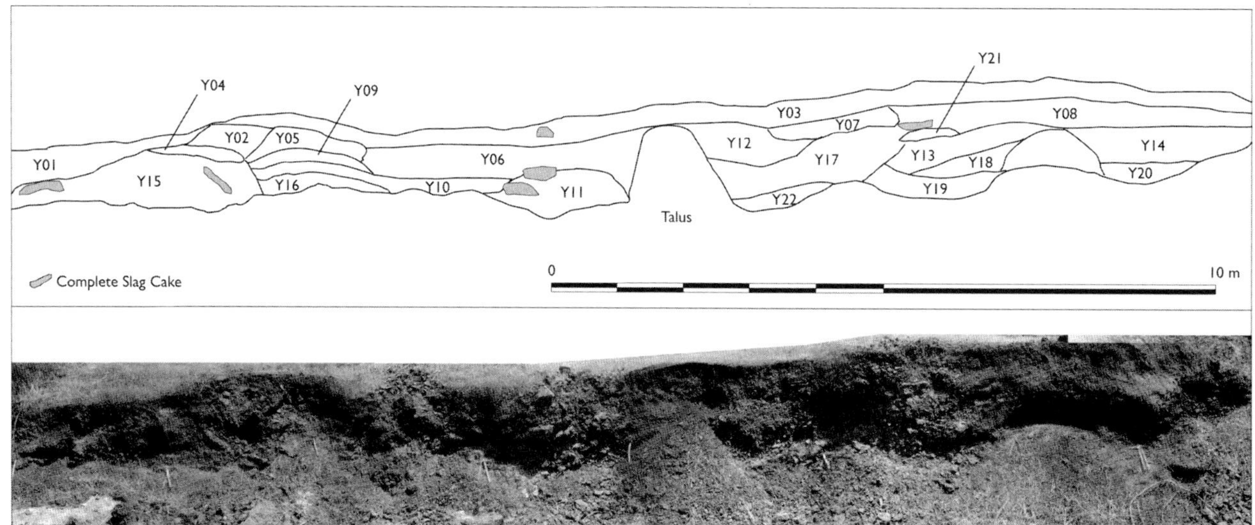

Fig. 3.53. Skouriotissa Vouppes *(TP007): section AU03. Above: section drawing. Below: photograph (Vasiliki Kassianidou)*

Table 3.18. Skouriotissa Vouppes *(TP007): charcoal analysis from section AU03*

	Layer Y06, A002	Layer Y09, A002	Layer Y11, A002	Layer Y12, A002	Layer Y20, A002	Layer Y21, A002	Layer Y22, A001
Alnus orientalis	1			1	1		
Coniferae				1			
cf. Labiatae				1			
Olea europaea						1	
Pinus brutia	1	6	3	12	1	4	4
Pinus sp.							2
Platanus orientalis						1	
Quercus sp.				1			
Bark		1		1			
Not identifiable						1	

Table 3.19. Skouriotissa Vouppes *(TP007): description of AU05 layers*

Layer	Layer material	Sherds	Comments
Y01	Slag – Small		Possible work floor. Furnace material is crushed and forms a uniform flat layer.
Y02	Slag – Large/Medium		
Y03	Slag – Small		Very small slag.
Y04	Slag – Cakes		
Y05	Slag – Small	1	
Y06	Slag – Cakes		Slag cakes mixed with medium pieces of slag.
Y07	Slag – Large/Medium		Charcoal is small but good for species ID.
Y08	Slag – Small		
Y09	Slag – Cakes		
Y10	Slag – Small		
Y11	Slag – Cakes		Inaccessible.
Y12	Slag – Cakes		Very small slag. Inaccessible.
Y13	Slag – Small		Crushed gossan. Possible work floor.
Y14	Slag – Cakes		Possible work floor.
Y15	Slag – Large/Medium	1	
Y16	Slag – Small		Crushed furnace material.
Y17	Furnace Material	6	Small slag and sediment.
Y18	Sediment	6	
Y19	Ground Ore/Flux	2	Small slag and sediment.
Y20	Slag – Cakes	30	No metallurgical finds were collected while cleaning the section, only pottery.
Y21	Slag – Small	10	Tumble from the wall. Layer is very rich in pottery, charcoal, tiles, etc.
Y22	Slag – Cakes	4	Small slag and sediment.
Y23	Slag – Cakes	3	
Y24	Slag – Medium/Small		Built stone and slag wall. Structure also contains tiles. Thick plaster between stones.
Y25	Slag – Small	2	
Y26	Slag – Cakes		Small slag and sediment. Surface layer – mixed.
Y27	Slag – Small		
Y28	Slag – Cakes		
Y29	Slag – Cakes		Inaccessible.
Y30	Slag – Small		Slag cakes and large pieces. Inaccessible.
Y31	Slag – Medium/Small		Inaccessible.
Y32	Slag – Large/Medium		Mainly medium pieces of slag; some cakes. Inaccessible.
Y33	Slag – Cakes		Sediment and small pieces of slag. Inaccessible.
Y34	Sediment		Inaccessible.
Y35	Slag – Cakes		
Y36	Slag – Small		
Y37	Sediment		Inaccessible.
Y38	Slag – Cakes		
Y39	Slag – Cakes		
Y40	Slag – Large/Small		
Y41	Slag – Cakes		Some small pieces of tap slag.
Y42	Slag – Medium/Small		Inaccessible.
Y43	Slag – Large/Medium		
Y44	Slag – Small		Very small pieces of slag.
Y45	Slag – Cakes		Inaccessible.
Y46	Slag – Cakes		
Y47	Slag – Cakes	4	Sherds collected during cleaning. Small metallic perforated disc: may be modern.
Y48	Slag – Cakes		Very small pieces of slag mixed with carbon rich sediment.
Y49	Slag – Cakes		
Y50	Slag – Small		Very small pieces of slag mixed with carbon rich sediment.
Y51	Slag – Cakes	1	Very small pieces of slag mixed with carbon rich sediment. Very rich in charcoal. Crushed furnace material.
Y52	Slag – Small		Small pieces of slag mixed with carbon rich sediment.
Y53	Slag – Cakes		
Y54	Slag – Cakes		
Y55	Slag – Cakes		Very small pieces of slag mixed with carbon rich sediment. Very rich in charcoal. Crushed furnace material.
Y56	Slag – Small		
Y57	Sediment		Very small pieces of slag mixed with carbon rich sediment. Very rich in charcoal. Crushed furnace material.

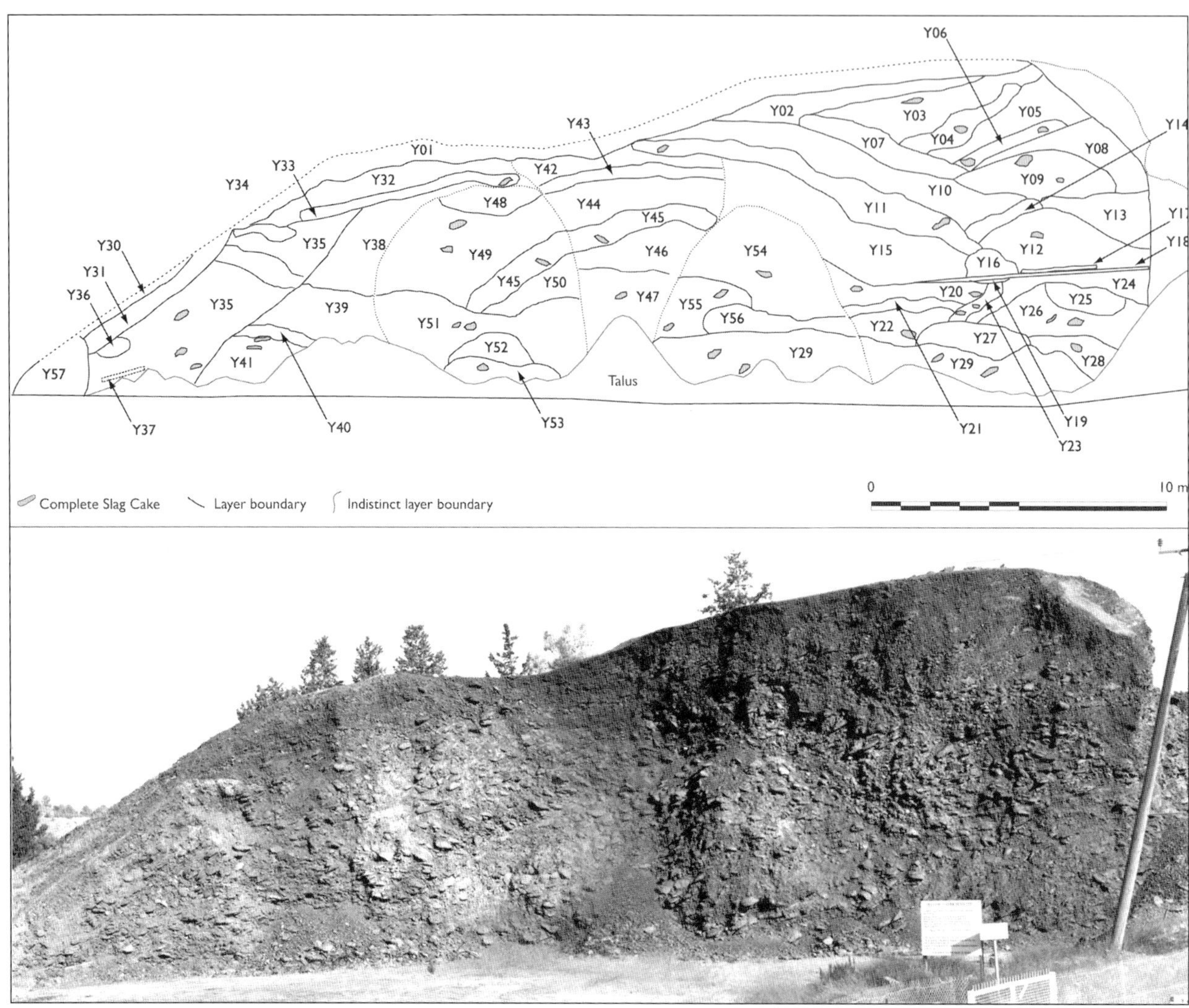

Fig. 3.54. Skouriotissa Vouppes *(TP007): section AU05. Above: section drawing (Myrto Georgakopoulou). Below: photograph (Gary Tompsett)*

Table 3.20. Skouriotissa Vouppes *(TP007): charcoal analysis from section AU05*

	Layer Y25, A002	Layer Y29, A002	Layer Y37, A002
Pinus brutia	1		1
Pinus nigra		1	

trucks carrying freshly extracted ore. This, together with the fact that the section is neither flat nor perpendicular, meant that it was unsuitable for rectified photography or for careful recording and sampling.

AU07 Between AU01 and AU02 is a stone wall and area of sediment, rich in slag and pottery fragments (AU07). The wall is built with undressed limestone and thick layers of plaster, and is oriented east-north-east to west-south-west. Among the stones were some that looked like artefacts but are now in secondary use. Among the courses of stone were pottery fragments, mainly tiles. The wall is covered with a layer of small pieces of slag.

The section was cleaned, drawn and sampled during the 2003 season (Plate 3.20; Table 3.21). After cleaning the talus in front of the wall, it was clear that it had been formed by collapsed building material, mainly plaster and stones, but also slag cakes and tiles. During cleaning we collected numerous pottery sherds, as well as glass, bone, an iron nail and a possible copper alloy artefact.

Because the remains of this building are now covered by the bulk of the slag heap, it is clear that its construction and use must predate the formation of this part of the heap. The presence of buildings within slag heaps is not unusual, and was also recorded at Mitsero *Kouloupakhis* (Kassianidou *et al.* 2003, 88; for an example from Spain see Rothenberg and Blanco Freijeiro 1981, 101–102).

Within this area (AU07 and PU07) we collected 102 pottery sherds and tile fragments. From AU07 came tile (TCP533–36, TCP538), Cooking Wares, one Early Roman fragment (TCP540), Heavy and Light Utility

Fig. 3.55. Skouriotissa Vouppes *(TP007): section AU06. Height at highest point on left is c. 14 m (Gary Tompsett)*

Table 3.21. Skouriotissa Vouppes *(TP007): description of AU07 layers. There was no pottery or tile*

Layer	Layer material	Comments
Clean: slag	Other	Very small pieces of slag mixed with carbon rich sediment. Very rich in charcoal. Crushed furnace material.
Clean: wall	Other	Very small pieces of slag mixed with carbon rich sediment.
Y01	Slag – Small	Slag cakes mixed with large pieces of slag.
Y02	Sediment	Very small pieces of slag mixed with carbon rich sediment. It is very rich in charcoal. Also contains crushed furnace material.
Y03	Other	
Y04	Slag – Medium/Small	Inaccessible.
Y05	Slag – Small	Inaccessible.
Y06	Other	Inaccessible.

wares, including one Late Roman fragment (TCP539), Late Roman Table Wares such as Cypriot Red Slip wares form 2, 9 and 9a and Phocaean Red Slip Wares, and a Late Roman transport amphora fragment (TCP537). In PU07 we collected tile (TCP557), Cooking Wares (TCP558), Heavy and Light Utility wares, Table Wares such as Cypriot Red Slip Ware form 9 and Phocaean Red Slip Ware, and some transport amphorae, e.g. Late Roman amphorae type 1.

Two of the Cooking Ware fragments of types CWPR11 and CWPR04a (TCP540) from AU07 are dated to the Early Roman period; some of the less precisely datable fragments may also date to this period. It is possible that these fragments reflect the actual use of the building. If Skouriotissa was indeed the mine visited by Galen, then this structure may have been part of the village that he said existed below the mine. The presence of significant quantities of Late Roman pottery shows that this area remained residential for many centuries, until it was eventually abandoned and completely covered by the slag heap. According to radiocarbon dating this must have taken place sometime after the 6th century AD.

A sample of charcoal from Layer Y05 was radiocarbon dated (Wk-26027), giving a date of AD 565–654 (95.4%). Since the sample preserved no bark or outer ring, the tree must have been cut after the date determined by radiocarbon. Y05 is the lowest slag layer at the base of this section of the slag heap and gives us an *terminus ante quem* for the abandonment of the building. It also provides us with solid evidence for the continuation of extensive copper production well into the 7th century.

Further charcoal was analysed from Layer Y06, the sediment below the wall. As with other sections, the best-represented taxon is the Cyprus pine, while oriental plane and alder are also present (Table 3.22).

AU08 AU08 is a small section perpendicular to the edge of AU07 where the wall ends. It was not recorded in detail, but pottery was collected from the collapse material in front of it (PU08). This included tile (TCP559), Cooking Wares, Cypriot Red Slip ware, Phocaean Table Ware form 3 from the mid-5th century AD onwards and several transport amphora fragments, such as a Late Roman Amphora type 1, dated to that period.

Table 3.22. Skouriotissa Vouppes *(TP007): charcoal analysis from section AU07*

	Layer Y06, A001	Layer Y06, A002	Layer Y06, A003	Layer Y06, A004
Alnus orientalis			1	
Pinus brutia	8	3	2	1
Platanus orientalis	1			
Bark			2	

Table 3.23. Skouriotissa Vouppes *(TP007): description of AU09 layers. There was no pottery or tile*

Layer	Layer material	Comments
CLEAN		Some slag cakes. Inaccessible.
Clean	Slag – Large/Medium/Small	
Y01	Slag – Small	
Y02	Slag – Cakes	
Y03	Slag – Small	
Y04	Furnace Material	

AU09 Between sections AU01 and AU07, but at a higher level, there is what seems to be a wall built of slag cakes. This is not vertical but rather inclined inwards at the top (Plate 3.21; Table 3.23) and wider at the bottom. The layer below it is rich in sediment and finely crushed slag.

The talus and the area in front of AU09 was full of pottery, and in fact has produced some of the best preserved examples of Late Roman pottery in the whole Survey Area, with the full range of functions and the widest ranges of types (Table 3.27; Table 3.28). These include tiles (TCP560, TCP568), Late Roman Cooking Wares (TCP564–566), Late Roman Light Utility Wares (TCP567), Late Roman Table Wares such as Cypriot Red Slip ware forms 2 and 8, Egyptian Red Slip ware A, form P (TCP541), Phocaean Red Slip ware and African Red Slip ware and finally Late Roman Transport amphorae such as Late Roman amphora type 1, Late Roman amphora type 4 from Gaza (TCP208), a fragment of a North Palestinian amphora (TCP563) and one of unknown provenance (TCP562). Among the African Red Slip wares is a fragment decorated with an engraved male figure, wearing a chiton and holding a staff (TCP561).

This construction is, perhaps, the best evidence for our interpretation that a considerable effort was made to support and hold back the enormous volume of slag that built up over the years from copper production at Skouriotissa. Perhaps it was even more crucial in this area, where there may have been a settlement under increasing threat from the expanding waste heap.

AU10 This is a small section created by the track cut through AU03 (Table 3.24). The section was not recorded in detail and samples of slag were, therefore, not collected. Although there is a lot of collapsed material, only four sherds were collected from the talus.

AU11 This is in a very disturbed area, just outside and north of the fence around AU04. It is not a very clear section. It was cut by a small track that also created AU12, so material may have spilled over from there. It consists mainly of sediment mixed with crushed slag, and contains a high proportion of pottery fragments. Above these is a thick layer of ash. Pottery was collected from the section (as PU12), but some tiles were left in situ. One fragment of Cypriot Red Slip Table Ware suggests a date during the Late Roman period.

AU12 AU12 lies on the other side of the track that created AU11. Interestingly, the section does not consist solely of slag, but has some other archaeological strata that, as with AU09, may be associated with structures. The slag occurs in a mixed layer of slag and sediment, which contains a high number of sherds. Above there is a layer of slag, and then a layer of tiles and stone. Above these is a thick layer of ash. Pottery was collected from the section (as PU12), but the tiles were left in situ.

AU13 AU13 is the east-facing section above AU01. It is not vertical and could not be accessed easily, so was not recorded in detail.

AU14 AU14 is a north-west-facing section at the very top of the slag heap, just above and to the east of AU01. The top surface, where there are two large water tanks, is easily accessible and was recorded as layer Y01. AU14 is, in fact, the highest preserved part of the Skouriotissa slag heap and, therefore, it presumably represents the latest phases of smelting activity in this location. The section was drawn and samples of slag were collected (Plate 3.22; Table 3.25).

The tile and two utility ware sherds collected did not help to date more precisely the smelting activities in this part of the slag heap. A single piece of charcoal collected from Layer Y22 was radiocarbon dated (Wk-26026), and produced a date of AD 359–540 (95.4%). Lying almost at the top of the slag heap in this part of the extensive deposit, it shows that in this area production ceased in the 6th century AD.

The charcoal taxa identified in the samples from this section are maple, Cyprus pine and turpentine/Atlas pistachio (Table 3.26).

Artefacts

In general the pottery collected from the slag heap was very well preserved (Table 3.27; Table 3.28). The surfaces

Table 3.24. Skouriotissa Vouppes *(TP007): description of AU10 layers*

Layer	Layer material	Sherds	Comments
Y01	Slag – Small		Small pieces of slag mixed with carbon rich sediment.
Y02	Slag – Small		
Y03	Slag – Medium/Small		Inaccessible.
Y04	Slag – Cakes		
Y05	Slag – Medium/Small		
Y06	Slag – Medium		Slag cakes mixed with large pieces of slag. Inaccessible.
Y07	Slag – Small		
Y08	Slag – Cakes		
Y09	Slag – Cakes	1	
Y10	Slag – Medium		
Y11	Slag – Cakes		

Table 3.25. Skouriotissa Vouppes *(TP007): description of AU14 layers*

Layer	Layer material	Sherds	Comments
Y01	Slag – Small		Inaccessible.
Y02	Slag – Small		Inaccessible.
Y03	Slag – Small		Slag cakes mixed with small pieces of slag. Inaccessible.
Y04	Slag – Small		
Y05	Slag – Medium		Slag cakes mixed with small pieces of slag. Inaccessible.
Y06	Slag – Small		Inaccessible.
Y07	Slag – Small		Inaccessible.
Y08	Slag – Medium		Inaccessible.
Y09	Sediment		Inaccessible.
Y10	Slag – Medium/Small		Stones mixed with sediment. Inaccessible.
Y11	Slag – Small		
Y12	Slag – Small		
Y13	Slag – Small	1	
Y14	Slag – Cakes	2	Very small pieces of slag mixed with sediment.
Y15	Slag – Medium		
Y16	Slag – Small		Inaccessible.
Y17	Sediment		Inaccessible.
Y18	Slag – Cakes		
Y19	Slag – Medium		
Y20	Slag – Medium/Small	5	Slag collected with matrix.
Y21	Slag – Large		Sediment. Charcoal sample good for species ID.
Y22	Slag – Large		
Y23	Slag – Small		Charcoal sample good for species ID.
Y24	Slag – Cakes		Very small slag. Layer rich in carbon.

and fractures were not weathered, and fragment size was large compared to that of the Survey Area overall. The two Early Roman Cooking Ware fragments (TCP540) and the Mid Roman amphora fragment (TCP555) provide evidence for the earlier phases of Roman activities at Skouriotissa, also indicated by the radiocarbon dates. A few fragments of African Red Slip were collected, but none could be assigned a form, and these, as well as some of the less

Table 3.26. Skouriotissa Vouppes *(TP007): charcoal analysis from section AU14*

TP007.AU14	Layer Y17, A003	Layer Y21, A002
Acer sp.	1	
Pinus brutia	1	
Pistacia terebinthus/atlantica		1

Table 3.27. Skouriotissa Vouppes *(TP007): pottery from AUs. See also Table 3.28. TCP numbers refer to Pottery Catalogue in Volume 1, Chapter 3.6*

Historical Antiquity (Archaic to Late Roman)

Fct	*Type*	*No.*	*Weight*
Ar	Ti	4	592g
HU	HU	18	1.019kg
LU	LU	21	161g
Tr	Am	2	130g
TW	TW	1	11g
U	U	2	15g

Hellenistic to Roman

Fct	*Type*	*No.*	*Weight*
CW	CW	5	47g
LU	LUR06	1	15g
Tr	Am07	1	11g
TW	RS	1	10g
TW	SRS	1	1g
TW	TW	1	16g

Early Roman

Fct	*Type*	*No.*	*Weight*
CW	CWPR04a	1	34g TCP540

Early to Late Roman

Fct	*Type*	*No.*	*Weight*
Ar	Ti	1	50g
Ar	TiP	2	490g
CW	CW	7	48g
CW	CWPR08a	2	11g
HU	HU	4	190g
LU	LU	9	84g
Tr	Am	1	275g
TW	ARS	1	2g
TW	RS	1	4g

Late Roman

Fct	*Type*	*No.*	*Weight*
Ar	Ti	1	130g
Ar	TiP	3	610g
Ar	TiSk01	7	1.41kg
Ar	TiSk02	9	2.42kg TCP533
Ar	TiSk03	5	820g
Ar	TiSk04	2	600g
Ar	TiSk05	2	370g TCP534
Ar	TiSkC01	14	1.919kg TCP527, TCP535
Ar	TiSkC02	2	220g TCP532
Ar	TiSkC04	2	195g TCP536
Ar	TiSkC05	1	85g TCP538
CW	CW	6	16g
CW	CWPR14	2	23g TCP530
HU	HUR10a	1	48g TCP529
HU	HUR35	1	76g TCP539
LU	LU	1	6g
LU	LUR07	1	58g TCP528
Tr	Am	3	210g
Tr	Am08	1	220g TCP537
Tr	LR1	10	547g TCP531
TW	CRS	1	9g
TW	CRS02	3	34g
TW	CRS08	1	30g
TW	CRS09	1	11g
TW	CRS09A	1	18g
TW	ERSAP	1	21g TCP541
TW	LRC	2	16g
TW	RS	3	55g

Roman to Modern

Fct	*Type*	*No.*	*Weight*
Ar	Ti	1	70g
LU	LU	1	11g

Historical (Archaic to Modern)

Fct	*Type*	*No.*	*Weight*
CW	CW	5	70g
HU	HU	13	1.061kg
LU	LU	9	75g

Unknown

Fct	*Type*	*No.*	*Weight*
Un	Un	2	7g

precisely datable fragments, may also date to the Early and Late Roman periods.

The remaining closely dated diagnostic pottery, collected in and around the slag heap, all dates to the Late Roman period. The Table Wares are, mainly, typical late 5th–7th century AD wares and shapes found elsewhere in the Survey Area, apart from a unique fragment of Egyptian Red Slip ware (TCP541). The slag heap also boasts the highest concentration of Late Roman amphora 1 in the Survey Area, and the only fragments of Late Roman amphora 4 from Gaza (TCP208). Although none of the few Palestinian Late Roman amphora 5 fragments collected from the Survey Area come from TP007, we did collect one fragment of a Late Roman North Palestinian amphora (TCP563). Generally, the Cooking Wares have corrugated surfaces typical of the Late Roman period.

The pottery from the slag heap represents the widest range of imported Table Wares and transport amphorae in the entire Survey Area, giving evidence for the close ties between the mining industry and the extra-island world. This special connection is also supported by the slightly higher proportion of transport amphorae at Skouriotissa, compared to any other Late Roman site in the Survey Area. Clearly, the activities taking place at the mine were connected to the East Mediterranean supply system of the Late Roman world. There are no other finds to indicate any special status of the architecture associated with AU07, although the large number of tiles, both pan and cover tiles, as well as two fragments of water pipe, suggest the presence of substantial architecture located in the vicinity of the smelting activity. Six types of pan tiles and five types of cover tiles appear commonly at TP007. Based on their contextual association with diagnostic wares, they are dated to the Late Roman period.

Three ground stone tools were recovered from the slag heap: a mortar from AU05 (TCL334); a hammer stone from AU07; and a quern from AU09. Of interest is the use of hard materials, such as chromite, in the manufacture of the mortar, and basal rocks for the quern and hammer stone. Similar stone tools have been recorded in contexts associated with ore crushing at the Late Bronze Age settlement of Apliki *Karamallos* (Kassianidou 2007) and the Archaic–Hellenistic smelting site of Ayia Varvara *Almyras* (Connolly, in Fasnacht *et al.* 1992, 71).

Table 3.28. Skouriotissa Vouppes *(TP007): pottery from PUs. See also Table 3.27. TCP numbers refer to Pottery Catalogue in Volume 1, Chapter 3.6*

Historical Antiquity (Archaic to Late Roman)

Fct	*Type*	*No.*	*Weight*
Ar	Ti	8	2.395kg
HU	HU	13	400g
LU	LU	25	291g
Tr	Am	2	140g
TW	RS	1	10g
U	U	1	240g

Hellenistic to Roman

Fct	*Type*	*No.*	*Weight*
CW	CW	11	80g
Tr	Am07	1	12g
TW	TW	1	1g

Early Roman

Fct	*Type*	*No.*	*Weight*
CW	CWPR11	1	25g

Early to Late Roman

Fct	*Type*	*No.*	*Weight*
Ar	TiC	2	260g
CW	CW	24	295g
CW	CWPR12	1	10g
HU	HU	8	583g
HU	HUR08	1	65g
LU	LU	16	255g
Tr	Am	4	395g
Tr	Am05	1	70g TCP542
TW	ARS	1	12g TCP561

Mid Roman

Fct	*Type*	*No.*	*Weight*
Tr	Am02	1	50g TCP555

Late Roman

Fct	*Type*	*No.*	*Weight*
Ar	Ti	2	580g
Ar	TiSk01	9	4.605kg TCP557
Ar	TiSk02	6	3.92kg
Ar	TiSk03	26	8.315kg TCP544, TCP568, TCP569
Ar	TiSk04	1	450g TCP550
Ar	TiSk05	1	430g
Ar	TiSk06	1	390g TCP551
Ar	TiSkC01	15	1.803kg TCP545, TCP559
Ar	TiSkC02	1	400g
Ar	TiSkC03	1	110g TCP560
Ar	TiSkC04	3	225g
Ar	TiSkC05	1	90g
CW	CW	8	180g
CW	CWCR01a	1	120g TCP565
CW	CWCR05	1	42g TCP564
CW	CWJ01	1	10g TCP552
CW	CWL01	1	95g TCP566
CW	CWL02	1	5g TCP558
CW	CWPR12	1	32g TCP547
HU	HUR21	1	83g TCP548
HU	HUR22	1	135g TCP549
LU	LU	5	65g
LU	LUR05	1	15g TCP567
Tr	Am	8	640g
Tr	Am09	1	35g TCP562
Tr	Am10	1	30g TCP563
Tr	Gaz	1	12g
Tr	LR1	18	1.145kg TCP546, TCP554
TW	CRS	11	251g
TW	CRS02	2	25g
TW	CRS09	1	10g
TW	CRS09A	1	8g
TW	LRC	1	3g
TW	LRC03	2	30g
TW	LRC10b	1	30g TCP553
TW	RS	5	80g
Un	Un	1	210g TCP543

Roman to Modern

Fct	*Type*	*No.*	*Weight*
Ar	Ti	2	155g
HU	Pit	1	370g

Historical (Archaic to Modern)

Fct	*Type*	*No.*	*Weight*
Ar	Ti	1	40g
Ar	WaP	2	115g TCP556
CW	CW	4	90g
HU	HU	4	280g
HU	HUR34	1	20g
LU	LU	4	140g

Modern

Fct	*Type*	*No.*	*Weight*
Ar	WaP	1	70g

Unknown

Fct	*Type*	*No.*	*Weight*
Un	Un	1	20g

Conclusion: Skouriotissa Slag Heap

Our work at the Skouriotissa slag heap has shown that most of the remains left behind by the ancient copper industry date to the Late Roman period. Furthermore, it is clear that in the vicinity of the slag heap there was once a settlement. Both the pottery collected and the radiocarbon dates we obtained clearly show that production was active and in full force at least until the 7th century AD.

Having obtained radiocarbon dates from a series of samples from different sections (AUs) of the slag heap, it is possible to follow the development of this anthropogenic mountain. In the earliest phase, production was clearly focused on what is now the northern end of the slag heap. The centre moved further and further away from the mine towards the south, eventually taking over the area where a settlement once used to thrive.

Samples of slag collected from the various sections have been analysed and the full results are presented in Volume 1, Chapter 3.9. Although analyses of Skouriotissa slag samples published in the past (e.g. Bruce *et al.* 1937, 647) found them to be rich in manganese, which is characteristic of Roman slag (Kassianidou and Van Lokeren 2003, 226), the vast majority is in fact not manganiferous. This inconsistency in chemical composition was also noted among the slag samples collected from the Roman slag heaps around Mitsero (Kassianidou and Van Lokeren

Table 3.29. Skouriotissa Kitromilia *(TP172): description of AU01 layers*

Layer	Layer material	Sherds	Comments
Clean		4	
Y01	Sediment		Inaccessible
Y02	Slag - Small		Very small pieces of slag
Y03	Slag - Small		Inaccessible
Y04	Slag - Small		Inaccessible
Y05	Slag - Small		Inaccessible
Y06	Slag - Medium		Also contains slag cakes. Inaccessible
Y07	Slag - Small		Inaccessible
Y08	Slag - Medium/Small		
Y09	Slag - Medium		
Y10	Slag - Cakes		
Y11	Slag - Large		
Y12	Slag - Small		Small pieces of slag mixed with carbon-rich sediment
Y13	Slag - Small		
Y14	Slag - Small		
Y15	Slag - Large		
Y16	Slag - Small		
Y17	Slag - Small		Small pieces of slag mixed with carbon-rich sediment
Y18	Slag - Small		Very small pieces of slag mixed with carbon-rich sediment
Y19	Slag - Small		
Y20	Slag - Small		Very small pieces of slag mixed with carbon-rich sediment
Y21	Slag - Small	1	Very small pieces of slag mixed with carbon-rich sediment. Very rich in charcoal. Crushed furnace material
Y22	Slag - Small		Very small pieces of slag mixed with carbon-rich sediment. Very rich in charcoal. Crushed furnace material
Y23	Slag - Medium/Small		
Y24	Slag - Medium		Sediment & crushed pillow lava. Very rich in pottery. Plastered stones.
Y25	Slag - Small		Very small pieces of slag mixed with carbon-rich sediment. Very rich in charcoal. Crushed furnace material
Y26	Slag - Medium/Small		
Y27	Slag - Small		Very small pieces of slag mixed with carbon-rich sediment. Very rich in charcoal. Crushed furnace material
Y28	Slag - Small		Very small pieces of slag mixed with carbon-rich sediment. Very rich in charcoal. Crushed furnace material
Y29	Slag - Small		Very small pieces of slag mixed with carbon-rich sediment
Y30	Slag - Cakes		Slag cakes mixed with large pieces of slag
Y31	Slag - Medium/Small		

2003, 226), and needs to be addressed. Furthermore, most of the analysed slag samples have a low copper content (1% or lower), indicating the efficiency of the smelting process. Finally, the slag samples have extremely low levels of zinc, another issue that needs to be discussed.

Anthracological study of the charcoal samples collected from the recorded sections was undertaken by Maria Ntinou (Volume 1, Chapter 3.10). Analysis shows that the preferred species for fuel was *Pinus brutia*, a tree which grows in this part of the Troodos Mountains and which would have been abundant in the past (Volume 1, Chapter 4.8). Through the analysis of the charcoal collected in the various sections of TP007, Ntinou reached the conclusion that, in the case of Skouriotissa, the fuel used for smelting was not only produced locally, but was the product of an industrial network of charcoal production and fuel provisioning, that connected the Skouriotissa mine with the Troodos pine forests to the south.

Skouriotissa *Kitromilia*: The Secondary Slag Heap (TP172)

A second, smaller slag heap is located some 500 m north-west of TP007, and was shown to us by the chief geologist of the Hellenic Mining Company. It is located just east of the modern cementation plant and the area is very disturbed by present-day activities. We cleaned and recorded the top part of the slag heap, which had been sectioned (AU01; Plate 3.23).

The layers of this slag heap mostly consisted of finely crushed slag mixed with furnace material and large amounts of charcoal (Table 3.29). We collected and analysed samples of slag and charcoal, but found very little pottery while cleaning, and only one Archaic–Late Roman sherd in the section (Table 3.30). Interestingly, the slag samples were mostly manganiferous, with four samples having a manganese content above 25%. The level of copper in most samples is well below 1%, while zinc is present at levels below 0.05%. The unstratified pottery included a Roman tile and a fragment of Late Roman Cypriot Red Slip.

The analysis of single charcoal fragments recovered from successive layers of this heap show, once more, the exclusive presence of the Cyprus pine (Table 3.31).

The relationship between this slag heap and the large one (TP007) is unclear. The fact that some of the slag samples from this heap were found to contain significant amounts of manganese, an element only associated with slags of the Roman period (see Volume 1, Chapter 3.9), shows that TP172 also dates to this period. A sample of charcoal coming from layer Y20 of the section was radiocarbon dated (Wk 25877) and produced a date of AD 546–646 (95.4%). It is therefore suggested that this deposit of slag may represent the very last phase of operation at the mine. In other words, this represents small-scale production of copper, after the abandonment of the workshops represented by the large slag heap.

Table 3.30. Skouriotissa Kitromilia *(TP172): pottery in AU01*

Historical Antiquity (Archaic to Late Roman)			
Fct	*Type*	*No.*	*Weight*
HU	HU	1	10g
LU	LU	2	4g
Early to Late Roman			
Fct	*Type*	*No.*	*Weight*
Ar	Ti	1	175g
Late Roman			
Fct	*Type*	*No.*	*Weight*
TW	CRS	1	6g

The Context and the Monastery of Panayia Skouriotissa

Systematic block survey in the immediate area of the slag heap was difficult owing to ground visibility, crops and the United Nations Camp. We investigated two Survey Units (SU0002, SU0008) some 200 m west of the northern end of the slag heap, lying at a lower level on the eastern side of the river. The pottery collected is chronologically very different from that in the slag heap, and much more mixed. A small concentration of Hellenistic–Early Roman amphora fragments came from SU0002. The Hellenistic–Early Roman presence, however, seems to be confirmed by a fragment of Eastern Sigillata ware.

The pottery from the units in the transect north of this area (TT3883500N) revealed a remarkable chronological mix and range, including a very high concentration of Hellenistic–Early Roman Table Wares and a rare fragment of a Hellenistic *unguentarium*. Some of the earlier Table Wares may have come from tombs, which are numerous in the area south of the slag heap and stretching to the village of Katydhata (Chapter 3.10, 3.14; see also 3.13). It is known that Skouriotissa was also mined during this period, and there must have been a settlement in the area. Distribution of pottery at the smelting site of Mavrovouni in the Lagoudhera Valley (Chapter 4.6) indicates that smelting took place in close proximity to the settlement.

One logical site for the settlement would be under the monastery of Panayia Skouriotissa, now the United Nations San Martin camp. This monastery is immediately adjacent to the western side of the monumental Roman slag heap (TP007). Its title derives from 'skouria' or slag, and so can be translated as 'Our Lady of the Slag Heap'. Judging by a fresco fragment the original church probably dates to the 15th century AD, although the monastery, built by Bishop Makarios, was not constructed until 1716 and most of the icons date to the 18th century AD. When the Russian monk Basil Bars'kyj visited in 1835 there were only three or four monks in residence (Bars'kyj 1996, 40). The church was rebuilt in 1845. We were shown four, rather crude, limestone column fragments in the grounds of the camp, three of them 40 cm in diameter and one of them including a basic capital with two torus mouldings (TP091). These were plough damaged and not in situ, but date to the Late Roman or Byzantine period and suggest a substantial structure in the vicinity, which might have been part of the settlement associated with the slag heap and mines.

Table 3.31. Skouriotissa Kitromilia *(TP172): charcoal analysis of section AU01*

	Layer Y18, A002	Layer Y21, A002	Layer Y26, A002	Layer Y27, A001
Pinus brutia	1	1	1	
Pinus sp.				1

The pottery from the three Survey Units closest to the southern edge of the United Nations camp (SU1022–24) also revealed a remarkable chronological mix and range, from the prehistoric period through the Iron Age to the Late Roman period. This mixture attests to the long occupation of the area south and west of Skouriotissa, which was probably associated with the mine. Some of the large number of Hellenistic and Early Roman Table Wares may have come from the tombs, as well as from a mining settlement located at the site of San Martin Camp. Several of the pottery types found in the slag heap were also collected from these units, including Late Roman amphorae type 1, Cypriot Red Ware forms 2 and 9, Phocaean Red Slip Ware form 3, and African Red Slip ware. The remaining units of this transect (TT3883000N), further away from the camp on the western side, also have a highly mixed pottery distribution, but lower densities, while the units on the eastern side mainly contain pottery that was less datable or post-Roman.

By 1912, the monastery was abandoned, apart from the church, and the following year it became part of the metallurgical history of the area, when it was taken over and developed by Godfrey Gunther as the headquarters of the Cyprus Mines Corporation (Lavender 1962, 66). Given its proximity to the Buffer Zone, it is now the San Martin Camp, which during our survey was the headquarters of the United Nations Argentinian contingent.

20th Century Mining Settlement

The Skouriotissa mining settlement (TP107), now a completely abandoned workers' housing complex, is known locally simply as 'Spitia' or 'Exinda Spitia' – the Sixty Houses. Local informants reported that the Cyprus Mines Corporation leased the land for the settlement from the church; with its abandonment, it has returned to the ownership of the local bishopric. Lavender (1962, 66) records that the construction of workers' housing in this area, across the river from the monastery that served as Gunther's headquarters, began in 1923 and continued through the 1920s and 1930s. The mining company constructed sanitary facilities in the village and piped water to communal facilities, but dysentery and other public health problems plagued Skouriotissa and the other workers' complexes owned by the Cyprus Mines Corporation at Mavrovouni and Xeros (Lavender 1962, 66).

The workers' village was occupied by Greek Cypriot and Turkish Cypriot workers, and their families. Two schools were provided, one for Greek Cypriot and another for Turkish Cypriot children (Lavender 1962, 230). The workers' village was a vehicle for various social welfare campaigns, notably those introduced by George and Elsie White who were hired by the Cyprus Mines Corporation in 1939 (Lavender 1962, 267). The Whites oversaw the creation of welfare centres that taught ante- and post-natal care, distributed milk to children (not previously a common part of the Cypriot diet) and also promoted the Boy Scout and Girl Guide movements (Lavender 1962, 267). According to a local informant, the settlement was abandoned after the Turkish invasion of 1974.

The extant remains of the mining village recorded by the field survey consisted of three groups of houses, built to a standard pattern but with slight variation between the three groups. The three groups were recorded collectively as BU0121 (House Group 1; 5 extant houses), BU0119 (House Group 2; 23 extant houses), and BU0120 (House Group 3; 8 extant houses). Each housing group is marshalled into a roughly gridded layout. The three groups are separated by two roads leading into the settlement from the south. Remains of shared, separate latrines survive in some locations, and stone lined cesspits survive where the superstructure of the latrine has been destroyed.

The mining village at Skouriotissa was occupied by Greek refugees towards the end of the Second World War. Lavender (1962, 291) records that the village was in need of extensive repair and renovation following the end of the war. It seems likely that the surviving buildings either date to the post-war period, or are earlier structures extensively renovated at that time. Lavender (1969, 291) describes the pre-war housing as consisting of two-roomed, mudbrick structures with a dirt floor and veranda. The current houses also follow this pattern, but all have cement floors.

The houses of Group 2 (BU0119) appear to have been occupied most recently, as they have evidence of connections to electricity and reticulated water. They also feature a hard, exterior, cement render covering the mudbrick, with decorative dado lines in the render on each elevation (Fig. 3.56). Other decorative features include red painted bargeboards and architraves, contrasting with the white painted render. The houses still follow a simple two-room form, each room with an attached external courtyard, one of which is covered with a shed roof, enclosing the external hearth and sink. Internally they have lath and plaster ceilings.

Group 1 and 3 houses feature a softer, external lime render, without decorative features. Group 3 houses feature cane ceilings, in the traditional style of the region. There is evidence of Italian style terracotta tiles roofs, but most have been removed, probably for re-use. The houses are surrounded with the remnants of useful garden plants, such as prickly pear, figs and grapes, and numerous eucalypts and cypresses.

BU0122, located to the south of the three groups of houses, was identified by a local informant as a former school building, now used as a farm store. It is a substantial structure of rendered mudbrick, with decorative red brick features and a hipped roof, now clad in corrugated iron, perhaps replacing earlier terracotta tiles.

Other features in the village area include a roadside shrine, installed within a recent sentry box (1940s–1960s), constructed at the crossroads in the village (BU0118). The shrine continued to be visited and maintained at the time of the field survey. While the land around the abandoned mining village continues to be farmed, its location in a

Fig. 3.56. Skouriotissa mining settlement (TP107): House Group 2 (BU0119) (Chris Parks)

'peninsula' of land (also containing the Skouriotissa mine) surrounded by the Buffer Zone, means that access to this area is now limited. The network of cobbled, cypress-lined roads leading to the mining settlement reflect its past importance to the region and its role in providing health care, schools and other services for workers and their families. These roads also provide relatively rare examples of cobbled surfaces that have not been replaced with tarmac.

The Skouriotissa mining settlement offers stark evidence of the new forms of social control that accompanied 20th century industrial developments. The regimented, grid-based layout of freestanding workers' housing is totally alien to the built-up forms of the TAESP landscape, which feature densely nucleated settlements and villages that developed organically, with houses closely abutting one another. It is interesting that the Skouriotissa mining settlement was known throughout its life of over 50 years as simply 'The Houses'. It did not develop into a new form of community: the traditional village territories that surrounded the mining area, which was only formally named Skouriotissa in 1931 (Given 2005, 52–53), continued to define concepts of community and belonging in the Karkotis valley landscape.

Conclusion

The earliest phases of production in Skouriotissa were almost certainly located on Phoukasa hill, now completely removed by opencast mining. The earliest evidence for copper production in the area was uncovered by chance, by the Cyprus Water Authority, while opening a long trench in one of the roads in Katydhata village, following completion of TAESP's field work (Kassianidou 2008, 255–56). During work in the vicinity of the church, a group of tombs was accidentally discovered and subsequently excavated by Giorgos Georgiou, archaeological officer of the Department of Antiquities. Two of the excavated tombs produced an array of pottery dated to the Prehistoric Bronze Age 2 period (19th–18th centuries BC).

What is extraordinary is that among the finds from this trench was a small quantity of slag (Kassianidou 2008, 256). It is unclear whether the slag was inside or outside the tombs, but it is apparently contemporary with the burials. If it did come from the tombs, it is the first clear evidence of slag being deposited together with other funerary gifts. Unfortunately, the excavation was not extended and these questions remain, for now, unanswered. The excavator kindly allowed us to study the slag. The fragments come from flat, circular, cakes c. 1 cm thick. They are very homogeneous and, therefore, very different from slag found on other Middle Cypriot sites, namely Alambra (Gale *et al.* 1996, 139) and perhaps Pyrgos (Belgiorno 2000, 31). It is, in fact, different from anything else we know from Cyprus. Perhaps chemical and microscopic analyses, now under way, will help to inform us about the technology that produced it.

Although we have not recorded any remains that date to periods prior to the Roman period, there is no doubt that mining and smelting took place in Skouriotissa, probably, from the Bronze Age. Direct evidence for earlier mining phases is provided by the three radiocarbon dates on wooden supports from Skouriotissa, mentioned above, which fall within the Archaic period. Furthermore, smaller slag heaps with a different type of slag identified as 'Phoenician' (because they were more oxidised and therefore believed to have been of an earlier date) were identified on the hill of Phoukasa (Bruce *et al.* 1937, 642); unfortunately these deposits no longer exist and thus could not be recorded.

It is clear that copper production on a truly industrial scale at Skouriotissa dates to the Late Roman period. During that time, in order to produce the two million tons of slag that form the main heap, thousands of people must have been employed in the mines and smelting workshops. We have also shown without doubt that the production of copper did not cease during the 4th century AD, but continued with the same intensity well into the 7th century, and perhaps later. During that time, copper must have formed the basis of the Cypriot economy, as it had done since the Late Bronze Age. It also lay behind the wealth and prosperity of the island, a fact vividly

Table 3.32. Skouriotissa Pseftas *(TS13): pottery from SU1006, SU1072–78. TCP numbers refer to Pottery Catalogue in Volume 1, Chapter 3.6*

Prehistoric Bronze Age

Fct	*Type*	*No.*	*Weight*
LU	RPO	2	20g

Cypro-Geometric to Classical

Fct	*Type*	*No.*	*Weight*
LU	WP	2	25g

Historical Antiquity (Archaic to Late Roman)

Fct	*Type*	*No.*	*Weight*
Ar	Ti	15	1.305kg
Ar	TiCS	2	150g
Ar	TiP	1	315g
HU	HU	35	897g
LU	LU	46	393g
Tr	Am	2	130g
TW	TW	4	25g

Classical to Hellenistic

Fct	*Type*	*No.*	*Weight*
TW	BG	2	10g
TW	BS	1	2g

Hellenistic

Fct	*Type*	*No.*	*Weight*
La	La03	1	5g TCP250
TW	BS	7	26g
TW	RS	11	34g

Late Hellenistic

Fct	*Type*	*No.*	*Weight*
TW	CS20	1	5g
TW	ESA15B	1	40g TCP246
TW	ESA16	2	3g
TW	ESA20	1	5g

Hellenistic to Roman

Fct	*Type*	*No.*	*Weight*
LU	LUR09	1	15g TCP189
Tr	Am01	1	50g
Tr	Am07	2	33g
Tr	Mav01	3	240g
TW	SRS	25	100g

Late Hellenistic to Early Roman

Fct	*Type*	*No.*	*Weight*
TW	CS	7	45g
TW	ESA	21	138g
TW	Sig	2	5g TCP251
TW	TW	1	10g

Early Roman

Fct	*Type*	*No.*	*Weight*
CW	CWPR04a	11	51g TCP248
La	La01	1	5g
TW	CS06	1	15g
TW	SigW	2	5g TCP247

Early to Late Roman

Fct	*Type*	*No.*	*Weight*
Ar	Ti	1	25g
CW	CW	53	299g
CW	CWCR02a	1	7g
CW	CWCR03	1	15g
CW	CWFPWh	3	130g
Tr	AmSk01	4	30g

Mid Roman

Fct	*Type*	*No.*	*Weight*
TW	CRS09A	1	16g

Late Roman

Fct	*Type*	*No.*	*Weight*
Ar	TiCS	1	27g
Ar	TiP	6	842g
Ar	TiSkC03	1	40g
HU	HUR20	1	42g TCP249
Tr	LR1	1	35g
TW	CRS	5	64g
TW	CRS02	1	10g
TW	LRC03	1	15g
TW	RS	1	8g

Roman to Modern

Fct	*Type*	*No.*	*Weight*
Ar	Ti	6	410g
CW	CW	9	60g
LU	LU	15	160g

Historical (Archaic to Modern)

Fct	*Type*	*No.*	*Weight*
HU	HU	94	2.84kg
LU	LU	122	1.42kg

Medieval to Modern

Fct	*Type*	*No.*	*Weight*
CW	BGW	1	7g

Byzantine to Medieval

Fct	*Type*	*No.*	*Weight*
TW	CGS05	1	10g

Medieval-Frankish

Fct	*Type*	*No.*	*Weight*
TW	CGS05	1	10g

Ottoman to Modern II

Fct	*Type*	*No.*	*Weight*
HU	BuH	4	147g
LU	BuL	22	277g

Modern

Fct	*Type*	*No.*	*Weight*
Ar	TiCh	4	89g
TW	Por	1	15g

Unknown

Fct	*Type*	*No.*	*Weight*
HU	HU	1	275g
Un	Un	1	55g

illustrated by the basilicas and other monuments of the Late Roman period.

3.13 Hellenistic and Roman Pottery at Skouriotissa *Pseftas*

Skouriotissa *Pseftas* (TS13; Plate 3.24) is an area of dense Hellenistic and Roman pottery on a series of anthropogenic terraces, some 100 m west of the Karkotis River and about 300 m west of the Skouriotissa mine. The Karkotis River drainage near Skouriotissa has been modified heavily since the 1963 aerial photographs were taken: roads have been constructed, the mine and San Martin United Nations camp have been extended, and agricultural terraces for cultivation and orchards have been created by bulldozing, importing fill, manuring and ploughing. To the east lies the Karkotis River and a disused rail track, paved with slag and built up with imported yellow soil. This track was once used to transport material from the mine to Morphou Bay. Because Pseftas is located in a politically sensitive area just south of the Buffer Zone, our time to survey there was limited, and we had few opportunities to take photographs.

We conducted block survey to ascertain the extent and character of the Hellenistic–Roman pottery scatter (Plate 3.24, Table 3.32). The fields on the eastern side of the road – located on an anthropogenic terrace – contained substantial amounts of pottery dominated by Hellenistic and Roman wares. The most significant amounts are from the Roman period, followed by Late Hellenistic–Early Roman material. A full array of functions was represented, including architectural, Cooking, Light and Heavy Utility wares (although proportionately less than might be expected of an in situ settlement), Table Wares, transport amphorae and lamps. The presence of several Hellenistic wares (including Late Hellenistic Eastern Sigillata A) confirms activity during that period. The fields on the western side of the road present a slightly different picture. Due to their position, near the foot of pillow basalt slopes to the north-west, they occupy a terrace composed of mixed fluvial and colluvial sediments. The quantities of pottery found here were far smaller. The assemblage's functional spectrum and temporal distribution were the same as that on the eastern side of the road, except for the absence of transport amphorae and lamps.

The distribution of pottery functions east of the road is quite similar to that of the Late Roman settlement at Nikitari *Sanidhia* (Chapter 2.15), except for the very low proportion of tile fragments collected at the latter. The general similarity to Sanidhia may indicate the presence of a settlement in this area, although the high proportion of Hellenistic and Early Roman Table Wares suggests that the assemblage is in a secondary depositional context. The range of chronotypes is no different from the range collected in other areas with a strong Hellenistic–Roman presence. A higher occurrence of specific chronotypes, however, may indicate the intrusion of foreign material into the assemblage, e.g. material from washed-out tombs (see Chapter 3.14 for further discussion of Hellenistic–Roman tomb assemblages in the Karkotis Valley). As with elsewhere along the Karkotis, artefact distribution patterns of this and earlier periods are particularly vulnerable to Roman and later land levelling (see Chapter 3.10 and Volume 1, Chapter 4.6 for a discussion of post-depositional processes in this area).

Chipped Stone and Ground stone

In spite of a background scatter of pottery extending in date to the Modern period, Pseftas provides a clear example of the local chipped stone industry of the Hellenistic and Roman periods. Only one piece of chipped stone was recovered from the olive mill (TP109; see below), but a more substantial sample was collected across the block survey (see Table 3.33), particularly from areas where there were high levels of Hellenistic–Roman pottery. A rubbing stone from SU1006 represents the only ground stone tool.

Table 3.33. Skouriotissa Pseftas *(TS13): chipped stone counts*

	TP109	*Survey Units*
Cores		9
Blanks	1	10
Debitage		14
Tools		15
Totals	**1**	**48**

A number of features add to the characterisation of the Pseftas lithic samples as Hellenistic–Roman. The entire sample is composed of local jasper and chalcedony materials, with a single core produced from silicified umber, a stone also available locally. All major artefact categories are represented, suggesting that core reduction took place locally; the core technology and tool types are also consistent. The industry is dominated by the use of a variety of simple flake cores, including two amorphous cores, one change-of-orientation core, a single platform core, four core fragments and a tested jasper nodule. All cores were used for the manufacture of flakes, with the change-of-orientation core also exhibiting irregular, elongated flake or blade scars.

Pseftas featured a moderate to heavy concentration of chipped stone, more intense on the west side of the road. Many of these flakes and utilized tools were made of local red jasper. The discovery of three large jasper cores (not collected) on a spur some 200 m north-west of Pseftas is consistent with the character of this assemblage. This spur has a series of jasper outcrops and very probably was a raw material source for the chipped stone tools produced in Pseftas. The tools are dominated by the ad hoc use of sharp unretouched flake edges (9 pieces; 56%). A single flake tool is represented by a notched piece, while five other retouched tools consist of *dhoukani* flakes made on local jasper (representing 31% of the tool sample). The more moderate level of *dhoukani* flakes and the presence of numerous utilized flakes, in comparison to relatively few flake tools, is a pattern consistent with samples collected from other Roman sites in the TAESP area, for example, at Phlasou *Dodekeskala* (Chapter 3.6) and Petra *Phoukasa* (Chapter 2.6).

Transects TT3883500N and TT3883000N, crossing the valley 300 m and 800 m south of Pseftas respectively, provide good parallels to this sample. Both samples are dominated by local jasper and chalcedony used for the production of flakes. Each assemblage included a *dhoukani* flake made of jasper, as well as one flake tool and one utilized flake from each respective transect. The cores recovered from Transect TT3883500N include one amorphous example and a splintered piece exhibiting flake scars. This transect also produced three ground stone tools, including two rubbing stones and a grinder, as well as an unworked piece of picrolite (from SU1007).

Adit and Olive Mill (TP109)

More specific indications of ancient activity at Pseftas include an adit and an olive mill installation, situated some

Table 3.34. Skouriotissa Pseftas *(TS13): pottery from TP109. TCP numbers refer to Pottery Catalogue in Volume 1, Chapter 3.6*

Cypro-Geometric to Classical

Fct	*Type*	*No.*	*Weight*
LU	WPC	1	50g

Historical Antiquity (Archaic to Late Roman)

Fct	*Type*	*No.*	*Weight*
Ar	Ti	5	1.11kg
HU	HU	9	1.42kg
LU	LU	6	252g

Hellenistic to Roman

Fct	*Type*	*No.*	*Weight*
Ar	TiP	3	3.18kg TCP621, TCP622
CW	CW	3	14g
TW	SRS	2	15g

Early to Late Roman

Fct	*Type*	*No.*	*Weight*
Ar	Ti	2	230g
Ar	TiC	1	75g
Ar	TiP	1	320g
CW	CW	4	16g
CW	CWPR13	1	4g

Late Roman

Fct	*Type*	*No.*	*Weight*
Ar	TiP	1	130g
Ar	TiSkC02	1	140g
Ar	TiSkC05	1	550g TCP623
CW	CWPDh	1	7g
Tr	Pal	1	12g
TW	CRS09	2	30g
TW	LRC10	1	43g

Roman to Modern

Fct	*Type*	*No.*	*Weight*
Ar	TiCS	2	65g

Historical (Archaic to Modern)

Fct	*Type*	*No.*	*Weight*
HU	HU	4	190g
LU	LU	8	46g

Ottoman to Modern I

Fct	*Type*	*No.*	*Weight*
LU	LUBW	1	20g TCP620

200 m to the north of the block Survey Area, at Katydhata *Psevtadhes* (TP109). The adit is cut into a basalt outcrop at the foot of a long spur, where it flattens out onto the deeper-soiled alluvial terraces along the Karkotis River. The jasper outcrops discussed above are 100 m further up the spur to the west. Those who dug this adit exploited the natural jointing in a dyke rising through the pillow lava. Its roof slopes into the ground at an angle of about 45°, the hole itself appears to be, at least, several metres deep; its full depth is uncertain due to natural and cultural infilling. The 2-m wide opening faces south-east, the same direction as the slope.

Leading out of the adit is a shallow, overgrown depression that is partially filled with soil and rocky debris. The small basalt boulders surrounding the entrance could have resulted from clearing the adit. In addition, numerous large diabase cobbles were brought up from the Karkotis River; these may have been used to crush the metal ore mined in the adit. Pottery was collected in four POSI units (Table 3.34).

Approximately 25 m east of the adit is a semicircular depression cut into the slope. This seems to be the remains of a plastered vat, with an estimated diameter of 2 m. Because much of it has silted up, only the uppermost 50–60 cm are visible, but it is clear that its lower part is cut out of the rock, and at least the top 20 cm are built up. Its bedrock walls have been lined with a lime plaster that includes many basalt pebbles (up to 8 mm in diameter). Beside the vat were three, large, stone slabs, one of which is certainly a millstone fragment (59 × 56 cm) with an 11 cm square socket in its centre.

The vat is most likely a receptacle for settling and storing pressed oil. It resembles the vat in the Roman-period olive oil processing complex at Amathus *Ayia Varvara*, which was also plastered, with a diameter of 1.75 m and a depth of 1.5 m, and a stone channel leading to it from the press room (Hadjisavvas 1992, 50). The size and shape of the socket in the millstone fragment suggest that it was used for crushing olives in a rotary mill before the pulp was pressed to extract the oil (Hadjisavvas 1992, 17–19).

Six ground stone tools were recovered at Psevtadhes, including four rubbing stones, an anvil/rubbing stone and a pounder. As noted for the ground stone artefacts collected at Skouriotissa *Vouppes* (Chapter 3.12), and considering the context, these tools could have been used for ore dressing (Connolly, in Fasnacht *et al.* 1992, 71–72).

The presence of mining features such as an adit is consistent with this area's proximity to the Skouriotissa mine. Because major exploitation of the copper ores at Skouriotissa took place during the Roman period, a search for metallic ores just across the river is not unexpected. The instability of the Geomorphological Unit in which the adit is situated would allow associated artefacts to move downslope. This south-easterly movement may be directly related to the significant quantities of Hellenistic–Roman pottery found during block survey in Pseftas; however, no pottery was collected from a unit further up the slope, and the size and state of preservation of the pottery collected near the adit do not indicate much movement. No Survey Units were established at Psevtadhes and thus the data cannot be quantified. Nonetheless, the presence of Late Roman pottery and the absence of Hellenistic to Early Roman wares so common in the general area do suggest a Late Roman date.

The olive mill installation indicates the presence of a small farmstead at some point in time, but the high proportion of large architectural fragments from the Roman period observed on site may indicate more substantial architecture in the area. The striking heterogeneity of the tiles (13 groups differentiated by fabric, style and decoration) and their abundant fresh breaks suggest that they may have been moved from elsewhere to aid construction of the nearby irrigation channel. The Late Roman slag heap at Skouriotissa *Vouppes* (TP007), which produced abundant tile fragments (see Chapter 3.12), is one potential source. The only conclusion possible is that a Roman period settlement existed somewhere nearby.

Transect survey south and south-east of Pseftas revealed moderate to heavy densities of Hellenistic–Roman pottery. All phases within the Hellenistic–Roman period are represented within these Survey Units, although pottery from the Late Roman period was least numerous. Functional types include a high proportion of Table Ware and Cooking Ware, as well as some architectural pieces, a few transport amphorae, *unguentaria* and a lamp. Some of these remains probably derived from a settlement in the general area, as suggested by the material at Pseftas, as well as by heavy concentrations of tiles near the Late Roman slag heap (TP007). The Hellenistic–Roman assemblages may also include material from washed-out tombs, which is logical given the frequent occurrence of contemporary funerary activity in the area (see Chapter 3.14).

Conclusions

The geomorphological context makes interpretation of the Hellenistic–Roman material at Pseftas difficult. Interestingly, this results not so much from post-Roman depositional processes, as from Roman-period soil movement and construction associated with the creation of fields and irrigation systems for intensive agriculture, presumably to support the massive copper production at Skouriotissa (Volume 1, Chapter 4.6).

The pottery scatter at Pseftas is mainly Roman, with substantial Late Hellenistic–Early Roman and some Hellenistic material. The full range of functions suggests a settlement resembling Sanidhia on the Koutraphas plateau (Chapter 2.15). The chipped stone represents a characteristically Roman pattern of local material (the jasper probably quarried from an outcrop 200 m away) and simple flake technology, with a range of utilized flakes and flake tools, including *dhoukani* flakes. It is possible that some of this represents tomb material, though the lithics suggest that at least some of it must be settlement debris. The large amounts of material being moved for land levelling and mining in the general region must have had some, if not considerable, influence on the sorting and dispersal of material.

An olive mill 200 m north of the pottery scatter seems to be roughly contemporary, and may have been part of an associated farmstead, or slightly larger settlement. An adjacent adit with a striking amount of ground stone, probably for ore dressing, is a reminder of the other half of the symbiotic relationship between agriculture and mining that characterized this region in the Roman period.

3.14 Mortuary Landscapes of the Karkotis Valley

Tombs were the focus of most early 20th century archaelogical endeavours in the Karkotis Valley (see Chapter 3.9). Other than a locality name, however, their exact locations were almost never recorded. In the course of transect and block survey, we recorded all tombs encountered as POSIs (see Plate 3.1 for a map of the

Table 3.35. Tombs in the Karkotis valley (see POSI catalogue in Appendix 2 for further details)

TP065	Evrykhou *Varkakioes* (Evrykhou Tomb 5)	Hellenistic–Roman. Collapsed. Unlooted. 10.3 × 2.0 m. Five niches, three tile-covered limestone sarcophagi. Coins, pottery, glass. (Jacobsen 2007)
TP101	Evrykhou *Pano Atsas* (Evrykhou Tombs 1–2)	Archaic–Classical. (Nicolaou 1984, 234)
TP138	Phlasou *Akhneradhoes*	Two possible tombs. (1) Oval depression 2.5 × 2.1 × 0.2 m. (2) Oval depression, 2.3 × 2.2 × 0.7 m, possible upcast to E. More possible tombs upslope to the SE.
TP178	Evrykhou *Ammos*	Two tombs, cut into 15-m long outcrop. Apparently looted and infilled. No artefacts.
TP247	Evrykhou *Phinikos* (Evrykhou Tomb 4)	Hellenistic–Roman. 8.3 × 1.95 m. Vaulted ceiling, three niches. Peak of use in Hellenistic period. Similar to TP065. (Nicolaou 1984)
	Evrykhou village (Evrykhou Tomb 3)	Archaic–Classical. (Nicolaou 1984, 234)
TP090	Skouriotissa *Kataliontis*	Possible Roman tomb.
TP093	Katydhata *Mutallou*	Rectilinear tomb. c. 2 × 1.4 m.
TP094	Katydhata *Mutallou*	Tomb with four chambers. Dromos lost. c. 3.3 × 1.3 m.
TP116	Katydhata *Mutallou*	Tomb opening.
TP037	Katydhata *Laonarka*	Tomb with rectangular chamber (c. 3.8 × 1.9 m) and niche (1.35 × 1.9 m), probably Roman.
TP063	Katydhata *Laonarka*	Cut into basalt outcrop. Chamber roughly circular, c. 2 m diameter. Dromos faces SW.
TP111	Katydhata *Laonarka*	Chamber roughly circular, c. 2.2 m diameter. Dromos faces NW.
TP126	Katydhata *Laonarka*	Roughly rectangular chamber c. 3.5 m long, probably opening to WNW. Roughly vertical sides.
TP127	Katydhata *Laonarka*	Rectilinear chamber tomb with dromos (Roman). Dromos c. 3.5 m long with steps. Rock-cut benches and sarcophagus fragments.
TP128	Katydhata *Laonarka*	Rectilinear chamber tomb with dromos (Roman).
TP166	Katydhata *Laonarka*	Collapsed dromos, facing NW. Chamber not visible.
TP203	Katydhata village	Middle–Late Bronze Age chamber tomb (Katydhata Village Tomb 1).

Karkotis Valley). Tombs excavated by the Cypriot Department of Antiquities in the Intensive Survey Zone were also issued POSI numbers in order to incorporate them into our interpretations of the Survey Area. Those tomb POSIs not directly associated with a Special Interest Area are summarised in tabular format (Table 3.35). Collectively, they permit a reconstruction of the ancient mortuary landscape in the Karkotis Valley.

Of particular interest is a Hellenistic–Roman mortuary complex that evidently stretched from Katydhata and Linou villages north toward Skouriotissa. Ohnefalsch-Richter excavated a range of Roman tombs in this area, which, among other finds, produced some striking examples of glass (Myres and Ohnefalsch-Richter 1899, 4; Ohnefalsch-Richter 1893, 407–408, pl. LXV). Early in the 20th century Markides excavated nine looted Roman tombs at *Apoti*, on the eastern side of the road between Katydhata and Skouriotissa (Markides 1916, 4; Vessberg and Westholm 1956, 22). South of this area TAESP recorded four tombs (TP090, TP093, TP094, TP116) that probably belong to the same necropolis. Two unlooted tombs, excavated by the Cypriot Department of Antiquities in the Evrykhou area, provide rare detailed comparative evidence for mortuary practices during the Hellenistic–Early Roman period (TP065, TP247).

Four tombs (TP037, TP126–28) cut into the bedrock of the western slope of the Katydhata Park Ridge, immediately north of Katydhata *Laonarka*, can be dated to the Roman period by means of their morphology and/or associated artefacts. Two of them (TP127–28) are intact chamber tombs with dromoi whose roofs have collapsed. Their rectilinear construction and use of benches in niches for the deceased strongly suggests a Roman date (Carstens 2006, 157–58; Parks 1999). The north-west-facing dromos of TP128 is c. 3.7 m long, and the three lichen-covered limestone blocks near the opening probably once composed its door slab. The doorway's vertical facade and edges were carved with particular care. The tomb's interior has a rectangular main chamber with four niches, each set c. 50 cm above the tomb floor, branching off to the sides.

The west-facing dromos of TP127 is c. 3.5 m long, and its walls appear to have been slightly domed (Fig. 3.57). Several steps are cut into the dromos, next to which sits a thick, irregular limestone block that probably was used as a door slab. The tomb's interior consists of two chambers with a combined length of c. 8 m; the inner chamber has raised platforms surviving on the north side and the end. Its roof work is regular: there was an effort to make the ceiling flat, with right angles at the corners. A limestone block (c. 0.50 × 0.42 × 0.10 m), just inside the tomb entrance, probably formed part of a sarcophagus; the fragment of roof tile found beside it may have been used as the lid.

Human bone, pottery and glass sherds were collected inside TP127. The bones all derive from one or more fully mature individuals. They consist of two diaphyseal fragments of tibiae, one fibula diaphyseal fragment, the glabellar portion of a frontal bone, a femoral head, and the body of a lumbar vertebra. The late Danielle Parks examined the glass vessels: they include base fragments from a very large candlestick *unguentarium* (TCS073; see Volume 1, Chapter 3.7 for Special Finds catalogue); the base and body of a medium candlestick *unguentarium*; the rim of a tall flask or candlestick *unguentarium*; the neck of a piriform (sack-shaped) flask; the base of a conical or cylindrical beaker; the neck and rim of a candlestick *unguentarium*; and the rim of a large beaker (c. 0.20 m in diameter) with thin, fairly straight walls and a rounded base (TCS074). On the whole, these vessels date to the 2nd or, more likely, the 3rd century AD.

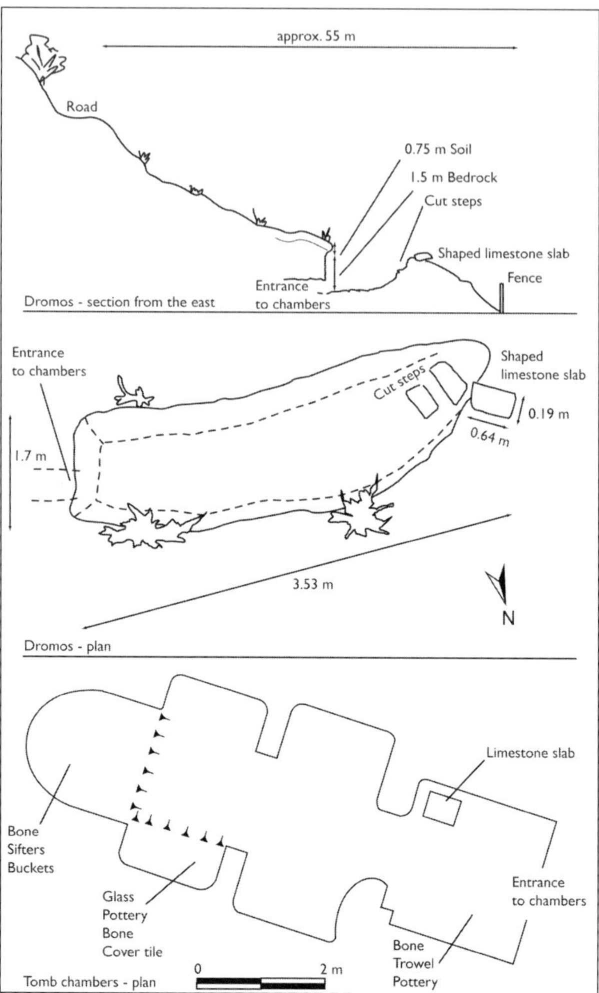

Fig. 3.57. Katydhata Laonarka *(TP127): drawing of Roman tomb (Rebekah Merriman, finalised by Luke Sollars)*

The pottery from TP127 dates to the Hellenistic–Roman period and includes remnants of corrugated Cooking Ware (Early Roman), Cypriot Sigillata (usually Early Roman in the TAESP Survey Area), a common Roman period pan tile, and a transport amphora. Also found in TP127 were two lamps, one Vessberg form 10–12 (40–150 AD), the other comprising two fragments of a Vessberg form 13–14. The imperfect congruence between the date ranges of the glass and pottery fragments can be explained by the dearth of pottery common to Roman tombs of the 3rd century (but cf. Tomb 5 in Evrykhou, our TP065; see below). On the whole, burials in TP127 seem to have begun in the 1st century and continued into the 2nd, if not the 3rd century AD. The small size of the artefact assemblage, particularly the pottery, and the evidence for looting, mean that these conclusions are necessarily tentative.

In addition to surviving tombs, the functional character of surface material can reveal the locations and nature of mortuary landscapes. In excavations of the Hellenistic–Roman period, Eastern Sigillata A vessels, *unguentaria* and lamps are found in both settlements and necropoleis, although they are proportionally rarer at settlement sites. The northern part of the Karkotis Valley revealed a high proportion of Eastern Sigillata A and lamps. In fact, the largest amount of Eastern Sigillata A in the entire TAESP Survey Area came from here: in Skouriotissa *Pseftas* (TS13); around Katydhata *Pano Limna* (TS15); and near TP090, a possible Roman tomb (SU1022–24). Concentrations of lamps were found at Pano Limna (TP119), in association with two tombs (TP090, TP127) and on Transect TT3883500N (in SU1015).

Unguentaria consistently appear in high numbers in Hellenistic–Roman tombs in Cyprus, but this class of vessel was usually made of glass during the Roman period and is, therefore, less likely to survive on the surface. Tombs of the Hellenistic period, however, often were re-used during the Early Roman period, and an unguentarium fragment was collected, together with an Eastern Sigillata A sherd and a lamp fragment, west of a probable Roman tomb (TP037) at Katydhata *Laonarka* (SU1064). The individual fragments did not necessarily come from these particular tombs: the area was littered with empty tombs, and much of the pottery collected must have washed out of them, obscuring the original landscape pattern.

In Evrykhou Tomb V (TP065), more than 40 of the 158 ceramic objects were lamps, while 13 were unguentaria (Jacobsen 2007). Lamps and unguentaria tend to be proportionally rare among survey finds; for example, only a single lamp fragment was published by the Sydney Cyprus Survey Project (Keswani *et al.* 2003, 213, no. 1625.3.1). The pottery volume of the Canadian Palaipaphos Survey Project lists 13 lamp fragments, but they are, as yet, unaccompanied by any contextual information (Lund 1993, 117–18). Lamps and to some extent unguentaria are thin-walled and so less likely to survive, but this circumstance also applies to Table Wares and Cooking Wares. Such rarity may thus reflect TAESP's collection strategy rather than any real absence. Fragments from lamps, which always are small and lack straight lines, might have been more easily overlooked by the survey teams; however, the clays used for lamps were fired to a light colour and often covered with a red slip, making them resemble Table Wares. Moreover, small Cooking Ware fragments, that should be much harder to see because of the dark soils, were consistently collected by the teams. No Late Roman lamps were collected from the many Late Roman settlements in the Survey Area; this is a period when lamps only rarely appeared in tombs and always individually. This situation suggests that in Survey Units where more than one lamp or unguentarium fragment was collected and where concentrations of imported Table Wares such as Eastern Sigillata A were found, the fragments most likely came from tombs.

TAESP has added significantly to the knowledge base of Bronze Age mortuary activities focused on Katydhata and Linou villages and their environs. The area encompassing these villages may also have been a centre of settlement during the PreBA 2. Iron Age tombs are much less numerous, which is consistent with an apparent decline in settlement activity at this time in the Karkotis Valley. The tombs were apparently restricted to the eastern and western edges of the valley, although previous research also indicates limited Iron Age mortuary activity in the Katydhata-Linou area.

Hellenistic–Roman tombs are most numerous in the areas that were occupied densely during these periods, i.e. the northern half of the Karkotis Valley Intensive Survey Zone (particularly around Katydhata and Skouriotissa villages and their environs) and the area around Dodekaskala (TS11) in the south-east. The large number of Hellenistic–Roman tombs also seems to mirror a population boom at this time. Overall, it seems possible that a great deal of Hellenistic–Roman pottery in the Karkotis Valley washed out of tombs and mingled with settlement assemblages. This is particularly true for the northern part of the Intensive Survey Zone, where the Hellenistic–Roman material tends to appear not in the valley bottom, but on its edges. Moreover, the Survey Units in this area have a proportionately higher amount of pottery typical of tombs versus settlements, despite the fact that the survey collection strategy was consistent across the entire Intensive Survey Zone.

3.15 The Karkotis Valley in Context

Our interpretation of the landscape, society and environment of the Karkotis Valley is based not just on intensive survey within the demarcated Intensive Survey Zone, but on the wider context of the valley. This information derives partly from work in adjacent Intensive Survey Zones, particularly in the Atsas Valley (Chapter 2.3), but also on the systematic extensive transects carried out by 'Team X'. The methodology of this team is explained in full in Volume 1, Chapter 2.2, but in summary, these 1 km-long transects were laid out on a 2-km grid outside the Intensive Survey Zones and consisted of normal Survey Units separated by 100 m, along with the usual recording of POSIs, Building Units, etc. In this section, we discuss two particularly relevant areas investigated by means of extensive survey: the hillslopes on each side of the Upper Karkotis Valley to the south of the Intensive Survey Zone; and the village of Evrykhou.

Upper Karkotis Valley

Two extensive transects passed through the western slopes of the Upper Karkotis Valley (TT489000C and TT489000D), while two were conducted on the valley's eastern slopes (TT491000D and TT3876000U; Plate 3.25). Like the intensive transects in the Karkotis Valley Intensive Survey Zone, their extensive counterparts in the Upper Karkotis Valley foothills ran near various villages (Korakou, Kalliana, Tembria), or even through them (Sina Oros). Extensive survey, however, produced vastly different artefact distributions, which may be associated with contrasts between the steeper valley slopes in the upper part of the valley and the floodplain further down. The topography of the land extensively surveyed was characterized by high ridges (over 600 m) and deeply incised tributaries of the Karkotis River. These tributaries had been tapped by concrete irrigation channels that watered agricultural fields nearest the villages (e.g. Kalliana on TT489000D).

Unlike the transects of the Karkotis Valley Intensive Survey Zone, very few cultural artefacts were found along the extensive transects. Two of them produced no pottery or chipped stone whatsoever (TT489000C; TT3876000U). Transect survey along TT489000D revealed very low densities of Historical, Antiquity and Modern sherds in a Survey Unit on a terraced fruit orchard. Four Survey Units on Transect TT491000D produced very low densities of tiles and pottery dating from the 18th century to the present, although the soil surfaces of these terraces seem to have been created or disturbed quite recently. These last two transects were located close to the modern villages of Kalliana and Sina Oros, respectively, so the pottery found there may indicate continuity of settlement and agricultural cultivation.

Despite the lack of cultural artefacts, evidence of land use was clearly apparent. Many gully slopes had been terraced for fruit, nut, olive and vine cultivation. On a slope near Korakou village (TT489000C), the vegetation was characterized as a 'garden landscape', because all of the plants had an identifiable use as food, fuel, construction, medicine, etc. (Forbes 1997). A set of paths provided access between the village and this 'garden landscape'.

Other networks of paths were observed along the sides of the valley, both on the west (TT489000C) and the east (TT3876000U: TP224–25). These paths were all simple cuts into the hillside, although TP224 and TP225 were c. 0.8 m wide. Most of the paths rose out of the valley and contoured around just below the ridgeline. Some of them may be for use by hunters, although shotgun cartridges were distributed less consistently and in lower densities than in the Karkotis Valley Intensive Survey Zone. There seems to be less hunting in the Lagoudhera Valley because it has fewer population centres and fewer cultivated agricultural fields in the valley bottom. Shepherds may also use the paths. Evidence of fairly recent animal grazing could be seen on south-facing slopes along Transect TT489000C, which were marked with braided paths and supported substantial brome grass (*Bromus scoparius* +/- *Bromus rubens* and *Bromus arvensis*). On a slope above Sina Oros village, near Transect TT491000D, we recorded a sub-circular rock pile, c. 6 m in diameter (TP214). Associated with a line of hawthorn trees and a possible path, the rock pile seems to be the remnants of a small hut, or shelter, with wide-ranging views of the Karkotis Valley.

The Upper Karkotis Valley has a complex system of irrigation channels, weirs and watermills that feed the channels and mills of the Intensive Survey Zone further downstream. One such mill is located near the village centre in lower Kalliana (BU0060). It is currently used to grind fishmeal, but in the past was used for cereals, cotton, beans, peas and sesame. Water is taken from the main aqueduct to the south at a higher level. The channel splits at Mylos tou Spyrou (BU0061), and the western branch leads to the penstock of BU0060.

Mylos tou Spyrou (BU0061) is a cotton mill located off the Galata to Kalliana road. It is known locally as the first cotton mill in the area and has not been used since 1947. In the 19th century, the Karkotis Valley was known for producing the best cotton in Cyprus, mainly due to the abundant water and the regular siltation of the fields after flooding (Gaudry 1855, 159–61). The Greek Cypriot owner was a man named Spyros Hadjivangelis. In 1901 the government engineer, Edward Nicolls, referred to it as the mill of Papa Milona (Nicolls 1901). The mill is located at the top of three terraces, with the millhouse on the second terrace and the wheel room on the third.

Evrykhou Village

Team X's transect TT491000C was located on the eastern side of the Upper Karkotis Valley, crossing a series of three gullies where the foothills meet the floodplain. In the spirit of Team X surveying wherever the transect leads, come what may, it passed directly through the centre of the village of Evrykhou. Apart from giving the team the opportunity for some humorous photography (Fig. 3.58), this was a

Fig. 3.58. Team X 'surveys' the village of Evrykhou (Stephen Digney)

Fig. 3.59. Evrykhou railway station (BU0048) (Chris Parks)

stimulating and interesting exercise that involved plenty of oral history, coffee and interaction with the villagers. Discoveries of Iron Age, Hellenistic and Roman tombs in the area (Chapter 3.14, Nicolaou 1984) have led to the villagers' long familiarity with antiquities, and there are many small local collections that have been declared to, and approved by, the Cypriot Department of Antiquities. This meant that people immediately identified with the team's goals and told them about tombs, grain and olive mills, churches and (one of the most commonly mentioned historical monuments) the colonial-period railway station. The experience was a salutary reminder that landscape archaeology does not stop on the outskirts of towns and villages.

In 1440, Evrykhou was a fief of the Count of Jaffa, with 74 serfs working the land (Grivaud 2002, 40; Richard 1962, 142–43), while the Venetian village list of 1565 records 90 *francomati* (free peasant farmers) (Grivaud 1998, 469). This made it a very substantial settlement in the Karkotis Valley, on a par with Kalliana across the valley to the west, and smaller only than Kakopetria/Galata further up the valley. The 1831 census records it as a mixed Greek Cypriot and Turkish Cypriot village (Sarınay 2000), and by the first British census of 1881 it was the largest village in the valley, with a population of 588 (Grivaud 1998, 469). Today it is the central village of the northern half of the Karkotis Valley, with banks, a regional high school, five churches, coffee shops with specific political affiliations, a police station and a rural hospital (Kinani 1992).

Land use around Evrykhou includes cultivation of olives, fruits and nuts in the valley bottom and in the main gullies that pass through the village. Within the village itself, vegetables and fruit are grown on small plots and gardens, giving occasional opportunities for survey and suggesting a close integration of village and countryside. Four Survey Units were completed around the village. Two sherds dating to the Late Chalcolithic/Philia period represent the earliest found along this transect and are the only examples in the Karkotis valley outside Koutroullis (Chapter 3.5). Low densities of tile, as well as pottery from the Hellenistic–Roman periods, appeared consistently across the transect. There was also a consistent representation, in low to moderate densities, of sherds from the 16th century through the Modern period, which suggests debris and dumping from the Medieval, Ottoman and Modern village. Densities were not as high as might have been expected for the centre and outskirts of a long-lasting settlement: the highest figure for the Medieval–Modern periods was 16 sherds/100 m^2, which is in line with the southern transects of the Karkotis Valley Intensive Survey Zone, rather than with the higher densities immediately around Phlasou and Katydhata. The transect also produced two lithic artefacts, consisting of a chunk and a *dhoukani* flake, both made of local jasper.

Evrykhou's village centre is dominated by the church of Ayia Marina, which was completed in 1872 (BU0057). In the back streets of Evrykhou, villagers informed us of an old olive oil mill (TP179) dating to the early 20th century (now demolished). The mill was used by residents of the surrounding villages for olive processing. All that remains of the mill is a well that once provided drinking water for its patrons.

Village residents often refer to the now-disused rail station located below the village at Evrykhou *Balioes* (Fig. 3.59; BU0048). The two-storey building is built out of ashlar masonry rusticated on the foundation and carefully margined and chiselled around the doors and windows. This structure is slowly deteriorating, and no trace of the railway or platform remains. It was built when the Cyprus Government Railway was extended from Morphou to Evrykhou in 1915, and followed the standardized 'Class 2' station design also used for Morphou (Turner 1979, 37).

Unlike the police station, which was an adapted village house, the Evrykhou railway station was unmistakably a government building, of the same brownstone type as the government offices in Nicosia. The station was closed in 1932, officially because of the unprofitability of this stretch of line and the wear and tear of the steep gradient on the engines (Turner 1979, 38). The villagers, however, gave us alternative explanations for the station's closure: it was the colonial government's revenge for Evrykhou's anti-British sentiments during the October 1931 rioting and burning down of Government House in Nicosia by Greek Cypriot protesters (Kinani 1992, 24); or even a punishment for villagers shooting tin cans during a visit from the Governor. After its closure, the building was used as a temporary hospital during a typhoid epidemic and, from 1937, as a Forest Department office (SA1/823/1933). It was burned down by EOKA B fighters in 1974 and is now derelict.

The striking number of watermills in the area immediately round Evrykhou is a result of both the plentiful supply of water and the demand from a substantial local population. Censuses from the Medieval and Ottoman periods indicate that in 1565 there were 385 *francomati* living in the villages stretching from Tembria, north to Katydhata, and in 1826 there were 228 heads of household (Papadopoullos 1965, 123–24; Grivaud 1998, 468–70). The continuous settlement and cultivation of this area of the Karkotis valley, as well as the economic activity across this region, are indicators that watermills and irrigation networks have been an important part of life since the medieval period. There is also evidence for the complexity of mill ownership. In 1715 Margarou, the daughter of a priest who lived in Korakou, gave to her husband the sixth part of the 'Mill of Loundzeris' in Evrykhou for three days and nights every 30 days, in exchange for a silver-plated knife (Theocharides 1993, 447). The detailed breakdown and ownership of very specific periods of use is quite characteristic; at the level of village water rights, they persist to the present day (Volume 1, Chapter 3.12; Kinani 1992, 27–28).

There are nine watermills in and around the adjacent villages of Evrykhou and Tembria. The construction materials and techniques are generally typical of the Karkotis Valley mills. Basalt, limestone and rubble masonry remain the main building materials used, again reflecting the use of the available surrounding local natural resources for construction. These mills are generally set in orchards and cultivated or uncultivated fields, but usually not in proximity to any significant grain crops. The largest and best preserved of these mills are BU0070 ('Lachistos Mill') on the outskirts of Evrykhou (see Chapter 3.3), and the Mylos tou Stylli (see Chapter 3.4) in Evrykhou village, still in operation.

The Koumnas mill (BU0046) is located on the west bank of the Karkotis River at a road junction between Evrykhou and Tembria, 700 m south-west of Evrykhou. The penstock is situated near an old bridge, perhaps built during the Late Ottoman period, probably serving as a communication link between the inhabitants of the surrounding villages and the mill before the construction of the modern road. Another mill, BU0097, is located on the outskirts of Evrykhou, on the corner of the road leading to the Stylianides Mill; it is now being used as a warehouse. Another interesting mill is located in uncultivated fields, in Tembria village (BU0064); it is mostly ruined, but there are remains of a wooden water chute, a feature normal in Turkey (Danisman 1977; Donners *et al.* 2002) but unusual in Cyprus and unique in our Survey Area. The ruinous state of the penstock suggests that rather than rebuilding the watermill, the owner decided to use the more economically viable solution of using a hollowed out tree trunk through which the water could be guided into the wheel chamber; the abundance of trees in the area would have made this a quicker and less expensive solution to keep the mill operational. The elevation of these watermills ranges from c. 400–500 m asl. They were clearly feeding water to each other, starting at a higher elevation and working to a mill at a lower altitude, in an attempt to maximize water power (see Volume 1, Chapter 3.11).

These complex irrigation networks in and around the villages of Tembria and Evrykhou serve a variety of fruit orchards and crops, as well as a number of watermills. Although evidence of agricultural activity around both villages is strong, historical landscape analyses indicate that grains were less cultivated in this area, due partly to the higher elevation of the landscape (Volume 1, Chapter 5.4). This factor suggests that the watermills were perhaps situated here to take advantage of the runoff and precipitation that could be maximized through the steeper valley slopes for greater energy to power the watermills, and that villagers obtained grain from the lower valleys or the plains below, before grinding them in the Tembria or Evrykhou mills.

3.16 Karkotis Valley: Conclusions

In this concluding section we address a series of specialist themes particularly important for our understanding of the Karkotis Valley and best understood by examining them across the Intensive Survey Zone as a whole: chipped stone and ground stone; copper slag; and olive trees. These and other issues are addressed more fully for the Survey Area as a whole in Volume 1, Chapters 3 and 4. We then provide brief summaries and conclusions for each of the four main period groupings: Prehistoric; Iron Age; Hellenistic–Roman; and Byzantine–Modern. For more detailed analyses of these periods, see Volume 1, Chapter 5.

Chipped Stone and Ground stone

The two southernmost transects of the Karkotis Valley Intensive Survey Zone have a low, patchy distribution of chipped stone material. The vast majority of the remains are indicative of tool manufacture. Only two *dhoukani* blades were present, and these are made of low quality local material. Only one ground stone tool (for pounding) was found along these two transects. The rest of the transects to the north have a more constant distribution of chipped stone, which is usually low–moderate, but becomes heavy in places. Evidence of tool manufacture (cores, blanks, debris) was most common, followed by smaller, but still significant, numbers of both flake/utilized tools and *dhoukani* blades. Flake and utilized tools were found in all but the southernmost transects. They often appeared in areas that also contained prehistoric pottery, but there was no direct correlation between quantities of these lithics and pottery.

Transect TT3880500N seems to represent the southern extent of a moderate concentration of *dhoukani* blades, lying along the east side of the river and continuing up to the northern extent of Katydhata village. This zone mostly coincides with the densest pottery concentrations from the Medieval–Modern periods and may represent the rough limits of active, recent agricultural cultivation. At the northern and southern ends of the Karkotis Valley, *dhoukani* blades also become common west of the river. The Karkotis Valley Intensive Survey Zone had the largest number of *dhoukani* blades of anywhere in the Survey Area, and the highest proportion of these made of exotic Lefkara chert.

The heaviest concentrations of ground stone tools seem to correlate closely with heavy concentrations of prehistoric pottery, namely at Koutroullis and Laonarka. Tools for grinding were by far the most numerous, followed by pounding tools, vessels and cutting tools. Again, these concentrations were the heaviest in the entire Survey Area.

Copper Slag

The southern three transects of the Karkotis Valley (Plate 3.3) show only patchy, low densities of slag distribution. The one exception is a Survey Unit just east of the river, whose abundant slag is suspect because of its location well within the river's floodplain. Slag continues to be distributed at low levels, but is more common around Phlasou village (including TS04 and TS11). Only in the Survey Units around Katydhata does slag begin to appear consistently, albeit still at low density. The more regular appearance of slag around the modern villages may be tied to its use in road paving and construction.

Slag becomes ubiquitous, and appears occasionally in moderate–heavy densities, from Transect TT3882500N and northward. The most logical explanation is the proximity of these areas to the massive slag heaps at Skouriotissa mine. Indeed, a distinct north-west by south-east chain of heavy slag concentrations parallels the current extent of the spoil heaps at Skouriotissa. Modern communication routes must also be factored into any understanding of slag distribution. For example, east of the road at Pseftas, slag was found in moderate quantities, mostly in small pieces. The heaviest concentration was noted along the terrace's eastern boundary, which may be due to the proximity of the railway track.

On the whole, slag appears more consistently across the Karkotis Valley Intensive Survey Zone than any other in the Survey Area. No slag was detected in the extensive transects at the southern part of the Karkotis Valley. Because these transects were conducted in the mountains and foothills on the valley's margins, slag distribution seems to be correlated with the broad floodplain of the valley bottom.

Olive Trees

On the basis of field survey of surviving old olive trees (Volume 1, Chapter 4.7), we were able to analyse the spatial distribution of old olive plantings in the Karkotis Valley (Plate 3.26). All observations on the distribution of old olive trees should be viewed as indications only, based upon surviving trees. The presence of a very old tree in a locality is direct evidence of past olive cultivation activity; but the absence of surviving trees, which could be due to a variety of circumstances, does not necessarily infer that they were never planted in that location. With this caveat in mind we were able to address the patterns of olive plantings over time in the Karkotis Valley and the relationship of these patterns with settlement growth, successive land husbandry regimes and the geomorphological processes of the valley.

Within the confines of the Survey Area, we found that the oldest recorded olive trees, those planted before and during the early 15th century AD, were concentrated in the northern part of the Karkotis Valley, between Linou and Skouriotissa. Moreover, all these occur on remnants of old elevated terraces more than 20 m above the present level of the watercourse and more than 250 m linear distance from the river. These early plantings are also exclusively on the eastern side of the Karkotis River, clustering close to the existing settlements of Katydhata and Linou.

A significant change in distribution appears to have begun in the late 15th century, with olive plantings extending from Evrykhou in the south to Skouriotissa in the north, and extending onto both sides of the river. In the late 15th century olive plantings were much closer to the present watercourse than those earlier in the century. A number of late 15th-century plantings are within 100 m of the river bank (100 m at Katydhata; 65 m at Kato Phlasou). The ones closest to the river occur on remnants of old elevated terraces, less than 10 m above the present level of the watercourse. Three trees more than 500 years old at Kato Phlasou are only 4–5 m above the present river bank.

In the early 16th century olive plantings on both sides of the river were also close to the present watercourse: trees at Katydhata, Phlasou and Evrykhou are within 60–80 m of the river, and the closest are now growing on terraces only c. 5 m above the present river bank. By the late 16th century, the spatial distribution of olive plantations in the Karkotis Valley that we see today had been established (Plate 3.26, b).

The sequential spatial distributions of old olive trees described above support historic records of estates at Linou and Phlasou. Phlasou was a royal estate in the mid-15th century, passed to a nobleman in the 1460s and recorded as a royal estate again in the mid-16th century. The 84 *francomati* recorded in 1565 suggest a substantial population (see Chapter 3.8). Linou is less well documented, but was clearly a well-established settlement by 1565 with 34 *francomati* (Grivaud 1998, 468). Both settlements clearly participated in the well-known prosperity of the 16th century (Grivaud 1998, 224), and it is unsurprising that these estates were able to make the relatively long-term investment involved in planting olive trees.

Additionally, the absence of olive trees planted before the late 14th and early 15th centuries suggests that any significant changes in the track of the river course, flooding and river terracing, which would have impacted adversely on olive plantations, occurred before this time. Since the late 15th century, the spatial distribution of surviving old olive trees suggests a degree of landscape stability. Any changes in the track of the river course, flooding and river terracing have not been basin-wide changes but, where they have occurred, have probably been local in their impact.

It is difficult to reconcile the persistence of olive trees from this period, when the high energy river flows associated with the perennial snowpack in the headwaters of the watershed in the Little Ice Age (16th–early 19th centuries) could well have produced basin-wide changes. A possible explanation is that the significant transport of boulders and sediment by these flows was limited to an entrenched river course, much as we see it today (Chapter 3.2).

Prehistoric Periods

With a few notable exceptions, relatively little prehistoric pottery was recovered west of the Karkotis River. We have certainly lost some prehistoric surfaces as a result of the river's later incision and deposition, but this does not apply to the older, higher terraces of the valley. The concentrations of Chalcolithic and Early Prehistoric Bronze Age 1 (Late Chalcolithic/Philia phase) sherds, chipped stone material and domestic debris in the vicinity of Koutroullis (Chapter 3.5) suggest a settlement of that date. This particular concentration represents the only activity during the Chalcolithic and PreBA 1 periods in the Karkotis Valley. There is continuing evidence of PreBA material at Koutroullis, but more in terms of a halo around this locality, with a denser and wider spread at Laonarka to the north.

Laonarka (Chapter 3.9) and the area around Katydhata village produced an enormous concentration of Prehistoric Bronze Age 2 pottery (and, to a lesser extent, Protohistoric Bronze Age pottery) in the vicinity of known tombs, but also where settlement evidence would be expected. There are also scattered PreBA 2 sherds across the valley outside the two main concentrations at Koutroullis and Laonarka. These resulted partly from the greater quantities of pottery being produced, broken and disposed of, and partly from more wide-ranging and intensive cultivation, and other activities outside the immediate surroundings of these two localities. All such activities seem to have been reduced significantly in scale during the ProBA, when evidence around Laonarka consists mainly of mortuary activity.

There appears to be a gap in the prehistoric pottery sequence between PreBA 1 and the beginning of PreBA 2 in the Karkotis Valley. Specifically, the Laonarka settlement and mortuary complex did not contain pottery earlier than the end of EC III, in contrast to the settlement at Koutroullis, which yielded nothing later than EC I. Given the generally expansionist trajectory of the PreBA in the Karkotis Valley, however, this apparent gap probably reflects the need for better pottery chronologies rather than any real interruption in occupation.

Iron Age

Overall, quantities of Iron Age pottery were much lower in the Karkotis Valley Intensive Survey Zone than pottery from the prehistoric periods. There is a thin scatter of Iron Age pottery across the entire valley, as well as two very obvious concentrations at Pano Limna (Chapter 3.11) and around Katydhata village (Chapter 3.10). Beyond these two concentrations, densities are never more than 2 sherds/100 m^2, and the pottery is scattered widely.

What does this mean in terms of Iron Age activity or post-depositional processes? With the development of agricultural terraces and irrigation networks, which were quite substantial during the Roman period, the surface archaeological record would have been lost due to excavation of soils on about half of the landscape and deposition of that soil over the other half. This is the nature of terrace construction, wherein a very small area of original surface might remain in situ, while the great majority is lost to excavation and burial. To find materials of this age and older, excavation on the lower half of any terrace would be required to reach pre-Roman landscapes that lie buried.

By comparison with other periods, densities in this area seem low, never rising above 5.6 sherds/100 m^2. This is characteristic of the Iron Age, however, and may be due, in part, to our inability to distinguish some utility wares from those of later periods: much of the rather similar 'Historical Antiquity' distribution actually may be Iron Age.

Such a broad scatter and low densities of material would be expected in the hinterland of a substantial settlement and sanctuary in and around Katydhata. It is most likely that these scatters derive from intensive cultivation, manuring, and general travelling and living. The proliferation of these activities is unsurprising, given the good water supplies and alluvial soil in the valley, as well as its proximity to the city-kingdom of Soloi 8 km to the north-west.

There are some substantial and continuous areas of Iron Age pottery to the south and south-west of Katydhata village. Interestingly, they do not coincide with the Bronze Age pottery distribution. The densest areas are immediately west and south of the southern tail of the modern village, rather than at the base of the ridgeline where geophysical investigation suggests Bronze Age occupation. Most of this area is free of erosion problems. The Iron Age pottery consists primarily of White Painted and Black-on-Red wares, of types that would seem to characterize a settlement (Heavy and Light Utility, Cooking Wares, Table Wares). Although no Iron Age mortuary remains were found at Katydhata, two Archaic–Classical tombs were excavated further up the eastern side of the valley in Evrykhou (Nicolaou 1984, 234).

The evidence is much more striking at Pano Limna, on the far side of the valley from Katydhata and 1 km to the west (Chapter 3.11). Block survey in the highest alluvial terraces on the western edge of the valley showed levels of Iron Age pottery similar to those at Katydhata. On the hillslope a large scatter of terracotta figurines indicates the presence of a sanctuary. The sanctuary had a striking view from its spur on the western side of the valley, across the arable land with its low spread of Iron Age pottery to the presumed settlement at Katydhata. Similarly, the sanctuary and the small settlement that probably accompanied it were clearly visible to those living, farming and working in the valley. The activities of making and dedicating these figurines were as visible a part of the landscape as dwelling, farming and travelling.

Hellenistic–Roman

Based on the size of the pottery assemblages and the regularity of their distributions, the Hellenistic–Roman periods represented a time of unprecedented human activity in the Karkotis Valley. The southernmost (upper) region of the Intensive Survey Zone had consistent distributions, at low–moderate densities, of Hellenistic–Roman pottery. These distributions, however, did not extend as regularly to the valley's western and eastern edges, where two rich tombs of this period have been excavated (Nicolaou 1984; Jacobsen 2007). The tombs contained jewellery and many glass vessels, suggesting a certain level of economic affluence in the upper part of the valley, although these types of finds very rarely survive on the surface. At Dodekaskala (Chapter 3.6), we can see a distinct peak that was most pronounced during the Roman and Late Roman periods, although the distribution is rather diffused compared to the clear sites in the northern (lower) end of the Intensive Survey Zone.

Between Dodekaskala and the southern limits of Katydhata village, distributions of Hellenistic–Roman pottery were low and actually dropped to their lowest point in the Intensive Survey Zone around Pano Phlasou and Linou villages. From Katydhata village and northward, pottery from the Hellenistic through Late Roman periods became more densely and consistently distributed. A significant concentration was evident at Pano Limna (Chapter 3.11), peaking in the Roman/Late Roman periods. Another notable concentration appeared at Pseftas (Chapter 3.13), located at the extreme northern end of the Karkotis Valley Intensive Survey Zone. These two substantial pottery scatters were both associated with architectural remains. A third concentration on the south-western side of Katydhata village is mainly associated with mortuary activity, as are several small peaks in the northern end of the Intensive Survey Zone around the Skouriotissa mine.

Most of the major concentrations of Hellenistic–Roman pottery 'ring' the Skouriotissa mine, which is unsurprising, given the intensive mining and smelting of copper ore that occurred there during the Roman period. This general area also saw the widest range of imports in the form of Table Wares and transport amphorae for food. The settlement was not located under the modern village of Katydhata, where numerous tombs have been found. Instead, the present day San Martin United Nations Camp, adjacent to the slag heap and on the site of the Skouriotissa monastery probably dating back to the 15th century AD, is a likely location for the Hellenistic–Roman settlement associated with the mine and many of the tombs in this area. The settlement may also have been located on the actual Phoukasa Hill, where the Roman mine was, but the hill has been completely obliterated by modern mining.

The only pottery concentration located further up the valley (Dodekaskala; Chapter 3.6) may be linked more directly to agricultural support of the mining process. The rich tombs and apparent scarcity of settlements, combined with the low-density scatter of pottery surrounding the modern villages such as Pano Phlasou, probably indicates a certain degree of settlement continuity in the Karkotis Valley. On the whole, the low, but constant, amounts of Hellenistic–Roman pottery found across the Karkotis Valley seem indicative of a manuring 'carpet'.

Levelling of vast tracts of fields is the main agency of mixing and confounding the archaeological record in the Karkotis Valley Intensive Survey Zone. This statement is not made lightly: to reach this conclusion has required exhaustive analyses of the geomorphological and geological record within the Survey Area and even the whole island itself. The character of the main channel and agricultural terracing in the Karkotis Valley between Skouriotissa and Kakopetria is unusual for Cyprus, and thus requires special attention. The main arguments, conclusions and implications of these analyses are presented here, supported by descriptions and analyses presented in Volume 1, Chapter 4.6.

Unlike the greater part of the Survey Area, this Intensive Survey Zone has been subjected to significant earthworks projects, one mining and the other agricultural. The temporal coincidence of these two activities is no accident. Rather, given the number of labourers involved in mining activities, a local habitation and food production 'footprint' is expected on the landscape. We conclude that the central Karkotis landscape was reshaped by Roman efforts to extract minerals and to grow food for the labour force. The land levelling and development of irrigation infrastructure best explain the landforms, and the assignment of this period to their construction also provides a simple answer. We base these conclusions on the following information (as presented here and in Volume 1, Chapter 4.6):

- the terrace landforms require special geomorphological explanation;
- a purely geological explanation of the nature of sedimentary deposits within these landforms is not fully satisfactory;
- compared with the rest of Cyprus, these are unique irrigation schemes on likewise unique landforms;

- the Karkotis is a perennially flowing river, even during the driest periods of regional palaeoclimate;
- the nature of fluvial and bedrock materials produce quality soils to support agriculture;
- the largest known copper ore body on Cyprus is in the river valley next to these extraordinary terrace ranks.

Further, as we demonstrate in Volume 1, Chapter 4.6, the efficient construction of level fields in the fluvial and colluvial deposits of this valley would require excavation and burial of original surface deposits. This would have removed any earlier (i.e. pre-Roman) artefacts, and thus rendered the surface almost, or entirely, devoid of pre-Roman cultural material. It is only after the land reaches its new shape that the generators of this new landscape may deposit cultural materials and have them survive, essentially in situ, for our survey to document. Until the 21st century, there has been little ability or desire to disturb, or significantly reshape, these Roman earthworks, which are a significant example of the Roman-period efforts to reshape the landscape into their own creation.

Byzantine–Modern

The patterns of pottery distribution on the valley floor and hillslopes of the Karkotis Valley provide us with a sense of the changing dynamics of communities and their environment across the second millennium AD. There was a sharp reduction in both numbers and spread of pottery in the Byzantine period, in contrast to the Late Roman period; this is a familiar phenomenon (Gregory 2003), and is discussed in more detail in Volume 1, Chapter 5.4. There was a steady rise in pottery densities from the 14th century onwards, peaking in the later Ottoman and British colonial period.

During the Medieval period there is a very clear focus on the estates of Phlasou and Linou, with a 14th-century outpost just north of and perhaps including Katydhata. From the 16th century there is a much broader spread across the entire landscape of the valley floor. This indicates the flourishing settlements of the upper Karkotis Valley, such as Korakou and Evrykhou, and widespread intensive cultivation.

Several of the Medieval–Modern centres of occupation in the Karkotis Valley are no longer inhabited. They were revealed by TAESP in various ways, including detection of localized, moderate concentrations of contemporary pottery (e.g. Dodekaskala), as well as through the use of ethnohistoric and ethnographic evidence (e.g. Agroladhou village) and standing architectural remains (e.g. Ayios Epiphanios and the modern miners' village at Skouriotissa). The modern villages of Phlasou, Linou and Katydhata have been occupied continuously since the Medieval period. They are characterized by heavier, more diffuse concentrations of pottery, which may be attributed to greater continuity of settlement and more intensive agricultural exploitation (including manuring and ploughing) of the surrounding fields.

Going beyond the surface artefacts, our fieldwork has raised a wide variety of themes and issues, which are discussed in full in Volume 1, Chapter 5.4. Seen in the long-term view of survey archaeology, for example, settlements are not so much sites as processes. This is particularly clear in the complex development and division of the village of Phlasou, articulated by its churches, threshing floors and the debris of day-to-day activity (Chapter 3.8). The 22 churches in the part of the Karkotis Valley lying within our Survey Area show highly complex and varied patterns of locations: some mark the focus of communities, some evoke the memories of past communities, while others are carefully sited on spurs to be visible from up the valley, but not from down it.

One of the key human activities in the Medieval–Modern periods that we investigated in the Karkotis Valley was agriculture. The Z-shaped terraces on the thin-soiled hillslopes challenge our assumptions that the deep-soiled valley floors were the 'best' for cultivation (Chapter 3.3). Features such as fields, terrace walls and even olive trees are far more than functional facilities: as Forbes (2007, 204) demonstrates for the Methana peninsula in Greece, these carry important affective associations, enshrining family relationships and memories. Even the apparently functional mechanism of a water-powered grain mill turns out to be the focus of a range of highly emotive activities, and entirely bound up in the biography of its miller (Chapter 3.4).

Conclusion

We faced some substantial challenges in the Karkotis Valley. The patchwork of small fields and terraces, along with the extensive manipulation of soils and surfaces in the Roman period, made for some very intricate geomorphology and patchy archaeology. The substantial villages of Phlasou, Linou and Katydhata have all existed since the Medieval period, and along with their modern expansions obscure much of the Intensive Survey Zone. To this may be added the issue of ground visibility, often poor because of intensive agriculture and lush vegetation fed by the unusually plentiful water supply.

These challenges, however, were more than offset by the richness and interest of the material we discovered and the issues we investigated; our methodology was flexible enough to cope with them, while remaining sufficiently consistent. We also dedicated a lot of time and resources to this area: 30% of our Survey Units lie within the Karkotis Valley, along with an impressive 70% of our counted pottery and 39% of our analysed lithics.

The breadth of issues addressed is clear from the synthetic discussions in Volume 1, Chapters 3, 4 and 5, in all of which the Karkotis Valley plays a prominent role. These include the earliest Chalcolithic settlement and extensive PreBA occupation, the monumental Late Roman slag heap of Skouriotissa, the careful positioning of an Iron Age sanctuary and Medieval churches, changing haloes of surface material round agricultural settlements, the levelling of fields in the Roman period, the complex irrigation system from the Medieval period to today, and the evidence for past human activities ranging from threshing and smelting, to cooking and burying the dead.

Our intensive survey has demonstrated that the Karkotis Valley was occupied deep into antiquity. The hospitality of the Karkotis Valley to human settlement is illustrated by the fact that every single transect revealed pottery from each of the four main pottery periods (i.e. Prehistoric, Iron Age, Hellenistic–Roman and Medieval–Modern). Since the 4th millennium BC, no human cultural phase goes unrepresented by artefactual evidence. This is due, in large part, to the two factors that set it apart from the rest of the Survey Area, and indeed from Cyprus as a whole. The Karkotis Valley contains one of the richest copper ore deposits on the island, and the most powerful river in the island, along with the agricultural soils and plentiful water supply that it brings down from the heights of Mount Olympus.

4. The Upper Lagoudhera Valley

Edited by Angus Graham

with contributions by Iain Banks (geophysics), Stephen Digney (team leader, Team X), Ruth Smadar Gabrieli (pottery), Michael Given (historical periods), Angus Graham (team leader), Marios Hadjianastasis (oral history), Vasiliki Kassianidou (archaeometallurgy), Abel Lufafa (geomorphology), Carole McCartney (lithics), Jay Noller (geomorphology), Maria Ntinou (charcoal analysis), Neil Urwin (botany) and Kristina Winther-Jacobsen (pottery)

4.1 Introduction

The Upper Lagoudhera Valley Intensive Survey Zone is located within the copper-ore-bearing zone of the Troodos Mountains (Fig. 4.1; see Plate 4.1 for a map). No archaeological study of this area of Cyprus has previously taken place, and the initial observations of the richness of the data, particularly relating to copper mining and smelting, presented a clear opportunity to add to our knowledge of these activities.

Our main research questions were intended to advance our understanding of this important economic and social activity, both on Cyprus and within the wider Roman world. They included: identifying the locations and methods of ore extraction; furthering our knowledge of mining and smelting communities; examining the relationship and communication between extractors and processors; finding out when these operations took place; and clarifying the smelting process and any technological changes over time. This latter aspect includes the important issue of the fuel used for smelting, and consequently the issue of sustainable land management. We also sought to understand copper production in the Lagoudhera valley in the context of production on Cyprus as a whole. This involved the investigation of the communication routes between Ayia Marina *Mavrovouni* and the wider network, including the work carried out by TAESP at Skouriotissa (Chapter 3.12) and that already done by the Sydney Cyprus Survey Project to the east of our area (Given and Knapp 2003).

It was, of course, not just the copper production activities that interested us, but also the other human activities such as agriculture and settlement. Investigating the nature and scale of the impact of human industries on the environment and how the environment has influenced these activities is essential to a holistic understanding of people in the landscape. This approach uses the longest possible timescale, from evidence of the earliest human activity in the Upper Lagoudhera Valley through to the complete reshaping of the land by massive earth-moving equipment, as we witnessed during the survey seasons of 2001–2003 (Table 4.1). The environment of the Upper Lagoudhera Valley is particularly interesting because it combines traits of the Karkotis Valley Intensive Survey Zone and the mountain landscape of the Asinou Valley Intensive Survey Zone.

The chapter begins with an analysis of the environmental setting of the entire Lagoudhera drainage system, from its upper reaches in the Troodos Mountains, down to the confluence with the Asinou River in the plains of the Mesaoria (Plate 4.1). The archaeological discussion and interpretation is structured primarily on a geographical basis from south to north, followed by two thematic sections. It begins in the south-west of the Upper Lagoudhera Valley, with the mining of copper ore on Alestos, a mountain which sits alone in the foothills of the Troodos Range (Chapter 4.3). This is followed by a discussion of the settlement at Litharkies, on the

Fig. 4.1. The modern copper and gold mine of Alestos from the north-east, with the edge of the modern sulphur mine of Memi on the left (Michael Given)

Table 4.1. The Upper Lagoudhera Valley: chronological summary

Period	Activity	Name/ID number	Chapter
Prehistoric	Chalcolithic sherds & pestle		4.6
Hellenistic–Roman	Roman mining settlement	Litharkies	4.4
	Roman smelting & settlement	Mavrovouni	4.6
	Ancient mines	Alestos	4.3
	Ancient mining adits	Ayios Kyriakos	4.5
Byzantine–Modern	Med–Mod villages	Ayios Yeoryios Kafkallou, Vyzakia, Xyliatos	4.9
	Med–Ott rural estate & threshing floor	Athassi	4.7
	Water mills	BU0104, BU0109	4.9
	Check dams	TP009, TP145, TP147, TP213, TP234	4.4, 4.7, Table 4.2
	Paths	TP086–87, TP222–23	4.4
	Med–Ott olive trees		4.5
	20th century mines	Alestos, Memi	4.3

south flank of the hill, and the area between that and the Lagoudhera Valley (Chapter 4.4).

We then move to the confluence of this valley and the Lagoudhera Valley, where there is an area of mining prospection/extraction on both sides of the Lagoudhera river bed at Ayios Kyriakos, along with evidence for widespread prospection and extraction to the east of the Lagoudhera Valley (Chapter 4.5). Downstream from Ayios Kyriakos is the copper-smelting site of Ayia Marina *Mavrovouni*, with a slag heap and area of dense pottery (Chapter 4.6). Further down the Lagoudhera Valley is the Medieval to Ottoman rural estate house at Xyliatos *Athassi* (Chapter 4.7). Following this we turn to Roman copper production (Chapter 4.8) and Medieval–Modern land use (Chapter 4.9) within the Upper Lagoudhera Valley as a whole. We then sum up the periods and main themes (Chapter 4.10).

4.2 Environmental Setting and Description

The survey transects of the Lagoudhera Intensive Survey Zone inspect the upper Lagoudhera watershed, drained by the near-perennially flowing Lagoudhera River (Plate 4.1). This watershed originates on the north slope of Adelphi (1613 m), a solitary peak in the Adelphi Range. Adelphi

Fig. 4.2. Lagoudhera Valley looking south from Vyzakia, with Memi and Alestos mines (Chris Parks)

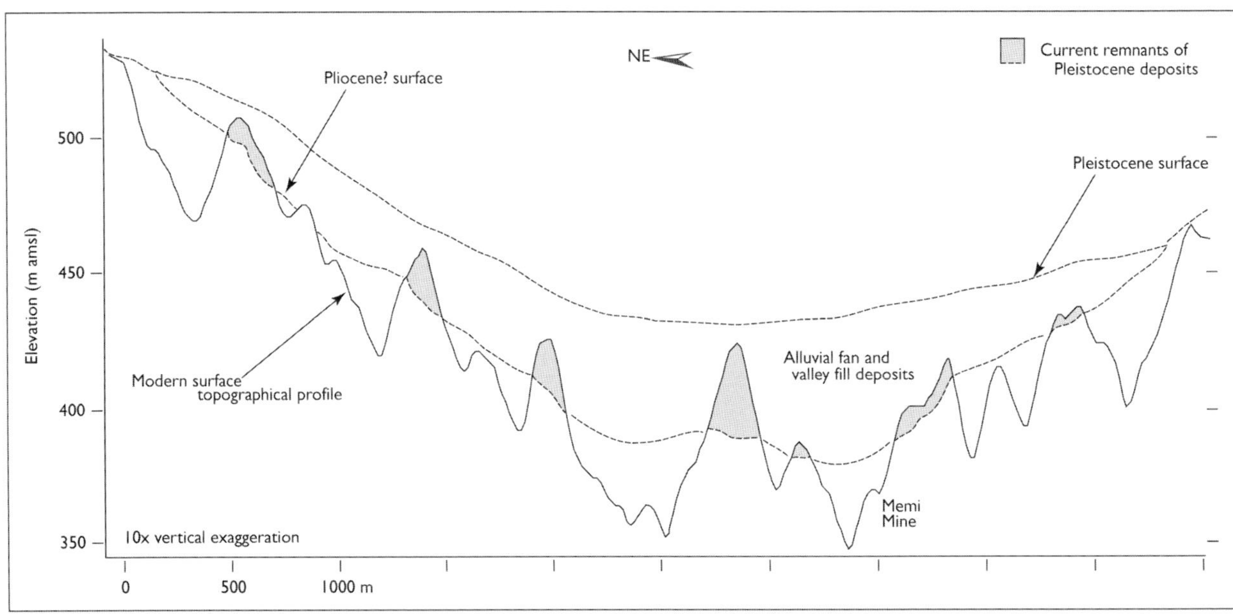

Fig. 4.3. Profile drawing of Upper Lagoudhera Valley (Jay Noller, finalised by Luke Sollars)

also drains south to the Akrotiri Peninsula, from which it is visible, via the Limnati and Kouris Rivers.

Locally, the entire Lagoudhera Intensive Survey Zone is commanded by the lone, cone-shaped, volcanic-looking Alestos peak (683 m) (Fig. 4.2). Pallouri is the name of the upland plain that extends from west of the village of Xyliatos and the confluences of two streams, the Argaki tis Yerokaminas and Argaki tis Klimarri, to the saddle between Alestos and the northern ridge of Adelphi, known as Moutti tou Kriniati (952 m). The Kannavia River runs from Adelphi north, around the slopes of Alestos, to join the Lagoudhera just north of the Intensive Survey Zone. Ayios Yeoryios Kafkallou, a sizeable village, is located on the bank opposite Alestos.

Erosion over the past half-million years has developed a valley system whose walls expose a 25–100-m thick deposit of marine and terrestrial sediments that once infilled a valley of significantly greater dimensions (Plate 4.1). The older valley may have developed and deepened when the Mediterranean Sea was significantly depressed during the Messinian Crisis of c. 5.5 Ma (Pliocene), and then infilled following sea level rise. This geological oddity has great significance for the cultural record of land use in and around the Lagoudhera Intensive Survey

Zone. Firstly, the accumulation in the ancient Lagoudhera Valley of sediments discharged from the Troodos means that soils developed on exposed surfaces are infinitely more conducive to agriculture than the bare rock outcrops that characterize other nearby valleys. Secondly, the relative uniqueness of the soils in this growing zone means more resistance to drought and greater crop yields, above and beyond that of others in nearby areas. Pallouri and the ridge along the north-western boundary of the Intensive Survey Zone are in this special zone.

Unfortunately, perhaps, for the agriculturalists, erosion has fairly well cleaned out the southern and eastern side of the ancient valley and dug deeper into bedrock (Fig. 4.3). This has resulted in the exposure of Troodos Ophiolite, notably the Upper and Lower Pillow Lavas and Basal Group rock formations. These rocks do not form good substrates for productive agriculture, as noted elsewhere in the TAESP Survey Area. Agricultural land use is limited to (1) terraced hillslopes, wherein the thin soils are thickened over cut-and-fill, stone-shored benches (treads), and (2) fluvial bottom lands where relatively recent (late Pleistocene–present) accumulations of sediments provide good parent material for development of productive soils.

Fortunately, for the metallurgist, erosion has cut below the ancient valley fill. For here, the rich copper and other ores were exposed and ripened for exploitation by miners. The Memi Mine is the latest of these excavations. Alestos has clearly stood above both generations of the Lagoudhera valley, and its Basal Group rocks represent an ancient fault block infused with metals that have been variously exploited, attested by the 20th century exploitation of ore clearly visible in the huge spoil heaps spilling down the north, south and south-east-facing slopes of the hills.

Like most rivers along the north slope of the Troodos, the Lagoudhera and its tributaries have had fluctuating bed elevations in response to changes in climate and land cover. Since the Late Pleistocene, the rivers and streams have a net trend of incision, with momentary stalls, which led to the development of the stair-step of fluvial terraces in valley bottoms. Brief episodes of flooding and debris flows deposited boulders in long, linear bars on floodplains and adjacent terraces. These bars would eventually be adapted for terrace walls and structures, as can be seen in Xyliatos *Ayios Kyriakos* (TS10; Chapter 4.5). As with the Karkotis Valley, boulder size diminishes from nearly a metre to centimetres in diameter with distance downstream along the Lagoudhera River.

Irrigation and Management of Water Supply

Modern (post-WW2) irrigation works consist of early concrete flumes and metal gates, which have been supplanted by localized black PVC pipe. The Pitsilia Integrated Rural Development Project was implemented during the early 1980s by the Republic of Cyprus to supply water to fields and villages, including most of this Intensive Survey Zone, from storage behind Xyliatos Dam, built in 1982–83 across the Lagoudhera River just 2 km upstream. Even from its first years, the dam consistently overflowed, leading to an increase in its capacity in 1998 (Kyrou and Rayssiguier 2001). A pumped-storage reservoir, completed during our survey (2002), is located at the northern edge of the Intensive Survey Zone and serves to augment the Xyliatos Irrigation District's agricultural and domestic water supply, as well as that of the Nicosia metropolitan area.

Early waterworks, including aqueducts, cisterns and wells, are noted in the Intensive Survey Zone (see below). Evidence of the multiple generations of water conveyance include a pre-1980s open channel, cut through rock, which was covered with concrete during the early 1980s and within which steel pipe was placed during the 1990s. Above the Xyliatos Irrigation District lines, deep groundwater boreholes and gas-powered pumps feed the now ubiquitous 'black' pipe sprinkler and drip irrigators in the fields of citrus, vegetables and vines.

Land Sculpting

Field terraces of the Lagoudhera Intensive Survey Zone include some of the best representatives of the different styles of Mediterranean hillslope agriculture, comparable with those documented in Greece (Rackham and Moody 1996) and the Levant (Ron 1966). Survey transects crossed all types of traditional terraces (Rackham and Moody 1996, 140–41), and some modern variants of hillslope terraces were also surveyed. Types of dry-stack stone terrace construction included stepped, braided and pocket terraces (after Rackham and Moody 1996, 141), as well as outcrop extensions and check dams. Interspersed among these stone, soil-conservation structures are field walls for property division and sets of parallel walls lining roads and footpaths: locally field walls also serve as soil conservation or water conveyance structures. Some buildings are incorporated into these stone structures.

The recent development of terraces for agriculture, particularly orchards, has used earth-moving equipment in this area since the mid 1980s, when new irrigation works were introduced (see below). According to two local informants, the valley to the north of the village of Xyliatos was bulldozed from 1988. Throughout the Upper Lagoudhera Valley we observed a rapidly changing landscape during the lifetime of the project. Survey transects traversed many terraces that were recently produced by huge earth-moving machinery (Fig. 4.4).

We also witnessed areas previously surveyed being modified in this way. During the 2001 season, an area surveyed along the transect immediately east of the Lagoudhera river bed was characterized by overgrown, abandoned nut and fruit orchards with rock outcrops. Two years later, it was being transformed into large flat treads, with steep risers, by earth-moving machinery. Similarly, an extensive area, half a kilometre east of Xyliatos, was

Table 4.2. Check dams in Lagoudhera Intensive Survey Zone

	Name	*No.*	*Elevation (m asl)*	*Description*
TP009	Xyliatos *Athasin*	3+	350	Gully with 3 (possibly 4) check dams; next gully to East has more.
TP076	Ayia Marina *Sykia tou Kaiserili*	2	440	Gully with 2 check dams. Upper: W 11 m. Lower: W 2.6 m. H 0.9 m.
TP079	Ayia Marina *Lovarkatis*	4	405	Filling gap in basalt dyke. W 7.2 m. H 3.0 m. Another 3 in gully.
TP145	Xyliatos Litharkies	3	500	Upper: W 10 m. H 1.0 m. Middle: W 8 m. H 0.5 m. Lower: W 10 m. H 0.5 m.
TP147	Xyliatos *Kokkinoplevra tou Alestou*	6	510	On steep ESE slope of Alestos. Upper dam: W 3m. Lower 5 dams are smaller, each forming cultivable area of c. 2 m^2.
TP151	Xyliatos *Kokkinoplevra tou Alestou*	1	635	In narrow steep gully on Alestos with 25° slope.
TP175	Xyliatos *Alestos*	7	530	Steep east-facing rocky gully on Alestos. Crudely built of boulders.
TP213	Xyliatos *Alestos*	8	520	Narrow gully on east-facing slope of Alestos. Built of cobbles & boulders of angular basalt. 2nd from top: W 7.4 m. H 0.9 m. 3rd: W 4.4 m. H 0.9 m. 5th: W 4.3 m. H 1.3 m.
TP234	Xyliatos *Kokkinoplevra tou Alestou*	15	480	Two 1st-order gullies with 7 and 8 check dams, just above where they converge. Built of angular basalt boulders. Lowest: W 7.5 m. H 1.1 m. Next up: 7.5 m. H 1.4 m. Associated paths.

Fig. 4.4. Bulldozing and bulldozed terraces on the flank of Alestos, with the spoil heaps from the modern mine above, taken from the south-east (Chris Parks)

transformed into huge terraces during the 2002 season. The newly available water supply is largely the impetus for these transformations. Additionally, this activity has been encouraged by the Government of Cyprus's Ministry of Agriculture through its Land Realignment and Consolidation Programme, wherein many small land holdings are aggregated into one, and land is levelled for modern mechanized agricultural production.

Vegetation

Ancient to modern agricultural and mining activities are well expressed by patterns in vegetation (Table 4.3). Cultivars ranging from cereals to vegetables to orchards of citrus, almond and olive are arranged along fluvial terraces and hillslope terraces. Wild and managed fields of cereals are present on broad hillslope terraces and some valley-bottom plots, and account for one-fifth of the land cover of the Intensive Survey Zone. The average size of Geomorphological Units on arable land was 2694 m^2, and in most cases they corresponded to arable field (property) boundaries on the cadastral map. This is a very small size for an average landholding and is an indicator of landholding miniaturization or fragmentation in the area, due mainly to land being divided between heirs (Christodoulou 1959, 83–85). Most of the ancient fields

Table 4.3. Percentage vegetation cover across the Lagoudhera Valley Intensive Survey Zone and the entire Survey Area

Land Cover Type	*Class*	*Lagoudhera %*	*Survey Area %*
Pine (dense)	1	1.9	5.5
Pine 30–60%	2	11.9	7.2
Pine 10–30%	3	13.5	20.4
Batha/Pine 10%	4	28.2	15.1
Forested	1-4	55.5	48.1
Garigue/Batha	5	5.5	5.6
Batha (Open Heath)	6	0.7	2.9
Grass/grassy batha/cereal crops	7	20.9	28.0
Intensive cereal crops	8	0.2	0.6
Vegetable crops	9	3.1	2.6
Non-conifers and orchards	10	8.2	3.6
Built-up	11	2.1	2.8
Disturbed surface (mines)	12	3.5	6.0
Water	13	0.2	0.0

are out of production as they are too small and on land inaccessible to modern machinery.

The whole area has been greatly modified over the last 20 years, especially through bulldozing, to expand the cultivable area. The size of bulldozed cuts increases with ease of excavation, from small lots in basalt to expansive fields in Pleistocene fluvial gravel deposits. Vegetables and other market crops are limited to the low-sloping treads of fluvial terraces, and account for 3% of the Intensive Survey Zone, a distant second to the Karkotis Valley. Market crops, more profitable in domestic and export markets, appear to be increasing at the expense of the older cereal fields. Orchards cover 8%, and are largely confined to modern bulldozed terraces and ridgetops. Mines and pines make up much of the remainder, as the thin, relatively unproductive soils and extensive mining landholdings obviate further agricultural development.

4.3 Ancient and Modern Mining on Alestos

During the 1930s about 10,000 tons of gold ore were obtained from Alestos (Bear 1963, 81). The hill has also long been known to be a source of chalcopyrite (copper iron sulphide), and the area close to the summit on the east side was extensively mined, using opencast methods, during the 20th century (Carr 1960, 46). The lease of the mine belonged to the Hellenic Mining Company, which in 1971–72, using the opencast method, extracted a total of 660,515 tons of copper ore (Mines 2010).

The 20th-century mining operations at Alestos (TP005) can be clearly seen from a great distance: huge spoil heaps cascade down the sides of the hill, and a large chunk of the east side of the summit has been removed (Fig. 4.5). The remnants of this opencast mine consist of an acidic lake

Fig. 4.5. Alestos opencast mine from the west-south-west (Chris Parks)

and the ruined infrastructure of the mining operation. The west-south-west face is very eroded, and the spoil heaps spill down the north, south and south-east-facing slopes of the hill. Modern mining has obliterated any ancient galleries that may have once existed in the core of the ore body. A number of adits, however, some of which are almost certainly ancient, survive on the south and south-east-facing slopes of the hill and are discussed below.

Our main aim was to investigate mining at Alestos and any possible communication routes between the mines, the Roman mining settlement of Xyliatos *Litharkies* (TS05), and the Roman settlement and smelting site of Ayia Marina *Mavrovouni* (TS02). To do this we surveyed one transect to the west of Litharkies and four transects between it and the Lagoudhera Valley to the east. We also carried out careful reconnaissance of the south and south-west-facing slopes of Alestos between the settlement and the summit.

Adits

On the south-facing slope of Alestos we recorded a number of adits and other evidence of exploration for ore bodies (Plate 4.2; Table 4.4). An informant from Xyliatos told us that the top of Alestos was covered in pits, c. 1 m in diameter, which may well have been adit entrances. The adits we recorded ranged from an area close to the summit, with two collapsed intersecting adits at 664 m asl (TP153), down to a prospection hole at 562 m (TP115). The largest adit found on the southern face is TP112. This adit, which is at least 18.5 m deep and filled with water, is far larger than the Iron Age adit at Almyras (Fasnacht *et al.* 1996, 115; Mines 2010) or any of those recorded by the Sydney Cyprus Survey Project (Knapp *et al.* 2003, 143).

About 20 m below and to the south-west of that adit is a smaller one (TP148). This has an external stone-built platform at its entrance, to allow some security when working on the 15° slope. Three sherds were found in the Survey Unit directly below TP112 and TP148: Roman tile, Roman Cooking Ware and Historical Antiquity Light Utility ware. These may support our hypothesis that the

Table 4.4. Ayios Yeoryios Alestos: *mining adits. D = Depth H = Height W = Width*

	Type	*Condition*	*Dimensions (m)*	*Notable features*
TP112	Adit with shaft	Good. Water at bottom	D: 18.5+ W: 0.7–1.1 H: 1.2 Inside entrance: W 2.8; H 1.55	Cut into basalt/gossan outcrop. Slopes gently (16°) for 8.3 m; then steeply for 10.3 m until water was reached. Cut in bedrock in front to allow access. Platform in front made of spoil.
TP115	Prospection cut	Partially filled by collapse from E side	H: 3.0 W: 3.0 D: 1.5+	Cut at ground level; sloped down to straight back; may have gone deeper.
TP148	Adit	Some collapse & fill; otherwise good	D: 1.7–4.0 m H: 0.5–0.9 m	Extends E and N inside. Stone platform to E with retaining wall; 2.6 x 2.5 m.
TP149	Modern quarry & possible gallery	Mostly cut away by quarry; overgrown	L: 10 m	Base visible in quarry floor; continues into quarry face.
TP153	2 adits	Collapsed; full of rubble	South: D: 1.8. W: 1.6. Entrance 0.7 x 0.7 East: D: 0.9. Entrance 0.7 x 0.7	One leads S, one leads E, with small flat area between the entrances. S adit has cut 1.8 x 0.45 leading to entrance.
TP180	Adit	Full of water; well-preserved	L of entrance: 0.9 H of steps: 0.2 & 0.24 W of adit: 1.4	Entrance passage with 2 steps. More steps in adit continuing below water line. Modern spoil heap 4 m below
TP181	Adit	Slightly collapsed; some collapse and fill; water	D: 3.0 W of entrance: 1.0. H: 0.8	On steep slope (22°). Goes at least 3 m into hillside; blocked with rubble. No spoil heap.
TP182	Prospection cut	Good	0.9 x 1.1	Small rectangular cut on steep slope (22°).
TP184	Adit	Some collapsed boulders from roof	Upper: 0.8 x 0.1. D: 2.8 Lower: 1.0 x 0.98. D: 2.8	Y-shaped adit with 2 entrances. On steep slope (32°). Heads towards TP180 15 m to W.
TP232	Adit?	Partly filled in; damaged by bulldozing	W: 1.6 H: 0.58+ L: 3.3	Rock cut in basalt-sheeted dyke; possible adit.

adits are ancient. Located c. 30 m to the east of TP112 is a modern quarry with the remnants of an adit at the rear (TP149). The quarry seems to have cut away the first 10 m of a gallery, whose base is visible under rubble. The area to the east of the modern quarry is now covered by spoil from the 20th-century mining operations.

Another small cluster of adits and exploratory cuts was recorded on a basalt slope forming a spur on the south-east side of Alestos (Fig. 4.6; Fig. 4.7). The largest of these adits (TP180) is at 577 m asl. It has a set of steps down to the entrance and appears to have cut through into a vertical exploratory cut (TP184) further upslope. The area at the front of TP180 was filled with water when surveyed in July 2003 and hints at past mining conditions. It is possible that winter and spring rains made it difficult to mine this adit at these times, which might have restricted activity to the summer or autumn months. About 7 m above TP180 is a smaller adit, only 3 m deep (TP181). A further 9.5 m above this adit is another exploratory cut (TP182). A path (TP186) running along a natural break in the rocky slope appears to link this area of mining activity with the modern spoil of the opencast mining to the west.

It is always very difficult to date such structures solely on shape and size, particularly when later miners return to an abandoned mine and use similar methods. While the archives of the Mines Service of the Republic of Cyprus state that the Alestos ore deposit was only exploited as an opencast mine in the 20th century, it is possible that exploration adits were created at some time in the 19th century before the opencast mine opened. According to Carr (1960, 44), the upper part of Alestos hill was explored by drilling and stripping east of the summit. The removal of soil and bedrock rubble implied by the term 'stripping' is clearly much more intensive than the exploration carried out in the adits we recorded. Their small size and the fact that they are clustered, rather than dispersed, may be used as arguments that they are ancient.

Platforms

We recorded seven flat platforms on Alestos (Table 4.5), from close to the summit (TP154 at 664 m asl) to much further down in the pine trees on the south-east flank (TP173 at 509 m asl). All the platforms have a dry-stack retaining wall on their downslope side and are cut into the bedrock at their rear. The flat areas all have a sub-rounded shape and are in the order of 2–3 m in diameter.

Some of these platforms recorded on Alestos may have been associated with the 20th-century mining infrastructure. Platforms were constructed as areas where miners could keep their equipment, preventing it from rolling down the mountain, and to dress (sieve and field-test) ore rock without the laborious transit to lower elevations. They are also positioned so miners could safely wait out the explosion of dynamite. An explosion within an adit would send rock flying out of the adit mouth and tumbling down the slope, so a miner has to be physically removed from the adit to avoid being hit by flying rocks; the platform provides security and comfort on the very steep slope. Although blasting was an available mining technology from the 16th century in Europe (Golas and Needham 1999, 306), it was not until the late 19th century

Fig. 4.6. Alestos: group of adits on the south-east shoulder of the mountain, looking east down the slope. In the foreground are the two entrances to TP184; the figure in the right background is standing on the levelled spoil heap of TP180; the figure on the left is standing in TP181 (Chris Parks)

Fig. 4.7. Alestos: entrance to adit TP180, with steps on the left; view from the north. Scale is 1 m (Chris Parks)

Table 4.5. Platforms on Alestos

	Dimensions (m)	*Height of retaining wall (m)*	*Location relative to nearest adits*	*Platform and retaining wall construction*
TP150	2.6 x 2.5	0.70	68 m NW of and 38 m above TP112 on the same colluvial facet	Dry stack angular basalt boulder wall. Upslope side is cut into bedrock.
TP152	1.7 x 2.6	c. 0.2	100 m SW of TP153	Curved dry stack wall closely packed and levelled with pebble- and cobble-sized stones. Upslope side is cut into bedrock.
TP154	2.8 x 2.2	0.45	12 m below TP153	4 courses of dry stack wall. Packed behind with pebble- and cobble-sized stones. Upslope side cut into bedrock.
TP173	2.9 x 2.4	0.50–0.55	220 m SE of and 68 m below TP180	2-m wide wall. 5 courses of cobble-sized angular gossan blocks with some pebble infill behind. Platform built up with soil.
TP183	2.8 x 2.2	0.72	36 m N of TP180 and 24 m from TP182	Boulder- and cobble-sized dry stack wall with pebble-sized stones used as fill behind. Upslope side cut into bedrock.
TP185	2.7 x 2.8	c. 0.3	51 m E of TP180 and 43 m from TP182	2 courses of boulder- and cobble-sized dry stack angular basalt wall built onto bedrock. Pebble-sized fill to produce a very flat platform surface. Upslope side cut into bedrock.
TP235	2.0 x 2.0	0.10–0.15	8 m W of TP115	1–2 courses of dry stack wall. Platform cut into bedrock at the rear. Upslope side cut into bedrock.

Fig. 4.8. Alestos: platform TP183 from the east-south-east. Scale is 1 m (Chris Parks)

Fig. 4.9. Fieldwalking at Xyliatos Litharkies, *with Alestos behind, from the south-west (Michael Given)*

that it became reliable for general use. In view of this, and the lack of significant lichenous cover on structural stones, it is likely that some of the platforms are 20th-century constructions. The platform at the entrance to adit TP148, however, is contemporary with the adit and is presumably ancient. TP173 in pine trees on the lower SE slopes of Alestos appears to have no association with the adits further up the slope and its function remains unclear.

Mining Operations

The water in both TP112 and TP180 suggests some of the difficulties of mining on Alestos. Mining as a seasonal activity has been suggested for sites such as Almyras (Fasnacht 1999, 182; Kassianidou 1998, 229). If TP112 was mined, even in the summer months, it would have required baling out before mining could commence. There are two apparent clusters of activity: TP112, TP148 and TP149, which are within 40 m of each other; and TP180–82 and TP184, again all in close proximity. A chalcopyrite seam has clearly been found and the area explored and exploited. The small fragments of bedrock on the spoil heaps of TP112 and TP180 suggest that some mineral dressing occurred at the mine.

Where the hillside was very steep, as in the case of TP148, a platform was constructed to facilitate the work by cutting into the bedrock upslope and using angular blocks to construct a retaining wall downslope. The other platforms around Alestos not directly associated with an adit are of similar construction. They clearly show the ease with which the basalt can be cut and a stable flat surface produced. The path linking the area of adits on a south-east-facing slope with an area further upslope, attests to the ease with which a 28° slope can be traversed using a natural break in slope.

The future of copper mining at Alestos is currently in the hands of Eastern Mediterranean Resources (EMED). Eastern Mediterranean Minerals (Cyprus) (EMM), a joint venture of the Hellenic Mining Company and Oxiana Europe, carried out exploratory drilling in 2000 on Alestos for gold deposits (Michalski 1998, 53.1; Mobbs 2000, 34.2). EMM, which held 88 km^2 of prospecting permits in Cyprus, has subsequently been bought by EMED, which resumed a drilling programme in the 'North Alestos' prospect in Autumn 2005 and recorded significant alteration and sulphides, which is typical of ores at the periphery of Cyprus-style copper deposits (Eastern 2005).

4.4 Roman Mining Settlement at Xyliatos *Litharkies* (TS05)

At Litharkies on the south flank of Alestos, high densities of tiles, Cooking Wares, Table Wares, utility wares and transport amphorae provide evidence of a settlement in the Early and Late Roman periods, in close proximity to the mines upslope. A large number of rock piles, lining agricultural terraces, most likely represents field clearance of remains of Roman structures. This is supported by the large amount of tile still found in the fields.

Our work in this area sought to define the precise location and extent of the settlement, and how this may have changed over time. Our aim was also to understand the social organisation of the ancient mining community at Alestos, the management of ore, food, water and fuel resources, and the relationship and communication between this community of extractors and that of the smelters at Ayia Marina *Mavrovouni* (Chapter 4.6).

Litharkies is bounded to the west by a flat area (TP212) at the crest of the ridge, and to the south by a dirt track. To the east, the boundary is formed by a stream bed, which had not much more than a trickle in it throughout July 2003, while the ridge directly to the south of the check dams (TP145) forms the northern boundary. We block surveyed 30 Survey Units within this area, though we had to leave a considerable amount of area unsurveyed due to poor ground visibility (Fig. 4.10).

Fig. 4.10. Litharkies in the middle ground, viewed looking south from Alestos (Chris Parks)

Fig. 4.11. Ayia Marina Lovarkatis *(TP079): check dam, 3 m high, built on a basalt dyke. An example of an outcrop-extension type of soil and water conservation structure (Chris Parks)*

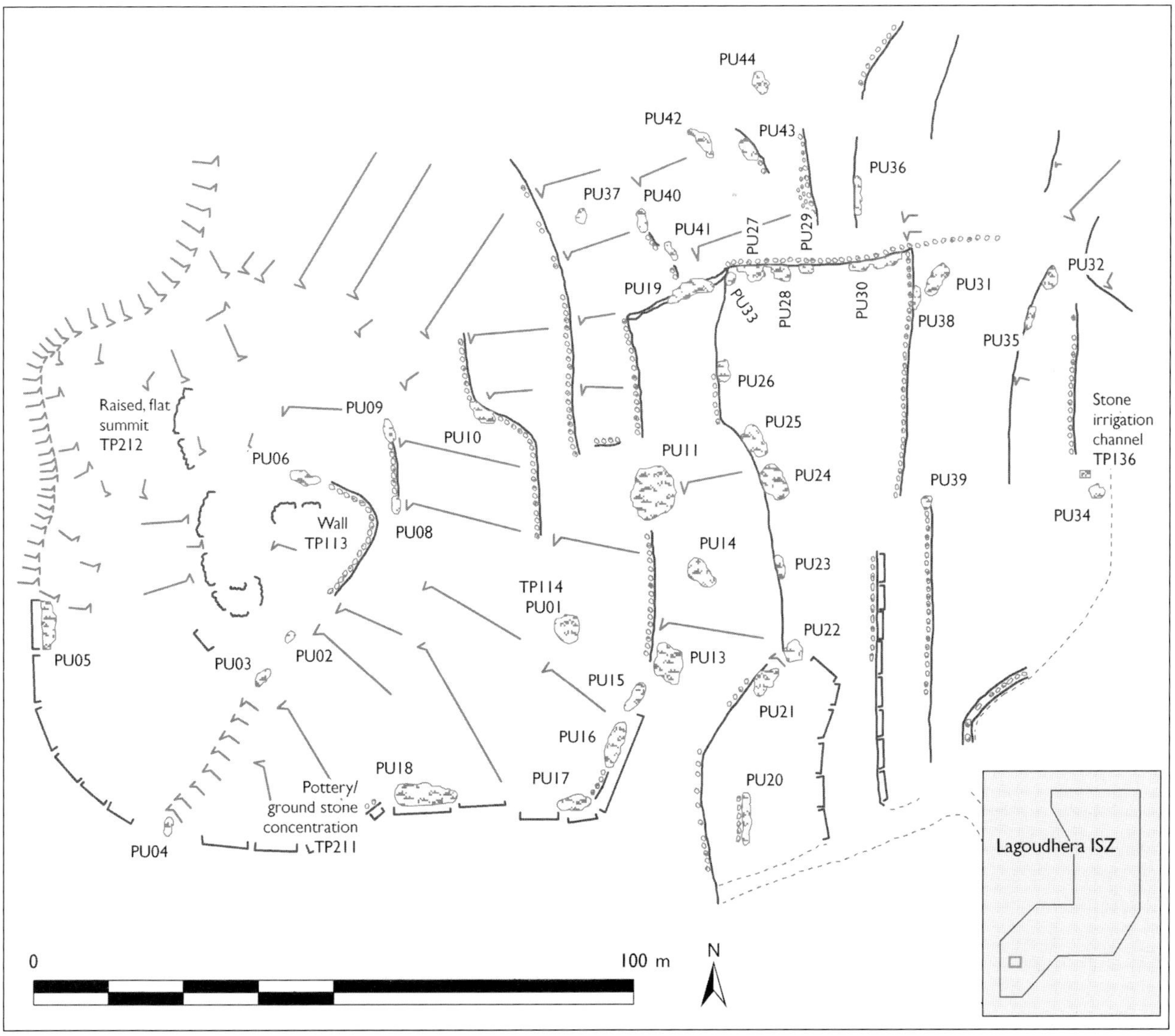

PU44
PU42
PU43
PU36
PU37
PU40
PU41
PU27
PU29
PU19
PU33
PU28
PU30
PU31
PU32
PU38
PU35
PU26
Raised, flat summit TP212
PU09
PU06
PU10
PU11
PU25
Stone irrigation channel TP136
PU24
PU39
Wall TP113
PU08
PU14
PU34
PU23
TP114 PU01
PU22
PU05
PU03
PU02
PU13
PU15
PU21
PU16
PU18
PU17
PU20
Pottery/ ground stone concentration
TP211
PU04
Lagoudhera ISZ
0
100 m
N

Fig. 4.12. Xyliatos Litharkies *(TS05): plan with rock piles (TP210) and high density tread. The hilltop is in the west, with a long slope down to the east. NB There are no PU01, 07, 12 (Rosey Blackwell, finalised by Luke Sollars)*

Table 4.6. Xyliatos Litharkies *(TS05): summary of collected pottery from rock piles (TP210) and two pottery scatters (TP211; TP212). See also Table 4.7. TCP numbers refer to Pottery Catalogue in Volume 1, Chapter 3.6*

Historical Antiquity (Archaic to Late Roman)

Fct	*Type*	*No.*	*Weight*
HU	HU	17	762g
LU	LU	15	372g

Hellenistic

Fct	*Type*	*No.*	*Weight*
TW	CC	1	2g

Hellenistic to Roman

Fct	*Type*	*No.*	*Weight*
CW	CW	4	27g
HU	Pit17	1	138g
Tr	Am	1	180g

Late Hellenistic to Early Roman

Fct	*Type*	*No.*	*Weight*
TW	ESA	1	14g

Early Roman

Fct	*Type*	*No.*	*Weight*
TW	CS40	1	20g TCP697
TW	CS58	1	14g TCP696

Early to Late Roman

Fct	*Type*	*No.*	*Weight*
Ar	Ti	12	4.48kg
Ar	TiP	7	3.26kg
CW	CWFPWh01	2	88g
HU	HUR01	1	59g
HU	Pit07	1	1.2kg TCP694

Late Roman

Fct	*Type*	*No.*	*Weight*
Ar	TiP	1	320g
Ar	TiSk02	1	530g
Ar	TiSkC02	2	2.165kg TCP698
Ar	TiSkC03	2	300g
HU	HU	2	72g
HU	Pit24	1	2.75kg TCP695

Roman to Modern

Fct	*Type*	*No.*	*Weight*
Ar	Ti	1	275g

Historical (Archaic to Modern)

Fct	*Type*	*No.*	*Weight*
HU	HU	9	1.688kg
HU	Pit12a	4	550g
LU	LU	1	8g

Medieval to Modern

Fct	*Type*	*No.*	*Weight*
U	UPSJu	1	25g

Fig. 4.13. Xyliatos Litharkies *(TS05): settlement area with rock pile (TP210.PU11) (Chris Parks)*

Present Day Environment

The area surrounding Litharkies can be divided into three hydrological catchments, two of which drain to its north-east and one to its north-west (see Plate 4.6). The two north-eastern drainages (of which the southern one is the Argaki tis Yerokaminas) both meet the Lagoudhera River south of Mavrovouni, while the north-western one is dominated by relatively high slopes and deep gullies, and runs into the Kannavia Valley.

The hydrology of the area is influenced by slopes. At the mainly rocky summits, the runoff and overland flow gains significant momentum by the time it reaches the middle portions of the slope. The bottoms of the gullies formed by this flow have, in most cases, been opportunistically used to trap sediment with check dams big enough for a single fruit tree. Almost all check dams are east-facing and have evidence of planting. One series of check dams (TP234) to the west of Litharkies is west-facing, and seems to be a recent attempt to stem the erosion that was evidently cutting deep gullies into the landscape. Another very striking check dam is 3 m high and exploits a large basalt dyke crossing part of the gully (Table 4.2, Fig. 4.11).

The whole area has been greatly modified over the last twenty years, especially through bulldozing to expand the cultivable area. The size of bulldozed cuts increases as one moves north, probably because of the change from basalt to the more easily excavated Pleistocene fluvial gravel deposits.

Rock Piles, Structural Remains and Water Resources

A series of 41 rock piles was recorded throughout the settlement area of Litharkies (TP210; Fig. 4.12; Fig. 4.13). They vary in size considerably, ranging from large piles over 7 m in length to much smaller ones of only 1.5 m in diameter. In height they ranged up to c. 1.6 m, forming the risers between the treads. The rocks are of the same lithology as those formations exposed on Alestos, and appear to have been derived from scree slopes, field clearance (soils derived from colluvium on Alestos) and rounded stones from the Pleistocene fluvial gravel deposits. PU21–30 and PU33 actually represent one continuous pile of rocks. Some of the rock piles have been disturbed by the recent laying of irrigation pipes.

As one would expect from field clearance, the pottery collected mainly consisted of larger fragments of tiles and Heavy and Light Utility wares (e.g. TCP694–95), though there were also a few fragments of Cooking Wares (Table 4.6). The pottery points to the Roman period, although there are single pieces of Hellenistic Table Ware and Medieval–Modern utility ware (UPSJu). The proximity of the largest rock piles to the high-density area of ceramic vessels and tile fragments, together with the results of the resistivity survey, support our interpretation that the stones were from structural remains of the Roman period.

In the south-west part of Litharkies we recorded three POSIs: a Roman well, or more probably cistern, with plaster lining (TP191); a pile of Roman pottery fragments (TP211); and part of a wall with in situ pottery (TP238). A rock pile in the same area supports this being part of the Roman settlement of Litharkies (TP210.PU18). These are all located on what was formerly a gently rolling south-east-facing slope, but following extensive bulldozing over the last 20 years (most recently in 2002) it is now an artificially flat area, that gives way to a sharp slope to the west. Material movement in this area is thus hard to interpret, although it could have been buried in the process of bulldozing, which may explain the lower densities found in the Survey Units here (SU2633–36). Nevertheless they contain LHER, Early Roman and Late Roman artefacts, with Early Roman being the most significant period (Table 4.7).

The well or cistern (TP191) has a diameter of 1.35 m and an extant height of 1.6 m, and the bulldozer cut reveals that the bedrock was cut to construct it (Fig. 4.14). Given that it is located some distance from the stream, it is more likely that it was a cistern than a well. There is a good parallel at the Roman farmstead of Petra *Phoukasa* (TP221) in the Atsas Valley (Chapter 2.6). This is a circular cistern, 2.5 m in diameter, on a knoll, with large quantities of Roman tile round it. The roof of the building would have acted as the collector for the cistern.

With an extant capacity of c. 2300 litres the Litharkies cistern would, most likely, not have provided sufficient capacity to last through the summer months. The Roman period is known as a warm and/or dry climatic anomaly. Although we cannot positively conclude what the discharge was at that time, it could have been drier and warmer, and consequently the thunderstorms may have been stronger and peak flood flows greater. This might suggest that little water flowed in the summer months in the stream to the east of TS05. It is possible that summer thunderstorms served to resupply the cistern. It may have been that there are more cisterns at Litharkies that we did not find because they have been infilled (Rackham and Moody 1996, 43–44). The south-east domestic quarter at Kourion, for example, has at least nine surviving cisterns (Buell and Mavromatis 2010). Alternatively, it may have been that the donkeys and workers returned with water from the Lagoudhera River after delivering ore to Mavrovouni for smelting.

Resistivity Survey

Geophysical survey was conducted at Litharkies on two separate terraces (Fig. 4.15). Grid 1 is on the terrace where it was not possible to carry out Survey Units, but where there were large rock piles (TP210.PU11, PU14, PU19) and large pieces of ground stone. Grid 2 is located on the terrace below, where the highest density of pottery and tile in Litharkies was recorded (SU2605, SU2632, SU2648). In both cases, the intention was to detect any traces of settlement that related to the artefactual material. The surveys were conducted using a Geoscan RM15 resistivity meter, taking readings at 1 × 1 m across 20-m grid squares. The data were downloaded into Geoplot v3 and the results processed in the same software.

Fig. 4.14. Xyliatos Litharkies *(TP191): plaster lining of cistern or well. Scale is 2 m (Chris Parks)*

In Grid 1 the quantities of surface stone and pottery suggest that there may have been a building of some form on the platform. The stone scatter created substantial noise across the plot, but there was an anomaly within the noise that formed a rectangular shape measuring roughly 7 × 3 m. This was formed by slightly lower readings than its surroundings, suggesting that it was indicating a negative feature, possibly the foundations of a building. There were also fainter anomalies that might have represented archaeological features, but as the soil conditions were very dry, it is difficult to determine whether they represent features, or were just created by the processing.

This 7 × 3 m rectangular shape is adjacent to the largest of the Litharkies rock piles (TP210.PU11; Fig. 4.13), which contained a piece of Late Roman pan tile and a fragment of Roman pithos rim (Pit07; TCP694). Rock piles PU14 and PU19 at the southern and northern ends of Grid 1 respectively had no pottery or tile recorded in them. PU14 had one ground stone fragment, and PU19 had three, of which one was a vasicular, basalt grooved rubbing stone (see discussion below).

Grid 2 consisted of two lower terraces to the east, though it only covered the northern half of the lowest, easternmost terrace. Both terraces had been ploughed and showed striking densities of artefactual material on the surface. The most obvious anomalies are the very dark patches (Fig. 4.15): one lies towards the southern end of the plot, while the second forms a short diagonal line near the north-western corner. These are likely to have been caused by solid material, perhaps the rubble of former

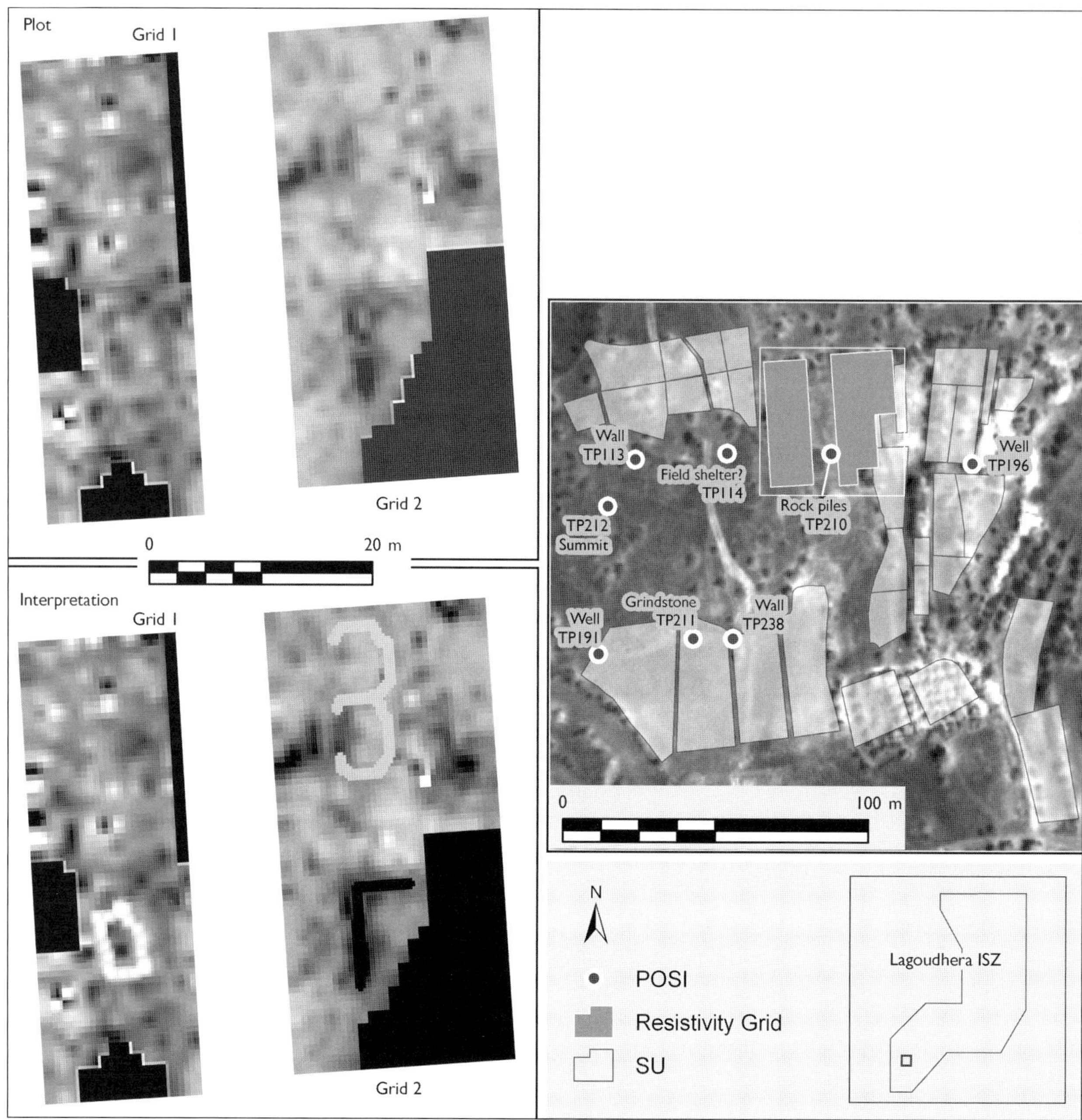

Fig. 4.15. Xyliatos Litharkies *(TS05): resistivity survey results, with detailed and interpretative plots. Grid 1 shows a roughly rectangular anomaly, c. 7 × 3 m. Grid 2 shows possible walls joining at right angles, and 2 conjoined roughly circular anomalies, one c. 7 m in diameter, the other c. 7 × 9 m. Corrected satellite image (2003) courtesy of the Cyprus Geological Survey Department (Iain Banks and Luke Sollars)*

walls. The intensity of the response was not particularly high in absolute terms, but the readings were substantially higher than the background. It is, therefore, reasonable to assume that the darker patches do relate to structural remains. This is particularly true of the anomaly at the southern end, which appears to form a right angle. This is more likely to represent anthropogenic activity rather than geological conditions.

There are also two lighter anomalies in Grid 2 that appear as circles (Fig. 4.15). The anomalies give the impression of a circle with a diameter of roughly 7 m, conjoined with a more oval shape that seems to have dimensions of c. 7 × 9 m. The width of the anomalies is no more than a metre or so, which would be consistent with a wall. The anomalies are light grey, suggesting that they are of average resistance, neither high nor low in the dataset. This suggests that the cause of the anomaly is neither particularly compact nor particularly loose. Accordingly, it is unlikely that the anomalies represent solid walls, particularly if the previous interpretations of the higher anomalies are correct. There are lighter grey areas around the anomalies, which makes it unlikely that they represent a ditch or other negative feature. The most likely explanation is that the anomalies represent walls, but that the walls consisted of a relatively conductive material, or that the material was relatively loose. If this is the case, then the anomalies might represent circular buildings such as huts, or they might represent a circular structure similar to the Archaic sanctuary at Pano Limna (Chapter 3.11). While one of the few pieces of Cypro-Geometric to Cypro-Classical pottery found at Litharkies came from this area, there are no figurines or anything else that would allow us to identify a sanctuary.

Pottery Distribution and Analysis

Litharkies is most striking for the concentration of Hellenistic–Roman pottery, which is immense when compared to all other individual SUs and SIAs in the Survey Area (Volume 1, Chapter 5.3). With a mean sherd density of 86.7 sherds/100 m^2 for the 30 units that make up the SIA, it is almost three times denser than the mean of the 16 units at Mavrovouni, and many times denser than anywhere else in the Survey Area. The density of Hellenistic–Roman material at Litharkies ranged from 2.5 to 490 sherds/100 m^2, and there were clearly areas representing differing activities to be investigated.

Six Cypro-Geometric to Cypro-Classical sherds from four different Survey Units show a range of wares, suggesting that they represent more than a single 'pot burst' (Plate 4.3). The only positively identified Hellenistic material, with the exception of two sherds of Cooking Ware, is Table Ware. Its density and distribution reveal that the north-western part of Litharkies was the focus of activity. The low hill that forms the focus of the settlement area (TP212) forms part of the shoulder and backslope of Litharkies Ridge. The slopes range from 10–12°, although the shoulders tend to flatten out towards the summit. This means that material at the summit is not subject to a significant rate of downslope movement, whether because of tillage, soil erosion, or hillslope creep, and is likely to be in situ. The area also affords a good view over Litharkies to the east and towards the Kannavia Valley to the west.

The highest densities of Late Hellenistic–Early Roman (LHER) pottery are found in the north-west area of Litharkies and on the northern half of a terrace in the centre of the area (where resistivity Grid 2 was carried out; see above). Unfortunately, the area between them could not be surveyed owing to poor visibility, though it was here that we carried out resistivity Grid 1. It was only at the northern end of the terrace that LHER and Early Roman (ER) pottery was found; this is where the three highest densities of ER pottery were all found (13.6–16.1 sherds/100 m^2; SU2605, SU2632, SU2648; see Plate 4.4). More broadly, running from south to north, the density of Hellenistic–Roman material in the five Survey Units on this terrace is c. 23, 123, 490, 239 and 294 sherds/100 m^2. It appears that the focus of activity in the Early Roman period continued from the Hellenistic period, with the focus in the northern half of Litharkies, but with a shift in the high-density concentration from the north-west to the centre. This terrace is under the influence of colluvial processes that could be moving materials into the area from upslope. Further movement of materials from the terrace should have been curtailed by the dry-stack terrace wall, hence explaining the lower densities in the terraces below.

Again, the three Survey Units with densest Late Roman pottery are in the northern half of this terrace (Plate 4.4). The density falls dramatically from north to south, along the tread in the space of 40 m, with the three northern Survey Units having a mean of 83.1 sherds/100 m^2, while the two to the south have a mean of 11.3 sherds/100 m^2. These are probably in situ, as slope gradients are low, the Survey Units are at a significant distance from steeper slopes on Alestos, and the water flow paths are too long for sufficient stream power to move the artefacts. These three units represent the heart of the artefactual evidence, and considering the density of large rock piles forming the field boundaries on this terrace and the one above and to the west, this seems the most likely area of settlement during the Early and Late Roman periods (see Fig. 4.12 above). The density spike in the broader Historical Antiquity period (750 BC–AD 650) is also coincident with this area. The piles of stone represent material that was originally brought into the area, principally from the rubbly scree slopes of Alestos, to be used for building and subsequently cleared to make way for cultivation. The resistivity survey on the treads in this area, strongly suggest the foundations of structures (see above).

The variety of forms of Table Ware, Cooking Ware and utility ware reveals a place of food storage, preparation and consumption (Table 4.7). The high density of tile is evidence of the structures around which these activities were centred. Late Roman assemblages tend to have a strong bias towards materials such as tiles that survive well, while the LHER corpus is mainly made up of more fragile Table Wares. With this in mind, it is clear that the northern part of this terrace has a stronger representation of LHER material compared to the Late Roman material.

The central Survey Unit on this terrace (SU2605) has both ER and LR material, and is notable for the wide variety of Cooking Wares (e.g. TCP426–28). Furthermore, all the common Table Ware types known throughout TAESP are represented in this unit (e.g. TCP429–33). This terrace had a range of transport amphorae fragments, including all three of the Mavrovouni-type amphorae, as well as Skouriotissa types 1 and 3 and HR amphora type 5. Within this range of local transport vessels it is remarkable that only three fragments of imported amphorae were identified: LR amphora 1; and HR amphora types 3 and 7 (e.g. TCP418, TCP461). This seems to suggest that the mining operation was sustained locally, rather than by imported food supplies.

A broad range of pan and cover tile fragments was found on the terrace consistent with tiles found at Skouriotissa (e.g. TCP415–17, TCP419–20). This does not necessarily mean

Table 4.7. Xyliatos Litharkies *(TS05): summary of collected pottery from block survey (SU2601–06, SU2632–39, SU2641–45, SU2648, SU2652–60); see also Table 4.6. TCP numbers refer to Pottery Catalogue in Volume 1, Chapter 3.6*

Cypro-Geometric to Classical

Fct	*Type*	*No.*	*Weight*
HU	HU	1	30g
HU	WPC	4	340g TCP471, TCP472
LU	LU	1	4g
TW	BORO	1	10g TCP478
TW	RS	1	2g

Historical Antiquity (Archaic to Late Roman)

Fct	*Type*	*No.*	*Weight*
CW	CW	1	5g
HU	HU	236	9.771kg
LU	LU	338	5.297kg
TW	BS	2	8g
TW	RS	1	1g
TW	TW	11	36g
Un	Un	1	55g

Hellenistic

Fct	*Type*	*No.*	*Weight*
CW	CWPR10	2	15g TCP474
PO	Ug	1	70g TCP463
TW	BS	23	87g TCP473, TCP475, TCP476, TCP477
TW	CC	2	13g
TW	RB	1	8g TCP480
TW	RS	9	42g

Late Hellenistic

Fct	*Type*	*No.*	*Weight*
TW	CS20	1	6g TCP453

Hellenistic to Roman

Fct	*Type*	*No.*	*Weight*
Ar	Ti	1	400g TCP458
Ar	TiP	9	2.43kg TCP415, TCP416, TCP417, TCP419
CW	CW	260	1.717kg
CW	CWJ04	1	4g TCP427
CW	CWPR	1	5g
CW	CWPR15	1	30g TCP428
CW	CWPR16a	3	50g TCP440
HU	HU	1	20g
HU	HUB02	2	275g TCP446
HU	HUR02	1	195g TCP444
HU	HUR11	1	50g
HU	HUR12	1	40g
HU	HUR15	1	29g
HU	HUR23	1	110g TCP445
HU	HUR24	2	140g
HU	HUR31	1	30g TCP410
HU	Pit11	6	1.48kg
HU	Pit14	1	165g TCP422
HU	Pit16	1	410g TCP464
HU	Pit17	1	345g TCP465
HU	Pit23	3	1.215kg TCP421
LU	LU	8	158g
LU	LUB02	1	34g TCP449
LU	LUR08	1	38g
Tr	Am	10	727g
Tr	Am03	1	60g
Tr	Am07	14	379g TCP461
Tr	Mav01	2	640g TCP479
Tr	Mav02	2	105g
Tr	Mav03	2	45g
TW	RS	1	10g
TW	SRS	28	203g
TW	TW	13	86g

Hellenistic to Early Roman

Fct	*Type*	*No.*	*Weight*
Tr	Am	1	70g
TW	RS	2	4g
TW	SRS	1	5g

Late Hellenistic to Early Roman

Fct	*Type*	*No.*	*Weight*
TW	CS	14	120g TCP438
TW	ESA	8	67g
TW	RS	8	20g
TW	Sig	24	75g TCP450

Early Roman

Fct	*Type*	*No.*	*Weight*
CW	CWPR04a	3	34g TCP457
CW	CWPR04b	1	6g TCP441
CW	CWPR04c	1	26g TCP466
La	La01	2	3g
TW	CS04B	1	9g
TW	CS11	10	81g TCP431, TCP455
TW	CS12	5	72g TCP436, TCP437, TCP456
TW	CS22A	7	16g
TW	CS28	1	3g
TW	CS29	3	27g TCP432, TCP454
TW	CS40	1	5g
TW	CS58	1	20g TCP448
TW	ESB	1	15g
TW	ESB09	1	2g TCP452
TW	SigW	3	28g TCP447, TCP481

Early to Late Roman

Fct	*Type*	*No.*	*Weight*
Ar	Ti	103	17.973kg
Ar	TiC	6	652g
Ar	TiCA	11	1.443kg
Ar	TiP	63	13.216kg
CW	CW	10	47g
CW	CWCR02b	1	11g TCP426
CW	CWCR03	2	12g
CW	CWFPWh	3	41g
CW	CWFPWh01	2	40g
CW	CWPR04	2	19g
CW	CWPR08a	1	10g
CW	CWPR13	5	49g
CW	CWPR16	2	41g
HU	HUR01	17	925g
HU	HUR03	1	75g
LU	LU	3	57g
LU	LUR01	1	20g
Tr	Am05	1	85g
Tr	Am13	5	145g
Tr	AmSk01	3	46g
Tr	AmSk03	1	46g TCP418

TW	ARS	4	17g

Late Roman

Fct	*Type*	*No.*	*Weight*
Ar	TiP	4	315g
Ar	TiSk04	1	130g
Ar	TiSkC02	5	395g
Ar	TiSkC03	30	2.92kg
			TCP420
Ar	TiSkC05	1	175g
CW	CW	17	112g
CW	CWCR01	2	38g
			TCP442
CW	CWPR04a	1	5g
CW	CWPR13	5	85g
			TCP439
HU	HU	1	38g
HU	HUR01b	1	85g
			TCP468
HU	HUR24	3	193g
			TCP423, TCP459, TCP462
HU	HUR28	1	100g
			TCP482
HU	HUR35	1	35g
HU	Pit01	2	450g
HU	Pit10	1	240g
LU	LU	1	15g
LU	LUR13	1	25g
			TCP434
Tr	LR1	5	183g
Tr	Pal	1	21g
TW	CRS	19	194g
TW	CRS01	1	9g
TW	CRS02	6	88g
TW	CRS09	7	99g
			TCP430
TW	CRS09X	1	15g
			TCP433
TW	LRC	9	46g
			TCP470
TW	LRC03	6	106g
			TCP429
TW	LRC03D	1	15g
			TCP467
TW	LRC10	1	15g

Roman to Modern

Fct	*Type*	*No.*	*Weight*
Ar	Ti	17	2.375kg
CW	CW	2	16g
HU	HU	43	3.865kg
HU	HU01	6	950g
			TCP411, TCP412
HU	HUC	7	147g
			TCP424, TCP425, TCP451
HU	HUR30	1	220g
			TCP414
HU	Pit08	1	72g
HU	Pit09	8	2.368kg
HU	Pit15	1	70g
			TCP460
LU	LU	10	307g
TW	TW	1	15g

Historical (Archaic to Modern)

Fct	*Type*	*No.*	*Weight*
HU	HU	263	21.032kg
HU	Pit12a	1	150g
			TCP413
LU	LU	159	2.386kg
Un	Un	4	434g

Medieval utility period I

Fct	*Type*	*No.*	*Weight*
U	UL01	1	70g
			TCP443

Medieval to Modern

Fct	*Type*	*No.*	*Weight*
CW	CW	1	10g
HU	HU	5	128g
LU	LU	5	50g
U	BuLK	1	24g

Medieval utility period III

Fct	*Type*	*No.*	*Weight*
U	ID04	1	19g

Medieval-Venetian to Early Ottoman

Fct	*Type*	*No.*	*Weight*
TW	MP01	1	7g

Ottoman to Modern II

Fct	*Type*	*No.*	*Weight*
LU	BuL	5	39g
TW	MP05	1	14g

Modern

Fct	*Type*	*No.*	*Weight*
Ar	TiCh	2	66g
HU	HU	1	100g
TW	G07	1	4g
TW	Por	2	11g

Unknown

Fct	*Type*	*No.*	*Weight*
Ar	Un	1	200g

there was close contact with Skouriotissa, since several of the same types of tiles were found at the Apollo Hylates Sanctuary at Kourion (Huffstot 1987, figs 185–86). It does, however, suggest the existence of a range of buildings with tiled roofs, either spatially or temporally differentiated. Unfortunately tiles are difficult to date very precisely.

We carried out ten Survey Units on the two terraces directly below and to the east of this one, which are the saddle and valley side-wall of a stream draining Mouti tis Kriniati (SU2606, SU2637–45; Plate 4.4). Compared to the terrace above, the sherd densities are lower, not because there was any movement down the valley with stream water, but because the main focus of activity was in the areas just above. These terraces show higher densities of Late Roman material, which was present in all but one of the Survey Units. The Early Roman material, on the other hand, is only conclusively found in two of the ten Survey Units, but LHER is found in half of them: it has a mean density for the two terraces of 2.1 sherds/100 m^2, compared to the overall Litharkies mean for LHER of 5.2.

The Roman material on these two terraces includes a full range of functions, including the only piece categorized as 'personal object' from Litharkies, a fragment of a Late Hellenistic–Early Roman unguentarium (TCP463). It was also in this area that the only sherd of Mid Roman date was found, a fragment of ARS50 Table Ware dated from the second quarter of the 3rd to the 5th century AD (Hayes 1972, 69–73, fig. 12). Notably, there are only two other fragments of ARS50 found in the whole of the Upper Lagoudhera Valley, and they were collected on the edge of

Table 4.8. Xyliatos Litharkies *(TS05): chipped stone category counts and percentages*

	Count	*%*
Blanks	11	32%
Cores	10	29%
Debris	8	24%
Tools	5	15%
Total	**34**	**100%**

the smelting settlement at Ayia Marina *Mavrovouni*. Only one other piece of Mid Roman Table Ware was collected in the Upper Lagoudhera Valley, a fragment of Phocaean Red Slip Ware (LRCA1kn5; TCP166) (Meyza 2000), found just south of the slag heap at Mavrovouni. The scarcity of Mid Roman ceramics is a general problem of Cypriot archaeology, but some of the long-lived utility wares may be hiding among the Late Roman chronotypes (see Volume 1, Chapter 5.3).

Chipped and Ground Stone

With 34 pieces, the total number of chipped stone artefacts collected from Litharkies is relatively high in comparison to samples collected from the Roman farmsteads of Linou *Vrysi tou Haji Christophi* (Chapter 2.5) and Petra *Phoukasa* (2.6), and the outskirts of an agricultural settlement at Phlasou *Dodekaskala* (3.6). The sample is more consistent with samples collected at the mining settlements of Skouriotissa *Pseftas* (Chapter 3.13) and Ayia Marina *Mavrovouni* (4.6).

The chipped stone sample from Litharkies is similar to these other Roman assemblages in that it is dominated by the use of jasper and chalcedony. The predominance of chalcedony artefacts (29 pieces; 85%), as well as a sample of 11 pieces of unworked chalcedony chunks, suggests that this material may be available in close proximity to the site. The distribution of artefacts across the major lithic categories belonging to Litharkies suggests that local jasper, and especially chalcedony, were knapped in the settlement for the production of simple, sharp, cutting edges. The industry is flake-based with blanks struck from simple flake cores, many of which were only tested, or very lightly utilized, prior to discard.

The tools are relatively infrequent and exhibit a low diversity, consisting of two simple utilized flakes, one of which is made on non-local chert, a marginally retouched flake, and one denticulated piece. These features are consistent with the samples collected from sites dating to the Late Roman period elsewhere in the TAESP Survey Area. A single *dhoukani* flake, made of non-local translucent chert, from SU2604 appears to be an exception to the dominant Late Roman character of Litharkies, and clearly corresponds to a peak in Medieval–Modern pottery in the same area.

In spite of the relatively large collective sample from Litharkies, the distribution of artefacts across individual Survey Units is generally low, between one and four artefacts (Plate 4.5). The densest concentration of artefacts lies in the eastern and south-eastern part of the settlement, particularly in SU2601 (the largest circle in Plate 4.5). This Survey Unit lies just to the south-east of the main arc of settlement evidence fanning out from TP210, in an area that provided comparatively few ceramic finds (Plate 4.4). The material from SU2601 consisted of four tested cores, four flakes, and five pieces of debris (of which three were produced on local chalcedony), as well as 11 pieces of unworked chalcedony. This distribution suggests that this area may have been a specific locality dedicated to knapping, on the south-western outskirts of the main settlement area.

Only six ground stone artefacts were collected from Litharkies, with an additional five examples photographed in situ. The sample certainly under-represents the total number of ground stone artefacts at Litharkies, but provides a number of interesting details that are instrumental to the interpretation of the site.

To the north and east of the rock piles of TP210, on or adjacent to the terraces where the geophysical survey was carried out, were a pounder/anvil (SU2632), a grinder fragment (SU2642), and a quern (SU2605), plus a crudely shaped mortar that we did not collect (SU2605). In the southern part of the rock piles were a pounder\hammerstone\grinder (SU2635) and a hammerstone\grinder (near SU2634; not collected). In functional terms, these types of ground stone tools (particularly pounders, hammerstones, grinders, anvils and mortars) could have been used either for food preparation or for ore dressing (e.g. Connolly 1992, 71–72; Kassianidou 2007). It is notable that ground stone samples from mining contexts elsewhere in the Survey Area, such as Ayia Marina *Mavrovouni* (Chapter 4.6), Katydhata *Psevtadhes* (TP109; Chapter 3.13), and Skouriotissa *Vouppes* (Chapter 3.12), provided collections with tool types similar to the Litharkies samples. In contrast, the Roman small-scale domestic sites of Linou *Vrysi tou Haji Christophi* (Chapter 2.5), Petra *Phoukasa* (Chapter 2.6) and Phlasou *Dodekaskala* (Chapter 3.6) produced far fewer ground stone artefacts overall, and these were dominated by 'domestic' types, such as rubbers, rather than the types noted above that have been highlighted in discussions of ore dressing tools.

Beyond such hand tools, a fragment of a millstone (perhaps broken during manufacture) was recorded in the same area (SU2633). This piece, along with the broken remnant of a large, roughly hewn deep basin (TP210. PU14) suggests the presence of a press, most likely for olives, located in the general vicinity of the tiled structures (Hadjisavvas 1992).

Two additional querns found in the rock piles (TP210. PU19, PU39) were for grinding grain, emphasising the importance of grain in the diet of a mining settlement in late antiquity (Given and Knapp 2003, 315–16). That this requirement was not simply met using local technology is shown by one of the querns, a fragment of a large grinding stone made of vesicular basalt belonging to a type imported in the Late Roman period (TCL504) (see Volume 1, Chapter 3.8). This corner fragment of a large square block shows diagnostic parallel grooves and intensive wear on its upper surface. It would have been one of a pair of grinding blocks, most likely the lower, and resembles the complete examples recovered from the Kyrenia shipwreck (Katzev 1969, 1970).

The Litharkies Landscape

The Survey Units carried out to the north-east of the main concentration at Litharkies have dramatically lower densities of Hellenistic–Roman pottery, suggesting that the stream bed marks the eastern limit of the settlement (Plate 4.6). The Litharkies ridge is clearly the western limit of the settlement area. A transect running about 80 m west of the ridge (TT501750E) revealed an area dominated by very steep slopes ranging from 18–23°, which explains the very shallow soil depth, as soil is eroded as soon as it forms. Over 80% of the area we traversed in this transect is under pine forest and has been severely dissected by erosion forming a series of gullies.

Two of these gullies contain a series of 15 check dams (TP234; see Table 4.2), which are west-facing and appear to be a recent attempt to stem the erosion that was evidently cutting deep gullies into the landscape. Most of the land behind the dams was not being used for cultivation. The gully has a path along it and across the flat treads behind the check dams. The south-facing slope of the gully is steep and incised by a number of smaller gullies. Despite its steepness there were narrow paths c. 20 cm wide, which, given the cartridge cases found in the area, were most likely formed by hunters.

The southern half of transect TT502000E, up to 300 m south of Litharkies, recorded only a small number of sherds, which may in part be due to the mechanized manipulation of the area. They include an Early Roman lamp, type 1 (Vessberg Form 10–12) dated AD 40–150, and a fragment of Hellenistic–Roman Cooking Ware, from two adjacent Survey Units. Light Utility ware fragments dated to Historical Antiquity were also found. Although the density of pottery is very low, it does point towards some contemporary activity in the landscape to the south of the settlement. The composition of the assemblage may suggest the possibility of tombs in this area, but the artefact variability may be the product of post-depositional processes. Consequently, it might also represent agricultural practices in the area, as represented much more clearly round the Roman farmsteads of the Atsas Valley (Chapter 2.5). A local informant recalls his father digging a well next to a spring and finding an older well with steps going down to a depth of 20 feet (Plate 4.6).

The area just north of Litharkies has two series of check dams, TP145 and TP147, both in gullies facing south-east (Table 4.2). The two Survey Units between the two series have Table Ware, Cooking Ware and Light Utility ware from the Early Roman, Hellenistic–Roman (HR), Historical

Table 4.9. Xyliatos Litharkies *(TP146): summary of pottery. TCP numbers refer to Pottery Catalogue in Volume 1, Chapter 3.6*

Hellenistic to Roman			
Fct	*Type*	*No.*	*Weight*
CW	CW	10	130 g
Early Roman			
Fct	*Type*	*No.*	*Weight*
CW	CWPR04c	16	140 g TCP659
LU	Jug	10	330 g TCP660

Antiquity and Roman periods, a composition that again may suggest the possibility of tombs in this area.

The possibility of a cemetery is further supported by a dense pottery scatter, most probably deriving from an Early Roman tomb, above TP147 (TP146; Table 4.9; location marked on Plate 4.6). The scatter extends c. 2 m across and 4 m downslope, and lies on the top and south-facing slope of a low ridge c. 2 m high. A metre above the scatter, on the top of the ridge, there is a depression c. 3 m square and 0.5 m deep. This has recently been planted with a young olive; it was clearly the digging for this that produced the small concentration of sherds. These include fragments of an Early Roman jug and Early Roman cooking pot, and fragments of Hellenistic–Roman (HR) Cooking Ware. The jug and cooking pots are typical grave goods of the Early Roman period.

If these sherds do represent a burial, it commands a prominent view of the valley south of Alestos, and at 513 m overlooks the settlement at Litharkies. The choice of such a vantage point is consistent with Hellenistic tombs found in the Karkotis Valley that were re-used in the Early Roman period (Volume 1, Chapter 5.3). Indeed, other sites suggest that a 'tomb with a view' is a common characteristic of chamber tombs (Parks 2004). The artefacts from the surrounding Survey Units may also reflect the journeys between the settlement and the mines. These various sherds are all traces of the experience of the landscape: on their way to and from work, the miners would have walked by their relatives, colleagues, friends, enemies or lovers, buried on the hillside.

The lower parts of the south-east-facing side of the Alestos hillside, 250 m east of Litharkies, are characterized by almond terraces, which give way to a gully and further upwards to an area forested mainly with pine (Transect TT502250E; location marked on Plate 4.6). The upper parts of the slope are represented by severely eroded bedrock, facilitating movement of materials downslope. On the three treads immediately above the stream bed, on the toeslope of Alestos, we recorded very low densities of Medieval–Modern, Ottoman–Modern II and Modern pottery. There was also a piece of Historical Antiquity Light Utility ware, and a body fragment of a Late Chalcolithic/Philia Light Utility Red Monochrome or Red Polished Ware, the

Fig. 4.16. Xyliatos Ayios Kyriakos *(TP086): section of path between two terrace walls (Chris Parks)*

earliest sherd in the Alestos area. These three treads have had both colluvial and alluvial processes affecting artefact distribution, as well as some anthropogenic impact from terrace construction, and so it is difficult to interpret the context of the material.

A similar pattern is found a further 250 m east of Litharkies (Transect TT502500E). The south-facing slopes of Alestos are greatly incised, forming a series of gullies. In some areas significant portions of the upper parts of the transect are bare rock that has been exploited for mining. These are source areas in the erosion process, and feed into deep gullies that in some cases have check dams. The lower section has an ephemeral stream that could move material further down. The stream bed below the north-east/south-west ridge has been filled in by a bulldozing operation that produced a riser 6 m high. Only a single sherd, dating to Historical Antiquity, was found in the whole of the transect. This is hardly surprising, given that the slope ranged from 18–25°. A series of eight 'pocket' check dams (TP213) (see Table 4.2, and Plate 4.6 for location), each supporting either an olive or almond tree, is testament to the efforts to conserve the sediments and soil on the hillside, but the check dams themselves had started to collapse through lack of repair.

Much of the area 750 m east of Litharkies had been bulldozed by summer 2003 (Transect TT502750E). It is composed of a series of three hills, the southernmost of which forms a cliff that leads into the Argaki tis Yerokaminas drainage. Its parent material, unlike the basalt slopes of Alestos, is predominantly Pleistocene fluvial gravels; easily excavated into terraces with high risers by bulldozing. One of the bulldozed cuts is 10–11 m high and almost vertical. The five sherds we found in this area were clearly affected by a combination of the colluvial and fluvial processes, and the more recent mechanized terracing.

Communication and Surveillance

About 750 m east of Litharkies the stream which borders the settlement is restricted to its narrowest point by almost vertical basalt outcrops on both sides (Plate 4.7). In this area the stream switches back in a tight meander bend and then turns northwards again, to join the Lagoudhera valley at Ayios Kyriakos (TS10). Ayios Kyriakos is in fact defined by the spur that has been cut at the confluence of the Lagoudhera and this stream, which has its origins south of Litharkies.

There are two paths in the area of this meander. TP222 is a narrow path c. 35 cm wide, and may well have been formed by hunters in the area, as it leads to an outcrop of bedrock that stands vertically above the stream bed and is covered in a number of cartridges. TP223 is a far more well-defined path. One section is built on the bedrock with a dry-stack retaining wall 3 m above the stream bed. This has produced a levelled section, 0.7–1.1 m wide and 7.2 m long, and would easily be wide enough for a loaded donkey. To the south-west the path continues close to the stream bed through the gully for about 30 m, at which point it was too overgrown to follow any further. From the north end of the built stretch, the path winds its way up the steep slope over the bedrock. A further section of dry-stack walling, c. 1.1 m long and 0.3 m high, is used to bridge a gap between two bedrock outcrops. The path continues to the end of the ridge, which has been cut by the stream. It then trends downslope again towards the stream bed, where it is abruptly cut through by recent bulldozing and lost.

Fig. 4.17. View from outcrop at TP174 to the west-south-west, towards outcrop TP170 and Litharkies (Chris Parks)

This section of path is over 100 m in length and provides an excellent example of movement through the landscape by means of a built communication infrastructure. There is no doubt that this path continues into the Lagoudhera valley at the point of the confluence and most likely links in with the path which runs between Ayios Kyriakos and Mavrovouni (TP086), or alternatively the section of path found slightly higher up the east-facing Lagoudhera Valley hillslope (TP099). Both of these have dry-stack retaining features providing level and stable surfaces.

Entering the Lagoudhera Valley the whole floodplain on the west side of the river is currently flat and easy to traverse. The existence of two paths (TP086 and TP087), however, suggests that people have not always used the floodplain area to move through the landscape, and that the river may have been wider. Path TP086 is about 4 m above this floodplain, allowing passage at all times of the year. The path has been cut into the riser and is about 1.5 m wide (Fig. 4.16). Most of the path is defined by dry-stack retaining walls, made from river stones with chinking. It is clearly marked on the cadastral map and fords the river to the west of the ruined church (Plate 4.7). Farmers said that it had been used by people with donkeys as recently as 10 years ago, though this may be a euphemism for the recent past.

Path TP086 splits in two, one part continuing on the same elevation until it drops down next to the adits at Ayios Kyriakos. The other part of the path (TP087) heads south-east, down an outcrop of columnar basalt. The path had been cut into this outcrop above the alluvial floodplain, and angular basalt boulders have been used to augment it and produce an even slope down to the river. Two of the pieces of columnar basalt outcrop are missing below the path and have been filled by blocks. There are blocks similar to these in the terrace wall just to the east of the path. The column missing at the north end of TP087 is also filled with angular basalt blocks, but they were heavily covered in lichens, indicating that this area had been repaired long ago, whereas the missing column to the south had no lichen and had clearly been repaired more recently. The path leads to an adit near the river (TP088). After fording the Lagoudhera river, the path (TP086 on the west side of the valley, now TP024) continues northwards, bisecting the smelting area of Ayia Marina *Mavrovouni* (TS02), running directly to the west of the slag heap (see Chapter 4.6).

While the date of these paths is far from certain, they do cross the Roman mining landscape and reveal that with some human input, in the form of dry-stack retaining walls, it becomes very easy to traverse through parts of the landscape that at first seem challenging.

High up on Alestos are two large basalt outcrops. At one of these, TP170 at 580 m asl, there was no evidence of material culture apart from a few cartridges, but the view from its summit is highly significant. Litharkies can clearly be seen to the south-west, as can the whole of the valley bottom on the south side of Alestos where the stream runs down to join the Lagoudhera Valley, just south of Ayios Kyriakos. This confluence itself is not visible, as the valley bottom turns northwards round Alestos and out of view. The Lagoudhera Valley can, however, be seen through a saddle in the ridge that separates Alestos from the Argaki tis Yerokaminas drainage. This outcrop has a commanding view and would have been able to provide any controllers of the mining operation a clear view of the workforce moving between Litharkies and Mavrovouni.

The other outcrop (TP174; 559 m asl) is further to the east around the steep slope of Alestos, and has a wide view from Memi and Ayios Kyriakos in the east to Litharkies in the west (Fig. 4.17). It is also intervisible with outcrop TP170. Again, no artefacts were recorded in the area. Sentries on these outcrops could effectively observe the mining community and any movements between the settlement and the smelting site. The 'Rock of Ayios Kyriakos' at Mavrovouni is another example of a rock outcrop ideally placed to provide visual control over an industrial workforce (TP017; see Chapter 4.6).

Litharkies: Conclusion

The peak of activity at Litharkies is firmly placed in the Roman period, and is almost certainly associated with mining Alestos for chalcopyrite, which was then processed to produce copper. Analysis of the pottery evidence suggests greater activity in the Early Roman period. This is in contrast to the assemblage at Ayia Marina *Mavrovouni*, which has more Late Roman material. This may represent a change in the organisation of mining and smelting in the area. It is possible that most of the workforce was located at Litharkies in the Early Roman period and that this arrangement of labour settlement was reversed in the Late Roman period.

As well as the remains of an actual tomb (TP146), a series of lamp and unguentarium fragments are evidence for the existence of a cemetery; these are very common in Late Hellenistic–Early Roman tombs, but proportionally quite rare in domestic contexts. The tile fragments and ground stone, by contrast, as well as the rock piles and resistivity results, all suggest settlement activity. The absence of Early Roman Heavy Utility wares, which would be expected in such a settlement, may be caused by the general difficulty of dating this type of pottery. Since Early Roman tombs are often re-used Hellenistic tombs, the Hellenistic pottery identified may also be part of tomb assemblages, suggesting that the exploitation of Alestos for copper may have started during this period.

Xyliatos *Litharkies* appears to have carried out at least some of the initial ore processing. Some of the ground stone may have been used for that purpose, but equally could have been used for domestic purposes. There is no evidence of the waste material from the crushing of ore and bedrock material. This may have occurred at the adits themselves, as the size of the spoil fragments would suggest. Paths marked on the cadastral map and those recorded in the Upper Lagoudhera Valley reveal that moving between the mining settlement and smelting site would not have been particularly difficult, and the built-up sections of path reveal how easily a robust communication network can be formed. A number of areas on the side of Alestos provide commanding views of the area of mining, as well as the communication route between Litharkies and the Lagoudhera Valley, and could have been employed to observe and control the workforce. For the miners working in the area of adits on the southern flank (e.g. TP112), the day began and ended with a walk past the tomb of a fellow member of the Litharkies community, perhaps a stark reminder of the dangers of working in such an environment.

It is not at all clear from the artefacts at Litharkies what the composition of the community was. We do not have any gender-specific material, or anything that would allude to the presence of children within the community, nor of social stratification. What we do have is evidence for the mundaneness of life at Litharkies: people cooking and eating, storing food, building the infrastructure for water storage, resting and sleeping in roofed houses, and finally dying and being buried by friends, family or workmates. What may be tools for grinding and pounding the rocks that they dug from the ground are found in amongst the settlement. The ceramic evidence to the north and south of Litharkies might suggest that they chopped or coppiced their fuel, and picked and harvested their food from the fertile land around them. Furthermore, the lack of imported amphorae supports this notion of local sustainability.

4.5 Ancient Mining Adits at Xyliatos *Ayios Kyriakos* (TS10)

Modern geological reports and exploitation have shown that the ore body of Memi (Fig. 4.18), the closest to the slag heap of Mavrovouni, consisted mainly of pyrites, an iron sulphide mineral. This is not an ore for copper or iron, but was mined in modern times for the production of sulphur (Carr 1960, 46). A mining lease was granted to the Hellenic Mining Company, which originally extracted the ore by an underground operation, in June 1954 (Pantazis 1969, 37). In the four years of operation before work ended, due to a fall in demand for pyrites, just over 10,000 tons of ore were mined and treated. This produced 4800 tons of pyrites, all of which was exported by shipping from Morphou Bay (Bear 1963, 72, table 24, pl. 1). In 1965 the operations were resumed and the ore body was exploited by the opencast method: according to a report by the Mines Service, a total of 2,028,898 tons of pyrite ore had been extracted by 1971. After another break in operations, mining resumed between 1987 and 1990, producing a further 95,901 tons of ore (Mines 2010).

We examined the original geological field maps at the Geological Survey Department, and found that the Memi area was noted for its two slag heaps and a broad open landscape of 'speckled' black and grey basalt, an oxidized caprock overlying the sulphide ore body. Although the main ore body of Memi mine is classified as non-cupreous disseminated pyrite (Pantazis 1969, 42), the pyrite was found to be associated with chalcopyrite at its southern periphery. Furthermore, small amounts of secondary minerals such as covellite, azurite and chalcanthite were also identified (Pantazis 1969, 43). According to Pantazis (1969, 37), 'around the ore-body, particularly on the eastern and western sides, there is a number of old galleries of which some are timbered; but these are small and appear to end at

Fig. 4.18. Memi mine looking south-south-east, with Xyliatos Ayios Kyriakos *(TS10) towards the right, in the valley behind the middle terrace of the mine, and Ayia Marina* Mavrovouni *(TS02) on the extreme right-hand edge (Chris Parks)*

the periphery of the main ore-body'. On the 1952 geological map, six pits, or adits, of pre-existing mining are noted. One of the pits, 10 feet in diameter, was located about 20 m east of SU0624; the geologists noted it was barren and excavated into Lower Pillow Lava formation basalt (Plate 4.8). No dimensions were recorded for the other five.

Clearly these adits, some of which survived the modern operations and were found and recorded by TAESP, were exploiting these small pockets of copper ores that were associated with the iron pyrites. The remnant of an adit (TP046) found on the north-facing side of Memi was not recorded on the archive map. Bedrock visible in the dirt road running around the north side of the hill suggests that the hillslope had been cut back during the 20th-century mining operations, and that the adit could have been several metres long. As noted above it is extremely difficult to date this structure. The possibility that it is modern cannot be ruled out, especially since the specific adit was not noted on the map: it may have been created in the first phase of the 20th century exploitation, when the ore was extracted by an underground operation.

To the north of Memi and 200 m east of the slag heap is a further area with geological indications of copper ore, as well as silica and iron oxide. This area (SU0658) had five fragments of Hellenistic–Roman Cooking Ware and two fragments of Late Hellenistic–Early Roman Table Ware, one Cypriot Sigillata and one Eastern Sigillata B. These suggest that there may have been some prospection and/or exploitation of the area contemporary with activities round the slag heap. A further 650 m to the north-east is an adit in an area of prominent copper staining, with a width of 1.5 m, height of 0.5 m and depth of 1.0 m (TP075).

Fig. 4.19. Xyliatos Ayios Kyriakos *(TS10): mining adits. From left to right: TP052, TP054, TP053 (Chris Parks)*

At Ayios Kyriakos, on the west flank of Memi mine, there is a group of six ancient adits (TP050–52, TP054–55, TP088), two prospection cuts (TP057–58) and two shafts (TP053, TP056) cut in the contact between the pillow lavas and the Pleistocene fluvial gravels (Table 4.10). These are situated on both sides of a steeply incised section of the river channel, 800 m south of the Mavrovouni slag heap (TP006). The area is characterized by pillow lavas covered by the Lagoudhera river gravels. The area along the bottom of the gorge is well watered and lush with bamboo, oleander, cistus and hawthorn.

All the adits were cut in the contact zone between the gravels and the pillow lavas, at a location where there were probably mineral veins (Fig. 4.19). The largest of the adits,

Table 4.10. Xyliatos Ayios Kyriakos *(TS10): mining adits. D = Depth H = Height W = Width*

	Type	*Condition*	*Dimensions (m)*	*Notable features*
TP050	Adit	Entrance altered by collapse. Filled with rubble, so original shape is not preserved		Terrace wall to SW creates a platform in front.
TP051	Adit	Filled with rubble, so exact shape is unclear	W: 1.7 H: 0.4 D: 1.0+	Terrace wall to SW creates a platform in front.
TP052	Adit	Wide entrance probably caused by collapse	Entrance H: 1.2–2.25 W: 2.1 D: 1.5	Bedrock platform in front defined by terrace wall to SW: could be original working surface.
TP053	Almost vertical shaft	Partly filled in. Floor surface obscured by pine needles	W: 1.7–2.4 H: 4.8–5.0	Small terrace wall, clearly a later construction, lines W end of shaft. Small hole at bottom.
TP054	Adit	Very well preserved. Trapezoidal with wider floor and rounded roof	W: 1.24 H: 1.7 D: 1.5	Ceiling has evidence of burning; uncertain whether from fire setting or later use.
TP055	Adit?	Filled with very fine sediment	Unclear	Small and not well shaped. May simply be a fallen pillow lava. Disused cement irrigation channel in front.
TP056	Shaft	Floor obscured by vegetation	D: 3-4–5.0 W at bottom: 1.1 W at top: 0.8	Parallel walls perpendicular to face on E side of the river, c. 7 m above the irrigation channel.
TP057	Prospection cut		W: 0.4 H: 0.05 D: 0.20–0.30	Vertical cut into the adjacent pillow lavas above and below at N side. Pillow lava material continues beyond this cut; therefore anthropogenic.
TP058	Prospection cut	Salt efflorescence on back wall	W: 0.3 H: 0.1–0.15 D: 0.3	Similar to TP057. Some spoil material in front of cut. Vertical cut on both sides. Cut goes through pillows and into pillow material.
TP088	Adit		D: 1.85–2.20 W across bottom: 2.0 H: 1.4	Green vein (copper sulphates?) that has been 'chased' into the rock.

TP050, is completely blocked with boulders fallen from the gravel deposits. The adit extends to a depth of at least 5 m. The roof has intense red and yellow ochre colours, as well as evidence of fire, something we observed in other adits. This pattern could be interpreted as showing evidence of fire setting, which was well known in antiquity and is described by Pliny the Elder (XXXIII, 21) and Agricola (1950, 118–20). Alternatively, the fire might have been lit by someone using the adit as a shelter.

The adits are trapezoidal in cross-section, the best-preserved example being TP054 (Fig. 4.20). As well as the adits we also recorded two perpendicular shafts with parallel sides, one on the west side of the gully (TP053) and one on the east (TP056). They are not cylindrical, nor perfectly vertical, giving the impression that they are following a vein rather than being used to access a lower level.

According to Bruce *et al.* (1937, 648–50), who recorded the remains of ancient galleries uncovered by the 20th-century operations at Skouriotissa and Mavrovouni, the nature and hardness of the host rock dictated to a great degree the size and shape of the gallery and whether or not timber was needed for extra support. In the case of hard rock, the underground galleries were small with a maximum width of 76 cm and a maximum height of 124 cm, while in softer rock and stronger ground they could be as big as 180 cm in width and height. The miners removed as much ore as possible leaving intervening pillars to support the weight of the overlying rock. When too much ore had been removed and the area was no longer safe it was abandoned and allowed to cave in. If the pillars were rich in minerals, then they would backfill the spaces and remove any remaining ore in the pillars.

The ancient galleries had a narrow base and would widen out in the middle, presumably in order to allow the miners to walk through loaded with baskets full of extracted ore (for section drawings see Bruce *et al.* 1937, 670, fig. 385). The adits recorded by TAESP have a wide base and thus are different from the ancient galleries described by Bruce. This difference may be due to the different functions of an adit and a gallery: the former is a horizontal or gently sloping passage driven from the surface to an ore body, while the latter is created underground and is accessed either through an adit, or through a shaft – a vertical or near-vertical passage linking the surface with an ore

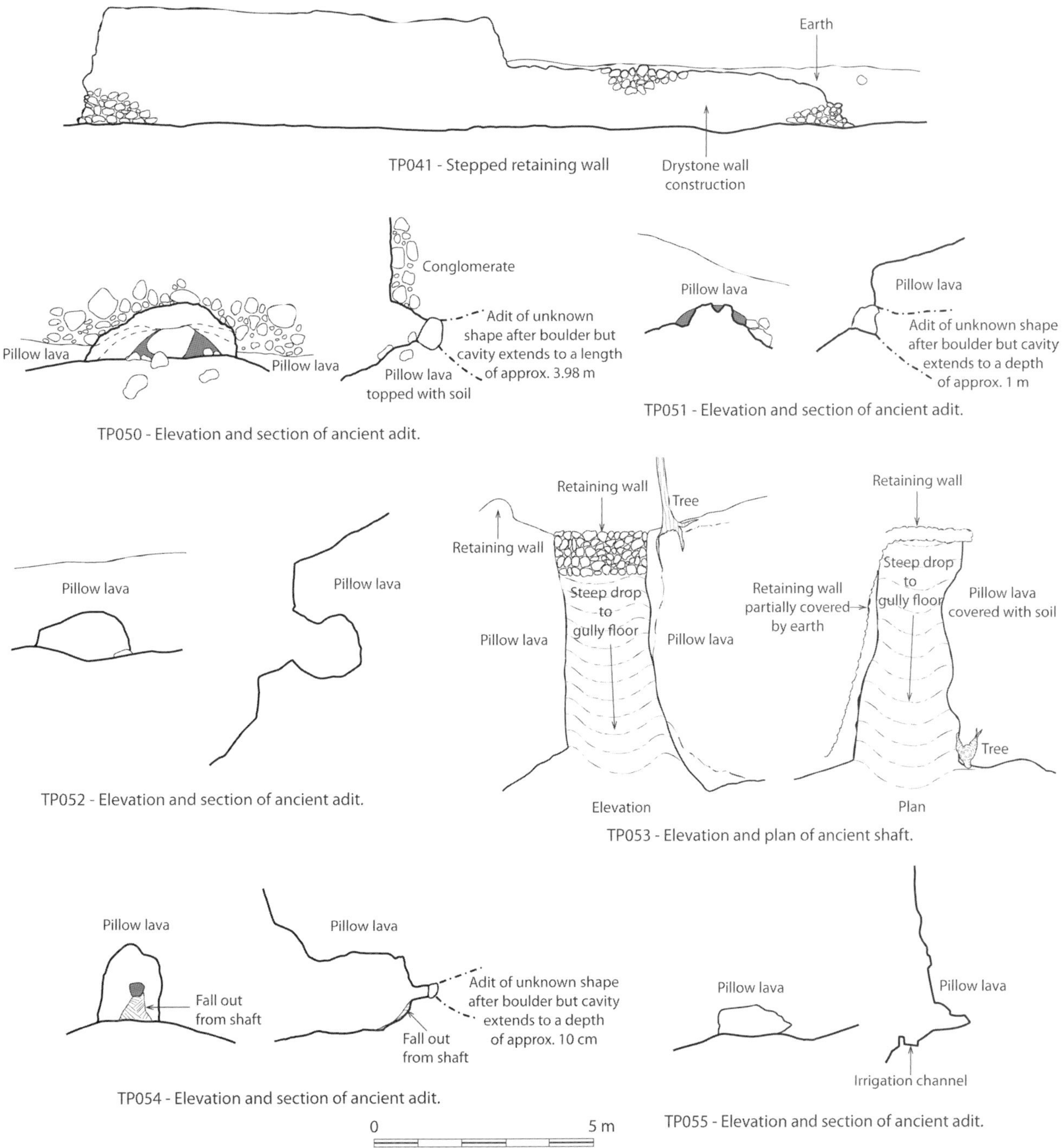

Fig. 4.20. Xyliatos Ayios Kyriakos *(TS10): plans and elevations of mining adits (Sophie Pullar, finalised by Jean Humbert)*

body (Kassianidou 2003a, 44). As the adit is basically the entrance to the mine, it needs to have a wider opening in order to allow miners to come in and out with ease.

Taking into consideration the size and shape of the adits and shafts, as well as the fact that they were noted by geologists before the beginning of modern operations, we believe them to be ancient, even though there was, unfortunately, no pottery to aid our dating. Their location at the periphery of the main pyritic ore body, where according to the geological reports small pockets of copper ores existed, also supports this idea. These adits cannot possibly have been modern, as they are too small and limited in depth. In fact, their size leads us to believe that they may be even earlier than the Roman slag heap (TP006).

While the modern mine of Memi produced predominately pyrite ore, small deposits of chalcopyrite and other copper minerals such as covellite certainly existed, but they were limited. According to Pantazis (1969), the amount of copper minerals present in the Memi deposit does not correspond to the size of the slag heap at Mavrovouni (Chapter 4.6), and the principal source of ore in the area must have been Alestos. It is possible that the adits at Ayios Kyriakos are prehistoric in date and were used to extract limited amounts of chalcopyrite. That said, no evidence of an earlier smelting site has been found in the area (though the possibility that such a workshop once existed and was subsequently destroyed by the opencast mine is not unlikely) and the evidence of prehistoric artefacts in the vicinity is limited (see below). It seems more likely that the adits are Roman in date as the chipped stone suggests significant Roman activity in the area. If this is the case, when the Roman miners exhausted the limited copper mineralization and realized that the main ore body was not appropriate for copper production, they abandoned their efforts.

We surveyed a series of units along the terrace on the western side of the incised river channel. The pottery was undistinguished, with the same low, even scatter of Hellenistic–Roman and Medieval–Modern sherds that this whole stretch shows from Mavrovouni southwards. There were no signs of increasing density adjacent to the adits, nor any peaks associated with specific periods such as Late Roman. The chipped and ground stone, however, showed a clear peak in the Survey Units closest to the adits, with a total of 93 chipped stone artefacts and six ground stone tools.

The six ground stone tools found in the area are dominated by grinding tools: two light duty polishing stones (SU1652, SU1654); a grinder (SU1664); and a rubbing stone (SU1666). There were also two pounding tools: a pounder/rubbing stone (SU1653); and a hammerstone (SU1657). These artefacts belong to types that could have been used for both domestic purposes as well as ore processing (Kassianidou 2007). Given their context near the adits at Ayios Kyriakos and the lack of evidence for any kind of settlement in the vicinity, their use in ore processing seems more likely.

The large sample of chipped stone collected from the block survey carried out in the area of the Ayios Kyriakos adits (TS10) may provide more information about dating than the small group of ground stone tools noted above. The assemblage is dominated by core reduction materials, with cores (13 pieces; 14%), blanks (10 pieces; 11%) and especially debris (50 pieces; 54%), accounting for over 78% of the total sample. All of this material was produced on local jasper and chalcedony. Only one core, a splintered piece, was made of Lefkara basal chert. This suggests the localized manufacture of flake tools from materials occurring in the pillow lavas of the immediate area. Given the clear raw material preference, the simple core technology employed, and the background scatter of sherds belonging to the Late Roman period, this sample fits well with others assigned to a Roman date and discussed elsewhere.

The percentage of tools belonging to the Ayios Kyriakos sample (22%) similarly fits within the moderate range established by other samples belonging to Roman settlements near copper mines, such as Skouriotissa *Pseftas* (Chapter 3.13), Phlasou *Dodekaskala* (3.6) or Mavrovouni (4.6). Of particular interest is the prevalence of expedient utilized flake implements, which clearly dominate the tools sample (60%). The dominance of this tool type along with flake tools (25%) and the relative paucity of *dhoukani* flakes (15%) is a feature of TAESP samples dated to the Late Roman period. In addition, two of the *dhoukani* flakes recovered were made of local jasper, a common feature of other assemblages assigned to the Late Roman period.

Within the set of tools from Ayios Kyriakos, however, are examples showing abrasion wear rather than the type of angular edge damages noted for utilized flakes elsewhere. These abrasion tools, when considered together with the presence of a perforator, a *pièce esquillée*, two side scrapers and a multiple tool (scraper/denticulate), provide a diversity of tool type that is perhaps more similar to prehistoric samples like that of Phlasou *Koutroullis* (Chapter 3.5). In spite of the probability that these samples are displaced from original locations to the surveyed terraces west of the Ayios Kyriakos adits, the absence of prehistoric ceramics argues against a prehistoric attribution. A single *dhoukani* flake made on non-local Lefkara chert may correlate best with the presence of Medieval–Modern ceramics and relate to agricultural practices associated with these periods.

There is further evidence of exploration c. 100 m downstream of this cluster of adits. This consists of a single adit (TP088) at the base of a sill on the west side of the river, which can be reached down a path (TP087). The adit cuts through the surrounding basalt rock to the bottom of the basalt outcrop, where a triangular hole had been cut out above the watermark visible on the outcrop. The watermark is c. 50 cm above the current channel: as long as the river deposition did not rise any higher than this, the adit would be preserved without filling in with sediment. It would be difficult for the river to remove sediments from such a feature once filled. So this adit must be relatively young, perhaps only since the end of the Little Ice Age, which would have produced much higher water levels and likely sediment deposition in the area. Since we have no evidence for copper mining in this period, the use of this adit must be otherwise explained.

The Ayios Kyriakos Landscape

Survey south of Ayios Kyriakos had the aim of placing the remnants of ancient mining activities into context, including the investigation of possible communication into the hills of the Troodos Range and the fuel used for smelting. The river valley has been heavily disturbed in recent years through bulldozing and dry-stack terracing of hillslope colluvium and fluvial terrace gravels. Bench terracing has disrupted hillslope sediments by cutting deeply to bedrock and mobilizing topsoil to new deposits. The soils present on the treads of the terraces are predominantly of local origin. Modern machinery makes it possible to import significant quantities of materials, e.g. one field was covered with imported crushed basalt bedrock and for this reason was not surveyed (GU1659–61).

As well as the adits at Ayios Kyriakos, we discovered two mining adits south of Ayios Kyriakos and to the east of the river (Plate 4.13; TP103, TP106). They lie in an incised valley south of Memi mine, where active fluvial processes are still occurring on the valley floor. Bulldozed terraces dominate both sides of this valley. The soft basalt into which they cut disintegrates into silt and sand, and so the bulldozing has created a thick new cover of uniformly coloured soil across the entire area. Bulldozing carried out in 1988 has produced risers up to 4 m in height. The basalt bedrock of the area is exposed in many dykes, which are rich in copper ore.

The adit at TP103 was cut by bulldozing in two places, revealing a gallery some 5 m long which bends evenly round 90° in the course of its length. At the east-facing exposed cut it is 0.90 m wide and 1.05 m high, and at the south-facing cut it is 0.48 m high and 0.69 m wide. We recorded ground stone and other hand-sized river cobbles inside it. TP106 has suffered substantial collapse, but it shows an opening in an almost-vertical outcrop of basalt, 0.80 m high and 0.85 m wide. It penetrates c. 1 m into the rock before it is obscured by rubble.

On the east bank of the Lagoudhera River, c. 650 m south of Ayios Kyriakos and in the immediate area of SU1689, is an area of dry-stack terracing with three substantial olive trees (Fig. 4.21). Their circumferences and estimated ages are: c. 7.09 m, late 16th century; c. 6.91 m, late 16th century; and c. 12.37 m, late 15th century (for methodology see Volume 1, Chapter 2.11). These dates fit well with the historical evidence for Xyliatos village, just 530 m to the south-east (Volume 2, Chapter 4.9). As many of these trees are on the 5 m floodplain of the current channel, they may clarify our understanding of the effects of the Little Ice Age and its wetter climate on the Lagoudhera landscape. Little Ice Age (Ottoman Period) floods could have been strong enough to affect the valley bottom up to the level of these trees, which obviously have survived such floods.

Fig. 4.21. Olive tree with circumference of c. 12.37 m, dating to the late 15th century, c. 650 m south of Xyliatos Ayios Kyriakos *(Michael Given)*

In the Gialias River, four watersheds to the east of the Lagoudhera, Devillers and Lécuyer (2008) demonstrated that Troodos rivers experienced infrequent flash floods (compared with today's regime) after the Byzantine Period and certainly following Venetian rule. They noted that the Gialias has deposited several metres of sediment in floods with temperate flows. That is, river flow (discharge) was over many months, rather than unreliable and of short duration as it is today. In any case, the deposition and erosion of sediments by the Lagoudhera River during the Little Ice Age occurred below the elevation of these three olive trees.

This area to the south of the adits at Ayios Kyriakos reveals a density of Hellenistic–Roman pottery of c. 0.5 sherds/100 m^2, which is in the same order of density as the block survey downstream north of the estate at Athassi (c. 0.6 sherds/100 m^2). It includes two fragments of Late Hellenistic–Early Roman Eastern Sigillata A Table Ware and two fragments of Skouriotissa cover tile, type 4. There is also evidence of human activity from the Medieval–Modern period (c. 2.6 sherds/100 m^2), but with only one fragment datable to the Medieval period (1191–1571 AD), and another datable to the 14th–15th centuries AD in the same Survey Unit on the west side of the river. These may have been from general cultivation or movement across the area during these periods, which is unsurprising given the estate at Athassi (Chapter 4.7) and established villages at Xyliatos and elsewhere.

4.6 Roman Smelting and Settlement at Ayia Marina *Mavrovouni* (TS02)

The material remains at Ayia Marina *Mavrovouni* (TS02) include a slag heap (TP006), a wide scatter of pottery and tile fragments, and a complex system of fields and field walls. The locality name 'Mavrovouni', meaning 'Black Hill', is a clear reference to the slag heap (Given *et al.* 2001, 433; 2002, 28). The locality lies immediately below the towering spoil heaps of Memi, the 20th-century pyrites mine (Fig. 4.22). Although it is now known that small amounts of copper sulphides were associated with the main pyrites ore body, they are not large enough to justify the amount of slag present at Mavrovouni (Pantazis 1969, 37). The nearest major source of copper ore for the smelting workshops of Mavrovouni is to be found on Alestos, which is clearly visible to the west (Fig. 4.23). The nearest slag heap to Alestos is at Mavrovouni, and even if a slag heap had been obliterated by the Alestos mine we would have found slag downslope. Thus, the relationship of the smelting operations with the Roman mining settlement of Litharkies (Chapter 4.4) is crucial to our understanding of Mavrovouni.

One of our major aims at Mavrovouni was to establish the chronology and character of both the settlement and the smelting activities that went on immediately adjacent to it. We also aimed to further our understanding of the smelting process, and to investigate how this compared to other smelting operations on Cyprus and how its technology

Fig. 4.22. The spoil heaps of Memi mine, with Mavrovouni directly in front, including the slag heap (TP006) and the Rock of Ayios Kyriakos (TP017) (Chris Parks)

Fig. 4.23. Ayia Marina Mavrovouni *(TS02): slag heap in the foreground, with the modern mine of Alestos appearing over the ridgeline (Chris Parks)*

Fig. 4.24. Slag heap and surrounding fields. Slag heap in the centre, with the Rock of Ayios Kyriakos (TP017) on the far left above the track (Michael Given)

changed over time. This involved examining a range of issues: the fuel used for smelting, and consequently the issue of sustainable land management; whether or not this activity was a year-round or seasonal one; who the smelters were and who else lived at Mavrovouni; the relationship and communications between extractors and processors; and finally the destination of the copper, the wider network of communication routes, and the role of the Litharkies/Mavrovouni complex in the island-wide copper production system.

The Slag Heaps

As indicated on the 1952 geological map, there were at least two slag heaps in the area prior to development of Memi Mine: one which we recorded (TP006); and another removed by the time of our survey. Pantazis estimated the volume of TP006 at 10,000 tons (1969, 37). This estimate was made after mining operations had already disturbed the area. Like other slag heaps on the island, it has been greatly reduced in size by modern quarrying; slag was used as road metal (Kassianidou *et al.* 2003, 82) and most of its central portion has been removed. The slag heap is now c. 30 × 45 m, with a remaining height of 4 m (about the 10,000 tons noted by Pantazis). The field mapping in 1952 measured the extent of this nearly elliptical pile of slag as 93 m along its northwest–southeast major axis, and 57 m along its northeast–southwest minor axis. It is noted as a hill on the 1920s cadastral map, meaning that its height was greater than 5 m.

By regarding the shape of the slag heap as an elliptical fustrum (truncated cone), knowing that the Romans often levelled their slag heaps to produce a working area, and with the density of the slag heap at 2.0 tons/m^3, we can estimate the mass of the slag heap to be about 36,000 tons at a height of 5 m. Based upon a slag to copper ratio of 12:1 this suggests a copper output of 3000 tons for TP006 (based on the area shown on the 1952 map, as indicated in Plate 4.8). This is considerably smaller than the slag heaps of Mitsero *Sykamies* and Mitsero *Kouloupakhis* (Given *et al.* 2003b, 100; Kassianidou *et al.* 2003, 85). The *Kouloupakhis* slag heap was found to be 24 m deep after drilling and has been estimated at 600,000 tons of slag (Rickard 1930, 299), with metallic copper production estimated at 30,000 tons. The slag heap at Skouriotissa is by far the largest on the island with its estimated 2 million tons of ancient slag (Chapter 3.12).

A second smaller slag heap was documented in 1952 in a field that now lies below the modern track. This slag heap was piled on the south-east side of a low-lying bedrock hillock, known locally as the 'Rock of Ayios Kyriakos' (TP017); its location is also demonstrated in the relatively high densities of slag fragments found in the adjacent Survey Units. The slag heap's footprint was elliptical in shape, measuring 34.5 m along its east–west major axis and 23 m along its north–south minor axis. Its height was not recorded. A pile of slag rubble of this extent could have been as much as 5 m tall without being noted on the cadastral map, and thus, would not have contained more than 4,000 tons of slag and produced 200 tons of copper. By the time geologist Pantazis recorded the site (1969), this hill and surrounding area would have already been scarred by the effects of the modern Memi Mine operations. It is clear from our estimates that a minimum of 3000 tons of copper was produced from these two operations, but it could have been considerably more had slag heap TP006 been higher than the minimum of 5 m.

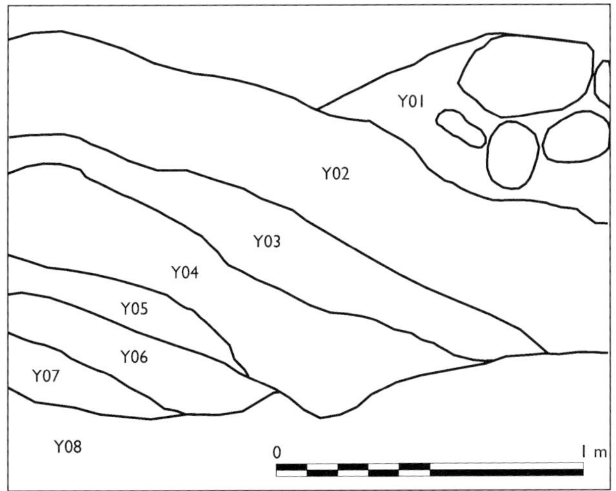

Fig. 4.25. Ayia Marina Mavrovouni *(TP006): section drawing of AU01 (Vasiliki Kassianidou)*

Modern quarrying has created a number of sections in the main slag heap (TP006.AU01–04), which we recorded using our standard archaeometallurgical recording procedures (Volume 1, Chapter 2.12). AU01 (Fig. 4.25; Table 4.11) is the south-facing section to the east of the large section defined as AU03. The top layer is full of diabase boulders, while the others consist of various sizes of slag fragments. The section does not reach the base of the slag heap and, therefore, it corresponds only to the later phases of the smelting activities at this site. Layer A1 contained a single Light Utility sherd from the very broad Historical (Archaic–Modern) period.

AU02 (Fig. 4.26; Table 4.12) is the east-facing section to the east of AU03. Samples of slag and charcoal were collected. The section does not reach the base of the slag heap and, thus, the material collected corresponds to the later phases of the smelting activities.

The south-facing AU03 (Fig. 4.27; Table 4.13) is the most extensive of the four sections, with 14 different layers. Their inclination shows that the slag was initially dumped from the west, and later from the east. A number of the layers (e.g. Layers 6, 10, 12) consist of slag crushed to small fragments, while others (e.g. Layers 7 and 9) consist of medium pieces of slag, and some of large pieces (e.g. Layers 1, 2, 3, 4, 5). A number of complete slag cakes are within these layers, or form distinctive layers, and it is their orientation which best indicates the direction of the dumping episodes. The section does not reach the base of the slag heap.

AU04 (Fig. 4.28; Table 4.14) is a north-facing section located behind AU03; it was created when a pit was dug to plant an olive tree. Although very small, AU04 is extremely interesting because it consists of layers that are rich in furnace material, furnace conglomerate and charcoal. This clearly was once the location of a smelting

Table 4.11. Ayia Marina Mavrovouni *(TP006): AU01 layers. There were no sherds*

Layer	*Material*	*Comments*
Y01	Slag – Medium	Slag and furnace material collected during cleaning of the section.
Y02	Slag – Small	
Y03	Slag – Medium	Also contains small pieces of tap slap.
Y04	Slag – Small	Also contains small pieces of tap slap.
Y05	Slag – Medium	Also contains small pieces of tap slap.
Y06	Slag – Medium	Also contains small pieces of tap slap.
Y07	Slag – Small	Pieces very small; mixed with fine charcoal dust & brown sediment.
Y08	Slag – Medium	Layer is loosely packed.

furnace that is now represented solely by the fragments of its upper structure.

The characteristics of a Roman period slag heap include very large slag cakes; slag which has a bluish tinge, which indicates the presence of manganese; large slagged igneous rocks; and very large fragments of slagged furnace wall made of refractory clay out of which the smelting furnaces were built (Kassianidou and Van Lokeren 2003, 223–24). The Mavrovouni slag heap has all of these characteristics, and therefore, it should be dated to the Roman period. Unfortunately, the single piece of pottery collected from the stratified layers does not offer any assistance in clarifying the issue of dating. A sample of charcoal collected from Layer 14 of AU03 was radiocarbon dated (Wk-25878) and produced a calibrated date of 416–533 AD (1σ) or 400–540 AD (2σ). Layer 14 lies at the base of the preserved section and is covered with another metre of slag. This means that it does not help us to date the beginning, or end, of the smelting operation, but it does show very clearly that copper was produced during the Late Roman period.

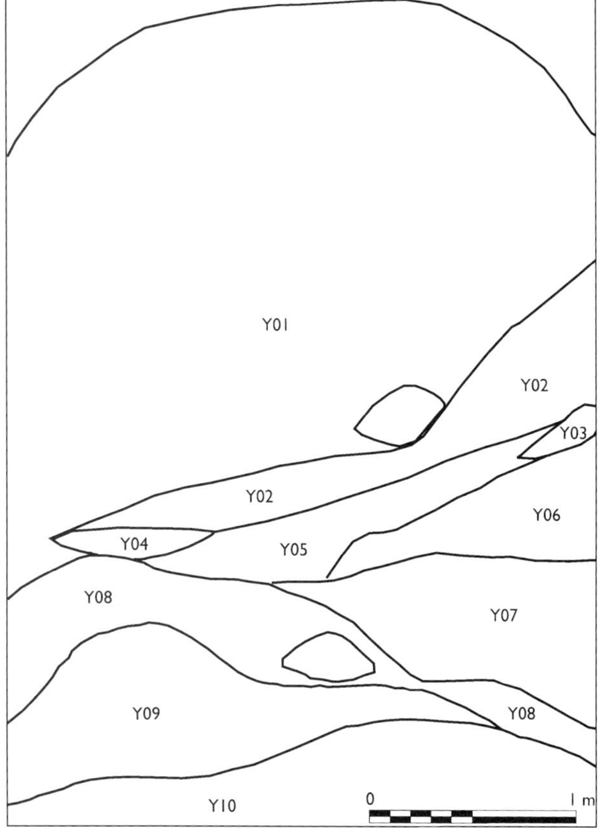

Fig. 4.26. Ayia Marina Mavrovouni *(TP006): section drawing of AU02 (Vasiliki Kassianidou)*

Charcoal analysis of samples from AU02, AU03 and AU04 were undertaken by Maria Ntinou (for further discussion see Volume 1, Chapter 3.10). The majority of the samples come from different layers of the AU03 section, from where single charcoal fragments were recovered. In both AU03 (Table 4.16) and the sample from AU02 (Table 4.15), *Pinus brutia* is the only taxon identified. However, two samples from AU04, from layers with furnace slag and charcoal in particular, provided abundant material and a greater number of taxa (Table 4.15). The Cyprus pine is the most well represented taxon, but other taxa are also present, namely maple, olive, lentisc, evergreen oak, oriental plane and oriental alder.

Samples of slag collected from the various sections have been analysed by Myrto Georgakopoulou, and the full results are presented in Volume 1, Chapter 3.9. The vast majority of the analysed samples have a copper content below 1%, indicating that the slag is the product of an advanced smelting technology. Furthermore, the analysis showed that apart from one sample, all the rest contain significant amounts of manganese. In these manganiferous samples the concentration ranges from 3.8% to 39.6%. Manganese is not found in the copper ores, and therefore its presence indicates that it was deliberately added as a flux. Since it has been shown that in Cyprus the use of manganese as a flux is a trait of the Roman period smelting technology (Kassianidou 2003b, 226), the chemical analysis confirms the notion that the slag heap dates to the Roman period. The most likely source of manganese was umber, a compound of iron and manganese, which is very common in the mining regions of the Troodos

Table 4.12. Ayia Marina Mavrovouni *(TP006): AU02 layers*

Layer	*Material*	Sherds	*Comments*
Y01	Slag – Large		Also contains complete slag cakes.
Y02	Slag – Medium		Lens of small pieces of furnace slag mixed with charcoal pieces and charcoal dust
Y03	Slag – Small		
Y04	Ground Ore/Flux		Large pieces of slag and complete slag cakes.
Y05	Slag – Medium		Very small pieces of tap slag mixed with charcoal and charcoal dust.
Y06	Slag – Small	1	Furnace slag. Much charcoal.
Y07	Slag – Small		Much charcoal. Possibly the remains of a collapsed furnace.
Y08	Slag – Small		
Y09	Slag – Small		Furnace Slag. Very rich in charcoal.
Y10	Slag – Medium		Lens of small pieces of furnace material mixed with small pieces of slag.

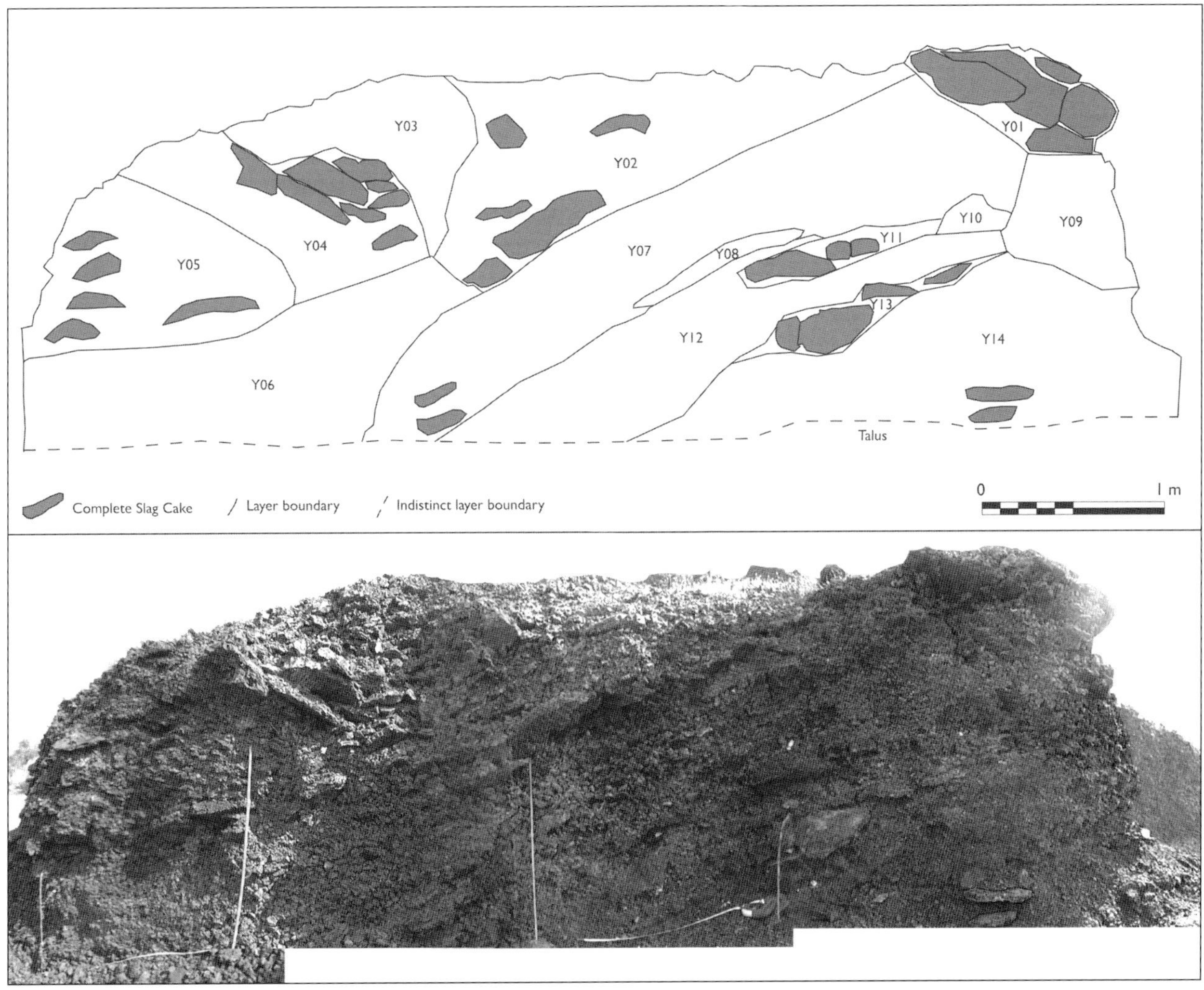

Fig. 4.27. Ayia Marina Mavrovouni *(TP006): section AU03. Above: section drawing (Vasiliki Kassianidou). Below: photograph (Chris Parks)*

Table 4.13. Ayia Marina Mavrovouni *(TP006): AU03 layers*

Layer	*Material*	*Sherds*	*Comments*
Y01	Slag – Large		Slag mixed with fine brown sediment and charcoal dust.
Y02	Slag – Large	1	Top layer. Very mixed: slag, large diabase boulders, soil.
Y03	Slag – Large		
Y04	Slag – Large		
Y05	Slag – Large		
Y06	Slag – Small		
Y07	Slag – Medium		Large pieces and complete slag cakes.
Y08	Furnace Material		Layer in front of the section. Fallen slag, stones etc.
Y09	Slag – Medium		Also contains small pieces of slag.
Y10	Slag – Small		Layer in front of the section. Fallen slag, stones etc.
Y11	Slag – Large		Lens of very small pieces of slag mixed with charcoal & fine charcoal dust.
Y12	Slag – Small		
Y13	Slag – Large		Mixed with charcoal.
Y14	Slag – Small		

tons of charcoal, based on the charcoal to slag ratio of 3:2 (Volume 1, Chapter 4.8). Assuming the charcoal was produced in the forests and a carrying capacity of 90 kg for donkeys (Adams 2007, 57–58; Bekker-Nielsen 2004, 74; Burnet 2004, 86; Landels 1978, 172), this would have required more than 660,000 donkey journeys of charcoal from the forests during the entire period of smelting. Had the smelting operation been all year-round, over a 450-year period, this would equate to only, approximately, four donkey loads of charcoal per day, producing c. 12 kg of copper per day. An average load of 60 kg per donkey and periods of more intense operation would of course increase the daily journey rate (cf. the official load limit of 100 Roman pounds in the *Codex Theodosianus*: Bekker-Nielsen 2004, 74).

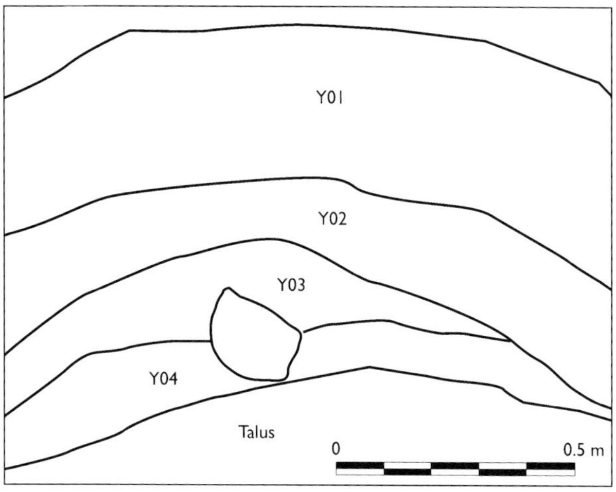

Fig. 4.28. Ayia Marina Mavrovouni *(TP006): section drawing of AU04 (Vasiliki Kassianidou)*

Pottery Distribution and Chronology

Two Chalcolithic sherds from the block survey south of the slag heap, on the west side of the river, represent the earliest archaeological data from within the Lagoudhera Valley. One was from a Red-on-White open vessel, cream-slipped and burnished with a broad swipe of washy red paint across the interior (TCP273). The other was part of a Red Monochrome closed vessel with a red, brick-like fabric and dark red burnished slip (TCP272). On the same east-facing terraced hillside were a re-used Chalcolithic stone pestle (TCL192) and a good density of chipped stone, though this is more likely to relate to Roman-period activity in the area (see below).

The southern end of the hillside, where the sherds were found, ends in a gentle spit above a bend in the Lagoudhera River, which comprises a typical Chalcolithic settlement location (Webb *et al.* 2009). Extensive survey of the

Table 4.14. Ayia Marina Mavrovouni *(TP006): AU04 layers. There were no sherds*

Layer	*Material*	*Comments*
Y01	Slag – Small	
Y02	Furnace Material	Ground ore and flux. Lens of what looks like burnt gossan, but also fine bits of fired clay (furnace material?) and charcoal.
Y03	Slag – Large	Also contains medium pieces. Not cut by the section.
Y04	Slag – Medium	Also contains small pieces.

Table 4.15. Ayia Marina Mavrovouni *(TP006): charcoal analysis from AU02 and AU04*

	AU02, Layer Y02, F. 15	*AU04, Layer Y04, A004*	*AU04, Layer Y02, A002*
Acer sp.		1	1
Alnus orientalis		1	
Olea europaea			1
Pinus brutia	1	37	57
Pinus sp.			2
Pistacia lentiscus			3
Platanus orientalis		1	
Quercus sp. evergreen type			6

Table 4.16. Ayia Marina Mavrovouni *(TP006): charcoal analysis from AU03*

	Layer Y01, F. 1	*Layer Y03, F. 12*	*Layer Y04, F. 20*	*Layer Y05, F. 9 & F. 21*	*Layer Y07, F. 5, F. 13 & F. 19*	*Layer Y09, F. 14*	*Layer Y10, F. 2*	*Layer Y12, F. 17*
Pinus brutia	3	1	1	3	3	1	1	1

Fig. 4.29. Path between Ayia Marina village and Mavrovouni, looking south-west to Memi mine (TP077) (Chris Parks)

whole hillside, however, revealed no further indication of Chalcolithic pottery. Chalcolithic settlements have been recorded at Kato Moni *Kambia*, Kato Moni *Monarga* and Orounda *Stavros tou Koundi* in the adjacent Peristerona River valley, 8 km to the north-east (Knapp *et al.* 1992, 332–33) and perhaps these sherds are connected with people from these settlements who came to the area for the oxidised iron minerals, which they used as pigments.

One of the most striking features of Mavrovouni was an impressively dense scatter of Late Hellenistic to Late Roman pottery, by far the densest pottery scatter in the Survey Area. We carried out block survey across this whole scatter, using our normal walker spacing and collection strategy, but in smaller Survey Units (TS02; Plate 4.8; Table 4.17) and in addition gridded the most interesting field (TP104; Table 4.18). Detailed discussions of the interpretation of the Mavrovouni assemblages can be found in Graham *et al.* 2006 and Winther-Jacobsen 2010 (p. 256, bottom); see also Volume 1, Chapter 5.3.

As with the rest of the Lagoudhera Valley, there is almost no Iron Age material at Mavrovouni, just two fragments south of the slag heap and three more just outside the main area of block survey. The Hellenistic Period is represented by only seven sherds, collected in seven Survey Units across the broad area stretching from just north of the slag heap, down to the adits at Ayios Kyriakos to the south. These occasional sherds consist of six fragments of Classical and Hellenistic Black Slip Table Ware and three pieces of Cooking Ware pot CWPR07, similar to some Hellenistic pots found in Evrykhou tomb IV (TP247; Chapter 3.14).

The material securely datable to the Late Hellenistic to Early Roman (LHER) period all consists of Table Wares; 16 out of the 20 sherds are restricted to the area with the high density of finds to the south of the slag heap, with another found north of the slag heap and two between Mavrovouni and Ayios Kyriakos. The highest density of LHER pottery from all the Survey Units is only 4.8 sherds/100 m^2. Only eight sherds from six Survey Units, which are all on the high density tread of Mavrovouni, are securely datable to the Early Roman period (Table 4.17). The four fragments of the thin-walled Cooking Ware pot (CWPR05) were found in the two fields immediately to the south of the slag heap. Light and Heavy Utility wares are more difficult to date, and within a general Roman context LHER utility wares become invisible. With only Table Wares from the LHER period and Table Wares and Cooking Wares from the Early Roman period being securely datable, the complete range of functions undertaken at the site during these periods is unclear: cooking and eating are certain, but storage and living are not.

The Late Hellenistic to Early Roman chronology of this area is based primarily on pottery, supported by a single Ptolemaic coin found in TP104. All the identified sigillata forms are unique occurrences, but several fragments are too small for secure assignment to the typologies. Eastern Sigillata A Form 22A (ESA22A) and Cypriot Sigillata (CS) Forms 4B and 12 are, however, all datable to within the 1st century AD, though some may be as early as the mid-2nd century BC. Based on results from Paphos, the identification of a Western Sigillata fragment also suggests a date no earlier than the Augustan period (Hayes 1991, 51). A few Black Slip and Red Slip ware body fragments and the Ptolemaic coin indicate a less restricted chronology, but so far none of the typical early sigillata forms such as ESA3–4 have been identified.

The main focus of human activity was indicated by a very high sherd density located south-east of the slag heap, mainly dating to the Late Hellenistic to Late Roman (LR) periods. The mean density for Hellenistic–Roman material in the 11 Survey Units between the slag heap and the north end of the tread is 4.5 sherds/100 m^2 (Plate 4.8). This contrasts with the mean to the south, which is almost seven times that at 30.5 sherds/100 m^2 (16 Survey Units); this becomes 16.9 sherds/100 m^2 without the very dense SU0622 in the calculations. Interestingly, the two Survey Units in the field adjacent to the south side of the slag heap have densities of just 4.7 and 13.8 sherds/100 m^2. The next field to the south-east (SU0622) has the fourth highest Hellenistic–Roman density in the whole of the Lagoudhera valley, at 234.6 sherds/100 m^2. This is a huge density: across the Survey Area as a whole, we view figures above 20 Hellenistic–Roman sherds/100 m^2 as being significantly above the broad scatters derived from manuring and similar practices.

In the south-west corner of the tread we surveyed a group of three Survey Units with densities ranging from 37.7 to 59.9 sherds/100 m^2. These two areas appear to be the two focal points of human activity at Mavrovouni. The area may extend west, but we were unable to survey the fields on this side of the tread because of low ground visibility. The large flat tread drops abruptly to a series of more recent fluvial terraces, approximately 40 m south-west of the Rock of Ayios Kyriakos (TP017); however, the southern boundary of the high density of Late Hellenistic to

Table 4.17. Ayia Marina Mavrovouni *(TS02: SU0012, SU0614–40, SU0659–61, SU0620–23, SU1646–51, SU1690–98): summary of collected pottery from block survey TS02. TCP numbers refer to Pottery Catalogue in volume 1, chapter 3.6*

Cypro-Geometric to Classical

Fct	*Type*	*No.*	*Weight*
HU	Per	1	70g TCP182
LU	LU	1	50g
LU	WP	1	10g

Historical Antiquity (Archaic to Late Roman)

Fct	*Type*	*No.*	*Weight*
Ar	Ti	75	8.55kg
Ar	TiP	5	760g
CW	CW	4	45g
HU	HU	1	10g
LU	LU	6	17g
Tr	Am	12	670g
TW	TW	6	58g

Cypro-Classical

Fct	*Type*	*No.*	*Weight*
TW	BS	2	25g
TW	RS	1	2g

Hellenistic

Fct	*Type*	*No.*	*Weight*
CW	CWPR07	3	50g TCP157, TCP159
TW	BS	5	36g

Hellenistic to Roman

Fct	*Type*	*No.*	*Weight*
CW	CW	22	165g
CW	CWPR02	1	10g TCP180
CW	CWPR09	1	17g TCP181
HU	HU	49	1.76kg
HU	HUR07	54	2.45kg TCP178
HU	Pit11	1	140g
LU	LU	34	248g
LU	LUR06	1	25g
LU	LUR08	1	22g
LU	LUR11	3	250g TCP173
Tr	Am	1	35g
Tr	Am01	1	50g
Tr	Am07	2	10g
TW	BS	1	2g
TW	SRS	46	316g
TW	TW	3	60g

Late Hellenistic to Early Roman

Fct	*Type*	*No.*	*Weight*
TW	CS	9	46g
TW	ESA	6	30g
TW	ESA22A	1	2g
TW	Sig	2	20g

Early Roman

Fct	*Type*	*No.*	*Weight*
CW	CWPR05	4	32g TCP174
TW	CS04B	1	20g TCP171
TW	CS12	2	15g TCP158
TW	SigW	1	7g TCP168

Early to Late Roman

Fct	*Type*	*No.*	*Weight*
Ar	Ti	10	600g
Ar	TiCA	13	1.047kg
Ar	TiP	7	695g
CW	CW	154	791g
CW	CWC	2	42g
CW	CWCR02a	3	55g TCP156
CW	CWPR04	1	10g
CW	CWPR08a	2	15g
HU	HUR01	10	385g TCP153, TCP154
HU	HUR10	1	37g
Tr	Am	3	115g
TW	ARS	4	35g

Mid Roman

Fct	*Type*	*No.*	*Weight*
TW	ARS50	2	15g

Late Roman

Fct	*Type*	*No.*	*Weight*
Ar	Ti	1	90g
Ar	TiP	4	530g
CW	CW	13	50g
CW	CWCR01	2	100g TCP022
CW	CWPR13	2	25g TCP176
CW	CWPR16	3	40g TCP175
HU	Pit01	2	720g TCP177
Tr	Am	1	90g
Tr	LR1	4	85g
TW	CRS	12	149g TCP152
TW	CRS01	1	5g TCP179
TW	CRS02	16	302g
TW	CRS02X	2	22g TCP165
TW	CRS08	1	15g TCP169
TW	CRS09	7	67g TCP025, TCP026
TW	CRS10A	1	30g TCP170
TW	CRS11	2	50g TCP162
TW	CRSK01	1	20g TCP024
TW	LRC	7	37g TCP167, TCP172
TW	LRC02A	3	35g
TW	LRC03	8	102g
TW	LRC03F	1	10g TCP023
TW	LRC10	1	20g TCP027
TW	LRCA1kn5	1	18g TCP166
TW	RS	10	75g

Roman to Modern

Fct	*Type*	*No.*	*Weight*
Ar	Brk	1	225g
Ar	Ti	27	1.467kg
CW	CW	6	42g
HU	Pit11	9	1.225kg TCP161
LU	LU	33	144g

Historical (Archaic to Modern)

Fct	*Type*	*No.*	*Weight*
Ar	Ti	61	3.13kg
CW	CW	118	460g
HU	HU	879	28.726kg
LU	LU	774	6.539kg
LU	LUB01	6	250g TCP163

Medieval

Fct	*Type*	*No.*	*Weight*
TW	G01	1	20g
TW	GS07	1	5g

Medieval to Ottoman

Fct	*Type*	*No.*	*Weight*
TW	G02	2	15g

TW	G05	2	20g

Medieval to Modern

Fct	*Type*	*No.*	*Weight*
Ar	Un01	2	100g
CW	Tia	2	55g
HU	HU	8	240g
LU	LU	42	685g
TW	G	1	2g
U	BUPSJa	1	170g

Byzantine to Medieval

Fct	*Type*	*No.*	*Weight*
TW	GS05	1	2g
TW	SP03	1	10g
			TCP150

Medieval-Frankish

Fct	*Type*	*No.*	*Weight*
TW	CGS05	10	105g
			TCP183
TW	CGS06	1	2g
TW	CGS07	7	60g
TW	G05	2	25g
TW	GS03	1	5g

Ottoman

Fct	*Type*	*No.*	*Weight*
TW	G03	4	97g
TW	MP01	4	15g

Ottoman to Modern I

Fct	*Type*	*No.*	*Weight*
LU	BGW	1	5g
TW	G01	2	5g
TW	G03	1	15g
TW	MP01	2	10g
U	URB01	1	85g
			TCP160

Medieval-Venetian to Early Ottoman

Fct	*Type*	*No.*	*Weight*
Ar	G06	1	10g
TW	CGS06	2	132g
			TCP155
TW	G03	11	119g
TW	GS07	1	5g
TW	MP01	7	108g
			TCP151
TW	MP02	1	15g
TW	MP03	1	10g

Ottoman to Modern II

Fct	*Type*	*No.*	*Weight*
CW	BGW	3	12g
HU	BuH	34	1.329kg
LU	BuL	54	744g
TW	BGW02	3	25g
TW	G03	2	15g
TW	G04	2	10g
TW	MP01	4	30g
TW	MP02	2	30g
TW	SP01	1	7g
TW	SP02	3	46g
			TCP164
TW	SP03	1	2g

Modern

Fct	*Type*	*No.*	*Weight*
Ar	Brk	41	1.289kg
Ar	Ti	5	380g
Ar	tiCH	20	697g
CW	BGW	2	43g
CW	BGW01	1	5g
CW	CW	2	57g
CW	Tia02	1	50g
HU	HU	32	1.565kg
LU	LU	1	10g
TW	G	1	10g
TW	G03	1	5g
TW	G07	1	5g
TW	Por	31	212g
TW	SP01	4	27g
TW	SP02	8	35g

Unknown

Fct	*Type*	*No.*	*Weight*
TW	G01	1	10g
Un	UN	3	199g

foothills. If very high manganese content was required, then manganese concretions produced through the weathering of umbers could have been used. Such deposits are found near Ayia Marina Xyliatou, c. 1.5 km to the north-east of Mavrovouni, and on the eastern slopes of Phoukasa Hill at Skouriotissa, c. 15 km to the north-west (Constantinou 1982, 19; 1992, 64–65).

A path (Fig. 4.29; TP077) connects Ayia Marina village to the north-east to the smelting site of Mavrovouni to the south-west, though a section is lost under the modern spoil heaps. This 1.3 m-wide pathway with its hard-packed surface is cut into the hillside and reinforced with angular basalt boulders on the downslope side. The path follows an easy route through the landscape, moving around the top of, and between, steep gullies in the area. While there is no firm evidence that this is the remains of a Roman route between the smelting site and the source of flux, the path does illustrate the ease of traversing a landscape that *prima facie* appears topographically challenging.

Smelting requires fuel. Large amounts of charcoal were used in the furnace in order to achieve the high temperatures needed and produce the reducing atmosphere (Craddock 1995, 189). Anthracological study of the charcoal samples by Maria Ntinou (Volume 1, Chapter 3.10) shows that the preferred species for fuel in Mavrovouni was *Pinus brutia*, a tree which grows in this part of the Troodos mountains and which would have been abundant in the past. In the Mavrovouni slag heap, charcoal from *Pinus brutia* represents 87.2% (109 of 125) of the total samples collected. Nevertheless, other plant species were also identified, namely maple, olive, lentisk, evergreen oak, oriental plane and oriental alder. The most common of these was the evergreen oak (4.8%), which was not identified in the Skouriotissa samples. Interestingly, the more varied samples came from the probable smelting furnace in AU04. These anthracological studies argue against our previous suggestion (Graham *et al.* 2006, 349) that more sustainable fuel resources, such as the readily available *Quercus coccifera*, hawthorn and olive, may have been used in greater proportion at Mavrovouni.

To produce the 40,000 tons of slag in the two Mavrovouni slag heaps would have required approximately 60,000

Table 4.18. Ayia Marina Mavrovouni *(TP104): summary of collected pottery from grid collection. TCP numbers refer to Pottery Catalogue in Volume 1, Chapter 3.6*

Historical Antiquity (Archaic to Late Roman)

Fct	*Type*	*No.*	*Weight*
HU	HU	24	565g
LU	LU	19	148g

Hellenistic to Roman

Fct	*Type*	*No.*	*Weight*
Ar	TiP	3	1.07kg
			TCP585, TCP613
CW	CW	30	349g
HU	HU	154	4.947kg
HU	HUB01	1	130g
			TCP596
HU	HUH01	1	90g
HU	HUL01	1	65g
			TCP616
HU	HUR11	1	37g
			TCP589
HU	HUR12	1	45g
			TCP594
HU	HUR13	1	30g
			TCP595
HU	HUR14	1	50g
			TCP587
HU	HUR15	1	40g
			TCP598
HU	HUR17	1	40g
			TCP611
HU	HUR18	1	20g
			TCP604
HU	HUR19	1	65g
			TCP605
HU	Pit11	1	130g
HU	UN02	1	135g
LU	LU	104	994g
LU	LUR04	1	70g
			TCP590
LU	LUR08	1	28g
LU	LUR12	1	37g
			TCP588
Tr	Am	8	710g
Tr	Am03	2	160g
Tr	Am04	1	80g
Tr	Am07	1	10g
			TCP597
Tr	Mav	1	140g
Tr	Mav01	13	1.688kg
			TCP586, TCP607, TCP608, TCP615, TCP619
Tr	Mav02	2	355g
			TCP593, TCP602
Tr	Mav03	1	80g
			TCP609
TW	RS	1	2g
TW	SRS	10	46g
TW	TW	1	2g

Late Hellenistic to Early Roman

Fct	*Type*	*No.*	*Weight*
TW	ESA	2	5g
TW	Sig	1	5g

Early to Late Roman

Fct	*Type*	*No.*	*Weight*
Ar	Ti	1	160g
Ar	TiCA	2	235g
Ar	TiP	17	2.6kg
CW	CW	42	162g
CW	CWFPWh	2	65g
CW	CWPR13	1	20g
HU	HUR01	4	190g
HU	Pit07	1	330g
			TCP599
LU	LU	1	40g

Late Roman

Fct	*Type*	*No.*	*Weight*
Ar	Ti	1	50g
Ar	TiP	4	380g
Ar	TiSk01	1	315g
Ar	TiSkC03	1	80g
			TCP612
CW	CWCR03	1	10g
			TCP618
CW	CWPR13	2	22g
			TCP592, TCP600
HU	Pit01	3	2.27kg
HU	Pit10	1	280g
			TCP610
Tr	Am	1	40g
Tr	LR1	1	65g
			TCP591
TW	CRS	1	50g
TW	CRS01	2	28g
TW	CRS02	5	81g
TW	CRS05	1	20g
TW	CRS08	1	12g
			TCP584
TW	CRS09	2	15g
TW	CRS09A	1	10g
			TCP601
TW	CRS11	1	40g
TW	LRC	3	8g
TW	LRC01A	1	8g
			TCP603
TW	LRC03	6	37g

Roman to Modern

Fct	*Type*	*No.*	*Weight*
Ar	Ti	28	1.692kg
CW	CW	2	29g
HU	HU	67	4.97kg
HU	Pit08	2	200g
			TCP606
HU	Pit09	2	270g
			TCP617
HU	Pit11	3	492g
			TCP614
LU	LU	13	180g

Historical (Archaic to Modern)

Fct	*Type*	*No.*	*Weight*
HU	HU	13	632g
LU	LU	8	67g
LU	LUR02	1	18g
LU	RS	1	50g

Medieval to Modern

Fct	*Type*	*No.*	*Weight*
Ar	Brk	1	120g
CW	BGW	4	12g
HU	HU	13	299g
LU	LU	6	108g
Un	Un	1	35g

Byzantine to Medieval

Fct	*Type*	*No.*	*Weight*
TW	GS02	1	20g

Medieval-Frankish

Fct	*Type*	*No.*	*Weight*
TW	CGS05	1	5g

Medieval-Venetian to Early Ottoman

Fct	*Type*	*No.*	*Weight*
TW	MP01	1	22g

Ottoman to Modern II

Fct	*Type*	*No.*	*Weight*
HU	BuH	7	342g
LU	BuL	7	148g
TW	G07	1	3g
TW	SP02	1	10g

Modern

Fct	*Type*	*No.*	*Weight*
TW	Por	1	2g

Unknown

Fct	*Type*	*No.*	*Weight*
Un	Un	1	75g

Table 4.19. Ayia Marina Mavrovouni *(TS02 and TP104): list of datable Table Ware types. For numbers prefixed 'TCP' see catalogue entries in Volume 1, Chapter 3.6*

	Sherds in High Density Area	*Sherds in rest of TS02*	*Date*
Black slip ware	3		Classical to Hellenistic
Sigillata	1	1	Late Hellenistic–Early Roman
ESA	7		Mid 2nd century BC–1st century AD
ESA22A	1		Late 2nd century BC–AD 10
CS	10		Late 2nd century BC–2nd century AD
CS4B	1		Early 1st century AD
CS12	1		Second half of 1st to first half of 2nd century AD
ARS	2		Mid 3rd–7th century AD
ARS50	2		370–450 AD
CRS	10		4th–7th century AD
CRS1	1	1	Late 4th to third quarter of 5th century AD
CRS2	19	3	Late 4th to third quarter of 5th century AD
CRS5	1		Mid–late 6th century AD
CRS8	1	1	Late 4th–7th century AD
CRS9 and 9A	7	1	550–600 AD
CRS10A	1		600–700 AD
CRS11	2		550–650 AD
LRC	7		Late 4th–mid 7th century AD
LRCA1kn5	1		370–450 AD
LRC1	1		Late 4th–third quarter of 5th century AD
LRC2A	4		425–450/before mid 5th century AD
LRC3	12	4	First half of 6th century AD

Late Roman material is reached before this topographical change. The density of material increases again on the lower treads to the south, but the densities of slag suggest that this may be down to later anthropogenic activity in cultivating these terraces.

The fields between the Rock of Ayios Kyriakos and the edge of the tread demonstrate a visible increase of post-Roman material. This is consistent with other archaeological data, in the form of painted plaster fragments and tiles in close proximity to a great rock pile, corroborating the textual evidence for the church of Ayios Kyriakos located in the southern end of the area (Goodwin 1984, 176). The church was presumably constructed at some point within the Medieval period, but there is no conclusive archaeological evidence for the dating (Given *et al.* 2002, 29).

Because of our interest in the people living and/or working at Mavrovouni and the general social implications, a very detailed analysis of the pottery was undertaken. Our representative collection methods (Volume 1, Chapter 2.3), combined with the sheer numbers of sherds found in this area, make this analysis very robust.

The Table Wares indicate continuous activity in the area from the end of the mid-Roman period through the entire Late Roman period (Table 4.19). The forms represented are mainly bowls and dishes, while closed vessels such as jugs are not represented, which is consistent with finds from contemporary sites such as Panayia Ematousa (Lund 2006a). Generally, the repertoire of Roman Table Ware forms is dominated by open shapes (e.g. Hayes 1985), while funerary assemblages are dominated by closed shapes (e.g. Jacobsen 2007).

The presence of an early CRS8 (TCP169) indicates a start in the 4th century at the latest. The late 4th to 3rd quarter of the 5th century AD is dominated by CRS2 (e.g. an imitation: TCP165). Other forms belonging in this period are African Red Slip ware (ARS) Form 50 and Phocaean Red Slip ware (LRC) Forms A1kn5 (TCP166), 1 (TCP603) and 2. The 2nd half of the 5th century to 1st half of the 6th century AD are dominated by LRC3 alone. In the 2nd half of the 6th century to AD 600, CRS9 takes over, followed by CRS5, CRS11 (TCP162) and CRS10A (TCP170), which takes us into the 7th century.

Of the three dominant Table Ware forms, the earliest, CRS2, appears to be the most common. Unfortunately there is much variety within the CRS typology, and sometimes is it difficult to classify a given fragment correctly, particularly when dealing with forms CRS2 and 9. Large amounts of material have been collected and published since the typology was established and later refined by John

Hayes (1967, 1972). Most recently Meyza has suggested a refined typology (2000), which has been used here to establish the 4th century AD chronology of the main area of high density.

If Cypriot Sigillata and Red Slip ware were produced at Soloi, as originally suggested by Hayes (1967, 74), we would expect this to be reflected in the distribution of the material in the hinterland, at sites such as Mavrovouni and indeed in the entire TAESP area. Unfortunately, undisturbed Hellenistic and Early Roman surfaces are rare in the Survey Area. Cypriot Red Slip ware is the most common Table Ware in the Mavrovouni area. Although the actual kiln sites have never been positively identified, recent archaeometric analyses confirm the close visual similarities, and indicate that production was located in the Paphos region (Daszkiewicz and Raabe 1995; Rautman *et al.* 1993, 260–61). The clay sources were very similar or the same, but the technology had changed, and although the chronological hiatus of the 3rd century AD has never been filled, Meyza has drawn attention to the general continuity of several forms (1995, 180–82). The Cypriot Red Slip wares found at Mavrovouni appear to span the entire period of production, from some of the earliest 4th century types until the 7th century, suggesting close permanent contact between Soloi and the Paphos regions during the Roman period.

Separating casseroles from cooking pots can be very difficult when fragments are small, but the majority of fragments collected at Mavrovouni appear to have come from cooking pots; only a single fragment of a frying pan with a wishbone handle was collected. With Mavrovouni situated not far from the Late Roman Cooking Ware production site at Dhiorios, we would expect a close resemblance, but this is not the case. No so-called Dhiorios pots were collected at Mavrovouni, and the only close parallel found was a pot from an AD 300–450 context at Maroni *Petrera* on the south coast (Tomber 2002, 51 no. 79, fig. 6.5).

Generally the Cooking Wares at Mavrovouni appear to be Late Roman rather than Early Roman (e.g. TCP156–57, TCP159, TCP174–76, TCP592, TCP600, TCP618). Firstly, there is even less resemblance to Early Roman material from the House of Dionysos at Paphos (Hayes 1991, 78–84). Secondly, the fabric is no longer as brittle as that found in the Early Roman period. Thirdly, most of the material from Mavrovouni has corrugated sides, which indicates a later Roman date (Hayes 1991, 124). Finally, though direct parallels are missing, the corrugation, proportions and body forms have a general morphological resemblance to Late Roman Cooking Wares.

The utility ceramics are predominantly made of self-slip fabrics. The material comprises an equal combination of open and closed forms, and there is even a fragment of a large lid. We collected a large number of forms, of which almost no two are alike (e.g. TCP153–54, TCP163, TCP173, TCP178, TCP587–90, TCP594–96, TCP598, TCP604–605, TCP611, and TCP616). Considering the existing variety within the typologies of Cypriot Table Wares, it is hardly surprising that pottery less subject to the dictates of fashion is even more variable. The exception is the large basin with triangular rim of the Roman period, the most common open form (TCP153–54). Bowls with similar rims have been found at the House of Dionysos at Paphos, where they are especially common in the 2nd century AD, but the rims are less thick (Hayes 1991, 66, fig. 24). Rim fragments closer to the fragments from Mavrovouni were found in Late Roman contexts at Dhiorios (Catling 1972, 32, no. P324, fig. 20, 38 no. P406, fig. 24) and at Panayia Ematousa (Jacobsen 2006b, 279–81, UC70.170)

The pithoi are all made of a coarse fabric, fired dark reddish-brown, very similar to the tiles. Even though the thick-walled fragments of pithoi are more likely to be preserved, the morphological range testifies to the need for storage at Mavrovouni. Six types of pithoi have been identified: one type possibly dates to the Roman period (TCP599), and two types date to the Late Roman period (TCP177 and TCP610). Parallels come from Dhiorios, Kalavasos *Kopetra*, Maroni *Petrera* and Panayia *Ematousa* (Catling 1972, fig. 33, no. P225; Jacobsen 2006b; Rautman *et al.* 1993, 237, fig. 3, no. 19; Tomber 2002, fig. 6.7, nos. 123, 125). It has not been possible to date the remaining three types represented (e.g. TCP161, TCP606, TCP614, TCP617). Though some post-Roman Table Ware has been collected at Mavrovouni, there was none of the post-Roman beetroot-shaped pithos.

Only a few fragments of the most common Late Roman amphora (LR1) (e.g. TCP591) have been recorded at Mavrovouni: the commoner types appear to be local (Jacobsen 2004). Three types of amphorae made of self-slip fabrics have been identified (Mav01–03), two of which certainly have twisted bases (e.g. TCP586, TCP593, TCP602, TCP607–609, TCP615, TCP619). Several diagnostic fragments have been collected and, though morphologically different, all three types appear to be rather heavy and thick-walled compared to the LR1 amphorae. The fabrics are closely related and the differences may only be a matter of different levels of clay refinement. Several other amphora fragments made of self-slip fabrics have been identified in the Survey Area, and a variety of twisted bases indicate that this is also a common feature. Three similar bases have been identified at Dhiorios (Catling 1972, 71), but no parallels have been identified among the published material from southern Cyprus.

A large number of Roman pan tile fragments, both red and yellow, was collected at Mavrovouni (e.g. TCP585, TCP612–13). The numbers, however, are minimal compared to those from the other Roman slag heap of Skouriotissa (Chapter 3.12). Establishing a typology of tiles is problematic. Roman tiles underwent few morphological changes, and the clay sources have continued to be used for tiles into the 20th century. Two types of cover tiles have been identified; both belong to a small, thick-walled gabled type (e.g. TCP612). The pan

Table 4.20. Ayia Marina Mavrovouni *(TS02): chipped stone category counts*

	Central (to S of slag heap) (SU0012, 0614–22) Mainly Roman	**Rubble piles & grid** TP025, TP104	**Ayios Kyriakos** (SU0622–25, 0631, 0639–61) Mainly Med–Mod	**North of slag heap** (SU0620–30, 0633–35, 1647–51, 1690–98)	**South** (SU1620–44)	**Totals**
Debris	5	2	3	53	8	**71**
Blanks	5	0	2	33	3	**43**
Cores	8	2	0	27	5	**42**
Tools	2	6	8	29	11	**56**
Totals	**20**	**10**	**13**	**142**	**27**	**212**

tiles which fit these cover tiles must have had very narrow raised edges, unlike any of the Roman pan tiles found on site. Pan tiles of that type have been found in the Survey Area at a modern tile kiln at Ayios Theodoros, and the production most likely belongs to the post-Roman period.

Chipped Stone and Ground Stone

The 212 pieces of chipped stone from Ayia Marina *Mavrovouni* (TS02) represent one of the largest collections in the Survey Area. A few were recovered from TP025 (a single tool) and TP104 (including two pieces of debris, two cores and five tools), but most came from Survey Units across the TS02 area (Table 4.20). Generally the chipped stone assemblage belonging to Mavrovouni can be summarized as flake-based and heavily dependent upon the use of the local raw materials jasper and chalcedony.

Because significant differences occur in the distribution of ceramic types across the area, the lithics are best understood in a series of sub-groupings pertaining to different zones (Plate 4.9; Table 4.20). The first consists of 20 chipped stone artefacts associated with the highest concentration of Roman pottery in the central area, just south of the slag heap. The second consists of 10 pieces associated with the rubble piles (TP025) and gridded field (TP104). The third, with 13 pieces, is further to the south, in the area with a greater concentration of Medieval–Modern pottery near the church of Ayios Kyriakos (TP047). The 'North' column in Table 4.20 shows that the greatest concentration of chipped stone in the TS02 area lies in the area immediately north of the slag heap and the ruined enclosure (TP023) and wall (TP022), with 142 pieces. By contrast, only 27 were collected from the Survey Units to the south of this area.

The chipped stone associated with the concentrations of predominantly Roman pottery south of the slag heap consist mainly of cores and debitage made on local jasper and chalcedony, suggesting that knapping took place in the vicinity. The only tools collected from these Survey Units are two flake tools (a notch and a marginally retouched piece) made on non-local translucent Lefkara cherts. A utilized flake was recovered from the rubble piles (TP025), along with a more significant sample including cores and debitage, as well as tools dominated by the use of local jasper and chalcedony. The tools from the gridded field (TP104) include a utilized flake, a notched flake, a multiple flake tool and two *dhoukani* flakes (one of which was made on non-local translucent Lefkara chert). These show an extended tool repertoire that is consistent with collections associated with Late Roman pottery elsewhere in the Survey Area.

The presence of simple flake tools and utilized flakes made from knapped stone in a context associated with smelting has also been shown at the Late Bronze Age site of Politiko *Phorades,* where it was suggested that such tools may have been employed in the cutting of plant materials for the production of *tuyères* or fire tinder (Knapp *et al.* n.d.). At Mavrovouni, however, the presence of the two *dhoukani* flakes is somewhat problematic given the paucity of other agricultural evidence (see below). *Dhoukani* flakes produced on jasper are a feature of Roman chipped stone samples elsewhere in the Survey Area, most notably at Skouriotissa *Pseftas* (Chapter 3.13). These two *dhoukani* flakes cannot, therefore, be simply dismissed as later intrusives, suggesting that some of the agricultural production that sustained the mining community might have been carried out locally. Threshing tools were not, however, exclusively used for cereal production. There are other significant possibilities in the context of a smelting site, such as the preparation of fodder for livestock, which would match our suggestion of manuring in the area (see below), or cutting straw for tempering pottery or mudbrick, and similar uses (Anderson 2006, 225–26).

Chipped stone collected from Survey Units in the central area of TS02, near to the ruined church of Ayios Kyriakos (nine pieces) and Survey Units abutting the slag heap (four pieces) which are dominated by Medieval–Modern ceramics, are more heavily dominated by tools than cores or knapping waste (Table 4.20). All but one of the artefacts (a utilized flake on Lefkara-basal chert) were made from local jasper and chalcedony. The tools, particularly in the area of the church of Ayios Kyriakos, are dominated exclusively by simple flake tools and utilized flake implements, such as those noted above in the areas with the greatest concentrations of Roman pottery. These artefacts are more in keeping with the character shown by samples collected at other sites assigned to the Roman period in the TAESP area, and corroborate the presence of

Roman ceramics mixed with Medieval–Modern material in the vicinity of Ayios Kyriakos.

The greatest concentration of chipped stone at Mavrovouni (142 pieces) lies just north of the slag heap, where there was considerably less pottery of Roman (Plate 4.8) and Medieval–Modern (Plate 4.14) date than to the south. This north/south contrast may be somewhat exaggerated by discovery biases: by the time the team were working north of the slag heap they had gained more experience and, in particular, were better at identifying chipped stone. The disparity between high chipped stone levels and low pottery levels north of the slag heap is, however, too great to be explained by this alone, and raises the possibility of a Roman-period chipped stone working area, separate from the settlement.

This assemblage of chipped stone north of the slag heap is again heavily dominated by the use of local jasper and chalcedony, with a large number of simple flake cores (27 pieces). These consist of: six reduced for the production of flake tools (including two marginally retouched flakes, three notches and one scraper); one *dhoukani* flake; and 17 predominantly expedient utilized flakes. A further three utilized flakes and two *dhoukani* flakes represent the only artefacts made on non-local cherts in this sample. While it is more likely that the latter, in particular, relate to subsequent agricultural activity in the TS02 area after the Roman period, the bulk of the core reduction material, and simple flake tools and implements, would not be inconsistent with samples dated to the Roman period elsewhere in the Survey Area, as in the central area of Mavrovouni.

An additional feature that is interesting in this regard is the similar contextual disparity between the concentration of Roman ceramics and the area with the greatest number of chipped stone artefacts shown also at Litharkies (Chapter 4.4). While the characterization of Mavrovouni as a smelting site is distinct from that of Litharkies as a settlement, the high concentrations of core reduction materials and debris away from the highest ceramic densities seem suggestive of a specific production area. Simple ad hoc flake tools, however, have also been recovered from more securely dated later period sites, such as Mandres, so this sample is best defined as a mix of artefacts equally characteristic of late antiquity as well as later historic periods.

The sample of chipped stone collected in the southern part of Mavrovouni represents Survey Units both immediately to the north and south of the path running between terrace walls (TP086). With 27 pieces, this sample is considerably smaller than that to the north of the slag heap, but is again notable for occurring in an area with comparatively little ceramic material. The proximity of these Survey Units to the ruined church of Ayios Kyriakos, as well as the presence of two *dhoukani* flakes made of non-local Lefkara cherts, suggests that at least some of this sample is related to post-Roman agricultural activity in the area. However, the probability that some of this material derives from the centre of Roman activity, having been transported for terrace building in the post-Roman periods, is suggested by the consistency of the material with the samples noted above.

The sample from the south of the Mavrovouni area has comparatively few cores and other knapping waste and is dominated by simple flake tools and utilized flakes that were produced on local jasper and chalcedony. One further possibility that needs to be considered with this sample in particular is the recovery of a few Chalcolithic sherds from along the river (see above), as well as a probable Chalcolithic pestle re-used, probably later, as a pounding tool. Since it is likely that prehistoric material located along the river could also have been transported upslope during terrace construction, it is worth noting the presence of two flake tools made on non-local Lefkara-basal chert, namely a burin and a scraper from SU1624. Flake tools made of non-local cherts do not occur frequently in contexts with Roman pottery and may indicate residual lithic material better associated with the prehistoric pottery.

Material from this apparently Roman chipped stone industry associated with copper production is distributed across the Lagoudhera landscape more widely. In the valley of a small tributary of the Lagoudhera River immediately south of Memi mine (TT503500E), a sample of 13 pieces of chipped stone is typical of the simple core technology utilized for the production of flake tools and implements from local jasper and chalcedony. Cores in this sample include a single platform core and tested nodule, along with a platform rejuvenation flake. Tools include a single utilized flake and a *dhoukani* flake made on jasper. This sample would be at home with other Roman samples at Mavrovouni, or in the Survey Area generally. No ground stone tools were recovered from this transect. Similarly, in a north–south transect running 700 m east of Mavrovouni (TT504000E), the three flakes, core fragment and 1 chunk were poorly diagnostic, but would fit with other evidence of a local jasper flake-based industry in the Survey Area. The two diabase hammer stones from the transect would also be at home in a metalworking context, such as that defined for the Mavrovouni area.

Only six ground stone tools were collected from Mavrovouni, though as at Litharkies it is likely that more examples could exist in the rubble piles and field boundaries. These tools consist of four pounding tools, one grinding tool and a flake from ground stone tool manufacture. The presence of these kinds of ground stone tools in the context of a smelting settlement is understandable, and it is notable that all of the ground stone was recovered in Survey Units either in the central area (SU0618–19, with one pecking\polishing stone each), or in the Survey Units located immediately to the south of the church of Ayios Kyriakos (a pounder and a grinder in SU1623, and a pestle re-used as a pounding tool in SU1625). The latter (TCL192) is probably Chalcolithic in origin, and exhibits extensive secondary chipping damage due to use in a heavy pounding activity.

Resistivity Survey

The resistivity survey at Mavrovouni was carried out in July 2002, and consisted of four separate grids, each located in a field with high levels of pottery (Plate 4.10). The aim of the survey was to detect any evidence that the pottery concentrations related to structural remains. Because of the amount of slag across the entire area, magnetometry was unsuitable. The survey was conducted using a Geoscan RM15 resistivity meter. Readings were taken at 1 m intervals, with the size of the grids depending upon the size of the fields. It was impractical in most instances to use 20 m grids because of the terraced nature of the fields. The readings were captured and filtered using Geoplot v3.

Grid 1 measured 13 × 14 m. The dummy readings represent the olive trees in the field. The readings were overall very low, which relates to the arid conditions. Except for spikes caused by contact problems, all of the readings were below 100 ohms, with the mean being around 38 ohms. The interpretations should be considered with this caveat in mind.

In terms of anomalies, it is apparent that there is higher resistance in the northern corner of the plot. The readings in this area are considerably higher than in the rest of the field, while the darker, roughly L-shaped band that represents the edge of this area produced the highest readings of all. The plot is not terribly clear, and any interpretation has to be tentative in the absence of testing through excavation. Nonetheless, this may represent a building: the darker band would represent the wall of the structure, while the generally higher readings within represent floor deposits that are more compacted than the soils elsewhere in the field.

Grid 2, which had fewer olive trees in it, measured 20 × 20 m. The range of readings was low, with only spikes above 100 ohms, the average being 39 ohms. There is again some evidence for a structure in the northern corner of the grid. This is clearer than the possible structure in Grid 1, forming a rectangular shape roughly 6 × 4 m. The interior has relatively low readings, which is less suggestive of a floor layer. There are two other anomalies, which may represent human activity. These are two linear bands of higher readings that run from the eastern to the western corner, taking a slight curve. The two anomalies appear to be related, as they are concentric. These may represent former wall lines, but could equally be purely geological in nature.

Grid 3 measured 20 × 20 m; the olive trees appear as patches of white dummy readings. The range of readings was very low, with only spikes above 50 ohms and an average reading of 21.6 ohms.

The low level of the readings, taken with the small range, means that there must be considerable doubt about any interpretations. There does, however, appear to be a rectilinear anomaly running across the centre of the plot, from the east to the west corner. This appears to divide into at least three smaller rectangular units. If this anomaly is real rather than an artefact of processing, then the anomaly may represent a building of some 15 × 3.5 m. The processing was not excessive; after the removal of spikes, a high pass filter and a low pass filter were applied, and the results interpolated on both x- and y-axes.

The other potential anomaly is a darker band running from the north to the south corner. It is darker in the north, becoming very faint towards the south. It also appears to be overlain by the potential building. If this anomaly represents an archaeological feature, it would be a wall, possibly earlier than the potential building.

Grid 4 measured 20 × 20 m. The readings were higher in this field than in Grid 3, although only spikes exceeded 100 ohms. The average in this case was 45 ohms, showing that the general moisture levels were, however, higher in this field than in Grid 3. The most obvious change in resistance runs along the northern edge of the plot at a slight angle. This is likely to represent walling, particularly as these readings are in strong contrast to the surrounding background; however, as the range in the data is only 22 ohms, there is still no certainty about the results.

The survey at Mavrovouni was complicated by the olive trees that covered many of the fields, and by the generally dry conditions. All of the results are compromised by the low ranges of readings, and none of the areas produced a resistance of greater than 100 ohms. Re-survey at a less arid time of the year might produce better results.

Despite this, some interesting indications of potential archaeological features were recorded. Grids 1, 2 and 3 all produced anomalies that might represent buildings, which may well accord with the levels of pottery recovered from fieldwalking. Grid 4 produced an anomaly that may represent a wall; while not direct evidence for occupation, it would relate to the use of the field by a settlement, and would therefore act as supporting evidence for the potential structures in the other fields.

Although no dressed stones or other building materials were identified at Mavrovouni, there was a series of rock piles on the field boundaries similar to those found at Xyliatos *Litharkies* (Fig. 4.30; Plate 4.11). The rock piles (TP025) and field boundaries are composed of huge numbers of river boulders (up to 1 m in diameter) and cobbles. We recorded 23 rock piles, typically between 1 and 3 m in height, and mostly relating to field boundary walls and/or corners. The largest is found to the north of the slag heap, while the greater volume of river boulders lies to the south. In addition to the huge mass of river boulders and cobbles in the rock piles a considerable volume is contained within the field walls, amounting to several hundred cubic metres of rock. The largest rock pile is c. 3 m high (Plate 4.11, no. 18). The L-shaped rock pile (no. 3) is adjacent to the location of the church of Ayios Kyriakos, as marked on the cadastral, and coincides with the main concentration of Medieval pottery. Tens of cubic metres of rock were used to form the raised path TP024 running through the middle of Mavrovouni and directly past the slag heap.

The geophysical survey suggests that there are structural elements that do not conform to the present alignment of

Fig. 4.30. Ayia Marina Mavrovouni *(TS02): rock pile (Chris Parks)*

field wall boundaries. The rubble piles in the adjacent field boundaries support the notion of the clearance of structures to make way for present agricultural activities. While it is possible that the rock piles represent the restructuring of the area from the former 16th-century settlement of San Chirico (Ayios Kyriakos) and its church (Chapter 4.9; Goodwin 1984, 176; Grivaud 1998, 204), the tiles document the presence of architecture in this area in Roman times and in the gridded circle survey (TP104) the density of Medieval–Modern pottery is far lower than that of Roman pottery.

Pollution, Working Conditions and Agricultural Production

Pollution is an important factor in the discussion of the health and the living and working conditions of the smelters and other inhabitants of Mavrovouni. Geoarchaeological and geochemical research carried out in Wadi Faynan, Jordan, has revealed that modern agricultural and pastoral activities are affected by copper concentrations produced by ancient copper smelting. The pollution affects the grain seed potential and is also absorbed by livestock (Barker *et al.* 1999, 262–69; 2000, 44–46; Pyatt *et al.* 1999). The same applies to ancient smelting sites in Cyprus (Pyatt 2001) where there is the added complication that one of the by-products of smelting chalcopyrite (copper iron sulphide) is sulphur dioxide (SO_2), a gas which is poisonous to plants, animals and humans. The repeated inhalation of sulphur dioxide by the smelters would have caused asthma-like symptoms amongst the workforce, producing fluid on the lungs (lung oedema) and a sore throat. The smelters would also have had sore red eyes as a result of working in such an environment (Sulphur 1994).

This pollutant raises the question of when such activities may have occurred. On days with a strong wind, or on hot days when convective mixing is strong, the SO_2 and other emissions would have mixed fairly quickly within the boundary layer of air (A. Manning pers. comm.). This would reduce their impact upon the nearby settlement and provide the smelters some respite when not at the furnace. The normal daytime anabatic (upslope) wind would, however, have blown from the north, so taking the sulphur dioxide directly into their living quarters. SO_2 is wet deposited (removed by rain); it can also be converted to sulphate particles by oxidation that are subsequently dry and wet deposited from the atmosphere. This, however, is not instantaneous and so even if they were smelting during the winter and spring months the SO_2 can travel many kilometres before it is deposited, and many more before the sulphate is removed from the air (A. Manning pers. comm.; Brueggemann and Spindler 1999). The excess calcium carbonate in the soils and aeolian dust of the island would have buffered the acidity of vapours and any deposits eminating from the smelting area, certainly within decades of such activities. Today the Mavrovouni tread and the west bank of the valley are intensively cultivated with vegetable plots, fruit trees and olive and almond groves. It is unclear how much residue, if any, remains in the Mavrovouni area as chemical analysis of the soils were not carried out.

There is ceramic evidence for storage at Mavrovouni, but this would be the case whether the crops were grown nearby or brought in. There are, however, no quern stones, cut stone crushers, or counter weights to provide firm evidence for local agricultural production, though some may be hidden in the rock piles and field boundaries.

To the north of the slag heap it is clear that we do not have evidence of living and eating. The density ranges from 1.4 to 11.1 sherds/100 m^2 in 9 of the 11 units surveyed. The mean for the 11 units is just 4.5 sherds/100 m^2. While this is considerably lower than the area on the spur to the south of the slag heap, it is nevertheless 3.7 times denser than the area surveyed on the west bank of the river. If smelting emissions left it unsuitable for cultivation during the Roman period, then manuring as a depositional process could be ruled out. It may well represent a 'halo' deriving from the dumping of waste from the nearby living areas. The ancient route to the north is, most likely, the one followed by the modern dirt track along the spur and then down to a ford across the Xyliatos stream to the east, just upstream of its confluence with the Lagoudhera River. Is it possible that potbursts over the years contributed to this assemblage? To the east of this area on the broad stable tread on the other side of the Xyliatos stream, the sherd densities appear to be too low to indicate manuring; they may have been uncultivated in the Roman period due to the effects of industrial pollution.

Looking across the river to the west bank south of the slag heap, between the Rock of Ayios Kyriakos (TP17) and the adits at Ayios Kyriakos (TS10), 26 of the 36 units surveyed have a low density of slag in them, only rarely rising above 2 fragments/100 m^2. The cobble and boulder terrace walls form a series of stepped parallel terraces up the hillside (Moody and Grove 1990, 183; Rackham and Moody 1996, 141). This is most likely due to people moving the silty loam soil from the floodplain up to the terraces for use as a filler. The soils of the floodplain have better tilth than the soils of the backslope and people were most likely trying to increase productivity of their terraces with this loamier soil. In this area it is noticeable that soil colour and texture do not vary much at all from the floodplain, to the top of the terraced region, so again this indicates that once the terraces are cut, people are hauling arable soils from the floodplain up to the terrace treads.

In the same area, 26 of the 36 Survey Units contain Hellenistic–Roman pottery (not the same 26 units as those with slag). The density ranges from 0.3–7.8 sherds/100 m^2, with a mean of 1.2 sherds/100 m^2 and a mode and median both of <1. The mean is greater due to the three highest density Survey Units. These units are all adjacent to each other and directly above the path (TP085) on the lowest tread of fields in the northern part of the surveyed area. Interestingly, the two highest slag densities occur in these fields. While colluvial processes may marginally have been a factor, the proximity of these fields to the path and the fact that they are the closest fields on this tread to the ford in the river, may explain the density spike. Was it an initial dumping area for earth and/or manure, which was then spread around the area? Did the heavier pottery fragments and slag pieces remain in higher densities here as a result of a two-stage depositional process? Was this material brought up the hillside to improve fertility, necessary as a result of possible contamination from the smelting operations downstream? Some of the Roman sherds may also represent activity along the communication route between Mavrovouni and Litharkies.

The density of Medieval–Modern pottery on the west bank is 2.2 sherds/100 m^2, which may result from systematic manuring. Again the density spike of two units with >10 sherds/100 m^2 is coincident with the Hellenistic–Roman material. The pottery evidence suggests that these two fields, with much higher densities, are the result of manure coming from Mavrovouni across the ford and via the path (TP085), to be dumped there prior to spreading across the fields. It is unclear when this practice started. Could it have been in the Roman period? Or was it simply that Roman sherds were mixed in with the Medieval–Modern material when dumping started during the lifetime of the church of Ayios Kyriakos and possibly the village of 'San Chirico' (Chapter 4.9)? During the Roman period manure would have been provided by donkeys kept for transport of ore from Litharkies and charcoal from the forests for the furnaces. In the Medieval–Modern period donkeys would have been used as both pack animals and transport.

In summary, it seems clear that the smelters would have suffered considerable discomfort, not only from the heat of the furnace work, but also the SO_2 and other noxious emissions. Despite the proximity of their living quarters mixing would have considerably diluted the emissions. It is far less clear how much these emissions affected the immediate and surrounding landscape in terms of their viability for cultivation, and we have a mixed picture with some sherd densities too low to suggest manuring, but others that do.

The Wider Support Network

The transects north and east of Mavrovouni contained little or no pottery contemporary with the smelting. The paucity of artefacts and the fluvial, colluvial and anthropogenic processes make it very difficult to interpret any level of activity in this area contemporary with the smelting operations.

The route in and out of Mavrovouni to the north was through the Lagoudhera Valley itself (Plate 4.12). On the east side of the river bed two flat treads allow easy movement up and down the valley. The six Survey Units (SU1690–95) on the east bank of the Lagoudhera, immediately north of its confluence with the Xyliatos River, lie on a Holocene fluvial terrace between the river and the dirt track. At this point the dirt track follows the line of the path from Vyzakia to Kannavia on the cadastral map, and is the most likely route used during the Roman period to connect with the wider transport network (Graham *et al.* 2006, 359–60). The tread adjacent to the dirt track has high quantities of slag on it, though this is probably the result of transporting from the slag heap for road metalling (see

Volume 1, Chapter 3.9). Next to these Survey Units is a series of rocks, in an approximately straight line, looking like a terrace wall (TP123). One of them has a rounded depression and was probably a door socket.

The modern dirt track leading north from Mavrovouni runs directly to the east of the two treads to Athassi, 800 m north of the slag heap. Here a gully cuts through the treads from the hills to the east, allowing only a narrow passage through the valley. Just north of this point we surveyed 12 units on both sides of the river (SU1699–1710). As well as Medieval–Modern material (Chapter 4.7), they produced several tiny fragments from Historical Antiquity and the Roman period. The density of Historical Antiquity material for 11 of them is less than 1 sherd/100 m^2; the 12th unit, however, lying directly below the dirt track on the east bank (SU1710), has a density of 10.2 sherds/100 m^2. This may represent pot bursts from the transport route to and from Mavrovouni. The Hellenistic–Roman sherd density is c. 0.6 sherds/100 m^2 over the whole area, with a ± 6% variance between the east and west banks of the river. This broad but very low-density deposition may well be a result of manuring and show some agricultural production contemporary with the smelting.

One model suggested for sustaining mining settlements in the Bronze Age is the agricultural support settlement (Keswani 1993). This model has also been suggested for the Roman period by the Sydney Cyprus Survey Project, with a Roman estate at Politiko *Phorades* located near the copper-rich Kokkinorotsos, as well as the larger ore deposits of Kapedhes and Agrokipia (Knapp *et al.* 2003, 135). TAESP has found clear evidence for a network of Roman farmsteads in the Atsas area, almost certainly linked to the contemporary intensive exploitation of the copper resources at the neighbouring mine of Skouriotissa (Chapter 2.7). This is further demonstrated by the same local amphora and tile fabrics being found in both smelting and agricultural sites (e.g. at Skouriotissa and Pano Limna: Chapter 3.11). Results from transect survey suggest that a similar network of Roman farmsteads was located on the Koutraphas plateau (Chapter 2.15). Lying just north of the Lagoudhera River valley and only about 8 km downstream from Mavrovouni, this area would provide easily accessible supplies for the smelting settlement, and would certainly negate any concerns about the productivity of the land surrounding the smelting operation due to pollution.

Mavrovouni: Conclusions

The broad range of vessels for storing, transporting, cooking and eating at Ayia Marina *Mavrovouni* indicates a settlement to the south of the slag heap, with very little evidence of activity directly north of the smelting area. The proximity to the slag heap implies that Mavrovouni was settled with people processing the ore. Mitsero *Kouloupakhis* provides a good parallel, with its concentration of pottery contemporary with and close to the slag heap (Kassianidou *et al.* 2003, 92).

The tiles remain the only firm contemporary evidence of architecture, but the rock piles and resistivity results strongly suggest Roman structures built from locally sourced river boulders and cobbles. The close proximity of the smelters' housing to the slag heap, perhaps just 100 m, and all the pollution emitted from the furnaces reveal something of the social organisation at Mavrovouni. Such proximity would have provided little respite for the workers. Allowing for the need for space around the furnaces and the desire not to restrict the up-valley breeze, the houses were as close as possible to the slag heap.

Known Late Roman sites in Cyprus are mainly associated with churches, e.g. Ayios Kononas in the Akamas peninsula (Fejfer and Mathiesen 1995) and Kalavasos *Kopetra* in southern Cyprus (Rautman *et al.* 2003). At Kopetra, however, as well as churches, there is evidence of architecture, agricultural production, metalworking and smelting. Although the majority of the enormous number of transport amphorae found at Kopetra came from Cyprus, this still indicates a much higher level of direct integration into the outside world than is apparent at Mavrovouni. The same can be argued for Ayios Kononas. Neither Ayios Kononas nor Kopetra were located directly by the sea, and the contact with the outside world is a deliberate organisational choice. Kopetra may be associated with the copper extraction at Kalavasos *Spilios* and Petra further up the valley (Rautman *et al.* 2003, 16).

Mavrovouni is associated with a similar resource, but the character of the ceramic assemblage and the absence of luxury items seem to suggest that production was controlled from the outside, and that any surplus from this production had no immediate impact on the local area. There is no archaeological evidence to provide a firm indication that agricultural production was taking place, though it cannot be ruled out. What seems more likely is that the agriculture took place on the Plains, for example in our Koutraphas Intensive Survey Zone (Chapter 2.15), with a direct route through the Lagoudhera Valley for bringing in food and transporting the matte for further refinement, use and export.

4.7 Medieval–Ottoman Rural Estate at Xyliatos *Athassi*

An isolated rural estate at Athassi (Fig. 4.31), 800 m north of Mavrovouni, which was abandoned some time before 1825, is mentioned as a taxable settlement from 1440 to 1565 (Grivaud 1998, 200). In 1461 it was part of the royal estate, and along with the nearby villages of Vyzakia and Cafcalo (now Ayios Yeoryios Kafkallou) was given by James the Bastard to his Sicilian henchman Nicolas Morabit, in thanks for his support in the campaign against James' half-sister, Queen Charlotte (de Lusignan 2001, 93, para. 403; Boustronios 1489, 27–28, para. 74; de Mas Latrie 1852–61, II, 251). It appears in three Venetian village lists in the mid-16th century, and in 1565 the estate had five *francomati* (free peasant farmers) (Grivaud 1998, 468).

The ruined estate house (TP014) has four rooms and evidence of a second storey, which is not preserved (Fig. 4.32; Fig. 4.34). The lower floor of the main building is constructed with basalt boulders and small rubble fill. The second storey consists of fired bricks to a height of approximately 19 courses, topped by mudbrick with fired brick corners. Two rooms abut the main structure, sharing its south wall. They are made of mudbrick on a basalt boulder base. The room to the north of the main structure also shares a wall with the main house, while its other three walls are constructed of mudbrick: the house is fronted by a terrace on its west.

A threshing floor (TP015) is built directly on bedrock and into the terracing c. 25 m above and east of the estate house (Fig. 4.34). It measures c. 7 m north–south and 4.5 m east–west. The surface is made up of large, flat paving stones not indigenous to the area, with some scratches on the stones from the *dhoukani* teeth. The centre of the floor is in good condition, but the north and western edges are eroding down into the terrace. It lies on the south edge of a gully and so is exposed to the wind for winnowing. This is clearly associated with the estate's production of grain. No lithics were recovered from here, which is in keeping with evidence elsewhere in the Survey Area that threshing sledges were not stored, and only occasionally repaired, at threshing floors.

We were able to survey seven units on stable treads directly above the river on the east side of the valley, just below and north of the estate house (SU1699–1704, SU1710), and another five on a series of stable terraces on the west side of the river, which had been mechanically modified at some point since 1963 (SU1705–1709). These units had a low, but continuous, density of Medieval–Modern pottery ranging from 0.5 to 4.0 sherds/100 m^2. The ground visibility of the treads immediately between the house and the river and further south was too low for them to be surveyed.

Taking all these Survey Units together, the Athassi area only yielded three fragments of Medieval Table Ware: a piece of Cypriot Incised Sgraffito Ware (from Paphos?) of the Byzantine-Medieval period (early 13th century?); a sherd of Monochrome Painted Ware of the Medieval-Frankish period (c. 14th–15th centuries); and a fragment of Cypriot Green Painted Ware from Lapithos of the Medieval-Venetian to Early Modern periods (c. 16th century or later). A handful of more recent sherds included Polychrome Painted Ware from Grottaglie in southern Italy and/or its imitation from Corfu (19th century or later), and fragments of Slip-painted Ware in yellow from Didymoteicho in northern Greece and/or from Çanakkale in western Turkey (c. late 19th–early 20th centuries) (Vroom 2005, 184–87).

Fig. 4.31. Xyliatos Athassi *(TP014), looking south (Chris Parks)*

A gully 200 m to the north-east of the estate house at Athassi has a series of three, possibly four, check dams, with terraced foothills on each side (TP009; Table 4.2). The walls join up basalt dykes on either side of the gully, but do not have the same vegetation as the dykes. The flat arable land built up behind the dams was sown with barley and almond trees. These and another series in the next gully to the east, as well as the terraced foothills with their stack retaining walls to the north of the estate house, may well have been part of the estate. Four Survey Units cross this terraced area (SU0600–0603). Only seven sherds were counted in these Survey Units. These included a Medieval-Frankish (14th–15th centuries) piece of Monochrome Painted Table Ware (MP04), and one Late Roman Table Ware fragment (CRS02). The remaining material could only be dated to the broad Archaic–Modern period. The area to the east and south-east (upslope) of the estate house is currently an almond grove; no pottery was recorded in these Survey Units to throw light on the life of the Athassi estate. Poor ground visibility (10–30%) and colluvial processes due to the steepness of the slope (17–25°), very likely contributed to this lack of material.

Across the valley and 240 m to the south-west is a two-roomed rectangular structure built into a riser, incorporating bedrock in the rear north-west corner of the larger room (TP045). It is built on unmaintained anthropogenic terraces. The walls are informally coursed, and are built of angular basalt and river boulders. Angular basalt, limestone, river pebbles and cobbles, tile and pottery are used as chinking. Flat stone, possibly used as a support course for a mud roof, caps the rear wall of the larger room, though a corrugated iron roof now covers the northern third of this larger room. There are three niches on the east wall and two on the west wall of the larger room. The west and south walls of the smaller room are in ruins, but the east wall is better preserved and has a small window in it. The larger room is possibly a living space while smaller room may have housed animals. This structure is unlikely to be part of the Athassi estate. It may well be representative of the investment in rural areas in the 1920s and 1930s, which resulted in series of substantial field houses spaced along the deeply incised valleys of the northern Troodos (Given 2000, 225). Because of very poor ground visibility the area around this house was not surveyed.

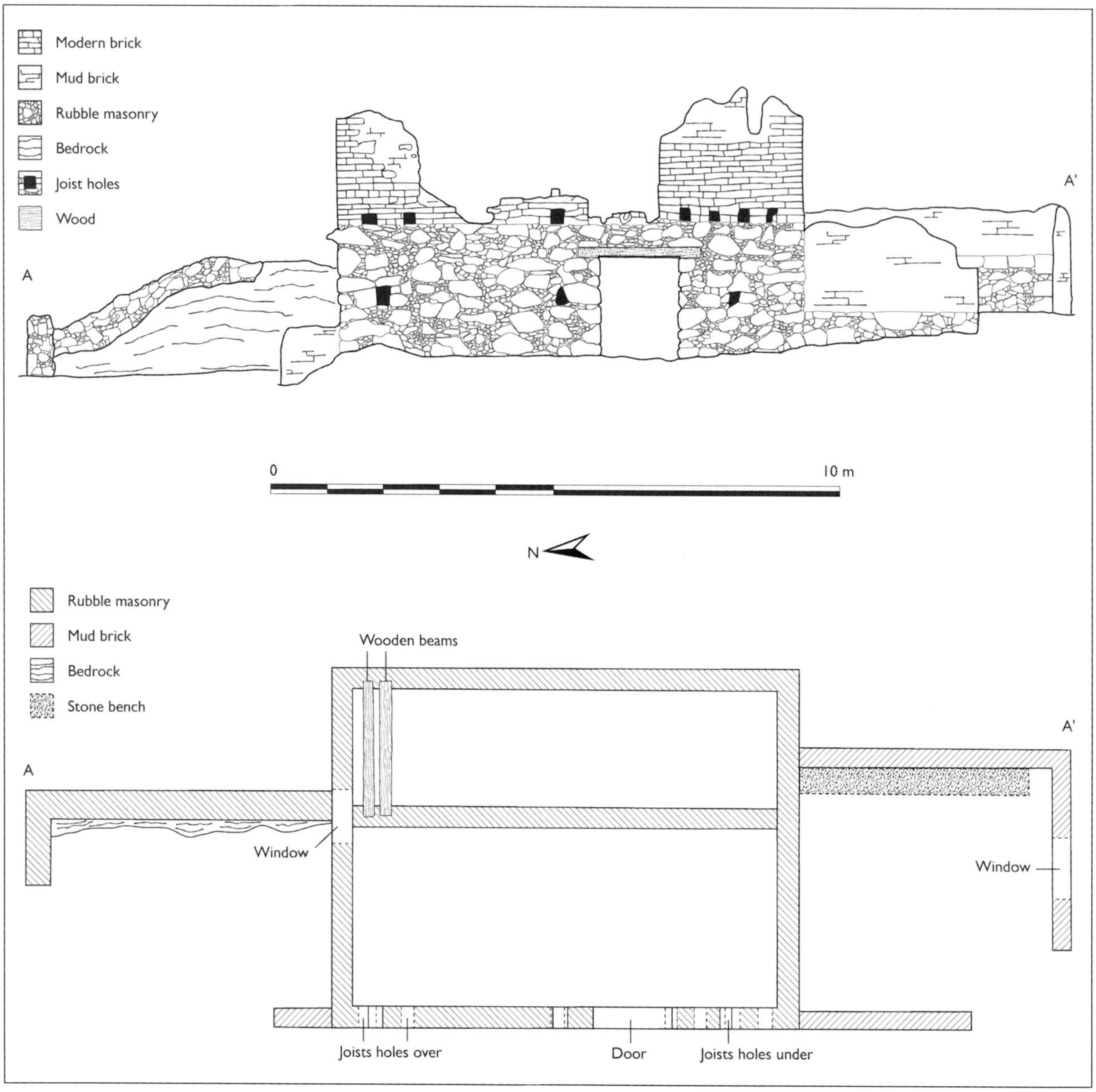

Modern brick
Mud brick
Rubble masonry
Bedrock
Joist holes
Wood
A
A'
0
10 m
N
Rubble masonry
Mud brick
Bedrock
Stone bench
Wooden beams
A
A'
Window
Window
Joists holes over
Door
Joists holes under

Fig. 4.32. Xyliatos Athassi *(TP014): plan and elevation of estate house (Cara McAllister, Lyndsay McGill and Chris Timmer)*

Fig. 4.33. Xyliatos Athassi*: estate house (TP014): west front (Chris Parks)*

4.8 Roman Copper Mining and Processing

The Litharkies-Mavrovouni mining and smelting operation is very small in scale compared to the enormous operations at Skouriotissa. At 10,000 tons the surviving Mavrovouni slag heap is a mere 0.5% of that at Skouriotissa. There is, however, a great deal of extant material culture (Plate 4.13) that provides important insights into the organisation of this key industry in the Roman period.

In the Early Roman period we have considerable evidence of life at Litharkies, including architecture and food preparation, cooking, eating and storing, and also death, with a tomb located between the probable site of the miners' settlement and their place of toil on the slopes of Alestos. The ceramic evidence from Litharkies

Fig. 4.34. Xyliatos Athassi*: estate house (TP014), with threshing floor (TP015) in the foreground, and another structure (TP045) on the far side of the valley with bulldozed terraces behind it (Michael Given)*

Table 4.21. Xyliatos Athassi *(TP015), and surrounding area, Medieval–Modern pottery (SU0600–0603, SU1699–1710). TCP numbers refer to Pottery Catalogue in Volume 1, Chapter 3.6*

Cypro-Geometric to Classical

Fct	*Type*	*No.*	*Weight*
LU	BS	2	2g

Historical Antiquity (Archaic to Late Roman)

Fct	*Type*	*No.*	*Weight*
HU	HU	13	68g
LU	LU	8	32g
TW	TW	2	5g

Hellenistic to Roman

Fct	*Type*	*No.*	*Weight*
TW	SRS	7	27g
TW	TW	4	12g

Early to Late Roman

Fct	*Type*	*No.*	*Weight*
CW	CW	7	34g

Late **Roman**

Fct	*Type*	*No.*	*Weight*
TW	CRS02	1	25g

Historical (Archaic to Modern)

Fct	*Type*	*No.*	*Weight*
CW	CW	3	12g
HU	HU	21	566g
LU	LU	141	402g

Medieval to Modern

Fct	*Type*	*No.*	*Weight*
CW	BGW	4	20g
HU	HU	9	261g
LU	LU	4	33g

Byzantine to Medieval

Fct	*Type*	*No.*	*Weight*
TW	CGS03	1	9g TCP274

Medieval-Frankish

Fct	*Type*	*No.*	*Weight*
TW	MP04	1	15g

Ottoman to Modern I

Fct	*Type*	*No.*	*Weight*
TW	BGW	1	2g
TW	G05	1	4g

Medieval-Venetian to Early Ottoman

Fct	*Type*	*No.*	*Weight*
TW	CGS06	1	5g

Ottoman to Modern II

Fct	*Type*	*No.*	*Weight*
HU	BuH	6	107g
LU	BuL	2	38g
TW	PP02	2	65g
TW	SP02	1	5g

Modern

Fct	*Type*	*No.*	*Weight*
HU	HU	6	220g
LU	LU	4	54g
TW	MP	3	85g
TW	MP01	1	20g
TW	Por	7	70g

Unknown

Fct	*Type*	*No.*	*Weight*
LU	LU	2	6g

and Mavrovouni appears to shed light on a key aspect of organisation with regard to the mining and smelting operations. At Litharkies there seems to have been greater activity in the Early Roman period, whereas Ayia Marina *Mavrovouni* appears to have been most active during the Late Roman period. This suggests that Litharkies may have housed the Mavrovouni smelters in the Early Roman period, and that Mavrovouni may have housed the Litharkies miners in the Late Roman period.

A large workforce of relatively low status is suggested by high ratios of Cooking Wares to Table Wares at both sites. Furthermore, the low ratio of slipped Table Wares may indicate that a larger proportion of food was eaten off Light Utility vessels. It is possible that the lowest status workers, criminals or perhaps slaves may have been used to carry out the repetitive, unskilled and dangerous work of the mining and smelting operation and eaten off what we term Light Utility wares.

The main site for ore extraction was clearly Alestos; however, some mining and exploration took place much nearer to Mavrovouni on the slopes of Memi. The surviving adits on Alestos provide evidence of exploratory cuts, as well as adits with working platforms constructed at their entrances to facilitate the work. The water-filled adit (TP112) is a clear reminder of the crucial unskilled activity of bailing out the adits and shafts (see Chapter 3.12). The size of the fragments in the spoil heaps of two adits would suggest that once the ore was brought to the surface it was crushed at the adit before being transported downslope. Ground stone found at Xyliatos *Litharkies* also suggests that some initial processing of the ore may have taken place at the settlement before shipment to Mavrovouni for further processing and smelting. We can clearly see segments of the well-trodden paths (TP086, TP099 and TP223) between the two centres of activity: with their stone-armoured features they reveal the investment made in the communication infrastructure (see Volume 1, Chapter 3.13). Two outcrops of rock would have been ideal locations for monitoring the traffic between Litharkies and Mavrovouni, though this suggestion is based upon other contemporaneous infrastructure and textual sources and not material culture at either outcrop.

Given the heat of the furnace and the poisonous emissions smelting chalcopyrite was an unpleasant business. Mavrovouni, like Litharkies, would have been made up of a mixture of free skilled workers and convicts or, perhaps, unskilled slave workers. The unskilled were most likely employed to drive the bellows, carry the slag and even crush it; there is evidence that in the Roman period significant effort was dedicated to crushing the slag to very small sizes (Kassianidou 2003b, 223). Specialized metallurgists would also have been working in the smelting workshops, overseeing the operation and making decisions regarding the charges of the furnaces and the quality of the product. Finally, administrators would have been in charge of running the operation, procuring the necessary supplies for the workforce and shipping the product to its destination.

Anthracological studies of the charcoal samples from sections of the slag heap clearly show *Pinus brutia* was the preferred species for fuel at Mavrovouni. Neil Urwin (Volume 1, Chapter 4.8) argues in the case of Skouriotissa that when timber resources were being exploited close to the smelting site, the timber may have been transported to a central charcoal-making facility at the smelting site. When the timber exploitation became more distant the wood may have been sent to a charcoal-making facility in the area before being shipped as charcoal to the smelting operation. Without any obvious haulage routes in the Lagoudhera Valley above Mavrovouni and given the small-scale nature of the operation, it seems more likely that charcoal would have been transported by donkey down the Lagoudhera Valley and perhaps also through the network at Litharkies.

Skouriotissa appears to have been controlled by an imperial administrator in the Early Roman period (Galen, *De Temp. Fac. Simp. Med.* 9; see Wallace and Orphanides 1990, 223), and a contemporary inscription records that the procurator employed a local company of contractors from three mining villages to work the Soloi mines (Michaelides 1996, 144; Mitford 1950, 13; 1980, 1298, 1372, n. 177). We cannot be sure, however, where the Litharkies-Mavrovouni operation fits in. Although Mavrovouni was most likely within 10 km of the island-wide Roman road network (Bekker-Nielsen 2004, 173–74) and only about 25 km from Soloi, the few imported amphorae, when compared to Skouriotissa, suggest that both Mavrovouni and Litharkies were somewhat disconnected from the extra-island network (see Volume 1, Chapter 5.3). The relatively small operation and disconnection may suggest that it was leased to a wealthy individual, a common practice (Kassianidou 2000, 751), and was outside direct imperial control.

We have suggested that the smelting operation at Mavrovouni was supported by a supply network of Roman farmsteads on the Mesaoria Plain (Graham *et al.* 2006, 358; see also Volume 1, Chapter 5.3). Although it cannot be firmly ruled out, evidence of agricultural production at Mavrovouni is far from clear. At both Litharkies and Mavrovouni Heavy Utility wares make up the largest group of pottery, suggesting considerable storage. It seems likely that both sites could have been supplied by farmsteads. That said, ceramic evidence in the transects to the east of Mavrovouni and to the north and south of Litharkies suggests that the communities may have used the resources around them, by chopping or coppicing their fuel, and picking and harvesting food to add to the grain brought in from the Plains to the north.

The metal produced at Mavrovouni was transported down the Lagoudhera Valley on the east side of the river. In the Late Roman period it would have connected with the island-wide road network that lay within 10 km and then headed to Soloi (Graham *et al.* 2006, 360; see also Volume 1, Chapter 3.13), presumably for shipment to a regional mint or other consumption site. It might have been a relatively small operation, but it was clearly a profitable one as the operation continued until the early 7th century when there is argued to be a general economic decline on the island, which is clear from the pottery (Lund 1993, 143).

4.9 Medieval–Modern Churches, Settlements, Water and Land Use

The exploitation of this often challenging landscape for agriculture in the Medieval–Modern periods is one of the most striking features of the Lagoudhera Valley Intensive Survey Zone. Evidence includes pottery scatters, ruined and working churches, soil management structures, settlements and structures, and a range of historical records. The aim of this section is to integrate these different types of evidence in order to understand the complex relationships between the landscape and the people who worked and lived in it. Geographically we range beyond the borders of the Lagoudhera Intensive Survey Zone to incorporate evidence from neighbouring villages and from the extensive survey transects carried out by Team X.

Churches, Settlements and Agriculture

The first historical reference to Xyliatos is as a village belonging to the royal estate in the late 15th century (de Mas Latrie 1852–61 III, 505). The name may derive from a settler named Xylias, though the ending implies landed property, perhaps woodland property (Xyliatos 1989). The name then appears in Venetian village lists as a *prastio* or hamlet, with a single *francomato* (free peasant farmer) in 1565 (Grivaud 1998, 468). It is clearly the same as the 'Filato' that appears on 16th-century maps (Stylianou and Stylianou 1980, 257, 273).

Interestingly, these dates fit very well with the group of three olive trees 530 m to the north-west of the village: the two smaller ones were planted in the late 16th century, and the larger one in the late 15th century (Chapter 4.5). The same phenomenon of a small group of olive trees associated with a Late Medieval estate also appears in the Karkotis Valley, for example Agroladou (Chapter 3.3) and Phlasou (Chapter 3.8).

Even though the 1565 census excludes serfs, women and children, Xyliatos is clearly a very small settlement, on a level with nearby Vyzakia (1 *francomato*) and Nikitari (2) (Grivaud 1998, 468–70). Based on numbers of *francomati* only, Ayia Marina 2 km to the north-east was the largest community (10 *francomati*), followed by Ayios Yeoryios Kafkallou (7) and Athassi (5). These low figures are in great contrast to the substantial villages of the plains and the Karkotis Valley, such as Pano Koutraphas (57 *francomati*) and Katydhata (54) (see Volume 1, Chapter 5.4).

Much of the territory round Xyliatos was held by summer transhumants from the village of Chandria, 10 km up the Lagoudhera Valley to the south-west (Xyliatos 1989, 293). This was an exactly parallel system to that of the villagers of Galata and Kyperounda using Mandres (Volume 1, Chapter 5.4; Volume 2, Chapter 2.10; Given 2000, 217–19).

Vyzakia, like Nikitari, sits on west-facing slopes above the Lagoudhera River. With its one *francomato* in 1565 it was clearly a settlement of a similar size to Xyliatos. In this case we know that previously it was a royal estate, given by James the Bastard to Nicolas Morabit in 1461 along with Athassi and Cafcalo (Chapter 4.7). The village's church of the Archangel Michael was built in c. 1500, and still survives with its characterful naïve paintings. The soldiers at the Betrayal of Christ are wearing Venetian swords and helmets, and it is a Venetian nobleman who is spearing Christ's side in the Crucifixion. The Catholic Venetians had been ruling Cyprus since 1489, and it is striking that this Orthodox church gives them such negative roles to play in the Passion of Christ (Stylianou and Stylianou 1985, 110–13).

In the late 15th century the village of Ayia Marina Xyliatou belonged to the royal estate (de Mas Latrie 1852–61, III, 505). It was clearly inherited by the Venetian governor and his Council of Ten, as in 1517 they sold it to the Cypriot nobleman Hector Cadith for 1547 ducats and shared the proceeds (Aristeidou 1994, 390–91). With 10 *francomati* in 1565, it was probably the largest village in the immediate area (Grivaud 1998, 468).

An informant from Xyliatos told us a story of the origins of Ayia Marina. Some Orounda residents found the icon of Ayia Marina south of Xyliatos, and were carrying it back to their village when the donkey that was carrying the icon fell down and would not get up. The Orounda residents put a different burden on the donkey and it was able to continue again, so they saw this as a sign that Ayia Marina wanted her icon to stay there. That was how the village of Ayia Marina came into being.

The pottery distribution map (Plate 4.14) shows a concentration of Medieval pottery at Mavrovouni, with substantial amounts of 14th, 15th and especially 16th-century material. The Medieval-Frankish assemblage has 5 of the 17 chronotypes found in the whole of the Survey Area, and they are all clustered in the south-west corner of Mavrovouni around the remains of the church of Ayios Kyriakos (see Chapter 4.6 above), representing a small settlement and cultivation round it. The Table Wares of the Byzantine to Medieval period include fragments of Slip-painted Ware (c. early 13th century), Cypriot Incised Sgraffito Ware, Brown and Green Sgraffito Ware (from Paphos?), and Monochrome (Pale) Yellow Glazed Ware (c. early 13th century?). Those of the Medieval-Frankish period contain, among others, Cypriot Brown and Green Sgraffito Ware (c. late 14th–15th centuries) and Cypriot Green Sgraffito Ware (late 15th–early 16th centuries). Both these last wares were probably produced in Lapithos.

This settlement may be the same as the 'San Chirico' of the 16th-century Venetian village lists, but the identification seems ambiguous (Grivaud 1998, 204, 470; Papadopoullos 1965). The 16th–17th century sherds (MedVOtt) are spread a little more broadly, with a concentration in the south near the church ruins. This includes a possible turquoise/blue glazed ware tile (G06), as well as some material on the west bank and further north in the area of the spoil heap. The site yielded, for instance, sherds of Table Wares, such as Monochrome Green Painted Ware (c. 16th century or later) and Monochrome Glazed Wares of the 16th–17th centuries (MedVOtt). Finally, it is noteworthy to mention some later pieces of Monochrome Painted Ware from Çanakkale (c. 19th century or later) and of Slip-Painted Ware in a green colour and in a yellow colour from Didymoteicho in northern Greece and/or from Çanakkale in western Turkey (c. late 19th–early 20th centuries) (Vroom 2005, 180–83, 186–87).

Three of the four Venetian village lists, excluding the 1565 census of *francomati*, list 'Alestos' as a *prastio* or hamlet (Grivaud 1998, 199, 468). A single piece of 16th/17th-century green monochrome painted Table Ware (MP01) at Litharkies is not significant enough to confirm this identification. A local informant had told us that a church was located on the east side of the stream at Litharkies on the Appis ridge. A visit to this area revealed considerable bulldozing and no evidence of a church.

More secure is the identification of Athassi in the north of the Upper Lagoudhera Intensive Survey Zone with 'Casal Athasi', first mentioned in 1440 and recorded as having 5 *francomati* in 1565 (Grivaud 1998, 200, 468). The 14th–16th-century material here is very scarce, and the surviving structures and threshing floors clearly date to relatively late in the Ottoman period (Chapter 4.7).

The census and taxation figures for the 1820s and 1830s give rather more detail about the population and economy of the area, which can usefully be compared with the artefact distribution maps (Volume 1, Chapter 5.4; Given and Hadjianastasis 2010, 51–53). The villages round Xyliatos are still clearly very small, as shown by the figures for the Christian poll-tax or *kharaj* (Papadopoullos 1965, 123–24; Sarınay 2000). Xyliatos, Nikitari and Ayia Marina were all purely Greek villages, with 4, 4 and 5 *kharaj*-payers respectively. Vyzakia and Mandres were counted together as a mixed village with 5 *kharaj*-payers, though there were presumably Turkish households as well. The wheat and barley that were extracted as tithes from Ayia Marina and Vyzakia in 1832 were typically between 5 and 10 times lower than what was paid in the larger villages of Pano Koutraphas and Evrykhou.

The Ottoman-period pottery in the Lagoudhera Intensive Survey Zone is clearly highly restricted in its distribution. There is a small and very low-density scatter round Athassi, presumably associated with the estate building, threshing floor and check dams found there (Chapter 4.7). The 13 Ottoman sherds at Litharkies could derive from cultivators based at Ayios Yeoryios Kafkallou, 1.5 km to the north-west, though none of them were found associated with the overgrown terraces. They include Light and Heavy Utility ware and two fragments of Cooking Ware. What is thought to be a collapsed field shelter at Litharkies, measuring 4.0 × 3.8 m and cut into a riser, suggests temporary occupation (TP114).

The distribution of Ottoman-period pottery round Mavrovouni (TS02) shows a low-density carpet of material, rarely rising above 2 sherds/100 m^2, stretching for a good kilometre along the fluvial terraces of the valley floor. The 650-m long strip of fertile fluvial terraces on the east side of the river, which also contains the Roman smelting site and settlement, is remarkable for its elaborate system of stone-clad retaining walls which articulate the different levels of the fluvial terraces. They are presumably Ottoman in date, if not earlier, and have been maintained until the present. The most striking of these is 9 m long and 2.5 m high, at the north tip of the Mavrovouni tread (Fig. 4.35; TP041). This huge wall has a terrace 9 m long and 3.5 wide above it, and appears a considerable investment in such a small space. However, it also serves to prevent erosion through slumping into the confluence between the Lagoudhera and Xyliatos Rivers. There is no evidence for any Ottoman settlement at Mavrovouni, and with the greater nucleation of this period, these fields were presumably cultivated by villagers from Xyliatos, Ayia Marina, or even by wage labourers based at Athassi.

The 1924 cadastral plan of Xyliatos village shows 14 threshing floors and an olive press opposite the church, which shows a significant if small-scale family-based arable economy in the village territory. The low density of material in the river cut valley directly below and to the east of Xyliatos reveals further presence of the Xyliatos villagers in the landscape. The low densities to the north and north-east were presumably due to the cultivators from Ayia Marina or possibly even Athassi.

The village of Ayios Yeoryios Kafkallou lies on a spur overlooking the Kannavia River, overshadowed by the mountain and copper mine of Alestos. To the west are the slopes of the Troodos range and the Adelphi forest. Extensive bulldozing in the area has produced terraces with unprotected risers of up to 3 m in height, which were already showing signs of erosion. In the centre of the village is the church of Ayios Yeoryios, which stands on a high point in the spur. As with Vyzakia and Athassi, the village was given by James the Bastard to Morabit in 1461, under the name 'Cafcallo'. These three settlements lie along the river valley within 4 km of each other.

During the Ottoman and British colonial period, Ayios Yeoryios had a very different trajectory from Vyzakia or Athassi. It does not appear in the 1825 poll-tax register (Papadopoullos 1965, 124–25), the 1832 cereals production register (Papadopoullos 1965, 187–88), or the 1833 property register (Sarınay 2000, 161, 192). By the late 19th century it had a permanent population of just five people (Grivaud 1998, 468). Its main function during the first half of the 20th century and very probably the 19th century was as a seasonal settlement for farmers from the mountain village of Kyperounda to grow cereals (Given 2000, 218). This is reflected in the disproportionate number of threshing floors marked on the 1925 cadastral plan, with 49 serving a handful of houses. In this respect it is very similar to the seasonal settlement of Mandres (Chapter 2.10). Where it differs is in having a much longer history and a church, dedicated to Ayios Yeoryios and rebuilt on a large scale in 1900. The two phenomena are clearly related: the rebuilding of the church marks the memory of long-standing community, rather than the periodic occupation of a seasonal village.

All these threshing floors clearly required substantial production of stone flakes for the threshing sledges. As we discuss in Volume 1, Chapter 3.8, most of these were made of Lefkara chert and imported, though there was also some expedient production for repairs using local jasper and chalcedony. One possible location for this was a jasper

Fig. 4.35. Ayia Marina Kato Kremasha *(TP041): field retaining wall (Chris Parks)*

quarry and workshop at Ayia Marina *Vrysi* (TP096). The substantial sample of 63 artefacts consists of 17 pieces of knapping debris, 13 unworked flake blanks, and flake cores including 4 alternating platform cores, 8 amorphous cores, 12 core fragments, a single splintered piece and two tested cores. All of this demonstrates the significant amount of knapping activity that took place at this site. The comparatively few tools recovered included five utilized flake implements and a single notched flake tool.

The few tools and the simple expedient flake technology are generally consistent with Roman-period production and with the Medieval–Modern *dhoukani* flake industry. An assemblage of Medieval–Modern *dhoukani* flakes would normally include exotic Lefkara cherts, but this clearly does not apply to a quarry and workshop site. In terms of position, Vrysi lies 1.2 km west of Ayia Marina village, 1.0 km east of the estate at Athassi, and 1.6 km north-east of the Roman smelting site of Mavrovouni, and so could have served all equally. Vrysi could have produced flakes for Roman Mavrovouni or for the Medieval–Modern villages and estates of the area; or, of course, for both.

Pastoralism was an important part of the economy and society of this region in the 19th and 20th centuries. Esme Scott-Stevenson, the wife of the first British Commissioner of Kyrenia in the late 1870s, travelled through the valley from Lagoudhera village, through Xyliatos and into the Mavrovouni mining area on the way to Ayia Marina:

> Lavouthera [Lagoudhera], a village set amidst medlars and mulberries, was the first place we passed through; from which, crossing the gorge by one of those old stone bridges with a single arch, so often met in Cyprus, we passed into another ravine, until we came to the village of Scusliliato [Xyliatos], a most quaint little place, each house having its thorn enclosure full of goats with kids, sheep with lambs – in fact, animals of every description with their little ones. From this we passed through a valley remarkable for the strata of coloured rocks which run across it. (Scott-Stevenson 1880, 248)

The western flanks of the hills to the south-west of Vyzakia were thick with shotgun cartridges. Evidence of clay pigeon shooting in the pines and gullied pillow lavas in this area attests to recreational shooting, as well as hunting for birds and ground quarry. There is a general low-density carpet of shotgun cartridges throughout the Upper Lagoudhera Valley. However, the Lagoudhera River valley itself and the southern flank of Alestos are clearly the two focal areas for hunting in these foothills, as they have the highest densities of cartridges. This may in part be due to the ease of access by dirt track from the tarmac roads between Vyzakia and Ayia Marina and from Ayios Yeoryios Kafkallou respectively.

Water Resources

Utilization of water as a resource is evident in wells, irrigation structures, mills, and soil and water conservation structures such as check dams. One striking example is a square well (TP074) at the base of a dry-stack wall in the north-east of the Intensive Survey Zone, 1.1 km north-east of Mavrovouni. Due to the amount of carbonate accumulated in the soil (K2), it is clearly many centuries to a thousand years old. It is built out of local basalt. We measured it on 4 July 2002, when the stream just below it was dry, and it held 2.0 m of water.

Today at Litharkies water for cultivation comes from two wells marked on the cadastral map close to the stream bed (TP195–96). It is delivered to the fruit trees and crops via plastic piping. The water level is only 2.5 m below ground. TP195 is a round to oval-shaped, stone-lined well capped with concrete and a square metal lid, measuring c. 0.85 × 1.0 m. It is in the same cadastral plot that our informant from Xyliatos told us of an ancient well with cedar planks. The upper part of TP196 is square and partly stone-lined with diabase river boulders and partly built in concrete and covered by a metal lid. The lower part of the well is cut into bedrock, at which point the well is round. The well measures 2.45 × 1.8 m. Its owner estimated it to be about 60 years old.

As we have seen, the Lagoudhera River was an important resource in the copper production process during the Roman period, and presumably was a source of potable water for the community centred around the church of Ayios Kyriakos and the Athassi estate. There is also evidence of its use as a source of power for two watermills in the valley between Athassi and Vyzakia (BU0104; BU0109). One of these (BU0104), located on the Madharis River in Vyzakia village, has a surviving millhouse and wheel chamber with a metal turbine 2.74 m in diameter (Fig. 2.23).

This part of the Lagoudhera Valley has clearly been intensively used since at least the 15th century, when a system of feudal estates was already in place. One key activity was cultivation, which in this challenging area needed particularly careful management of soil and water. This was variously accomplished by systems of retaining walls on the well-watered fluvial terraces, check dams on the thin-soiled hillslopes, wells for fields and channels for the seasonal watermills, and most recently by piped irrigation dependent on the 1982–83 Xyliatos Dam. The settlement pattern has developed from a substantial number of small-scale feudal estates such as Xyliatos and Athassi to a greater nucleation of villages, though with more dependence on seasonal settlements such as Ayios Yeoryios Kafkallou and field shelters.

4.10 Conclusion

The Lagoudhera Intensive Survey Zone has revealed human activity at varying intensities and with many different motivations since the Chalcolithic Period. After a brief chronological survey, we address the three most significant aspects of the relationship between the valley and its inhabitants: water, copper and agriculture.

Other than two Chalcolithic sherds and a re-used Chalcolithic stone pestle found near Mavrovouni, there is no material from the prehistoric periods or the Iron Age. The first major development that we have evidence for comes in the Hellenistic and especially the Roman period, with a major mining and smelting operation that extended across much of the valley. Mining adits on Alestos (Chapter 4.3) and at Ayios Kyriakos (4.5) are hard to date, but their morphology and context suggest they are Roman, or even (in the case of Ayios Kyriakos) earlier. The miners in the Alestos adits were extracting chalcopyrites, and were clearly based at the substantial mining settlement of Litharkies lying on the mountain's southern flank.

Judging by its pottery, the settlement of Litharkies dates mainly to the Hellenistic and Early Roman periods (Chapter 4.4). Rock piles, large numbers of tile fragments and geophysical results all suggest the presence of substantial structures, while the pottery shows that food storage, preparation and consumption were all carried out there. Surprisingly low proportions of Table Wares suggest that the workers were of low status, and ate their food from Light Utility vessels. After initial crushing and sorting at the adits on Alestos itself, there might have been a certain amount of further ore processing at Litharkies, before the ore was transported down a series of paths to the valley bottom at Mavrovouni for smelting.

There were originally two slag heaps at Mavrovouni, though one has been removed and the second one greatly reduced (Chapter 4.6). Our recording and sampling from the surviving sections has allowed us to analyse the fuel, flux and technology of the copper production process in the Roman period. Both heaps originally contained some 40,000 tons of slag, requiring perhaps 60,000 tons of charcoal and 660,000 donkey journeys to bring in this charcoal from the forests to the south. Compared to the massive operation at Skouriotissa, this is relatively small-scale. Even so, it is clear that it was sufficient to cause substantial pollution, both of the soil and the air. This may be why we did not find the expected spread of low-density pottery from manuring along the fluvial terraces both north and south of the site. It seems that food had to be brought in from, for example, the agricultural production areas of the Koutraphas plateau down the valley to the north.

In the Medieval period there are several small documented villages such as Xyliatos, which was a royal estate in the 15th century (Chapter 4.9). This fits very well with the date of three 15th–16th-century olive trees we recorded 500 m outside the village. At Mavrovouni a scatter of 14th–16th-century pottery, painted plaster fragments and tile fragments shows the location of the church of Ayios Kyriakos and an associated settlement that may be the San Chirico of the 16th-century Venetian village lists.

Villages such as Xyliatos, Vyzakia and Ayia Marina continued into the Ottoman and Modern periods, though the settlement round Ayios Kyriakos did not. Ayios Yeoryios Kafkallou, with its great numbers of threshing floors, is a seasonal settlement for summer cultivation, similar to Kato Koutraphas *Mandres* on the plains, which is examined in detail in Chapter 2.10. Athassi, which again is recorded in the 15th and 16th centuries, survives today in the form of a large, ruined estate house, with four rooms on the ground floor built of basalt boulders and rubble fill and the remains of a second storey of fired brick (Chapter 4.7). Behind it is a threshing floor, and several of the gullies in the area round it have substantial check dams to provide adequate soil for cultivation. There is an impressive series of terrace walls along the fluvial terraces between Athassi and Mavrovouni, one of them up to 2.5 m high, and the whole area shows a complex network of paths facilitating communication both along the valley and across the ridgelines to neighbouring valleys.

In the 20th century industrial mining and intensive agriculture have greatly altered the landscape of the Upper Lagoudhera Valley, removing and masking earlier activity in the valley. The mine at Alestos produced gold in the 1930s, and then in subsequent decades opencast methods extracted chalcopyrites. The opencast mine of Memi, adjacent to Mavrovouni, produced pyrites. In recent decades agriculture has been greatly intensified by means of irrigation from the Xyliatos Dam, built in the 1980s, and by the bulldozing of artificial step terraces, often with soils composed largely of crushed bedrock and with risers so steep as to be potentially unstable.

Through this long history, the two most intense periods of occupation of the area are during the Roman and Modern periods, with the Roman Empire in pursuit of copper and present day Cypriots on a quest to expand the available cultivable land for vegetables, orchards and the oil from the olive tree. All these pursuits require water.

For the Roman-period miners at Litharkies, drinking water in the cistern may have been supplemented by the collection of water from the Lagoudhera River each time the ore shipment team returned from Mavrovouni, or perhaps more frequent thunderstorms at that period refilled the cistern. The location of the smelting at Mavrovouni was, in part, down to the need for water from the Lagoudhera River, for both metallurgical and domestic purposes.

The construction of dry-stack terrace walls and check dams, some of which are several hundreds, if not a thousand, years old (Given *et al.* 2003c), served to retain water as well as soil on the hillsides and in the gullies so that crops could be grown. Wells many hundreds of years old also reveal the need to access sub-surface water resources. In the Ottoman period water was used as a source of energy, with two mills upstream of Vyzakia. In recent decades irrigation methods have moved from concrete flumes to the black plastic piping we see throughout the Lagoudhera Valley today. Without the Lagoudhera River, the smelting site at Ayia Marina *Mavrovouni* would not have been viable and the cultivated terraces would have been far less productive than they are today.

Our major analytical focus in the Lagoudhera Valley has been the labour of the copper miners and smelters of the Roman period. We see the same desire for the elemental resources of the Troodos foothills reflected in the very visible remains of 20th-century mining at Alestos and Memi. The Upper Lagoudhera Valley has by far the most intensive occupation and human activity of the whole of the Survey Area, at least in terms of archaeological survey, containing 25 (81%) of the 31 densest Survey Units (i.e. those with Roman pottery above 10 sherds/100 m^2). All of these Survey Units are from the mining settlement of Litharkies and the smelting settlement at Mavrovouni.

Even if this copper production was a relatively small-scale operation, it was certainly a long-lived one, with evidence from both Mavrovouni and Litharkies from the Hellenistic period to the 7th century AD. The demand for copper clearly made it a profitable one. All the activity in the area during this period would have been associated with the production of copper: exploration, extraction, crushing ore, transporting ore, coppicing, harvesting, felling of timber, production of charcoal, transport of charcoal, delivery of flux, building and cleaning of furnaces, cultivation, smelting, transporting matte, collection and production of stone tools, building of paths and houses, delivery of foodstuffs, collection of water, etc. We can still see fragments of the communication network between the centres of activity, Mavrovouni and Litharkies, and the people in the hills and valleys surrounding the operation from our transect survey of the area.

Since that industrial episode in the social history of the Lagoudhera Valley, we have 1200 years where the focus became agriculture. Documentary sources provide glimpses of land ownership over the last 500 years, which we can tie into the archaeology recorded at the Athassi estate, the church at Mavrovouni and the extant villages in the area. Surviving olive trees and the terraces and check dams also attest to the cultivation of the area. In the 20th century the cultivation of the land continued, while the quest for mineral resources returned to Memi and Alestos. In the 21st century Memi lies quiet, but Alestos continues for the time being. The major activity in the area is the transformation of the hillslopes into wide terraces for future cultivation. As we surveyed, this mechanized process was transforming the landscape in an attempt to increase the area of cultivable land: a result of pressures elsewhere on the island from the increasing tourist industry.

The survey of the Lagoudhera Valley Intensive Survey Zone has provided a wealth of data with which to understand both the human activity that has shaped the landscape, and the natural landscape that has attracted people to exploit what it has to offer.

5. The Mountains

Edited by Erin Gibson

with contributions by Iain Banks (geophysics), Stephen Digney (team leader, Team X), Ian Evans (architecture), Sevina Floridou (architecture), Ruth Smadar Gabrieli (pottery), Erin Gibson (team leader), Michael Given (historical periods), Marios Hadjianastasis (oral history), Tracy Ireland (historical archaeology), Carole McCartney (lithics), Jay Noller (geomorphology), Colin Robins (geomorphology), Charlotte Schriwer (architecture), Luke Sollars (mountain settlements), Neil Urwin (botany), Joanita Vroom (pottery) and Kristina Winther-Jacobsen (pottery)

5.1 Introduction

We intentionally incorporated the survey of mountains into our research design in order to challenge previous assumptions concerning the presence of human activity in 'isolated' landscapes. Three main types of survey took place in the mountains: systematic intensive survey in the Asinou Valley Intensive Survey Zone; systematic extensive survey; and purposive survey that drew upon the rich oral history of the region. We also carried out more detailed investigation of structural remains, including the mapping and surveying of Places of Special Interest located using both purposive and intensive survey methods. Surveying this challenging mountain environment tested our traditional survey methods, definitions of human activity, and the material remains involved. Unlike any previous survey, TAESP has produced new interpretations of the northern foothills of the Troodos Mountains that revolutionise our perceptions of 'isolation' in the mountains (Table 5.1).

The Asinou Valley Intensive Survey Zone is located in the northern foothills of the Troodos Mountains within the boundary of the Adelphi State Forest. Summits along the valley margins range from 550 m in the north-east to 900 m in the south-west, while the Intensive Survey Zone covers a range of elevations from 350 to 600 m (Plate 5.1). The Asinou and Argaki ton Rotson Rivers bisect the Intensive Survey Zone and provide a year-round water supply to the valley and its past inhabitants. The mountainous forest landscape of the Asinou Valley Intensive Survey Zone is unique amongst those areas investigated by TAESP. Its distinctive landscape and environment made it possible to address a range of research questions previously unexplored in Cypriot survey archaeology.

While abandoned villages and churches were known to exist along the alluvial terraces of the Asinou River (Grivaud 1998, 200), few people ever explored the mountains of the Adelphi Forest with the aim of identifying the material remains of past human activity. TAESP aimed to challenge the view of mountain landscapes as being empty of material culture and settlement (see Given 2007) by employing intensive survey methodologies. The most prominent architectural feature of the Asinou River Valley is the church of Panayia Phorviotissa at Asinou, which dates to the beginning of the 12th century AD (Gibraltar *et al.* 1933; Stylianou and Stylianou 1985, 114). One goal of the survey was to put this popular and well-documented church into its archaeological and landscape context. Another was to investigate the colonial forestry policy that was first established in the late 19th century, and the effect it had on the people who used the valley (cf. Given 2002).

Collecting material culture, land use and settlement data produced a picture of the mountains that reflects the diversity of the landscape, while highlighting the limitations of pottery-based survey methodologies. Understanding the landscape required looking beyond pottery distributions to the less archaeologically visible

Table 5.1. The Asinou Valley: chronological summary

Period	Activity	Name/ID number	Chapter
Hellenistic–Roman	Late Roman multi-room structures	Trimitheri, Khalospita	5.4
	Roman pottery scatter	Lower Asinou Valley	5.4
Byzantine–Modern	Byz–Mod church, Byz–Ott monastery	Panayia Phorviotissa, Asinou	5.5
	Med–Ott settlement, church & paths	Vouni	5.3
	Med–Ott settlement & church	Khalospities	5.5
	Ott–Mod village & threshing floors	Asinou	5.5
	Ott–Mod settlements & church	Mandres tous Jerenides, Mutallia, Ayios Yeoryios	5.5
	Ott–Mod settlement & threshing floors	Karterouni	5.8
	Med–Ott settlement & churches	Aspri, Ayia Paraskevi	5.9
	Rural structures in foothills	Pano Atsa, Palloura	5.3
	Rural structures in mountains	Trimitheri, Laxia tou Laona, Khalospita	5.4
	Water mill	TP0054	5.8
	Paths	TP097, TP228, TP230	5.6
	Terraces & check dams	TP198, TP229–31, Stavros	5.7
	Resin tapping & pitch kilns	TP049, TP214, Palaeomandres	5.7
	Forest boundaries and cairns	TP062, TP068	5.8

remains of resource extraction, seasonal settlement and communication within the valley.

The Asinou Valley Intensive Survey Zone was surveyed from 2001–2003. During this time two major factors influenced the recovery of archaeological surface material in the mountains: pine needles and steep slopes. In many instances pine needles obscured the visibility of the ground surface, thus limiting the likelihood that field survey would recover surface artefacts. In 2001 we carried out several trials to address the limitations of pine needle cover. The first of these was the largely unsuccessful raking of 1-m diameter circles, positioned 40 m to the east or west of the transect line. In a second attempt circles were brought within the Survey Units following the transect line. Similar raking of these carefully laid out circles every 10 m proved less logistically challenging in terms of people needed, but was still very time consuming.

The final method proved to be less time consuming and logistically challenging than either of the above, and thus feasible within the constraints of a field season. It involved all five fieldwalkers raking an area of approximately 1 m in diameter, every 10 m within Survey Units, if more than 20% of the ground surface was obscured by pine needles. Whether or not the Survey Unit was raked was documented on the Survey Unit sheet. Interestingly, despite the amount of effort used to address the possible bias raised by pine needle cover, during the three seasons of survey in the mountains only one pottery sherd was ever recovered from a raked circle.

Steep slopes also limited the ability and feasibility of surveying some parts of the mountain landscape. Not only did slope affect the distribution of archaeological remains, as it did throughout the TAESP landscape, but steep slopes and the physically demanding mountain landscape influenced our ability to locate material remains of past human activity. This is nicely illustrated in an excerpt from the field notebook for the first day of surveying in the mountains:

- Day 5, 2003
- Using circle method
- Visibility poor 20–30% covered in pine needles, small shrubs and scary looking spiders.
- Finding it difficult to concentrate on finding pottery when trying to avoid plummeting off mountain.
- No pottery found; 4 shotgun cartridges.

The experience gained by the teams throughout the course of each season did not influence the quality of the results, but certainly affected the comfort in which they were collected. While on Day 5 fieldwalkers were concerned about plummeting off the mountainside, one week later they were actively climbing those same mountains, raking with ease and locating evidence for resource extraction.

This chapter draws upon the topographic and environmental variation expressed within the mountain landscape. The sections that follow are organized according to a variety of themes: settlement in the Adelphi foothills; settlement continuity from the Roman to Modern periods; Medieval to Modern settlement intensification; communication routes and interaction; land use; boundaries, shifting settlement and climate change; and mountain settlement and continuity. These themes are designed to explore the complexity of the mountain environment and mountain economy. This chapter includes intensive data from transect and block survey within the Asinou Valley Intensive Survey Zone and extensive survey data from POSIs within the mountains but outside the Intensive Survey Zone. The foothills zone divides the plains and the mountainous environment defined by the Adelphi State Forest. Although the foothills zone is included within this chapter, this distinct environmental and topographic zone is linked with both the plains to the north and the mountains to the south through communication routes and extraction activities (see also Volume 1, Chapter 3.13).

5.2 Environmental Setting and Geomorphology

More than half of the TAESP Survey Area is located in the foothills, mountains and intermontane valleys of the Troodos Mountains. The Asinou Valley Intensive Survey Zone encompasses 5% of the mountain area, from the base of the foothills near the 400-m contour line, which skirts the northern boundary of the Adelphi State Forest and separates forest from the agricultural plains to the north, to a peak elevation of 1000 m. This intriguing zone of activity is presently composed of pine-dominated Mediterranean open forest, having varied between woody plants during temperate climate periods and shrubby plants during arid and glacial conditions.

Valleys of the northern Troodos Mountains are V-shaped, incised through the highly fractured intrusive and extrusive volcanic rocks of the Troodos Ophiolite. Intracontinental rifting initiated uplift of the ophiolite during the Late Triassic period (Gass 1975; Robertson and Woodcock 1979). With time, channel incision and erosion produced a concentric outcrop pattern in which the oldest lithologic units of the ophiolite sequence are the most central (Gass 1975). Laterally alternating dyke swarms and pillow lavas – the Upper Cretaceous Sheeted (Diabase) Dyke formation and the Basal Group basalts, respectively – characterize substrata in most of the Asinou Valley Intensive Survey Zone (Geological 1995).

Owing to tectonic uplift of the Troodos, the rivers responded by cutting deep, steep-sided river valleys. As a result, the most characteristic landforms of bedrock in the Asinou Valley are either long linear spurs with narrow ridges and steep, contiguous side slopes, or conical hills with pyramid-shaped slopes (Plate 5.2). All landforms are marked to varying degrees by sheet, rill and gully incision, and hillslopes may contain vegetated or bare shallow colluvial hollows, or deep, rocky gullies. Hillslope gradients generally range from 0–10° along valley bottoms, and from 0–40° along ridgelines and hillslopes.

Along the length and breadth of hillslopes, upland soils vary in character and depth related to the dynamic equilibrium between soil production and soil erosion (Robins 2005). Two general classes of upland soils are recognized: residual and colluvial. Residual soils form fully in situ from the rock (residuum) and display mineralogical and textural differences caused by lateral variations among igneous bodies. Residual soils vary greatly in rock colour, texture, and hydrology; variations are apparent within even small outcrops and road-cuts. Where residual soils are transported by creep, raindrop-splash, and/or sheet erosion, they accumulate in thin (<25–50 cm) layers of gravelly colluvium, which mantle the landscape between ridge shoulders and the narrow deposits of alluvium along valley bottoms. Colluvial soils either show only weakly developed horizons, or else lack distinct horizons entirely. Compared to residual soils, colluvial soils have more muted colour and textural variations.

Owing principally to the nature of needle and branch fall from the pine forest, both types of upland soils have substantial accumulations of organic matter. Thick (5–10 cm) surface organic soil horizons (also called mor) are typically comprised of mosses, lichens, mycorrhizal fungi and decomposing plant matter. Decomposed organic matter (DOM) accumulates in the uppermost soil horizon (up to 2.5% by weight) below the forest-floor layer of pine needles and plant detritus. This amount is in stark contrast to the <0.2% by weight DOM at 30–50 cm depth in the lower horizons. The DOM is available for nutrient uptake by plants. As this layer is only 10–15 cm deep, the health of this ecosystem is vulnerable should the inputs of organic matter cease, as occurs with tree harvesting and forest fire. Further, the mantle of needles prevents the erosive actions of two of the key agents of downslope soil movement – raindrop-splash and sheet erosion.

It is evident from the gravely nature of these silty loam and silty clay loam soils that mass creep of colluvial soils entrains the coarse fragments from upper layers of fractured bedrock. The curved trunks of many modern trees further suggest gradual but persistent soil creep. Talus slopes and rocky gullies are common on especially steep slope faces. Ridge summits are typically rocky with their fine sediments probably removed by raindrop impact, runoff, wind, and mass creep. Isolated boulders and exposed bedrock blocks are common on ridge summits within the survey zone, and often show weathering rinds and lichen assemblages. These features are indicative of long periods of in situ weathering and therefore suggest landscape stability. Hilltops may constitute stable surfaces for coarse boulders and bedrock blocks, while finer materials achieve stability only on foot slope or toe slope terrain. Natural hillslopes of the Asinou Valley, therefore, are dynamic landforms that may experience both gradual soil creep and episodic, sudden rock or debris flows.

Intermontane valleys, such as that of Asinou, are developed at confluences of mountain rivers over generally weaker bedrock of the Basal Group formation. The valley has a prominent Pleistocene catastrophic landslide deposit composed of large, brecciated bedrock debris. This landslide represents (late?) Pleistocene (c. 125,000–10,000 BP) collapse of a mountain top bordering the southern Asinou Valley. The landslide was reworked by streams and the Asinou River, leaving fluvial deposits of coarse cobbles and boulders in a sandy matrix. Since the catastrophe, the Asinou River has been in a general state of incision.

The Asinou Valley Intensive Survey Zone is unique because it focuses on rugged terrain with steep slopes, variable soil thickness and other artefact contexts, and significant gradients in climate and vegetation. A still commonly held theory claims that Cyprus was once widely covered by forests, maquis, or scrub woodland, but that it declined into progressively sparser assemblages of grasses and dwarf woody colonizers under persistent, heavy grazing and other unsustainable land use practices (Thirgood 1987). Such changes in the amount and rate of organic matter additions to the soil would have had a negative feedback on soil health and accelerated the supply of soil and sediment from hillslopes to rivers. One of the aims of this chapter is to examine the intervention of humans in this progression of rock, to soil, to river, which was set into motion long, long before the island was first inhabited.

5.3 Settlement in the Adelphi Foothills

The Adelphi foothills are a transitional zone, or ecotone, between the Adelphi forest and the fertile agricultural plains of Kato Koutraphas *Mandres* (Volume 1, Chapter 4.1). This physical location at an ecotone ensures access to resources from the plains, such as cereal crops, while also enabling exploitation of forest resources, such as timber, fuel, resin, game animals and wild plants, for medicine and food. All pre-industrial rural communities, of course, need land for foraging and pasture just as much as they need formal arable land (Forbes 1997). The environment of the foothills is an area with a distinct set of resources, but it also optimizes this relationship by serving as the 'best of both worlds' in terms of resource base, where cereal cultivation, although limited, is possible alongside scattered areas of open forest.

Settlement within the foothills reflects this diverse environment. Located at the current boundary between privately owned land and state forest, the abandoned settlement of Nikitari *Vouni* and the isolated multi-roomed structures of Ayios Theodoros *Pano Atsa* and Ayios Theodoros *Palloura* were investigated in order to better understand settlement and interaction in this zone of transition.

Medieval/Ottoman settlement of Nikitari Vouni (TP031)

The abandoned settlement of Vouni ('hill') lies 2 km south-west of Nikitari village, at an elevation of 420 m. It sits in the saddle of a spur extending from the northern flank of Moutti tou Dhia in the Troodos foothills. Located on bedrock of pillow basalt, the shallow residual soils directly around the settlement are subject to a certain amount of movement through colluvial processes. These processes may have moved artefacts, but not far enough to lose contextual information.

This foothill settlement, like Ayios Theodoros *Pano Atsa* and Ayios Theodoros *Palloura* to the west, is ideally situated for the exploitation of resources from both the plains and the forest, while the immediate environment is able to support a rich variety of resources. There is terracing on the hillslope to the south of the village, and large olive trees and hawthorns on the spur to the north. The settlement now consists of at least 10 ruined structures, including the church of Ayios Georgios, though none of the walls stand more than two courses above current ground level (Fig. 5.1). The main cluster of these structural remains is obscured by rubble upturned by the bulldozing of a rough modern road to its east.

The surviving structures appear to have consisted of rectangular rooms clustered in L-shaped or linear arrangements. Levelled areas exist outside and downslope from the structures, as flat living and working surfaces around the dwellings. Two poorly built structures (PU01 and PU08) were clearly built of stone robbed from two other structures: L-shaped PU02–PU06 and rectangular-shaped PU07 respectively. This re-use suggests at least two phases of building at the site.

There are two significant structural outliers at Vouni. West of the road and downslope from the main cluster is a clearly defined two-room rectangular structure (PU09/PU10). It is better preserved than those nearer the road and has several lengths of clear wall face. East of the road and above the settlement to the south lies the church of Ayios Georgios (Fig. 5.2; just south of the area shown in Fig. 5.1). This has recently been cleaned and partially renovated by local villagers. They have erected a cross and rudimentary altar of concrete blocks, leaving three to four courses of stonework visible.

We used 2-m diameter gridded circles (see Volume 1, Chapter 2.3) to survey the abandoned village, and recovered both pottery and lithics. The pottery recovered belonged to four main groupings: Heavy Utility; Light Utility; Table Ware; and Cooking Ware, including two fragments of a *tianistra* or frying pan.

The Medieval–Modern period is well represented at Vouni (Table 5.2). The majority of pottery recovered was Medieval–Modern period, Light Utility or Heavy Utility ware. The scarcity of Table and Cooking Ware suggests that they are either often indistinguishable in their fragmented form from Light Utility ware, or that similar vessels may have served many functions in the village, including cooking and eating; or, of course, they might have been selectively removed on abandonment. Interestingly, pottery was distributed across the spur, rather than concentrated around the structural remains. More extensive structural remains may have once existed in the area and those preserved today only represent the most recent occupation of the area.

The three lithics recovered at Vouni support the hypothesis that this settlement was located between forest and plains

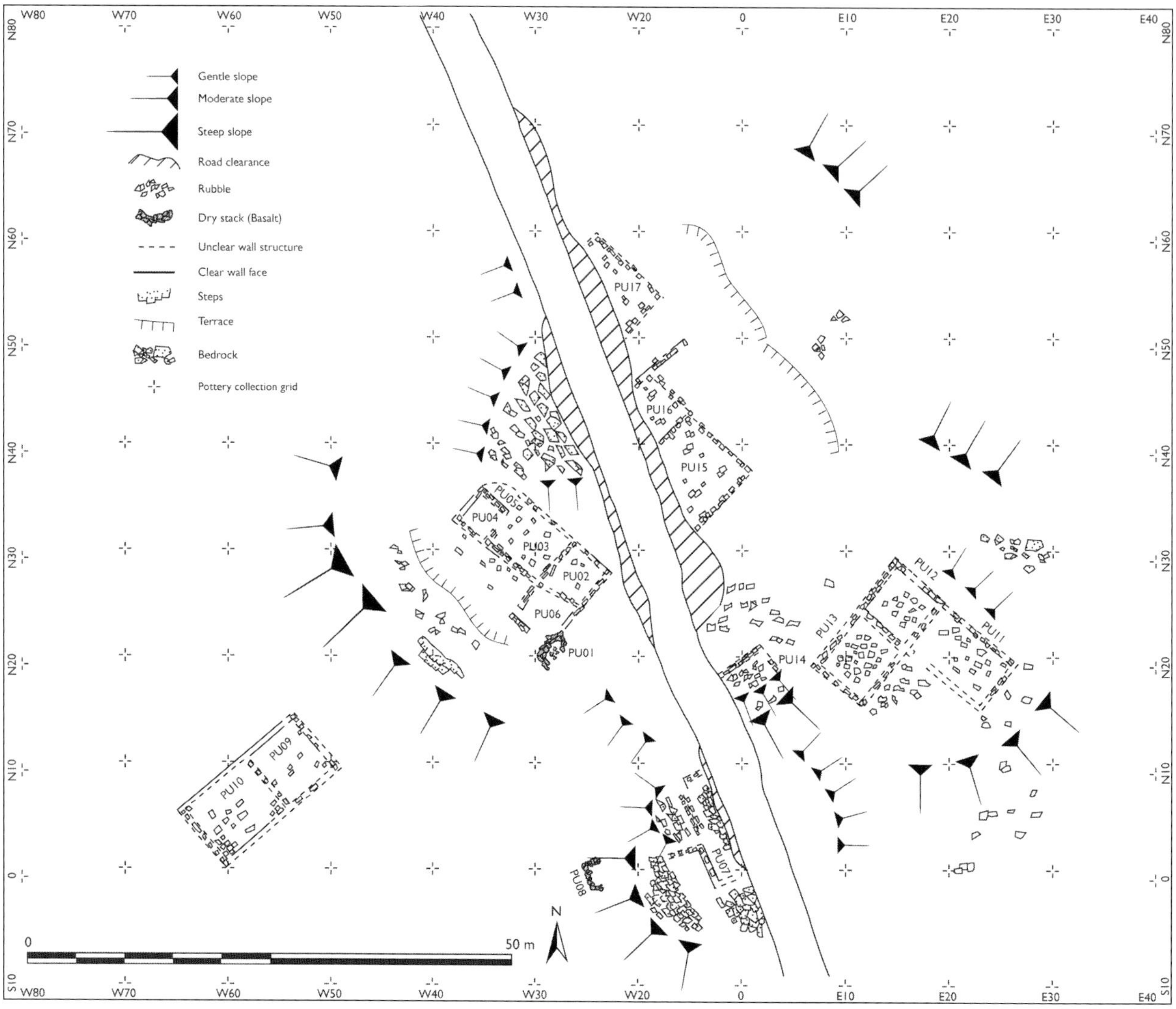

Fig. 5.1. Nikitari Vouni *(TP031): plan of settlement (Erinna Christou, finalised by Jean Humbert)*

Fig. 5.2. Nikitari Vouni *(TP031): Ruins of the church of Ayios Georgios, looking north, with the main part of the village just in view in the saddle beyond (Chris Parks)*

Table 5.2. Nikitari Vouni *(TP031): pottery*

Historical (Archaic to Modern)

Fct	*Type*	*No.*	*Weight*
CW	CW	2	1g
LU	LU	3	6g

Medieval to Modern

Fct	*Type*	*No.*	*Weight*
CW	BGW	2	22g
CW	Tia	2	35g
HU	HU	15	687g
LU	LU	59	804g

Ottoman to Modern I

Fct	*Type*	*No.*	*Weight*
TW	MP01	2	32g

Medieval-Venetian to Early Ottoman

Fct	*Type*	*No.*	*Weight*
TW	CGS06	2	17g

Modern

Fct	*Type*	*No.*	*Weight*
CW	BGW	2	5g
LU	LU	7	32g

Fig. 5.3. Path immediately east of Nikitari Vouni *(TP031), looking north-east towards the Mesaoria Plain (Chris Parks)*

to extract a variety of resources from both ecosystems. One chunk of chalcedony, a chip of jasper and a tool re-sharpening fragment, made from red jasper, show that local stone was used in the production of chipped stone tools. This expedient production of sharp cutting edges using local stone is prevalent within the mountains during the Medieval–Modern period (Volume 1, Chapter 3.8), and may indicate a more mobile population that travelled to the mountains to extract forest resources and required a flexible, diverse, and disposable toolkit. Survey Units on the plains to the north-east of Vouni showed similar evidence of local jasper use. Here a small sample of 12 chipped stone pieces represent a simple core technology aimed at flake production, with all artefacts (seven cores, three flakes and two pieces of debris) produced from local jasper.

Terraces located on the eastern and western slopes of the spur are not stone armoured, but were built drawing upon the natural topographic contours of the landscape. Although there is no evidence for what was grown on them, their limited nature suggests that they may have been used for local gardening, vines and orchards. A path surveyed by Gibson (2005, 160–61) and shown on cadastral map XXVIII-48 runs south-west to north-east through the village (Fig. 5.3). The close association of the path and the settlement suggests that they were used contemporaneously. Instead of agricultural production being focused at the settlement itself, it is more likely that people moved to and from the settlement, to the plains in the north-east or to the forest in the south-west (Gibson 2005, 160–61; see also Volume 1, Chapter 3.13).

There is no real indication of when Vouni was abandoned. The varying degree of structural preservation shown at the site and the presence of Medieval–Modern pottery suggests that there were two phases of occupation. The first rectangular and L-shaped structures were built on the spur between the 16th–18th centuries AD (PU02–07). Smaller, less well-built, temporary or seasonal structures (PU01, PU08) were constructed during the later part of the 18th and 19th centuries using stone from previous larger and better-built structures. Obviously by the time that these smaller structures were erected the permanent settlement had fallen into disuse. The absence of the settlement and church from

Fig. 5.4. Ayios Theodhoros Pano Atsa *(TP241) from the south (Michael Given)*

cadastral plans produced in the 1920s suggests that by this time the settlement had been abandoned completely. This abandonment may be related to the demarcation of the Adelphi State Forest in the early 20th century (Gibson 2005, 127; Sollars 2005, 136).

Rural Structures of Pano Atsa and Palloura

Ayios Theodoros *Pano Atsa* is a multi-roomed structure located 3 km to the east of Nikitari *Vouni*, just north of the Adelphi State Forest boundary (Fig. 5.4). The villagers of Ayios Theodoros refer to it as a *mandra* or goatfold ('Mandra tou Fatchitas').

Located on the eastern side of a spur facing south-east across the foothills, this structure has a panoramic view across the foothills and plains, and south-east into the mountains. The structure is made of mudbrick on top of a neatly faced stone foundation with tile chinking. There are five rooms, and the main room has two doors. The absence of an enclosure and the well-built construction indicate that this building was not originally intended for use as a goatfold.

A similar four-roomed structure called Ayios Theodoros *Palloura* (TP255), known locally as 'Mandra tou Araklethi', is located some 600 m south-east of Pano Atsa. The complex is composed of four large rooms with a three-course-high stone foundation. Unlike Pano Atsa, there is no evidence of mudbrick used in its construction. A possible stone enclosure measuring 8 × 4 m is attached to the main complex, though recent cultivation and bulldozing has destroyed one of its walls, and there are additional structures to the east and west. A poorly preserved oven is located to the south-west of these structures. The overall extent of the structural remains at this complex is uncertain because of the bulldozing disturbance, poor preservation and overgrown grass.

Neither structure could be dated from pottery found within their overgrown rooms, or from pottery or tile used as chinking in their walls. Both Pano Atsa and Palloura are located outside the Adelphi State Forest. The position of forestry cairns in close proximity to both structures suggests that they were still in use when the forestry boundary was formed. Given that villagers from Ayios Theodhoros and Nikitari still remember them as 'Mandra tou Araklethi' and 'Mandra tou Fatchitas' they probably continued in use into the 20th century.

Although both are remembered as animal folds, Palloura and Pano Atsa lack the characteristic features of *mandres*. Typically *mandres* are roughly built structures with goat pens made of thorns and limited domestic facilities (Given 2000, 227–29; Sollars 2005). The neat stonework, large room size, oven and uncertain presence of enclosures suggest that these structures were not built with the sole purpose of tending goats. Instead, the oven and large rooms imply a more permanent and economically substantial basis (Given 2004, 88). The large rooms found at both Palloura and Pano Atsa were most likely used for storage rather than as living space, although they could have been used as milking rooms for goats.

It is also possible that resources from the plains and mountains were stored within these structures during the Medieval–Modern periods (Gibson 2005, 164). Ethnographic and archival evidence indicate that plains-dwellers came to the Adelphi forest in the early 20th century to collect dead wood. After the forest demarcation, villagers were required to obtain permits to collect wood in the forest. In a British colonial archival document from 1922 the people of Ayios Theodoros, Kato Koutraphas

Mandres, Evrykhou and those villages within the Adelphi Forest were given permission to collect dead and dry wood from within the forest boundary (SA1/1922/1, Red 69; SA1/672/1921). According to informants from the area, collecting wood from the forest to sell to villages on the plains was a common occurrence throughout the Intensive Survey Zone. One interviewee, who lived in Kato Koutraphas *Mandres*, remembers travelling from his village into the forest to collect pinewood that he and his father then transported by donkey to Zodia, near Morphou, where it was sold.

A similar pattern of resource collection and storage may have occurred during the earlier Medieval and Ottoman periods. Fourteenth-century accounts from Psimolophou estate, for example, suggest that there was a substantial infrastructure to facilitate the extraction of resources from the forest. Men were hired to watch over the estate's supply of building wood in the forest, while forest roads were constructed to extract the wood (Richard 1947, 148–49). The similar (but smaller) Medieval to Ottoman period mountain estates at Asinou and Aspri may have exerted control over the extraction and distribution of resources, such as timber, within the foothills and mountains of the Adelphi Forest.

5.4 Roman–Modern Settlement Continuity

The Asinou Valley Intensive Survey Zone can be divided into two main regions. The Lower Asinou Valley is characterized by abandoned structures and pottery scatters distributed along the fertile, cultivated river terraces. The forest boundary, marking the separation between state forest and private land, skirts the cultivable parts of this valley. The Upper Asinou Valley is more isolated, with clusters of structural remains, evidence for forest resource use, and cultivation of small terraces. Both areas share similar trends in settlement history, resource use, communication, and long-term settlement activity from the Roman to Modern periods. The entire Asinou Valley Intensive Survey Zone can be characterized in terms of long-term settlement continuity from the Roman period until the mid-20th century. These findings challenge common perceptions that mountain landscapes are devoid of human presence.

Other than occasional chance finds (e.g. Hadjisavvas 1987), Roman occupation of the mountains – especially the deep forested mountain valleys – has until now seen no focused programme of research. The following discussion thus begins by highlighting the earliest settlement patterns, looking specifically at settlement evidence in the Lower (Nikitari *Khalospities)* and Upper Asinou Valley (Nikitari *Trimitheri* and Nikitari *Khalospita*).

Lower Asinou Valley

Roman material in the Lower Asinou Valley is distributed across what are today small open tracts of land near the church of Panayia Phorviotissa and up the valley toward Paleomandres (Plate 5.3). The sherd density, however, is relatively low (maximum of 7 sherds/100 m^2). The Table and Cooking Wares found throughout the Lower Asinou Valley suggest a residential function, as do the tile fragments. The absence of storage vessels in the assemblage suggests that there may have been a more temporary occupation in the valley during the Roman period. Although some potentially contemporaneous utility ware body sherds were identified, they did not include any of the specifically Roman utility ware chronotypes that were found in the rest of the Survey Area. Roman utility vessels, however, are more difficult to distinguish from later examples because the reddish-brown fabrics dominate in the mountains in both periods (see Volume 1, Chapter 3.3). Table Ware located in the Lower Asinou Valley dates to the Late Roman period, and no imported Table Ware from outside the island was identified within the survey zone.

It is impossible to interpret the clusters of Roman activity in the Lower Asinou Valley from the pottery alone. Generally the Roman period fragments collected were small. Two handles from frying pans with wishbone handles were collected at Nikitari *Khalospities* (TS12), the cluster of settlement evidence in the south-westernmost part of the Lower Asinou Valley. Distribution of this particular type of cooking vessel in the remote area of the Danish survey on the Akamas peninsula was investigated by Lund (2002), who suggested that this type of vessel was used by mobile shepherds. A similar phenomenon may be envisioned for the Asinou valley, although frying pans with wishbone handles were also collected at permanently settled sites in the TAESP area, such as Mavrovouni (Chapter 4.6) and Litharkies (Chapter 4.4). Although a clear Roman presence is evident from the scattered pottery found in the Asinou Valley, the Roman farmsteads that characterize other parts of the TAESP landscape did not exist in this area.

Upper Asinou Valley

With its interlocking paths, terraces and structures exhibiting occupation since the Roman period, the Upper Asinou Valley is unique within the Survey Area. In all cases Roman pottery was located in association with architectural remains. Parts of these structures show evidence of Roman occupation followed by later re-use in Medieval to Modern times. Nikitari *Trimitheri* and Nikitari *Khalospita* provide the best evidence for long-term occupation, while similar structures were located up river at Mandres ton Rotson and Khandakia (Sollars 2005, 134–35).

The three-room structure at Nikitari *Trimitheri* (TP220) is composed of varyingly preserved walls and rooms (Fig. 5.5). At 7 × 5 m, Room 1 is the largest, and has rectangular walls preserved to a height of 1.0–1.5 m. Room 2 is square with walls preserved to 0.8 m in height (Fig. 5.6). Logging activity and road building have disturbed parts of Rooms 2 and 3, while three pine trees in Room 3 show that there has not been any occupation in the dwelling for at least the

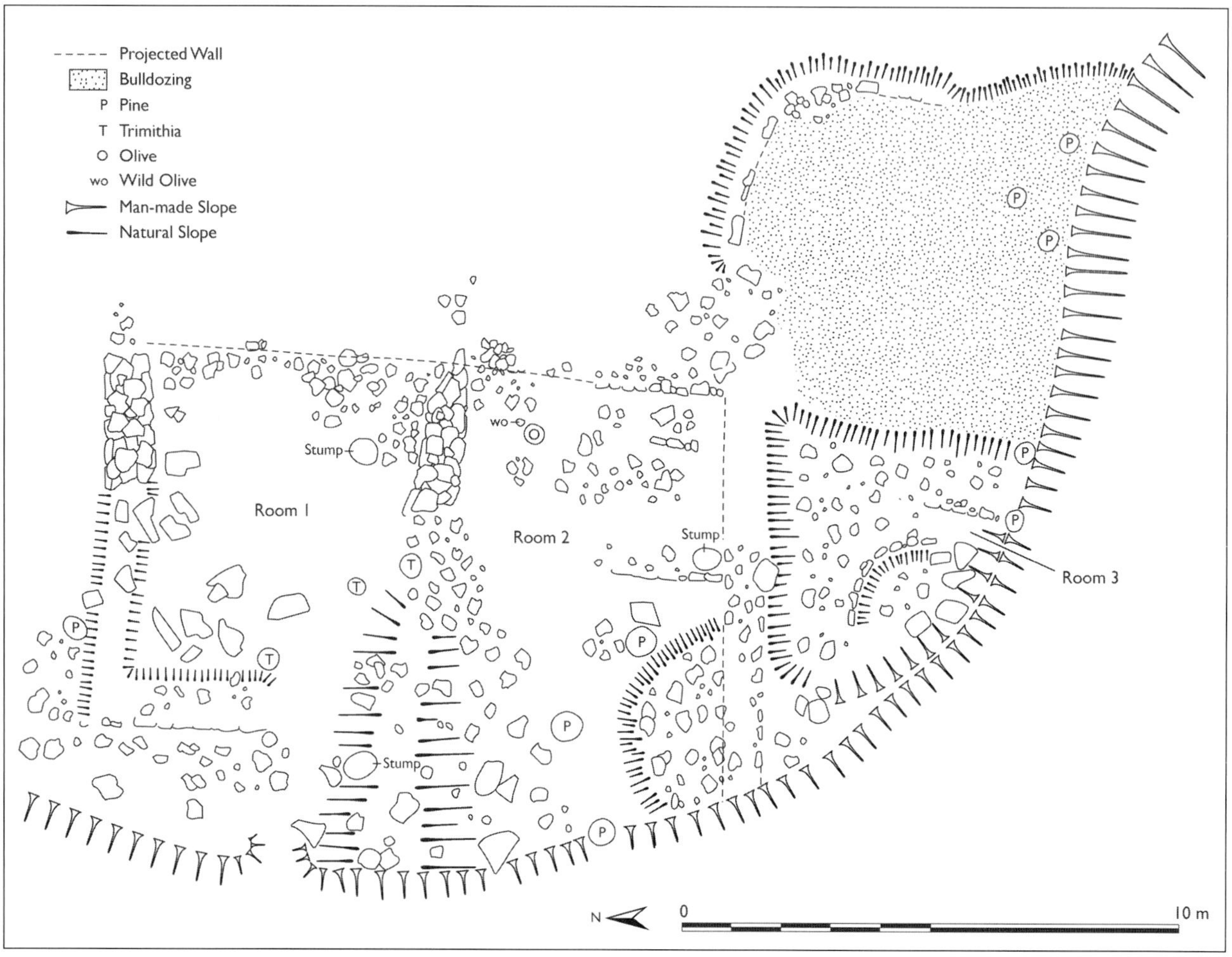

Fig. 5.5. Plan of Nikitari Trimitheri *(TP220) (Sarah Janes, finalised by Jean Humbert)*

Fig. 5.6. Nikitari Trimitheri *(TP220) from the south-south-east, with Room 2 in the foreground and Room 3 behind with the three pine trees (Chris Parks)*

past 40 years. The modern road, too, has disturbed the third room. To its east are the remains of a pit-like depression 1 m in diameter, which may be the remains of an additional structure or storage area. Terrace walls are visible both to the south-east and downslope of this building complex.

Pottery and tile collected from the walls and rooms of this structure date from the Late Roman to Modern periods (Table 5.3). Rooms 2 and 3 had definite evidence of Late Roman pottery, including a corrugated body fragment of a thin-walled cooking pot and a rim fragment of a Cypriot Red Slip Ware form 9, dating to the 2nd half of the 6th century AD. Evidence for Roman presence at Trimitheri comes mainly from these two pottery fragments, though the floor levels of the structure are not exposed.

The bulk of the pottery consists of Heavy Utility sherds dating broadly to the historical periods (Archaic–Modern). Most of these sherds were located in Room 1, the north-westernmost room and wall of the complex. This room was the best preserved and probably represents the most recent use of the structure as a goatfold (Panayiotis Loppas, interviewed by Gibson, 2004). The 14 pan tile fragments, which come particularly from the walls of Rooms 1–3, have no distinguishing features on their reverse, are of reddish-brown fabric, and are of the same type that was produced in the Early Roman period (see Volume 1, Chapter 3.3). The presence of Late Roman Table Ware and Cooking Ware in the south-eastern part of the structure supports the notion of an original Late Roman occupation in the south-eastern rooms, with later Medieval–Modern re-use throughout the

Table 5.3. Nikitari Trimitheri *(TP220): pottery from block survey. TCP numbers refer to Pottery Catalogue in Volume 1, Chapter 3.6*

Early to Late Roman			
Fct	*Type*	*No.*	*Weight*
Ar	Ti	14	3.943kg
Late Roman			
Fct	*Type*	*No.*	*Weight*
CW	CW	1	17g
TW	CRS09	1	37g TCP705

Historical (Archaic to Modern)			
Fct	*Type*	*No.*	*Weight*
HU	HU	14	6.205kg
LU	LU	1	9g
Medieval to Modern			
Fct	*Type*	*No.*	*Weight*
HU	Pit09	1	2.925kg
HU	Tri	1	630g TCP704

Unknown			
Fct	*Type*	*No.*	*Weight*
Un	Un	1	110g

structure, including the re-use of tile for roofing and the reconstruction of walls.

Nikitari *Laxia tou Laona* (TP200) is a 5 × 11 m ruined stone structure some 600 m south of Nikitari *Trimitheri*. It has been dug into the hillside up to a depth of 1 m on its westernmost side, with Medieval–Modern pithos sherds on the ground and in the northern wall. We only carried out a preliminary survey, and found no evidence for Roman period occupation. Instead it is likely that the structure was occupied at a similar time period to Trimitheri's re-use.

The terrace walls (TP229, TP230, TP231) and paths (TP228, TP230) in the Trimitheri area are distinctive. The high stone-armoured terraces were used for agriculture, but also seem to have had a broader role in stabilizing the landscape. High terrace walls (especially TP229) located along the margins of the river channel served to restrict the river's course during periods of flooding. Similar terraces and retaining walls were located upriver along the Argaki ton Rotson (Sollars 2005, 142), suggesting that agricultural activity continued into the highest reaches of the Asinou River Valley.

The morphology of these terraces is discussed in detail in Chapter 5.5. It is important to note here, however, that these terraces differ in morphology from the Medieval–Modern terraces located in the Lower Asinou Valley. Although there are complications and limitations to dating terraces, it seems probable that these terraces are related to more ancient agricultural activity preserved in the Upper Asinou Valley.

A small structure (TP227, also called Nikitari *Trimitheri*) located north of the Argaki ton Rotson River provides additional evidence for early terracing in the Upper Asinou Valley. The structure is made up of a series of terrace walls composed of large river boulders. A terrace serves as the back wall, while two other walls produce a square feature only 2.5 m across. Unlike Trimitheri and Laxia tou Laona, this precariously positioned structure, that incorporates terracing and rock outcrops into its walls, was clearly not designed for long-term occupation. Instead this temporary shelter was most likely constructed from previously abandoned terrace walls. This structure and its terrace walls are located to the west of a well-constructed, stable communication route (TP228) that follows the Argaki ton Rotson River.

The relationship between communication routes, terracing and settlement in the Trimitheri area suggests that this region was a focal point for interaction (see also Chapter 5.6). Here people settled, cultivated crops and communicated with those living to the north-east and south-west along the Argaki ton Rotson River. In at least two cases paths (TP228, TP230) within the Trimitheri locality were located along the tops of terraces. The limited evidence for terracing in their direct vicinity makes it difficult to assess whether or not the communication route was constructed during the same period as the terraces. On the other hand, morphological similarities between terraces, paths and stone retaining walls, such as that which follows the course of the Argaki ton Rotson River within the Khalospita locality (2.2 km to the south-south-west), suggest that these features were built contemporaneously (see Volume 1, Chapter 3.13).

Settlement evidence at Nikitari *Khalospita* (TP250) indicates a pattern of occupation similar to that of Trimitheri (TP220), with some Roman pottery and a larger Medieval–Modern component. There are two main rectangular structures along a low spur runing east–west. The first is composed of two poorly preserved rooms (7 × 4 m) filled with rubble, but with clear walls made of unworked basalt with some pottery chinking. Towards the nose of the same spur is the second structure, which consists of at least four rooms, with Corinthian style pan and cover tiles.

Pottery located from Nikitari *Khalospita* consists of both Roman and a later Medieval–Modern component. Sollars (2005, 117) located three sherds of self-slip Roman or pre-Roman period Cooking Ware, while the TAESP sample included Heavy Utility, Light Utility, Table and Cooking Ware from the 15th–20th centuries. It seems evident that Trimitheri, Khalospita and similar structures located farther up the Asinou Valley (Sollars 2005, 134–35) had two main periods of occupation: Roman and Medieval–Modern. The Roman-period occupation was either short-lived or is now buried beneath the more recent occupation. There is a dramatic shift between the sparse evidence for Roman activity and the prolific Medieval–Modern occupation in both the Lower and Upper Asinou Valley. Medieval estates that drew upon the rich resource base of the mountains prompted the settlement intensification that distinguishes the Medieval–Modern period from all others in the Survey Area.

5.5 Medieval–Modern Settlement Intensification

The scattered evidence for Hellenistic and Roman activity in the Asinou Valley contrasts with the intensified settlement activity of the Medieval–Modern period. In the highest reaches of the Asinou Valley, structures built and inhabited in the Late Roman period – such as Khalospita and Trimitheri – were resettled during the Medieval–Modern periods, with rooms expanded and old pottery and tile re-used and incorporated into the new buildings. In the latter stages of the 20th century, these structures were again re-used as the temporary dwellings of goatherds.

In the lower Asinou Valley, where there was scattered evidence for Roman activity, Medieval–Modern settlement activity was clustered in two main areas: around the church of Panayia Phorviotissa and its associated monastery buildings (TS08); and in the fertile agricultural fields near Khalospities (TS12) (Plate 5.4). Village lists from the 16th century record the settlement of Asinou as a *casale* – a term used to describe a nucleated village made up of several households owned by a feudal lord whose land is either worked by serfs two to three days per week, or whose land is cultivated by peasants for their own crops (Coureas 2005, 113).

Fig. 5.7. Church of Panayia Phorviotissa (TP030) from the west-south-west, showing the block-surveyed orchard (TS08) below and to the left of it (Chris Parks)

Fig. 5.8. Church of Panayia Phorviotissa: south side (Chris Parks)

Asinou Church and Monastery (TP030, TP117)

The most prominent architectural feature of the Asinou Valley is the church of Panayia Phorviotissa (TP030), also called 'Asinou Church', located in a prominent position on a spur 130 m to the south-east of the Asinou River (Fig. 5.7). Dedicatory inscriptions within the church suggest that it was built between the years of 1099 and 1105/6, and was donated by a 'magistros' (judge or taxation officer) named Nicephorus. The church, according to these inscriptions, was originally built as a family chapel on Nicephorus' estate at Asinou (Papacostas 1999, 480; Stylianou and Stylianou 1985, 114–17), but soon after its construction it became a monastery with Nicephorus as its first abbot. This monastery lasted until the 17th century.

There is little consensus concerning the origins and meaning of the name 'Phorviotissa'. While Buckler (Gibraltar *et al.* 1933, 346–47) believes it is the family name of Nicephorus, Stylianou and Stylianou (1985, 114) suggest that the church is named after the medicinal plant milkwort. In yet another interpretation the name is associated with pasture and horse breeding (Gibraltar *et al.* 1933, 328, 347; Zampelas 2002, 65; Frigeriou-Zeniou 1997, 193). Frigeriou-Zeniou's (1997, 193) analysis of paintings within the narthex of the church – especially depictions of two possible hunting dogs and the monks' clothing – suggests that the monastic community was involved in breeding and training horses for hunting in the 14th century.

Panayia Phorviotissa is a rectangular church built on a stone platform, with the characteristically steep roof of the mountain regions covering its domes (Fig. 5.8). There are at least two major periods of painting, one initiated in 1106 and another in 1350 (Stylianou and Stylianou 1985, 114–40; Winfield 1969; Hadjichristodoulou and Marianthefs 2002, 9–10). Graffiti on the eastern jambs of the north and south doors dated to 1450 and 1446 commemorate the death of two individuals. A small painting of Christ Emmanuel with a list of bishops dating from 1620 provides a relative date for a third period of painting. Unlike many of the simple undecorated exteriors of churches elsewhere in Cyprus, the exterior of Panayia Phorviotissa shows evidence that it was covered with a layer of painted plaster (Papacostas 2006, 227). This plaster is still preserved in places on the exterior of the church.

Structurally, the church underwent several phases of construction. In the dedicatory painting it is shown without a narthex; its roof has the steep pitch and tile cover still seen today. Stylianou and Stylianou (1985, 114) believe that the narthex was constructed in the late 12th century. The gothic arch in the narthex is an unusual architectural feature among Byzantine churches on the island. The first evidence for the use of gothic arches in rural church architecture on Cyprus comes from Panayia Phorviotissa and Panayia tou Arakos, Lagoudhera. Papacostas (2006, 227) suggests that it was a feature introduced from Palestine where it is found in 11th-century architecture.

The church shows signs of being reinforced in the past, with extra buttressing added to the inside of the apse, and buttresses, along with a flying buttress, added to the exterior north wall of the church (Winfield 1969, 7). There is a blocked doorway on the south wall of the narthex (Fig. 5.8), and the masonry of the north wall shows evidence of a wall fracture repaired with limestone (Winfield 1969, 7). In some cases the renovated walls of the church are composed of a combination of ashlar blocks, rounded stone and pottery. According to Winfield (1969, 5), the original structure was composed of roughly hewn stone set in a mud mortar – the use of mud is unusual as medieval architecture employed lime mortar whenever possible. It is likely that the use of mud instead of lime influenced the stability of the structure.

A courtyard or enclosure wall with evidence for different phases of building surrounds the church. The ground surface within the courtyard is irregular. While the area has not been bulldozed, some rubble and bedrock are exposed. Much of this rubble may be the remains of building material used in the construction and reconstruction of the church. An informant from Nikitari Village remembered a past cemetery with wooden crosses in the south-western part of this enclosure.

We carried out resistivity survey within the courtyard to determine whether or not the church was a replacement of an earlier building. The survey was carried out using a Geoscan RM15 resistivity meter; readings were taken at 1-m intervals across four 20 × 20 m grids. The results of the survey are initially striking because of the outline of the existing church, which dominates the plot and draws the eye. Many of the dark patches in the plot, however, probably represent bedrock lying close to the surface (Plate 5.5).

There are two major anomalies of interest on the north side of the church. The first is a lighter, linear band running from the north-east corner of the enclosure towards the south-west, which may indicate the remains of a foundation trench. Although it is important to acknowledge the limitations of the equipment and its effectiveness in arid conditions, this area of high and low readings may represent the foundations of an earlier building that appears to have similar dimensions to the existing church, but with a very different and presumably non-ecclesiastical alignment. Faint linear anomalies on the north-east side of the church, also running from north-east to south-west, may relate to the larger anomaly or may represent traces of other buildings.

The monastery of Panayia Phorviotissa existed from the 12th until the 17th or 18th century, and apparently was abandoned by the time of Bars'kyj's visit in 1735 (Bars'kyj 1996, 74; Klirides 1968, 84; Stylianou and Stylianou 1985, 114). At its dissolution the property was acquired by the

Fig. 5.9. Nikitari Kapsalia *(TP117) from the south-south-east: site of monastery in foreground with 17th-century olive trees, and the church beyond (Chris Parks)*

Bishopric of Kyrenia. This included a *metohi* in Nikitari with eight rooms; an olive mill in the monastery; part of a relic of Ayios Ioannis Lampadhistis in the church; 80 *skales* (5 ha) of fields round the monastery with 35 olive trees; 182 *skales* (11.4 ha) of fields in different locations; 4 *zevgaria* ('yokes') of vineyards in Kakopetria; 50 goats; 1 mule; 1 donkey; and two pairs of oxen (Klirides 1968, 83–84).

Pottery evidence combined with architectural data, obtained through mapping and geophysical survey, creates a convincing case for the remains at Nikitari *Kapsalia* (TP117), located 150 m to the south of the Asinou Church, as being the last site of the monastic buildings (Fig. 5.9). As noted above, earlier remains of monastic buildings or structures associated with the monastery were probably located in the south-westernmost fields directly to the north of the church, which then shifted southwards to Kapsalia.

The structures at Kapsalia (on Fig. 5.10 labelled A, B and C from west to east) are located on a spur and in close proximity to a path. Structure A is large and rectangular and cut into the slope at its southern end. Its western wall is clear and several large sherds of storage jars were found in its northern end. The least clear of the three structures (B) has only faint remains of walls and much rubble. Structure C is rectangular and cut into the slope, furthest to the east of the three structures and located against a forest track. The east, west and north wall lines and an entrance are discernable.

In an effort to determine the age of these structures and so their relationship to Panayia Phorviotisa, we measured the patches of the lichen *Rhyzocarpon tinei*, which only grows on stable surfaces (Volume 1, Chapter 2.4). *Rhyzocarpon tinei* measured on stones located in the easternmost structure (C) indicate that these stones have not moved in the past 300 years. This long-term stability corresponds to the age of the olive trees that grew immediately beside the structures (though they were cut down in late 2005 or early 2006).

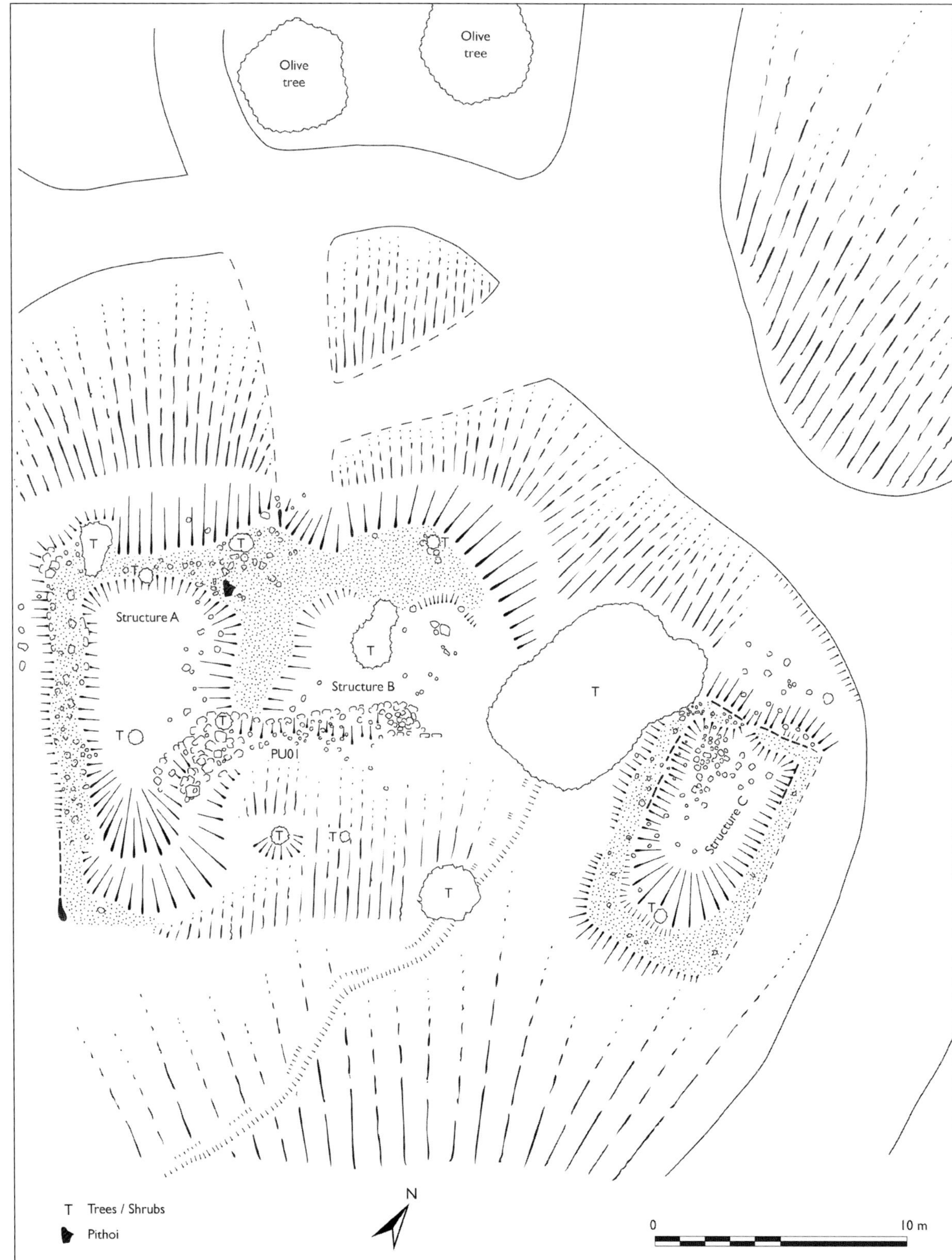

Fig. 5.10. Nikitari Kapsalia *(TP117): plan of monastery site (Julie Candy, finalised by Jean Humbert and Luke Sollars)*

Resistivity survey was carried out at Kapsalia to determine the extent of the architectural remains in the area (Plate 5.6). Shallow soil made it difficult to produce readings and the results are therefore provisional. The north-western corner of the plot is the worst affected by ground conditions. The only potential anthropogenic anomaly is a rectangular form lying roughly west-south-west across the line of the hillslope and measuring 15 ×

6 m. If this anomaly is accepted as being a real reflection of sub-surface conditions, then the best interpretation of the shape is that it represents the remains of a large building, possibly made of stone, although the readings from the 'walls' are only slightly higher than those of the surrounding soils. Such a structure supports the hypothesis that this area is the site of buildings associated with the monastic community at Panayia Phorviotissa.

In monastic estates such as that at Makhairas, the abbot managed the estate and led the monastery, while income came from estate lands (Coureas 2003, 107; cf. Given *et al.* 2002). A similar situation probably took place in the Asinou Valley, where the monastery of Panayia Phorviotissa held estate land and extracted its income from the terraced fields and their workforce. Produce collected by monks from estate lands throughout the valley must have been stored in a grange located in close proximity to the monastery (cf. Ionas 1998, 56; Coureas 2005, 113–15). It is uncertain if the structures located by TAESP include the remains of this grange. The location of two stone lined pits (*lakkoi*), apparently used by the monks to store grain, was identified by an informant on the eastern side of the paved road to the south of Panayia Phorviotissa. He recalls that one of these pits measured some 18 m in depth.

Asinou Church and Monastery: The Landscape Context (TS08)

To place the church and monastery in their landscape context we surveyed intensively the two most accessible and visible areas in their vicinity. The first was a sloping almond orchard to the north-west of the church. This orchard is composed of fluvial and colluvial sediments with soils terraced for agriculture. The overall stability of the slope was not affected by the tilling of individual terraces, and it is likely that material found within the orchard had changed position little since its original deposition.

While most of this pottery dates from the Medieval–Modern period, there was some Fine Ware and tile from the Late Roman period in the southernmost Survey Units closest to the church enclosure wall (Plate 5.7). This may be associated with the pre-ecclesiastical structure tentatively suggested by the resistivity survey.

A similar pattern of occupation is seen in the fields to the south of the church. Here the pottery distribution consists of small quantities of Roman Cooking Ware and tile within a larger Medieval–Modern assemblage. Interestingly, the remains of three Roman pan tiles appear to be associated with the structural remains of Kapsalia (TP117) located upslope and south-west. As mentioned previously, this is a pattern typical of the Lower Asinou Valley, with scattered evidence for Late Roman activity.

Medieval–Modern period pottery dominates the assemblage from TS08 (Table 5.4), with the greatest density located in the orchard to the north-west of the church. The largest quantity was recovered from SU0355, the south-westernmost Survey Unit. All pottery functions found within this unit have substantial quantities of material: tile; Cooking Ware; Table Ware; Heavy and Light Utility wares. Other units within the orchard showed similar concentrations of Heavy and Light Utility vessels, yet had little Table or Cooking Ware. The greatest densities of Medieval-Frankish and Medieval-Venetian/Early Ottoman pottery within TS08 also come from this Survey Unit and those within its vicinity (Vroom 2005, 120). These wares have open vessel shapes including small bowls, dishes and chalices suitable for eating and drinking

The highest density of pottery from the Ottoman to Modern period, especially from 1571 to the early 20th century, comes from Survey Units located to the south of Asinou Church, in the fields associated with the structural remains of Nikitari *Kapsalia* (TP117). Densities for the Medieval–Modern period as a whole in these Survey Units reach 29.6 sherds/100 m^2, including 3.4 from 1571–early 20th century (OttMod1) and 8.0 for the mid-Ottoman period to the mid-20th century (OttModII).

The assemblage of pottery in all but one of these southern Survey Units includes Cooking Ware, Heavy Utility, Light Utility, Utility and Table Ware. There is evidence of imported Table Ware from northern Greece and/or Çanakkale, southern Italy and/or Corfu (Vroom 2005, 184–87). The high quantities of Glazed, Painted and Sgraffito Ware here contrast starkly with the assemblage found elsewhere in the Asinou Valley. Such a broad pottery assemblage suggests settlement activities including cooking, eating, agricultural production and storage.

Pottery located to the north and south of the church suggests consistent patterns of human activity in the area of Panayia Phorviotissa in the Late Medieval, Ottoman and Modern periods. While occupation of the area to the north of the church (e.g. SU0355) is clearly Late Medieval, that to the south (e.g. SU2302) is later Ottoman and Modern. Pottery analysis suggests that in their respective time periods both these areas served as loci for agricultural production, cooking, eating and dwelling.

It is possible that earlier structures associated with Asinou Church were located to its north. From the dated pottery it seems that such a shift in settlement took place between the 16th and 18th centuries AD. The church architecture, courtyard and enclosure walls all show evidence of several periods of reconstruction. A shift in settlement may have corresponded to a period of renovation and/or renewed interest in the church, such as the third period of painting in 1620 described by Stylianou and Stylianou (1985, 114–40). At some point during the Early Ottoman period, the focus of settlement shifted south to the area around Nikitari *Kapsalia*.

Lithics found in TS08 point to the type of production activities that took place to the north and south of the church. A piece of ground stone made of gabbro located in the fields to the south of Asinou Church is likely associated with the Medieval–Modern pottery assemblage and probable monastery at Nikitari *Kapsalia*. Located near the three 300-year old domesticated olive trees, this

Table 5.4. Nikitari Kapsalia *(TS08): pottery from block survey associated with Asinou monastic settlement (SU0355–64, SU1361–66, SU1371, SU2301–05); see also Table 5.5. TCP numbers refer to Pottery Catalogue in Volume 1, Chapter 3.6*

Historical Antiquity (Archaic to Late Roman)

Fct	*Type*	*No.*	*Weight*
Ar	Ti	28	3.627kg
Ar	TiP	4	575g
HU	HU	5	272g
LU	LU	2	14g

Hellenistic to Roman

Fct	*Type*	*No.*	*Weight*
TW	SRS	1	2g
TW	TW	1	1g

Early to Late Roman

Fct	*Type*	*No.*	*Weight*
Ar	Ti	1	310g
Ar	TiCA	1	115g
Ar	TiP	17	2.01kg
CW	CW	2	8g
LU	LU	1	5g
TW	ARS	1	1g

Late Roman

Fct	*Type*	*No.*	*Weight*
Ar	TiP	2	140g
TW	CRS	1	11g
TW	CRS01	1	5g

Roman to Modern

Fct	*Type*	*No.*	*Weight*
Ar	Ti	22	1.01kg
Ar	TiP	5	810g
CW	CW	2	85g
LU	LU	13	70g

Historical (Archaic to Modern)

Fct	*Type*	*No.*	*Weight*
Ar	Ti	80	6.315kg
Ar	TiCS	1	310g
CW	CW	21	95g
HU	HU	123	4.722kg
LU	LU	99	673g
Tr	Am	1	70g
TW	TW	1	5g

Medieval to Modern

Fct	*Type*	*No.*	*Weight*
Ar	Brk	4	890g
Ar	TiF	4	410g
CW	BGW	16	352g
CW	Tia	7	477g
			TCP402, TCP405
CW	Tta	1	20g
HU	HU	148	16.245kg
HU	Pit	2	810g
HU	Pit02	1	300g
			TCP137
LU	ID04A	2	22g
LU	LU	157	2.202kg
TW	BGW	2	50g
TW	UnG	2	5g
U	Uja	2	52g
			TCP401
U	UL02	1	375g
U	UPSJu	2	25g

Medieval-Frankish

Fct	*Type*	*No.*	*Weight*
TW	CGS05	13	112g
TW	MP01	2	10g
TW	SP03	2	23g

Medieval utility period III

Fct	*Type*	*No.*	*Weight*
CW	Tia02	1	40g
CW	Tia03	1	5g
CW	Tia04	1	24g
LU	ID02A	7	173g
			TCP407
U	ID02	1	5g
U	ID03	1	26g
U	ID04	8	196g
U	Uja	1	25g
			TCP406
U	UPSJ01	1	55g
			TCP400

Ottoman to Modern I

Fct	*Type*	*No.*	*Weight*
TW	CGS06	1	7g
TW	G01	3	30g
TW	G02	1	4g
TW	G03	4	25g
TW	G07	1	5g
TW	MP01	2	7g
TW	SP01	2	15g
U	ID02	4	79g
U	UBR01	1	32g
U	ULSJ01	3	105g
			TCP403, TCP408

Medieval-Venetian to Early Ottoman

Fct	*Type*	*No.*	*Weight*
TW	CGS06	6	125g
			TCP138, TCP399
TW	G01	3	10g
TW	G02	1	2g
TW	G03	2	11g
TW	G04	2	15g
TW	G05	4	41g
TW	G08	1	5g
TW	MP01	25	252g
TW	MP02	1	20g

Ottoman to Modern II

Fct	*Type*	*No.*	*Weight*
HU	BuH	14	415g
HU	HU	2	43g
HU	Pit	1	430g
LU	BuL	13	99g
LU	LU	21	212g
TW	G07	1	5g
TW	MP01	1	5g
TW	Por	1	2g
TW	PP	1	15g
TW	PP07	1	2g
TW	SP02	1	5g
U	UPL01	1	30g
			TCP404

Modern

Fct	*Type*	*No.*	*Weight*
Ar	TiCh	12	310g
CW	Tta	2	65g
			TCP409
HU	Pit03	2	3.8kg
LU	LU	4	37g
LU	UFR01	1	52g
TW	MP01	1	50g
TW	Por	4	13g

Unknown

Fct	*Type*	*No.*	*Weight*
Un	UN	1	32g

grinding tool is a late representation of a much longer-lived technological tradition. Today Cypriots use similar grinding tools to crack green olives. This artefact, like many in the Asinou Valley, represents the continued use of stone tools beyond the prehistoric well into the historic and modern periods.

The only chipped stone located in the Asinou Valley Intensive Survey Zone was found in the Survey Units north of Panayia Phorviotissa church. A utilized flake, core, cortical flake and *dhoukani* blade were among these lithics. Of this small collection, half was made from local chalcedony, while the *dhoukani* flake and utilized

Table 5.5. Nikitari Rotsos *(TS17): pottery from block survey (SU1360, SU2325–29)*

Historical Antiquity (Archaic to Late Roman)

Fct	*Type*	*No.*	*Weight*
HU	HU	1	20g
LU	LU	1	5g

Early to Late Roman

Fct	*Type*	*No.*	*Weight*
Ar	Ti	2	228g
CW	CW	2	3g

Late Roman

Fct	*Type*	*No.*	*Weight*
TW	RS	1	2g

Roman to Modern

Fct	*Type*	*No.*	*Weight*
Ar	Ti	3	35g

Historical (Archaic to Modern)

Fct	*Type*	*No.*	*Weight*
HU	HU	9	420g
LU	LU	4	15g

Medieval to Modern

Fct	*Type*	*No.*	*Weight*
CW	BGW	1	2g
HU	HU	22	2.676kg
LU	LU	12	120g
U	ID02	1	15g

Ottoman to Modern I

Fct	*Type*	*No.*	*Weight*
U	ID02	1	8g

Medieval-Venetian to Early Ottoman

Fct	*Type*	*No.*	*Weight*
TW	CGS06	1	6g
TW	MP01	1	7g

Modern

Fct	*Type*	*No.*	*Weight*
Ar	TiCh	1	57g
LU	LU	2	20g

flake were made from the non-local Lefkera chert. Lithic analyses suggest that the utilized flake of Lefkera chert represents a *dhoukani* flake that at the time of deposit had not yet acquired use-wear. If this is the case, then it appears that individuals chose to use imported lithic material for the threshing of grain, while local material was used for a variety of tasks related to the expedient production of a cutting tool.

We carried out additional block survey in a series of agricultural fields 300 m to the south-west of the church (Nikitari *Rotsos*; TS17). This survey incorporated several terraced landforms that, though continually disturbed by ploughing, are relatively stable because of their shallow slopes and continued maintenance.

Overall very little pottery was located in these fields, in spite of their stability and good ground visibility. A limited Roman presence is represented in the westernmost Survey Units by two Roman pan tile and Cooking Ware fragments and two Late Roman Light and Heavy Utility sherds. The greatest densities of Medieval–Modern pottery (5.3 sherds/100 m^2) were recovered from the north-easternmost fields closest to the church and monastery buildings of TS08. Made up of mainly Heavy and Light Utility ware, as well as two pieces of Venetian to Early Ottoman period Table Ware, this pottery provides the most substantial evidence of settlement within TS17.

It is likely that nutrient management strategies played a role in pottery distributions in these terraced fields. Such low pottery densities are consistent with manuring practices in vineyards and orchards where manure is applied directly under the tree or vine, not broadcasted over the full field as is required for cereal and vegetable cultivation.

Medieval–Ottoman Settlement and Church at Nikitari *Khalospities* (TS12)

Nikitari *Khalospities* (TS12) encompassed the remains of the church of Ayios Ioannis (TP039); the terraced fields to the south-west of the Asinou River that were surveyed in order to put the church and structures in context (Plate 5.8); and the structures of Pera Yitonia (TP061).

The remains of the church of Ayios Ioannis (TP039) are located on the north-west bank of the Asinou river channel, to the north-east of the settlement at Pera Yitonia (TP061). According to a local informant, the church was constructed for the people living to the north of the Asinou River (possibly at Nikitari *Pera Yitonia*) when they were unable to cross to visit Asinou Church. The surviving structural remains consist of a well-built limestone ashlar wall four courses high, 10 m long and oriented at 46° (instead of the expected 90°). The blocks are carefully cut, and the wall is filled with rubble, mortar and tile. Although the wall's full width is obscured by river sediment, it appears that it is at least 1 m wide.

Considering the position of the church, it is interesting to note that river cobbles were not used in its construction. Instead the only visible wall uses carefully cut ashlar blocks. The unusual position of this church within a river terrace currently being eroded by the Asinou River suggests that the church has been involved in a series of past floods that buried the structure in the river terrace. These floods may be related to the climatic variability during the Medieval Warm Period and Little Ice Age as discussed in Chapter 5.8.

To put the church into its landscape and settlement context, we surveyed the anthropogenic terraces to its south paralleling the Asinou River. Much of the sediment within the current river terrace has been incised, transported and redeposited along the river. Those sediments in older terraces (farther from the river) have been moved minimally, as the stone-armoured terraces have helped to trap sediment and minimize the influence of sheetwash. Artefacts may have moved within the boundaries of terraces because of tilling, but sediment would not have moved between terraces.

In general, those terraces closest to the river (SU0300–0302; SU0365–66), and therefore the youngest, contain mostly Medieval–Modern pottery, while those furthest

Table 5.6. Nikitari Khalospities *(TS12): pottery from block survey (SU0300–302, SU0365–66, SU0382, SU0386, SU1353–59, SU1367–70). TCP numbers refer to Pottery Catalogue in Volume 1, Chapter 3.6*

Hellenistic to Roman

Fct	Type	No.	Weight
TW	SRS	2	5g

Early to Late Roman

Fct	Type	No.	Weight
CW	CWFPWh	1	20g

Late Roman

Fct	Type	No.	Weight
TW	CRS	1	10g
TW	CRS01	1	13g

Roman to Modern

Fct	Type	No.	Weight
Ar	Ti	4	135g
CW	CW	1	10g

Historical (Archaic to Modern)

Fct	Type	No.	Weight
Ar	Ti	1	15g
CW	CW	3	20g
HU	HU	24	4.203kg
LU	LU	35	301g

Medieval utility period I

Fct	Type	No.	Weight
CW	UFR02	13	310g TCP126

Medieval to Modern

Fct	Type	No.	Weight
Ar	Ti	5	520g
CW	CW	2	35g
CW	Tia	1	15g
HU	HU	54	10.37kg
LU	LU	98	1.525kg
U	UPSJu	20	605g

Medieval-Frankish

Fct	Type	No.	Weight
TW	CGS05	6	250g TCP140,TCP143
TW	CGS06	4	45g TCP145

Medieval utility period III

Fct	Type	No.	Weight
CW	Tia	17	1.015kg TCP139
CW	Tia02	2	80g

Ottoman to Modern II

Fct	Type	No.	Weight
HU	BuH	1	7g
HU	BUP	1	400g TCP125
LU	G07	1	10g

Modern

Fct	Type	No.	Weight
Ar	Brk	1	80g
CW	BGW	7	155g
CW	Tia	11	540g
HU	Dana	2	1.55kg TCP141
HU	HU	40	8.72kg
HU	LU	1	75g TCP148
HU	Pit03	1	3.85kg TCP142
HU	Pit04	2	515g TCP146
HU	Pit05	1	140g TCP147
HU	Pit06	1	145g TCP144
LU	LU	45	704g
LU	UFR01	2	35g
TW	Por	1	9g

from the river (SU1353–59) show more evidence of pre-Medieval pottery alongside the odd Modern sherd. There appears to be a pattern in the types of activity represented (Plate 5.9). Two Survey Units to the east (SU0365–66) contained a full range of material including tile, Table Ware, Cooking Ware, Utility, Heavy and Light Utility vessels, but the assemblage is dominated by utility wares. The density of pottery within these functional categories suggests that a settlement with large-scale agricultural production existed nearby. These differ from those to the west that show strikingly smaller densities of pottery and tile throughout all categories.

Storage pithoi, fragments from water jugs and *tianistra* or frying pans (e.g. TCP139) in SU0365 indicate that this area was used for both storage and cooking (Table 5.6). Two *dana* fragments (e.g. TCP141) located on this terrace suggest that wine or oil was collected in these large Heavy Utility basins during the Modern period (Ionas 1998, 56–57).

It is interesting to note the limited presence of Table Ware within this assemblage, which contrasts with that observed in the fields surrounding Asinou church where a similar broad assemblage included a high percentage of Table Ware (Plate 5.10). This can particularly be seen in the northernmost Survey Units at Asinou, where the Table Ware density remains relatively high in spite of the lower overall Medieval–Modern density. It seems that the community based at the monastery used a higher proportion of glazed and painted Table Wares than did the Khalospities community.

While there is evidence that food was cooked at Khalospities, there is little to suggest that it was eaten using Table Ware. It is tempting to suggest that those who lived in or around the church and monastery had better access to more specialized pottery than those who lived away from the church and worked the estate land. It is possible that those who worked in areas of agricultural production ate more expedient meals from less specialized vessels (our Utility and Light Utility) or vessels made in different materials, as was the case in mountainous Aetolia in central Greece (Vroom 1998, 151–58).

Settlement and food production are focused in the north-eastern Survey Units on the terraces closest to Ayios Ioannis Church. The church likely represents the only remaining standing structural remnants of a much larger settlement that was inhabited from the Medieval–Modern periods. This is very much the dominant period represented by the pottery in the area, with a very impressive 123.9 sherds/100 m^2 in SU0365.

Survey Units located 200 m to the south-west of these terraced fields are dispersed, with densities never rising to more than 0.6 sherds/100 m^2 for either the Hellenistic–Roman or Medieval–Modern periods (Plate 5.3; Plate 5.4). Overall the most notable feature in this area is the

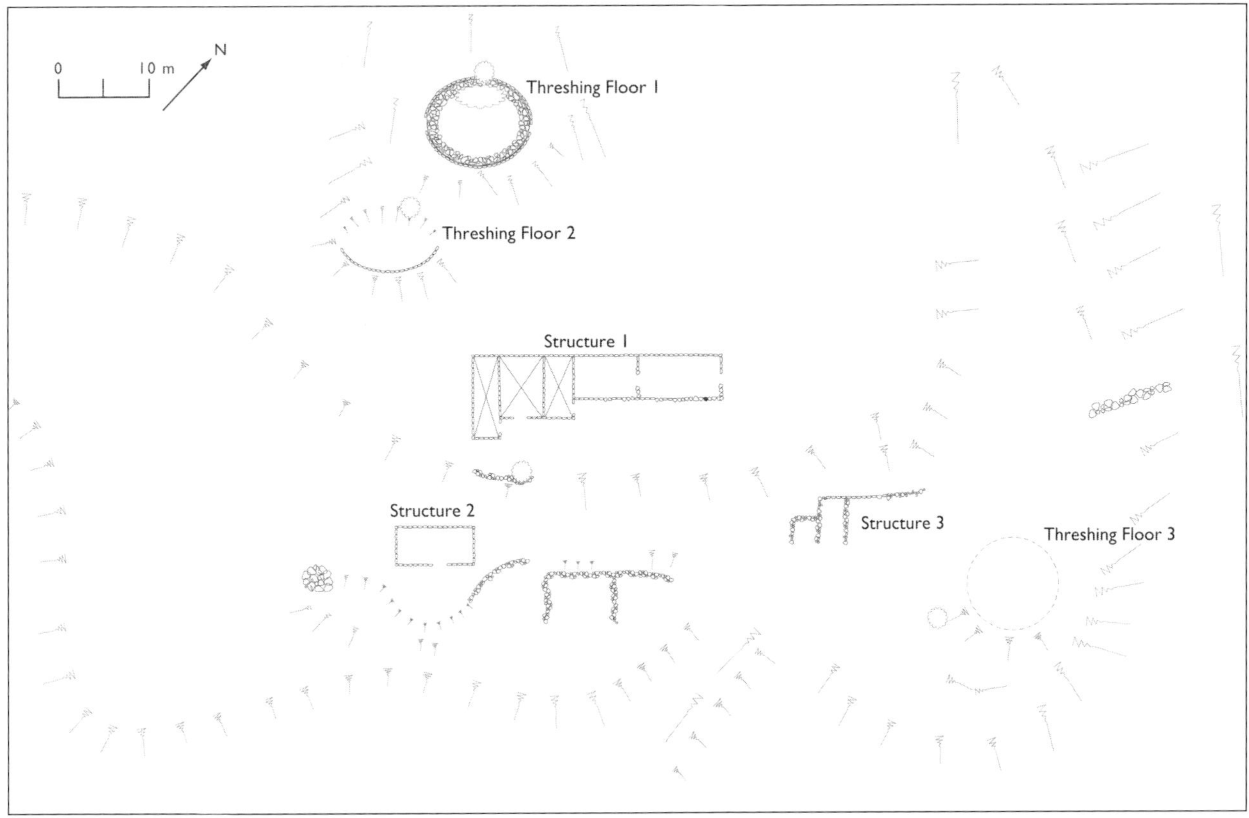

Fig. 5.11. Nikitari Pera Yitonia *(TP061): sketch plan (Luke Sollars)*

low amount of pottery recovered despite its good ground visibility, minimal sheet erosion and the fact that the fields had been recently tilled. Like TS17, either cultivation of these fields did not take place, or it took place with only highly localized distributions, characteristic of manure applied directly to tree or vine. It is likely that intensive occupation and cultivation only took place on the terraced fields near the Asinou River.

The abandoned settlement at Nikitari *Pera Yitonia* is located on a spur to the south-west of Ayios Ioannis church, north of the Asinou River. It was investigated both by TAESP (TP061) and by Sollars (2005, 123–28). The pottery associated with the settlement and its area dates to the Medieval–Modern periods, although the structures themselves are most likely to be 19th and early 20th century.

The structural remains at Pera Yitonia include at least three well-spaced, complex structures on a spur (Fig. 5.11). These buildings range in preservation from derelict to completely ruined. Their long axes are aligned north-east/south-west across the spur, so that the long sides of the buildings faced south-east across the valley. Terraced areas between the structures run along the contour and in places were divided up and down the slope. At least three threshing floors were identified, two north-west of Structure 1 and one south-east of Structure 3 (Fig. 5.12).

It is evident from the coarse ware used as chinking in the structures' walls, that the buildings and their predecessors date from the 16th–20th centuries. Structure 1 appears to be the most recently occupied, and was probably abandoned during the second half of the 20th century. The Ottoman pottery used as chinking in Structures 1 and 2 indicates a date no earlier than the 16th century. Structure 3 is less well made than the other two, but whether this denotes an earlier phase of occupation or a later, less permanent one is not clear.

Threshing Floor 1 was approximately 10 m in diameter and cut into hillslope above Structure 1. Basalt blocks were used as retaining walls and the floor was paved, with an outer band of basalt blocks and river boulders. Located just downslope of the first, Threshing Floor 2 featured a retaining wall built around its downslope side, while a third threshing floor on the north-western portion of the spur was poorly preserved.

The complex remains at Pera Yitonia highlight the diversity of settlement in the Asinou Valley, which drew on the flexibility of a landscape that could accommodate the resources of both the forest and the plains. It was this flexibility that enabled the population to thrive during the Medieval–Modern periods.

Asinou Village (TS03)

Asinou village is an abandoned settlement located on a high spur, looking north-east towards the 12th-century

Fig. 5.12. Nikitari Pera Yitonia *(TP061): structures and threshing floors (Chris Parks)*

Fig. 5.13. Asinou village from the south-south-west, with Asinou church visible to the right on a spur farther down the valley (Chris Parks)

church of Panayia Phorviotissa (Fig. 5.13). The remnants of the village comprise an integrated group of built units (BU0047) that demonstrate a highly complex history of re-use and re-cycling of structural elements, suggesting that the village was built, rebuilt and modified over a long period of time. Associated with it are a freestanding house and *mandra* (BU117), as well as an oven and two threshing floors or *alonia.*

The diversity of construction styles, building techniques and materials at Asinou Village indicates that it was constructed during multiple periods. The availability of different building materials, changing knowledge and traditions may have played a role in the formation of this village. Basalt was used in the initial construction, while later infill and additions to the stone-built elements were made in mudbrick. It is possible that in the past the stone walls supported mudbrick superstructures. At the time of the survey, a number of the structural units retained their recently constructed roofs, some of corrugated iron, and others of reeds, gorse, timber and earth, in the vernacular rural style of the region (Volume 1, Chapter 3.11). Two of these structural units showed signs of very recent occupation and abandonment, so changes to the village continued until very recently.

Just south-east of the village proper is a ruined one-and-a-half storey house with an associated *mandra* (BU0116; TP082; Fig. 5.14; Fig. 5.15). In form it is a '*makrinari*', based on a long, relatively narrow rectangular room (Ionas 1988, 47). One-and-a-half storey houses are often seen constructed in the region to take advantage of a sloping site, and they offer the advantage of an animal enclosure underneath the living space, which contributed to heating in the winter (Ionas 1988, 54). This house is constructed on a high, stone socle, topped with mudbrick. The flat mud roof of the ground floor partially survives, supported by timber beams and a reed ceiling. Entrance to the first floor was through a door in the north-west face, while the entrance to the ground floor was through a south-eastern door (visible

Fig. 5.14. Asinou village from the east-south-east, with the makrinari *house and* mandra *in the foreground (BU0116; TP082) (Chris Parks)*

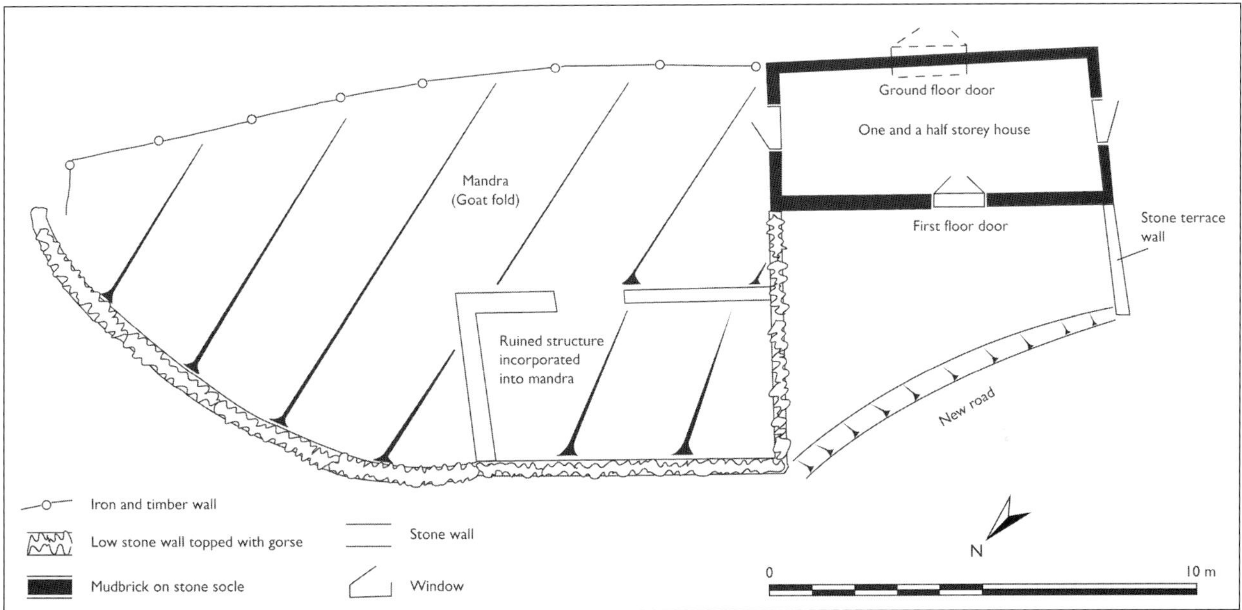

Fig. 5.15. Asinou village: plan of the makrinari *house showing re-use and* mandra *(BU0116; TP082) (Caroline Torres, finalised by Luke Sollars)*

in Fig. 5.14). An adjoining *mandra* was opportunistically constructed from the remains of an earlier stone structure, along with timber, gorse, and corrugated iron: coupled with information from a local informant, we can assume that the structure was used by goatherders during the 20th century.

The 1925 cadastral plan of the village shows three ovens, three threshing floors and four animal enclosures. Only one oven survived at the time of our survey, newly constructed on the site of an earlier one shown on the 1925 plan (Fig. 5.16). The plan shows two threshing floors in a characteristically breezy location, 100 m up the spur to the south of the village, and another one on the point of the spur immediately north-east of the village (TP016). The furthest south and best preserved is paved with stone and measures 11.4 × 7.7 m, with a rubble retaining wall along part of its lower side. Bulldozing has largely destroyed the other two threshing floors. The presence of three ovens and three threshing floors in the 1920s plan implies that the village may have housed at least three family groups at the time. Other evidence from Cyprus suggests that in the recent historic period threshing floors were individual family assets, rather than communal facilities (Given 2000, 215).

According to a local resident whose memories reach back to the 1940s, the village of Asinou produced *halloumi* cheese, grew barley in the fields immediately adjacent to the village and threshed it on the threshing floor. Other goatfolds and associated threshing floors were located in the nearby abandoned settlement of Pera Yitonia (see

Fig. 5.16. Asinou village: reconstructed oven (Chris Parks)

previous section) and elsewhere in the Upper Asinou Valley (e.g. Karterouni: see below). The same informant stressed that people living in the Asinou valley did not have wheat bread, nor were local mills operational during his lifetime. Firewood, barley and *halloumi* produced in the Asinou Valley were sold for cash in nearby Petra and Kakopetria.

One of the most intriguing aspects of Asinou village consists of the striking changes in style and building techniques, and the re-use of built elements. Plate 5.11, based on our structural analysis, shows the materials and techniques, and suggests the construction sequence and phases of development represented in the surviving built fabric.

Seven phases of construction and adaptation were delineated through the structural analysis of the village's built fabric (Plate 5.11):

Fig. 5.17. Asinou village: wall construction of Phase D and re-used block (BU0047.SE017) (Chris Parks)

Fig. 5.18. Asinou village (TS03): interior with corner fireplace (BU0047.SE043) (Chris Parks)

Fig. 5.19. Asinou village (TS03): hearth in centre of long wall of makrinari *style room, with niche visible behind (BU0047.SE002) (Chris Parks)*

- Phase A construction is characterized by the use of basalt with a distinct reddish hue and only a very small proportion of ceramic inclusions in the masonry.
- Phase B construction is characterized by blue basalt and some rough limestone, as well as a large proportion of pottery inclusions, including the extensive use of pottery and tile chinking.
- Phase C construction is similar to B and features the highest proportion of keyed walls, discussed further below.
- Phase D represents infill development between the major structural units of Phases A, B and C. It is distinguished from subsequent phases of infill by its use of stone, including a single, finely made limestone masonry block (Fig. 5.17) that appears to be re-used from an earlier structure.
- Phase E is characterized by the use of mudbrick additions, abutting earlier stone structures.
- Phase F represents changes or repairs to the mudbrick additions of Phase E, including the bricking up of a window and the construction of a mudbrick superstructure on an older stone socle.
- Phase G covers the most recent additions to the village complex, featuring concrete floors and concrete foundations for the mudbrick walls.

Stone walls keyed together at their corners indicate that they were built at the same time to produce a planned dwelling space or animal enclosure. The stone walls in the north-western portion of Asinou village are keyed at the corners (Phase A and C walls), suggesting that this part of the village was planned and constructed as one or two dwelling spaces and that the walls have been maintained in this form, if not in continual use, since their construction. The stone walls of the central and southern portions of the village (Phase A and B), however, generally abut one another and thus may reflect different periods of construction. The abutting stone walls imply that new dwelling spaces were constructed up against existing dwellings or relict dwellings, a practice commonly observed in Cypriot villages (Ionas 1988, 45). New dwelling spaces were also constructed using 'relict walls', that is the opportunistic incorporation of some surviving built fabric to create a new built form.

As mentioned above, two distinct types of basalt characterize Phase A and B construction. The 'red' and 'blue' basalt may derive from different sources in the same quarry area or different quarries altogether. Other than the 'blue' being placed later, we cannot distinguish the period of quarrying.

Four of the roofed spaces in the village have distinctive corner hearths constructed of mud and stone (Fig. 5.18). In contrast to the corner hearths, one room in the south of the village complex has a fireplace constructed in the centre of the long wall of a *makrinari* style room (Fig. 5.19; BU0047.SE002). The style and construction method of this hearth suggests a different approach or tradition in hearth making (Ionas 1988, 84–86). The central hearth is more elaborate and would have taken more time to construct than the simpler corner hearths, which took advantage of the meeting of two walls to support a simple lintel for the fireplace. It is possible that the central hearth predates the corner hearths and represents an earlier period of occupation in the village.

Both corner and central style hearths are also found in the abandoned village of Kato Koutraphas *Mandres* (Chapter 2.10). There, four corner hearths and two central hearths survive: the example of a central hearth found in BU0037 at Mandres is very similar in style to the single central hearth found at Asinou. The Asinou hearth, however, does not represent the earliest occupation of the dwelling space in which it is located, as it was built partially to obscure an earlier stone niche built into the masonry wall during its original construction. Such niches were used to hold lamps or other items. Thus, at least two phases of occupation can be demonstrated in this space.

Of the 98 sherds collected from Asinou village, 22 could be dated to the Ottoman–Modern II period (18th century to mid-20th century), and five to the Modern period (after 1878) (Table 5.7). Apart from an ancient amphora handle, the remainder could only be dated generally to the Medieval–Modern periods. In functional terms the assemblage is as expected for a small-scale rural settlement,

Table 5.7. Asinou Village (TP081, TP082): pottery

Historical Antiquity (Archaic to Late Roman)

Fct	*Type*	*No.*	*Weight*
Tr	Am	1	75g

Medieval to Modern

Fct	*Type*	*No.*	*Weight*
Ar	Brk	6	280g
Ar	Ti	8	700g
CW	BGW	5	105g
CW	Tia	4	185g
CW	Tta	1	45g
HU	HU	26	4.21kg
LU	LU	18	852g
TW	G01	2	50g
U	UPSJa	1	30g

Ottoman to Modern II

Fct	*Type*	*No.*	*Weight*
HU	BuH	4	425g
LU	BuL	2	28g
TW	G01	3	50g
TW	MP	1	7g
TW	MP01	2	60g
TW	SP01	8	90g
TW	SP02	1	12g

Modern

Fct	*Type*	*No.*	*Weight*
HU	Pit03	4	2.125kg
LU	LU	1	45g

with fragments of tile, Cooking Ware, Table Ware and Utility Ware.

The analysis of the built fabric at Asinou village strongly suggests that there were a number of periods of abandonment, or at least reduced occupation within the village, prior to the development of the village into its present form. The British colonial census of 1881 does not record any population at Asinou village (Census 1882), and so it is possible that the current built fabric reflects the re-occupation of the site from the late 19th to the mid-20th century. We know from local informants that most of the remaining inhabitants left in the 1940s. Thus the architectural remains utilized in the latest phase of village development may date from the 18th and early 19th centuries.

Asinou village is notable in the context of the Survey Area as a whole for the diversity of its construction materials and building styles and for the complexity of the extant built form, featuring many phases of construction, adaptation and re-use of relict walls. These features contrast with, for instance, the abandoned village of Kato Koutraphas *Mandres* (Chapter 2.10) where there is a far greater consistency in the construction materials and styles of the village's buildings, as well as a clearly discernable pattern of village expansion followed by contraction and abandonment. Asinou, in contrast to Mandres, is located on agriculturally marginal land where only small mountain terraces can be cultivated. This agricultural marginality, combined with the fluctuating use of this mountainous area for resource extraction and goatherding, as discussed elsewhere in this chapter, appears to have led to greater variation in, and mobility of, the groups living and working in this region. This is directly reflected in the repeated abandonment and re-use of Asinou's buildings, and in the diversity of construction styles and construction materials, which suggests discontinuities in local knowledge and tradition.

Settlement in the Upper Asinou Valley

As in the Lower Asinou Valley, Medieval–Modern settlement evidence from the Upper Asinou Valley is generally located in close proximity to the river. The natural river terraces have not been modified to make the large cultivated fields that are present further down the river. Instead, these terraces appear as small stone-lined features following the contours, and serving a dual purpose: they provide an additional cultivable surface, and at the same time control soil erosion on the steep river banks. Like the larger river terraces located in the Lower Asinou Valley, these terraces are associated with settlement activity, evidence for which comes from structural remains at localities such as Mandres tous Jerenides, Mutallia, Trimitheri and Khalospita.

Remains located at Trimitheri, Khalospita and Mandres tous Jerenides include terracing and multiple roomed structures. Similar structures were located farther up the Asinou Valley by Sollars (2005). There is a larger settlement or village at Nikitari *Mutallia*, indicated by structural remains and an overgrown church called Ayios Yeorgios. As will be discussed further below, these scattered settlements found in the Asinou Valley may have been *metochia*: seasonal or subsidiary settlements or monastic dependencies (Davies 2004, 112).

Mandres tous Jerenides (TP038) consists of four clusters of ruined structures in a forest clearing 5.5 km to the south-west of the village of Nikitari (Fig. 5.20). The northern two clusters lie on a sloping bench of ground located between two gullies, while the southern two lie on a short spur to the south of the southern gully. Here residual and colluvial soils have developed on Basal Group rocks, and present-day vegetation is typical of Mediterranean open forest: pine with grasses, cistus, terebinth, alium and wild olive. There is only one large domesticated olive to the east of one structure in the northern cluster of the settlement.

The northern clusters of structures are generally very well built, with squared stones, pottery and stone chinking and mud bonding. At least one piece of 19th-century pottery was identified in the chinking. This cluster includes a large and well-preserved three-room structure with an adjacent oven at its northern end (Fig. 5.22). The walls of the southern room abut a room to the north but were not joined, suggesting that there were two phases of building at the site. Structures are built into the slope and

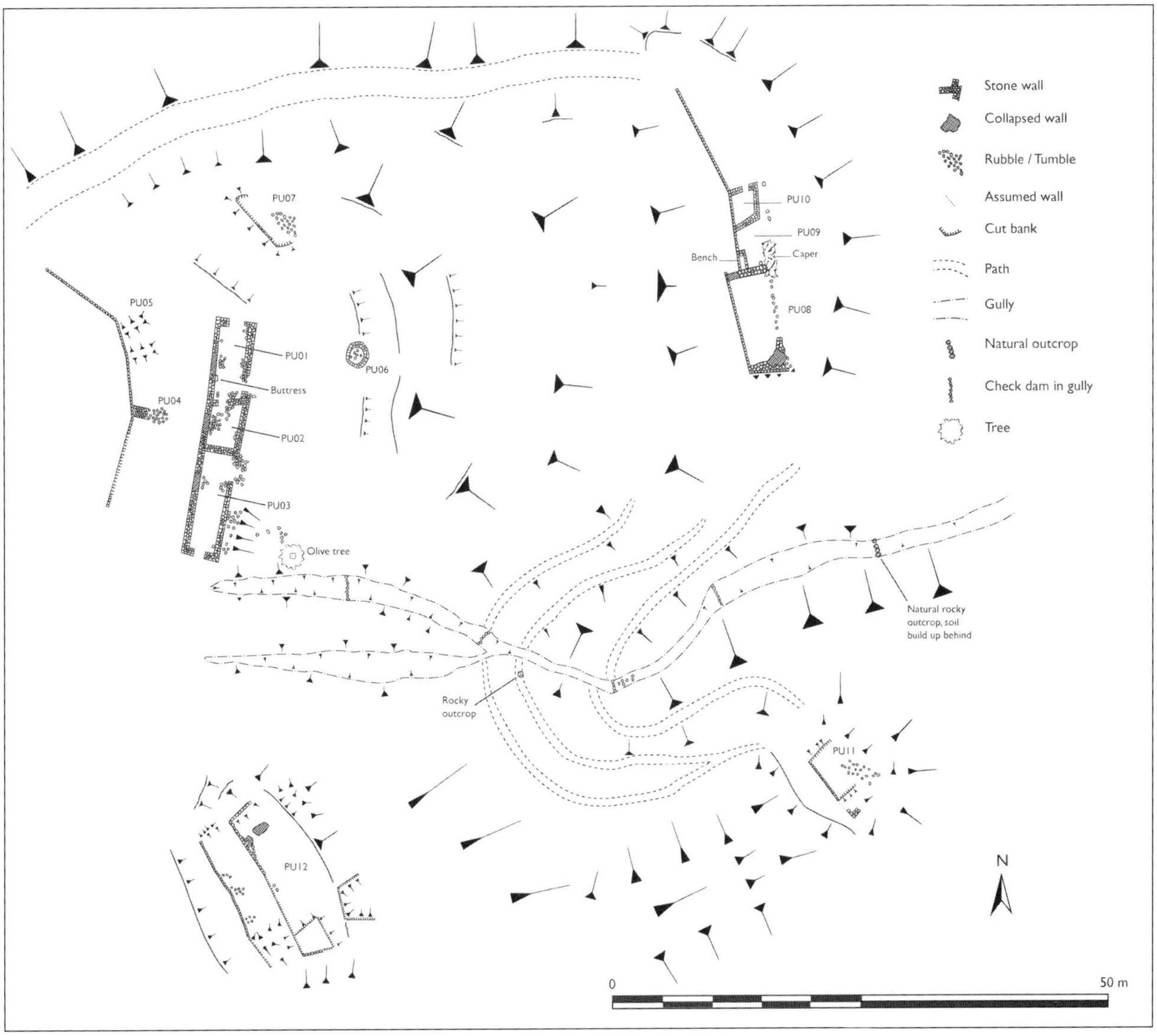

Fig. 5.20. Nikitari Mandres tous Jerenides *(TP038): plan (Rebekah Merriman, finalised by Jean Humbert and Luke Sollars)*

Fig. 5.21. Nikitari Mandres tous Jerenides *(TP038): northern cluster, with PU09 in the foreground, the oven (PU06) and PU01–PU03 below the trees (Chris Parks)*

Fig. 5.22. Nikitari Mandres tous Jerenides *(TP038): three-room structure from the south (PU01–PU03, with PU03 closest) (Chris Parks)*

in some instances may have re-used terrace walls in their construction.

The southern clusters of buildings are smaller, less well preserved and have rough stonework. The irregular stones are weathered and covered with lichen. There is considerably less rubble on the ground within these clusters. It is possible that the linear mounds and banks associated with structural rubble are the decayed remains of mudbrick used in their construction. The lowest group of structural remains is precipitously located at the end of the spur, overlooking the Argaki ton Rotson. It is clear from the workmanship and absence of holding pens that these structures, like many in the Upper Asinou Valley, were not originally built to house livestock.

A series of check dams within the two gullies run west to east through the settlement (Fig. 5.23). The limited sediment accumulation within the majority of these check dams suggests that they were constructed within the past 100 years, as part of the erosion control measures implemented by the Forestry Department (Gibson 2005, 127; Unwin 1933). In some cases the top surfaces of these check dams were worn and show evidence of having been used informally as a means of crossing the gully system. Five pine trees with resin tapping scars are located to the north-east of Mandres tous Jerenides (TP049), and suggest one type of resource extraction that was carried out by the settlements occupants.

A 1925 cadastral plan marks the settlement as comprised of four sheepfolds and an oven – likely the most recent use of these structures. The cadastral plan was made during the period when the settlement at Mandres tous Jerenides was used seasonally by pastoralists who sold cheese to the villages of Kakopetria, Galata, Ayios Theodhoros, and Evrykhou (Chrysostomos Georgiou, interviewed by Hadjianastasis, 2004). The local priest of Asinou church suggested that Nikitari *Mandres tous Jerenides* was the winter settlement for the shepherds of Spilia (Pater Kyriakos, interviewed by Sollars, 2002).

The village of Nikitari *Mutallia* (TP125) and its ruined church of Ayios Yeorgios (TP124) are located on the opposite side of the river from Mandres tous Jerenides, on the southern tip of a spur. This village is composed of extensive remains of multi-roomed structures and one sub-circular oven. Poor preservation of these structural remains and thick undergrowth made it impossible to determine their exact shape, or the spatial relationships between them.

The church of Ayios Yeorgios is overgrown and measures c. 12 × 5 m. Walls within the church stand to 1 m in height and are composed of four or five courses of stonework. The upper courses of the wall show signs of having been re-lain from fallen masonry. There is evidence that the church was used recently: a headscarf hangs from a pine tree growing within the church ruins, while a small plastic icon lies at its foot.

Dating the structural remains at Mutallia was difficult because of poor preservation and sparse pottery. The different degrees of preservation of the church and settlement suggest more than one phase of stonework. It appears that the architectural remains at Ayios Yeorgios, Mutallia and Mandres tous Jerenides exhibit two main periods of occupation. Structural evidence supports an older phase (with poorly preserved remains) and a more recent reoccupation (with better preserved remains). Similar phases of occupation and the presence of a ford, or crossing place, in the river in this locality support contemporaneous occupation of these two settlements and one church.

Fig. 5.23. Nikitari Mandres tous Jerenides *(TP038): check dams in the gully between the two clusters (Chris Parks)*

Fig. 5.24. Church of Ayios Yeorgios (TP124) at Nikitari Mutallia. *The recently dedicated scarf suggests the ruined structure's continuing use (Luke Sollars)*

Asinou Estate drew its income, at least partially, from resources found in the Upper and Lower Asinou Valley, which probably explains the small seasonal or secondary structures located in the Upper Asinou Valley. These include TAESP's Trimitheri and Khalospita, and those located by Sollars (2005): Khandakia; Mandres ton Rotson; and Lakxia tou Agrioklimatou. The steep valley sides and rugged terrain of the Upper Asinou Valley limited the type of agricultural production possible in the region. These structures and small settlements were presumably involved in the extraction of forestry resources and pastoralism, while small-scale terracing supplied subsistence agriculture to the inhabitants. Timber from the Troodos Mountains was in high demand during the Medieval period, especially in the 14th century when pine trees supplied masts for sailing ships (Coureas 2005, 105). Goatherding, as discussed in Chapter 5.7, was an economic activity maintained into the 19th and 20th centuries.

While poor preservation makes assessing the presence of communal facilities at Mutallia difficult, substantial architectural remains, church, ovens and its central position on a ford in the Asinou River suggest that this village was a focal point for activity in the Upper Asinou Valley. It may have served as a collection point for resources extracted by the inhabitants of the smaller scattered structures and settlements in the upper reaches of the Asinou Valley, before they were transported to the plains to be bartered or sold. Facilities at Mutallia provided the population from the scattered settlements with housing, religious facilities and a sense of community.

It is possible that Mutallia was involved in the administration of the Asinou estate. Resources collected here may have been taxed before being moved down river to the grange at Asinou. A complex infrastructure was necessary for the Asinou estate to collect produce and taxes from their lands (cf. Coureas 2005, 115). Itinerant monastic officers or 'wayfarers' visited daughter houses to assist in the harvest, while at the same time supervising its collection and measuring the quantities (Coureas 2003, 97–98, 105–107). It is thus possible that officers from the Asinou estate travelled to the small settlements and structures (or *metochia*) within the Upper Asinou Valley to witness the extraction of resources (Gibson 2005, 178–81).

Additional evidence for such a connection between the Asinou estate and these probable *metochia* comes from communication route data (see also Chapter 5.4). Paths located within the locality of Mandres tou Jerenides follow contour lines, skirting the lower clusters of structures, to cross the gully over a series of check dams. One path diverges to Ayios Theodoros to the north-west, while another path skirts above the Argaki ton Rotson River to the region of Nikitari *Khalospities*.

Interpreting Byzantine–Modern Settlement

Architectural remains, land use activity, communication route data and pottery distributions provide evidence that the Asinou Valley Intensive Survey Zone was a landscape where people grew crops, hunted, extracted forest resources, communicated with neighbouring villages, transported produce and herded goats. Regardless of the degree of activity that is archaeologically visible in this landscape, it is obvious that this Intensive Survey Zone lacks the pottery found in other survey zones within the TAESP landscape. There are several potential reasons for this difference:

- problems in dating Byzantine pottery
- isolation of the region
- homogeneity of TAESP Medieval pottery
- people chose not to settle in this area
- mountain population did not use pottery
- problems with survey techniques

As with elsewhere in Cyprus, there is no pottery evidence to suggest that the Asinou area was occupied in the Byzantine period. Some suggest that the Byzantine period was aceramic, but the most likely scenario is that pottery from the Byzantine period has not been identified accurately and currently is mixed in with Late Roman assemblages (see Volume 1, Chapter 5.4; Gregory 2003; Vroom 1998). The small quantity of Late Roman pottery suggests that either some of the pottery currently dated to the Medieval period should be reassigned to the earlier Late Roman/Byzantine period, or, conceivably, that there was little occupation of this region until the 13th century AD.

In general, Medieval pottery from the Survey Area is distinct from other areas in Cyprus. The pottery from the 12th–14th centuries has a different surface appearance, and types of pottery typical of the Medieval period elsewhere in Cyprus (such as pots and pans from the Levant, glazed pots and pans with pinched spouts in 14th-century assemblages) were not found in the Survey Area. The distinct nature of TAESP's Medieval assemblage suggests a degree of isolation that may be related to limited communication networks or to cultural traditions (Chapter 5.4).

It is possible that people coming to the Lower and Upper Asinou Valleys chose not to settle. This is certainly possible in the lower reaches of the Asinou Valley during the Roman period, where frying pan handles may be related to herders moving through the area (Chapter 5.4). The presence of Roman cooking pots within the structural remains in the Upper Asinou Valley, however, suggests that people did in fact settle and their habitation may be related directly to agriculture, pastoralism or the extraction of forest resources. Architectural remains and land use activities in association with small quantities of Medieval–Modern pottery recovered throughout the Asinou Valley suggest that people did live in this region during this later period.

The use of pottery is not universal and it varies by region and tradition. It is impossible to compare the assemblage of pottery here with that from mountainous areas elsewhere in Cyprus as the Asinou Valley Intensive Survey Zone was the first intensive survey of a mountain landscape on the island. Perhaps the people who lived and moved around the mountains turned to other types of vessels for storage and cooking. Accounts from the *casal* of Porchades (Parsata) near Lefkara indicate that goatskin bags were used to carry wine (Coureas 2005, 107). Certainly goatskin bags, wooden utensils, and carved wooden vessels would have been more expedient and lighter to carry. To address this question one would have to compare survey data from the Asinou Valley Intensive Survey Zone with other intensive survey data from mountainous environments (Gibson 2005, 184; see also Given 2000, 218–27; Vroom 1998).

Manuring may not have played an important role in the management of fields in the Asinou Valley Intensive Survey Zone, even though it is typically the way that household sherds were carried to the cereal fields of the plains and valleys. Perhaps the greater moisture of Troodos soils, compared to that of the plains, produced rotted or 'ghost' sherds that are difficult to identify or pick out of the soil without disintegration (see Bintliff *et al.* 1999; but cf. Davis 2004). Our survey teams identified no such sherds, however, even after three field seasons in the area and some very detailed scrutiny of the ground surface during intensive collecting.

The greatest challenge faced in the Asinou Valley Intensive Survey Zone was surface visibility (see Chapter 5.1). The survey team became more aware of different types of evidence of human activity because of the low quantities of pottery and lithics. Evidence for resource extraction and settlement from architectural remains, resin tapping scars, pitch kilns and check dams became the predominant focus of this aspect of the survey, highlighting diverse human actions in the mountains and forests.

Intensive survey in the mountains highlighted the limitations of focusing on pottery in the survey of past landscapes. Even intensive surveys that aim to record multiple and different types of evidence for human activity still tend to focus on pottery and chipped stone assemblages. By acknowledging the full diversity of human settlement evidence and human activity in the landscape it becomes possible to re-interpret landscapes previously assumed to be too remote or abandoned. Further work is needed to develop survey techniques and methodologies capable of capturing the full diversity of human action, including communication routes, resource extraction, landscape management and land use. Comparisons between survey zones will only be possible when all evidence of human action is collected.

Communication and land use data suggest a more intensive picture of occupation in the mountains than suggested by pottery alone. Two transects (TT496975E and TT495260E) that bisect the Asinou Valley Intensive Survey Zone illustrate the diversity of material remains within the Asinou landscape and the importance of adopting a holistic approach to locating and interpreting past human activities.

Transect TT496975E is located in the Lower Asinou Valley and crosses the fertile terraced fields along the Asinou River (Plate 5.12). Like many transects in this area, pottery was located in Survey Units closest to the river – those involved in agricultural production. A forest cairn (TP062) and the remains of Ayios Ioannis church (TP039) provide information on British colonial land use and Medieval settlement.

Distinctly different evidence for settlement and past human activity is found within transect TT495260E, located 3.5 km to the south-west in the Upper Asinou Valley. This area had little pottery, but an abundance of architectural remains, evidence of past land use and communication routes. Only four sherds of pottery were found within 29 Survey Units. These four sherds (two Archaic–Modern Light Utility wares, one Medieval–Venetian to Early Ottoman Table Ware sherd, and one sherd of Heavy Utility Archaic–Modern), if taken alone, are not representative of past activity in the Upper Asinou Valley. Instead the landscape is scattered with paths, structures, terrace walls, retaining walls and check dams. A similar non-ceramic picture emerges from extensive transects in the mountainous landscape outside the Asinou Valley Intensive Survey Zone, where evidence of past settlement came mainly from paths (TP193; TP233; transect TT495000C), resin tapping scars (transect TT495000C), architectural remains and terracing (TP194).

5.6 Communication Routes and Interaction

There are two main types of communication routes located within the Asinou area: paths involved in the daily movement of people from village to village and between villages and their outfields, which are discussed here; and longer distance routes that follow ridgelines. In many cases paths were found in association with settlements, soil conservation activities and resource extraction (for map see Plate 5.4).

Poorly preserved structural remains at Nikitari *Gnaphion* (TP098) were recovered alongside a path (TP097) that fords the Asinou River below Panayia Phorviotissa. 'Gnaphion' means tannery, and it is entirely possible that the ruins at Gnaphion represent the physical remains of a tannery, located on the banks of the Asinou River in close proximity to the estate church. The path – approximately 65 cm wide and partly dug into the bedrock – runs along a north–south route and appears to connect Panayia Phorviotissa with the structural remains at Gnaphion (TP098) to the north-west. It appears to continue along a north-easterly route connecting the Asinou valley to the northern plains. The presence of grey and reddish lichen on the surface of the hewn bedrock portion of the path suggests that it has been stable for some time. Troodos trails are typically devoid of decades- to centuries-old lichens as they are abraded by transportation (walkers, donkeys). The absence of the much slower-growing lichen *Rhyzocarpon tinei* suggests that that this path was abandoned within the past 100 years.

The degree to which routes of communication, terracing, and structural remains are entwined within the Asinou valley is best exemplified in the Trimitheri locality, where paths run across the terraces, drawing upon the stability of their surface (TP228, TP230). The routes of these paths suggest

Fig. 5.25. Path between Ayios Theodhoros and Asinou Valley (Erin Gibson)

that this region was a focal point for interaction: as well as living there and cultivating the land, the inhabitants communicated constantly with their neighbours to the north-east and south-west along the Argaki ton Rotson watercourse (see Chapter 5.4). A nearby path located at Nikitari *Khalospita* is striking for its width, stability and the care taken to preserve its stability. Retaining walls constructed along the river prevent its erosion. In places this path is over 1 m in width, with a stable surface that is certainly wide enough to enable loaded pack animals to pass each other.

Paths found in association with the check dam system in the Stavros locality (Chapter 5.7) illustrate how these conservation measures were linked within the daily practices of the population. Here paths and resources are tightly interwoven, with paths connecting gullies and winding between check dams. It some cases paths run along the top of check dams, suggesting that they were constructed at the same time as the dams or after they had fallen out of use. In cases where check dams and paths are found in the same vicinity but are not physically associated, the check dams may predate the construction of the paths. Understanding the relationship between paths and resource extraction, such as check dams, is important in order to clarify the link between daily movement, resource extraction and land use in the survey zone (Gibson 2007).

The quantity and stability of paths located within the Survey Area suggests dense occupation and long-term commitment to communication. It is likely that the intensification of Medieval period settlement in the Asinou valley went hand in hand with the expansion and formalisation of paths by estate owners who had an economic commitment to transport produce safely from estate land to storehouses, while ensuring that taxes from serfs and *francomati* were collected adequately. Psimolophou estate accounts from 1318 record 9.16 besants spent on 16 axes for digging forest roads for carrying estate building wood (Richard 1947). The foundation rules written by the hieromonk, abbot and patron of the Makhairas monastery, one Neilos, discuss itinerant monastic officers supervising the harvesting and transport of crops from daughter houses to the grange or warehouse (Coureas 2003, 97–98). Both accounts suggest that the construction and maintenance of roads and paths were under the jurisdiction of estate lords. Supplying and maintaining the infrastructure necessary for the cultivation, extraction and transportation of crops and resources from estate lands to the central manor was in the best interest of the estate (Given 2000, 218–27).

It is likely that in some instances paths constructed in the Roman period, in areas such as Trimitheri and Khalospita in the upper reaches of the Intensive Survey Zone, were re-used in the Medieval and Ottoman periods. In some cases these paths are still in use today. The path that connects the Kourdhali River Valley via Ayios Theodhoros to the Asinou River Valley was probably established prior to the Ottoman period (Fig. 5.25): it is still used today as a nature trail. Such trails act as reminders of the continued importance of communication routes within the landscape, memory and economy of the local population.

5.7 Land Use

Land use data give a picture of the Asinou Valley that is not otherwise seen in pottery distributions. Two aspects are important here: soil conservation and management, and resource extraction (for maps see Plate 5.3 (Hellenistic–Roman) and Plate 5.4 (Medieval–Modern)).

Soil Conservation and Management

Terraces and check dams are the two most prominent types of evidence for past soil conservation and management measures. Changes in land management practices, during both modern and ancient times, clearly reflect the dominant geomorphological and environmental processes shaping the northern flank of the Troodos Mountains. Archaeological and geomorphological survey within the Asinou Valley and the surrounding region provides a unique perspective on the processes shaping both the natural and human landscapes of Cyprus.

Terraces constructed within the area vary in size and morphology. They include large, bulldozed earth and gravel mounds; long, narrow, hand-dug, linear terrace cuts with path-like morphologies that contour hillsides; small scalloped excavations into bedrock; and pre-19th-century stacked stone terraces near abandoned or ruined settlements. In extensive transects carried out 2 km to the south-east of Nikitari village, we discovered the remains of a series of five terraces (TP198). These heavily lichenated stone terraces were constructed by adapting natural topographic features of the area. This building technique is common in much of the terracing located within the Asinou Valley, where steep mountainsides and bedrock outcrops are reformed to produce a stable cultivatable surface.

In most instances terrace walls in the Trimitheri locality are composed of large rounded boulders from the river. These terraces are unlike those located downstream in the vicinity of Asinou village (Chapter 5.5), where smaller cobbles and angular colluvium are used for terracing. Such differences in construction style at Trimitheri may indicate cultural preferences, different traditions and techniques of terracing, or merely the available building material to construct terraces. Similar terraces made from large boulders are found in the Akamas Peninsula in association with Late Roman settlement evidence (Fejfer 1995, 66; Gibson 2005). It is therefore possible that both the terraces and structure at Trimitheri represent Late Roman occupation and cultivation.

At Trimitheri the high, stone-armoured terraces were used for agriculture, while also acting as a means of stabilizing the landscape. High terrace walls (especially TP229), located along the margins of the river channel, probably served to restrict the river's course during flood. Other terrace walls (TP230, TP231) contributed towards controlling erosion, managing moisture and deepening soil, while creating a surface for agricultural production at a convenient location (Wilkinson 2003, 191).

Interestingly, terraces are located throughout the mountains in the Upper Asinou Valley, not just at Trimitheri as mentioned above, but also in the Rotzion locality, located just upstream. Here retaining walls and check dams were noted by the colonial Forest Department (Unwin 1933). Outside the Intensive Survey Zone and to the south-east of the Asinou River Valley (at Lakxia tou Kathiliki), terraces were found with associated retaining walls. Because of the limited extent of these terraces and check dams, it is likely that they represent local or subsistence-based agricultural production.

Check dams similarly serve to control erosion, preserve moisture and provide a surface for cultivation (for map see Plate 5.4). These stone-armoured dams are usually located within gullies where erosion would have been highest. Within the Asinou area the age and stability of these dams vary widely, from those constructed by the forestry department as part of erosion control measures in the early 20th century, to those with deep accumulations of soil that date to the Ottoman period. Check dams are scattered throughout the Intensive Survey Zone, providing evidence of widespread subsistence-based resource conservation. The focus of this activity is in the Lower Asinou Valley, in the area to the south-east of the church of Panayia Phorviotissa and Nikitari *Kapsalia* (TP117).

Stone check dams of varying ages are found in small, second- or third-order gullies. These dams are made of cobble- to boulder-sized stones stacked perpendicular to the direction of water flow and typically have reservoirs of less than 1 or 2 m^3. The younger generation of check dams was built near forestry trails to control soil erosion (Given *et al.* 2003c; Unwin 1933), while the older dams may have been involved in subsistence-based agricultural production, supporting individual family olive trees or small vegetable gardens.

Within the Asinou Valley Intensive Survey Zone, check dams served two main functions: to control erosion and to increase agricultural production. Check dams can be used to control erosion within gullies because they are small and span the full width of the gully channel. Because these dams are relatively low, the amount of sediment trapped is almost always less than 3 m^3. In many instances the sediment of check dams in the upper reaches of gullies overflow their reservoirs. The channel floors immediately downstream of such check dams have been scoured by the flow of the stream that has increased capacity for carrying sediment. This means that the overall amount of erosion controlled by these dams is lessened once they are full. For this reason, check dams are more appropriate for providing a growing surface for small-scale agriculture. The sediment that accumulates as a result of check dam construction can be used to support crops such as olive trees and vines etc. (e.g. TP143). This theory is supported by a local informant, who told us that in the recent past families tended check dams over time to ensure they accumulated enough sediment for cultivation, thus providing a long-term family resource.

Evidence for a similar tradition of land management may be present at Nikitari *Stavros* (TS19; Fig. 5.26). Check dams at Stavros are situated within shallow gullies, which show variability in their degree of erosion: some are shallow and vegetated by grasses, cistus, etc., while others have been completely stripped of vegetation and sediment. Gullies with slopes on an average of 15° are characteristic of check dams found throughout the Asinou Valley Intensive Survey Zone.

Fig. 5.26. Gully with check dams at Nikitari Stavros *(TP161; TS19) (Chris Parks)*

There are several phases of check dam development within each gully at Stavros. While some dams are clearly old, with pithos sherds used as chinking between large lichenated stones (Fig. 5.27), others have little evidence of sediment accumulation and represent more recent conservation measures (Fig. 5.26). The presence of both types of check dam within the same gully, and the extent of this system of stone structures, is important for interpreting land management in the Lower Asinou Valley. It is evident that there was long-term management and commitment to agricultural production in the *Stavros* locality, dating from the Ottoman period and continuing up into the Modern period. Using check dams to stabilize the landscape and produce agriculturally productive land is a technology, or tradition, unlimited to any one time period.

The close proximity of the Stavros check dams to the settlement at Panayia Phorviotissa and monastery at Kapsalia suggests that the check dams were constructed during the Medieval–Modern period, when settlement activity in this area was most active. A path linked Kapsalia to the check dam system of Stavros, further supporting the contemporaneity of these features. Unstable gullies are common throughout the Asinou Valley; the gully systems found around the church and monastery were chosen specifically for conservation and agricultural production.

The relationship between the settlement activity at the church of Panayia Phorviotissa and the check dams to its south-east parallels the Byzantine church of Mitsero *Lambadhiotissa*, which was studied in its landscape context by the Sydney Cyprus Survey Project. The church was closely associated with large check dams that supported agricultural land (Given *et al.* 2003c). Charcoal from these check dams dated the earliest of them to the Late Roman period. They were definitely being used at the same time as the Byzantine church, indicating long-term soil conservation measures and settlement intensification in the region during these and later periods. Although the check dams found at Stavros did not support the same quantity of agricultural land as they did at Mitsero, they provide evidence that a similar pattern of settlement intensification and expansion of agricultural land included the construction of check dams.

Fig. 5.27. Check dam at Nikitari Stavros *(TP161; TS19), with pithos sherd built in (Chris Parks)*

The construction of check dams was a significant part of the British Colonial Government's effort to conserve forests. In 1933 the International Union of Forest Research Organizations published a paper in which Cyprus' Conservator of Forests, A.H. Unwin (1933, 577), described the counter erosion measures adopted by the Cyprus Forestry Department. Dry stone walls (i.e. check dams) were constructed across narrow gullies near the sources of streams to limit erosion. The number of check dams and distance between them was dependent on the slope of the gully, with the interval ranging between 10 and 100 m. As described by Unwin (1933, 578), 'in each case, the stone wall has been built back into solid earth or into the weathered rock on each side of the gully. In many cases earth and small stones have been raked together', filling the space behind the wall to slope slightly back into the bed of the gully behind. These check dams were often planted with trees in the autumn and early winter. He reports that between 1878 and 1932 these terraces improved conditions so that 'trees growing on slopes on either side of the terraces, show quicker growth than before', while Aleppo pine, cypress and acacia reproduced naturally (Unwin 1933, 576). Interestingly, Unwin suggests that 'people of the hill country appear to have a natural aptitude for the making of dry stone walls', quite possibly because the tradition of constructing check dams had existed since the Late Roman period.

Resource Extraction

In the Asinou Valley, archaeological evidence of past resource extraction comes from both inside and outside the modern forest boundary, and includes pitch kilns, resin tapping scars, forestry cairns and watermills. Shotgun cartridges, tinfoil wrappers and chains from chainsaws were found within the boundaries of the Adephi State Forest and provide information about current resource use within the forest landscape. There are four main types of resource extraction that are relevant here: cultivation; pastoralism; hunting; the extraction of forest resources.

Threshing sledge blades and threshing floors provide evidence for the cultivation and processing of grain within the Lower Asinou Valley. Pera Yitonia and Asinou village are the only two areas within the Asinou Valley where threshing floors were located. Grain was probably cultivated along the fertile river terraces that run parallel to the Lower Asinou River, and small quantities could have been grown on the Stavros check dams. As mentioned previously, the terraces located in the Upper Asinou Valley may have been used for the cultivation of grain as well, although no evidence for the threshing proccss was identified.

Very few olive trees are located in the Asinou Valley today. The contemporary cultivation of olives is confined to the agricultural fields on the northern banks of the Lower Asinou River opposite Panayia Phorviotissa, or to very young trees located on the top of check dams and at abandoned settlements. The oldest trees are associated with the monastery buildings at Nikitari *Kapsalia* (TP117) where, as discussed previously, a piece of ground stone was found associated with monastery buildings and old olive trees. This association suggests that the grinding stone is related to the processing of olives, perhaps a precursor of the stone tools still used today for the cracking of green olives.

Evidence of pastoralism comes from cadastral map place names, archival documentation and ethnographic accounts. Goatfolds are marked on cadastral maps throughout the Upper and Lower Asinou Valleys. These designations indicate how the structures were used during the 1920s when the cadastral plans of the region were produced.

There is little direct archaeological evidence of pastoralism, however, when structures such as Nikitari *Palaeomandres* (TP048) are viewed in a more holistic landscape context, it is possible to look beyond the immediate past to the role of such a structure prior to the 19th and 20th centuries. Palaeomandres is a two-roomed structure, 8 m long and between 3 and 5 m wide, with rubble walls. It overlooks the Asinou Valley and is situated 15 m to the south-east of the Ayios Theodoros–Asinou communication route.

While no pottery was located in the structure to suggest its age or function, it is probably related to the Ayios Theodhoros–Asinou River Valley communication route (Gibson 2005). Ethnographic information suggests that the structure was used in the 19th–20th centuries when goats were moved between Ayios Theodhoros and Mandres tous Jerenides. According to an informant from the former village, during the 19th and 20th centuries Asinou village sold *halloumi* cheese to Nikitari and other villages on the plains, while Nikitari *Mandra tous Jerenides* sold its cheese to the villages of Kakopetria, Galata, Ayios Theodhoros and Evrykhou. The locality name *Palaeomandres* (old goatfolds) suggests that at the time the cadastral plan was produced the goatfold was already old. Palaeomandres, like many structures called '*mandra*' or 'goatfold' on the cadastral plans, was re-used during the last 200 hundred years, but its foundations were, most likely, established much earlier (Chapter 5.8).

It is important to realise that flocks were a flexible and moveable asset that could adapt to changing environmental conditions. During the 17th century, monasteries in Ermionidha in southern Greece raised goats and sheep as a form of 'agribusiness' (Forbes 2000, 55–61). In Ottoman Cyprus pastoralism was both a household activity and a larger specialized economic activity. Monasteries and estates had large herds managed by specialist herders (Ionas 1994, 435; Given 2000, 221–22). It is possible that pastoralism during the Medieval–Ottoman period was controlled by the Asinou estate, which could sell wool and cheese to local and regional markets for profit. After the monastery fell out of use goats became part of the household economy. The re-use of structural remains both in the Upper and Lower Asinou Valley during the later 19th and 20th centuries for goatfolds supports this theory.

A fresco (Plate 5.13) dated to 1332–1333 AD in the narthex of the church of Panayia Phorviotissa shows two hunting dogs tied to a stake and two moufflon in a mountainous, but non-forested, background (Stylianou and Stylianou 1985, 134–35). This scene suggests hunting took place in the Asinou Valley during the 14th century, and possibly that the landscape was not forested as today.

Hunting moufflon with dogs was a popular pastime of the rich within the Byzantine and Lusignan period elsewhere in Cyprus (Richard 1985, 280). Stylianou and Stylianou (1985, 134) have suggested that the founding of the monastery of the Mother of God of Kykkos in the 12th century was closely related to moufflon hunting by the Duke-Governor of the island, Manuel Butumites. Similarly, Wilhelm von Boldensele wrote in 1333:

> There are in the mountains of Cyprus wild sheep, with hair like that of goats and dogs, which are said to be found nowhere else. It is a very swift animal and its flesh is good and sweet. When I was out hunting I saw several caught by dogs, especially by the tame leopards of Cyprus (in Cobham 1908, 16).

There is a similarly interesting account from Ludolf von Suchen who visited Cyprus between 1336 and 1341, where he discusses how Hughues d'Ibelin, the Count of Jaffa and Ascalon, had more than 500 hounds:

> Every two dogs have their own servant to guard and bath and anoint them… When they go to the chase they live sometimes for a whole month in their tents among the forests and mountains, straying from place to place, hunting with their dogs and hawks, and sleeping in their tents in the fields and woods, carrying all their food and necessaries on camels and beasts of burden (in Cobham 1908, 20).

Evidence of contemporary hunting practices within the Asinou Valley came mainly from shotgun cartridges. While the distribution of these shotgun cartridges is focused in the lower Asinou Valley, they are also found both inside and outside the Adelphi State Forest Boundary – regardless of hunting restrictions. The material remains of modern hunting include tin foil and spam cans, characteristic traces of the modern huntsman's lunch, which were often located along mountain ridges. Extensive survey in adjacent mountain areas both to the north and south of the Asinou Valley Intensive Survey Zone also recovered shotgun cartridges along ridgelines. Travelling along mountain ridges was often the most expedient means of moving throughout the mountain landscape where gullies and steep slopes were common. Shotgun cartridge data collected through extensive transects proved that hunting is, and was, widespread throughout the mountains.

The extraction of forest resources forms a large percentage of the data recovered from the intensive and extensive survey of the mountain landscape. Evidence for resin tapping came from throughout the Asinou Valley (e.g. TP049) and the mountains. Resin was extracted from the sapwood of pine trees. In some cases trees were felled to take the resin, though evidence for tapping in the mountains shows that resin was extracted from standing trees, leaving an easily distinguishable scar (Ellis Burnet 2004; Gibson 2005). A cluster of five trees located near the settlement of Mandres tous Jerenides are between 100 and 150 years old (Fig. 5.28; TP049). These trees show excellent examples of resin tapping scars on their uphill side, a feature common throughout the survey zone. Evidence for resin extraction high in the mountains was found through extensive transects, where a scar was found at 700 m elevation.

Fig. 5.28. Pinus brutia *with resin tapping scar (TP049). Scale: 10 cm (Michael Given)*

Pitch was made by heating the heavier resin extracted from pine trees, or by burning sapwood slowly in a kiln. This pitch was widely used to preserve wood, especially doors and roof timbers. It was also used to seal and waterproof a variety of vessels, such as storage jars, goatskin bags used for wine, and to seal the hulls of ships (Thirgood 1987, 118). According to a local informant, five or six families living in Asinou village and Karterouni village still tapped trees for resin in the 1920s.

Two of the best-preserved pitch kilns are located at Nikitari *Palaeomandres* (Fig. 5.29; TP105). Both kilns are positioned at roughly the same elevation, on opposite sides of a dry gully where seasonal runoff is unlikely to affect them. The north-easternmost kiln is the larger of the two, measuring 3.5 m wide and 2.4 m long with a semicircular centre. Fire-cracked rock was visible in the northern wall inside the kiln. The second smaller kiln, located on the south-west side of the gully, is 2.0 m in diameter.

The pitch kilns at Palaeomandres are located adjacent to a path (TP100) that appears to connect Mandres tous Jerenides with the village of Ayios Theodhoros in the

Fig. 5.29. Nikitari Palaeomandres *(TP105): two pitch kilns 17 m apart, with dry gully running between them (Michael Given)*

Kourdhali River Valley to the west. Part of this same path crosses the Asinou River to the north-east and follows the river course down into the Lower Asinou Valley. The pitch kilns were intentionally placed in this central position.

The remains of an additional pitch kiln, or charcoal burner (Sina Oros *Mouti tou Stavrou*; TP214), was located through extensive transects. This sub-circular rock pile, 6 m in diameter, is located on a knoll overlooking the modern village of Sina Oros and is associated with abandoned terracing and olive trees between 100 and 200 years old.

It is probable that three unnaturally circular and heavily eroded clusters of rock, built on natural rock outcrops, are the remains of charcoal making areas or small pitch kilns (Nikitari *Stavros*, TP137; Nikitari *Khandakia*, TP144; Nikitari *Pykroathasoudhi*, TP141). All of these were located in isolated positions away from communication routes, and settlement evidence suggests that these structures were not designed to be used repeatedly, but rather employed for the expedient manufacture of pitch or charcoal.

Wood resources such as *Pinus brutia*, *Quercus alnifolia* (golden oak) and *Pistacia terebinthus* (terebinth) were widely used throughout the Asinou area for charcoal, fuel and tool making (Given 2002, 7–8). Although much of the evidence for timber use in the Survey Area comes from when Cyprus was a regional supplier of charcoal in the 19th and 20th centuries, pine from the Adelphi forest was widely used throughout all periods of forest occupation (Given 2002, 16; Thirgood 1987, 105–14). We know from our interviews with local people that *Pinus brutia* was cut, collected and sold as firewood to villages on the plains. The British Colonial Government harvested pine trees in the Adelphi forest during both World Wars.

Firebreaks and access routes were built in the forest as part of the new development policy that began in the 1920s, but which only became firmly established in the 1950s (SA1/1159/1920, Red 27). In 1933 relief labour constructed forest access roads in Asinou. These roads were meant to serve three main purposes: provide access to the forest to cut the cost of extracting timber and transporting it to markets; make it easier to fight fires in the forest; and offer tourist access to the church of Panayia Phorviotissa (SA1/444/1933). There is a section of this well-made tourist road in the Moutti tou Dhia locality (TP188), while a bridge belonging to this same road is located to the north-east of Panayia Phorviotissa.

5.8 Boundaries, Shifting Settlement and Climate Change

Impact of the State Forest on Settlement Pattern

During the 19th century, many of the once permanent mountain villages such as Nikitari *Asinou* (TS03) and Nikitari *Mutallia* (TP125) became seasonal settlements. This shift from permanent to seasonal settlement is entwined in changes in interaction that occurred alongside the Forest Delimitation of the late 19th century (SA1/444/1933; Gibson 2005, 166–67). The Forest Law of 1879 and the Forest Delimitation Law of 1881 established that goats were no longer allowed to graze in the State Forest without a permit (Given 2002). Forest cairns placed along this boundary signalled to villagers where the forest started and ended. Although the law was passed, it was very difficult to impose, and in 1933 the government was still trying to get the goats out of the Asinou Valley (SA1/444/1933). It was not until the 1930s, when new forestry roads were built and

Fig. 5.30. Ayios Theodhoros Karterouni *(TP062): forest cairn (Michael Given)*

Fig. 5.31. Ayios Theodhoros Karterouni *(TS14) from the south-west, with the main cluster of buildings near the top of the slope and the terraces below them (Michael Given)*

the old roads improved, that access to the forest enabled Forest Guards to implement laws passed 40 years earlier.

Settlements within the Adelphi forest were abandoned during the British colonial period, the result of a combination of social, economic and political factors. The delimitation of the forest was followed, 50 years later, by the Ten Year Forest Development Plan that aimed to protect the forest from grazing and felling, while restocking the forest with 'all the trees which the ground could carry' (SA1/556/1942: Red 8–9). Today young pine seedlings are still intensively grown on bulldozed, scooped or scalloped terraces within the Adelphi forest.

Accessing the natural resources and agricultural produce of rural Cyprus was a priority to the British Colonial Government during the late 19th and 20th centuries (Angelides 1996, 210–11). In general this complex transportation network, consisting of new roads and railways, provided rural villagers throughout Cyprus with access to larger urban and international markets, while also offering them other options for employment within the cities (Ionas 1994, 446).

The imposition of boundaries separating forest from agricultural land through the construction of forest cairns had dramatic effects on the way that people lived and interacted. We located two of the masonry forest cairns that probably belong to the original Adelphi State Forest boundary (TP062; TP068). The best-preserved cairn has a base diameter of 76 cm (TP062) and is preserved to a height of 30 cm, although stones scattered around the cairn suggest that originally it was between 60 and 70 cm in height. The cairn was made of angular basalt, and traces of soft white plaster were found on the surface. Similar masonry forest cairns were also found around the abandoned village of Karterouni (Fig. 5.30).

This abandoned village (TS14) is located at 730 m asl in the south-west of the Survey Area, on the steep valley sides to the east of the Kourdhali River (Fig. 5.31). The village stands in what used to be an enclave in the Adelphi forest, surrounded by original masonry forest cairns (Fig. 5.30).

The main cluster of buildings (TP067) stands close to the centre of the enclave, and consists of several abandoned structures in varying conditions, constructed from rough basalt blocks using mud bonding with stone and pottery chinking (Plate 5.14). One two-storey structure with a tile roof is almost completely intact. The quantity of modern detritus in and around it suggest that this was the last building to be abandoned, which, we know from oral sources, happened in the 1970s. The majority of structures are less well preserved, and while many still have walls standing to their full height, none have surviving roofs. Farther up the slope from the central cluster of buildings were several similarly constructed, and decayed, outliers. The door of one of these, right on the edge of the cleared area and below a forestry cairn, opened into a large enclosure.

The enclosure suggests a pastoral aspect to the village's past economy, while high terraces that break the slope below the central cluster of structures indicate an agricultural component. The terraces below the road and near the river are evidence of the determined exploitation of limited agricultural land. The success of this exploitation is demonstrated by the three threshing floors cut into the end of the spur, located close to the village and its terraces, and in a position where they could catch the valley's breezes (TP072).

A botanical survey of the area identified remnant populations of several species of plants that could be used for animal fodder. Milk vetch and ball cotton clover are widespread in the settlement, and would have provided protein-rich fodder in the spring and summer. Low growing brome grasses and other small plants provide light grazing in the spring, while rockrose and hawthorn could be grazed throughout the year. Tall grasses are abundant at Karterouni, while near the Kourdhali River green grasses and clover can be found even in the summer. The leaves of fig, poplar and plane trees, almond husks and prunings are available for use as animal fodder in Karterouni, and may have been used during the summer to supplement the animal diet.

There are several types of wild food available within the immediate vicinity of the village of Karterouni. These could be used to supplement the diet in times of crop failure. Essential sugars would be provided by figs, *Cytinus hyocistus*, grapes, blackberries, hawthorn and terebinth berries. Winter wild oats and wall barley could supplement a poor cereal harvest, while asphodel and reedmace could also be used. Milk vetch could be used to enhance the diet, but only if its toxins were removed. Asparagus, fennel, capers, campion and thistles were also widely available in the Karterouni settlement and could be used as supplementary food sources (see also Forbes 1997).

Because of poor ground visibility, no pottery analysis was carried out at Karterouni, and there is no clear evidence available to suggest a foundation date. The standard of construction hints at an early modern period, but this could simply be a result of continued occupation. The village does not appear on Venetian village lists (Grivaud 1998, 466–70) suggesting, perhaps, that it was founded after the end of the 16th century. Interestingly it was not included in the 1881 census either. Other villages, such as Nikitari *Vouni* (TP031), similarly located at the boundary between private agricultural land and the Adelphi forest, are also omitted from these village lists. It is evident, however, that at the time of the delimitation of the forest, the settlement at Karterouni had a significant enough population to warrant making it an enclave in the forest. As often occurred during the British colonial period, administrative boundaries were based on existing landholdings and village limits were simply formalised by the British.

Settlement and Climatic Variability

Climatic events and variability are increasingly easy to read and associate with social events from the Medieval period to the present. During this time, particularly the Medieval Warm Period or Medieval Optimum (8th/10th–14th centuries AD) and Little Ice Age (16th–19th centuries AD), climatic variability led to short- and long-term changes in moisture and temperature. As discussed in Volume 1, Chapter 4.4, climatic zones of Cyprus were enhanced or muted depending upon the regional and hemispheric nature of this variability. Such climate changes, as perceived by Cypriots, may have influenced their choices in settling and using the mountain landscape.

The church of Panayia Phorviotissa and its monastic buildings were constructed during the Medieval Optimum period and remained occupied, along with most of the settlement in the Asinou Valley Intensive Survey Zone, through the Little Ice Age. There are three main pieces of evidence that suggest landscape responses to climate change during this period in the Asinou Valley: sedimentation at Ayios Ioannis church; the Stavros check dams; the Palaeomylos watermill.

The church of Ayios Ioannis (TP039), located on the north-west bank of the Asinou River, is unusually positioned within a terrace of the river. As explained in Chapter 5.5, the only visible remains of the church is one wall made of ashlar stone blocks that have been eroded out of the river terrace. It is likely that the church and settlement in the area of Nikitari *Khalospities* (TS12) date to the same period. Thus the position of this church suggests that a sequence of alluviation and erosion episodes took place in the vicinity following the church's construction. The increased alluviation documented by Lécuyer *et al.* (2001) at Potamia *Agios Sozomenos* was related to the Little Ice Age. It seems that the Asinou River responded similarly to the increased discharge in the valley. The church of Ayios Ioannis may have been constructed at the same time as the 12th-century Panayia Phorviotissa, 1 km downstream. If the church of Ayios Ioannis was indeed constructed during the Medieval Optimum period, it was then buried by sediment carried in by the Asinou River during the Little Ice Age in the Later Medieval and Ottoman periods.

It is possible that climatic fluctuations increased the amount of erosion experienced on the steep mountainous hillsides of the Asinou Valley. Check dams may have been used to increase slope stability and conserve soil. If new settlers moved into the valley because of drought in the plains, then check dams planted with olive trees and other crops served as a means of countering increased population pressure, while offering additional resources in times of famine. Crops grown on the extensive check dams in the Stavros locality may have provided surplus food for the monastic estate at Panayia Phorviotissa to trade, or sell, to less drought-resistant estates in the plains and elsewhere.

The remains of the watermill at Palaeomylos ('old mill') (BU0054) lie on a terrace above the Asinou River, to the north-east of the Asinou Valley Intensive Survey Zone (Fig. 5.32). This structure is unlike the other watermills studied within the TAESP area, both in form and construction. It is built using basalt masonry and chinking with pink mortar. Instead of the usual vertical shaft, there is a hopper or chute that is square in plan and slopes down at a 15–20° angle. The height of the penstock is 2.1 m. The millrace is 7 m long, and the channel is covered with lime and crushed brick, as well as soot plaster for waterproofing. There is very little evidence of a millhouse or wheel chamber around the mill, and there is no archaeological evidence of any other mills in its vicinity. According to a local informant, the Asinou mill was small and seldom used, as there often was not enough water for it to run. In recent memory most people living in Asinou took their wheat to be milled in Petra or Evrykhou.

Today the location of the Palaeomylos mill seems unusual, as there is rarely any visible water in the vicinity.

Fig. 5.32. Nikitari Palaeomylos *(BU0054): Asinou watermill, looking along leat to opening of chute (Chris Parks)*

It is possible that this mill was built during the Little Ice Age when there was an increase in the amount of water passing through the Asinou River. Flour mills powered by water or animal were often part of the communal facilities provided by estate lords during the Medieval period – Kythrea, Palaekythro and Psimolophou all had flour mills (Richard 1985, 270; Coureas 2005, 113). While the Asinou estate was much smaller than these estates, the increase in cultivation in the Asinou Valley during the Medieval and Ottoman periods may have necessitated a local mill built and controlled by the estate and monastery of Asinou. As the climate changed and river discharge lessened, the mill may have fallen out of use during the 19th century. It would have been necessary to process cereals elsewhere in the plains, such as the mill between Nikitari and Vyzakia (BU0073). The path at Nikitari *Gnaphion* (TP097) may be the remains of a communication route that was involved in the transportation of cereals from the Asinou Valley to be milled and/or traded at Palaeomylos or on the plains at Petra.

Under the climatic conditions of the Medieval and Ottoman period where one generation endured drought and the next excess rain, areas such as the foothills and mountain valleys would be suitable targets for settlement. This diverse mountain environment and broad resource base included grazing land for pastoralism, agricultural fields for cereal cultivation, and forest for hunting, timber extraction, and gathering upland plants. This provided the inhabitants with a sustainable economy compared with contemporary life on the plains. The concentration of archaeological evidence that includes pottery, architectural remains, check dams, terraces and communication route data supports the assertion that estates and other communities moved from the plains to the Asinou Valley to settle during the Medieval to Ottoman period. It was a combination of diverse landscape, resources and technologies that enabled the monastic estate of Asinou and the estate at Aspri (see Chapter 5.9 below) to flourish until at least the mid-17th century.

5.9 The Wider Mountain Landscape

Extensive survey across the whole mountain landscape of the Survey Area offers an overall picture of activity outside the Asinou Valley Intensive Survey Zone (for methodology see Volume 1, Chapter 2.2; for map see Plate 5.1). The information collected in seven extensive transects places the data collected in the Asinou Valley in its broader mountain context.

Extensive survey recovered the most direct evidence of settlement activity in transect TT3879000V, which crossed from the Kourdhali River Valley eastward into the Asinou River Valley. A possible farmstead was located by a bend on the river, at the foot of a steep hillslope (Ayios Theodhoros *Tholos*; TP194). A series of ruined, overgrown terraces were associated with three piles of rock that may have been the remains of structures. This complex included a well or cistern, while paths and tracks cross at a ford on the river. These remains are similar to those located within the Upper Asinou Valley and may also date to Medieval–Modern times. Farther along this transect a 1 m-wide path (Ayios Theodhoros *Kankellia*; TP193) was cut into the hillside, and may connect Ayios Theodhoros to the plains in the north (see Volume 1, Chapter 3.13).

Extensive transects confirmed the picture of activity found within the Asinou Valley Intensive Survey Zone. Paths follow the contours of the mountains (Ayios Yeoryios *Plevra tis Mosphilias*; TP233) or climb ridgelines to cross between valleys (TT495000C). They are between 1 and 2 m wide and cut into the soil and bedrock of the hillside, providing evidence of long distance communication within and beyond the Asinou Valley. They suggest extensive interaction within the mountains in areas previously considered to be 'remote' or 'isolated'. The presence of resin tapping scars at elevations that exceed 700 m (TT495000C) confirms that human activity was not confined to cultivation in fertile river valleys; instead much, if not all, of the mountain landscape was exploited.

Located 4.5 km to the south-west of Panayia Phorviotissa is the Medieval–Modern mountain settlement of Ayios Yeorgios *Aspri* (TP066). This abandoned village on a spur at 960 m asl forces us to rethink interpretations of estate landscapes and medieval period occupation of the mountains (Fig. 5.33). It appears as 'Asprus' on a Venetian village list of 1565, and was home to six adult male

Fig. 5.33. Ayios Yeoryios Aspri *(TP066): ridgeline with the water tank at the left, the site of the church on the right, and the houses in between them (Chris Parks)*

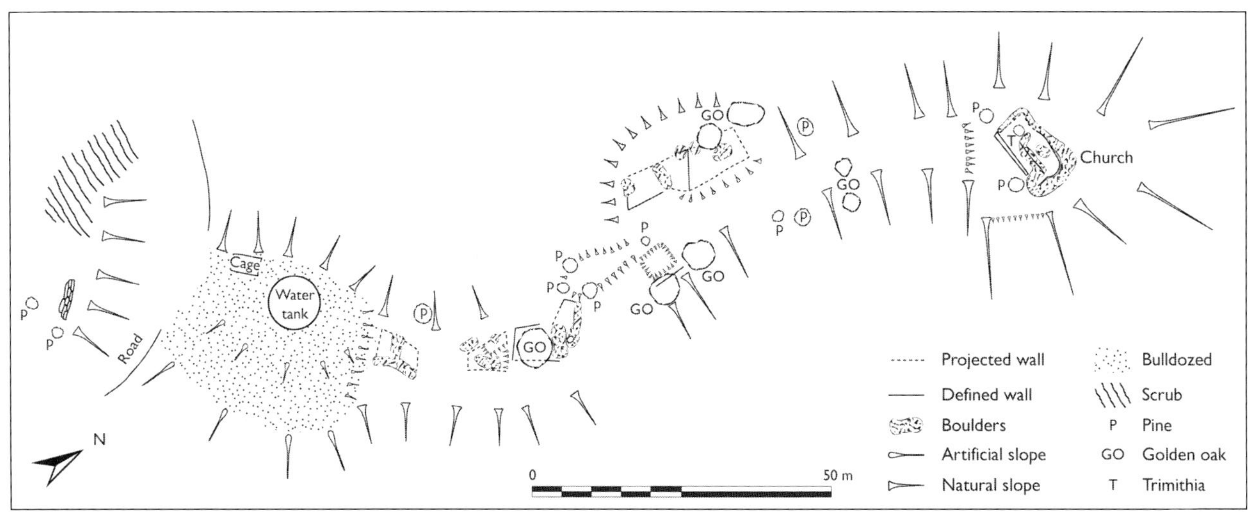

Fig. 5.34. Ayios Yeoryios Aspri *(TP066): plan (Sarah Janes, finalised by Jean Humbert and Luke Sollars)*

francomati (Grivaud 1998, 470). The remains of several buildings were identified along the flanks of the spur, and a church stood at its north-eastern end; none of the structures survive to more than two or three courses above current ground level (Fig. 5.34).

Clear wall lines in the church indicate that it was composed of a nave with an apse at the east end, a narthex at the west end, and a southern side aisle. Other structures, built on the sides of the spur below the central ridge, had rooms that were less distinct than those in the church. Some structures were built on platforms that had been cut into the bedrock. It is likely that in the past the settlement continued along the spur, across a now-bulldozed area and present location of a water tank, toward the current forestry road. A simple platform was defined by the remains of a retaining wall to the south-east of this road and may indicate that the settlement continued a little way up the slope.

To sample the pottery from Aspri, 26 organic POSI units were placed in and around the church at the north-east end of the spur, the settlement area located half way long the spur, and the bulldozed area just north-west of the forestry road. The material from the church area consists of Heavy Utility, Utility Ware, Light Utility and some Table Ware, all dating generically to the Medieval–Modern period. Two units, near a bulldozed tread at the base of the spur near the water tank, produced a range of Medieval–Modern pottery, including Monochrome wares with yellow glaze and green glaze, dating to the 16th and 17th centuries, and Medieval Utility II wares with incised decoration of types 3 and 4 (15th to early 20th centuries).

Late Medieval and Early Ottoman material is clearly distributed from the base of the spur to its point by the church, and correlates well with the ruined structures. This date is supported by the lichen, *Rhyzocarpon tinei*, that has colonized the exposed rubble of the church. By extrapolating points of disturbance of the church's fabric from an analysis of the frequency and diameter of lichen patches (Volume 1, Chapter 2.4), it was determined that the structure was built in the Early Medieval period. It was abandoned and began to decay during the Ottoman occupation and finally collapsed between 200 and 300 years ago. It is likely that both church and the settlement were abandoned by the end of the 17th century, like many such settlements in Cyprus.

Judging by the location, the economy was presumably based on pastoralism and exploitation of forest resources. While there are no clear signs of coppicing on the spur, the surrounding slopes are covered in golden oak, making it quite possible that charcoal burning was an aspect of the local economy. A local informant told us that in the 1940s the region was used by goatherds who re-used the Medieval–Ottoman period structures, as well as using sgraffito sherds found in the ruins as lamps.

Directly above Aspri is the small, ruined church of Ayia Paraskevi (TP249), sitting just below a prominent ridgeline, close to a confluence of at least four paths. Today half the church apse is discernable and three rough lines of rubble indicate the position of the walls. Ayia Paraskevi overlooks the settlement of Aspri and before the church fell into ruins it would have been visible to the settlement's inhabitants below. This intervisibility, the degree of preservation of structural remains at Ayia Paraskevi and the presence of Medieval–Modern period lugged church tiles, suggests that the settlement and the church were contemporaneous.

It is likely that the monastic estate at Kapsalia predates Aspri. The estate, associated with Panayia Phorviotissa, was established soon after the church was constructed in the 12th century. There is no pottery evidence to suggest that Aspri predates the 15th century. Interestingly it is during this period that occupation at Kapsalia increases – with much evidence for activity between the 15th and 20th centuries. Thus it is likely that the Asinou and Aspri estates were used contemporaneously from the 15th century until their abandonment. There is much potential for studying the interwoven and complex interrelationships that existed between these estates and their inhabitants in this mountainous landscape. It is possible that other small estates existed in the mountains but have been overlooked or misinterpreted, such as the clusters of settlement at Mandres tous Jerenides, Mutallia and Ayios Yeorgios (TP038; TP124; TP125).

5.10 The End of 'Isolation' in the Mountains

The quantity of pottery and chipped stone discovered in the mountains makes the area look minor and insignificant when compared to others within the TAESP landscape. During the course of the project we came to realise that it is the diversity of this mountain landscape and the way people lived in, adapted and modified it, which make it unique. It was the scarcity of traditional survey material that made those who surveyed in the mountains more sensitive to the diverse evidence of past human activity. Through the act of surveying and systematically moving through the landscape we became aware of the intricacies of occupation within the Asinou Valley and its surrounding area. Human activity was seldom represented in pottery or lithic scatters, but rather in how villagers moved to and from fields, collecting wood, tapping resin from trees high in the mountains, or in the small paths found amidst tended check dams, overgrown terraces, retaining walls along streams and isolated structures along ridgelines. These are the remains of mountain activities that changed our perception of the mountains as 'isolated', while demonstrating archaeologically that the mountains have been settled since the Roman period.

Intensive regional survey projects have become too comfortable in their methods. If the aim of survey archaeology is to understand the social and cultural aspects that lie behind material remains, then survey techniques must press forward to look beyond the easily quantifiable pottery and lithic scatters now so integral to the discipline. We must expand our techniques to weave alternative methods of survey and recording within our well-practised collection strategies. Fully integrating the study of land use, resource extraction and communication into intensive survey will challenge many of our preconceived ideas of isolated or abandoned landscapes.

The entire Asinou Valley Intensive Survey Zone is characterized by long-term settlement continuity from the Roman period until the mid-20th century. Roman material was scattered throughout the Lower Asinou Valley (e.g. Nikitari *Khalospities)* and the Upper Asinou Valley, where it was associated with the structural remains at Nikitari *Trimitheri* and Nikitari *Khalospita*. While this scattered occupation in the Asinou valley supports a definite Roman presence in the mountains, it is evident that this occupation differed strikingly from the Roman farmsteads and settlements located elsewhere in the TAESP landscape.

The best examples of long-term occupation come from Nikitari *Trimitheri* and Nikitari *Khalospita*. Similar structures were located by Sollars (2005, 134–35) at Mandres ton Rotson and Khandakia. These structures show evidence of Late Roman period activity followed by Medieval–Modern period re-use, when rooms were expanded and old pottery and tile incorporated into walls and foundations. Even as late as the early to mid-20th century, these structures served as temporary dwellings for goatherds.

In the lower Asinou Valley, Medieval–Modern settlement activity clustered around the church of Panayia Phorviotissa, its monastery buildings (TS08) and the fertile agricultural fields near Khalospities (TS12). This constitutes the core of the monastic estate. Check dams at Stavros produced cultivable surfaces while stabilizing the erosion on the hillsides to the south-east of the church. Modification of river terraces in the lower Asinou Valley provided agricultural land for the cultivation of cereals, olives and possibly vines. Cereals could be threshed at Pera Yitonia and later above Asinou village, while pottery at Khalospities and Kapsalia suggest large-scale storage of food resources.

A village (Mutallia) with subsidiary structures (Mandres tous Jerenides) and the church of Ayios Yeorgios were constructed up the Asinou River, while even further up the river valley and deeper into the forest structures at Trimitheri, Khalospita and its vicinity were re-used (Sollars 2005). These structures and settlements were probably monastic dependencies whose economies involved extracting forest resources and participating in pastoralism on behalf of the monastic estate. The scattered stone terracing located up the Asinou River suggests subsistence-based agricultural production. The small Medieval to Ottoman period estate at Aspri was in existence at the same time as the estate at Asinou, and similarly had an economy focused on pastoralism, upland horticulture and forestry extraction.

It is not surprising that the extraction of forestry resources formed a large part of the evidence for activity in the mountain landscape. It is striking, however, that resin tapping, pitch kilns and possibly even charcoal kilns were found so widely dispersed throughout the landscape. In some instances, such as at Palaeomandres, there were large pitch kilns located in close proximity to a major communication route, while in other cases small kilns were found in remote areas (Moutti tou Stavrou, Stavros, Khandakia and Pykroathasoudhi). It is possible that the production of charcoal and pitch may have been an expedient technology in which kilns were constructed where and when necessary. The construction of kilns for the production of resin or charcoal was part of the everyday knowledge of individuals who lived in the mountains. The repeated presence of resin tapping scars found on trees located adjacent to paths supports such a 'tradition' of forest resource extraction. Like the production of pitch and charcoal, extracting resin was part of the daily routine of people living, working and interacting in the forest.

During the Modern period many previously abandoned structures such as Mandres tous Jerenides were, according to local informants, re-occupied seasonally for pastoralism by people from Ayios Theodhoros. The Asinou Valley and its mountain landscape were occupied until the mid-20th century when the last of the occupants of the enclaves in the forest at Karterouni and Asinou village moved out of the mountains.

Today small garden plots are still scattered along the terraces of the Asinou River, where their owners, who live in nearby Nikitari, tend them. Chain saw blades, foil wrappers and shot gun cartridges scattered throughout the forest today provide evidence that even though the mountain forest is within the boundaries of the Adelphi State Forest and protection of the Forestry Department, the mountains remain part of local peoples' lives. The paths that may date to the first occupants of the mountains are still in use, and are still maintained by those who use them. The living memory of the forest, how it was used and feelings of resentment towards the colonial administration that expelled people and their goats from their mountain settlements and forest resources, are still felt by those who live in the villages of Ayios Theodhoros, Nikitari and Sina Oros.

This survey of the mountain landscape should dispel the common misconception of the mountains as isolated and devoid of an archaeological past. Indeed, we have found Roman occupation of the most remote regions of the Intensive Survey Zone. Just as importantly, however, this survey of a mountain landscape has highlighted the diversity of human activity and the limitations of traditional survey designs in locating such evidence. Human experience – the daily trudging up hillsides – cannot be underestimated as a means of coming to terms with a landscape. It is only by moving through the mountains that we gained an appreciation for the subtleties of the interaction and activities that took place within it and became better able to locate evidence for these activities.

6. Conclusions and Period Summaries

Michael Given, A. Bernard Knapp and Jay Noller

The preceding discussion and analysis of the TAESP landscape is based on a very substantial data set. Some figures give an idea of the scale and intensity of our fieldwork. During six seasons, we surveyed 1119 Survey Units and 256 Places of Special Interest. In these we counted 99,972 sherds, of which we analysed 30,710. We collected and analysed 1285 lithics, took 12,522 photographs and created 32,459 database records. This work was done over six seasons by 94 different people, who ate a total of 15,573 person-meals.

For survey projects analysing broad-brush data patterns across large and varied landscapes, this sort of scale is, or should be, the norm. But this volume demonstrates that we have combined all that number crunching with a close engagement with a specific landscape. This included individual survey teams puzzling over apparent patterns, anomalies and challenges; directors and specialists visiting the teams and making connections and comparisons; and everyone trying to put the artefact data and density maps from the labs back into the landscape. As we explain in the discussion of our research philosophy (Volume 1, Chapter 1.4), our everyday discussion and interaction in the field was how we integrated our own daily practice and teamwork with the landscape we were investigating.

The main conclusions to all this work come in Volume 1. Chapter 5 of that volume consists of full analyses of each period. Chapter 6 consists of thematic and diachronic analysis, particularly the material culture of survey (Volume 1, Chapter 6.1), human practice and experience (6.2), movement and interaction (6.3), the changing dynamic between people and the environment (6.4), and an overall evaluation of our work and conclusions (6.5). These analyses are based on the integrated fieldwork, specialist work and research presented in this volume, and on the more detailed specialist work presented in Volume 1, Chapter 3 (Material culture of the TAESP landscape) and Chapter 4 (Environmental record of the TAESP landscape).

This chapter is intended to give the reader an overview of each of our four main periods: Prehistoric; Iron Age; Hellenistic–Roman; and Byzantine–Modern. It gives cross-references to the detailed discussions of the material earlier in this volume, and to the specialist analyses and thematic syntheses in Volume 1. Where chapter references are not prefixed by a volume number, they refer to the current volume.

Prehistoric

One of the key issues from early prehistory that our work has addressed is seasonality (Volume 1, Chapter 5.1). We see this clearly in the presence of Late Epipalaeolithic (or Aceramic Neolithic?) harvesting activities on the Koutraphas plateau (Chapter 2.13). The very broad spread of chipped stone tools suggests cutting and shredding by mobile foragers. During the Neolithic, there is generally little activity in the Survey Area, perhaps because of the low quality jasper available there: there are no available exposures of chert-bearing formations, or of pillow basalts, as they are buried by the expansive fluvial fans of the northern flank of the Troodos. Although we do find some querns and rubbers (suggesting agricultural or clearance activities?), the major settlements of the Neolithic presumably focused more on regions with good quality chert.

During the Bronze Age, the area around Koutraphas shows little sign of occupation, perhaps because of its distance from known settlements or places of industrial activity (e.g. Skouriotissa or Tamassos). The main signs of Bronze Age activity are the ground stone and pottery around Nikitari *Petrera* (Chapter 2.14). The scatter of material at this site – saddle querns and grinders, a few chipped stone items, a senet gaming board, some Light and Heavy Utility wares – are the only signs of possible human settlement.

In later prehistory, however, we find some key sites and site clusters in the Karkotis Valley. Phlasou *Koutroullis* is a rare example of a Late Chalcolithic/Prehistoric Bronze Age 1 transitional site (Chapter 3.5), characterized by its concentration of pottery and chipped stone, and large assemblage of ground stone tools. Part of its importance surely lay in its location atop a ridge, giving it a commanding view over the entire Karkotis Valley, right down to Morphou Bay. The rich ceramic collection, including large storage jars and Table Wares, and a ground stone assemblage dominated by tools for grinding and pounding, portray an early village site connected to the surrounding regions (not least in the large percentages of non-local Lefkara cherts; see Table 3.5). The grinding and pounding tools may also point to wider avenues of communication, specifically as they relate to copper ore processing: the major ore sources around Skouriotissa lie only 3 km to the north. Proximity to Skouriotissa, in other words, may have been one reason why people chose to settle at Koutroullis.

Occupation in this area continues into the Prehistoric Bronze Age, when a substantial settlement and cemetery complex was established at Laonarka (Chapter 3.9). Together Koutroullis and Laonarka point to intensive prehistoric activity in the Karkotis Valley. The Laonarka area, at the southern end of the Karkotis valley, is separated from the Mesaoria by enclosing hills; it seems to have formed a somewhat self-contained area on the terraces of broad alluvial fan east of Karkotis River. At Laonarka itself, there were notable concentrations of flake and utilized chipped stone tools, at least one ground stone tool elsewhere associated with ore crushing, and a range of Red Polished III sherds of domestic types. Taken together with the dense halo of prehistoric pottery and chipped stone in and around the site, Laonarka was very likely a sizeable settled village. There were enough sherds of the standard Protohistoric Bronze Age wares to indicate some level of continuing occupation over nearly 1000 years.

Kato Koutraphas *Mandroudhes*, by contrast, is a small rural village that lies on the interface of the igneous and sedimentary zones (Chapter 2.9). Significant amounts of both Prehistoric and Protohistoric Bronze Age pottery (Utility, Table and Cooking Wares), together with a small amount of chipped stone (one piece of imported Lefkara chert) and an impressive range of ground stone tools used in grinding and processing cereals, all indicate continuous, or at least intermittent, habitation over a long period at this small but notable agricultural village. Its array of fine Table Wares (White Slip, Plain White Handmade) and distinctive pithoi with 'pie-crust' decoration, as well as non-local chert, suggest that this village, and the plains on which it lies, may have enjoyed more than just an isolated existence.

Artefact density analyses show that the complexity of prehistoric activity in the TAESP area cannot be reduced to a list of 'sites'. Already in the Prehistoric Bronze Age it is clear that the land was used much more intensively than in the past, with more production and consumption of pottery, chipped stone and especially ground stone material. Even at this time we can observe 'haloes' of material around the major settlements in the fertile and well-watered Karkotis Valley. The scatters in the Plains may be slighter, but they are still significant signs of habitation, production and interaction, whether on a local or regional level. These include obvious 'sites' such as Mandroudhes (Chapter 2.9) and Petrera (2.14), which any reasonably systematic survey could find. But there are also indications of wider Prehistoric Bronze Age activity in this area, such as Lemonas (which only appeared as significant in our GIS analysis; Chapter 2.7) and other unfocused but still important material round Mandres (2.11).

The TAESP landscape does not seem to have been so densely occupied or closely interconnected during the prehistoric periods as it was in later, Hellenistic–Roman and Medieval–Modern times. One possible explanation for this is that settlement and human activity were concentrated in the Karkotis Valley, thanks to the perennial river, but the evidence there has mostly been buried by Roman-period land levelling (Volume 1, Chapter 4.6); the evidence for prehistoric activity in the rest of the Survey Area is more visible but relatively light, due presumably to the ephemeral rivers and consequent poorer water supply. On the other hand, the identification of what appear to be substantial settlements at Koutraphas and Laonarka, smaller but long-settled sites such as Mandroudhes, and activity areas if not farmsteads at sites such as Petrera and Lemonas, show that the people and communities in the TAESP area were already linked in a way never before understood in this 'remote' region. It is difficult to piece together the total social landscape of prehistory in this region, but clearly the agricultural, if not the industrial, basis that characterized the materiality and connectivity of this area in later periods had already been laid down by the beginning of the Bronze Age.

Iron Age

One of the most interesting issues from the Iron Age (Volume 1, Chapter 5.2) is the role and location of the rural sanctuaries of Pano Limna (Chapter 3.11) and Khalospitia (2.4). Both are close to the mines at Skouriotissa, and Pano Limna in particular is directly across the valley from the Roman (and presumably earlier) mining headquarters and smelting operation. The figurines from these sanctuaries, particularly the ring dancers circling trees, show a concern with vegetation, as is common throughout Cyprus in the 6th century BC. It is interesting to put this beside the analysis of the charcoal from the slag heaps of TAESP and the Sydney Cyprus Survey Project, which indicates substantial wood harvesting in the Iron Age (Volume 1, Chapter 3.10). There seems to be a close association between wood use and a growing ritual focus on trees and vegetation.

There remains the problem of locating Iron Age settlements. We recorded one substantial cemetery near

Khalospitia sanctuary (Chapter 2.4), and the Cyprus Survey recorded other Iron Age tombs in our Survey Area. But even in the Karkotis Valley, the maximum Iron Age sherd density is 5.6 sherds/100 m^2. Compared to other periods before and after, this is very low indeed; and many areas, such as the Mandres and Koutraphas Intensive Survey Zones, are completely devoid of Iron Age material. This problem lies mainly in our inability to recognize Iron Age utility wares, particularly those of the Geometric and Archaic periods. Perhaps greater specialist input into this issue would have given a very different picture of the Iron Age in our area, yet even the easily recognisable painted wares are very rare. This problem is not unique to our Survey Area, and is clearly an issue that demands further research across the island.

Hellenistic–Roman

The contrast with the Hellenistic–Roman period could not be greater (Volume 1, Chapter 5.3). This period is rich in evidence for copper production, agriculture, domestic and craft activities, interaction within and beyond the Survey Area, and a striking complexity of social organisation. A large proportion of the material dates to the Late Roman period (AD 400–650), though in most areas there does seem to be substantial continuity from the Hellenistic and Early Roman periods.

The most striking evidence for the scale of activity during this period is the massive slag heap at Skouriotissa, with some two million tons of slag and all the associated mining, processing, organisation and wealth (Chapter 3.12). Analysis of the slag both here and in the contemporary but much smaller slag heap of Mavrovouni shows that by this time the smelting process was highly efficient, with 1% or less of copper remaining in the slag (Volume 1, Chapter 3.9). The geochemical halo of copper in the topsoil around Skouriotissa is pronounced, attesting to the dispersal of the metal by natural processes as well as traction and aerosolic dispersion by the human activities of transport and smelting respectively (Volume 1, Chapter 4.6). The source of fuel was almost entirely *Pinus brutia* (Volume 1, Chapter 3.10), demonstrating constant interaction between the mine and the 500 km^2 of forest in the Troodos Mountains which we estimate would have been needed to supply the mines with charcoal during their lifetime (Volume 1, Chapter 4.8).

The organisation of the mining and smelting operation is particularly clear in the Lagoudhera Valley. Here, the settlement of Litharkies (Chapter 4.4) supported the mining operation on Alestos (4.3), while the ore was transported to the smelting site and settlement of Mavrovouni, 2.3 km to the north-east and immediately adjacent to a good water supply (4.6). The settlement at Mavrovouni was as close as 100 m from the smelting site: workers would certainly have been substantially affected by the heat, as well as by fumes from sulphur dioxide and other emissions (4.8). A similarly close association between slag heaps and structures is seen at other slag heaps, including Skouriotissa, where, as the slag heap grew it swamped the neighbouring buildings (3.12).

Another indication of working conditions comes from a huge dump of locally produced transport amphorae at Skouriotissa; the 21 m^3 of sherds that we sampled were a tiny fragment of the original deposit (Chapter 3.12). These were probably used for the collection of copper salt solutions for medicinal purposes, and are strongly reminiscent of Galen's graphic description from the 2nd century AD of slaves running through the fume-filled galleries carrying amphorae of medicinal solutions.

The thousands of workers at the mines and smelting workshops clearly needed a reliable food supply, and one of our most significant findings relating to Roman-period copper production is its reliance on a complex system of agricultural production and supply. This reliance is clearest at Skouriotissa, where intensive cultivation across the lower part of the Karkotis Valley, based on small settlements such as Pano Limna (Chapter 3.11), produced a carpet of pottery across the valley; carpets of sherds like this would have been the result of manuring the fields, an activity associated with intensive cultivation. Cultivation presumably continued down the valley to the coastal plain round Soloi, but data from within our Survey Area show that it was also complemented by agricultural production in poorer and drier soils and at greater distances. This includes intensive cultivation farther north and up the valley, although not in a continuous carpet as happened closer to the mine; it also includes what seems to be a network of farmsteads and settlements across the drier and thin-soiled Atsas Valley (Chapters 2.5–2.7). The discovery of the same types of local amphorae and roof tiles in all of these areas emphasizes the close links between them.

On the plains farther east, agricultural production in the Hellenistic–Roman period seems to have been organized slightly differently. The farmsteads of Sanidhia and Katalasharis on the Koutraphas plateau (Chapter 2.15) have no roof tiles, unlike the Atsas Valley examples, and may only have been worked seasonally, like Mandres in the 19th and early 20th centuries. They may well have provided food to the miners and smelters at Litharkies and Mavrovouni, just 7.5 km up the most obvious communications route, the Elaia and Laghoudhera Valleys. Here, agricultural production was on a much smaller scale than at Skouriotissa, but without the advantage of excellent agricultural land immediately adjacent to it.

During this period, the coincidence of resource opportunity, subsistence demand and personal wealth in the Karkotis Valley led to the widespread transformation of the modestly graded, valley-side slopes of variable soil character, into a mosaic of level fields with nearly uniform soils. The unique hydrological character of the Karkotis, a perennially secure source of water, presented drinking, irrigation and energy resource opportunities. Alluvial sediments of the valley, ideal for well-drained agricultural soils, are metres thick along the valley axis, but thin outward to near nil at the foot of the surrounding ophiolitic bedrock hills. Unfortunately, the bedrock valley is narrow and constrains the alluvial deposits to a limited breadth along the valley floor. These resources must surely have been put to agricultural use for the production of food and fibre for the industrial activities at the north end of the central Karkotis. The small mountains of slag indicate that substantial numbers of people were required to extract and process metal ores, as well as to procure the necessary fuel for their smelters and food for themselves. The abundance of extractable metals would have brought material wealth to finance engineered projects (1) to level and augment soils for enhanced cropping capability; and (2) to gain water-use efficiency for food production, principally through irrigation and the milling of grains.

Land levelling of the Karkotis valley sides was an immense undertaking. Just within the Karkotis Intensive Survey Zone (with an area of 919 ha), the c. 450 ha of arable fields would have required in the order of 10 million metric tons of earth excavation, movement, mixing and depositing. An estimated total of 675 ha of fields were levelled in the Karkotis Valley during antiquity. The mass moved for agriculture here is a large number, one that is on a par with the estimated original mass of the Great Pyramid at Giza.

Unfortunately for survey archaeology, the land-levelling scheme all but obliterated any extant pre-Roman cultural materials from the surface, by either excavational erosion or depositional burial. Our method of surface inspection is blinded by this ancient land surface alteration. Despite its use elsewhere on Cyprus, modern deep-ploughing technology has yet to be applied in the Karkotis Valley; the use of such an apparatus would likely have stirred up to the surface deep layers of soil and their older artefacts. Hence our survey methods only provide a look at what has accumulated on these originally 'sterile' surfaces since the time of their construction. Since the broad-spread of artefacts dates only as far back as the Hellenistic–Roman period, we must conclude that this was the time of valley-wide land levelling.

One of our major contributions to the scholarship of the Hellenistic–Roman periods is our identification of a substantial chipped stone industry (Volume 1, Chapter 3.8). This is based on consistent evidence from 12 settlement and mining locations, all dated by means of pottery, and from five quarried jasper outcrops probably associated with them. Unlike in the Medieval–Modern period, knappers were mostly content to use the often poor quality, locally available jasper and chalcedony. Cores were not heavily exploited, and the industry mainly consisted of the production of utilized flake tools. A particularly interesting class of tools consists of *dhoukani* flakes for threshing sledges, again consisting mainly of local jasper rather than the imported Lefkara cherts favoured in later periods. The ground stone tools from the Roman period (Volume 1, Chapter 3.8) include larger items such as olive mills, demonstrating a development in the scale of production from household to community. Another specific function consists of grinders and rubbing stones in copper production areas, clearly intended for ore crushing and processing.

Our determination to apply intensive survey to the difficult terrain of the Troodos Mountains paid off with another important finding: there was significant activity in the mountains during the Hellenistic–Roman period. This is a direct refutation of the long-standing belief that the mountains were devoid of life before the Medieval period (e.g. Mitford 1980, 1309). In the Asinou Valley Intensive Survey Zone, our main focus of mountain survey, there were significant amounts of Roman material in the lower part of the valley, although with no real focus (Chapter 5.4). Farther up the valley, in its supposedly 'remote' and 'isolated' stretches, we discovered several well-preserved Roman structures, typically of three or four rooms (Chapter 5.4). These were associated with high terraces along the margins of the river channels, and seem to be contemporary. This is one of the best areas for the growth and regeneration of *Pinus brutia*, the main fuel source of the mines at Skouriotissa, and lies centrally in the area we estimate to have supplied the mines (Volume 1, Chapter 4.8). The most likely interpretation is that these were involved in charcoal production, with a little subsistence agriculture on associated terraces.

From all of this it is clear that the TAESP landscape in the Hellenistic–Roman period was an intimately connected one, from the massive industry at the mines and smelting workshops of Skouriotissa, to the farmsteads with their olive mills and transport amphorae, and the charcoal workers in the pine forests of the Troodos Mountains. These links between people and communities were far more than a 'settlement hierarchy', although that certainly can be identified. This social landscape consists of a host of interconnected activities, with people communicating through the supply of food and raw materials, the production of tools and containers, and a complex web of social intercourse and political direction. Other than a few rich tombs at Evrykhou (Chapter 3.14), there is no evidence that the wealth produced by the mines was invested in our area. It is more the richness of human activity and interaction that characterizes this landscape in the Hellenistic–Roman period.

Medieval–Modern

After a substantial lacuna in our knowledge during the 8th–11th centuries, the Medieval–Modern periods show a similar richness in material, information and complexity to the Hellenistic–Roman era. The most obvious feature of the Medieval period (Volume 1, Chapter 5.4) consists of the estates, from substantial ones in the Karkotis Valley to single structures in the mountains. In the 14th and 15th centuries, the pottery distribution data in the Karkotis Valley show distinct foci of activity round Phlasou and Linou, and perhaps Katydhata. This contrasts with the

16th century, when the pottery is much more widespread and continuous. Such a pattern is indicative of broad and intensive cultivation, even if it is hard to pinpoint the actual estates and settlements because of their modern successors.

At the other end of the scale, the mountainous part of our Survey Area is notable for its high numbers of small Medieval and earlier Ottoman estates and settlements, some of them monasteries or their dependencies. Aspri is a relatively substantial example, with a cluster of houses and a church at 960 m asl (Chapter 5.9). The paths we recorded in this area are hard to date, but there were clearly constant connections across all of this supposedly difficult and 'remote' terrain (Chapter 5.10).

Most of these small mountain settlements were abandoned by the 19th or early 20th centuries, but in the plains and bigger valleys the larger Medieval estates and villages became villages of freeholder peasants during the Ottoman period, and most are still villages today. Viewed in the longer term, it is clear that these settlements followed complex processes of development and movement. This is particularly clear with Phlasou in the Karkotis Valley (Chapter 3.8). Phlasou was a substantial Medieval estate, whose focus gradually moved towards the river and its watermills, and then split into several components; the movement and search for a focus continued into the early 20th century.

Thanks to our intensive survey data, we can develop our interpretation well beyond the simple identification of 'sites'. Across this entire period it is very clear that the activities of settlement and cultivation leave a readable imprint on the landscape, most strikingly in the 'haloes' of contemporary low-density pottery round settlements and in areas of cultivation (Volume 1, Chapter 5.4). This is most significant for the analysis and reconstruction of human experience in the landscape, allowing us to map human activity and regular patterns of movement. Round the Medieval estate and later village of Kato Koutraphas we have been able to combine our survey results with documentary data in an analysis of routine practice, soundscapes and community territory (Volume 1, Chapter 5.4).

Another challenge to the static 'settlement pattern' model comes from the indicators of seasonal activity that link the mountains and plains in our area. The best information comes from the abandoned 18th–early 20th-century settlement of Mandres, which was used in the growing season by cultivators from various mountain villages (Chapter 2.10). A similar phenomenon clearly links uplands and lowlands across our Survey Area; there are other seasonal settlements at Asinou (Chapter 5.5) and Ayios Yeoryios Kafkallou (Chapter 4.9). A crucial component of this landscape was the regular movement and communication between these mountains and plains settlements.

The Medieval–Modern periods in the Survey Area are particularly rich in information about agriculture and food processing, including artefacts, structures and the wider landscape. In the many areas of higher relief, terraces and check dams are a ubiquitous feature. The faint Z-shaped terraces on the steep and thin-soiled hillslopes of the Karkotis Valley show a striking contrast to the presumably contemporary intensive cultivation and irrigation of the valley floor (Chapter 3.3). Similarly, the monumental check dams of the Lagoudhera Valley, one of them 3 m high (Chapters 4.2, 4.4), contrast with the short rows of stones across gullies in the Asinou Valley, which provided pockets of cultivatable and erosion-free soil for the monks of Asinou monastery (Chapter 5.7).

Threshing and grinding grain in this period both have clear and informative archaeological correlates, including threshing sledge blades, threshing floors, grinding stones and watermills. Unlike the situation in the Hellenistic–Roman period, the threshing sledge blades are almost all made with imported Lefkara chert, with only replacements being made from the poorer quality local jasper and chalcedony (Volume 1, Chapter 3.8). Here is another complex pattern of regional interaction and communication. Watermills, which are common throughout the Ottoman period, lie along the stretches of river with the highest water flow, rather than being associated with centres of population or production. As with the movement to and from seasonal settlements, this encouraged communication up and down the valley, especially from villages lower down in the more arid plains.

It is clear from all of this that static models of settlement pattern or settlement hierarchy are wholly inappropriate to the Medieval–Modern periods, and indeed to any other period. Our analysis shows complex networks of human activities, experiences and relationships, rooted in particular places and maintained and developed by continual movement and interaction.

We can also see specific episodes and structures that cut across these patterns of place and interaction, which reshape the old patterns and create new ones in a continuing dynamic. In the Medieval–Modern periods the most significant of these are imperialism and large-scale mining. It is particularly clear in the British colonial period (Volume 1, Chapter 5.4). In the late 19th century, the new forest boundaries cut across old axes of movement travelled by goatherders and other exploiters of forest resources (Chapter 5.8). Similarly, the new Nicosia–Troodos road built at the beginning of the 20th century cut across the habitual movements of villagers up and down the valleys, and even by-passed the villages themselves, which until then had been the main nodes of communication (Chapter 2.17; Volume 1, Chapter 3.13).

The large-scale copper mining of the early and middle 20th century had a dramatic effect on agriculture, settlement and all the routine practices and social relations that depended on these. Daily and seasonal patterns of agricultural activity had to be accommodated to the demands and opportunities of the mines, and villages such as Katydhata developed new roles and identities that juxtaposed newcomers and new activities with old agricultural and family-based values. The identical units and grid lines of the miners' settlement at Skouriotissa, purpose-built in the 1920s, tried to create a new and regimented society, in opposition to the organic and kin-based plans of older villages and houses (Chapter 3.12).

Modern imperialism and industrial mining clearly have had a massive impact on local society. It is not just in the Modern period, however, that there are such tensions between local activities and central forces. The TAESP landscape at all periods shows a richness and complexity of social interaction, expressed in the artefacts, features and buildings that structured routine practices and patterns of movement. Our intensive survey and interdisciplinary analysis has allowed us to transcend traditional site-based understandings to address human practice, interaction and social relations expressed across the entire landscape.

Appendix 1. Catalogue of Places of Special Interest

For full descriptions see the TAESP database (TAESPdata 2007). For a discussion of recording methods, see Volume 1, Chapter 2.3. Grid references are in the UTM grid. Elevations are in metres above sea level. Numbers prefixed 'CS' refer to Cyprus Survey records held in the Department of Antiquities. Pottery periods refer just to pottery formally collected in POSI Units; see Table 1.2 for explanation of the abbreviations. For the pottery catalogue (ID numbers prefixed 'TCP'), see Volume 1, Chapter 3.6; for the special finds catalogue ('TCS'), Chapter 3.7. For discussion of the lithics ('TCL'), see Chapter 3.8; for the archaeometallurgical finds ('TCA'), Chapter 3.9. Chapter references are all to Volume 2 unless otherwise stated. Each entry has the following format:

TPxxx Village *Locality* Northing/Easting Elevation Cadastral plan no. Summary. POSI Unit nos. Pottery periods. Catalogue numbers. (Cross-reference)

TP001 Ayios Epiphanios *Apatoes* 489230/3880230 340m XVIII-36. Shallow depressions; terrace wall of large boulders

TP002 Ayios Epiphanios *Paleokklishia* 489100/3880950 300m XXVIII-36-W2. Ruined church (BU0103) and Medieval village of Ayios Epiphanios (Ch. 3.7)

TP003 Phlasou *Kourtellolaona* 490830/3880330 370m XXVIII-45. Ovoid mound with defined edges. Appears artificial. c. 10 x 15 m.

TP004 Evrykhou *Atsas* 492710/3880650 310m XXVIII-37. Stone bridge on stretch of disused road (Ch. 2.7)

TP005 Ayios Yeoryios *Alestos* 502100/3877000 600m XXIX-50. Modern opencast mine with acid lake. Ruined remnants of mining operation. (Ch. 4.3)

TP006 Ayia Marina *Mavrovouni* 503260/3878020 390m XXIX-50. Slag heap, extensive Roman pottery, rubble piles. TCA003–10 (Ch. 4.6)

TP007 Skouriotissa *Vouppos* 489560/3883500 220m XXVIII-28-E1. Large slag heap with remains of workshop floors. PU01–12. HA, HR, ER, ROM, MR, LR, RM, HIS, Mod, UN. TCP527–69. TCS067–70. TCL334. TCA011–17. (Ch. 3.12)

TP008 Kato Koutraphas *Mandres* 495860/3881540 280m XXVIII-39. Two threshing floors with 2 associated buildings. BU0013–15. HIS. TCL335. (Ch. 2.10)

TP009 Xyliatos *Athassi* 503000/3878980 350m XXIX-50. Series of 3 (possibly 4) check dams (Ch. 4.7)

TP010 Phlasou *Shaabanbeys* 489610/3880010 300m XXVIII-44-E1. Sediment profile showing flooding episodes

TP011 Phlasou *Limnes* 489590/3880420 320m XXVIII-36 Village Plan: Kato Phlasou. Series of 4–5 very old olive trees on terrace (Vol. 1, Ch. 4.7)

TP012 Phlasou *Kalophlitidhes* 490160/3880000 320m XXVIII-44-E1. Cement water reservoir

TP013 Phlasou *Tenekidhes* 490080/3879990 320m XXVIII-44-E1. Modern brick structure (storage?)

TP014 Xyliatos *Athassi* 502910/3878800 360m XXIX-42. Abandoned 4-room house with 2 storeys (BU0147) (Ch. 4.7)

TP015 Xyliatos *Athassi* 502920/3878810 360m XXIX-42. Threshing floor (Ch. 4.7)

TP016 Nikitari *Alonia* 497080/3877820 530m XXVIII-56. One paved threshing floors and 2 possible others (Ch. 5.5)

TP017 Ayia Marina *Mavrovouni* 503300/3877790 420m XXIX-50. Rock of Ayios Kyriakos. Basalt outcrop with modern and possibly ancient use. PU01. HA, HIS. (Ch. 4.6)

TP018 Kato Koutraphas *Mnimata* 495820/3881310 280m XXVIII-39. Outlying buildings c. 300 m south of Mandres (BU0005–0006). (Ch. 2.10)

TP019 Ayios Theodhoros *Vatherou* 492340/3879160 380m XXVIII-45. Tile and brick kiln. PU01. (Vol. 1, Ch. 3.11)

TP020 Kato Koutraphas *Mandres* 495800/3882360 260m XXVIII-31. Three-arched colonial road bridge. BU0114. HR. (Ch. 2.11)

TP021 Kato Koutraphas *Mandres* 495720/3881570 280m XXVIII-39. Central agglomerated village area. PU01–11, BU0011–12, BU0017–43, BU0050–52. HEL, ROM, LR, RM, HIS, MM, MEDVOTT, OTT, OTTMODI–II, MOD. TCP570–71. TCS071. TCL336–53. (Ch. 2.10)

TP022 Ayia Marina *Mavrovouni* 503200/3878010 360m XXIX-50. Small, stone-built structure, 2 niches in west wall. PU01. LR, HIS. TCP572

TP023 Ayia Marina *Mavrovouni* 503200/3878000 360m XXIX-50. Possible stone-built enclosure adjacent to TP022

TP024 Ayia Marina *Mavrovouni* 503240/3877920 360m XXIX-50. Stone-built wall of large boulders associated with possible path. PU01. (Ch. 4.6)

TP025 Ayia Marina *Mavrovouni* 503300/3877750 380m XXIX-50. Rubble piles. PU01–10, PU12–19. HA, HR, ROM, LR, HIS, MM, OTTMODII, MOD, UN. TCP573–75. (Ch. 4.6)

TP026 Kato Koutraphas *Kaphkalla* 495620/3881720 280m XXVIII-39. Outlying structures c. 100 m west of Mandres. BU0008–10, BU0115. (Ch. 2.10)

TP027 Kato Koutraphas *Vromoneron* 496000/3881600m XXVIII-39. Outlying structures and threshing floor 300m east of Mandres. BU0016. (Ch. 2.10)

TP028 Kato Koutraphas *Lakxies tis Korphis* 495660/3881410 280m. XXVIII-39. Outlying structure 200 m south-west of Mandres. BU0007. (Ch. 2.10)

TP029 Linou *Chankarena* 490030/3881440 280m XXVIII-36-E1. Road trench with stratigraphy and pottery & slag inclusions. HIS, MM

TP030 Nikitari *Kapsalia* 497580/3878280 440m XXVIII-55. Panayia Phorviotissa church and enclosure; geophysics. BU0058. (Ch. 5.5)

TP031 Nikitari *Vouni* 497820/3879970 420m XXVIII-48. Abandoned settlement with church. 50 PUs on grid with nos. in format 'PUE10N10'. HIS, MM, OTTMODI, MEDVOTT, MOD. (Ch. 5.3)

TP032 Ayios Epiphanios *Kangelia* 489410/3880480 300m XXVIII-36-E2. Artificially cut terrace showing 1.5 m section with pottery

TP033 Nikitari *Paleolinos* 497900/3878350 570m XXVIII-56. Ruins of Stavros Church on hilltop

TP034 Nikitari *Paleolinos* 497820/3877930 500m XXVIII-56. Check dam system covering at least 5 gullies

TP035 Katydhata *Laonarka* 489980/3882030 300m XXVIII-28. Bronze Age settlement; pottery and geophysics. Twenty-four PUs on grid with numbers in format 'PUE0N0'. PeB, RM, HIS. TCP576. (Ch. 3.9)

TP036 Phlasou *Phinikia* 489630/3880330 340m XXVIII-36. High revetting wall near well. PU01. HIS.

TP037 Katydhata *Laonarka* 489760/3881830 270m XXVIII-28. Rock-cut tomb, possibly related to 1918 Markides excavations. (Ch. 3.14)

TP038 Nikitari *Mandres tous Jerenides* 495240/3876500 620m XXVIII-63. Four clusters of ruined structures, possible threshing floor and well, check dams. (Ch. 5.5)

TP039 Nikitari *Pera Yitonia* 496960/3877890 400m XXVIII-55. Ashlar wall from church of Ayios Ioannis. (Ch. 5.5)

TP040 Katydhata *Laonarka* 489920/3882080 310m XXVIII-28. Fox-hole, originally thought to be a tomb. PU01. HIS, MOD

TP041 Ayia Marina *Kato Kremasha* 503190/3878240 360m XXIX-50. Terrace with 2.5 m high retaining wall (Ch. 4.9)

TP042 Ayia Marina *Kato Kremasha* 503460/3878240 440m XXIX-50. Possible collapsed structure

TP043 Ayios Epiphanios Village 489210/3880520 310m XXVIII-36-E2. Village Plan: Ayios Epiphanios. Foundations of building (Ch. 3.7)

TP044 Katydhata *Laonarka* 489970/3882040 290m XXVIII-28. Shaft (?) truncated by modern cut, back-filled in antiquity.

TP045 Ayios Yeoryios *Athassi* 502750/3878800 360m XXIX-50. Two-room, rectangular all-stone structure (Ch. 4.7)

TP046 Ayia Marina *Mavrovouni* 503500/3877670 380m XXIX-50. Collapsed adit (Ch. 4.5)

TP047 Ayia Marina *Mavrovouni* 503300/3877730 360m XXIX-50. Ruins of the church of Ayios Kyriakos (Ch. 4.6)

TP048 Nikitari *Palaeomandres* 495560/3877690 660m XXVIII-55. Two-room ruin on spur (Ch. 5.7)

TP049 Nikitari *Jenerides* 495450/3877180 640m XXVIII-55. Five adjacent pine trees with resin tapping (Ch. 5.7)

TP050 Xyliatos *Ayios Kyriakos* 503260/3877230 390m XXIX-50. Ancient adit (Ch. 4.5)

TP051 Xyliatos *Ayios Kyriakos* 503270/3877230 390m XXIX-50. Ancient adit (Ch. 4.5)

TP052 Xyliatos *Ayios Kyriakos* 503270/3877220 390m XXIX-50. Ancient adit (Ch. 4.5)

TP053 Xyliatos *Ayios Kyriakos* 503270/3877230 390m XXIX-50. Almost vertical ancient shaft (Ch. 4.5)

TP054 Xyliatos *Ayios Kyriakos* 503280/3877230 380m XXIX-50. Ancient adit (Ch. 4.5)

TP055 Xyliatos *Ayios Kyriakos* 503290/3877230 380m XXIX-50. Small ancient adit (Ch. 4.5)

TP056 Xyliatos *Ayios Kyriakos* 503300/3877230 390m XXIX-50. Ancient shaft (Ch. 4.5)

TP057 Xyliatos *Ayios Kyriakos* 503340/3877320 400m XXIX-50. Ancient prospection cut (Ch. 4.5)

TP058 Xyliatos *Ayios Kyriakos* 503340/3877320 400m XXIX-50. Ancient prospection cut (Ch. 4.5)

TP059 Nikitari *Kapsalia* 494820/3876370 700m XXVIII-62. Track crossing saddle

TP060 Nikitari *Ayios Theodhoros* 500020/3879710 420m XXIX-41. Rubble pile marked as ruined church of Ayios Theodhoros, with tile and Medieval–Modern pottery

TP061 Nikitari *Pera Yitonia* 496800/3877920 510m XXVIII-55. Abandoned village on north side of Asinou Valley. (Ch. 5.5)

TP062 Nikitari *Ambelia* 497000/3878300 490m XXVIII-55. Masonry forest cairn (Ch. 5.8)

TP063 Katydhata *Laonarka* 489880/3882000 300m XXVIII-28. Rock-cut tomb (Ch. 3.14)

TP064 Korakou *Amaxostrata* 489620/3878730 340m. Small isolated building. PU01. UN

TP065 Evrykhou *Varkakioes* 490260/3878640 400m XXVIII-52. Hellenistic and Roman tomb: Evrykhou Tomb 5 (Ch. 3.14)

TP066 Ayios Yeoryios *Aspri* 497170/3874160 960m XXXVII-7. Abandoned Late Medieval village with church. PU01–13, PU15, PU17–18, PU20, PU24–26. HIS, MM, MEDUIII, MEDVOTT, OTTMODII, UN. TCP577–83. (Ch. 5.9)

TP067 Ayios Theodhoros *Karterouni* 493360/3873340 730m XXXVII-14. Karterouni abandoned settlement. BU0127–30, BU0143–46. (Ch. 5.8)

TP068 Ayios Theodhoros *Philanti* 493230/3873740 690m XXXVII-14. Masonry forest cairn (Ch. 5.8)

TP069 Ayios Theodhoros *Teratsia* 493030/3873170 730m XXXVII-14. Masonry forest cairn

TP070 Ayios Theodhoros *Ayios Yeoryios* 492920/3873320 750m XXXVII-14. Ruined church of Ayios Yeoryios

TP071 Ayios Theodhoros *Ayios Yeorgios* 492880/3873420 760m XXXVII-14. Ruined settlement on spur above Ayios Yeoryios church

TP072 Ayios Theodhoros *Karterouni* 493260/3873340 690m. Threshing floors at Karterouni (Ch. 5.8)

TP073 Ayios Theodhoros *Karterouni* 493130/3873320 700m. Ford and track at Karterouni (Ch. 5.8)

TP074 Ayia Marina *Tholos* 503940/3878800 400m XXIX-42. Stone lined well (Ch. 4.9)

TP075 Ayia Marina *Motis* 504020/3878370 460m XXIV-50. Adit in bulldozed terrace (Ch. 4.5)

TP076 Ayia Marina *Sykia tou Kaiserili* 504020/3878040 460m XXIX-50. Two check dams in a gully

TP077 Ayia Marina *Sykia tou Kaiserili* 504000/3877920 440m XXIX-50. Path/roadway (Ch. 4.6)

TP078 Ayia Marina *Sykia tou Kaiserili* 504060/3878040 470m XXIX-50. Collapsed field house

TP079 Ayia Marina *Lovarkatis* 504060/3877690 410m XXIX-50. Check dam within a series of check dams in gully (Ch. 4.4)

TP080 Ayia Marina *Lovarkatis* 504050/3877680 410m XXIX-50. Possible field shelter/pen

TP081 Nikitari *Asinou* 497090/3877850 510m XXVIII-55. Abandoned village. PU01–04. HA, MM, OTTMODII, MOD. (Ch. 5.5)

TP082 Nikitari *Asinou* 497100/3877840 510m XXVIII-55. Two-storey house (*dhipato*) with attached goatfold (*mandra*). BU0116. OTTMODII. (Ch. 5.5)

TP083 Nikitari *Asinou* 497170/3877920 520m XXVIII-55. Potential threshing floor east of abandoned village (Ch. 5.5)

TP084 Katydhata *Lymnoes* 489450/3881660 220m XXVIII-36. Very old olive tree with 3 terraces cut into risers of larger terrace. (Vol. 1, Ch. 4.7)

TP085 Katydhata *Kouglides & Appithkies* 489720/3881820 270m XXVIII-28. Stone and sherds from Archaic–Roman settlement reported by Cyprus Survey (CS 2755)

TP086 Xyliatos *Ayios Kyriakos* 503220/3877420 380m XXIX-50. Path between 2 terrace walls (Ch. 4.4)

TP087 Xyliatos *Ayios Kyriakos* 503250/3877360 370m XXIX-50. Path; lower construction of TP086 (Ch. 4.4)

TP088 Xyliatos *Ayios Kyriakos* 503180/3877330 320m XXIX-50. Adit beside path TP086 (Ch. 4.5)

TP089 Skouriotissa *Psevtadhes* 489120/3883470 180m XXVIII-28-E1. Exposed section in terrace riser. PU01. GU1016. GAC, HEL, ROM, HIS

TP090 Skouriotissa *Kataliontis* 489600/3882920 230m XXVII-28-E1. Possible tomb sealed by slag cake in earthen terrace rising (Ch. 3.14)

TP091 Skouriotissa *Monastery* 489400/3883180 220m XXVIII-28-E1. Four column fragments at Camp San Martin (Ch. 3.12)

TP092 Katydhata *Pikrosykia* 488920/3882240 250m XXVIII-28. Modern shrine, surrounded by possible tombs. BU0125

TP093 Katydhata *Mutallou* 489900/3882870 240m XXVIII-28. Rectangular tomb (Ch. 3.14)

TP094 Katydhata *Mutallou* 490030/3882740 250m XXVIII-28. Tomb with four chambers (Ch. 3.14)

TP095 Potami *Kambos tou Lemonari* 501340/3884220 270m XXIX-17. Ground stone concentration with chipped stone scatter. PU01–03. TCL354–98. TCA018. (Ch. 2.13)

TP096 Ayia Marina *Vrysi* 503950/3878770 400m XXIX-42, 50. Jasper quarry. PU01. OTTMODII. TCL399–405. (Ch. 4.9)

TP097 Nikitari *Gnaphion* 497530/3878350 450m XXVIII-55. Path/track (Ch. 5.6)

TP098 Nikitari *Gnaphion* 497440/3878310 450m XXVIII-55. Stone pile: possible structure. BU0054. (Ch. 5.6)

TP099 Xyliatos *Louvas* 503180/3877180 390m. Possible path (Ch. 4.4)

TP100 Ayios Theodhoros *Khalkokolymbos* 495110/3877700 640m XXVIII-54. Path from Asinou to Theodhoros (abandoned segment) (Ch. 5.6; Vol. 1, Ch. 3.13)

TP101 Evrykhou *Pano Atsas* 493440/3880710 320m XXVIII-38. Excavated Archaic and Classical tombs (Evrykhou Tombs 1 and 2) (Ch. 3.14)

TP102 Katydhata *Pamboulia* 490040/3882480 250m XXVIII-28. Series of threshing floors on terraces (Ch. 3.10)

TP103 Xyliatos *Elaea tou Kaloyirou* 503480/3876780 440m XXIX-58. Probable adit (Ch. 4.5)

TP104 Ayia Marina *Mavrovouni* 503240/3877780 380m XXIX-50. 36 gridded circles (with PU nos in the format 'PUE00N00'); 26 grabs from the grid squares (PU01–PU25, PU31). HA, HR, LHER, ROM, LR, RM, HIS, MM, MEDB, MEDF, MEDVOTT, OTTMODII, MOD, UN. TCP584–619. TCS006–07, TCS072. TCL406–10. (Ch. 4.6)

TP105 Nikitari *Palaeomandres* 496200/3877490 530m XXVIII-55. Two rock-built circular pitch kilns (Ch. 5.7)

TP106 Xyliatos *Elaea tou Kaloyirou* 503560/3876940 430m XXVIII-58. Possible adit (Ch. 4.5)

TP107 Skouriotissa *Psevtadhes* 488980/3883360 200m XXVIII-28W1. Abandoned miners' village. BU0118–22. (Ch. 3.12)

TP108 Potami *Kollajes* 502980/3883040 260m XXIX-26. Cairn, querns, tombs and ground stones. PU01–03. TCL411

TP109 Katydhata *Psevtadhes* 489030/3884030 190m XXVIII-20. Cave, possible adit. PU01–04. BU0164. GAC, HA, HR, ROM, LR, RM, HIS, OTTMODI. TCP620–23. TCL412–17. (Ch. 3.13)

TP110 Katydhata *Alonia* 489970/3882260 260m XXVIII-28-E2. Large covered pit, perhaps a cistern

TP111 Katydhata *Laonarka* 489830/3882150 280m XXVIII-28-E2. Chamber tomb with dromos (Ch. 3.14)

TP112 Xyliatos *Kokkinoploura tou Alestou* 502030/3876470 570m XXIX-57. Proper adit with clearly cut shaft (Ch. 4.3)

TP113 Xyliatos *Litharkies* 501890/3876100 510m XXIX-57. L-shaped wall

TP114 Xyliatos *Litharkies* 501920/3876100 510m XXIX-57. Possible collapsed field shelter. PU01. (Ch. 4.9)

TP115 Ayios Yeoryios *Alestos* 501790/3876460 560m XXIX-57. Possible prospecting hole (Ch. 4.3)

TP116 Katydhata *Mutallou* 490100/3882730 260m XXVIII-28. Tomb opening (Ch. 3.14)

TP117 Nikitari *Kapsalia* 497600/3878030 490m XXVIII-55. Reported site of Asinou monastery buildings; 2 ancient olives; geophysical survey. PU01. MEDVOTT. (Ch. 5.5)

TP118 Katydhata *Pano Limna* 488900/3882020 250m XXVIII-28-W2. Pottery scatter and melted mudbrick (Ch. 3.11)

TP119 Katydhata *Pano Limna* 488800/3882020 260m XXVIII-28. Archaic sanctuary and Roman settlement. Organic collection grid: 88 PUs with nos. in format 'PUA07'. BA, PeB, GAC, HA, HR, HLER, ER, ROM, LR, RM, HIS, MM, MEDB, OTTMODI, MEDVOTT, MOD, UN. TCP624–42. TCS008–44. TCL418. (Ch. 3.11)

TP120 Katydhata *Livadhia* 489390/3882120 230m XXVIII-28-E2. Terrace wall made of slag cakes (Ch. 3.10)

TP121 Xyliatos *Saramalin* 503200/3876820 410m XXIX-58. Hillslope path, running north/south above Lagoudhera River

TP122 Kato Koutraphas *Mandres* 495750/3881540 280m. Threshing floors. TCL419–77. (Ch. 2.10)

TP123 Xyliatos *Psilliteri* 503040/3878260 350m XXIX-50. Boulder with possible door socket depression and line of associated stones (Ch. 4.6)

TP124 Nikitari *Mutallia* 495300/3876350 610m XXVIII-63. Ruined church of Ayios Yeoryios (Ch. 5.5)

TP125 Nikitari *Mutallia* 495290/3876380 610m XXVIII-63. Ruined settlement close to ruined church of Ayios Yeoryios (Ch. 5.5)

TP126 Katydhata *Laonarka* 489840/3882120 280m XXVIII-28-E2. Collapsed chamber of tomb (Ch. 3.14)

TP127 Katydhata *Laonarka* 489800/3882110 270m XXVIII-28-E2. Roman chamber tomb with dromos. PU01. HR, LHER, ER, ROM. TCS073–74. (Ch. 3.14)

TP128 Katydhata *Laonarka* 489810/3882120 260m XXVIII-28-E2. Chamber tomb with dromos (Ch. 3.14)

TP129 Katydhata *Pano Limna* 488790/3882070 250m XXVIII-28. Set of collapsed and/or robbed tombs. PU01–12. PeB, GAC, HA, HR, ROM, LR, ROM, LR, RM, HIS, UN. (Ch. 3.11)

TP130 Evrykhou *Kountouros* 493240/3881270 290m XXVIII-38. Ground stone. TCL478

TP131 Evrykhou *Pano Atsas* 493280/3881130 300m XXVIII-38. Small hill with platforms. PU01. (Ch. 2.7)

TP132 Phlasou *Strongilo* 490020/3880420 310m XXVIII-44-E1. Field with threshing floors recognized on the aerial photo; ploughed (Ch. 3.8)

TP133 Phlasou Village 489810/3879970 310m XXVIII-36-E2. Village Plan: Kato Phlasou No. 2. Disused water cistern

TP134 Kato Koutraphas *Konizos* 496980/3883110 240m XXVIII-31. Three lines of ruinous terrace walls

TP135 Phlasou *Koutroullis* 489920/3879540 340m XXVIII-44-E1. Section with Bronze Age pottery eroding out of the section (CS 2957). PU01–10. CHAL, LChPh, PeB, GAC, HA, HEL, ROM, LR, RM, HIS, MM. TCP643–58. TCL479–99. (Ch. 3.5)

TP136 Xyliatos *Dhyopevkous* 501980/3875920 520m XXIX-57. Disused stone irrigation channel and terrace wall

TP137 Nikitari *Stavros* 497890/3878290 490m XXVIII-56. Rock cluster (Ch. 5.7)

TP138 Phlasou *Akhneradhoes* 490600/3879480 370m XXVIII-45. Two possible tombs (Ch. 3.14)

TP139 Phlasou *Paleomylos* 489280/3879360 420m XXVIII-44-E2. Church of Ayios Yeoryios on spur (BU0088); Iron Age tomb (Ch. 3.3)

TP140 Pano Koutraphas Village 499280/3883440 230m. Village Plan: Pano Koutraphas. Demolished village, including abandoned watermill (BU0096) (Ch. 2.16)

TP141 Nikitari *Pykroathasoudhi* 497820/3877630 590m XXXVIII-55. Clusters of rocks, possibly from charcoal burning or pitch kilns (Ch. 5.7)

TP142 Xyliatos *Mutallin tis Trimithias* 501970/3875590 560m XXIX-57. Pile of stones with right angle

TP143 Ayios Yeoryios Kaphkalo *Khalospita* 497800/3877420 600m XXVIII-64. Possible check dams

TP144 Nikitari *Khandakia* 497780/3877340 580m XXXIII-63. Cluster of rocks, possibly from charcoal burning or pitch kilns (Ch. 5.7)

TP145 Xyliatos *Litharkies* 502000/3876180 500m XXIX-57. Series of 3 check dams (Ch. 4.4)

TP146 Xyliatos *Litharkies* 502000/3876240 510m XXIX-57. Small but dense scatter of pottery below a possible tomb. PU01. HR, ER. TCP659–60. (Ch. 4.4)

TP147 Xyliatos *Kokkinoplevra tou Alestou* 502020/3876280 510m XXIX-57. Series of 6 check dams (Ch. 4.4)

TP148 Xyliatos *Kokkinoplevra tou Alestou* 502020/3876450 570m XXIX-57. Adit with external stone-built platform (Ch. 4.3)

TP149 Xyliatos *Kokkinoplevra tou Alestou* 502060/3876450 570m XXIX-57. Modern quarry and possible adit (Ch. 4.3)

TP150 Xyliatos *Kokkinoplevra tou Alestou* 501980/3876510 610m XXIX-57. Stone wall of angular basalt boulders; small platform (Ch. 4.3)

TP151 Xyliatos *Kokkinoplevra tou Alestou* 501980/3876540 640m XXIX-57. Possible check dam high up on Alestos

TP152 Xyliatos *Kokkinoplevra tou Alestou* 501950/3876580 650m XXIX-57. Small platform with dry stone retaining wall (Ch. 4.3)

TP153 Xyliatos *Alestos* 501980/3876670 660m XXIX-57. Two adits on the top of Alestos (Ch. 4.3)

TP154 Xyliatos *Alestos* 501970/3876680 670m XXIX-57. Small platform with dry stone retaining wall and cut into bedrock (Ch. 4.3)

TP155 Nikitari *Stavros* 497920/3877900 520m XXVIII-56. Series of check dams (Ch. 5.7)

TP156 Nikitari *Stavros* 497920/3877920 500m XXVIII-56. Series of check dams (Ch. 5.7)

TP157 Nikitari *Stavros* 497920/3877950 500m XXVII-56. Series of check dams (Ch. 5.7)

TP158 Nikitari *Stavros* 497900/3877830 520m XXVIII-56. Possible check dam (Ch. 5.7)

TP159 Nikitari *Palaeolinos* 497380/3877990 490m XXVIII-56. Two stone check dams

TP160 Nikitari *Stavros* 497880/3877850 530m XXVIII-56. Possible wooden check dam (Ch. 5.7)

TP161 Nikitari *Stavros* 497880/3877800 530m XXVIII-56. Series of 13 check dams (Ch. 5.7)

TP162 Nikitari *Palaeolinos* 497840/3877920 530m XXVIII-56. Series of 5 check dams

TP163 Nikitari *Palaeolinos* 497820/3877940 500m XXVIII-56. Thirteen check dams

TP164 Nikitari *Palaeolinos* 497800/3877940 510m XXVIII-56. Series of 7 check dams

TP165 Nikitari *Palaeolinos* 497760/3877950 510m XXVIII-56. Check dam

TP166 Katydhata *Laonarka* 489830/3882140 280m XXVIII-28-E2. Collapsed dromos (Ch. 3.14)

TP167 Nikitari *Palaeolinos* 497740/3877870 470m XXVIII-56. First order gully with 5 check dams

TP168 Nikitari *Palaeolinos* 497720/3877880 510m XXVIII-56. Series of 6 check dams in wide gully

TP169 Nikitari *Palaeolinos* 497720/3877920 470m XXVIII-56. Gully with 5 check dams

TP170 Xyliatos *Alestos* 502280/3876580 580m XXIX-57. Rocky outcrop on Alestos with view (Ch. 4.4)

TP171 Skouriotissa *Phoukasa* 490700/3882580 280m XXVIII-29. Amphora pile in Skouriotissa mine. PU01. HA, ROM. TCP661–87. (Ch. 3.12)

TP172 Skouriotissa *Kitromilia* 489320/3883580 190m XXVIII-28-E1. Slag heap. HA, ROM, LR. (Ch. 3.12)

TP173 Xyliatos *Alestos* 502460/3876600 510m XXIX-57. Small oval platform (Ch. 4.3)

TP174 Xyliatos *Alestos* 502500/3876620 560m XXIX-57. Bedrock outcrop with view (Ch. 4.4)

TP175 Xyliatos *Alestos* 502500/3876620 530m XXIX-58. Series of 7 check dams

TP176 Phlasou *Koutroullis* 489920/3879620 350m XXVIII-44-EI. Very large rectangular threshing floor (Ch. 3.5)

TP177 Phlasou *Koutroullis* 489920/3879620 350m XXVIII-44-E1. Groups of ground stone. PU01–03. LChPh, MM. TCL500–503. (Ch. 3.5)

TP178 Evrykhou *Ammos* 490820/3878440 400m XXVIII-53. Two tombs, looted and infilled (Ch. 3.14)

TP179 Evrykhou Village 491030/3877550 450m XXVIII-53. Village Plan: Evrykhou. Two olive oil mills and well (Ch. 3.15)

TP180 Xyliatos *Alestos* 502370/3876790 580m XXIX-57. Large adit with steps and large modern spoil heap (Ch. 4.3)

TP181 Xyliatos *Alestos* 502360/3876790 580m XXIX-57. Adit without spoil heap (Ch. 4.3)

TP182 Xyliatos *Alestos* 502360/3876810 590m XXIX-57. Small exploratory cut into the bedrock (Ch. 4.3)

TP183 Xyliatos *Alestos* 502370/3876830 580m XXIX-57. Semicircular platform (Ch. 4.3)

TP184 Xyliatos *Alestos* 502360/3876800 590m XXIX-57. Adit with 2 entrances, possibly connected to TP180 (Ch. 4.3)

TP185 Xyliatos *Alestos* 502320/3876790 610m XXIX-57. Small platform (Ch. 4.3)

TP186 Xyliatos *Alestos* 502340/3876780 600m XXIX-57. Path on steep slope (Ch. 4.3)

TP187 Kato Phlasou *Koutroullis* 489970/3879680 360m XXVIII-44-E1. Stone-built retaining wall and threshing floor (Ch. 3.5)

TP188 Nikitari *Moutti tou Dhia* 496230/3877250 550m XXVIII-55. Section of road and supporting structure (Ch. 5.7)

TP189 Nikitari *Khandakia* 496180/3877170 580m XXVIII 63. Possible remains of stone-built structure

TP190 Nikitari *Moutti tou Dhia* 495720/3877780 630m XXVIII-55. Possible dry stone walling

TP191 Xyliatos *Litharkies* 501870/3876040 510m XXIX-57. Internal cement lining of well (Ch. 4.4)

TP192 Nikitari *Pykroathasoudhia* 495800/3876470 740m XXVIII-55. View from mountain in all directions

TP193 Ayios Theodhoros *Kankellia* 493480/3879000 520m XXVIII-46. Path cut into hillside (Ch. 5.9)

TP194 Ayios Theodhoros *Tholos* 492700/3878830 360m XXVIII-45. Possible farmstead: terraces, rubble piles and paths (Ch. 5.9)

TP195 Xyliatos *Litharkies* 502090/3876180 490m XXIX-57. Stone-lined well (Ch. 4.9)

TP196 Xyliatos *Litharkies* 502000/3876100 500m XXIX-57. Stone-lined well cut into bedrock (Ch. 4.9)

TP197 Katydhata *Pano Limna* 488880/3882270 250m XXVIII-28. Possible tomb with spoil heap (Ch. 3.11)

TP198 Ayios Yeoryios *Moni* 500600/3878930 440m XXIX-41. Terrace system (Ch. 5.7)

TP199 Ayios Yeoryios *Moni* 500760/3879000 420m XXIX-41. Path with traces of old terraces

TP200 Nikitari *Laxia tou Laona* 495220/3874660 710m XXXVII-06. Stone structure with unclear walls and pottery (Ch. 5.4)

TP201 Linou *Vrysi tou Haji Christophi* 492140/3882280 240m XXVIII-29. Spring. PU01–02. HA, ROM, LR, RM. (Ch. 2.5)

TP202 Linou *Vrysi tou Haji Christophi* 492100/3882300 250m XXVIII-29. Roman farmstead with 2 rooms, tile fragments and millstone. PU01–07. HA, HR, LHER, ROM, LR, HIS. TCP688–93. (Ch. 2.5)

TP203 Katydhata Village 489770/3882290 260m. Middle–Late Bronze Age chamber tomb (Katydhata Village Tomb 1) (Ch. 3.14)

TP204 Potami *Strata Oritissas* 501250/3884560 260m XXIX-17. Check dam made of large boulders, 7 m wide (Ch. 2.16)

TP205 Petra *Potima* 492100/3882920 210m XXVIII-29. 6th-century AD sherd in alluvial deposit. PU01. LR

TP206 Linou *Vrysi tou Haji Christophi* 492470/3882450 240m XXVIII-29. Jasper cores and flakes with carbonate coating. PU01. (Ch. 2.7)

TP207 Linou *Atsadhes* 492260/3882580 240m XXVIII-29. Jasper core and flakes. PU01. (Ch. 2.7)

TP208 Evrykhou *Tanayies* 492650/3882050 260m XXVIII-29. Phorades-type slag and pottery. PU01. PeB, GA, HA, HIS. (Ch. 2.7)

TP209 Evrykhou *Tanayies* 492800/3882170 270m XXVIII-30. Village of Lemonas. (Ch. 2.7)

TP210 Xyliatos *Litharkies* 501950/3876100 500m XXIX-57. Series of rock piles. PU02–06, PU08–11, PU13–29, PU38–39. HA, HEL, HR, ROM, LR, RM, HIS, MM. TCP694–95. TCL504. (Ch. 4.4)

TP211 Xyliatos *Litharkies* 501900/3876040 520m XXIX-57. Small concentration of pottery, tile and grindstone. PU01. HA, LHER, ER, ROM, LR, HIS. TCP696–98. (Ch. 4.4)

TP212 Xyliatos *Litharkies* 501880/3876080 520m XXIX-57. Raised flat area of summit of a small hill. PU01. HA, ROM, HIS. (Ch. 4.4)

TP213 Xyliatos *Alestos* 502490/3876930 520m XXIX-58. Eight check dams (Ch. 4.4)

TP214 Sina Oros *Mouti tou Stavrou* 491020/3873960 680m. Sub-circular pile of rocks and collapsed wall. (Ch. 3.15)

TP215 Evrykhou *Khalospitia* 493100/3882640 260m XXVIII-30. Archaic sanctuary. PU01–03. BA, PeB, PoBAR, GAC, AC, HA, HEL, HR, HER, ROM, LR, HIS, MM, MEDUIII, OTTMODI, MOD, UN. TCP699–701. TCS045–57. (Ch. 2.4)

TP216 Petra *Lithosourka* 492300/3883040 240m XXVIII-29. Extensive area of rubble piles, tile and pottery. PU01. HR, ROM, LR. TCP702–703. TCS075. (Ch. 2.7)

TP217 Petra *Meras* 491320/3883230 220m XXVIII-29. Scatter of worked red and brown jasper

TP218 Petra *Meras* 491320/3883220 100m XXVIII-29. Buried check dam and mining spoil

TP219 Nikitari *Trimitheri* 495340/3875100 700m XXVIII-63. Check dam in gully

TP220 Nikitari *Trimitheri* 495240/3875330 650m XXVIII-63. Three (possibily 4) structures on slope. PU01–10. ROM, LR, HIS, MM, UN. TCP704–705. (Ch. 5.4)

TP221 Petra *Phoukasa* 491480/3882990 230m XXVIII-21. Roman farmstead with cistern, pottery and tile (Ch. 2.6)

TP222 Xyliatos *Dhoxamenes* 502750/3876740 460m XXIX-58-WI. Path (Ch. 4.4)

TP223 Xyliatos *Dhoxamenes* 502710/3876720 240m XXIX-58-WI. Path with small retaining walls (Ch. 4.4)

TP224 Tembria *Esso Ambelika* 491360/3876010 600m XXVIII-61. Path (Ch. 3.15)

TP225 Tembria *Esso Ambelika* 491050/3875980 540m XXVIII-61. Path (Ch. 3.15)

TP226 Vyzakia *Konnidhes* 502830/3882810 310m XXIX-26. Abandoned settlement

TP227 Nikitari *Trimitheri* 495250/3875630 650m XXVIII-63. Possible stone structure (Ch. 5.4)

TP228 Nikitari *Trimitheri* 495260/3875640 650m XXVIII-63. Path following contour of mountains above river (Ch. 5.4)

TP229 Nikitari *Trimitheri* 495280/3875520 650m XXVIII-63. Possible retaining wall (Ch. 5.4)

TP230 Nikitari *Trimitheri* 495270/3875520 640m XXXVIII-63. Long stretch of wall and associated path (Ch. 5.4)

TP231 Nikitari *Trimitheri* 495270/3875610 640m XXVIII-63. Stone terrace wall remnant (Ch. 5.4)

TP232 Ayios Yeoryios Kaphkalo *Leftolaonon* 498570/3876430 610m XXVIII-64. Rock-cut (possible adit)

TP233 Ayios Yeoryios *Plevra tis Mosphilias* 498560/3876330 580m. XXVIII-64. Path/road

TP234 Xyliatos *Kokkinoplevra tou Alestou* 501790/3876200 480m XXIX-57. Series of 15 check dams in 2 first order gullies (Ch. 4.4)

TP235 Xyliatos *Kokkinoplevra tou Alestou* 501810/3876460 570m XXIX-57. Circular platform (Ch. 4.3)

TP236 Petra *Phoukasa* 491520/3882920 220m XXVIII-21. Jasper outcrop and lithics workshop. PU01. HA, LR, HIS. (Ch. 2.7)

TP237 Petra *Phoukasa* 491400/3883020 220m XXVIII-21. Jasper outcrop and lithics workshop. PU01–04. HA, HR, ROM, LR, RM, HIS, MM. (Ch. 2.7)

TP238 Xyliatos *Litharkies* 501920/3876040 520m XXIX-57. Cut with wall visible and in situ pottery (Ch. 4.4)

TP239 Kato Koutraphas *Mandroudhes* 495030/3880660 320m XXVIII-38. Bronze Age settlement with pottery and ground stone. 26 gridded PUs with nos. in format 'PUE0N0', followed by four grabs (PU01–04). BA, PeB, PoB. TCP706. TCL505–23. (Ch. 2.9)

TP240 Nikitari *Khalospidhia* 497060/3882100 290m XXVIII-31. Hillslope with outcrops and unworked fragments of red jasper (Ch. 2.11)

TP241 Ayios Theodhoros *Pano Atsa* 494050/3879710 410m XXVIII-46. Rural structure with 4 rooms; 'Mandra tou Fatchitas' (Ch. 5.3)

TP242 Pano Koutraphas *Petrera* 499010/3883500 230m XXVIII-24. Bronze Age pottery and ground stone scatter (Ch. 2.14)

TP243 Katydhata *Laonarka* 489970/3882010 280m XXVIII-28. Bronze Age settlement. 23 gridded PUs with nos. in format 'PUE0N0', followed by 3 grabs (GRAB1–3). PeB, GAC, HA, HIS, MM, MOD, UN. TCL524. (Ch. 3.9)

TP244 Kato Koutraphas Village 497900/3884600 190m XXVIII-24. Church of Panayia Chryseleousa; two threshing floors (Ch. 2.16)

TP245 Pano Koutraphas *Sanidhia* 499500/3884230 270m XXVIII-24. Dense concentration of Roman pottery (Ch. 2.15)

TP246 Phlasou *Langouphes* 489660/3879420 320m XXVIII-44-E2. Section with flood deposits and Bronze Age pottery. PU01–05. PeB, PoBAR, LR, UN. (Ch. 3.5)

TP247 Evrykhou *Phinikos* 490080/3878780 380m XXVIII-44-E2. Excavated Hellenistic–Roman tomb (Evrykhou Tomb 4) (Ch. 3.14)

TP248 Evrykhou *Kamilaries* 493430/3882340 280m XXVIII-30. Archaic cemetery. PU01. AC. TCP707–708 (Ch. 2.4)

TP249 Ayios Yeoryios *Ayia Paraskevi* 496830/3873680 1120m XXXVII-15. Ruined church of Ayia Paraskevi (Ch. 5.9)

TP250 Nikitari *Khalospita* 496020/3873310 900m XXXVII-15. Two ruined structures with Medieval–Modern pottery and pithos. PU01. HIS, MM, MEDUIII, MEDVOTT, OTTMODI. TCP709–12. (Ch. 5.4)

TP251 Ayios Epiphanios *Paleoekklishia* 488950/3881040 310m XXVIII-36-W2. Ruined Medieval church of the Panayia (Ch. 3.7)

TP252 Katydhata *Pano Limna* 488840/3882080 260m XXVIII-28. Late Roman architecture and pottery in section. PU01–06. GAC, HA, LHER, ROM, LR, HIS. (Ch. 3.11)

TP253 Korakou *Agroladou* 489360/3878400 380m XXVIII-52 XXVIII-52-E1. Village Plan: Agroladhou. Site of Agroladou village. BU0087. (Ch. 3.3)

TP254 Ayios Epiphanios *Arabajis* 489080/3880600 300m. Wall eroding out of terrace riser with Medieval pottery and bone (Ch. 3.7)

TP255 Ayios Theodhoros *Palloura* 494600/3879530 420m XXVIII-46. Stone-built structure of 4+ rooms. (Ch. 5.3)

TP256 Pano Koutraphas *Katalasharis* 499000/3884640 230m XXVIII-24. Roman and Ottoman–Modern pottery concentration (Ch. 2.15)

Appendix 2. Catalogue of Special Interest Areas

This appendix acts as both summary and concordance. Special Interest Areas (SIAs) are located by Intensive Survey Zone (ISZ), grid reference (Easting/Northing, in the UTM grid), elevation (metres above sea level), and the sheet and plan number of the 1:5000 cadastral map on which they appear (e.g. XXVII-28). Each entry lists the principal periods, Survey Units, Geomorphological Units, Places of Special Interest (prefixed 'TP') and Building Units that constitute the SIA. See also the catalogue of Places of Special Interest (Appendix 1) and the select catalogue of Building Units (Volume 1, Ch. 3.11). Cross-references are given to the main discussion elsewhere in the publication (in this volume unless otherwise stated).

TS01 Skouriotissa *Vouppes*

Modern copper mine and Roman slag heap. Karkotis ISZ. (Ch. 3.12)

489550/3883500. 220m. XXVIII-28

TP007 Large slag heap with workshop floors

TP171 Amphora pile

TP172 Slag heap

BU0093 Church in UN camp, built 1716

TS02 Ayia Marina *Mavrovouni*

Roman slag heap, pottery, field walls, Medieval–Ottoman church. Lagoudhera ISZ. (Ch. 4.6)

503400/3877400. 400m. XXIX-50

SU0012, SU0600–608, SU0614–40, SU0660–61, SU1620–51, SU1690–1710

GU0600–607, GU0617–40, GU0658–60, GU1629–39, GU1641, GU1667–78

TP006 Slag heap, Roman pottery, rubble piles

TP017 Rock of Ayios Kyriakos: basalt outcrop

TP022 Small, stone-built structure with 2 niches

TP023 Possible stone-built enclosure

TP024 Stone-built wall of large boulders

TP025 Rubble piles

TP041 Platform with 2.5 m-high retaining wall

TP042 Possible collapsed structure

TP047 Ruins of the church of Ayios Kyriakos

TP086 Path between two terrace walls

TP087 Path; lower construction of TP086

TP088 Adit beside path TP086

TP104 36 gridded circles in SU0622

TS03 Nikitari *Asinou*

Ottoman–Modern settlement. Asinou ISZ. (Ch. 5.5)

497600/3878400. 500m. XXVIII-55, XXVIII-56

TP016 1 paved threshing floor and possibly 2 others

TP081 Abandoned village

TP082 Two-storey house with attached goatfold

TP083 Possible threshing floor

BU0047 Village house. Stone & mudbrick.

BU0116 Village house. Stone & mudbrick.

TS04 Phlasou *Koutroullis tou Ayiou Yeoryiou*

Block survey for field team training. Medieval–Modern. Karkotis ISZ.

489900/3880300. 320m. XXXVIII-36-E2

SU0082–84, SU2001–11, SU2013–22, SU2026

GU0067–69, GU2001–2004, GU2008–10, GU2013–16, GU2018–19

TP132 Ploughed field, once with threshing floors

TP133 Disused water cistern

BU0080 Church of Ayios Dhimitrianos, 1906

BU0084 Church of Ayios Yeoryios, 1722

TS05 Xyliatos *Litharkies*

Hellenistic–Roman settlement, with rubble piles, tiles, pottery, geophysics. Lagoudhera ISZ. (Ch. 4.4)
501950/3876080. 520m. XXIX-57
SU2601–609, SU2632–60
GU2601–10, GU2623–84, GU2696–701
TP112 Adit with clearly cut shaft
TP113 L-shaped wall
TP114 Possible collapsed field shelter
TP145 Series of 3 check dams
TP146 Pottery scatter: tomb?
TP147 Series of 6 check dams
TP148 Adit with external stone-built platform
TP149 Modern quarry and possible adit
TP150 Stone wall with small platform
TP151 Possible check dam
TP152 Small platform with dry stone wall
TP153 2 adits on the top of Alestos
TP154 Small platform with wall and cut into bedrock
TP191 Internal cement lining of well
TP195 Stone-lined well
TP196 Well, stone-lined and cut into bedrock
TP210 Series of rock piles throughout block survey
TP211 Concentration of pottery, tile and grindstone
TP212 Raised flat area of summit of a small hill
TP213 8 check dams
TP234 Series of 15 check dams in 2 first order gullies
TP235 Circular platform
TP238 Cut with wall and in situ pottery

TS06 Phlasou *Koutroullis*

Chalcolithic/Early Bronze Age settlement: section, ground stone, pottery. Karkotis ISZ. (Ch. 3.5)
489920/3879620. 350m. XXVIII-44-E1
SU2006, SU2012, SU2078–84, SU2104
GU2033–35, GU2077, GU2080–86, GU2102–103
TP135 Section with Bronze Age pottery (Cyprus Survey CS2957)
TP176 Very large rectangular threshing floor
TP177 3 groups of ground stone on summit of ridge
TP187 Stone-built retaining wall and threshing floor
TP246 Section showing flood deposits with artefacts

TS07 Kato Koutraphas *Mandres*

Abandoned 19th–20th-century seasonal settlement, with threshing floors. Mandres ISZ. (Ch. 2.10)
495750/3881300. 280m. XXVIII-39
SU0009–11, SU0321–27, SU0330–54, SU1379–90, SU2024, SU3012–16, SU3022–23
GU0316–21, GU0324–38, GU1352, GU1363–68, GU3008–10, GU3053–56
TP008 2 threshing floors with associated buildings
TP018 Outlying structures
TP021 Central village area: houses, streets and ovens
TP026 Outlying structures
TP027 Outlying structures and threshing floor
TP028 Outlying structure
TP122 Threshing floors at Mandres
BU0005–43, BU0050–52, BU0115: houses, mostly with stone foundations and mudbrick walls

TS08 Nikitari *Kapsalia*

Byzantine and later church of Panayia Phorviotissa & surroundings. Asinou ISZ. (Ch. 5.5)
497580/3878280. 440m. XXVIII-55
SU0355–64, SU1361–66, SU1371, SU2301–305
GU0339–40, GU1339, GU2301–303
TP030 Church of Panayia Phorviotissa with enclosure
TP117 Ruined structure, probably Asinou monastery; 2 ancient olives
BU0058 Church of Panayia Phorviotissa, AD 1105.

TS09 Katydhata *Laonarka*

Prehistoric Bronze Age settlement, with previously excavated tombs. Karkotis ISZ. (Ch. 3.9)
489970/3882030. 300m. XXVIII-28
SU0071–78, SU0099–104, SU1012–14, SU1053–71, SU1079–81, SU1089–92, SU1094, SU1097–99, SU2189–91
GU0060–63, GU0073, GU0093, GU1051–57, GU1062–65, GU1073–74, GU1080, GU2148–49, GU3047
TP035 Bone and Bronze Age pottery at foot of hill
TP037 Rock-cut tomb
TP040 Military fox-hole
TP044 Ancient shaft (?) truncated by modern cut
TP063 Rock-cut tomb
TP085 Archaic–Roman worked stone and sherds found by Cyprus Survey (CS 2755)
TP126 Collapsed chamber of tomb
TP127 Roman chamber tomb with dromos
TP128 Chamber tomb with dromos
TP166 Collapsed dromos
TP203 Middle–Late Bronze Age chamber tomb (Katydhata Village Tomb 1)
TP243 Gridding of Bronze Age pottery scatter

TS10 Xyliatos *Ayios Kyriakos*

River gully with ancient adits and shafts. Lagoudhera ISZ. (Ch. 4.5)
503270/3877220. 390m. XXIX-50
SU1652–66, SU1676–89
GU0661–62, GU1642–46, GU1656–66
TP050–53, TP054–55: ancient adits
TP053, TP056: ancient shafts
TP057–58: ancient prospection cuts
TP099, TP121: paths

TS11 Phlasou *Dodekaskala*

Roman and Medieval–Modern pottery scatter; church & ruined monastery. Karkotis ISZ. (Ch. 3.6)
490580/3880100. 340m. XXVIII-45
SU0001, SU0003–0007, SU0013–20, SU0087–98,

SU1001–1004, SU1301–304, SU1601–605, SU2962–65
GU0001–0006, GU0009–13, GU0075–92, GU1001–1002, GU1601–605
BU0094 Church and site of monastery of Panayia Kousouliotissa.

TS12 Nikitari *Khalospities*
Medieval–Modern pottery scatter beside site of Ayios Ioannis church. Asinou ISZ. (Ch. 5.5)
497010/3878020. 400m. XXVIII-55
SU0300–302, SU0365–69, SU0382, SU0386, SU1353–59, SU1367–70
GU0300, GU0358, GU0361, GU1013–15, GU1352–28, GU1330–38
TP039 Ashlar wall from church of Ayios Ioannis

TS13 Skouriotissa *Pseftas*
Hellenistic–Roman pottery scatter. Adit; ancient olive mill. Karkotis ISZ. (Ch. 3.13)
489060/3883800. 180m. XXVIII-20-W2
SU1005–1006, SU1072–78. GU1003–1004, GU1058–61
TP109 Cave (possible adit) and olive mill

TS14 Ayios Theodhoros *Karterouni*
Ottoman to 20th-century village in forest with houses, threshing floors, paths, terraces and forestry cairns. (Ch. 5.8)
493360/3873340. 730m. XXXVII-14
TP067 Karterouni abandoned settlement
TP072 Threshing floors at Karterouni
TP073 Ford and track at Karterouni
BU0127–46: village houses, mainly built of stone

TS15 Katydhata *Pano Limna*
Archaic sanctuary and Roman settlement. Karkotis ISZ. (Ch. 3.11)
488850/3882020. 250m.
Cadastral maps XXVIII-28, XXVIII-28-W2
SU1082–84, SU2124–41
GU1066–67, GU1077, GU2115–20
TP092 Modern shrine, surrounded by possible tombs
TP118 In situ pottery scatter and melted mudbrick
TP119 Collection grid
TP129 Series of collapsed and/or robbed tombs
TP197 Possible tomb with spoil heap
TP252 Late Roman architecture and pottery appearing in bulldozed section

TS16 Phlasou *Strongilo*
Fields used for ploughsoil experiments. Karkotis ISZ. (Volume 1, Ch. 2.9)
489620/3879880. 300m. XXVIII-44
SU0392–95

TS17 Nikitari *Rotsos*
Block surveyed units along river with Medieval–Modern pottery. Asinou ISZ. (Ch. 5.5)
497320/3877960. 420m. XXVIII-55
SU1360, SU2325–29. GU1329, GU2323–26, GU2331
TP159 2 stone check dams

TS18 Linou *Vrysi tou Haji Christophi*
Roman farmstead with spring, millstone & artefact scatter. Atsas ISZ. (Ch. 2.5)
492120/3882290. 240m. XXVIII-29
SU2160–65. GU2133–36
TP201 Spring
TP202 Roman farmstead with 2 rooms, tile fragments and millstone

TS19 Nikitari *Stavros*
System of check dams near Stavros church, probably Ottoman. Asinou ISZ. (Ch. 5.7)
497740/3877870. 470m. XXVIII-56
No SUs. GU2327–30, GU2332–37, GU2339
TP034 Check dam system covering at least 5 gullies
TP143 Possible check dams
TP155 Series of check dams
TP156 Series of check dams
TP157 Series of check dams
TP158 Possible check dam
TP160 Possible check dam (wooden)
TP161 Series of 13 check dams
TP162 Series of 5 check dams
TP163 Series of 13 check dams
TP164 Series of 7 check dams
TP165 Check dam
TP167 First order gully with 5 check dams
TP168 Series of 6 check dams in wide gully
TP169 Gully with 5 check dams

TS20 Petra *Phoukasa*
Jasper working and Late Roman farmstead. Atsas ISZ. (Ch. 2.6)
491480/3882990. 230m. XXVIII-21
SU2187. GU2147
TP221 Probable Roman farmstead with cistern, pottery and tile
TP236 Jasper outcrop: lithic workshop
TP237 Outcrop of pillow lava

TS21 Potami *Kambos tou Lemonari*
Early Neolithic ground stone and chipped stone concentration. Koutraphas ISZ. (Ch. 2.13)
501420/3883980. 270m. XXIV-17
SU1328–52. GU1317–24

Bibliography

Adams, C.E.P.

2007 *Land transport in Roman Egypt: a study of economics and administration in a Roman province*. Oxford Classical Monographs. Oxford: Oxford University Press.

Agricola, G.

1950 *De re metallica: translated from the first Latin edition of 1556*. New York: Dover Publications.

Anderson, P.C.

2006 Non-mechanised processing and storage of cereals, grasses and pulses used for fodder, fuel, food and crafts: examples from N. Tunisia, Atlas Region, Northwestern Tell. In F. Ertuğ (ed.), *Proceedings of the IVth International Congress of Ethnobotany (ICEB2005), Yeditepe University, Istanbul, 21–26 August 2005*, 223–31. Istanbul: Eğe Yayınları.

Angelides, S.

1996 The Cyprus economy under British rule. In V. Karageorghis and D. Michaelides (eds.), *The development of the Cypriot economy from the Prehistoric period to the modern day*, 209–28. Nicosia: University of Cyprus; Bank of Cyprus.

Aristeidou, E.

1994 *Anekdhota engrafa tis kipriakis istorias apo to arkhio tis Venetias. Tomos B' (1509–1517)*. Texts and Studies in the History of Cyprus 19. Nicosia: Cyprus Research Centre.

Åström, P.

1972 *The Late Cypriote Bronze Age: architecture and pottery*. Swedish Cyprus Expedition 4: 1C. Lund: Swedish Cyprus Expedition.

1973 Comments on the corpus of Mycenaean pottery in Cyprus, *Acts of the International Archaeological Symposium, 'The Mycenaeans in the Eastern Mediterranean', Nicosia*, 122–27. Nicosia: Department of Antiquities, Republic of Cyprus.

1989 *Katydhata: a Bronze Age site in Cyprus*. Studies in Mediterranean Archaeology 86. Partille: Paul Åströms Förlag.

Bakirtzis, C.

1989 *Byzantini tsoukalolayina*. Arkhaioloyikon Dheltion, Dhimosievmata 39. Athens: Tameion Arkhaioloyikon Poron kai Apallotrioseon.

Barker, G., R. Adams, O.H. Creighton, D. Crook, D.D. Gilbertson, J.P. Grattan, C.O. Hunt, D.J. Mattingly, S.J. McLaren, H.A. Mohammed, P. Newson, C. Palmer, F.B. Pyatt, T.E.G. Reynolds, and R. Tomber

1999 Environment and land use in the Wadi Faynan, Southern Jordan: the third season of geoarchaeology and landscape archaeology. *Levant* 31, 255–92.

Barker, G., R. Adams, O.H. Creighton, P. Daly, D.D. Gilbertson, J.P. Grattan, C.O. Hunt, D.J. Mattingly, S.J. McLaren, P. Newson, C. Palmer, F.B. Pyatt, T.E.G. Reynolds, H. Smith, R. Tomber, and A.J. Truscott

2000 Archaeology and desertification in the Wadi Faynan: the fourth (1999) season of the Wadi Faynan landscape survey. *Levant* 32, 27–52.

Barlow, J.A.

1991 New light on Red Polished ware. In J.A. Barlow, D. Bolger, and B. Kling (eds.), *Cypriot ceramics: reading the prehistoric record*, 51–57. University Monographs. Philadelphia: University of Pennsylvania Press.

Bars'kyj, B.

1996 *A pilgrim's account of Cyprus: Bars'kyj's travels in Cyprus. Essay, translation, and commentaries*. Altamont, New York: Greece and Cyprus Research Center.

Bear, L.M.

1963 *The mineral resources and mining industry of Cyprus*. Bulletin 1. Nicosia: Geological Survey Department.

Bekker-Nielsen, T.

2004 *The roads of ancient Cyprus*. Copenhagen: Museum Tusculanum.

Belgiorno, M.R.

2000 Project 'Pyrame' 1998–1999: archaeological, metallurgical and historical evidence at Pyrgos (Limassol). *Report of the Department of Antiquities, Cyprus*, 1–17.

Bettison-Varga, L., R.J. Varga, and P. Shiffman

1992 Relation between ore-forming hydrothermal systems and extensional deformation in the Solea graben spreading center, Troodos ophiolite, Cyprus. *Geology* 20, 987–90.

Bevan, A.

2002 The rural landscape of Neopalatial Kythera: a GIS perspective. *Journal of Mediterranean Archaeology* 15, 217–55.

Bintliff, J.L., P. Howard, and A. Snodgrass

1999 The hidden landscape of prehistoric Greece. *Journal of Mediterranean Archaeology* 12, 139–68.

Boustronios, G.

1489 *The chronicle of George Boustronios 1456–1489*. Melbourne: University of Melbourne Cyprus Expedition.

Boutin, A., A.B. Knapp, I. Banks, M. Given, and M.T. Horowitz

2003 Settlement and cemetery in and around Katydhata village: from prehistory to the Roman era. *Report of the Department of Antiquities, Cyprus*, 335–49.

Briois, F., B. Gratuze, and J. Guilaine

1997 Obsidiennes du site néolithique précéramique de Shillourokambos (Chypre). *Paléorient* 23, 95–112.

Brook Ramsey, C.

2010 OxCal. Programme, V.4.1.7. Oxford: Radiocarbon Accelerator Unit, University of Oxford. Accessible at http://c14.arch.ox.ac.uk/embed.php?File=oxcal.html.

Bruce, J.L., C.P. Manglis, and D.M. Creveling

1937 Antiquities in the mines of Cyprus. In E. Gjerstad, J. Lindros, E. Sjöqvist, and A. Westholm (eds.), *The Swedish Cyprus Expedition: finds and results of the excavations in Cyprus, 1927–1931. Volume 3*, 639–71. Stockholm: Swedish Cyprus Expedition.

Brueggemann, E., and G. Spindler

1999 Wet and dry deposition of sulphur at the site Melpitz in East Germany. *Water, Air, & Soil Pollution* 109, 81–99.

Brumfield, A.

2000 Agriculture and rural settlement in Ottoman Crete, 1669–1898: a modern site survey. In U. Baram and L. Carroll (eds.), *A historical archaeology of the Ottoman Empire: breaking new ground*, 37–78. New York: Kluwer Academic/Plenum.

Buchholz, H.-G.

1991 Tamassos – Frangissa (1885). *Centre d'Études Chypriotes, Cahier* 16, 3–15.

Buell, M., and C. Mavromatis

2010 Kourion Mapping Project. *Report of the Department of Antiquities, Cyprus*, 261–94.

Buitron-Oliver, D.

1996 *The sanctuary of Apollo Hylates at Kourion: excavations in the archaic precinct*. Studies in Mediterranean Archaeology 109. Jonsered, Sweden: P. Åström.

Bustron, F.

1884 *Chronique de l'île de Chypre*. Extrait des Mélanges Historiques 5. Paris: Imprimerie nationale.

Carr, J.M.

1960 Geology and mineral resources of the Asinou–Kato Moni Area. In J.M. Carr and L.M. Bear (eds.), *The geology and mineral resources of the Peristerona–Lagoudhera area*, 21–46. Geological Survey Department, Cyprus, Memoir 2. Nicosia: Geological Survey Department.

Carstens, A.M.

2006 Cypriot chamber tombs. In L.W. Sørensen and K.W. Jacobsen (eds.), *Panayia Ematousa II. Political, cultural, ethnic and social relations in Cyprus: approaches to regional studies*, 125–79. Monographs of the Danish Institute at Athens 6.2. Athens: Danish Institute at Athens.

Catling, H.W.

1964 *Cypriot bronzework in the Mycenaean world*. Oxford monographs on classical archaeology. Oxford: Clarendon Press.

1972 An early Byzantine pottery factory at Dhiorios in Cyprus. *Levant* 4, 1–82.

Census

1882 *Report on the census of population, 1881, Cyprus*. London: Colonial Office.

Christodoulou, D.

1959 *The evolution of the rural land use pattern in Cyprus*. World Land Use Survey, Regional Monograph 2. Bude: Geographical Publications.

Cobham, C.D., ed.

1908 *Excerpta Cypria: materials for a history of Cyprus*. Cambridge: Cambridge University Press.

Connolly, A.

1992 Part B: The 1991 study season classification of ore dressing stone tools from Almyras. *Report of the Department of Antiquities, Cyprus*, 71–72.

Constantinou, G.

1982 Geological features and ancient exploitation of the cupriferous sulphide ore bodies of Cyprus. In J.D. Muhly, R. Maddin, and V. Karageorghis (eds.), *Early metallurgy in Cyprus, 4000–500 BC*, 13–24. Nicosia: Pierides Foundation and Department of Antiquities.

1992 Ancient copper mining in Cyprus. In A. Marangou and K. Psillides (eds.), *Cyprus, copper and the sea*, 43–74. Nicosia: Government of Cyprus.

Coureas, N.

2003 *The foundation rules of medieval Cypriot monasteries: Makhairas and St Neophytos*. Nicosia: Cyprus Research Centre.

2005 Economy. In A. Nicolaou-Konnari and C. Schabel (eds.), *Cyprus: society and culture 1191–1374*, 103–56. Leiden: Brill.

Craddock, P.

1995 *Early metal mining and production*. Edinburgh: Edinburgh University Press.

Cullis, C.G., and A.B. Edge

1922 *Report on the cupriferous deposits of Cyprus*. London: Crown Agents for the Colonies.

Danisman, H.H.G.

1977 A survey of turbine-type water-mills in the Bolu region of the central Anatolian plateau. *METU Journal of the Faculty of Architecture* 3, 17–37.

Daszkiewicz, M., and J. Raabe

1995 Cypriot Sigillata and Cypriot Red Slip ware: a preliminary report on technological investigations. In H. Meyza and J. Mlynarczyk (eds.), *Hellenistic and Roman pottery in the Eastern Mediterranean: Advances in Scientific Studies. Acts of the II Nieborów Pottery Workshop, Nieborów, 18–20 December 1993*, 183–84. Warsaw: Research Centre for Mediterranean Archaeology, Polish Academy of Sciences.

Davies, M., and K. Buckley

1987 *Port Arthur Conservation and Development Project archaeological procedures manual*. Occasional Paper 13. Hobart: Department of Lands Parks and Wildlife, Tasmania.

Davies, O.

1928–30 The copper mines of Cyprus. *Annual of the British School at Athens* 30, 74–85.

Davies, S.

2004 Pylos Regional Archaeological Project, part VI: Administration and settlement in Venetian Navarino. *Hesperia* 73, 59–120.

Davis, J.L.
2004 Are the landscapes of Greek prehistory hidden? A comparative approach. In S.E. Alcock and J.F. Cherry (eds.), *Side-by-Side Survey: Comparative Regional Studies in the Mediterranean World*, 22–35. Oxford: Oxbow Books.

de Lusignan, S.
2001 *Lusignan's chorography and brief general history of the island of Cyprus (A.D. 1573).* Sources for the History of Cyprus 10. Albany: University at Albany, State University of New York.

de Mas Latrie, R.
1852–61 *Histoire de l'Ile de Chypre sous le règne des princes de la maison de Lusignan*. Paris: Imprimerie Impériale.

des Gagniers, J., and T.T. Tinh
1985 *Soloi: dix campagnes de fouilles (1964–1974). I: introduction historique; la Basilique*. Sainte-Foy: Presses de l'Université Laval.

Devillers, B., and N. Lécuyer
2008 Le Petit Âge Glaciaire en milieu semi-aride: le bassin versant du Gialias (Chypre) et ses relations avec l'occupation des sols. *Zeitschrift für Geomorphologie* 52, 207–24.

Dewar, R., and K.A. McBride
1992 Remnant settlement patterns. In J. Rossignol and L. Wandsnider (eds.), *Space, time, and archaeological landscapes*, 227–55. New York Plenum Press.

Donners, K., M. Waelkens, and J. Deckers
2002 Watermills in the area of Sagalassos: a disappearing technology. *Anatolian Studies* 52, 1–17.

Eastern
2005 Eastern Mediterranean expands its operations from Cyprus to the Caucasus. *Minews* http://www.minesite.com/storyFull.php?storySeq=3161

Elliot, C.
1985 Appendix V: ground stone tools from Kition Areas I and II. In V. Karageorghis (ed.), *Excavations at Kition, vol. V: the pre-Phoenician levels, Part II*, 295–315. Nicosia: Department of Antiquities, Cyprus.

Ellis Burnet, J.
2004 *Forest bioresource utilisation in the Eastern Mediterranean since antiquity: a case study of the Makheras, Cyprus*. BAR International series 1243. Oxford: Archaeopress.

Falconer, S.E., P.L. Fall, T.W. Davis, M.T. Horowitz, and J. Hunt
2005 Initial archaeological investigations at Politiko-Troullia, 2004. *Report of the Department of Antiquities, Cyprus*, 69–85.

Fall, P.L., S.E. Falconer, M.T. Horowitz, J. Hunt, M. Metzger, and D. Ryter
2008 Bronze Age settlement and landscape at Politiko-Troullia, 2005–2007. *Report of the Department of Antiquities, Cyprus*, 183–208.

Fasnacht, W.
1999 Excavations at Agia Varvara-Almyras: a review of twelve years of research. *Report of the Department of Antiquities, Cyprus* 1999, 179–84.

Fasnacht, W., J. Kunz, C. Deslex, K. Zubler, P.O. Boll, A. Connolly, and T. Maradi
1996 Excavations at Ayia Varvara-Almyras: fifth preliminary report. *Report of the Department of Antiquities, Cyprus*, 95–125.

Fasnacht, W., K. Zubler, D. Gerbothé, R.S. Morris, V. Kassianidou, A. Connolly, and T. Rehren
1992 Excavations at Ayia Varvara Almyras. Fourth preliminary report. *Report of the Department of Antiquities, Cyprus*, 59–74.

Fejfer, J., ed.
1995 *Ancient Akamas: settlement and environment*. Aarhus: Aarhus University Press.

Fejfer, J., and H.E. Mathiesen
1995 The site of Ayios Kononas. In J. Fejfer (ed.), *Ancient Akamas: settlement and environment*, 73–86. Aarhus: Aarhus University Press.

Finlayson, B., and C. McCartney
1998 Chipped stone report. In E. Peltenburg (ed.), *Excavations at Kissonerga-Mosphilia 1979–1992, Lemba Archaeological Project, Cyprus, Vol. II.1B (Part 2)*, 249–94. Occasional Paper 19. Edinburgh: University of Edinburgh, Department of Archaeology.

Flourentzos, P.
1989 A group of tombs of Middle Bronze Age date from Linou. In P. Åström (ed.), *Katydhata: a Bronze Age site in Cyprus*, 61–70. Studies in Mediterranean Archaeology 86. Göteborg: P. Åströms Förlag.

Forbes, H.
1997 A 'waste' of resources: aspects of landscape exploitation in lowland Greek agriculture. In P.N. Kardulias and M.T. Shutes (eds.), *Aegean strategies: studies of culture and environment on the European fringe*, 187–213. Lanham: Rowman and Littlefield.
2000 The agrarian economy of the Ermionidha around 1700: an ethnohistorical reconstruction. In S.B. Sutton (ed.), *Contingent countryside: settlement, economy and land use in the southern Argolid since 1700*, 41–70. Stanford: Stanford University Press.
2007 *Meaning and identity in a Greek landscape: an archaeological ethnography*. Cambridge: Cambridge University Press.

Fortin, M.
1980 Fondation de villes grecs à Chypre: légendes et découvertes archéologiques. In B. Caron, M. Fortin, and G. Maloney (eds.), *Mélanges d'études anciennes offerts à Maurice Lebel*, 25–44. St-Jean-Chrysostôme, Québec: Éditions du Sphinx.

Fox, W.A., and D.A. Pearlman
1987 Threshing sledge production in the Paphos District, Cyprus. In D.W. Rupp (ed.), *Western Cyprus: connections*, 227–34. Göteborg: Paul Åströms Förlag.

Frankel, D., and J.M. Webb
2001 Population, households, and ceramic consumption in a prehistoric Cypriot village. *Journal of Field Archaeology* 28(1–2), 115–29.
2006 Neighbours: negotiating space in a prehistoric village. *Antiquity* 80(308), 287–302.
2012 Pottery production and distribution in prehistoric Bronze Age Cyprus: an application of pXRF analysis. *Journal of Archaeological Science* 39, 1380–87.

Frankel, D., J.M. Webb, and C. Eslick
1996 Anatolia and Cyprus in the third millennium BCE: a speculative model of interaction. In G. Bunnens (ed.), *Cultural interaction in the ancient Near East*, 37–50. Abr Nahrain Supplement 5. Louvain: Peeters.

Frigeriou-Zeniou, S.
1997 Moni ton Phorvion à Asinou de Chypre. In A.D. Lazarides, V. Barras, and T. Birchler (eds.), *Boukoleia: mélanges offerts à Bertrand Bouvier*, 191–99. Geneva: Editions des Belles-Lettres.
Gale, N.H., S. Stos-Gale, and W. Fasnacht
1996 Metal and metalworking. In J.E. Coleman, J.A. Barlow, M.K. Mogelonsky, and K.W. Schaar (eds.), *Alambra: a Middle Bronze Age settlement in Cyprus. Archaeological investigations by Cornell University 1974–1985*, 129–42. Studies in Mediterranean Archaeology 117. Jonsered: Paul Åströms Förlag.
Gale, N.H., and Z.A. Stos-Gale
1986 Oxhide ingots in Crete and Cyprus and the Bronze Age metals trade. *Annual of the British School at Athens* 81, 81–100.
1999 Copper oxhide ingots and the Aegean metals trade: new perspectives. In P.P. Betancourt, V. Karageorghis, R. Laffineur, and W.-D. Niemeier (eds.), *Meletemata I: studies in Aegean archaeology presented to Malcolm H. Wiener as he enters his 65th year*, 267–77. Aegaeum 20. Liège: Université de Liège.
Gass, I.G.
1975 The Troodos massif: its role in the unravelling of the ophiolite problem and its significance in the understanding of constructive plate margin processes. In A. Panayiotou (ed.), *Ophiolites: Proceedings of the International Ophiolite Symposium Cyprus 1979*. Nicosia: Ministry of Agriculture and Natural Resources.
Gaudry, A.
1855 *Recherches scientifiques en Orient entreprises par les ordres du Gouvernement, pendant les années 1853–1854. Partie agricole*. Paris: Imprimerie Impériale.
Geological
1995 *Geological Map of Cyprus*. Nicosia: Geological Survey Department.
Gibraltar, H., V. Seymer, W.H. Buckler, and G. Buckler
1933 The church of Asinou, Cyprus and its frescoes. *Archaeologia* 83, 327–50.
Gibson, E.
2005 *Negotiating space: routes of communication in Roman–British Colonial Cyprus*. PhD, University of Glasgow.
2007 The archaeology of movement in a Mediterranean landscape. *Journal of Mediterranean Archaeology* 20, 61–87.
Given, M.
2000 Agriculture, settlement and landscape in Ottoman Cyprus. *Levant* 32, 215–36.
2002 Maps, fields and boundary cairns: demarcation and resistance in colonial Cyprus. *International Journal of Historical Archaeology* 6, 1–22.
2004 *The archaeology of the colonized*. London: Routledge.
2005 Mining landscapes and colonial rule in early 20th century Cyprus. *Historical Archaeology* 39(3), 49–60.
2007 Mountain landscapes in early modern Cyprus. In S. Davies and J.L. Davis (eds.), *Between Venice and Istanbul: colonial landscapes in early modern Greece*, 137–48. Athens: American School of Classical Studies at Athens.
Given, M., D. Coleman, S. Moore, and J. Noller
2003a Agricultural landscapes. In M. Given and A.B. Knapp (eds.), *The Sydney Cyprus Survey Project: social approaches to regional archaeological survey*, 305–11. Los Angeles: University of California at Los Angeles Cotsen Institute of Archaeology.
Given, M., H. Corley, and L. Sollars
2007 Joining the dots: continuous survey, routine practice and the interpretation of a Cypriot landscape (with interactive GIS and integrated data archive). *Internet Archaeology* 20. http://intarch.ac.uk/journal/issue20/taesp_index.html
Given, M., J. Ellis Burnet, R. Schon, V. Kassianidou, S. Van Lokeren, L. Wells, N. Meyer, D. Coleman, T.E. Gregory, R.S. Moore, and J.S. Smith
2003b SIA 4: Mitsero Mavrovounos. In M. Given and A.B. Knapp (eds.), *The Sydney Cyprus Survey Project: social approaches to regional archaeological survey*, 96–109. Monumenta Archaeologica 21. Los Angeles: University of California at Los Angeles Cotsen Institute of Archaeology.
Given, M., and M. Hadjianastasis
2010 Landholding and landscape in Ottoman Cyprus. *Byzantine and Modern Greek Studies* 34, 38–60.
Given, M., V. Kassianidou, A.B. Knapp, and J. Noller
2002 Troodos Archaeological and Environmental Survey Project, Cyprus: report on the 2001 season. *Levant* 34, 25–38.
Given, M., and A.B. Knapp
2003 *The Sydney Cyprus Survey Project: social approaches to regional archaeological survey*. Monumenta Archaeologica 21. Los Angeles: Cotsen Institute of Archaeology, University of California at Los Angeles.
Given, M., A.B. Knapp, I. Evans, E. Gibson, T. Ireland, V. Kassianidou, J. Noller, H. Saunders, L. Sollars, N. Urwin, K.W. Jacobsen, and S. Zesimou
2001 Troodos Archaeological and Environmental Survey Project: First Preliminary Report (June–July 2000). *Report of the Department of Antiquities, Cyprus* 2001, 425–40.
Given, M., J. Noller, and L. Wells
2003c SCY114: Mitsero Lambadhiotissa: check dams and Byzantine church. In M. Given and A.B. Knapp (eds.), *The Sydney Cyprus Survey Project: social approaches to regional archaeological survey*, 187–92. Los Angeles: University of California at Los Angeles Cotsen Institute of Archaeology.
Gjerstad, E.
1926 *Studies on prehistoric Cyprus*. Uppsala Universitets årsskrift, 1926. Filosofi, språkvetenskap och historiska vetenskaper; 1. Uppsala: Lundequistska.
Gjerstad, E., J. Lindros, E. Sjöqvist, and A. Westholm
1935 *The Swedish Cyprus Expedition: finds and results of the excavations in Cyprus, 1927–1931. Volume 2*. Stockholm: Swedish Cyprus Expedition.
1937 *The Swedish Cyprus Expedition: finds and results of the excavations in Cyprus, 1927–1931. Volume 3*. Stockholm: Swedish Cyprus Expedition.
Golas, P.J., and J. Needham
1999 *Chemistry and chemical technology: mining*. Science and Civilisation in China 5.13. Cambridge: Cambridge University Press.
Goodwin, J.C.
1984 *An historical toponymy of Cyprus*. 4th edition. Nicosia: Private publication.
Graham, A., K.W. Jacobsen, and V. Kassianidou
2006 Agia Marina-Mavrovouni: preliminary report on the Roman settlement and smelting workshop in the central northern foothills of the Troodos Mountains, Cyprus. *Report of the Department of Antiquities, Cyprus*, 345–67.

Gregory, T.E.

2003 The Byzantine problem. In M. Given and A.B. Knapp (eds.), *The Sydney Cyprus Survey Project: social approaches to regional archaeological survey*, 283–84. Los Angeles: University of California at Los Angeles Cotsen Institute of Archaeology.

Grivaud, G.

1998 *Villages désertés à Chypre (fin XIIe – fin XIXe siècle)*. Meletai kai Ipomnimata 3. Nicosia: Archbishop Makarios III Foundation.

2002 Palaichori, a mountain village through the ages. In S. Sophocleous (ed.), *Palaichoria: centuries of heritage*, 23–73. Palaichori: Association for the Protection of the Monuments of Palaichori.

Gunnis, R.

1936 *Historic Cyprus: a guide to its towns and villages, monasteries and castles*. London: Methuen.

Hadjichristodoulou, C., and D. Marianthefs

2002 *The church of Our Lady of Asinou*. Guides to the Byzantine Monuments of Cyprus. Nicosia: The Bank of Cyprus Cultural Foundation and The Holy Bishopric of Morphou.

Hadjisavvas, S.

1987 A Roman imperial tomb on Troodos. *Report of the Department of Antiquities, Cyprus*, 253–57.

1992 *Olive oil processing in Cyprus from the Bronze Age to the Byzantine period*. Studies in Mediterranean Archaeology 99. Nicosia: P. Åströms Förlag.

Hayes, J.W.

1967 Cypriote sigillata. *Report of the Department of Antiquities, Cyprus*, 65–77.

1972 *Late Roman pottery*. Corrected edn. London: British School at Rome.

1985 Sigillate orientali, *Enciclopedia dell'arte antica: classica e orientale. Atlante delle forme ceramiche II. Ceramica fine romana nel bacino mediterraneo (tardo ellensimo e primo impero)*, 1–96. Rome: Instituto della Enciclopedia Italiana.

1991 *Paphos. Vol. 3: the Hellenistic and Roman pottery*. Nicosia: Department of Antiquities, Cyprus.

Hayes, P.P., and O. Thomsen

1995 On the archaeological usefulness of local knowledge. In J. Fejfer (ed.), *Ancient Akamas: settlement and environment*, 49–62. Aarhus: Aarhus University Press.

Healy, J.F.

1978 *Mining and metallurgy in the Greek and Roman World* London: Thames and Hudson.

Hjohlman, J.

2002 *Farming the land in Late Antiquity: the case of Berbati in the northeastern Peloponnese*. PhD, University of Stockholm.

Huffstot, J.

1987 Roof tiles. In D. Soren (ed.), *The sanctuary of Apollo Hylates at Kourion, Cyprus*, 263–99. Tucson: University of Arizona Press.

Ingham, F.T.

1959 Economic geology. In F.T. Ingham and R.A.M. Wilson (eds.), *The geology of the Xeros-Troodos area, with an account of the mineral resources*, 137–77. Geological Survey Department of Cyprus Memoir 1. Nicosia: Geological Survey Department.

Ionas, I.

1988 *La maison rurale de Chypre (XVIIIe–XXe siècle): aspects et techniques de construction*. Nicosia: Cyprus Research Centre.

1994 Subsistence economy in Cyprus. *Epetiris tou Kendrou Epistimonikon Erevnon* 20, 433–53.

1998 *Pottery in the Cyprus tradition*. Publications of the Cyprus Research Centre 23. Nicosia: Cyprus Research Centre.

2001 *Paradhosiaka epangelmata tis Kyprou*. Publications of the Cyprus Research Centre 37. Nicosia: Cyprus Research Centre.

Jacobsen, K.W.

2004 Regional distribution of transport amphorae in Cyprus in the Late Roman period. In J. Lund and J. Eiring (eds.), *Transport amphorae and trade in the Eastern Mediterranean: International Colloquium at the Danish Institute at Athens, 26–29 September*, 143–48. Monographs of the Danish Institute at Athens 5. Odder: Narayana Press.

2006a Transport amphorae. In L.W. Sørensen and K.W. Jacobsen (eds.), *Panayia Ematousa I. A rural site in south-eastern Cyprus*, 303–36. Monographs of the Danish Institute at Athens 6.1. Athens: Danish Institute at Athens.

2006b Utility ceramics. In L.W. Sørensen and K.W. Jacobsen (eds.), *Panayia Ematousa I. A rural site in south-eastern Cyprus*, 244–302. Monographs of the Danish Institute at Athens 6.1. Athens: Danish Institute at Athens.

2007 Pots for the dead: pottery and ritual in Cypriote tombs of the Hellenistic and Roman period. In D. Malfitana, J. Poblome, and J. Lund (eds.), *Old pottery in a new century: innovating perspectives on Roman pottery studies. Proceedings of the International Workshop, Catania 22–24 April 2004*, 389–96. Monografie dell'Istituto per i Beni Archeologici e Monumentali CNR. Rome: L'Erma di Bretschneider.

Karageorghis, V.

1977 A 'favissa' at Kakopetria. *Report of the Department of Antiquities, Cyprus*, 178–201.

Karageorghis, V., and M. Demas

1988 *Excavations at Maa-Palaeokastro 1979–1986*. Nicosia: Department of Antiquities.

Karouzis, G.

1984a Agroladhou. In A. Paulides (ed.), *Megali Kypriaki Enkyklopaideia 1*, 142. Nicosia: Philokypros.

1984b Ayios Epiphaneios (Solias). In A. Paulides (ed.), *Megali Kypriaki Enkyklopaideia 1*, 99. Nicosia: Philokypros.

Kassianidou, V.

1998 Small-scale mining and smelting in ancient Cyprus. In A.B. Knapp, V.C. Pigott, and E.W. Herbert (eds.), *Social approaches to an industrial past: the archaeology and anthropology of mining*, 226–41. London: Routledge.

2000 Hellenistic and Roman mining in Cyprus. In G.K. Ioannides and S.A. Hadjistilli (eds.), *Acts of the Third International Congress of Cypriot Studies*, 745–56. Nicosia: Society of Cyprus Studies.

2003a Archaeometallurgical procedures. In M. Given and A.B. Knapp (eds.), *The Sydney Cyprus Survey Project: social approaches to regional archaeological survey*, 44–48. Los Angeles: University of California at Los Angeles Cotsen Institute of Archaeology.

2003b Archaeometallurgy: data, analyses, and discussion. In M. Given and A.B. Knapp (eds.), *The Sydney Cyprus Survey Project: social approaches to regional archaeological survey*, 214–21, 223–27. Los Angeles: University of California at Los Angeles Cotsen Institute of Archaeology.

2004 Recording Cyprus's mining history through archaeological survey. In M. Iacovou (ed.), *Archaeological field survey in Cyprus: past history, future potentials*, 95–104. Athens: British School at Athens.

2007 Ground stone tools from Apliki Karamallos. In B. Kling and J.D. Muhly (eds.), *Joan du Plat Taylor's excavations at the late Bronze Age mining settlement at Apliki Karamallos, Cyprus*. Studies in Mediterranean Archaeology 134; Sävedalen: Paul Åströms Förlag.

2008 The formative years of the Cypriot copper industry. In I. Tzachili (ed.), *Aegean metallurgy in the Bronze Age*, 249–67. Athens: Ta Pragmata.

2009 Oxhide ingots in Cyprus. In F. Lo Schiavo, J.D. Muhly, R. Maddin, and A. Giumlia Mair (eds.), *Oxhide ingots in the Central Mediterranean*, 41–81. Rome: A.G. Leventis Foundation; CNR-Instituto di Studi sulle Civiltà dell´Egeo e del Vicino Oriente.

2012 The origin and use of metals in Iron Age Cyprus. In M. Iacovou (ed.), *Cyprus and the Aegean in the Early Iron Age: the legacy of Nicolas Coldstream*, 229–59. Nicosia: Cultural Foundation of the Bank of Cyprus.

Kassianidou, V., R. Clough, B. Creevey, T.E. Gregory, N. Meyer, R.S. Moore, R. Schon, J.S. Smith, N. Urwin, L. Wells, and H. Wright

2003 SIA 3: Mitsero Kouloupakhis. In M. Given and A.B. Knapp (eds.), *The Sydney Cyprus Survey Project: social approaches to regional archaeological survey*, 82–96. Los Angeles: University of California at Los Angeles Cotsen Institute of Archaeology.

Kassianidou, V., and S. Van Lokeren

2003 Archaeometallurgy: data, analyses, and discussion. In M. Given and A.B. Knapp (eds.), *The Sydney Cyprus Survey Project: social approaches to regional archaeological survey*, 214–27. Los Angeles: University of California at Los Angeles Cotsen Institute of Archaeology.

Katzev, M.

1969 The Kyrenia shipwreck. *Expedition* 11, 55–59.

1970 Kyrenia 1969: a Greek ship is raised. *Expedition* 12, 6–14.

Keswani, P.S.

1993 Models of local exchange in Late Bronze Age Cyprus. *Bulletin of the American Schools of Oriental Research* 292, 73–83.

2004 *Mortuary ritual and society in Bronze Age Cyprus*. Monographs in Mediterranean Archaeology. London: Equinox.

2005 Death, prestige, and copper in Bronze Age Cyprus. *American Journal of Archaeology* 109, 341–402.

Keswani, P.S., S.W. Manning, E. Ribeiro, J.S. Smith, R.S. Moore, T.E. Gregory, D. Coleman, A.B. Knapp, and V. Kassianidou

2003 The material culture of the SCSP landscape. In M. Given and A.B. Knapp (eds.), *The Sydney Cyprus Survey Project: social approaches to regional archaeological survey*, 202–65. Los Angeles: University of California at Los Angeles Cotsen Institute of Archaeology.

Kinani, T.

1992 *Evrykhou: istoria kai paradosi*. Evrykhou: Ekdosi Lykeiou Soleas.

Klirides, N.

1968 *25 monastiria tis Kipro. Volume 2*. Nicosia: no publisher given.

Knapp, A.B.

2008 *Identity, insularity and connectivity: prehistoric and protohistoric Cyprus*. Oxford: Oxford University Press.

Knapp, A.B., S. Bain, D. Coleman, P. Grave, V. Kassianidou, S. Manning, N. Meyer, R.S. Moore, J. Noller, E. Ribeiro, J. Smith, N. Urwin, S. Van Lokeren, and H. Wright

2003 SIA 7: Politiko Kokkinorotsos. In M. Given and A.B. Knapp (eds.), *The Sydney Cyprus Survey Project: social approaches to regional archaeological survey*, 130–46. Los Angeles: University of California at Los Angeles Cotsen Institute of Archaeology.

Knapp, A.B., S.O. Held, E. Zangger, and I. Johnson

1992 The Sydney Cyprus Survey Project (SCSP): first preliminary season (1992). *Report of the Department of Antiquities, Cyprus*, 319–36.

Knapp, A.B., V. Kassianidou, P. Duffy, M. Donnelly, and J. Noller

n.d. *The excavations at Politiko Phorades (1996–2000): the archaeology and archaeometallurgy of a Bronze Age smelting site*. Unpublished manuscript.

Koucky, F.L., and A. Steinberg

1974 Ancient mining and mineral dressing on Cyprus. In T.A. Wertime and S.F. Wertime (eds.), *Early pyrotechnology: the evolution of the first fire using industries*, 149–80. Washington DC: Smithsonian Institution Press.

1982 The ancient slags of Cyprus. In J.D. Muhly, R. Maddin, and V. Karageorghis (eds.), *Early metallurgy in Cyprus, 4000–500 BC*, 117–142. Nicosia: Pierides Foundation.

1989 Ancient mining and mineral dressing on Cyprus. In L.E. Stager and A.M. Walker (eds.), *American Expedition to Idalion, Cyprus, 1973–1980*, 275–327. Chicago: Oriental Institute of the University of Chicago.

Kousoulia

2004 Panay. Kousoulia. *Syndesmos Apodhimon Linous-Phlasous, Etisia Khoroesperidha*. Linou-Phlasou: Syndesmos Apodhimon Linous-Phlasous.

Koutraphas

1987 Koutraphas. In A. Paulides (ed.), *Megali Kypriaki Enkyklopaideia*, Vol. 7, 302–303. Nicosia: Philokypros.

Kyriakidou-Nestoros, A.

1989 *Laografika Meletemata*. Athens: Eteria Ellinikou Logotekhnikou kai Istorikou Arkheiou.

Kyrou, K., and J. Rayssiguier

2001 Increase in storage capacity at Xyliatos dam, Cyprus. *International Journal on Hydropower and Dams* 4, 124–27.

Landels, J. G.

1978 Engineering in the ancient world. Ancient Culture and Society. London: Chatto & Windus.

Lavender, D.

1962 *The story of the Cyprus Mines Corporation*. San Marino: Huntington Library.

Lécuyer, N., G. Grivaud, D. Michaelides, A. Nicolaides, H. Amouric, L. Decock, B. Devillers, V. François, F. Hadjichristophi, M. Loiseau, B. Simon, and L. Vallauri

2001 Potamia-Agios Sozomenos (Chypre). La constitution des paysages dans l'Orient médiéval. *Bulletin de Correspondance Hellénique* 125, 655–78.

Loulloupis, M.C.

1989 A rural cult place in Soloi area. In V. Tatton-Brown (ed.), *Cyprus and the East Mediterranean in the Iron Age*, 68–95. London: British Museum Publications.

Lund, J.

1993 Pottery of the Classical, Hellenistic and Roman periods. In L.W. Sørensen and D.W. Rupp (eds.), *The Land of the Paphian Aphrodite II*, 79–155. Studies in Mediterranean Archaeology 104:2. Göteborg: Paul Åströms Förlag.

2002 Frying pans and other cooking wares from the Akamas (Western Cyprus). In F. Blondé, P. Ballet, and J.-F. Salles (eds.), *Céramiques hellénistiques et romaines. Productions et diffusion en Méditerranée orientale (Chypre, Égypte et côte syro-palestinienne)*, 43–58. Travaux de la Maison de l'Orient Méditerranéen 35. Lyon: Maison de l'Orient Méditerranéen.

2006a Ceramic fine wares from the 4th century BC to the 7th century AD. In L.W. Sørensen and K.W. Jacobsen (eds.), *Panayia Ematousa I. A rural site in south-eastern Cyprus*, 182–230. Monographs of the Danish Institute at Athens 6.1. Athens: Danish Institute at Athens.

2006b On the circulation of goods in Hellenistic and Early Roman Cyprus: the ceramic evidence. In L.W. Sørensen and K.W. Jacobsen (eds.), *Panayia Ematousa II. Political, cultural, ethnic and social relations in Cyprus: approaches to regional studies*, 31–49. Monographs of the Danish Institute at Athens 6.2. Athens: Danish Institute at Athens.

Maier, F.G.

2000 The sanctuary of the Paphian Aphrodite in the Roman period. In G.K. Ioannides and S.A. Hadjistylli (eds.), *Third International Congress of Cypriot Studies, Nicosia 16–20 April 1996*, 495–505. Nicosia

Markides, M.

1916 Excavations at Skouriotissa and Katydhata. *Annual Report of the Curator of Antiquities*, 4–20.

Masson, O.

1979 Variétés chypriotes. *Report of the Department of Antiquities, Cyprus*, 218–22.

Mattingly, D.J., and R. Witcher

2004 Mapping the Roman world: the contribution of field survey data. In S.E. Alcock and J.F. Cherry (eds.), *Side-by-Side Survey: Comparative Regional Studies in the Mediterranean World*, 173–86. Oxford: Oxbow Books.

McCartney, C.

2003 The chipped stone. In E. Peltenburg (ed.), *The colonisation and settlement of Cyprus: investigations at Kissonerga-Mylouthkia, 1976–1996*, 203–20. Lemba Archaeological Project 3.1. Studies in Mediterranean Archaeology 70.4. Sävedalen: Paul Åströms Förlag.

2005 Preliminary report on the re-survey of three Early Neolithic sites in Cyprus. *Report of the Department of Antiquities, Cyprus*, 1–21.

McCartney, C., and B. Gratuze

2003 The chipped stone. In E.J. Peltenburg (ed.), *The colonisation and settlement of Cyprus: excavations at Kissonerga-Mylouthkia, 1976–1996*, 11–34. Studies in Mediterranean Archaeology 70:4. Sävedalen: Paul Åströms Förlag.

McCartney, C., and I. Todd

2005 Chipped stone. In I. Todd (ed.), *Excavations at Kalavasos-Tenta 2. Vasilikos Valley Project 7*, 177–264. Studies in Mediterranean Archaeology LXXI:7. Sävedalen: Paul Åströms Förlag.

McQuitty, A.

1995 Watermills in Jordan: technology, typology, dating and development. *Studies in the History and Archaeology of Jordan* 5, 745–51.

Menardos, S.

1970 *Toponymikai kai laographikai meletai*. Publications of the Cyprus Research Centre 31. Nicosia: Cyprus Research Centre.

Merkelbach, J.

1991 *Die protokolle des kadiamtes Nikosia 1105/06 (1693–1695)*. Frankfurt: Peter Lang.

Merrillees, R.S.

1984 Ambelikou-Aletri: a preliminary report. *Report of the Department of Antiquities, Cyprus*, 1–13.

Meyza, H.

1995 Cypriot Sigillata and Cyprot Red Slip Ware: problems of origin and continuity. In H. Meyza and J. Mlynarczyk (eds.), *Hellenistic and Roman pottery in the Eastern Mediterranean: Advances in Scientific Studies. Acts of the II Nieborów Pottery Workshop, Nieborów, 18–20 December 1993*, 179–202. Warsaw: Research Centre for Mediterranean Archaeology, Polish Academy of Sciences.

2000 Cypriot Red Slip: development of the ware (an attempt at refinement). In G.K. Ioannides and S.A. Hadjistyllis (eds.), *Acts of the Third International Congress of Cypriot Studies (Nicosia, April 1996). Vol. A, Ancient Section*, 507–29. Nicosia: Society of Cypriot Studies.

Michaelides, D.

1996 The economy of Cyprus during the Hellenistic and Roman periods. In V. Karageorghis and D. Michaelides (eds.), *The development of the Cypriot economy from the prehistoric period to the present day*. Nicosia: University of Cyprus; Bank of Cyprus.

Michaelides, A.M.

1981 *Lemesos, e palia politeia*. Nicosia: Agnes M. Michaelides.

Michalski, B.

1998 The mineral industry of Cyprus. *US Geological Survey Minerals Yearbook*: 53.1–53.2. http://minerals.usgs.gov/minerals/pubs/country/1998/9209098.pdf

Mines

2010 The Mines Service of Ministry of Agriculture, Natural Resources and Environment. http://www.moa.gov.cy/moa/Mines/MinesSrv.nsf

Mitford, T.B.

1950 New inscriptions from Roman Cyprus. *Opuscula Archaeologica* 6, 1–95.

1980 Roman Cyprus. In H. Temporini and W. Haase (eds.), *Aufstieg und Niedergang der Römischen Welt: Geschichte und Kultur Roms im Spiegel der neurern Forschung*, 1285–384. Berlin: Walter de Gruyter.

Mobbs, P.M.

2000 The mineral industry of Cyprus. *US Geological Survey Minerals Yearbook*: 34.1–34.3. http://minerals.usgs.gov/minerals/pubs/country/2000/cymyb00.pdf

Monmonier, M.

1996 *How to lie with maps*. 2nd Edition. London/Chicago: The University of Chicago Press.

Moody, J., and A.T. Grove

1990 Terraces and enclosure walls in the Cretan landscape. In S. Bottema, G. Entjes-Nieborg, and W. Van Ziest (eds.), *Man's role in the shaping of the Eastern Mediterranean landscape* 183–91. Rotterdam: Balkema.

Morris, R.S.

1984 The Stylianides Mill – Evrykhou. *Kipriakes Spoudhes* 57, 161–172.

Myres, J.L., and M. Ohnefalsch-Richter
1899 *A catalogue of the Cyprus Museum: with a chronicle of excavations undertaken since the British occupation*. Oxford: Clarendon Press.

Nicolls, E.
1901 *Report on Nicosia–Troodos carriage road*. Nicosia: Public Works Department. Unpublished document in Cyprus State Archives: SA1/1922/1899.

Nicolaou, I.
1984 A Hellenistic and Roman tomb at Eurychou-Phoenikas. *Report of the Department of Antiquities, Cyprus*, 234–56.

Noller, J.S., ed.
2010 *Study of the geomorphology of Cyprus: final technical report to the Geological Survey Department, Republic of Cyprus*. Nicosia: Geological Survey Department.

Noret, J.
1993 Vita Sancti Auxibii. In P. Van Deun and J. Noret (eds.), *Hagiographica cypria*, 137–202. Turnhout: Brepols.

Ohnefalsch-Richter, M.H.
1893 *Kypros, the Bible and Homer: Oriental civilization, art and religion in ancient times*. London: Asher.

Panayiotou, A.
1990 Skouriotissa metalleio. In A. Paulides (ed.), *Megali Kypriaki Enkyklopaideia 12*, 229–34. Nicosia: Philokypros.

Panayiotou, M.
2001 O teleftaios alevromylos doulevi me nero, ston Stylli tou Mylona. *Selides magazine*, 146–49.

Pantazis, T.M.
1969 The Memi mine. *Bulletin of the Geological Survey Department* 4, 37–44.

Papacostas, T.
1999 Secular landholdings and Venetians in 12th-century Cyprus. *Byzantinische Zeitschrift* 92, 479–501.
2006 Architecture et communautés étrangères à Chypre aux XIe et XII siècles. In S. Fourrier and G. Grivaud (eds.), *Identités croisées en un milieu méditerranéen: le cas de Chypre*, 223–40. Mon-Saint-Aignan: Universités de Rouen et du Havre.

Papadopoullos, T.
1965 *Social and historical data on population (1570–1881)*. Nicosia: Cyprus Research Centre.

Papapetrou, P.
2008 *Metalloryxon mnimes*. Nicosia: Pancyprian Federation of Labour.

Paraskevopoulou, M.
1982 *Researches into the traditions of the popular religious feasts of Cyprus*. Nicosia: Privately published.

Parks, D.A.
1999 *Burial customs of Roman Cyprus: origin and development*. PhD dissertation, University of Missouri, Columbia.
2004 *Funerary landscapes of Roman Cyprus*. Unpublished paper given at Society for American Archaeology, Montreal, Quebec.

Paulides, A.
1990 Solea i Solia. In A. Paulides (ed.), *Megali Kypriaki Enkyklopaideia 12*, 240–46. Nicosia: Philokypros.

Peltenburg, E.J.
1991 Toward a definition of the Late Chalcolithic in Cyprus: the Monochrome pottery debate. In J.A. Barlow, D. Bolger, and B. Kling (eds.), *Cypriot ceramics: reading the Prehistoric record*, 9–20. University Museum Monograph 74. Philadelphia: University Museum.
1996 From isolation to state formation in Cyprus, c. 3500–1500 B.C. In V. Karageorghis and D. Michaelides (eds.), *The development of the Cypriot economy: from the prehistoric period to the present day*, 17–44. Nicosia: Bank of Cyprus, University of Cyprus.

Pettegrew, D.K.
2001 Chasing the classical farmstead: assessing the formation and signature of rural settlement in Greek landscape archaeology. *Journal of Mediterranean Archaeology* 14, 189–209.

Phlasou
1989 Phlasou. In A. Paulides (ed.), *Megali Kypriaki Enkyklopaideia 13*, 258–59. Nicosia: Philokypros.

Pliny the Elder
1938 *Natural history*. 10 vols. Loeb Classical Library. London: William Heinemann.

Pyatt, F.B.
2001 Copper and lead bioaccumulation by *Acacia retinoides* and *Eucalyptus torquata* in sites contaminated as a consequence of extensive ancient mining activities in Cyprus. *Ecotoxicology and Environmental Safety* 50, 60–64.

Pyatt, F.B., G. Barker, P. Birch, D.D. Gilbertson, J.P. Grattan, and D.J. Mattingly
1999 King Solomon's miners: starvation and bioaccumulation? An environmental archaeological investigation in Southern Jordan. *Ecotoxicology and Environmental Safety* 43, 305–308.

Quilici, L.
1971 Lo scavo all'intorno della cinta urbana, I. *Studi Ciprioti e Rapporti di Scavo* 1, 63–162.

Raber, P.A.
1984 *The organization and development of early copper metallurgy in the Polis region, Western Cyprus*. PhD dissertation, Pennsylvania State University.

Rackham, O., and J. Moody
1996 *The making of the Cretan landscape*. Manchester: Manchester University Press.

Rautman, M., B. Gomez, H. Neff, and M.D. Glascock
1993 Neutron activation analysis of Late Roman ceramics from Kalavasos-Kopetra and the environs of the Vasilikos Valley. *Report of the Department of Antiquities, Cyprus*, 231–64.

Rautman, M., M.C. McClellan, L.V. Benson, S.C. Fox, M.D. Glascock, B. Gomez, H. Neff, W. O'Brien, and D.S. Reese
2003 *A Cypriot village of late antiquity: Kalavasos-Kopetra in the Vasilikos Valley*. Supplementary Series 52. Portsmouth, R.I.: Journal of Roman Archaeology.

Reinach, S.
1891 *Chroniques d'orient: documents sur les fouilles et découvertes dans l'Orient héllenique de 1883 à 1890*. Paris: Librairie de Firmin-Didot.

Richard, J.
1947 Casal de Psimolofo et la vie rurale en Chypre au XIVe siècle. *Mélanges d'Archéologie et d'Histoire publiés par l'Ecole Française de Rome* 59, 121–53.
1962 *Chypre sous les Lusignans: documents chypriotes des archives du Vatican (XIVe et XVe siècles)*. Bibliothèque archéologique et historiquc, Vol. 73. Paris: Institut français d'archéologie de Beyrouth.
1985 Agricultural conditions in the Crusader states. In N.P. Zacour and H.W. Hazard (eds.), *A history of the Crusades, volume 5: The impact of the Crusades on the Near East*, 251–94. Madison: University of Wisconsin Press.

Rickard, T.A.
1930 Copper mining in Cyprus. *Transactions of the Institution of Mining and Metallurgy* 39, 285–315.

Rizopoulou-Egoumenidou, E., and D. Myrianthefs
2003 Trade and use of millstones in Cyprus during the recent past (18th–20th centuries). In M. Barboff (ed.), *Meules à grains: actes du colloque international La Ferté-sous-Jouarre 16–19 mai 2002*, 175–83. Paris: Éditions Ibis Press.

Roberts, L., ed.
2000 *Latin texts from the first century B.C. to the seventeenth century A.D.* Sources for the History of Cyprus, Vol. 8. Albany: Greece and Cyprus Research Center.

Robertson, A.H.F., and N.H. Woodcock
1979 Tectonic setting of the Troodos massif in the east Mediterranean. In A. Panayiotou (ed.), *Ophiolites: Proceedings of the International Ophiolite Symposium Cyprus 1979*, 36–49. Nicosia: Ministry of Agriculture and Natural Resources.

Robins, C.R.
2005 *Spatial analysis of soil depth variability and pedogenesis along toposequences in the Troodos Mountains, Cyprus.* MSc, Oregon State University, Corvallis, OR.

Ron, Z.
1966 Agricultural terraces in the Judean Mountains. *Israel Exploration Journal* 16, 33–49; 111–22.

Rothenberg, B., and A. Blanco Freijeiro
1981 *Studies in ancient mining and metallurgy in south-west Spain.* London: Institute for Archaeometallurgical Studies, University College London.

Sarınay, Y., ed.
2000 *Osmanlı İdaresinde Kıbrıs (Nüfusu-Arazi Dağilimi ve Türk Vakıflar).* T.C. Başbakanlık, Devlet Arşivleri Genel Müdürlüğü, Osmanlı Arşivi Daire Başkanlığı 43. Ankara: T.C. Başbakanlık, Devlet Arşivleri Genel Müdürlüğü.

Schriwer, C.
2006 *'From water every living thing': watermills, irrigation and agriculture in the Bilad al-Sham: perspectives on history, architecture, landscape and society, 1100–1850 AD.* PhD dissertation, University of St Andrews.

Scott-Stevenson, E.
1880 *Our home in Cyprus.* London: Chapman and Hall.

Sebbane, M.
2001 Board games from Canaan in the Early and Intermediate Bronze Ages and the origin of the Egyptian senet game. *Tel Aviv* 28, 213–30.

Simmons, A.H.
1999 *Faunal extinction in an island society: pygmy hippopotamus hunters of Cyprus.* New York: Kluwer/Plenum.

Smith, J.S.
1997 Preliminary comments on a rural Cypro-Archaic sanctuary in Polis-Peristeries. *Bulletin of the American Schools of Oriental Research* 308, 77–98.

Smith, M.
1996 B. The Chipped Stone Assemblage. In D. Frankel and J.M. Webb (eds.), *Marki Alonia: An Early and Middle Bronze Age Town in Cyprus, Excavations 1990–1994*, 102–109. Studies in Mediterranean Archaeology 123:1. Jonsered: Paul Åströms Förlag.

Sollars, L.
2005 *Settlement and community: their location, limits and movement through the landscape of historical Cyprus.* PhD dissertation, University of Glasgow.

Soren, D.
1987 *The sanctuary of Apollo Hylates at Kourion, Cyprus.* Excavations at Kourion, Cyprus. Tucson: University of Arizona Press.

Steel, L.
2009 Exploring regional settlement on Cyprus in the Late Bronze Age: the rural hinterland. In I. Hein (ed.), *The formation of Cyprus in the second millennium BC: studies in regionalism during the Middle and Late Bronze Ages*, 135–145. Österreichische Akademie der Wissenschaften, Denkschriften der Gesamtakademie. Vienna: Österreichische Akademie der Wissenschaften.

Steel, L., and C. McCartney
2008 Survey at Arediou *Vouppes* (*Lithosouros*), a Late Bronze Age agricultural settlement on Cyprus: a preliminary analysis of the material culture assemblages. *Bulletin of the American Schools of Oriental Research* 351, 9–37.

Stewart, C.
1991 *Demons and the Devil; moral imagination in modern Greek culture.* Princeton: Princeton University Press.
1994 Magic circles: an approach to the Greek ritual. *Journal of the Anthropological Society of Oxford* 25, 91–101.

Stos-Gale, Z.A., G. Maliotis, N.H. Gale, and N. Annetts
1997 Lead isotope characteristics of the Cyprus copper deposits applied to provenance studies of copper oxhide ingots. *Archaeometry* 39, 83–124.

Stylianou, A., and J.A. Stylianou
1980 *The history of the cartography of Cyprus.* Nicosia: Cyprus Research Centre.
1985 *The painted churches of Cyprus: treasures of Byzantine art.* London: Trigraph.

Sulphur
1994 ICSC 0074 – Sulphur Dioxide. http://www.ilo.org/public/english/protection/safework/cis/products/icsc/dtasht/_icsc00/icsc0074.htm

Swiny, S.
1980 Bronze age gaming stones from Cyprus. *Report of the Department of Antiquities, Cyprus*, 54–78.
1986 *The Kent State University expedition to Episkopi Phaneromeni.* Studies in Mediterranean Archaeology 74. Nicosia: Paul Åströms Förlag.
1989 Some metal objects from Linou Ayii Saranta Tomb 5. In P. Åström (ed.), *Katydhata: a Bronze Age site in Cyprus*, 69–70. Studies in Mediterranean Archaeology 86. Partille: Paul Åströms Forlag.

Swiny, S., and C. Mavromatis
2000 Land behind Kourion: results of the 1997 Sotira Archaeological Project Survey. *Report of the Department of Antiquities, Cyprus*, 433–52.

Swiny, S., G.R. Rapp, and E. Herscher
2003 *Sotira Kaminoudhia: an early Bronze Age site in Cyprus.* American Schools of Oriental Research archaeological reports 8. Boston: American Schools of Oriental Research.

TAESPdata
2007 Troodos Archaeological and Environmental Survey Project data archive. http://ads.ahds.ac.uk/catalogue/resources.html?taesp_ahrc_2007

Theocharides, I.P.
1993 *Othomanika engrafa 1572–1839.* Nicosia: Kykko Monastery Research Centre.

Theocharides, I.P., and S. Andreev
1996 *Traghodhias 1821 sinekhia othomaniki piyi yia tin Kipro.* Nicosia: Kykko Monastery Research Centre.

Thirgood, J.V.
1987 *Cyprus: a chronicle of its forests, land, and people*. Vancouver: University of British Columbia Press.

Tomber, R.S.
2002 The ceramic finds from Maroni Petrera. In S.W. Manning and A. Manning (eds.), *The Late Roman church at Maroni Petrera. Survey and salvage excavations 1990–1997, and other traces of Roman remains in the lower Maroni Valley, Cyprus*, 41–55. Nicosia: A.G. Leventis Foundation.

Tufte, E.R.
1997 *Visual explanations: images and quantities, evidence and narrative*. Cheshire, Connecticut Graphics Press.

Turner, B.S.
1979 *The story of the Cyprus Government Railway*. London: Mechanical Engineering Publications.

Unwin, A.H.
1933 Counter-erosion methods in Cyprus with dry stone walls. *International Union of Forestry Research Organizations, Congrès de Nancy, 1932: Proceedings*, 570–78. Nancy: Berger-Levrault.

Urwin, N.
2003 Geobotany. In M. Given and A.B. Knapp (eds.), *The Sydney Cyprus Survey Project: social approaches to regional archaeological survey*, 299–301. Monumenta Archaeologica 21. Los Angeles: University of California at Los Angeles Cotsen Institute of Archaeology.

Varnava, P.
1993 *Ta metalleia tis Kypro (istoriki anadhromi)*. Nicosia: Pancyprian Federation of Labour.

Vessberg, O., and A. Westholm
1956 *The Swedish Cyprus Expedition: finds and results of the excavations in Cyprus 1927–1931*. Stockholm: Swedish Cyprus Expedition.

von Wartburg, M.-L.
1983 The Medieval cane sugar industry in Cyprus: results of recent excavations. *The Antiquaries Journal* 63, 298–314.
2000 Cane sugar production sites in Cyprus. Real and imagined. *Report of the Department of Antiquities, Cyprus*, 381–402.

Vroom, J.
1998 Early Modern archaeology in Central Greece: the contrast of artefact-rich and sherdless sites. *Journal of Mediterranean Archaeology* 11(2), 131–64.
2005 *Byzantine to modern pottery in the Aegean: an introduction & field guide*. Utrecht: Parnassus Press.

Wallace, P.W., and A.G. Orphanides, eds.
1990 *Sources for the history of Cyprus. Volume 1: Greek and Latin texts to the third century AD*. Albany: Institute of Cypriot Studies, University at Albany, State University of New York.

Webb, J.M.
1996 Stone artefacts. In D. Frankel and J.M. Webb (eds.), *Marki Alonia: An Early and Middle Bronze Age Town in Cyprus, Excavations 1990–1994*, 72–89. Studies in Mediterranean Archaeology 123:1. Jonsered: Paul Åströms Förlag.

Webb, J.M., and D. Frankel
1999 Characterizing the Philia facies: material culture, chronology and the origin of the Bronze Age in Cyprus. *American Journal of Archaeology* 103(1), 3–43.

Webb, J.M., D. Frankel, P. Croft, and C. McCartney
2009 Excavations at Politiko *Kokkinorotsos*: a Chalcolithic hunting station in Cyprus. *Proceedings of the Prehistoric Society* 75, 189–237.

Whitelaw, T.M.
1991 The ethnoarchaeology of recent rural settlement and land use in northwest Keos. In J.F. Cherry, J.L. Davis, and E. Mantzourani (eds.), *Landscape archaeology as long-term history: northern Keos in the Cycladic Islands*, 403–452. Los Angeles: UCLA, Institute of Archaeology.

Whitelaw, T.M., P. Doukellis, and L.G. Mendoni
1994 An ethnoarchaeological study of rural land-use in northwest Keos: insights and implications for the study of past Aegean landscapes. In P.N. Doukellis and L.G. Mendoni (eds.), *Structures rurales et sociétés antiques. Actes du colloque de Corfou (14–16 mai 1992)*, 163–86. Centre de recherches d'Histoire Ancienne 126. Paris: Belles Lettres.

Whittaker, J.C.
1999 Alonia: ethnoarchaeology of Cypriot threshing floors. *Journal of Mediterranean Archaeology* 12, 7–25.
2000 Alonia and dhoukanes: the ethnoarchaeology of threshing in Cyprus. *Near Eastern Archaeology* 63, 62–69.

Wilkinson, T.J.
2003 *Archaeological landscapes of the Near East*. Tucson: University of Arizona Press.

Wilson, A.
2012 An exploration of the relationship between shifting power, changing behaviour and new water technologies in the Roman Near East. *Water History* 4, 1–9.

Winfield, D.C.
1969 *The church of the Panagia Phorviotissa at Asinou*. Nicosia: Department of Antiquities, Republic of Cyprus.

Winther-Jacobsen, K.
2010 *From pots to people: a ceramic approach to the archaeological interpretation of ploughsoil assemblages in Late Roman Cyprus*. BABESCH Supplement 17. Leuven: Peeters.

Xyliatos
1989 Xyliatos. In A. Paulides (ed.), *Megali Kypriaki Enkyklopaideia*, Vol. 10, 293. Nicosia: Philokypros.

Young, J.H., and S.H. Young
1955 *Terracotta figurines from Kourion in Cyprus*. Philadelphia: University Museum, University of Pennsylvania.

Zampelas, M.
2002 *Churches and monasteries of Cyprus*. Nicosia: Zampelas Art.

Zwicker, U.
1986 Ancient metallurgical methods for copper production in Cyprus, Part 2: sulphide ore and copper-arsenic-alloy production. *Bulletin of the Cyprus Association of Geologists and Mining Engineers* 3, 92–111.

Zwicker, U., H. Rollig, and U. Schwarz
1972 Investigations on prehistoric and early historic copper-slag from Cyprus (preliminary report). *Report of the Department of Antiquities, Cyprus*, 34 45.

Index

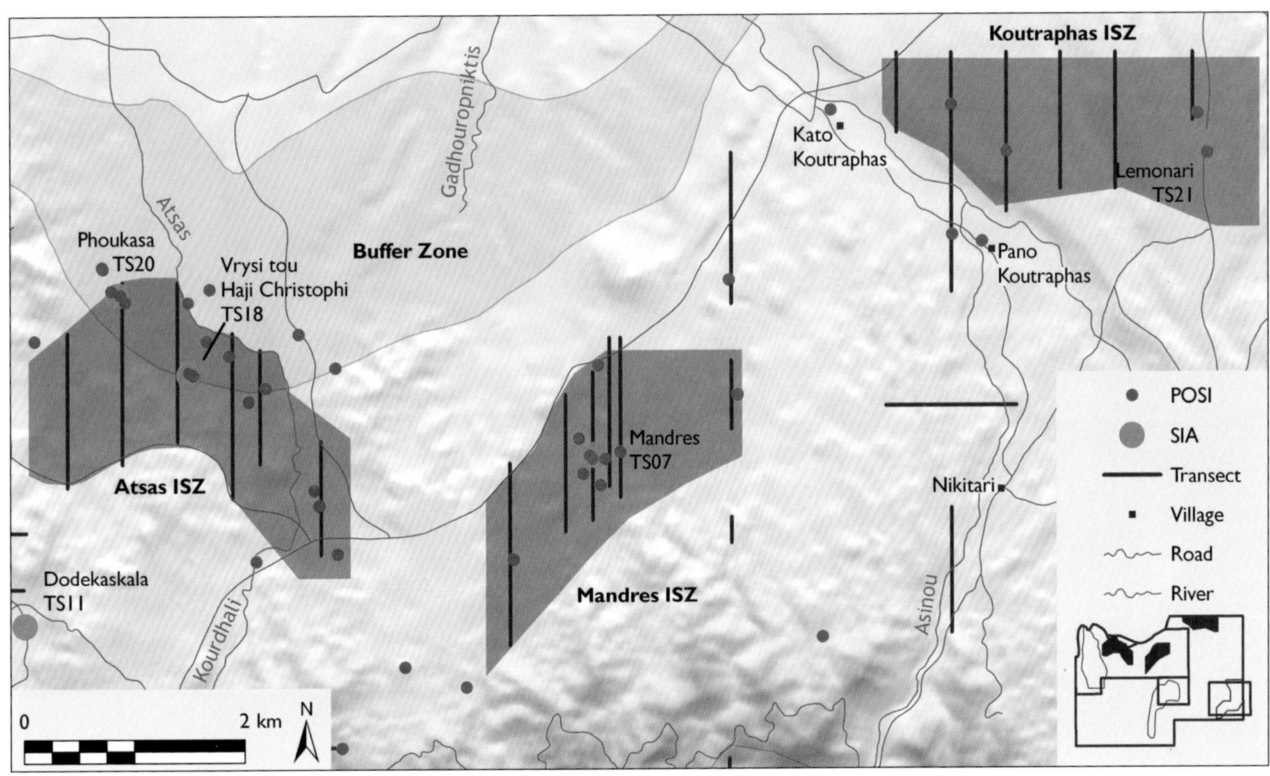

Plate 2.1. Topographical map of the Plains, with the Atsas, Mandres and Koutraphas Intensive Survey Zones (Luke Sollars)

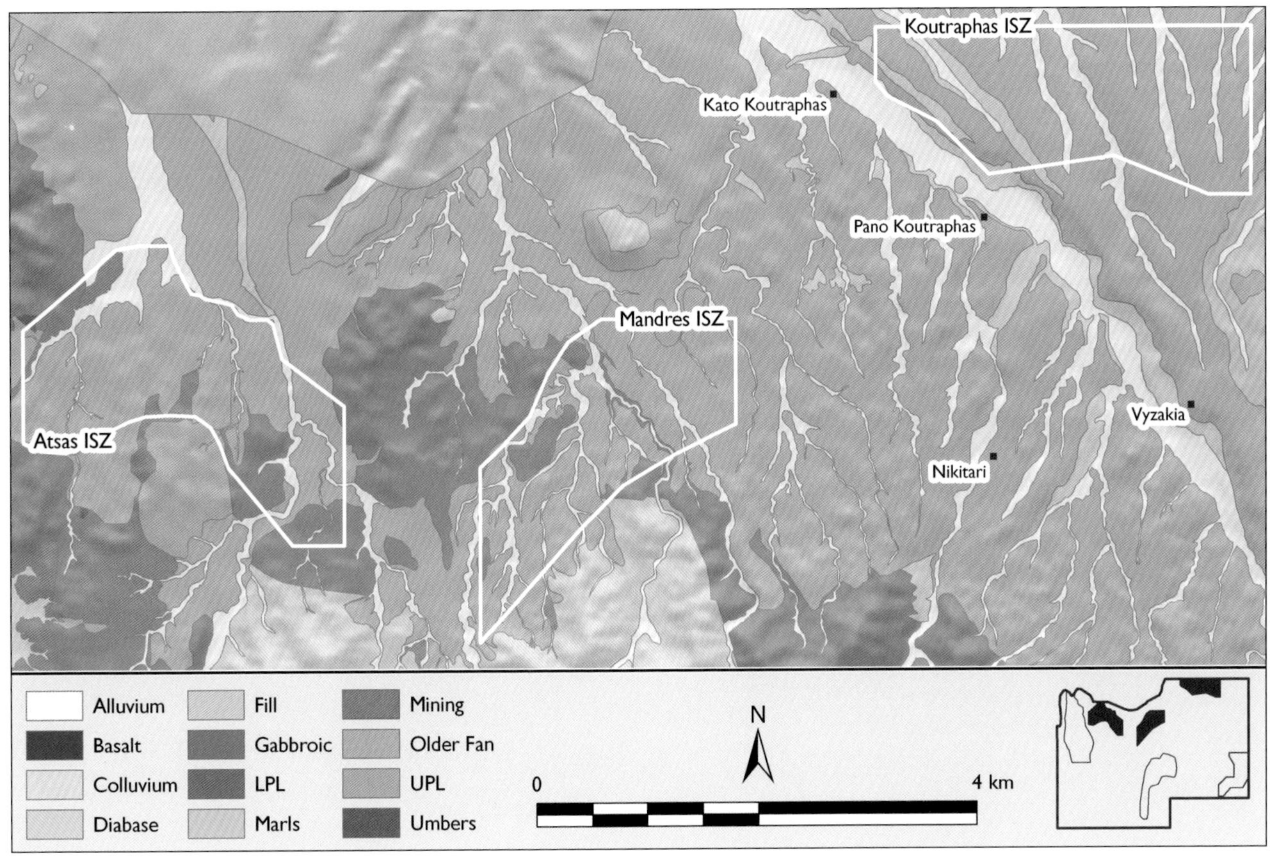

Plate 2.2. The Plains: geological map. No data for the grey area in the north-west (Jay Noller, finalised by Luke Sollars)

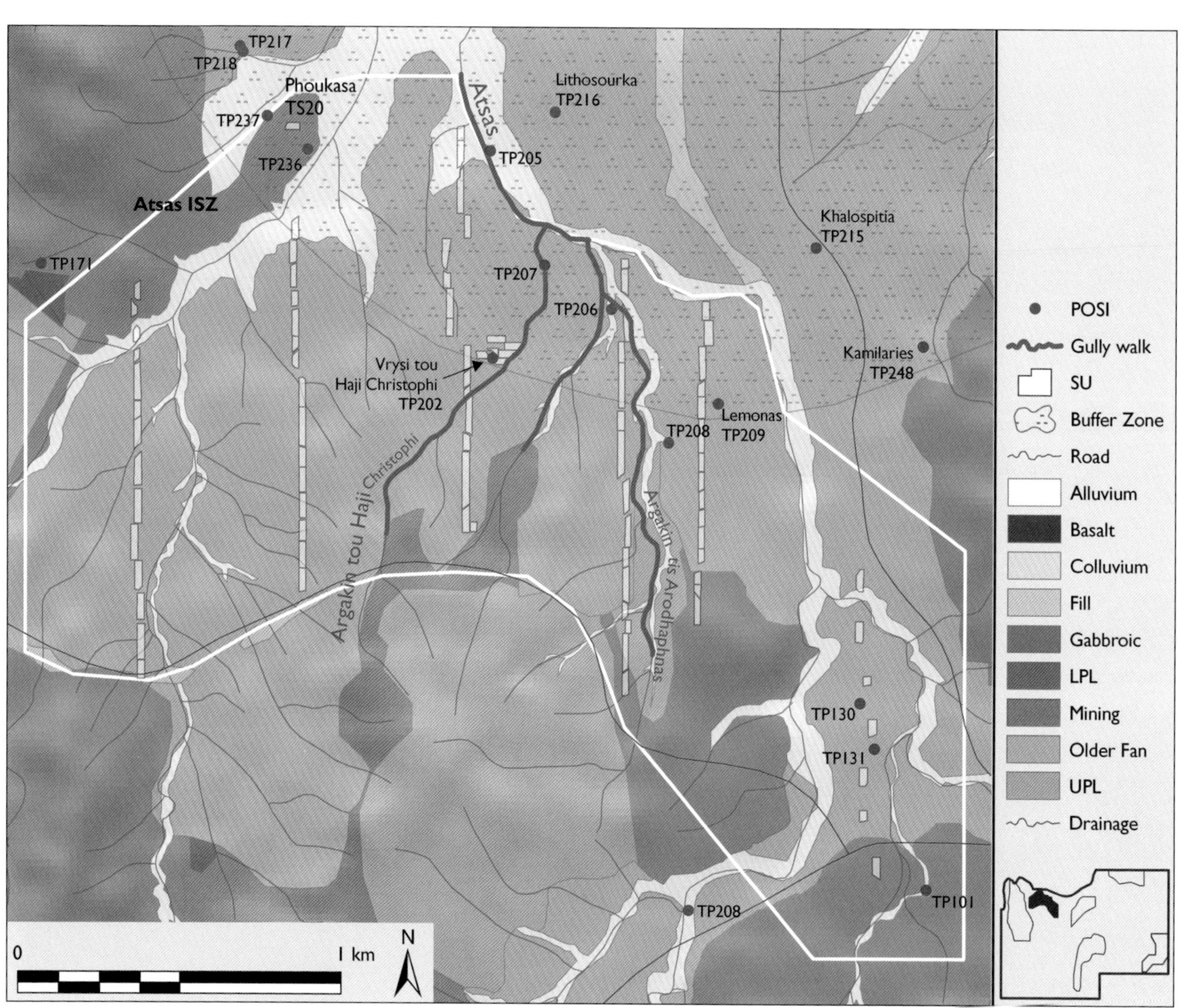

Plate 2.3. Atsas Intensive Survey Zone: topographical and geological map (Jay Noller, finalised by Luke Sollars)

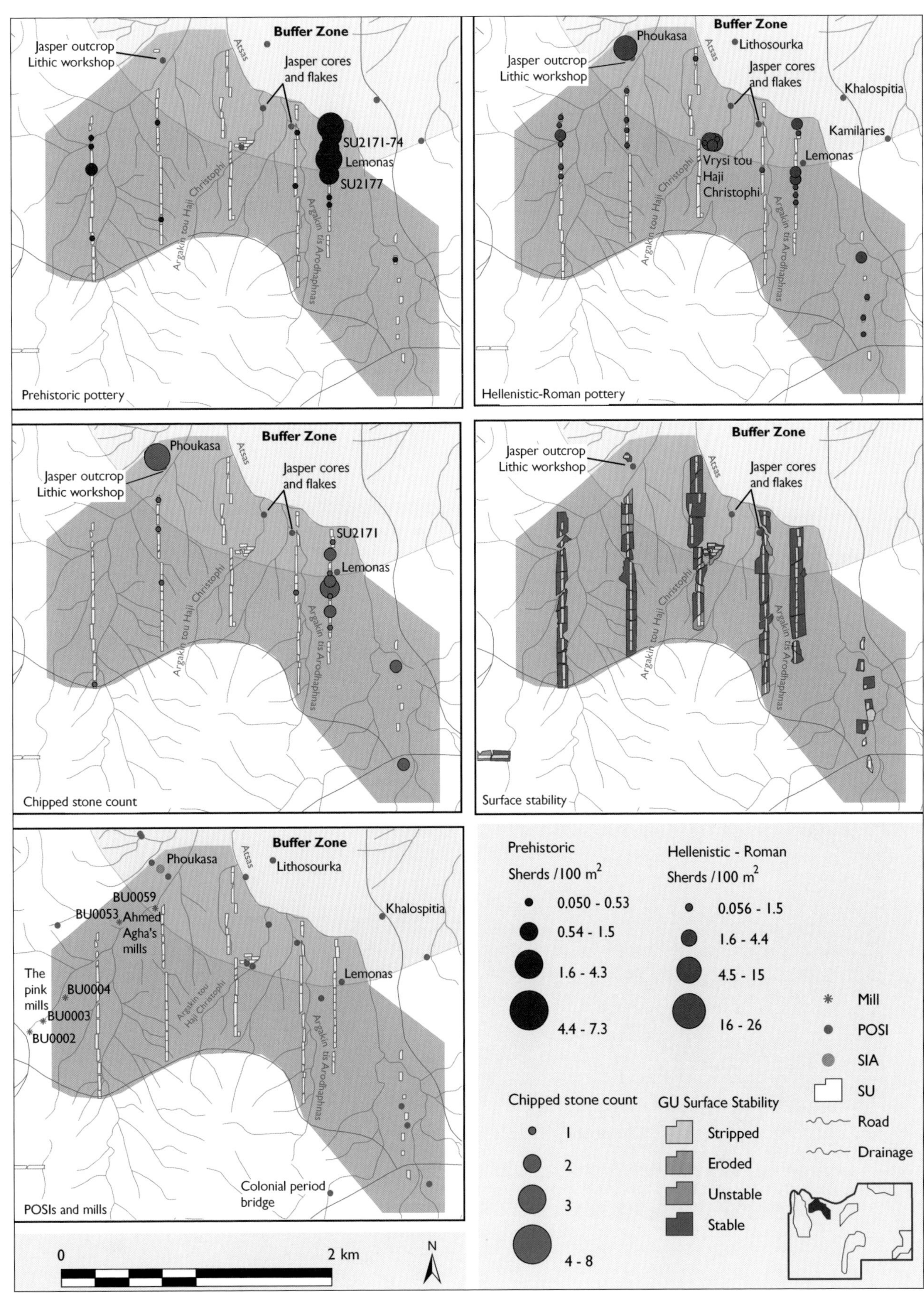

Plate 2.4. Atsas Intensive Survey Zone: prehistoric pottery; Hellenistic–Roman pottery; chipped stone count; surface stability; POSIs and mills (Luke Sollars)

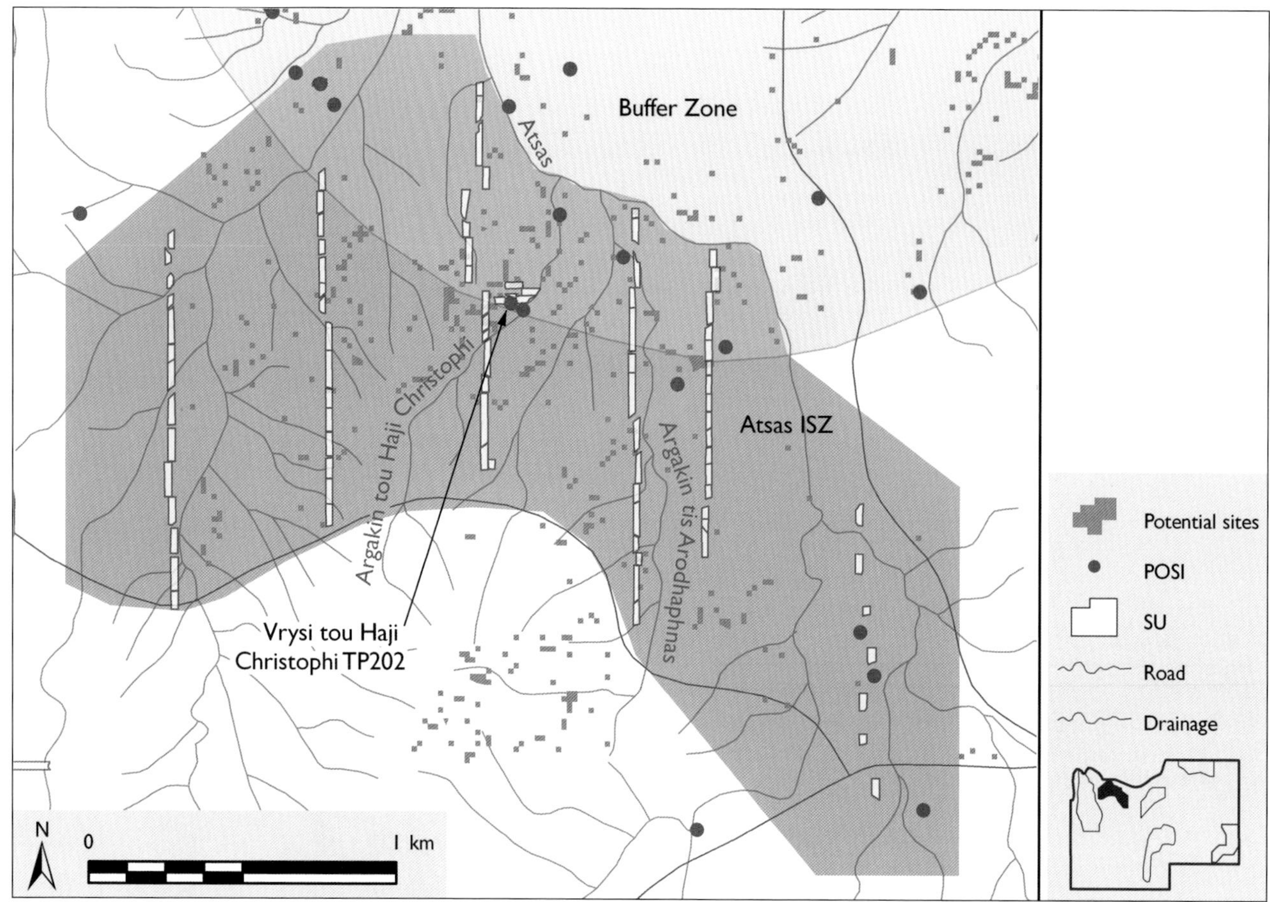

Plate 2.5. Atsas Intensive Survey Zone, showing potential sites predicted on the basis of geobotanical analysis of TP202 (NU052) (Neil Urwin)

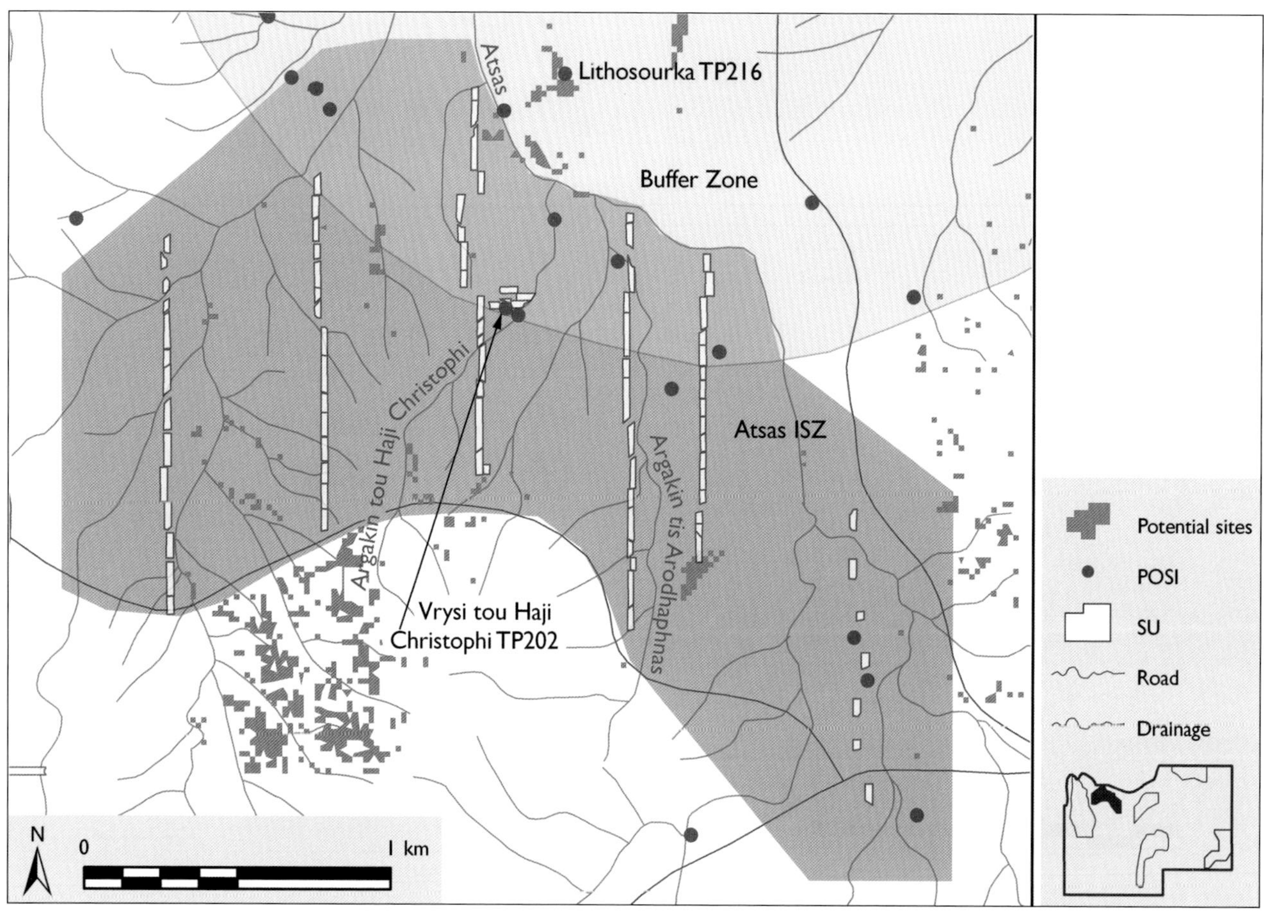

Plate 2.6. Atsas Intensive Survey Zone, showing potential sites predicted on the basis of geobotanical analysis of TP216 (NU053) (Neil Urwin)

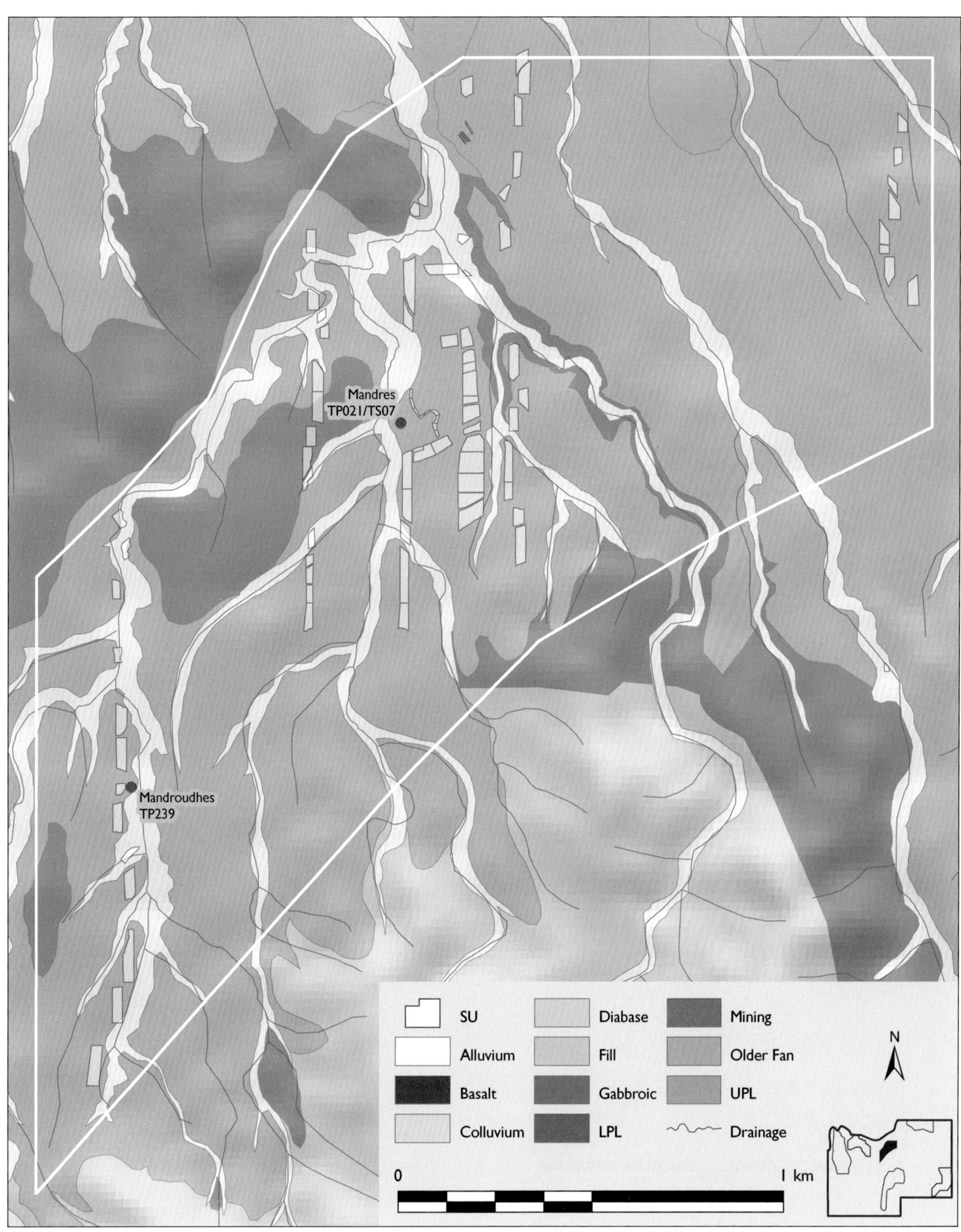

Plate 2.7. Mandres Intensive Survey Zone: geological map (Jay Noller, finalised by Luke Sollars)

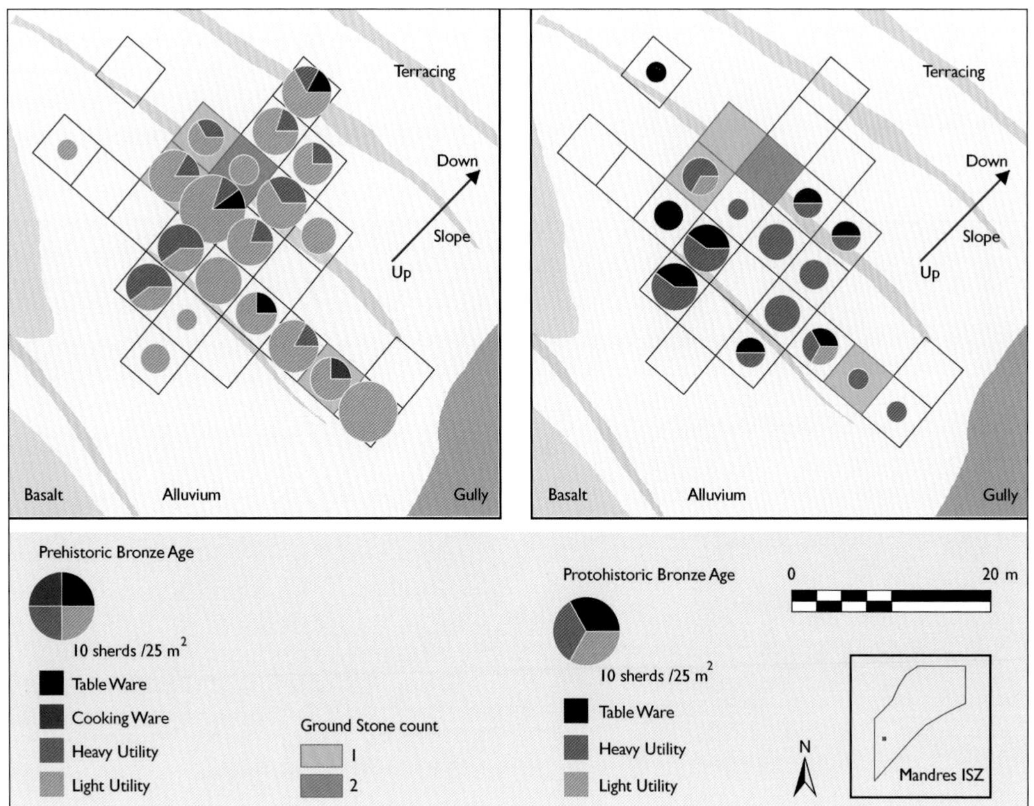

Plate 2.8. Kato Koutraphas Mandroudhes *(TP239): distribution of ground stone, Prehistoric Bronze Age pottery and Protohistoric Bronze Age pottery (Luke Sollars)*

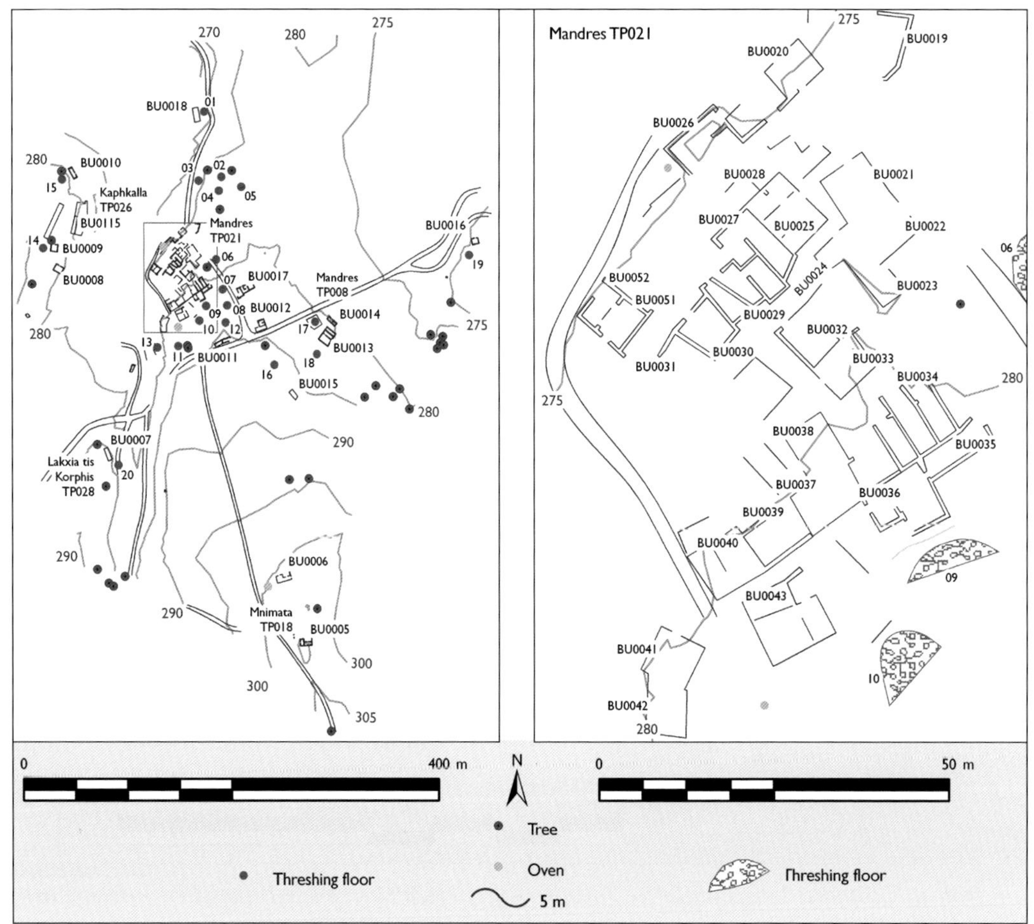

Plate 2.9. Kato Koutraphas Mandres *(TS07): map of settlement with Building Units, threshing floors, ovens and roads. General trend of slope is from south to north. Threshing floor numbers are POSI Units within TP122: for '07' read 'PU07'*

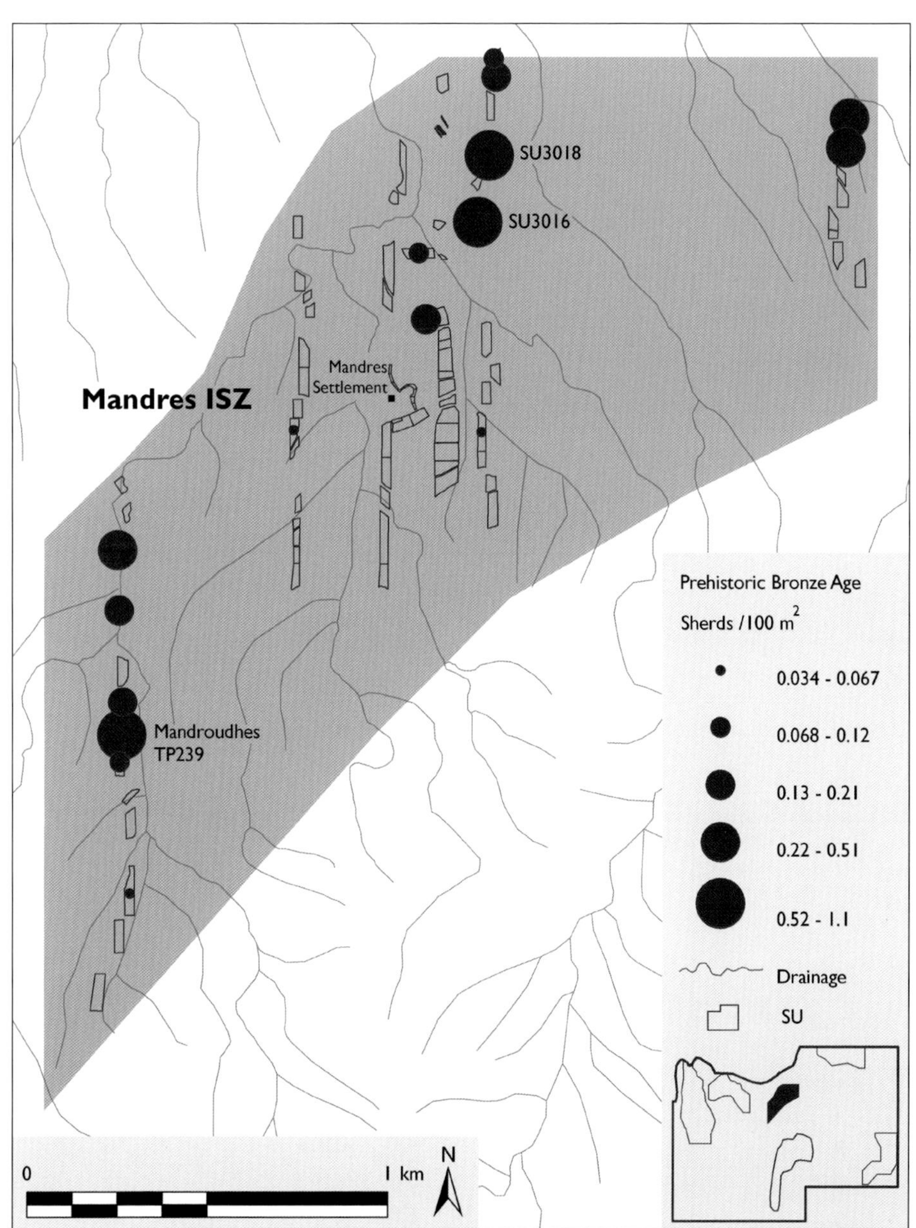

Plate 2.10. Mandres Intensive Survey Zone: distribution of Prehistoric Bronze Age pottery (Luke Sollars)

Plate 2.11. Koutraphas Intensive Survey Zone: Survey Units and surface stability (Luke Sollars)

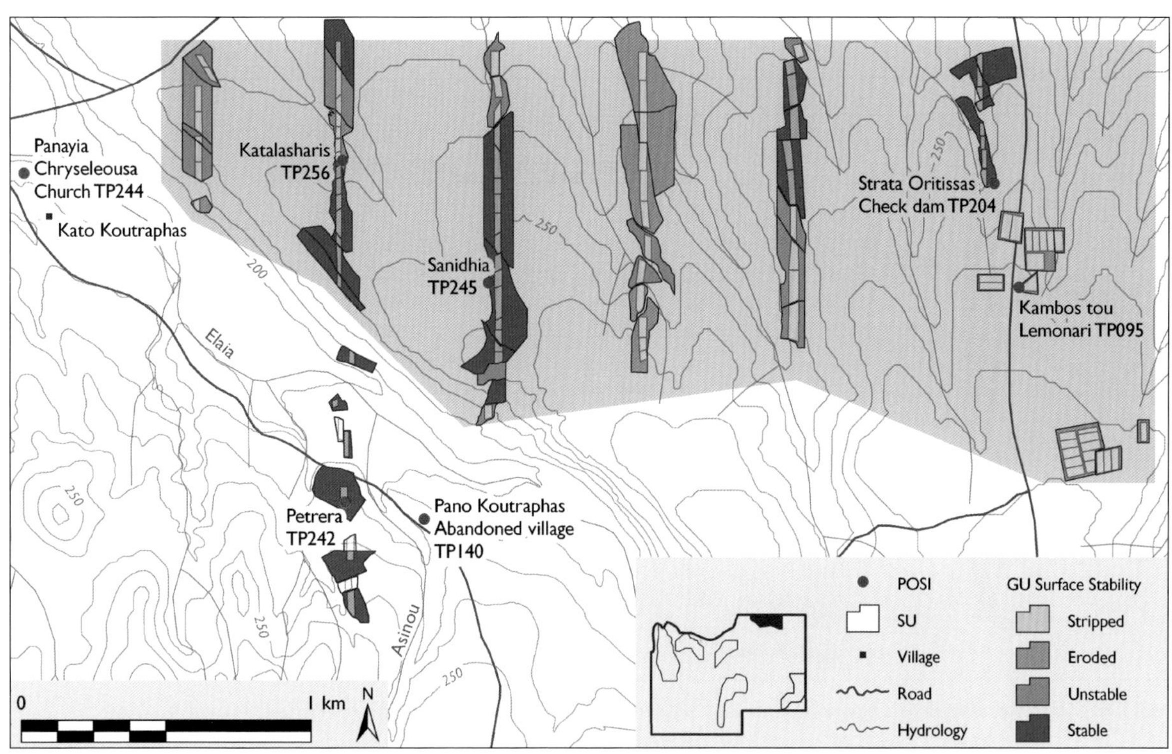

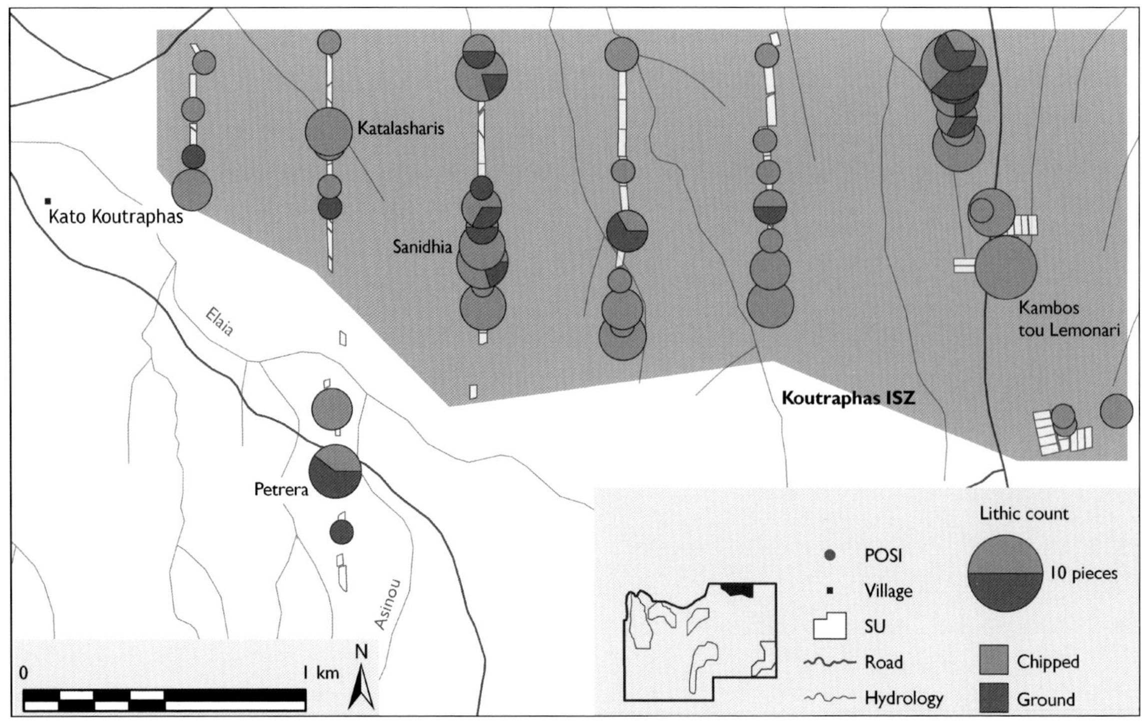

Plate 2.12. Koutraphas Intensive Survey Zone: distribution of chipped stone and ground stone tools (Luke Sollars)

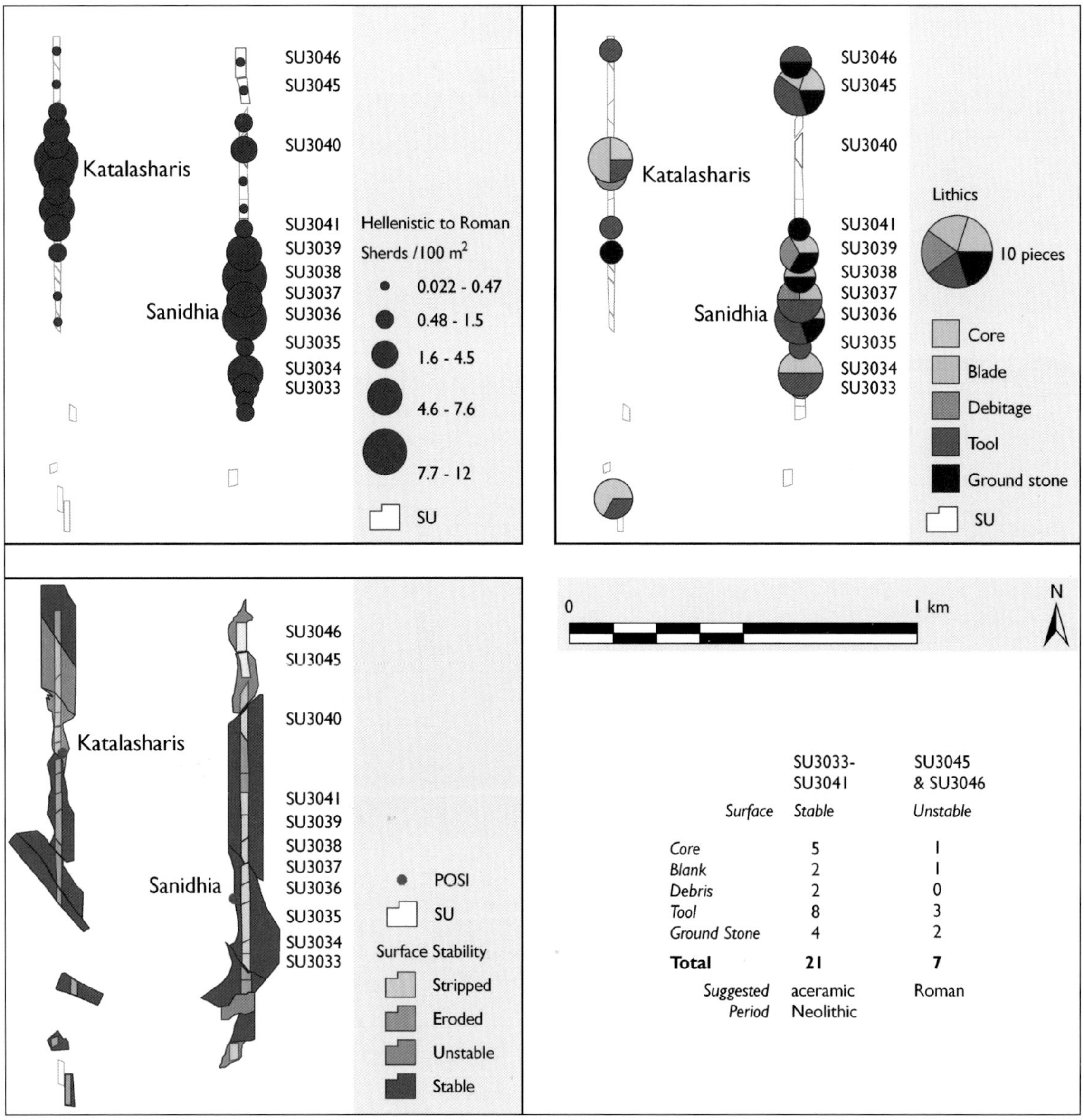

Surface	SU3033-SU3041 Stable	SU3045 & SU3046 Unstable
Core	5	1
Blank	2	1
Debris	2	0
Tool	8	3
Ground Stone	4	2
Total	**21**	**7**
Suggested Period	aceramic Neolithic	Roman

Plate 2.13. Ground stone, chipped stone and Roman pottery around Pano Koutraphas Sanidhia *(TP245) (Luke Sollars)*

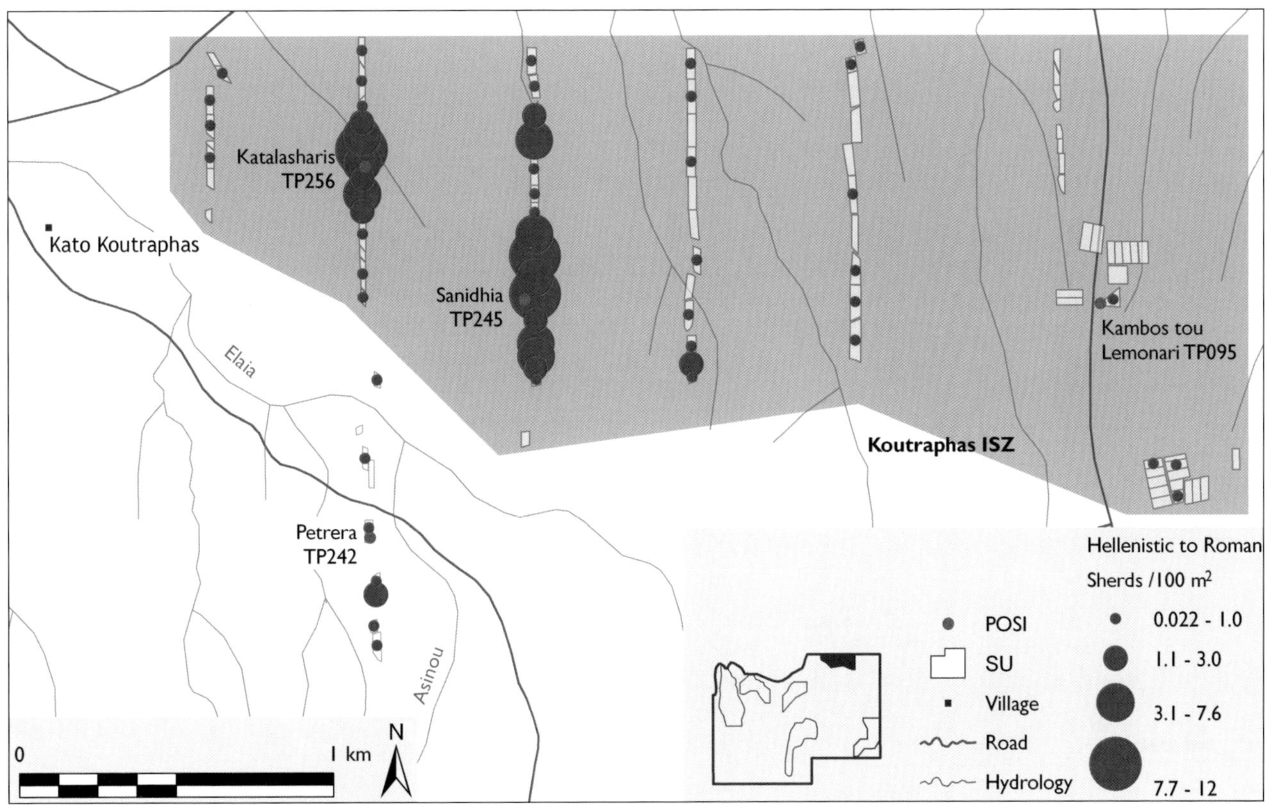

Plate 2.14. Koutraphas Intensive Survey Zone: Hellenistic–Roman pottery distribution (Luke Sollars)

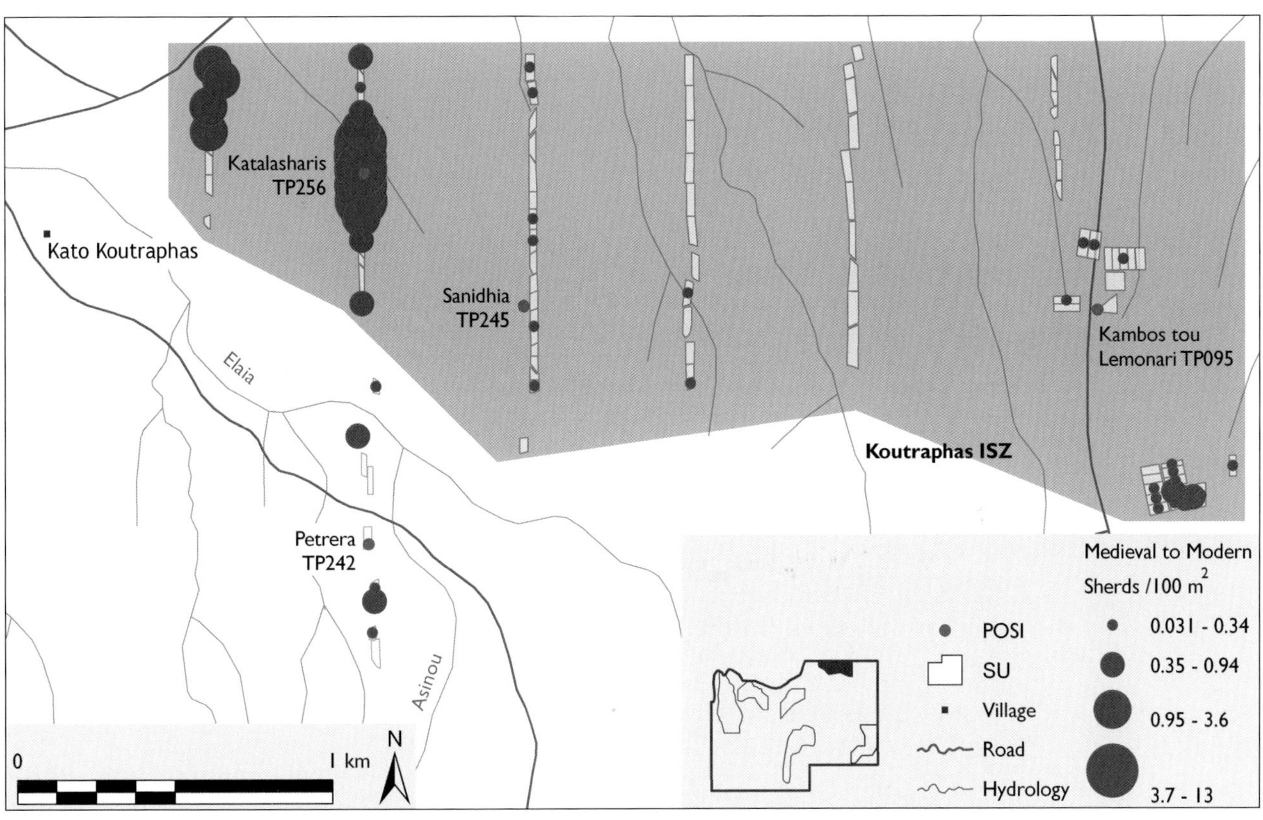

Plate 2.15. Koutraphas Intensive Survey Zone: Medieval–Modern pottery distribution (Luke Sollars)

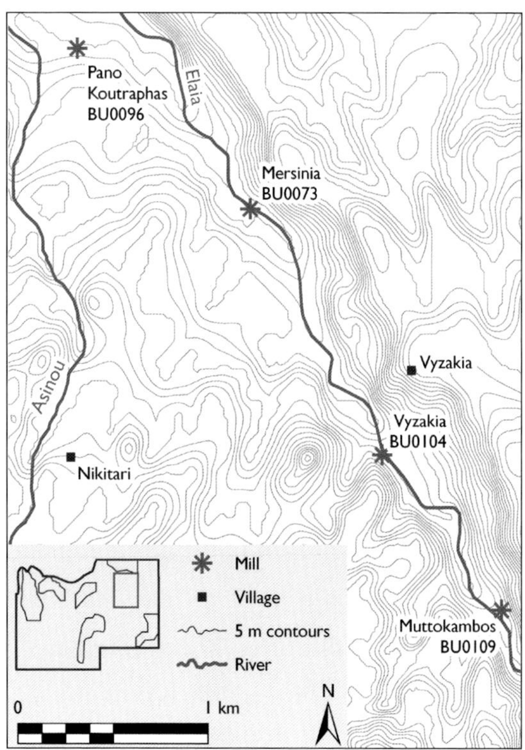

Plate 2.16. Map of watermills between Koutraphas and Lagoudhera Intensive Survey Zones (Luke Sollars)

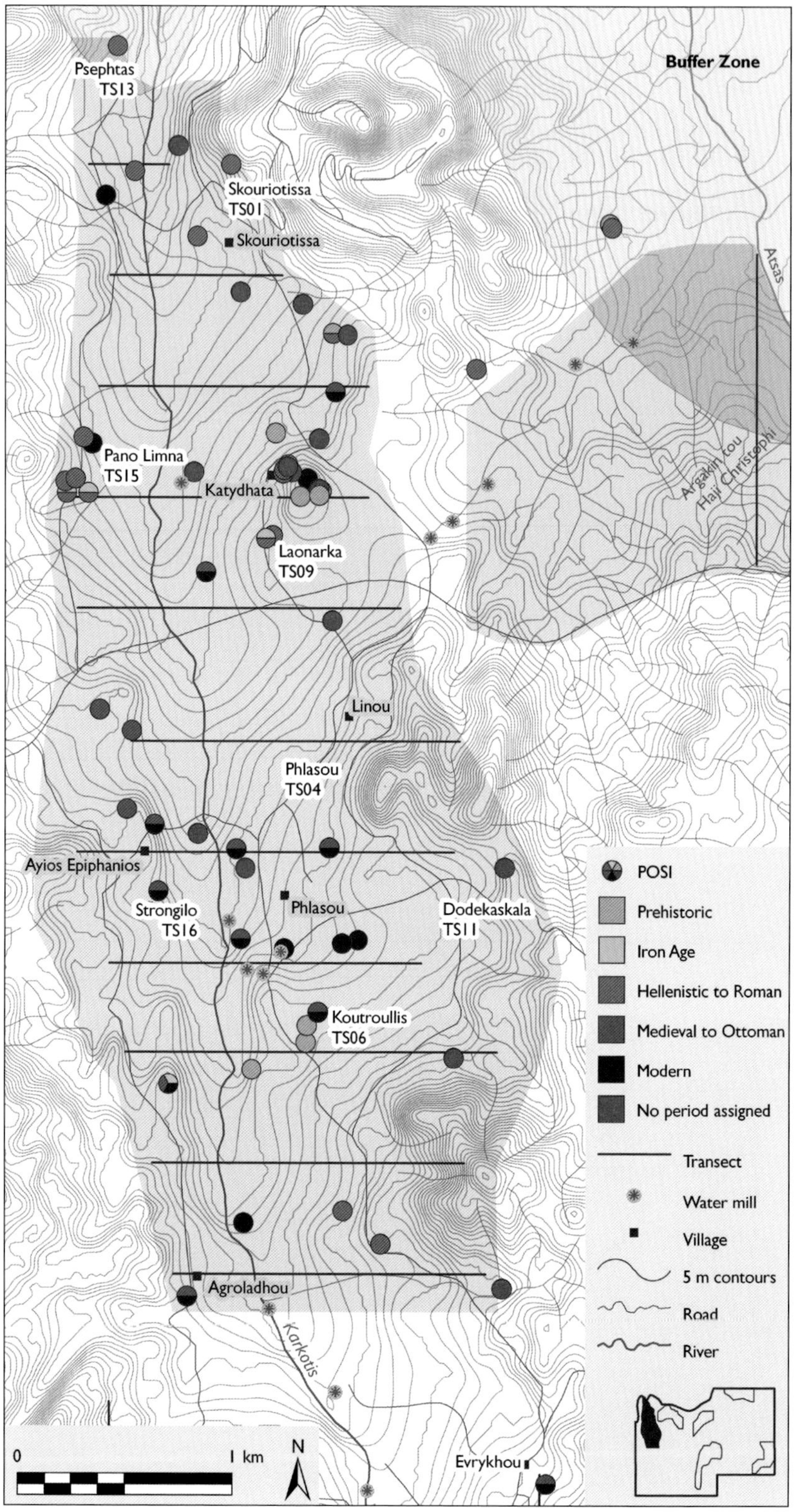

Plate 3.1. Karkotis Valley: topography, survey transects and POSIs by period (Luke Sollars)

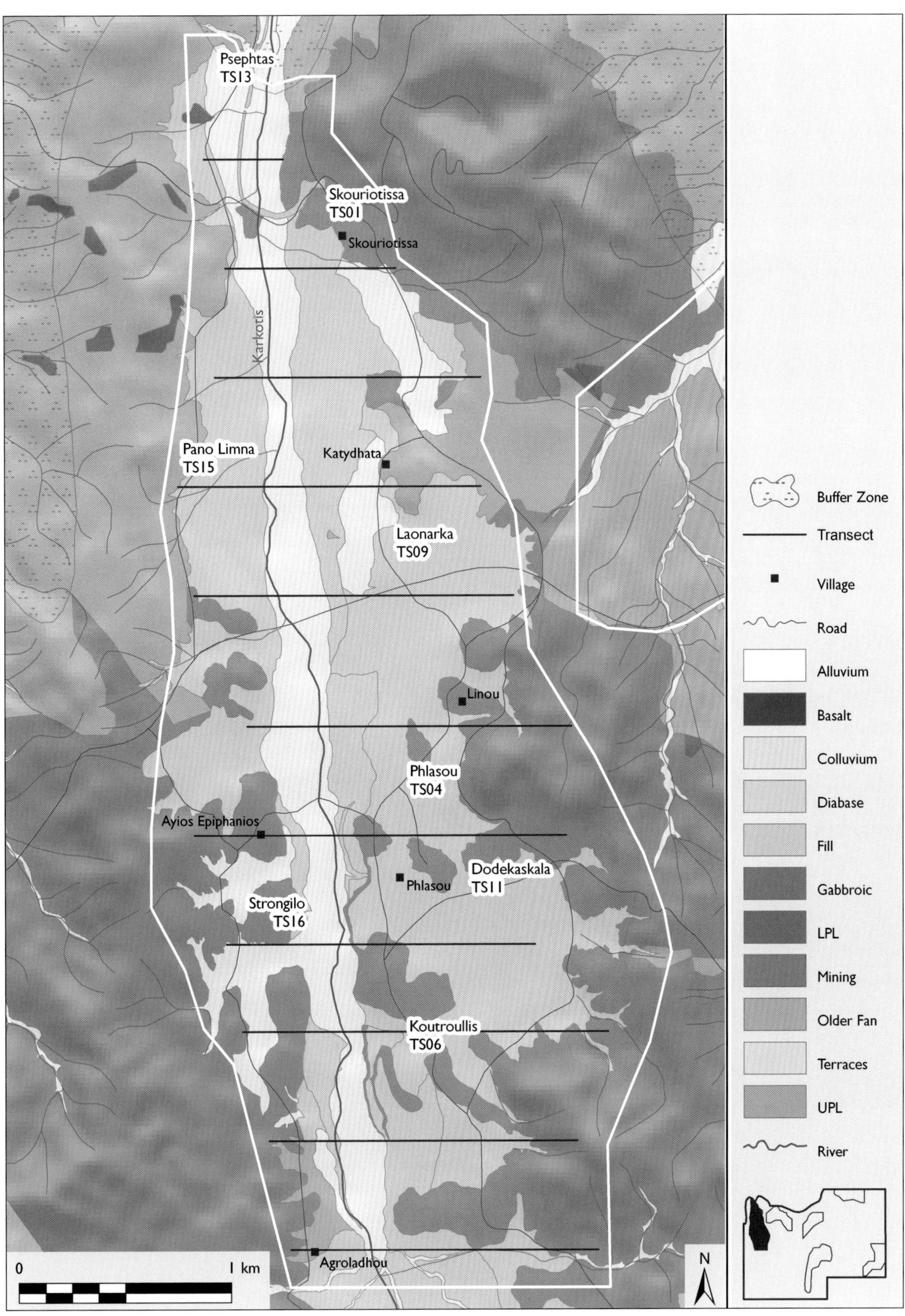

Plate 3.2. Geological map of Karkotis Valley (Jay Noller, finalised by Luke Sollars)

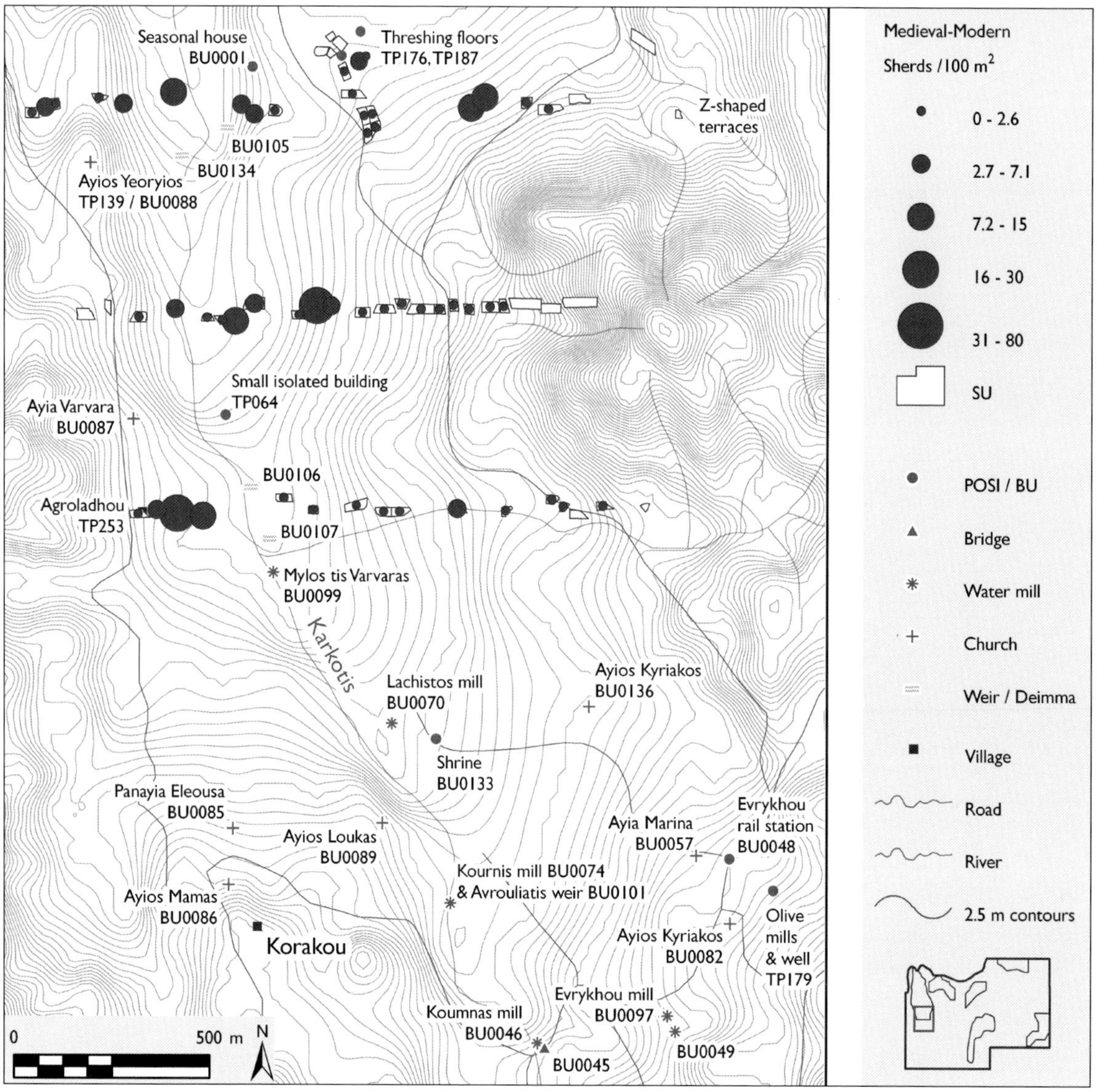

Plate 3.3. South Karkotis Valley: Medieval–Modern pottery, Building Units and POSIs (Luke Sollars)

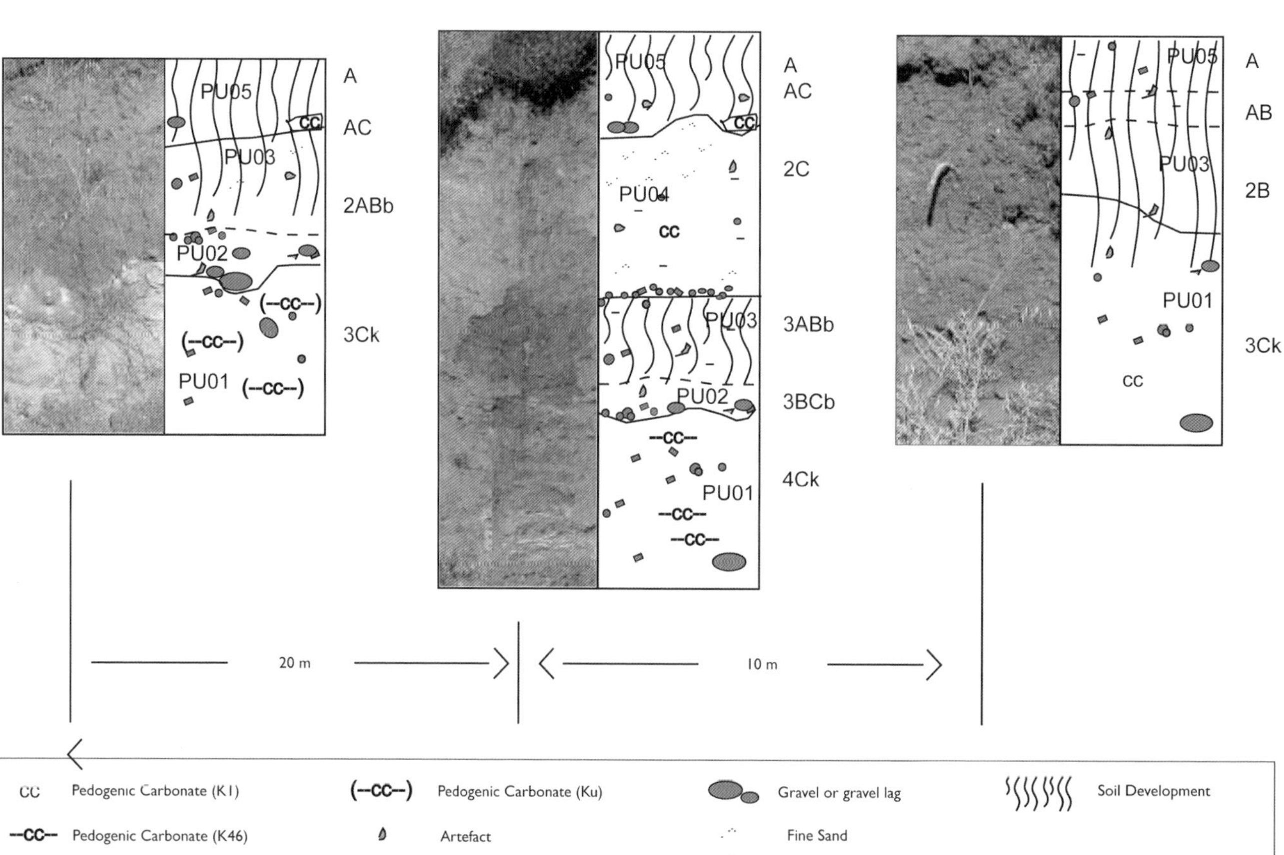

Plate 3.4. Phlasou Langouphes *(TP246): stratigraphic and soil cross-sections through flood deposits (Jay Noller and Colin Robins)*

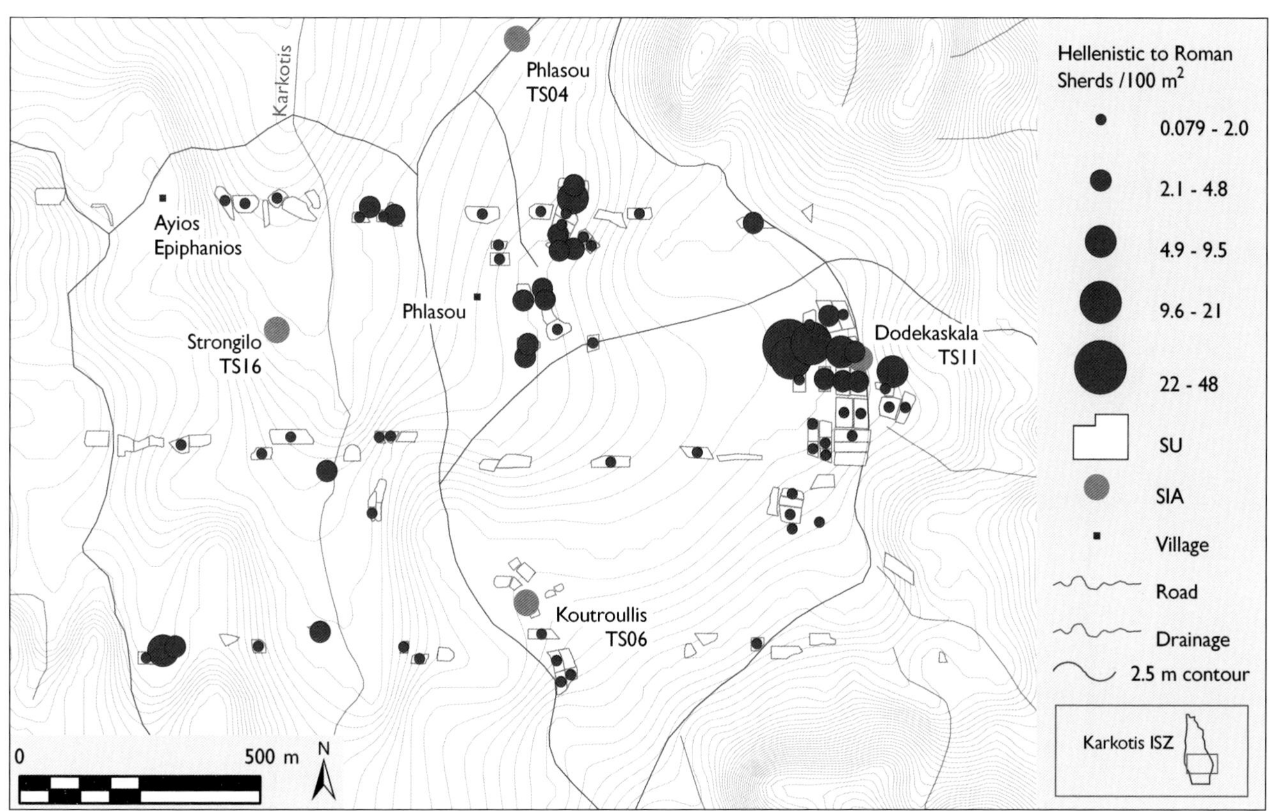

Plate 3.5. Central Karkotis Valley: distribution map of Hellenistic–Roman pottery (Luke Sollars)

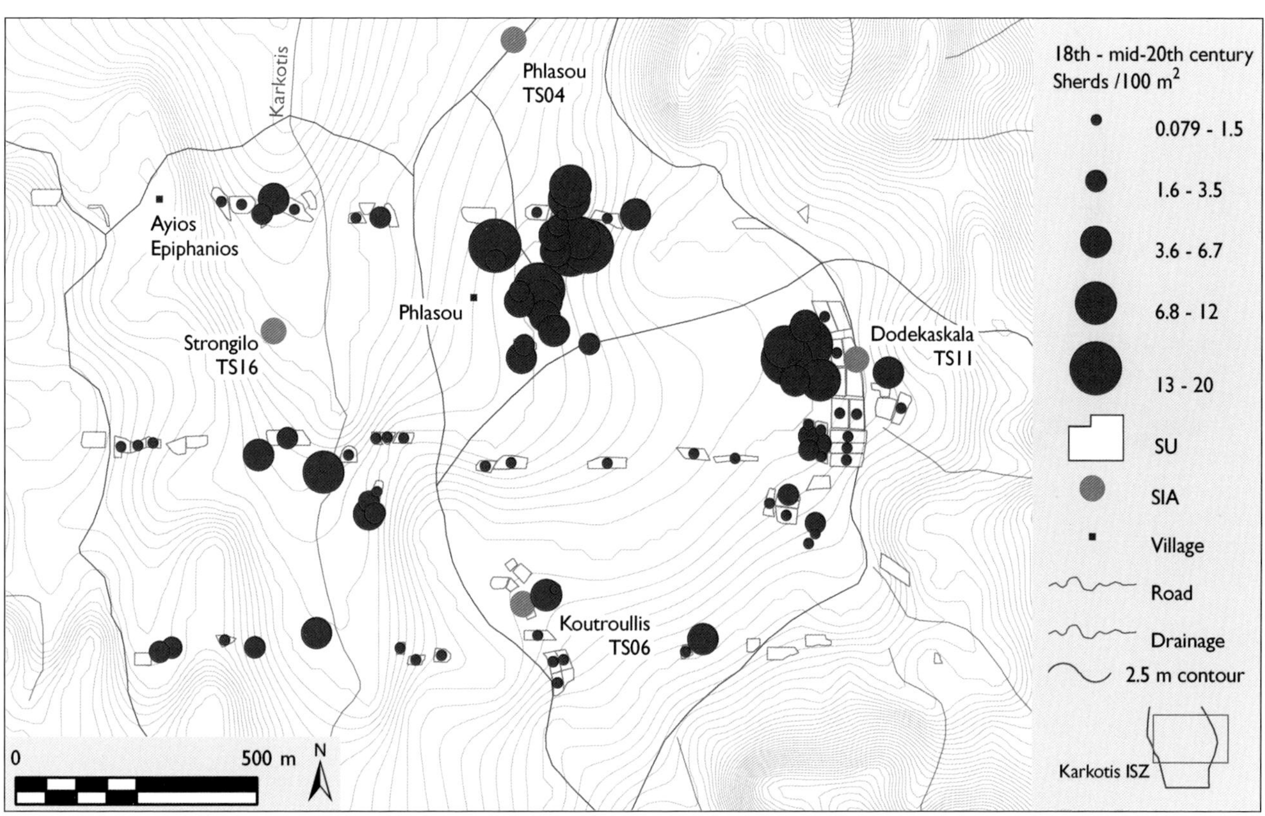

Plate 3.6. Central Karkotis Valley: distribution map of 18th–mid-20th-century pottery (OttModII) (Luke Sollars)

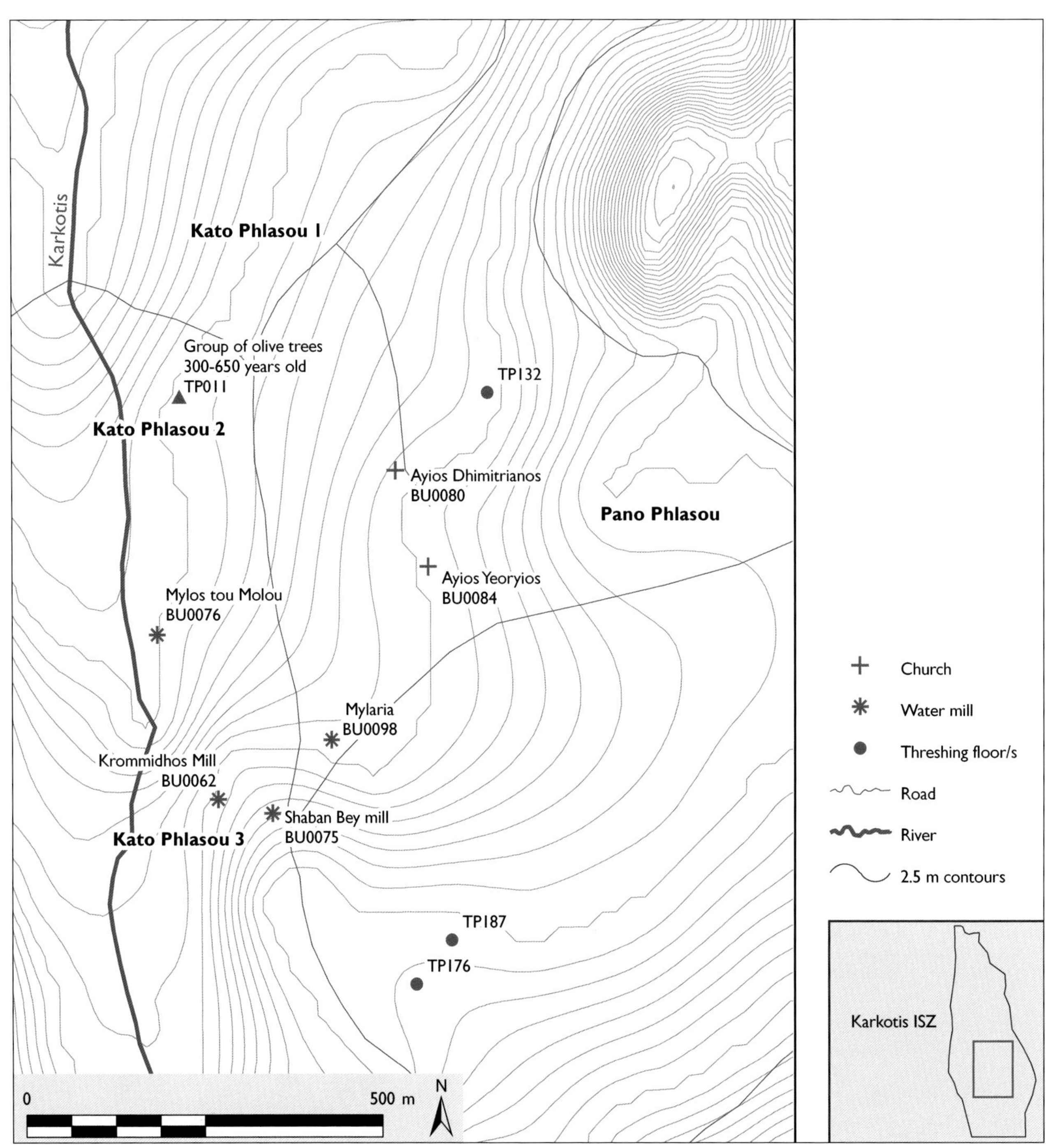

Plate 3.7. Topographic map of Kato Phlasou and Pano Phlasou (Luke Sollars)

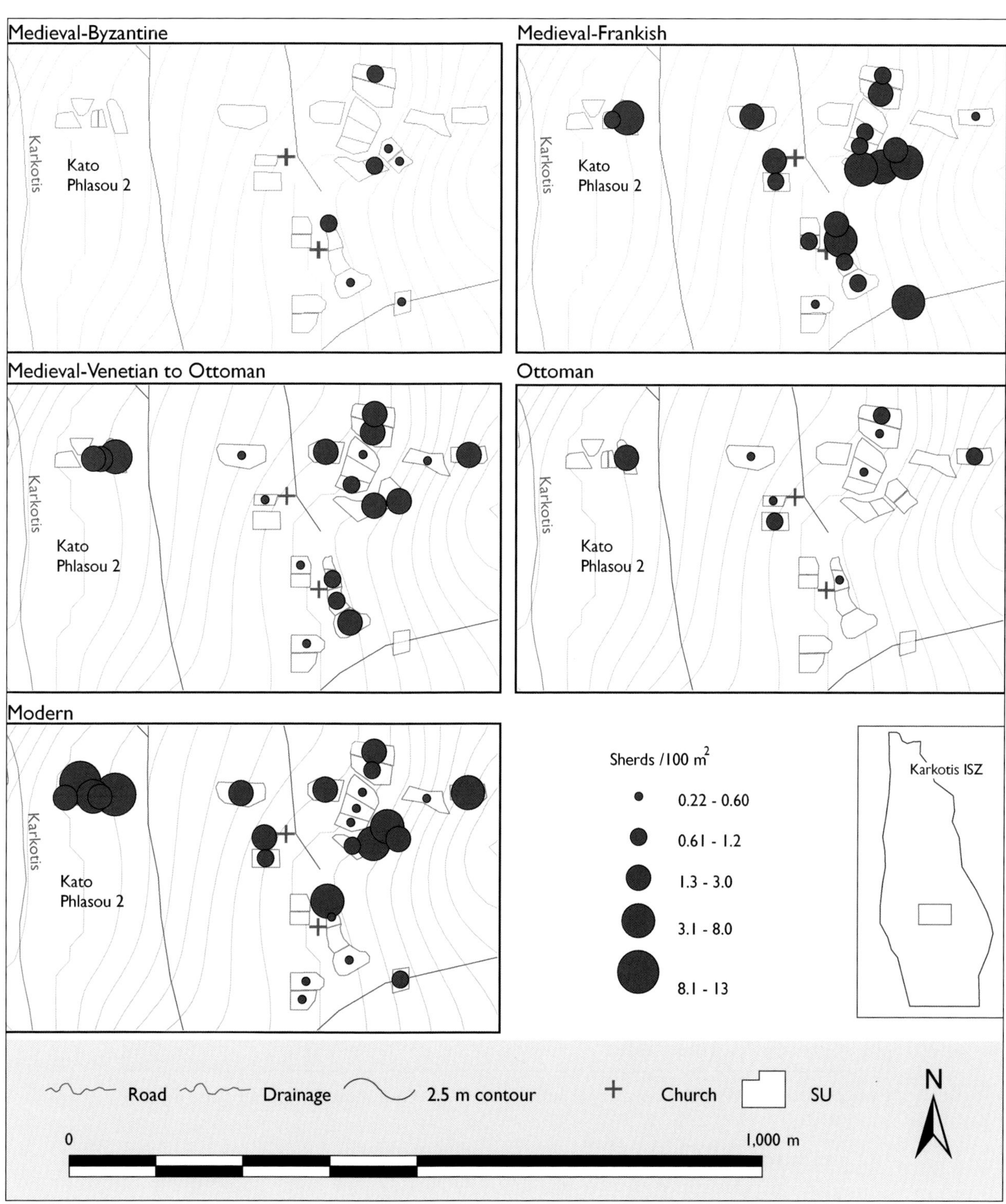

Plate 3.8. Medieval–Modern pottery distributions around Phlasou (Luke Sollars)

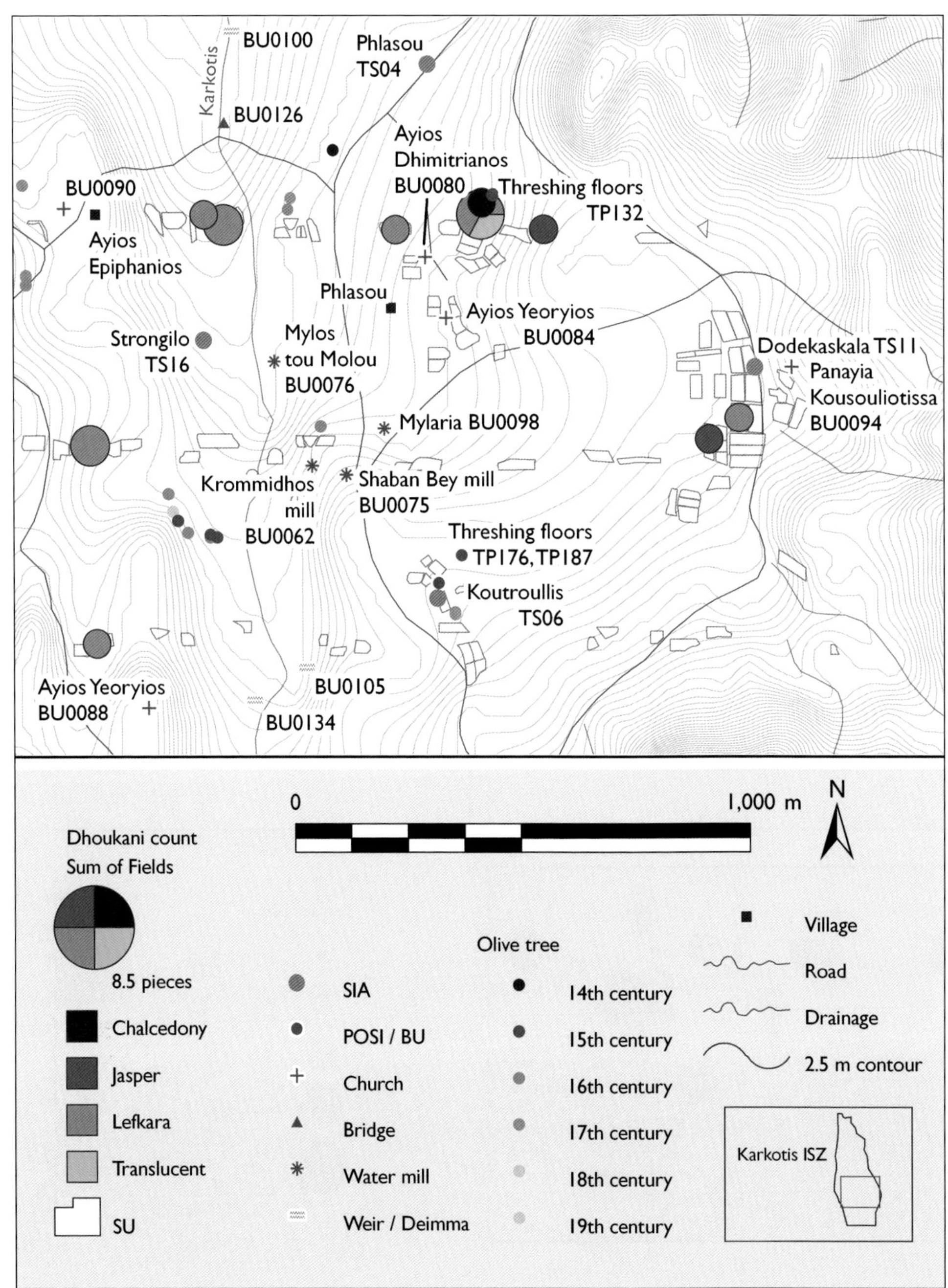

Plate 3.9. Distribution and materials of dhoukani *flakes in the central Karkotis Valley (Luke Sollars)*

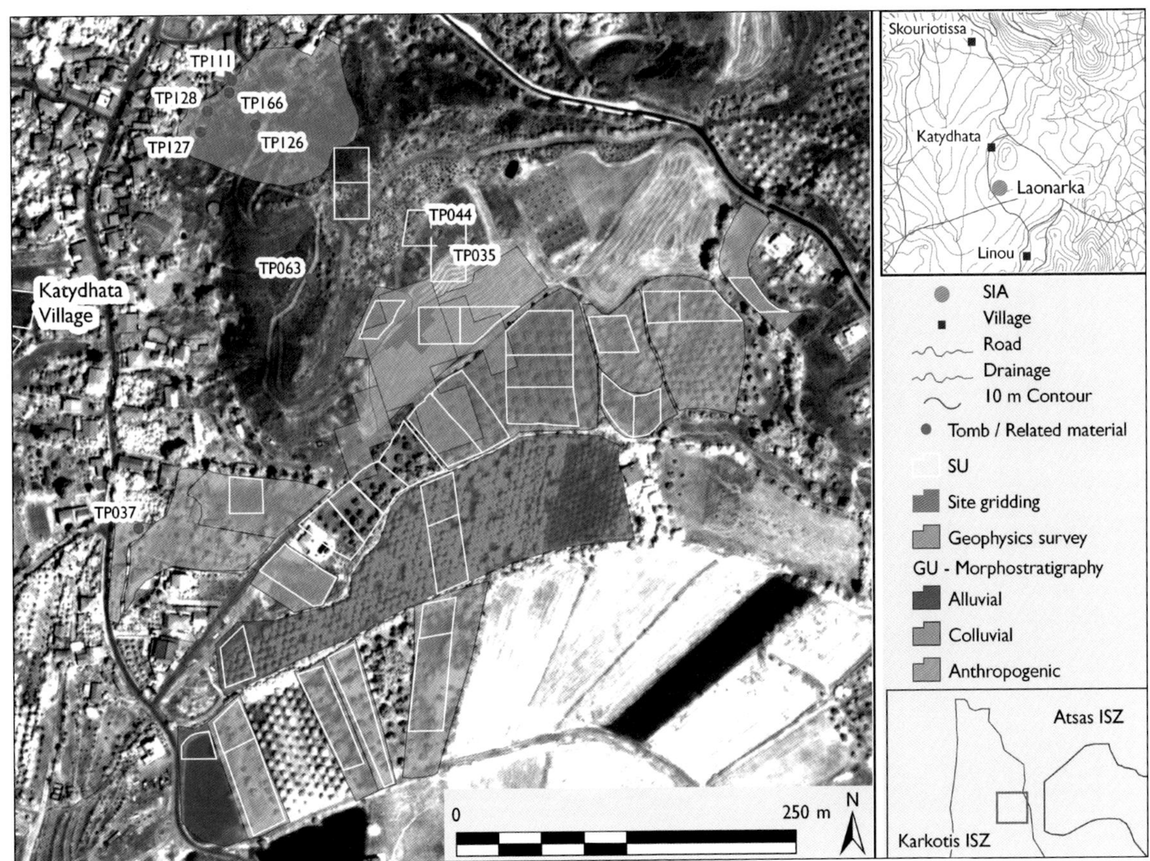

Plate 3.10. Katydhata Laonarka *(TS09): topographical map. Corrected satellite image (2003) courtesy of the Cyprus Geological Survey Department (Luke Sollars)*

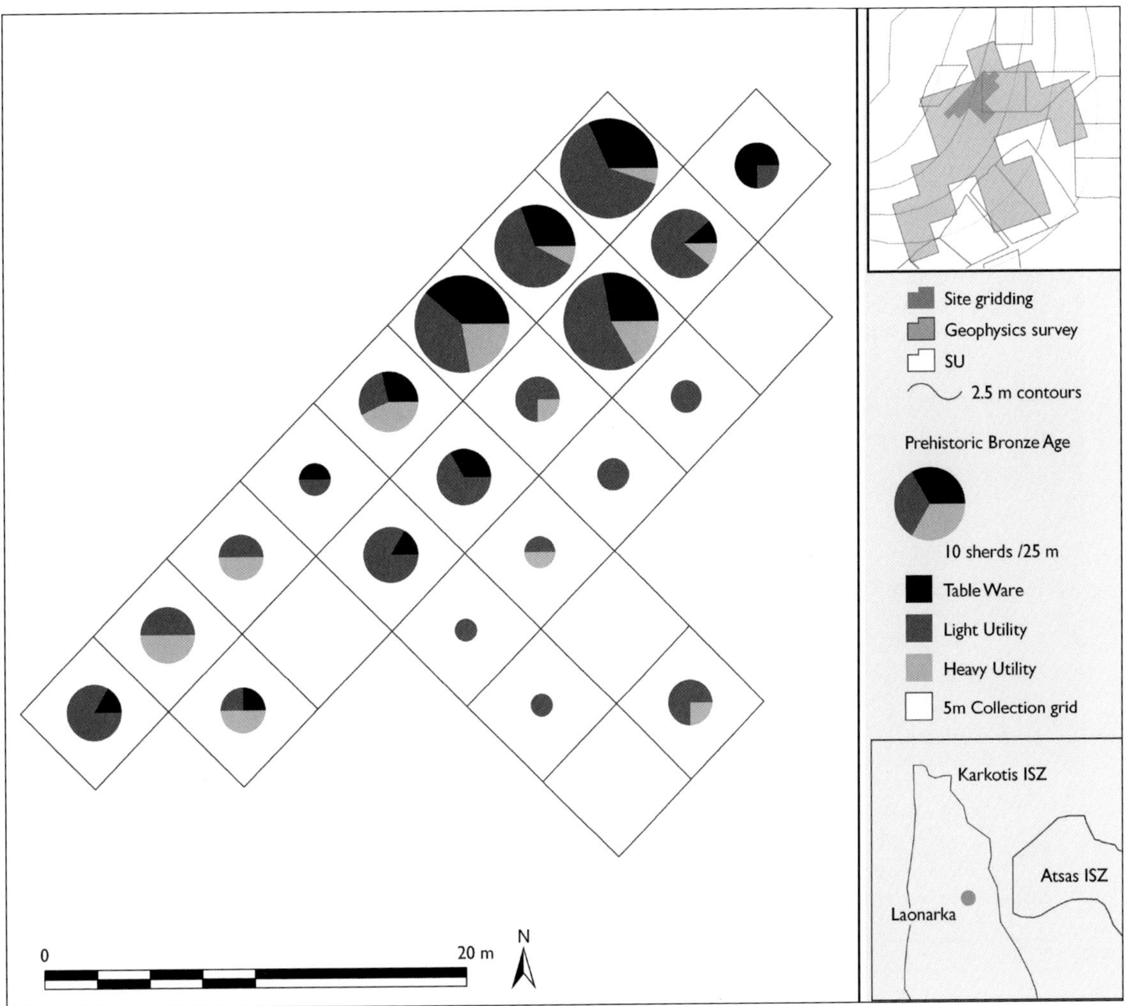

Plate 3.11. Katydhata Laonarka *(TS09; TP243): pottery collection grid with density of Prehistoric Bronze Age pottery (see Plate 3.10 for location) (Luke Sollars)*

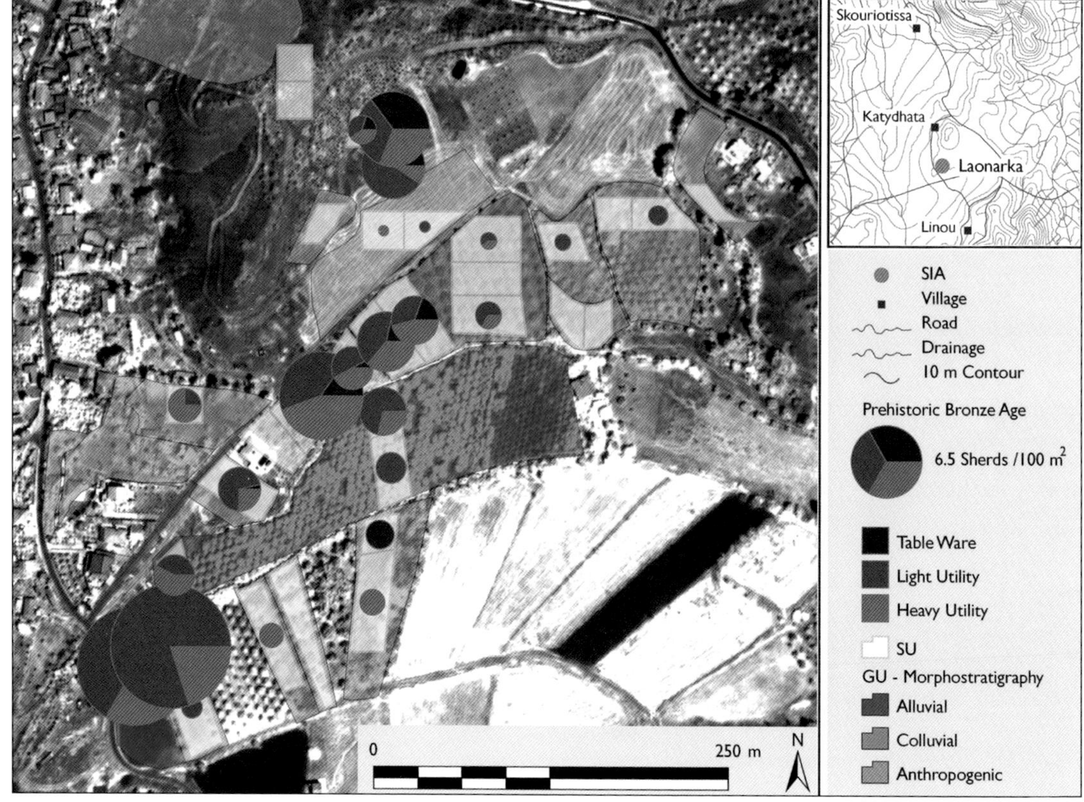

Plate 3.12. Katydhata Laonarka *(TS09): block survey and geomorphology, with Prehistoric Bronze Age pottery distribution divided by function (Luke Sollars)*

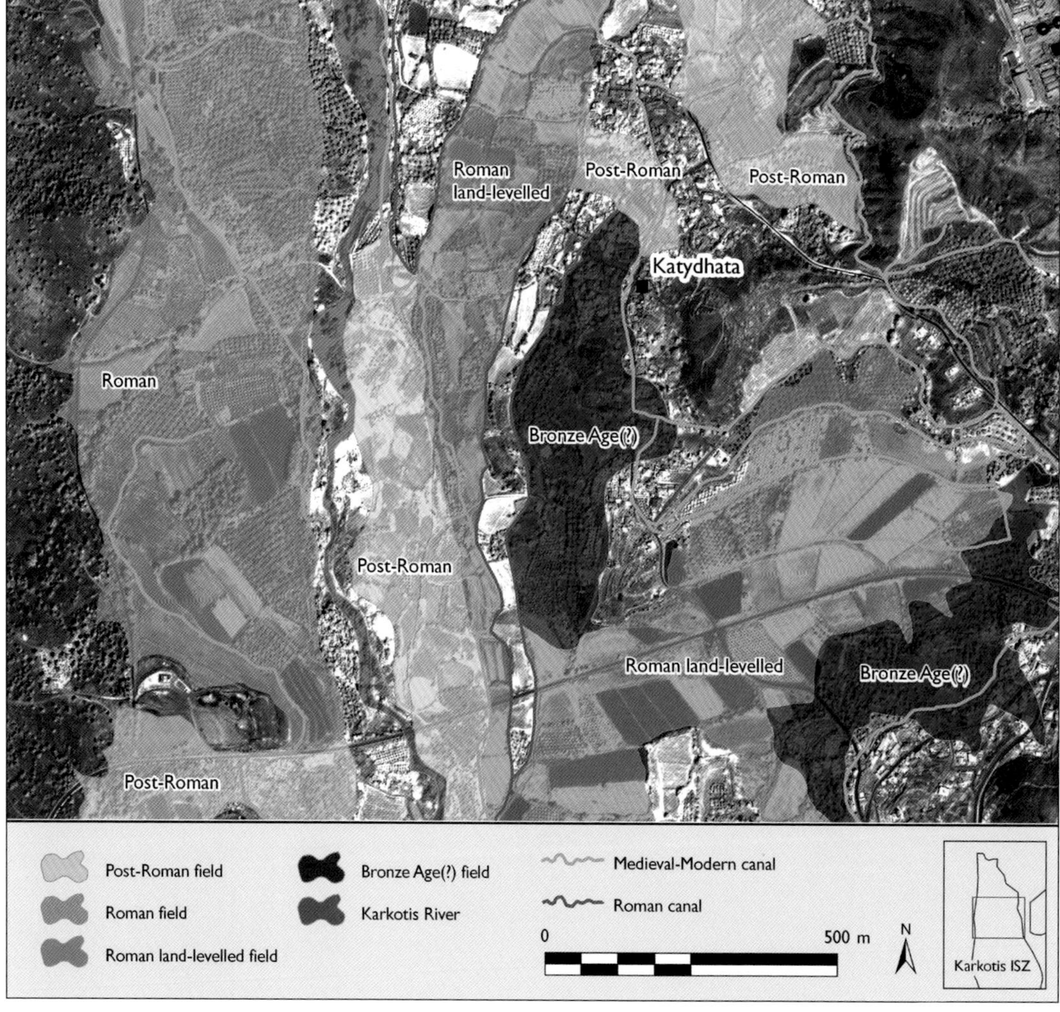

Plate 3.13. Postulated ages of fields on terrace ranks within the Karkotis Valley. Green colours indicate areas of land levelling (each shade is a separate rank). 'Roman' canals are now disused; 'Medieval–Modern' canals are in use, or have been in use till recently, and may have Roman predecessors. Corrected satellite image (2003) courtesy of the Cyprus Geological Survey Department (Jay Noller, finalised by Luke Sollars)

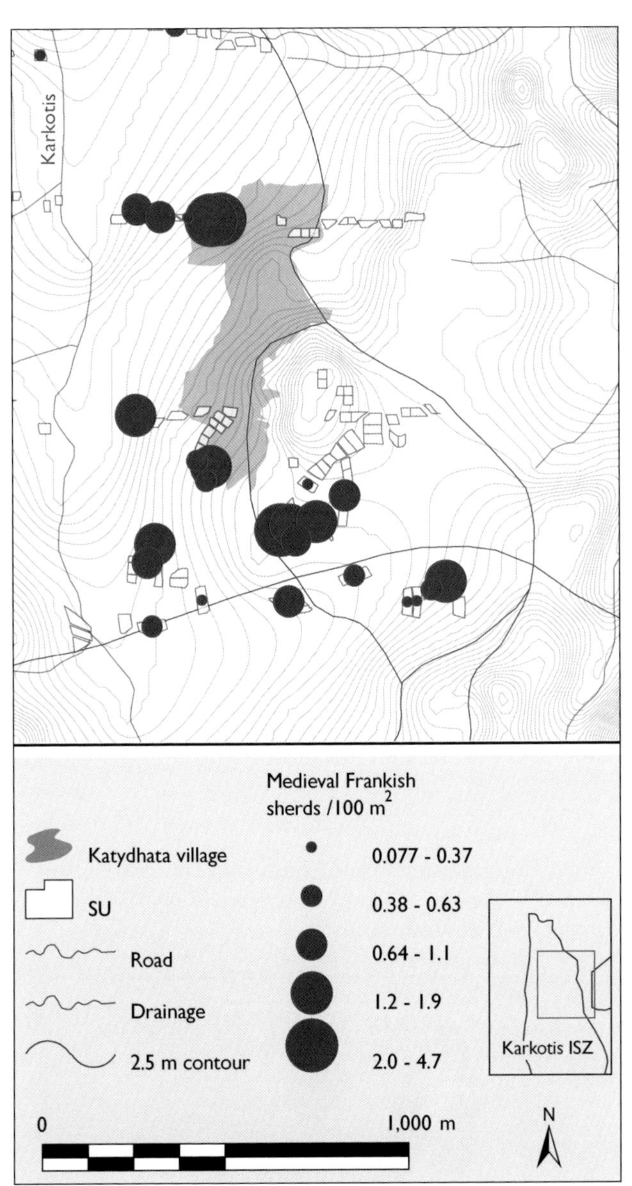

Plate 3.14. Distribution of Medieval-Frankish pottery (MedF) round Katydhata (Luke Sollars)

Plate 3.15. Katydhata Pano Limna *(TS15) and its surrounding area: topographical and environmental map (Luke Sollars)*

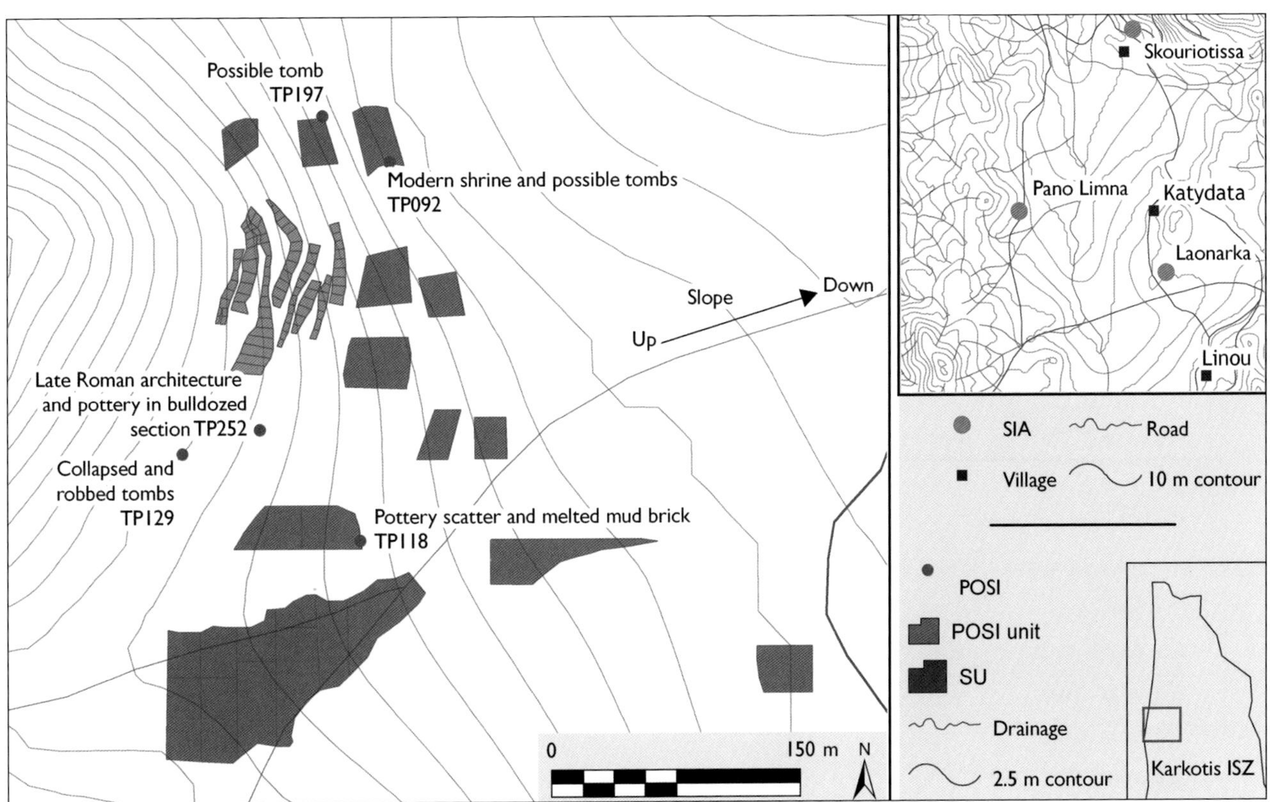

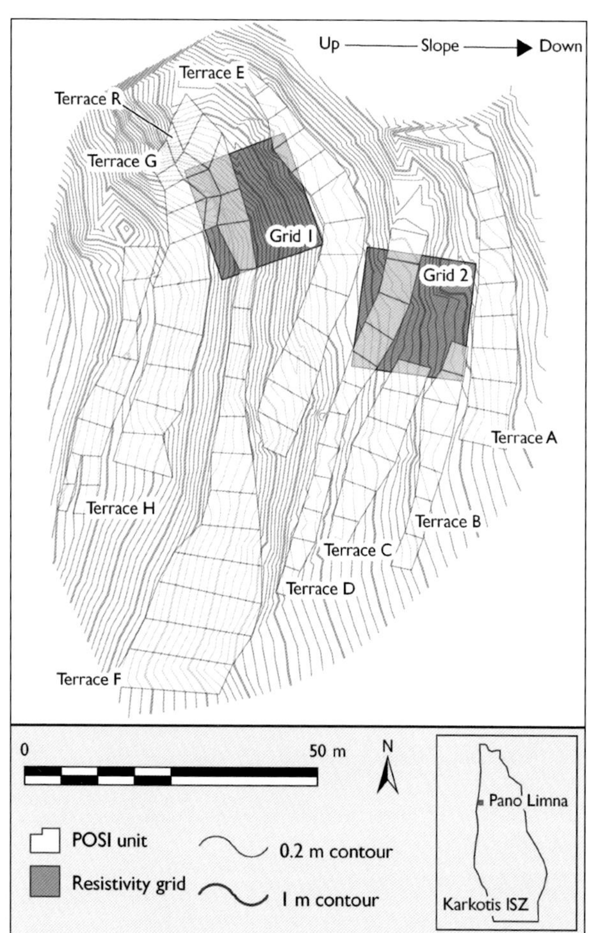

Plate 3.16. Katydhata Pano Limna *(TS15): topographic map with contours, collection grid, terrace identifiers, geophysical grid (Luke Sollars)*

Plate 3.17. Katydhata Pano Limna *(TP119): distribution map of Geometric–Classical pottery and figurines, and Roman pottery (Luke Sollars)*

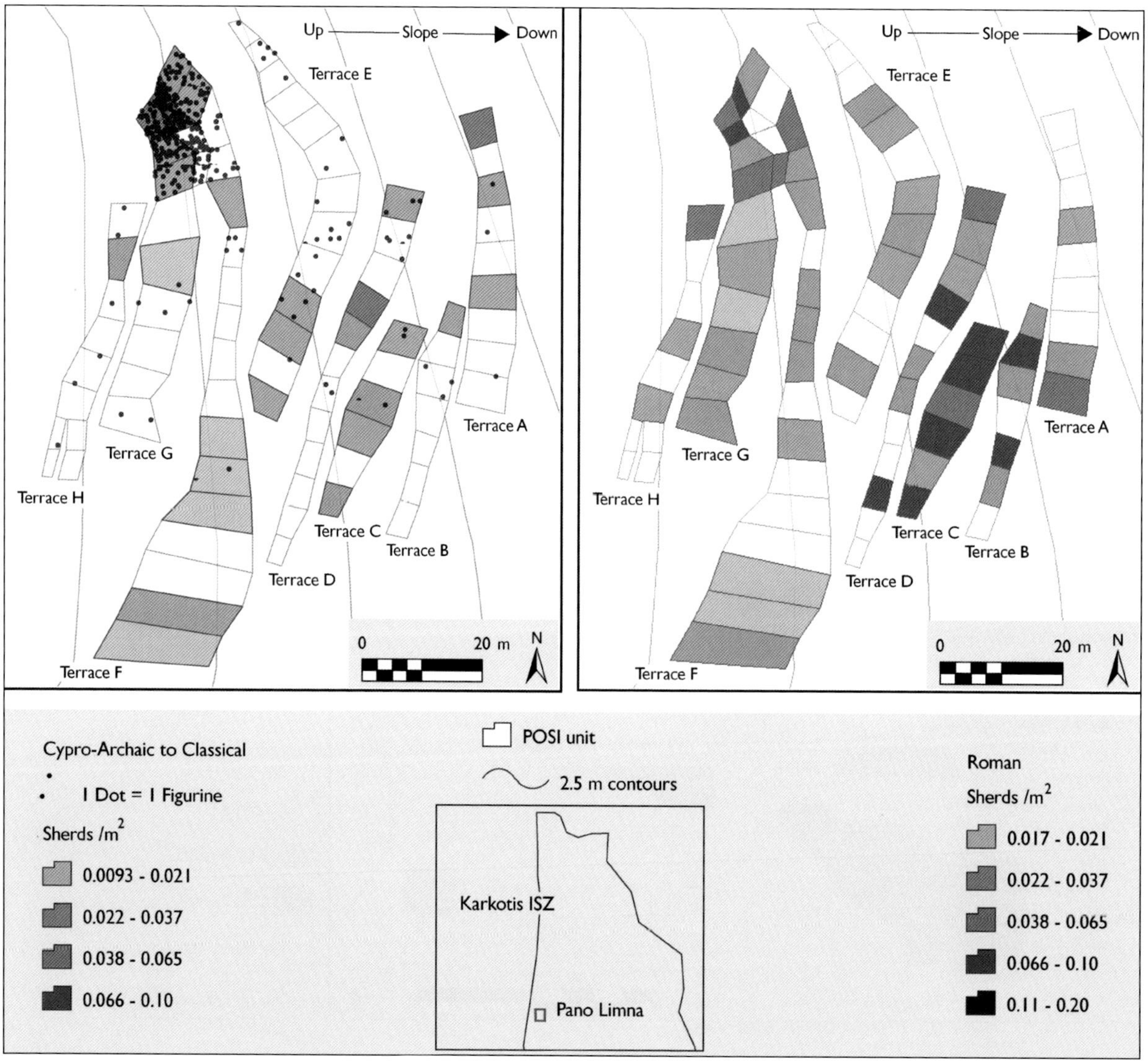

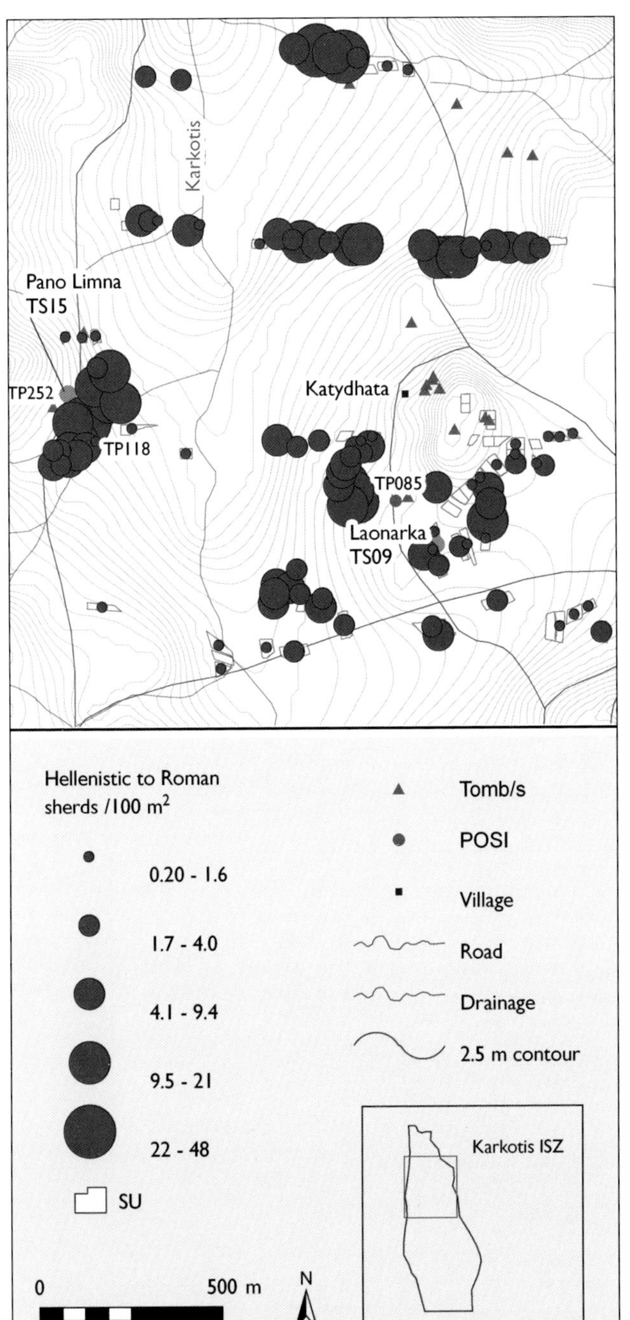

Plate 3.18. Katydhata Pano Limna *and area (TS15): distribution map of Hellenistic–Roman pottery and POSIs (Luke Sollars)*

Plate 3.19. The pottery dump in situ in 1996 and the remains of the modern house mentioned by Bruce (Photograph courtesy of Dr G. Malliotis, Hellenic Mining Company)

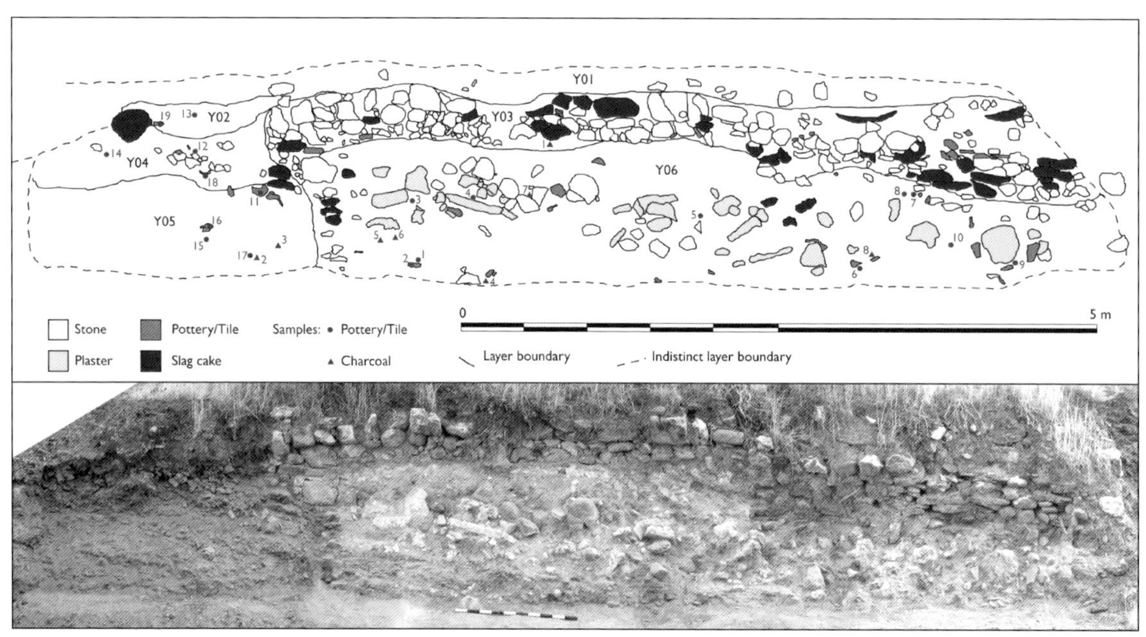

Plate 3.20. Skouriotissa Vouppes *(TP007): section AU07. Above: section drawing. Below: photograph (Thomas Tselios)*

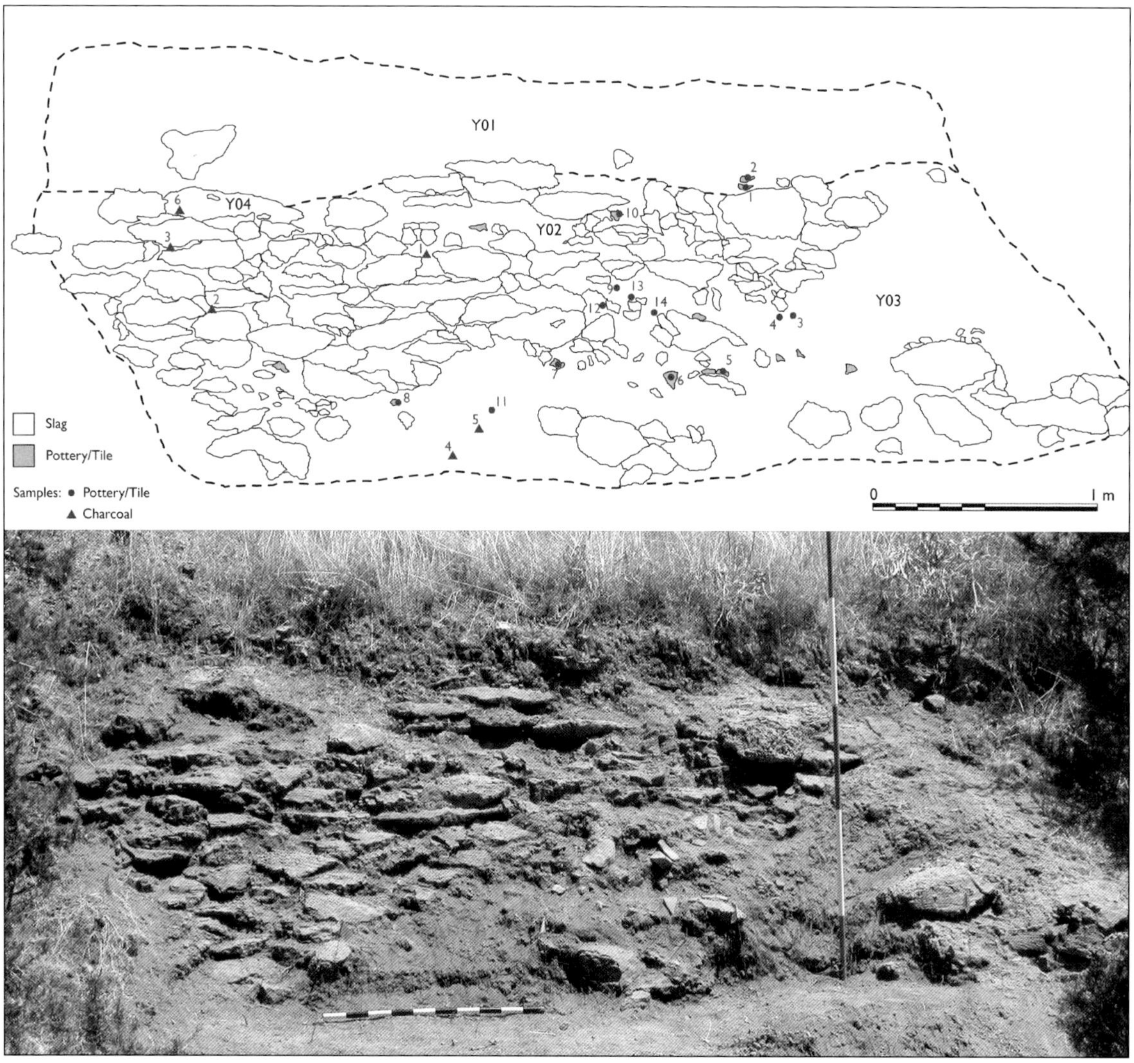

Plate 3.21. Skouriotissa Vouppes *(TP007): slag wall (AU09). Above: drawing. Below: photograph (Thomas Tselios)*

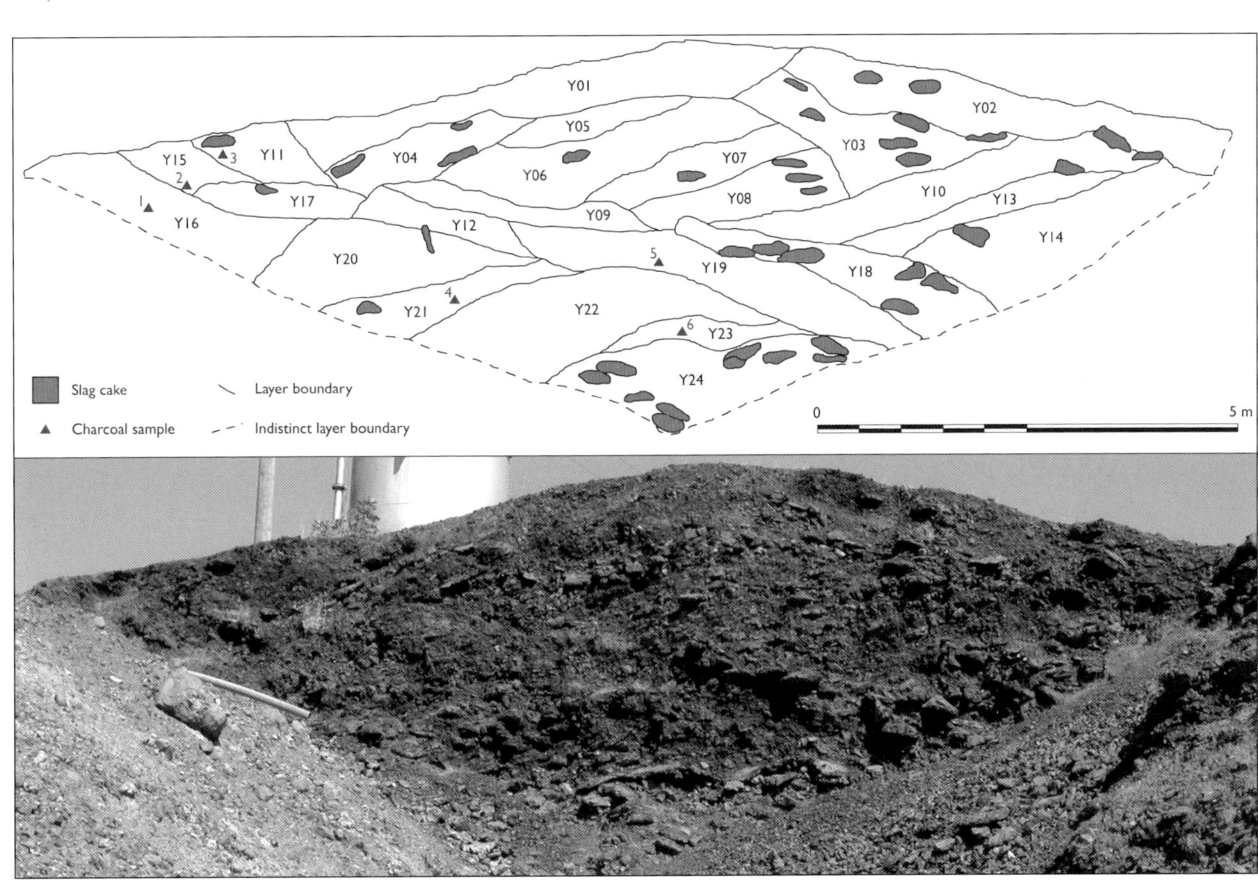

Plate 3.22. Skouriotissa Vouppes *(TP007): section AU14. Above: drawing. Below: photograph (Thomas Tselios)*

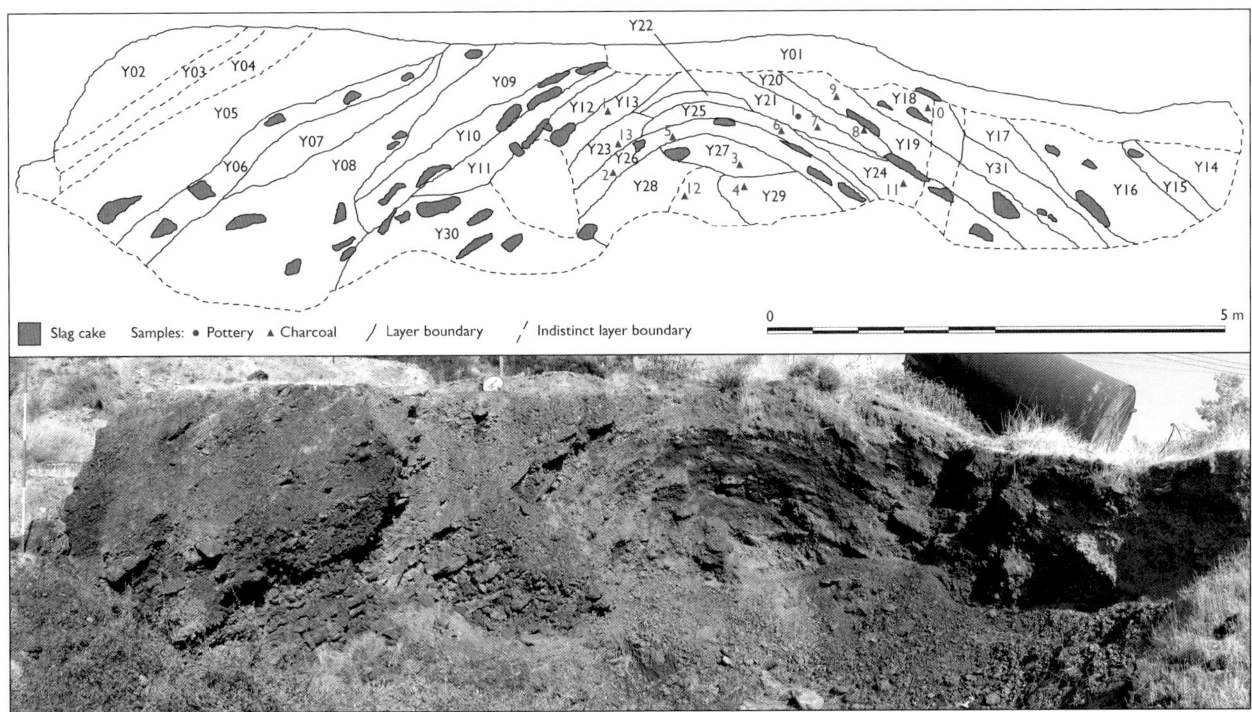

Plate 3.23. Skouriotissa Kitromilia *(TP172): section of smaller slag heap. Above: drawing (Thomas Tselios). Below: photograph (Chris Parks)*

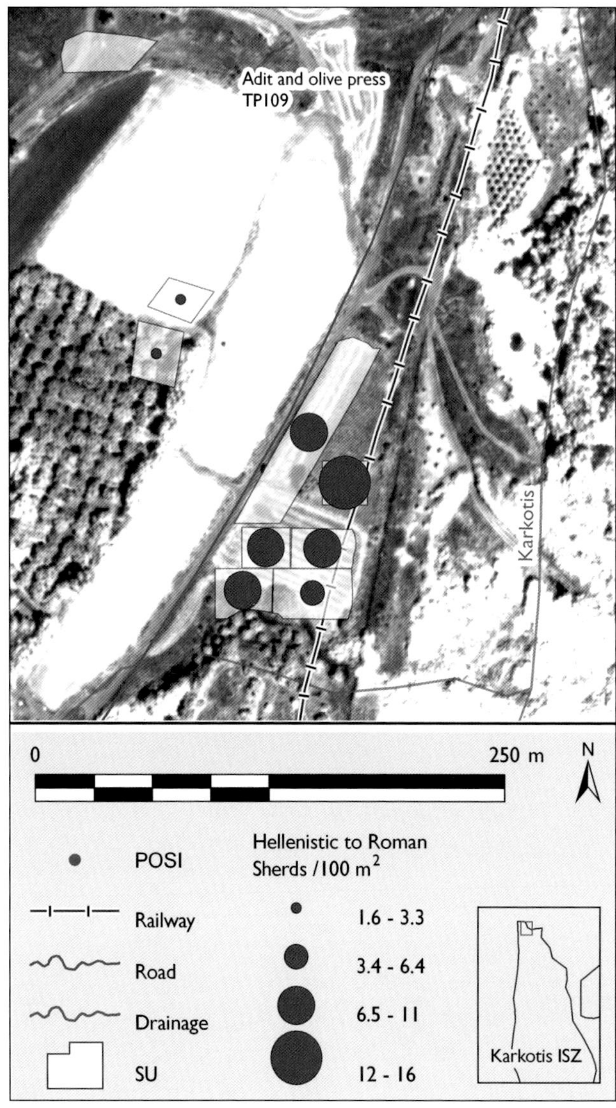

Plate 3.24. Skouriotissa Pseftas *(TS13): Hellenistic–Roman pottery (Luke Sollars)*

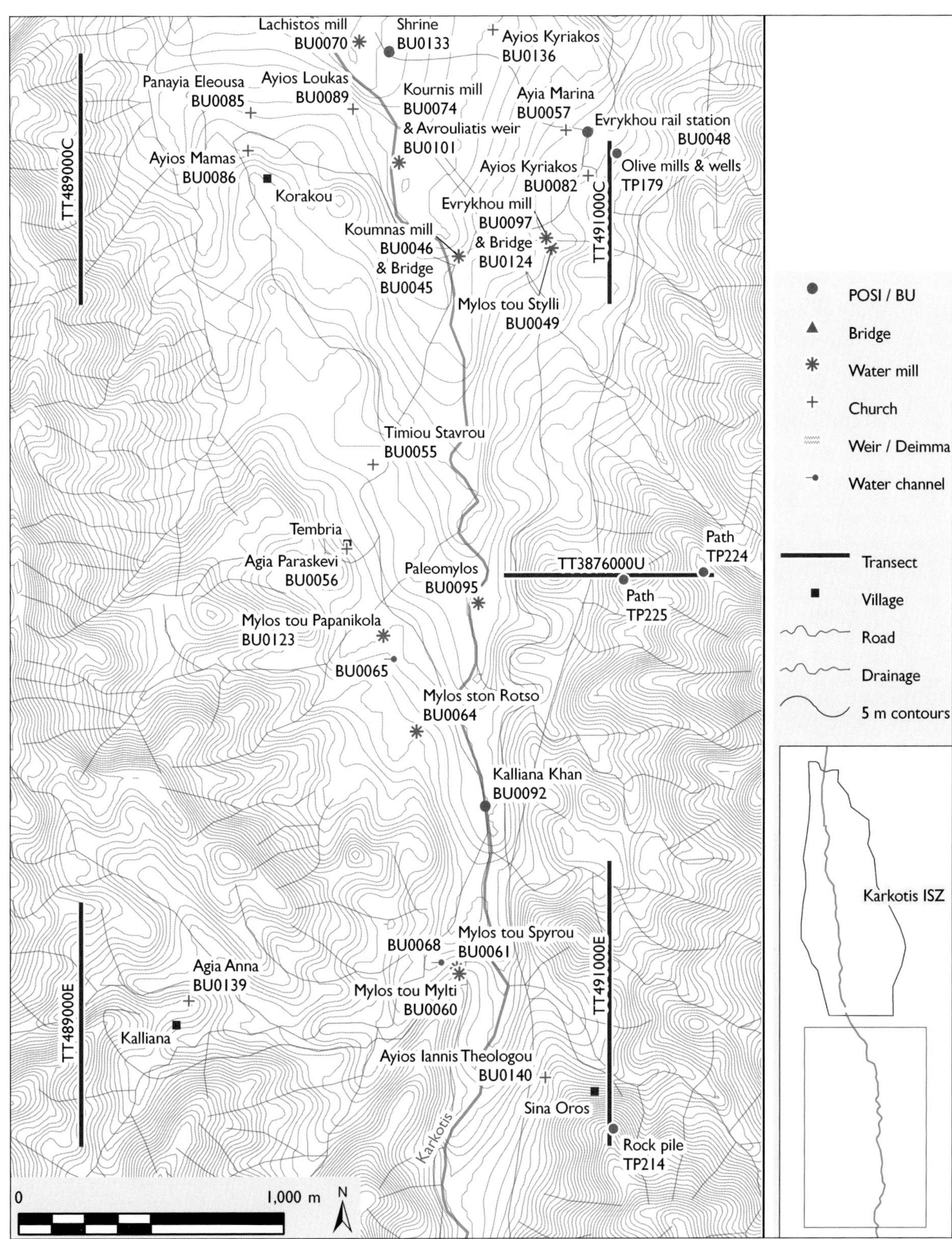

Plate 3.25. Area south of the Karkotis Valley Intensive Survey Zone: extensive transects, POSIs and BUs (Luke Sollars)

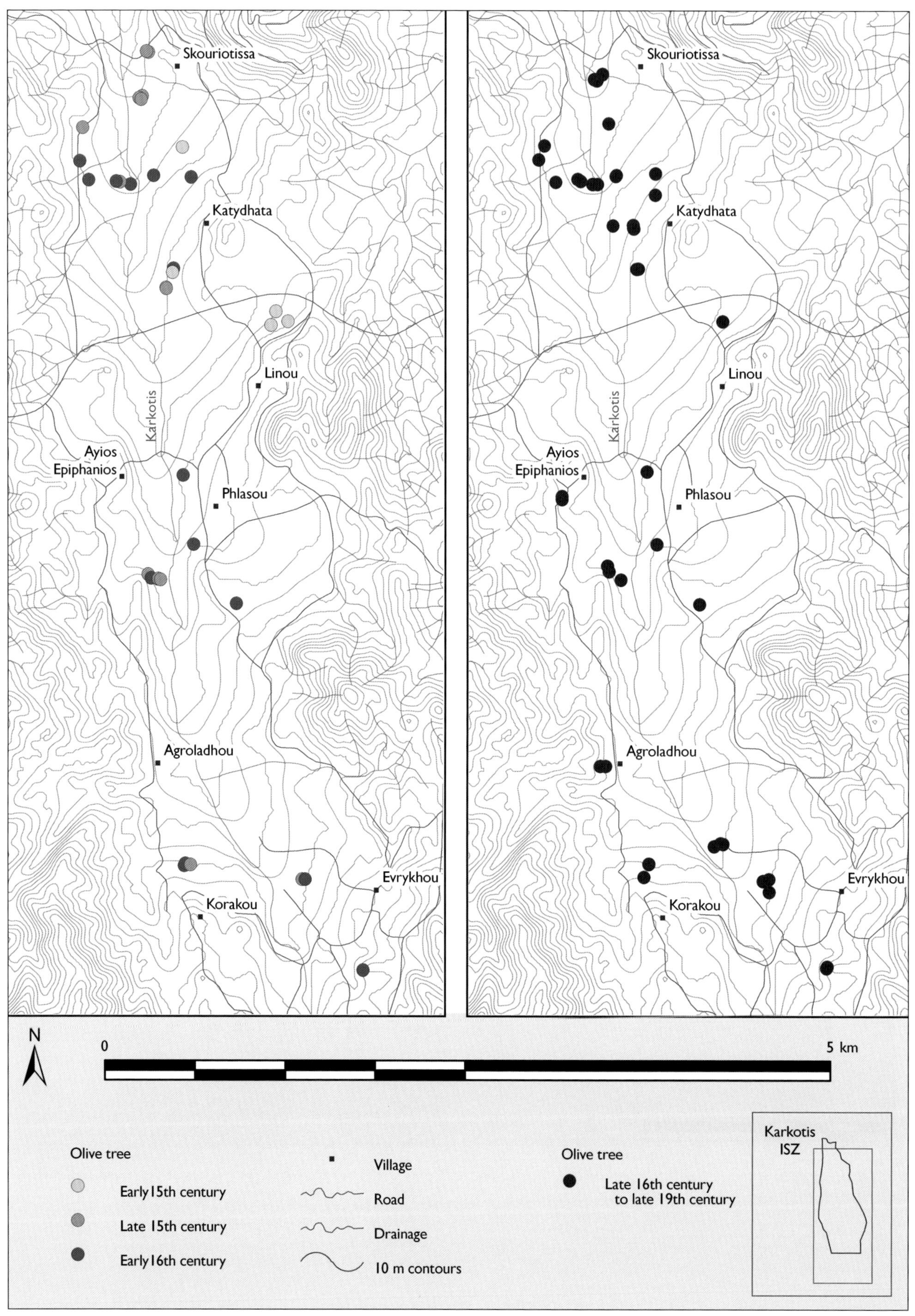

Plate 3.26. Extant olive plantings from (a) early 15th century–early 16th century, and (b) late 16th century–late 19th century (Luke Sollars)

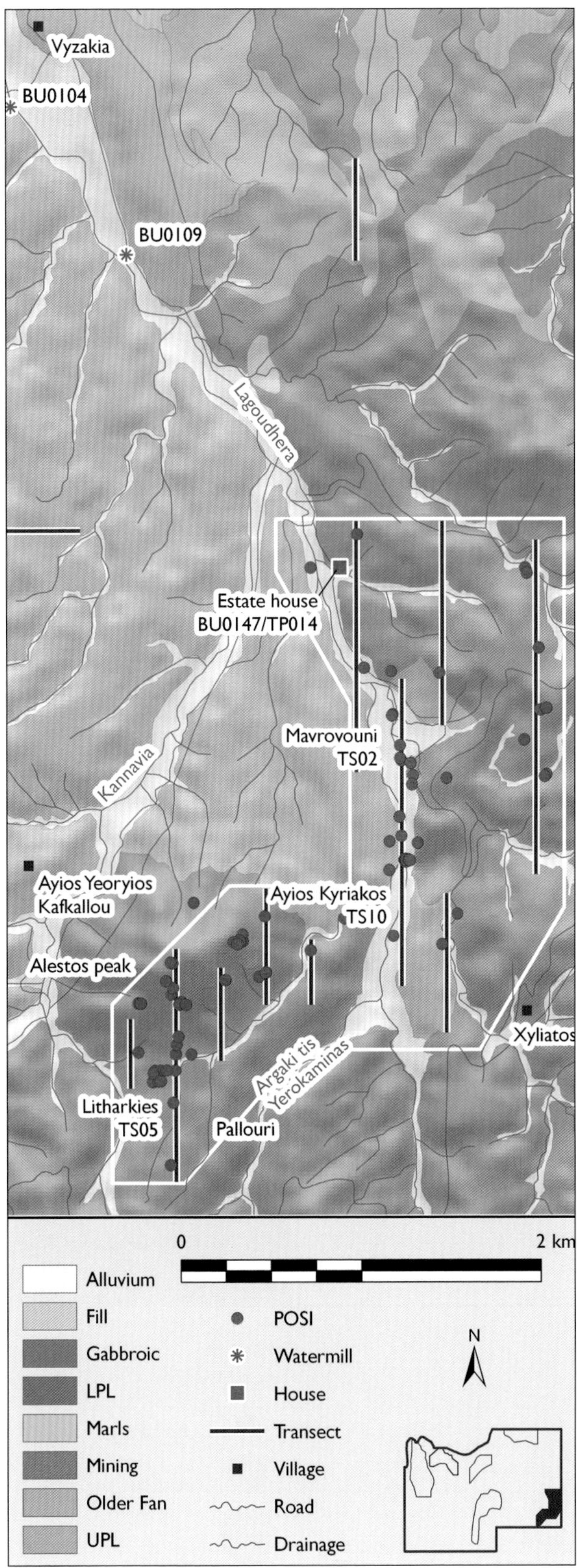

Plate 4.1. Topographical and geological map of Lagoudhera Valley (Jay Noller and Luke Sollars)

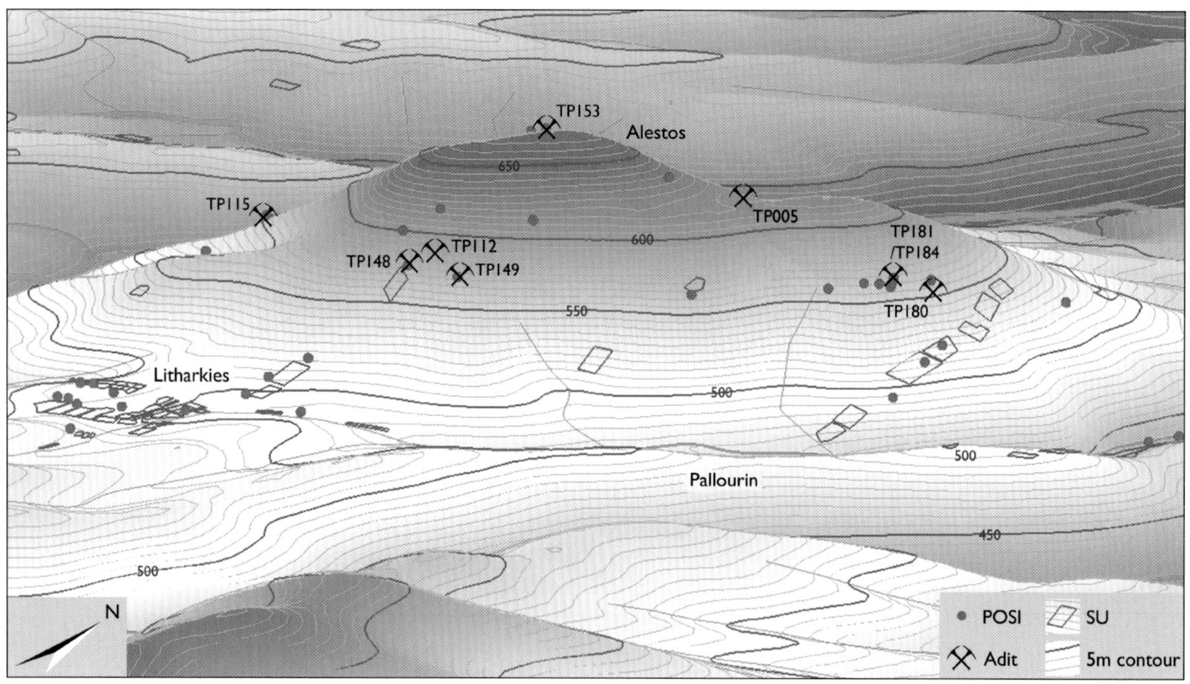

Plate 4.2. Digital Elevation Model of the south and south-east slopes of Alestos, looking north-west. From Litharkies to TP180 is 850 m. Altitudes in metres (Jay Noller, finalised by Luke Sollars)

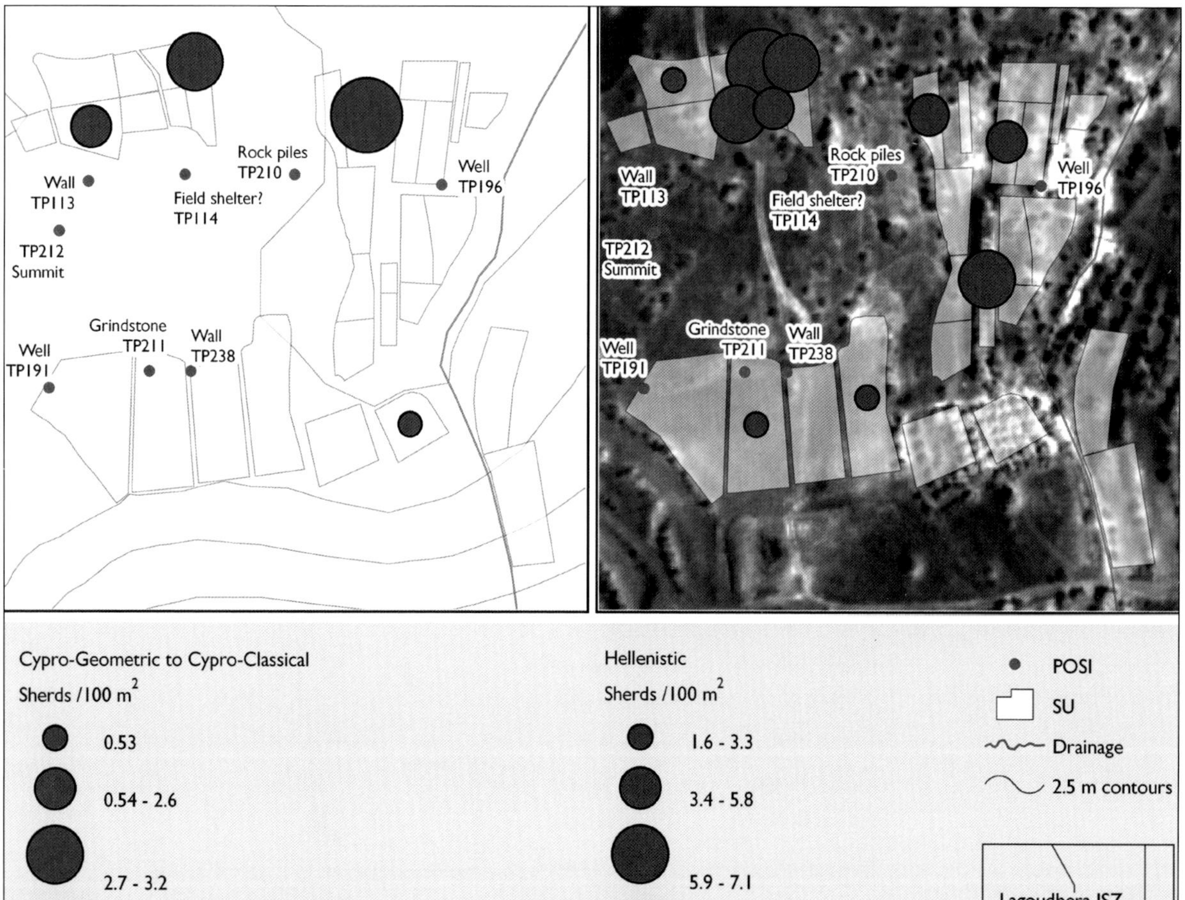

Plate 4.3. Xyliatos Litharkies *(TS05): map of Geometric–Archaic–Classical and Hellenistic pottery. Corrected satellite image (2003) courtesy of the Cyprus Geological Survey Department (Luke Sollars)*

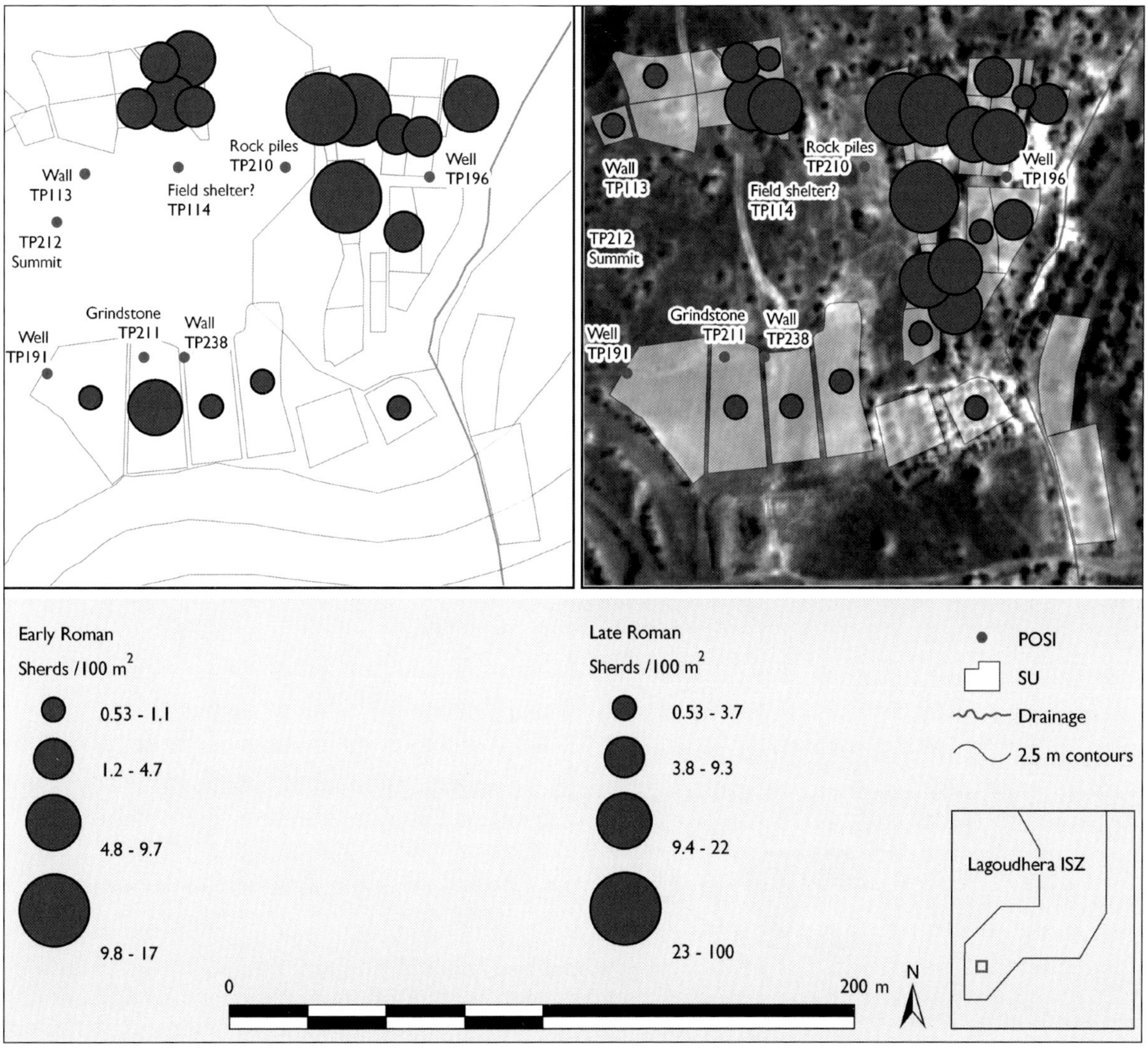

Rock piles
TP210
Well
TP196
Wall
TP113
Field shelter?
TP114
TP212
Summit
Grindstone
TP211
Wall
TP238
Well
TP191
Early Roman
Sherds /100 m2
0.53 - 1.1
1.2 - 4.7
4.8 - 9.7
9.8 - 17
Late Roman
Sherds /100 m2
0.53 - 3.7
3.8 - 9.3
9.4 - 22
23 - 100
POSI
SU
Drainage
2.5 m contours
Lagoudhera ISZ
0
200 m
N

Plate 4.4. Xyliatos Litharkies *(TS05): map of Early Roman and Late Roman pottery. Corrected satellite image (2003) courtesy of the Cyprus Geological Survey Department (Luke Sollars)*

Rock piles
TP210
Well
TP196
Wall
TP113
Field shelter?
TP114
TP212
Summit
Grindstone
TP211
Wall
TP238
Well
TP191
Chipped Stone Count
1
2
3
4 - 24
POSI
SU
Drainage
2.5 m contours
Lagoudhera ISZ
0
80 m
N

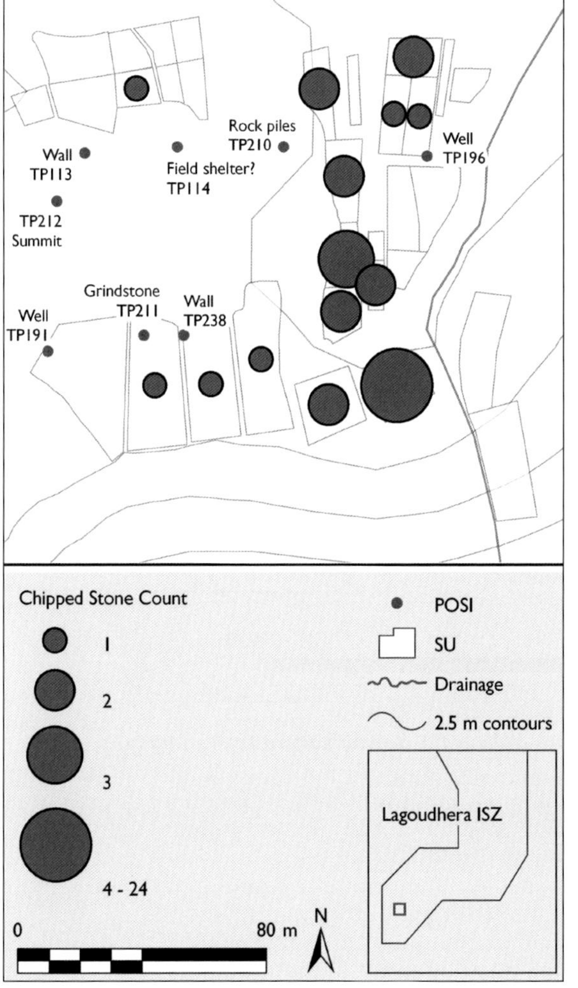

Plate 4.5. Xyliatos Litharkies *(TS05): distribution map of chipped stone (Luke Sollars)*

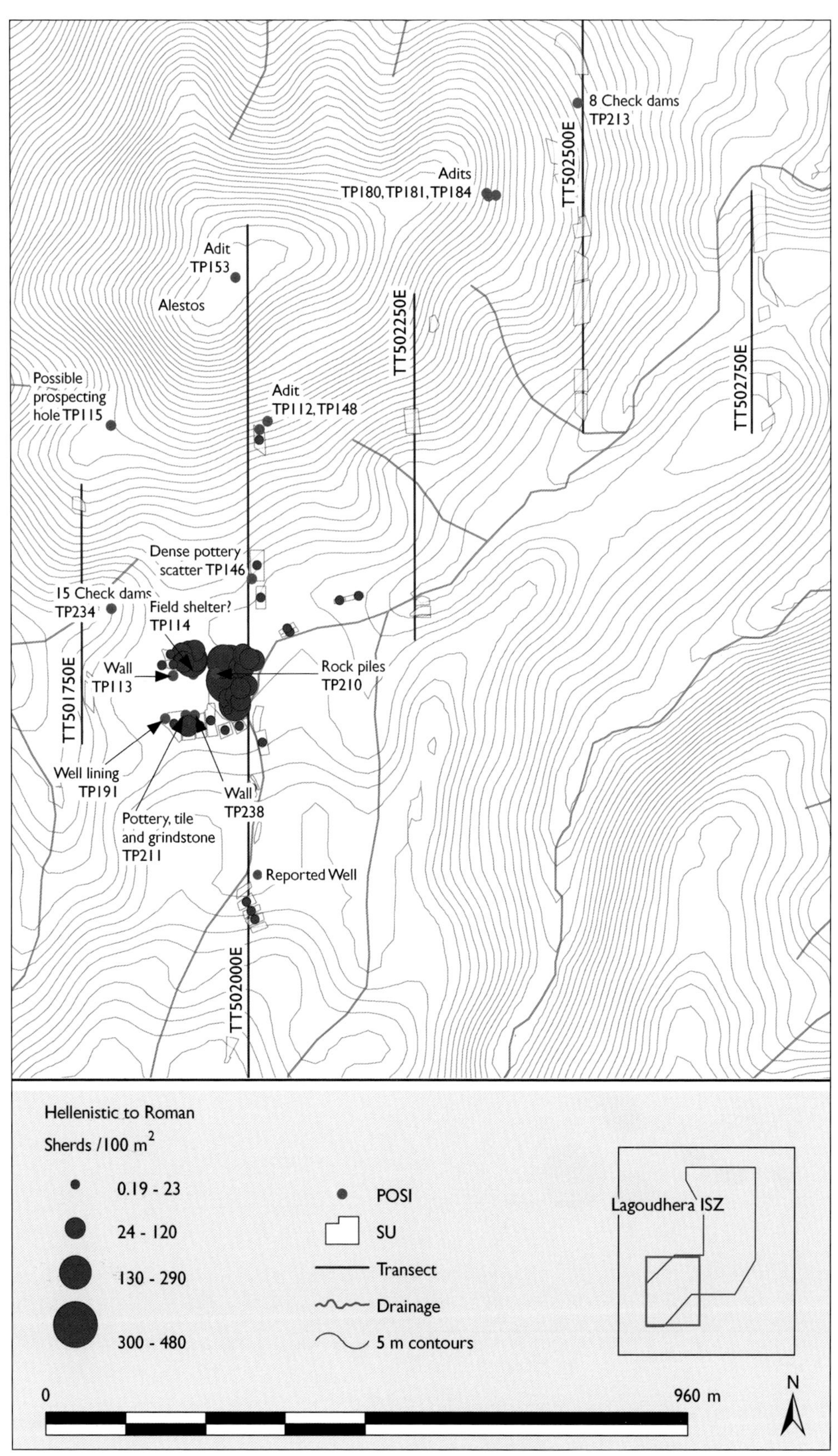

Plate 4.6. Xyliatos Litharkies *and its context, with Hellenistic–Roman pottery (Luke Sollars)*

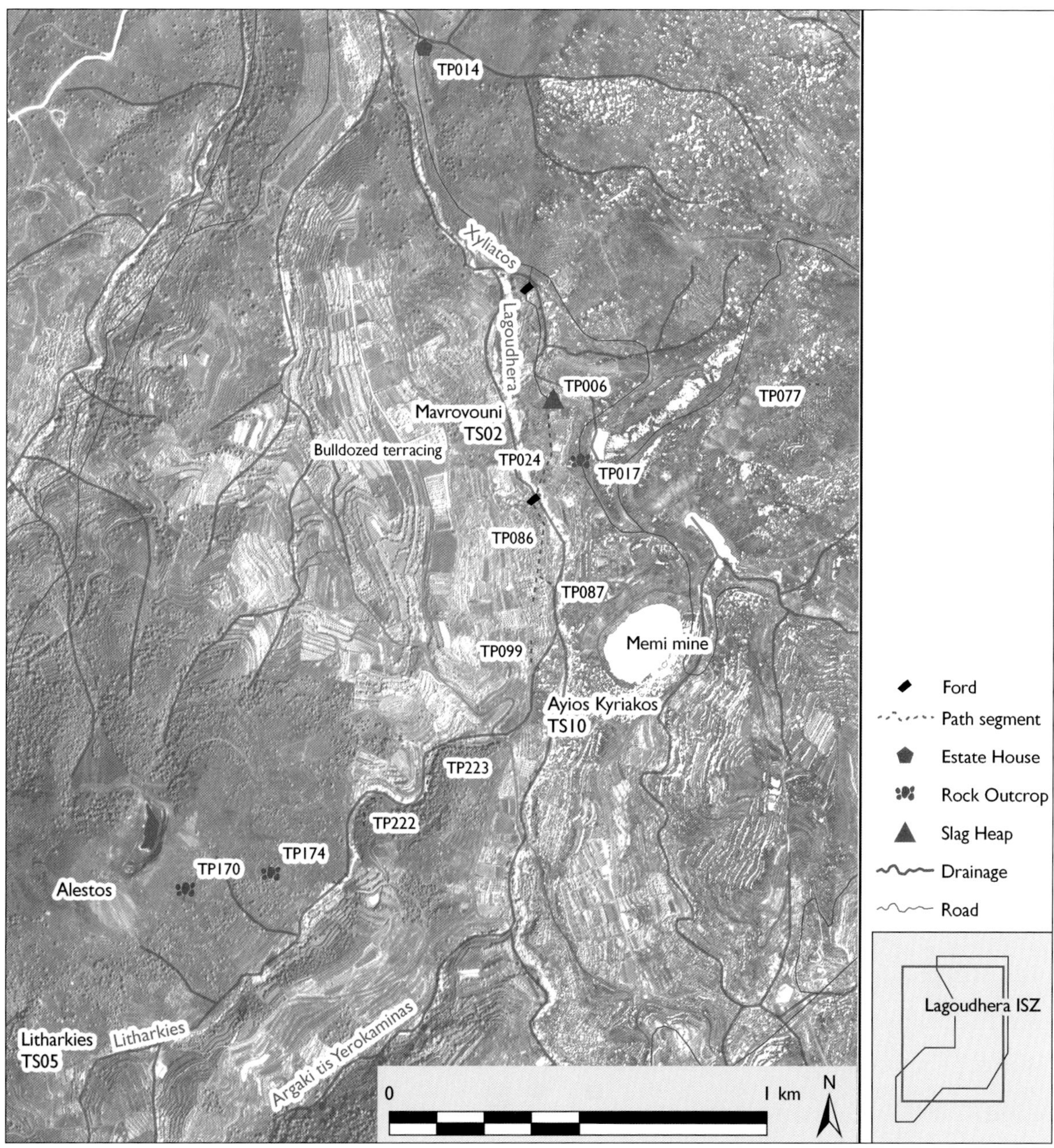

Plate 4.7. Lagoudhera Valley: main paths and Special Interest Areas. Corrected satellite image (2003) courtesy of the Cyprus Geological Survey Department (Luke Sollars)

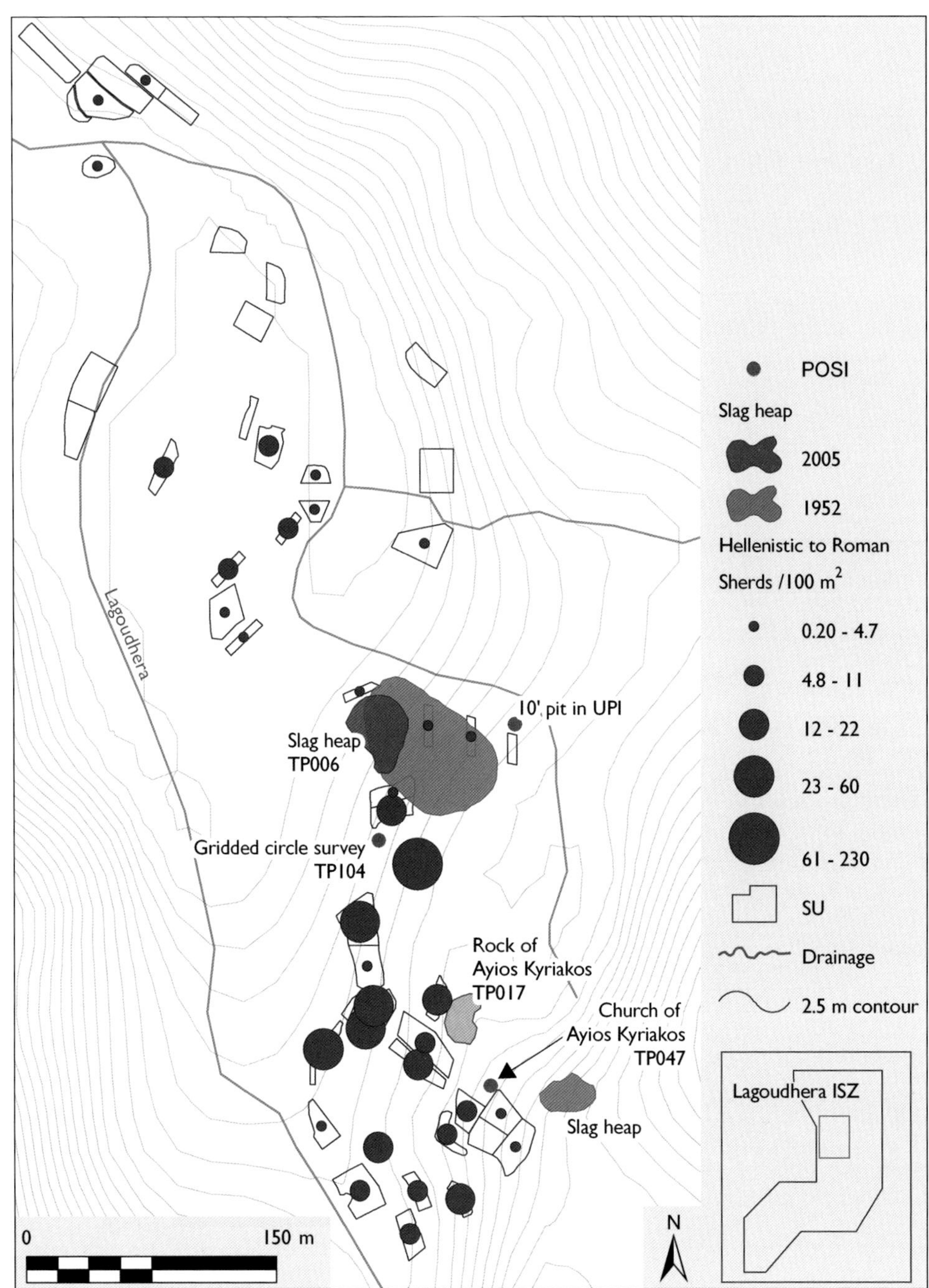

Plate 4.8. Ayia Marina Mavrovouni *(TS02): map of Hellenistic–Roman pottery from block survey, with areas of slag heaps and pit as recorded in 1952 Geological Survey Department archive map (Luke Sollars)*

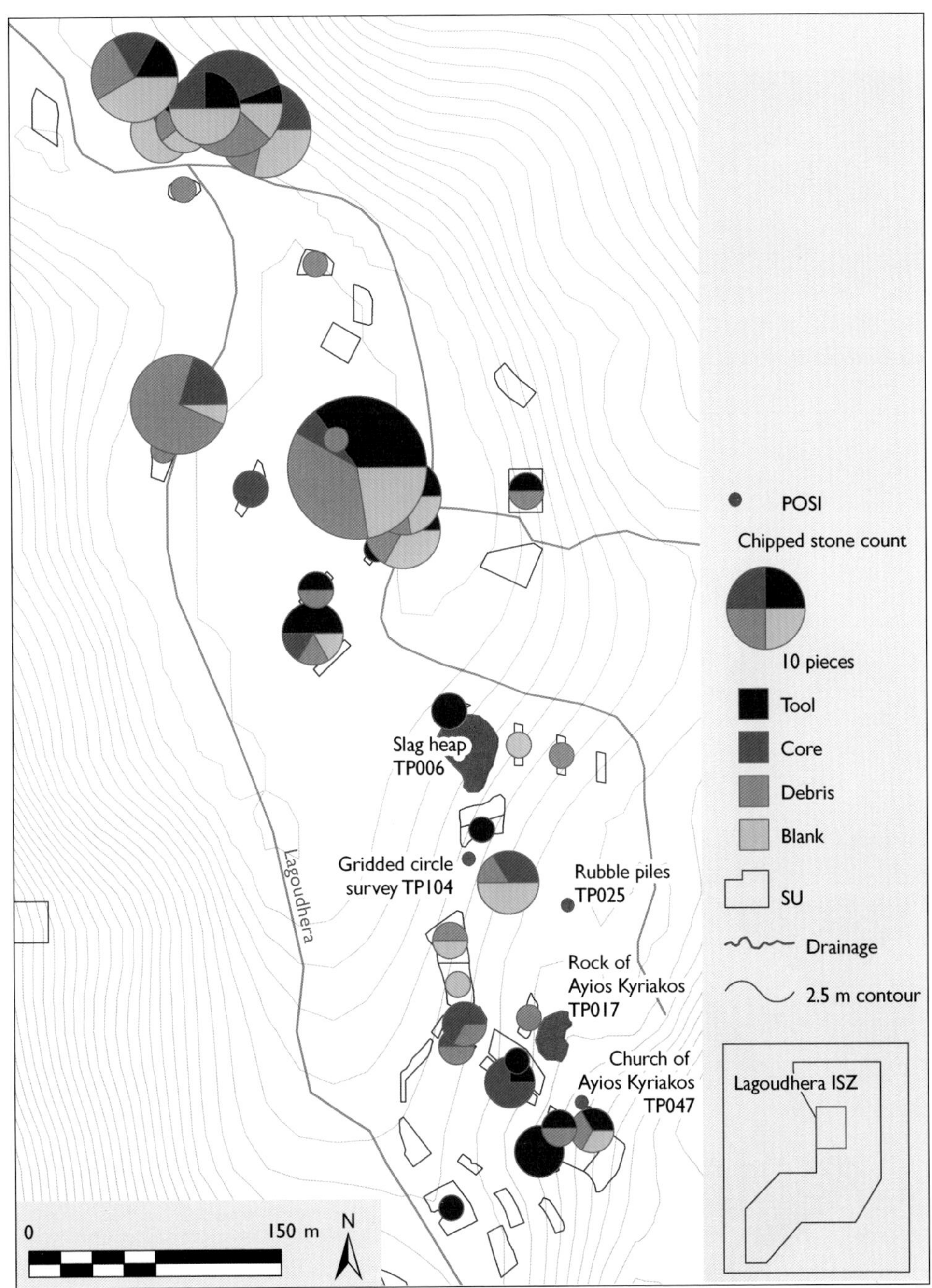

Plate 4.9. Ayia Marina Mavrovouni *(TS02): distribution map of chipped stone (tools, cores, debris, blanks)*

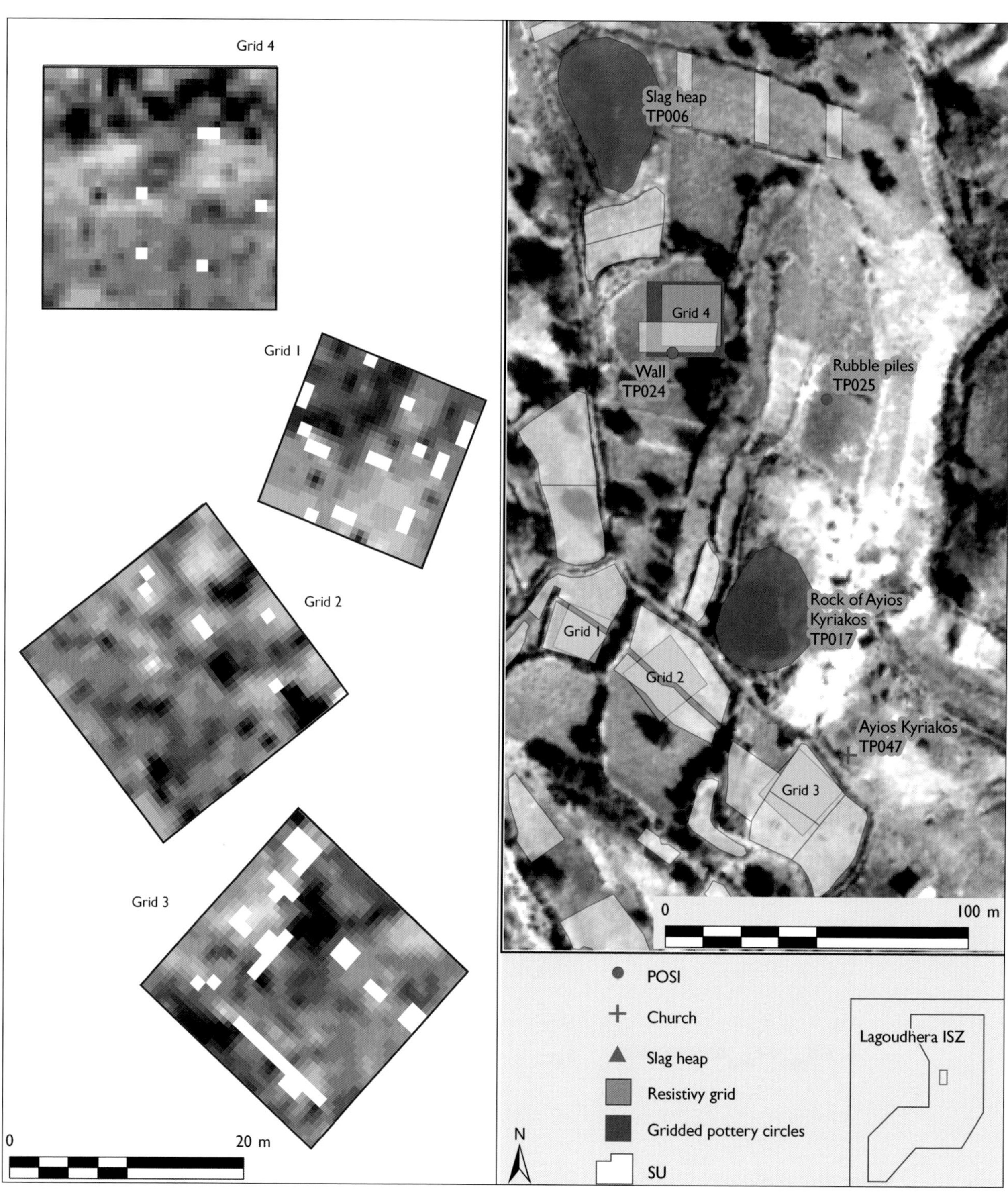

Plate 4.10. Ayia Marina Mavrovouni *(TS02): resistivity survey results. White patches in the resistivity grids refer to dummy readings. Based upon the aerial photograph taken by the Department of Lands and Surveys with the sanction of the Government of the Republic of Cyprus; State copyright reserved (Iain Banks and Luke Sollars)*

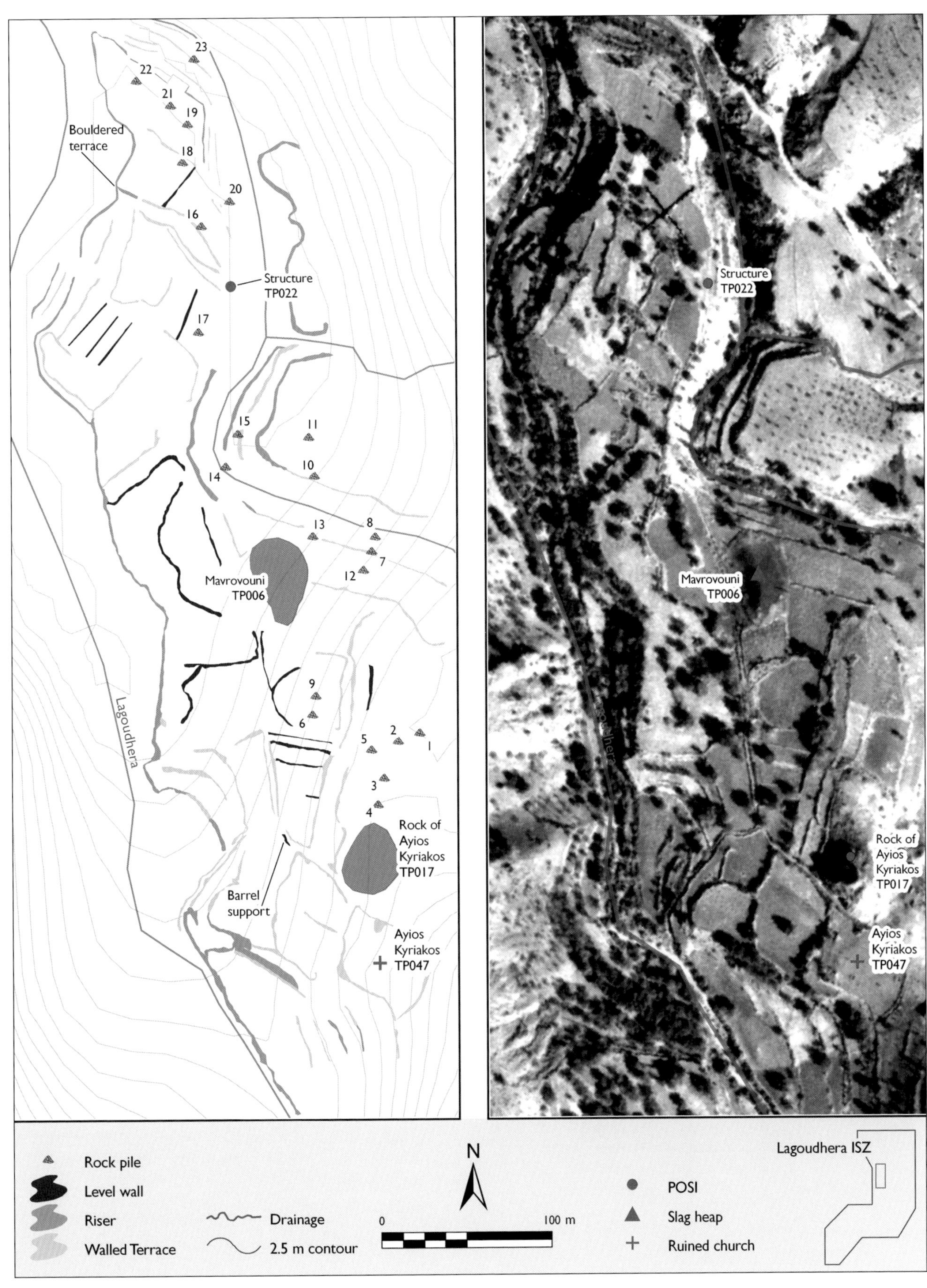

Plate 4.11. Ayia Marina Mavrovouni *(TP025): map of rock piles and walls (Paula Barry, finalised by Luke Sollars)*

Plate 4.12. View in springtime down the Lagoudhera Valley from the Rock of Ayios Kyriakos (TP017), with Mavrovouni slag heap (TP006) in the centre and the village of Vyzakia in the distance. Taken on 25 March 2006; the dirt track on the left was constructed after our fieldwork, and follows the line of the raised path TP024. (Michael Given)

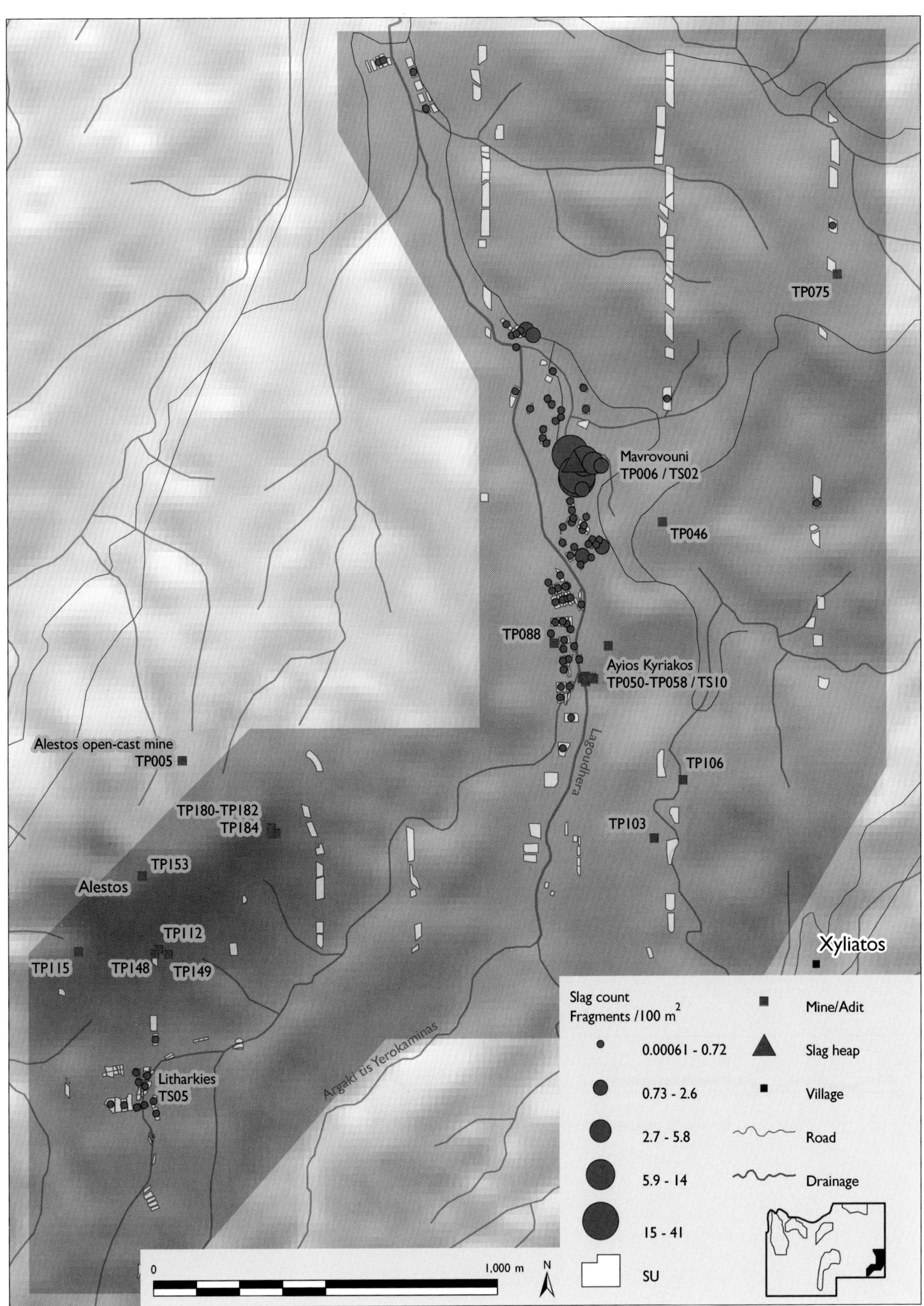

Plate 4.13. Map of archaeometallurgical features and slag in the Lagoudhera Valley and area to the east (Luke Sollars)

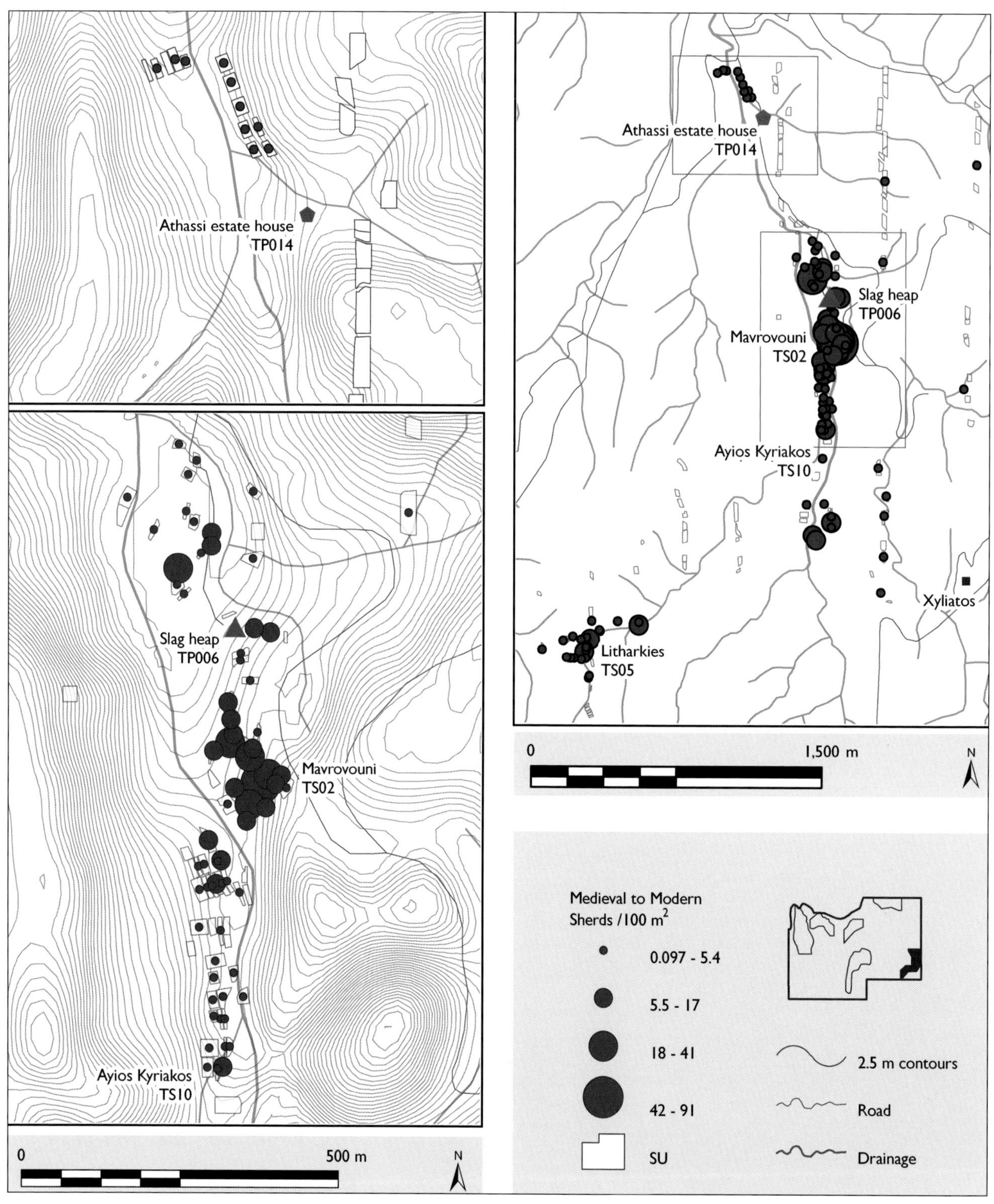

Plate 4.14. Upper Lagoudhera Valley: map of Medieval–Modern pottery distribution (Luke Sollars)

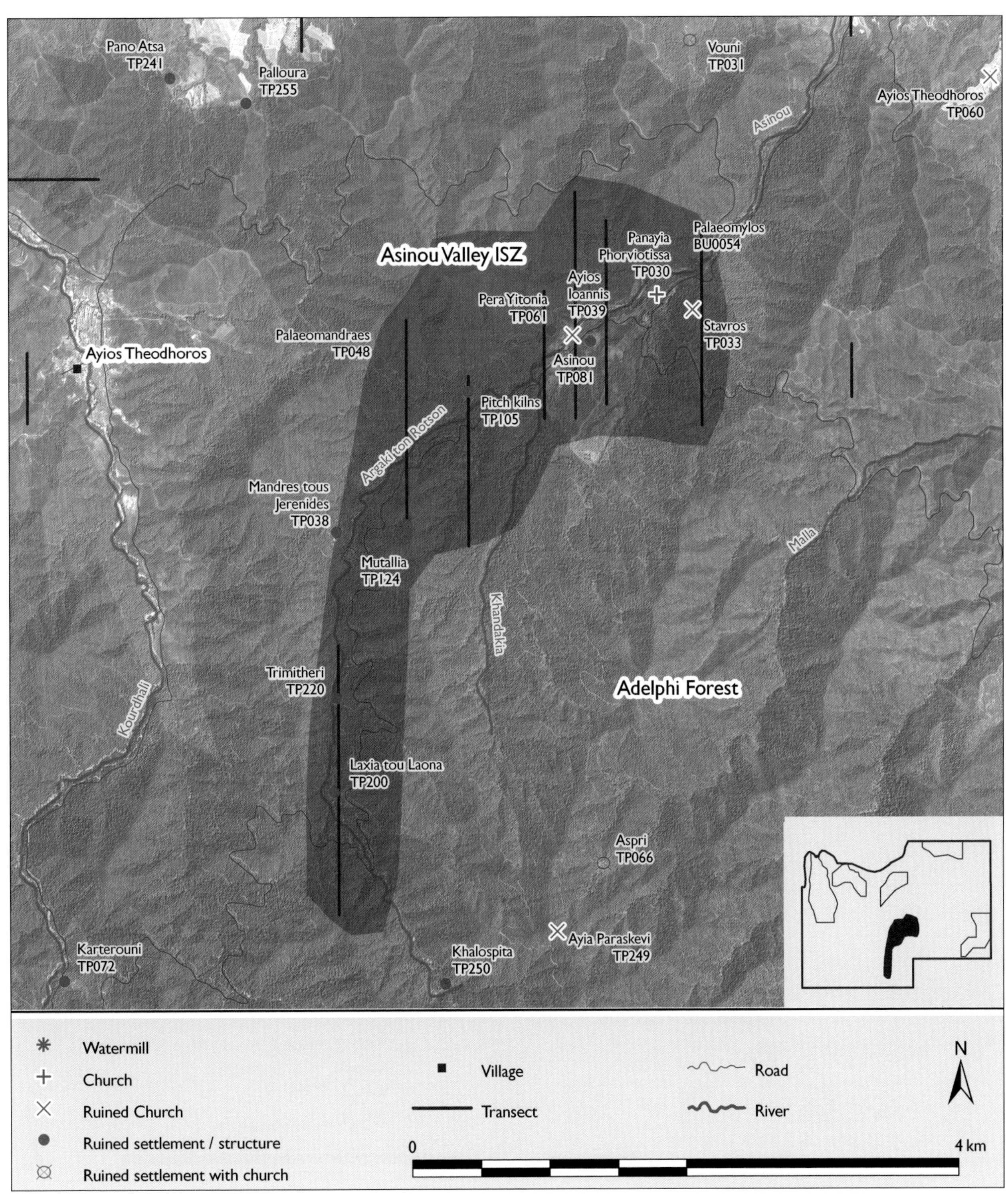

Plate 5.1. Map of the Mountains area, with Asinou Valley Intensive Survey Zone, topography and forest cover. Corrected satellite image (2003) courtesy of the Cyprus Geological Survey Department (Luke Sollars)

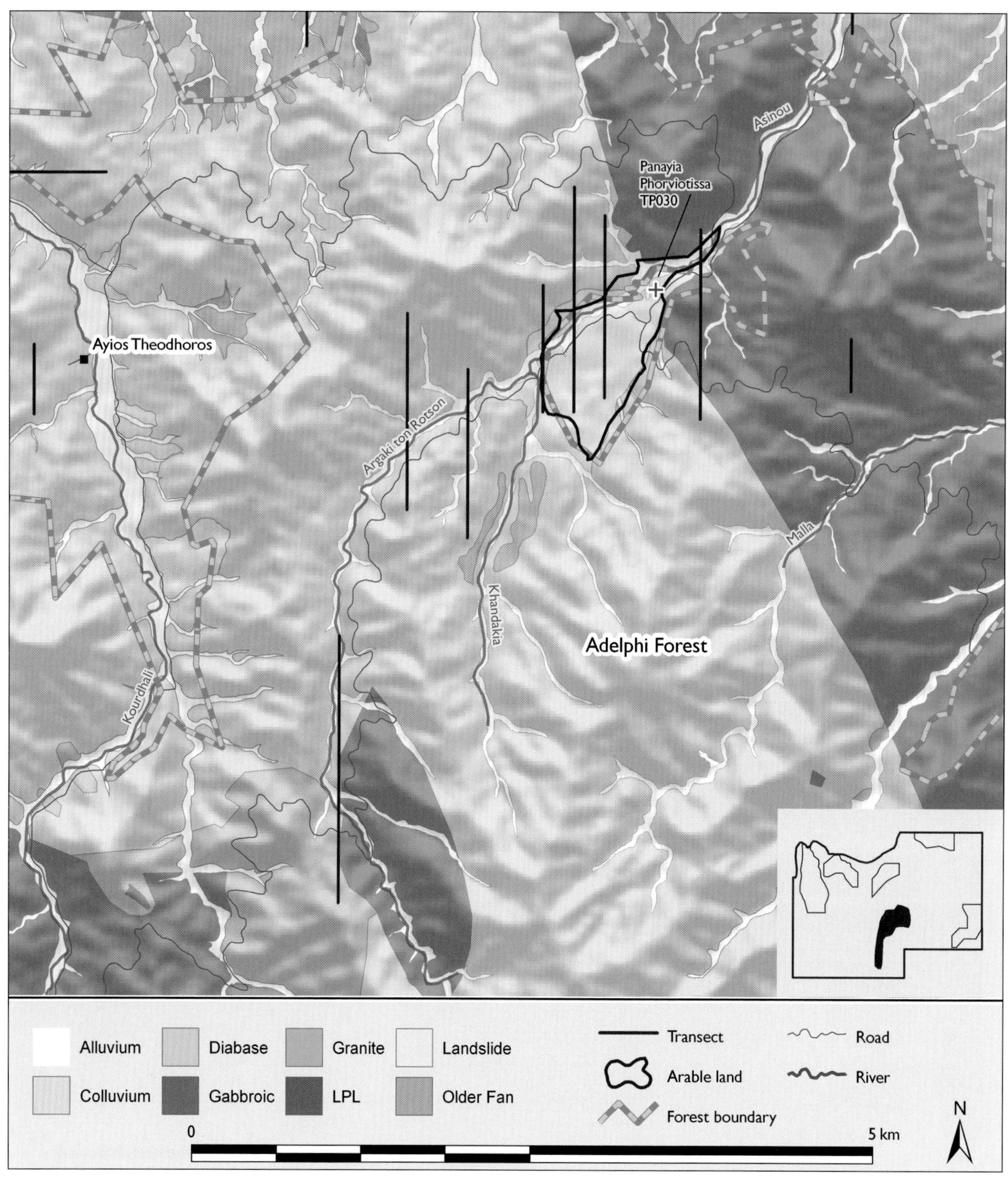

Plate 5.2. Map of the Mountains area, with geology, forest boundary and 20th-century cultivated land (Jay Noller and Luke Sollars)

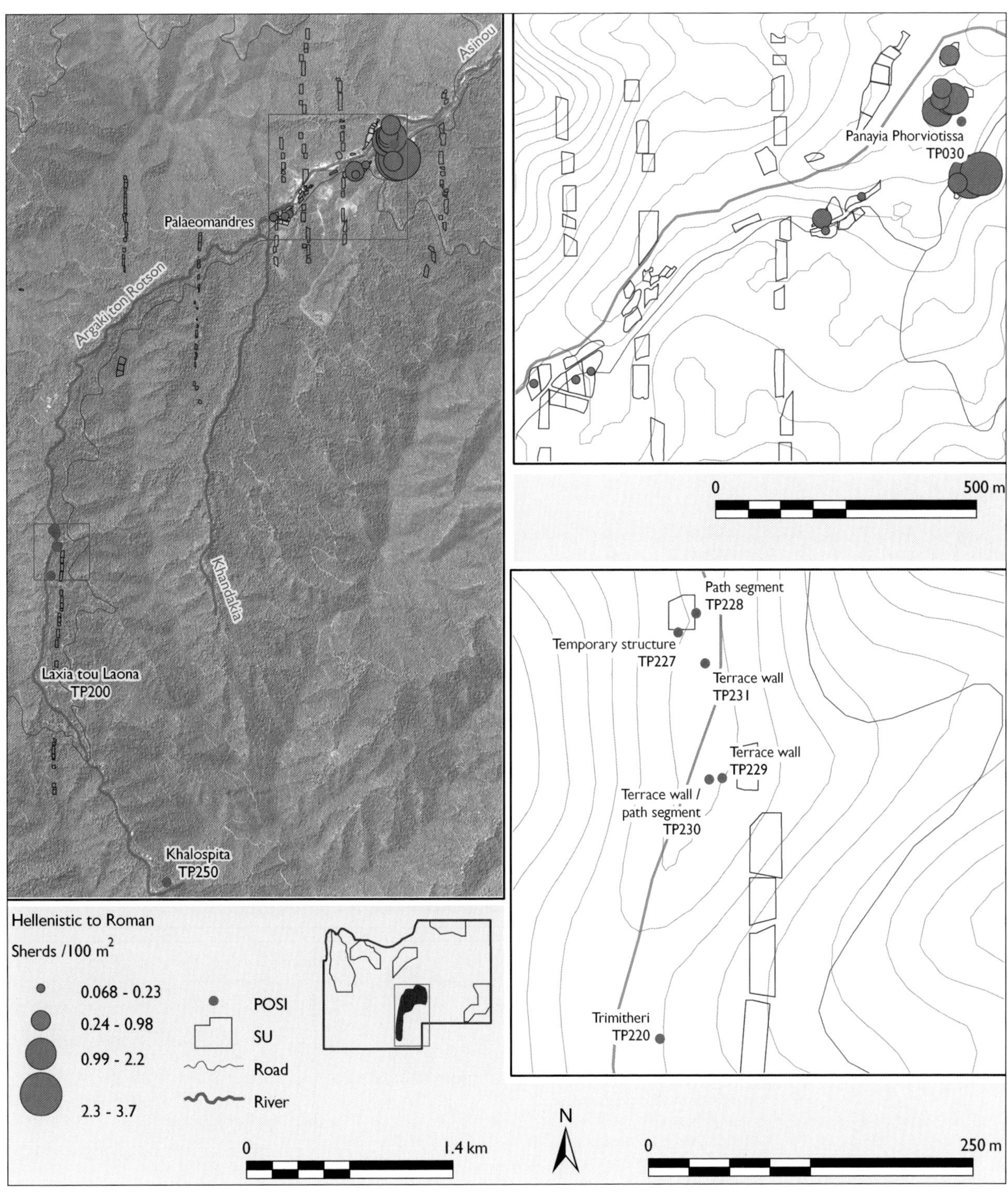

Plate 5.3. Asinou Valley: Hellenistic–Roman pottery and POSIs. Corrected satellite image (2003) courtesy of the Cyprus Geological Survey Department (Luke Sollars)

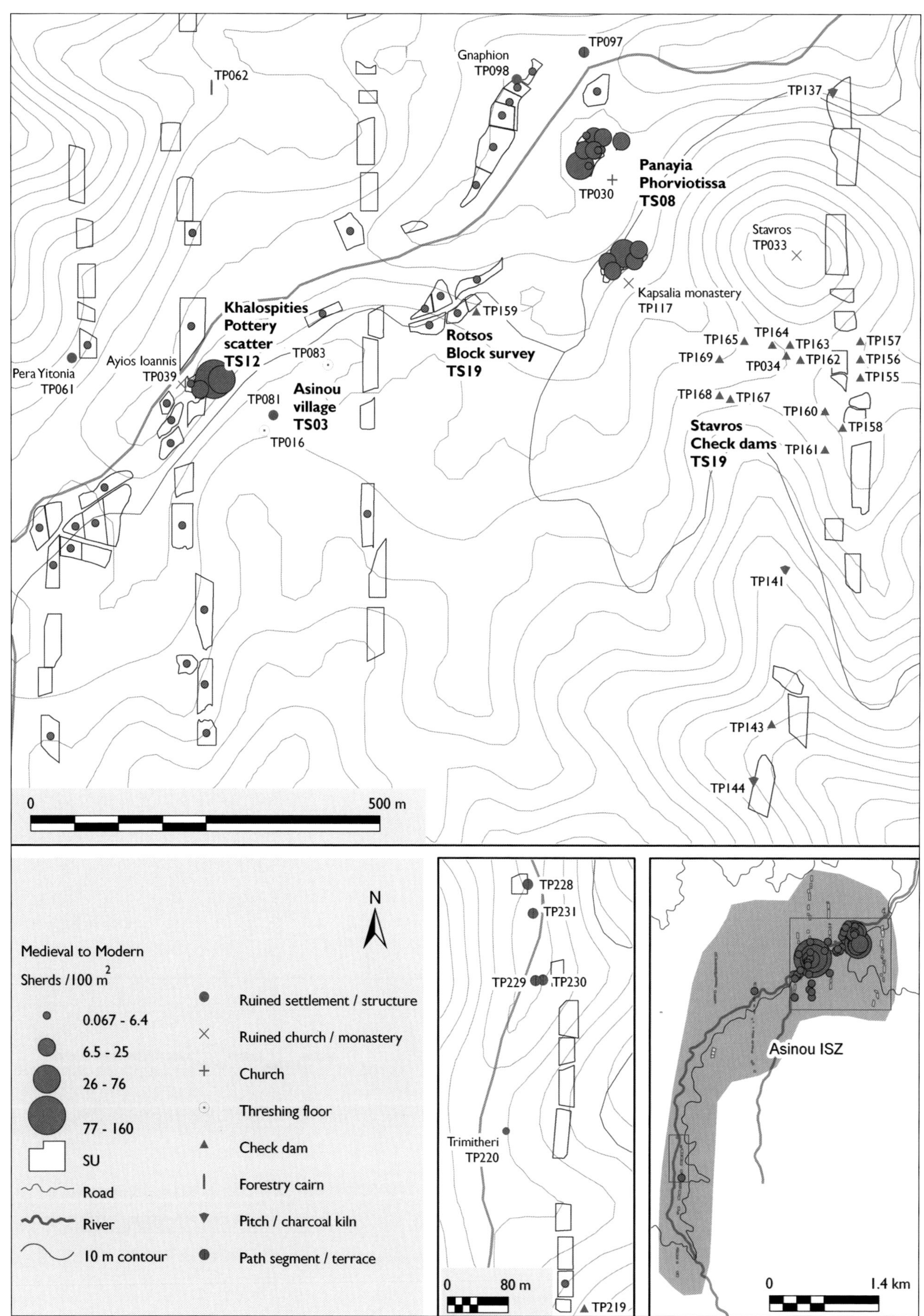

Plate 5.4. Asinou Valley: Medieval–Modern pottery and POSIs (Luke Sollars)

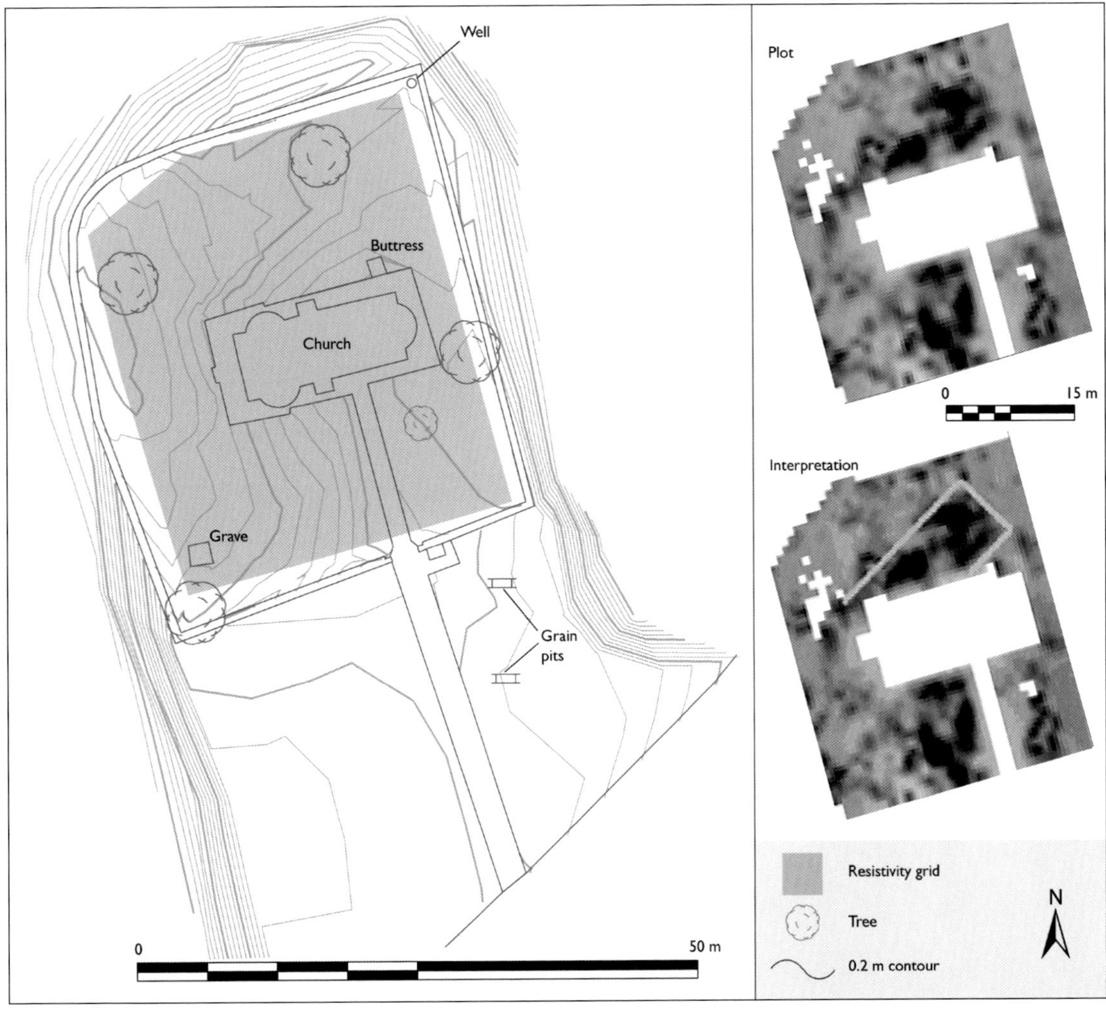

Plate 5.5. Courtyard of Panayia Phorviotissa (TP030): plan with resistivity survey and interpretation (Iain Banks and Luke Sollars)

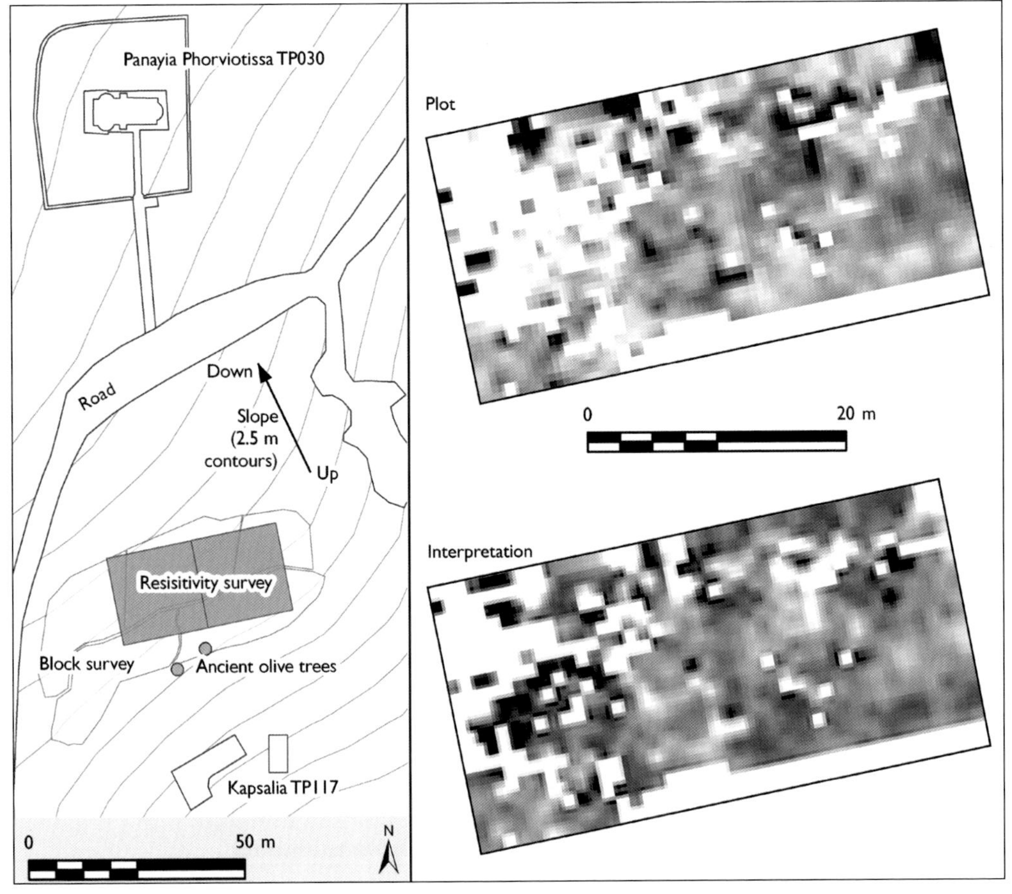

Plate 5.6. Nikitari Kapsalia *(TP117): resistivity survey (Iain Banks and Luke Sollars)*

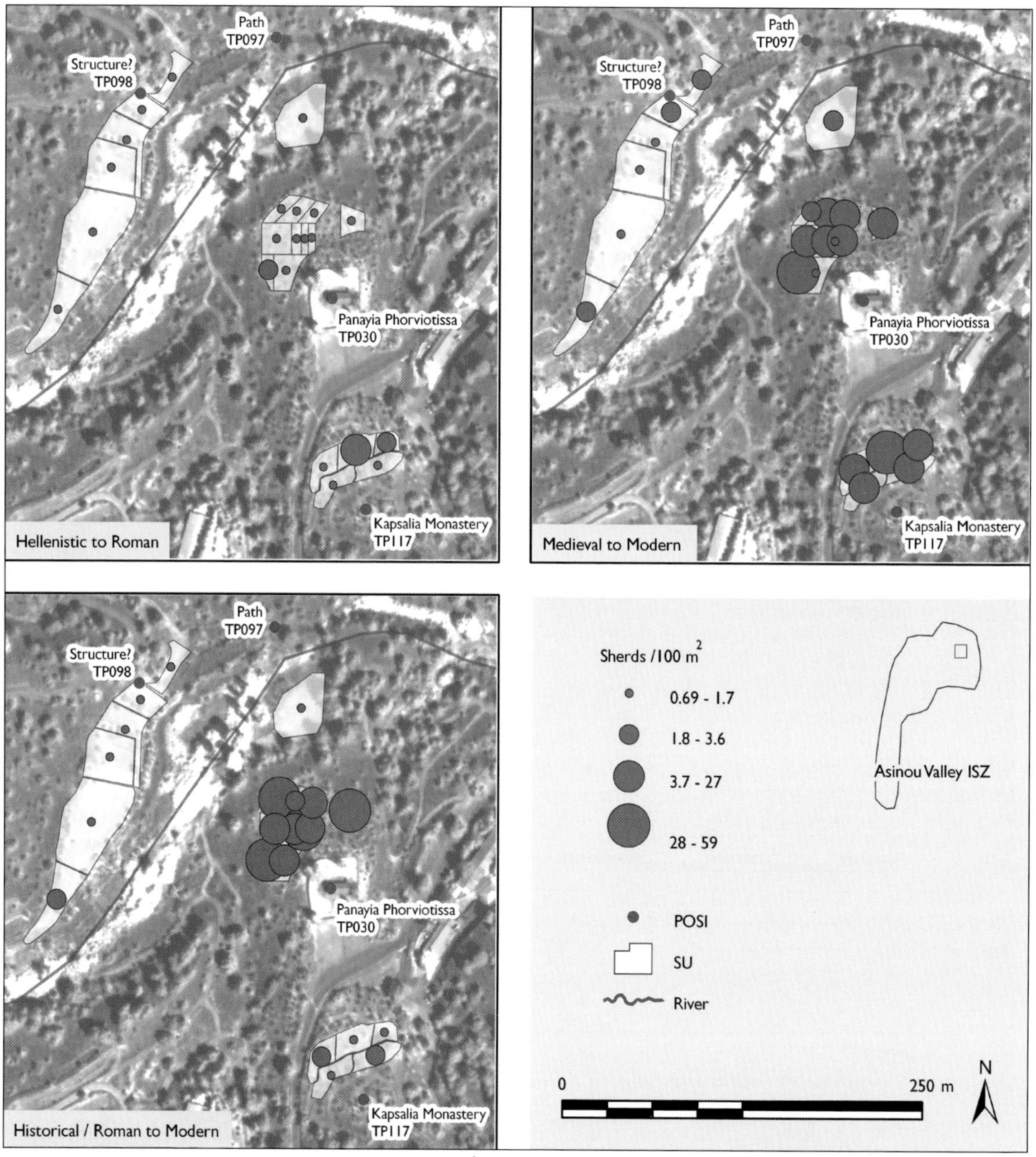

Path
TP097
Structure?
TP098
Panayia Phorviotissa
TP030
Kapsalia Monastery
TP117
Hellenistic to Roman

Path
TP097
Structure?
TP098
Panayia Phorviotissa
TP030
Kapsalia Monastery
TP117
Medieval to Modern

Path
TP097
Structure?
TP098
Panayia Phorviotissa
TP030
Kapsalia Monastery
TP117
Historical / Roman to Modern

Sherds /100 m^2
0.69 - 1.7
1.8 - 3.6
3.7 - 27
28 - 59
POSI
SU
River
Asinou Valley ISZ
0
250 m
N

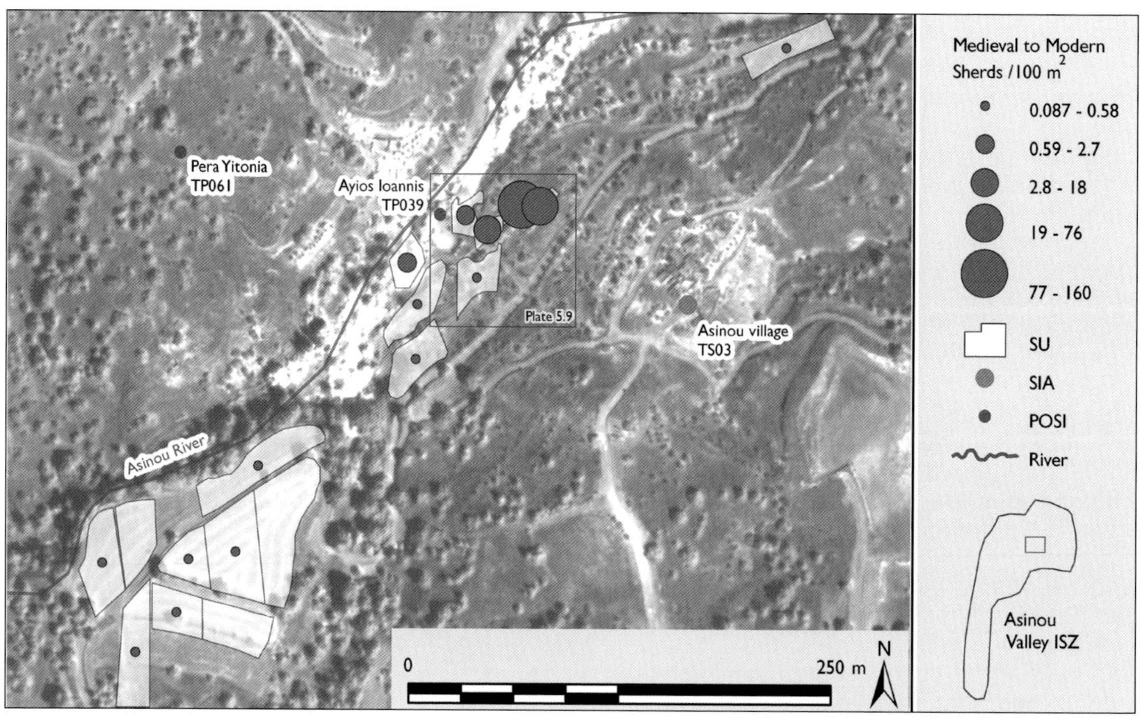

Plate 5.7. (top left) Block survey around Panayia Phorviotissa (TS08): Hellenistic–Roman; Medieval–Modern; Historical and Roman–Modern pottery. Corrected satellite image (2003) courtesy of the Cyprus Geological Survey Department (Luke Sollars)

Plate 5.8. (below left) Nikitari Khalospities *(TS12): Medieval–Modern pottery and POSIs. Corrected satellite image (2003) courtesy of the Cyprus Geological Survey Department (Luke Sollars)*

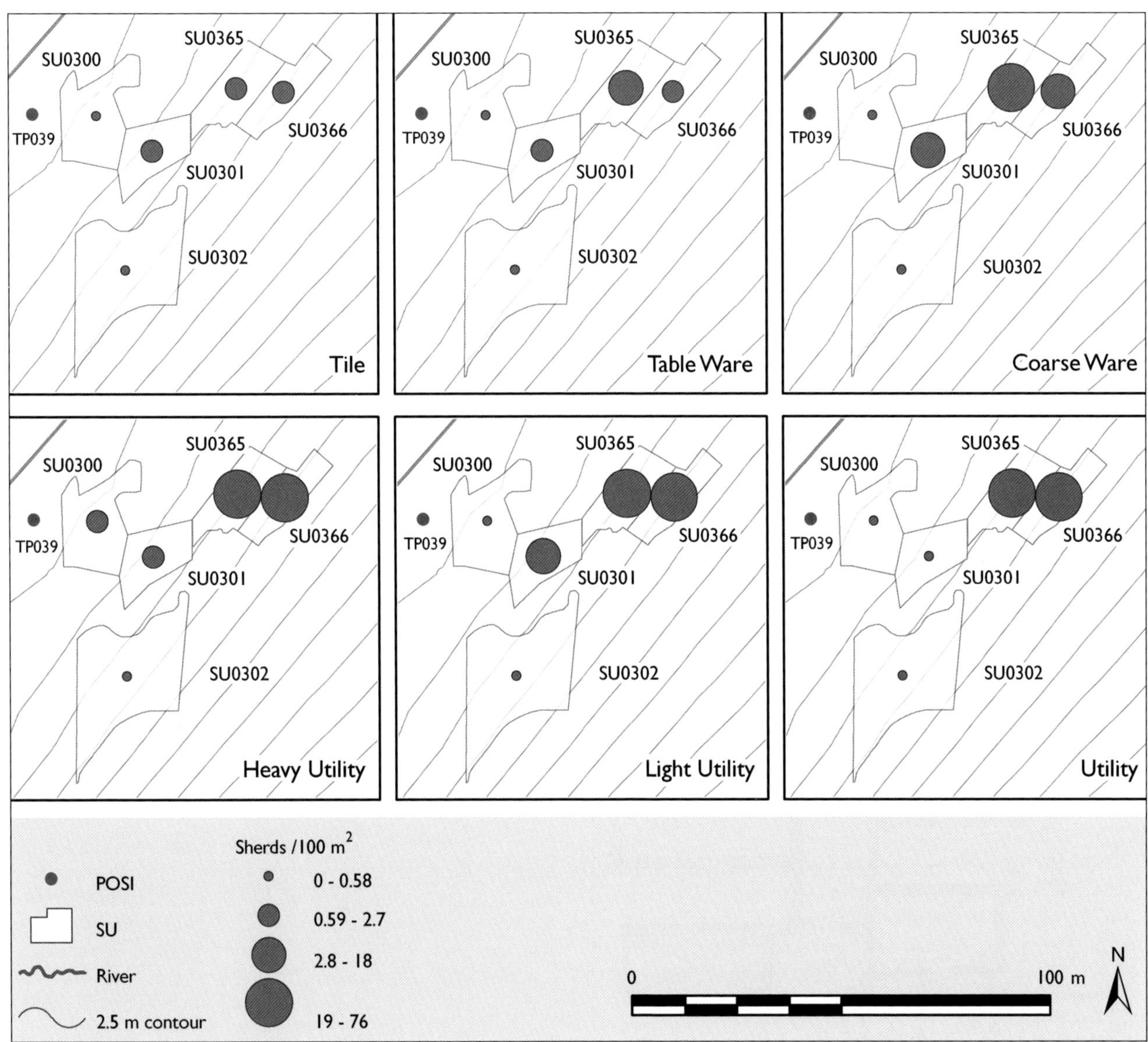

Plate 5.9. (above) Nikitari Khalospities *(TS12): functional categories of Medieval–Modern pottery (Luke Sollars)*

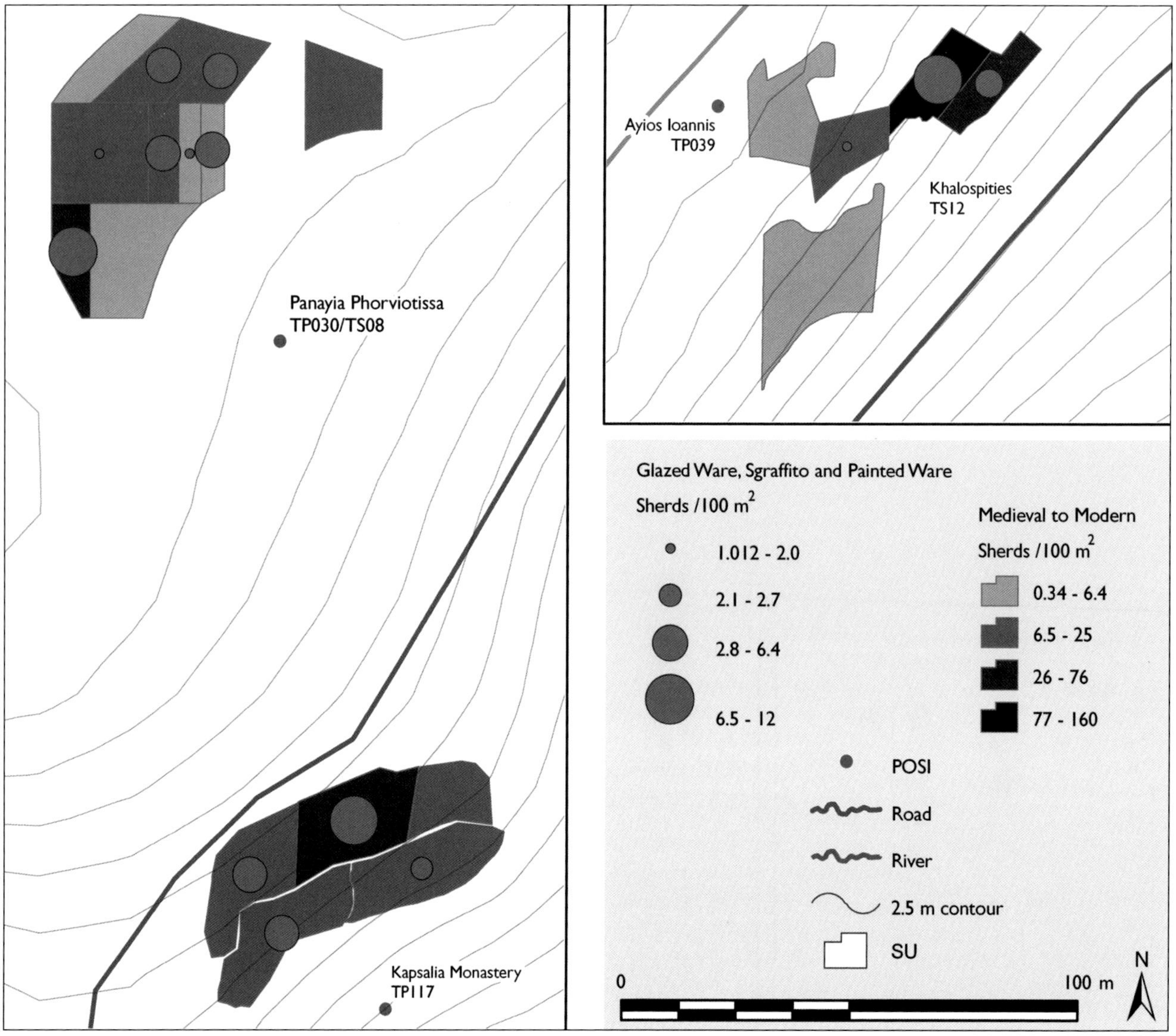

Plate 5.10. *(above) Panayia Phorviotissa (TS08) and Nikitari* Khalospities *(TS12): Density of Glazed Ware, Sgraffito and Painted Ware (see Plate 5.4 for context) (Luke Sollars)*

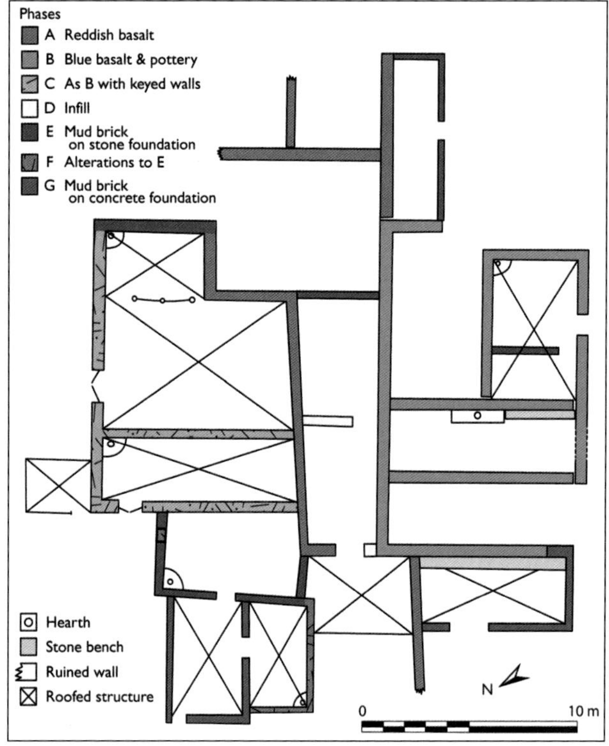

Plate 5.11. (left) Asinou village: phasing plan of central agglomeration (BU0047) (Tracy Ireland, finalised by Luke Sollars)

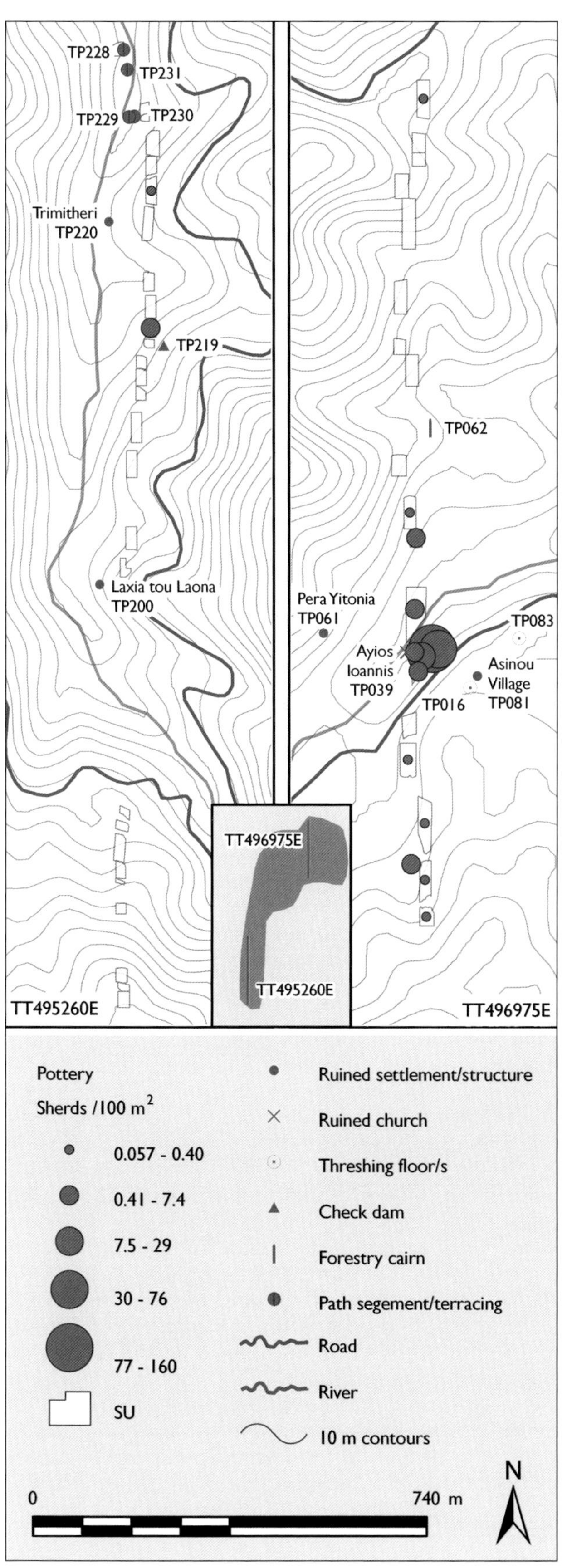

Plate 5.12. Comparative maps of TT496975E and TT495260E (Luke Sollars)

Plate 5.13. Hunting dogs tied to stake with two moufflon in mountain background, from narthex of Panayia Phorviotissa (Sophia Kalopissi-Verti)

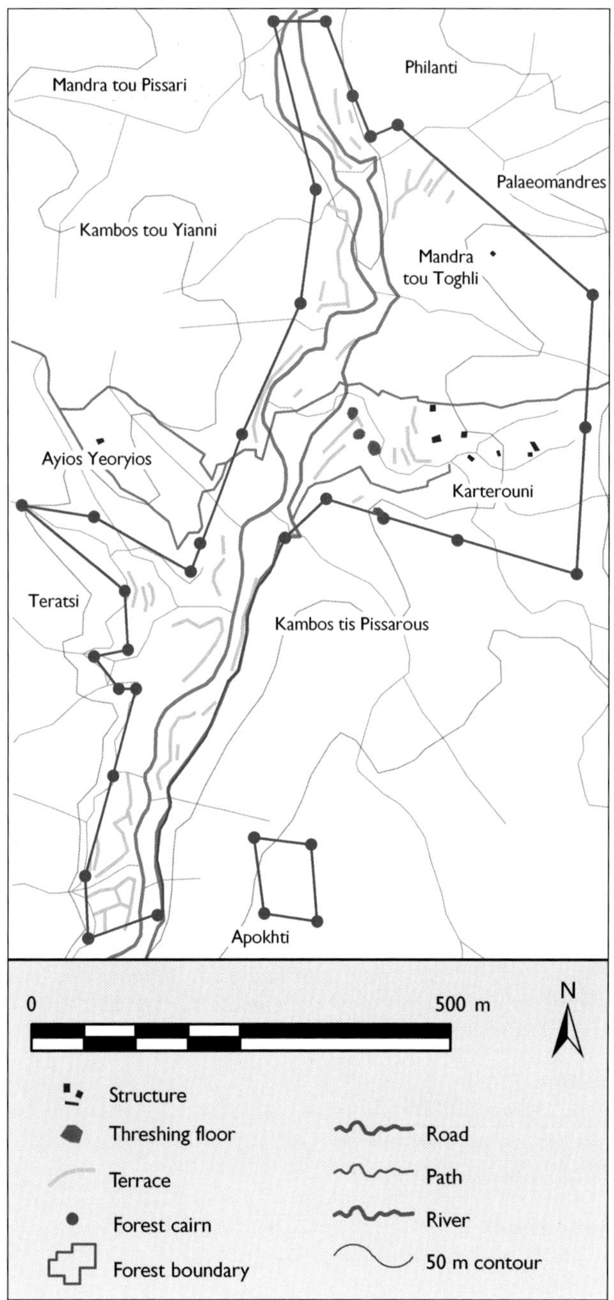

Plate 5.14. Ayios Theodhoros Karterouni *(TS14): map (Luke Sollars)*